YOWAMUSHI PEDAL

WATARU WATANABE

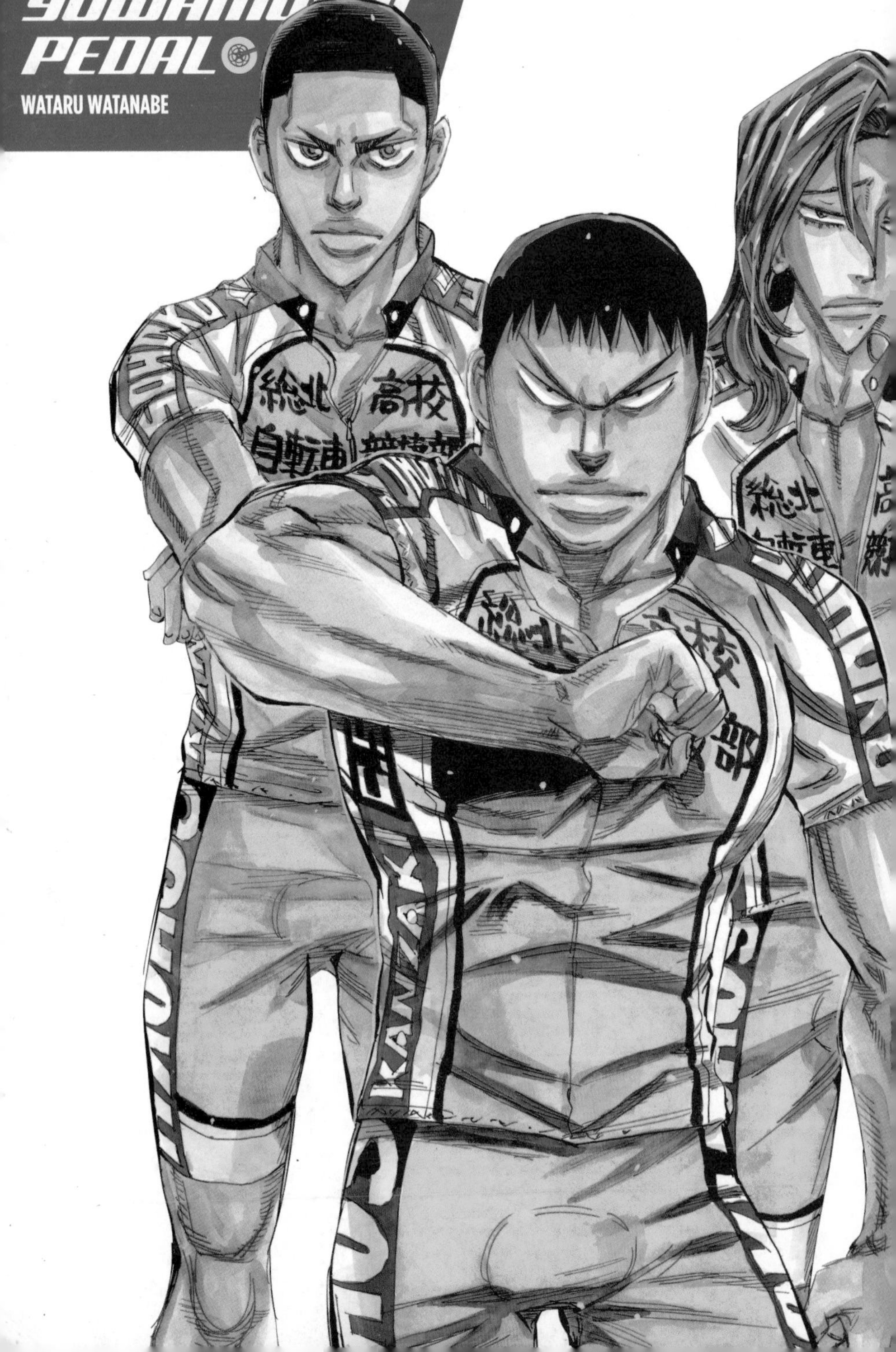
総北 高校
自転車
総北
高校
部
KANZAKI

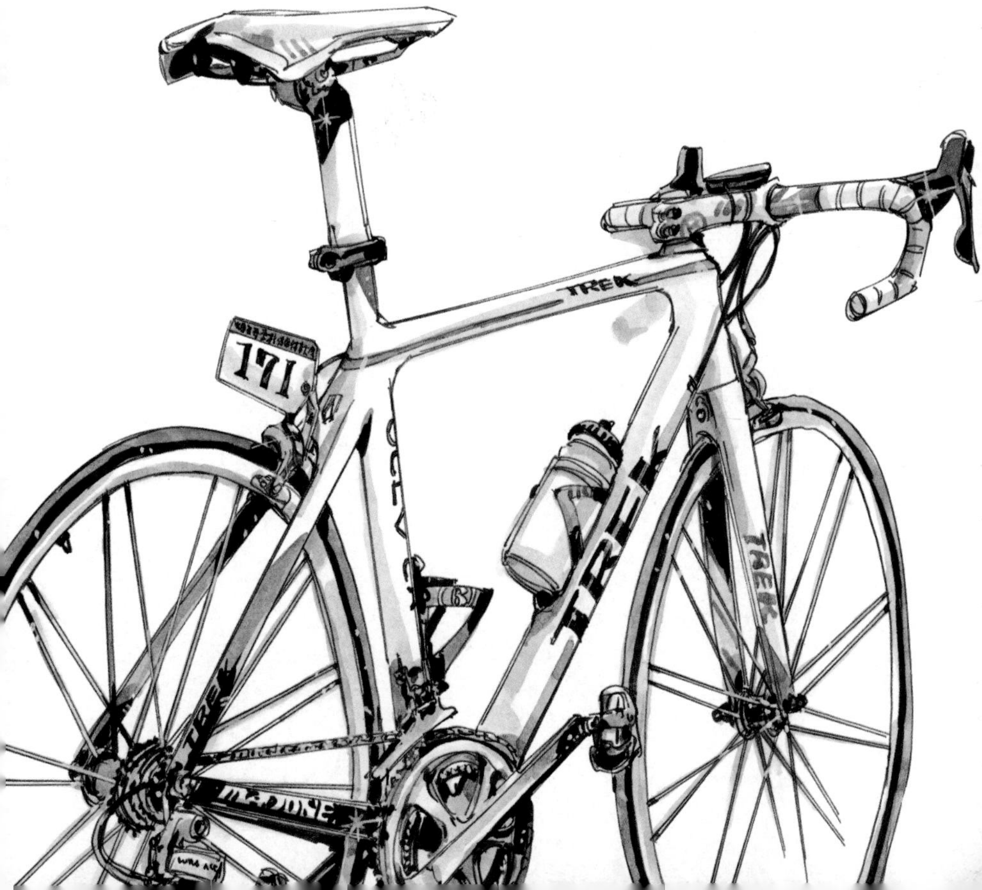
TREK
171
TREK
MADONE

11

WATARU
WATANABE

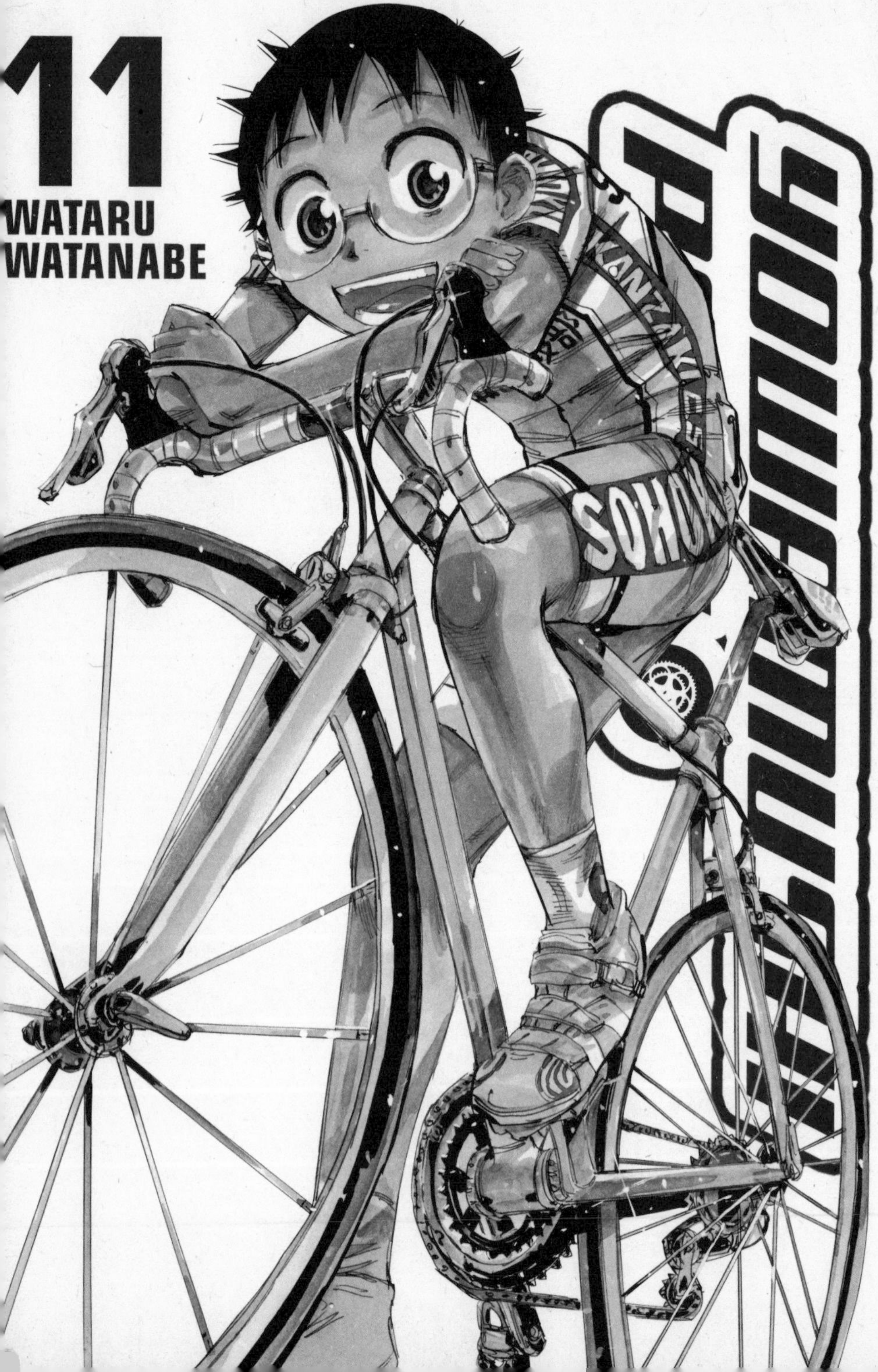

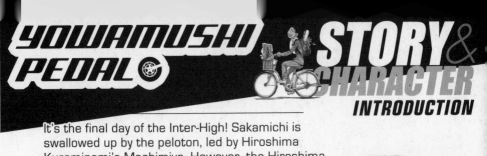

YOWAMUSHI PEDAL

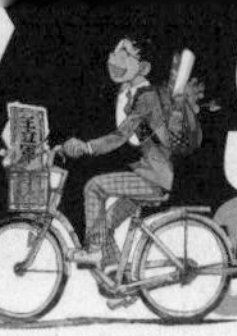

STORY & CHARACTER INTRODUCTION

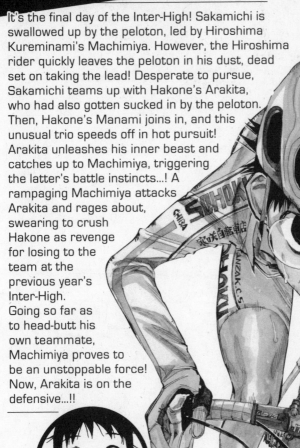

It's the final day of the Inter-High! Sakamichi is swallowed up by the peloton, led by Hiroshima Kureminami's Machimiya. However, the Hiroshima rider quickly leaves the peloton in his dust, dead set on taking the lead! Desperate to pursue, Sakamichi teams up with Hakone's Arakita, who had also gotten sucked in by the peloton. Then, Hakone's Manami joins in, and this unusual trio speeds off in hot pursuit! Arakita unleashes his inner beast and catches up to Machimiya, triggering the latter's battle instincts...! A rampaging Machimiya attacks Arakita and rages about, swearing to crush Hakone as revenge for losing to the team at the previous year's Inter-High. Going so far as to head-butt his own teammate, Machimiya proves to be an unstoppable force! Now, Arakita is on the defensive...!!

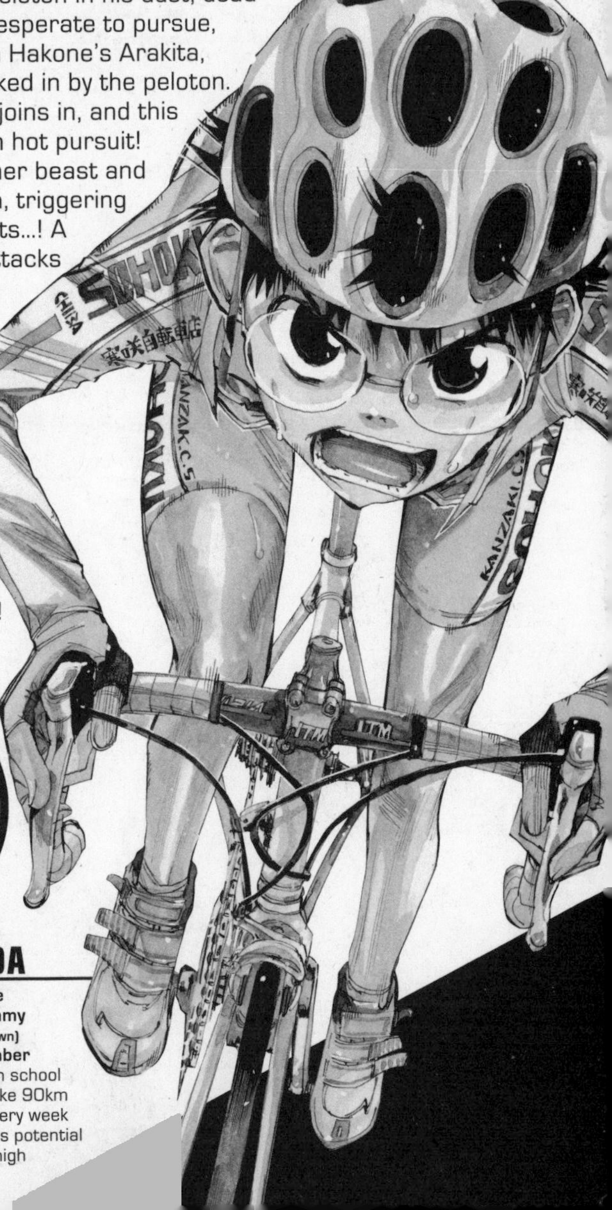

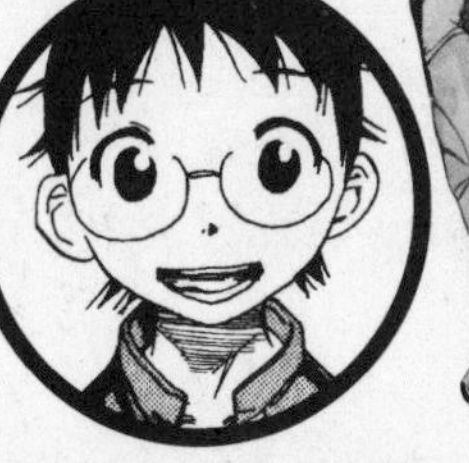

SAKAMICHI ONODA

Preferred Bike: **Chromoly Frame Road Bike, Mommy Bike** (maker unknown)

Cycling Style: **High Cadence Climber**

Sakamichi is an anime-loving high school student who rides his mommy bike 90km round- trip up extreme slopes every week to visit Akiba. Hearing that he has potential as a cyclist, Sakamichi joins his high school's Bicycle Racing Club.

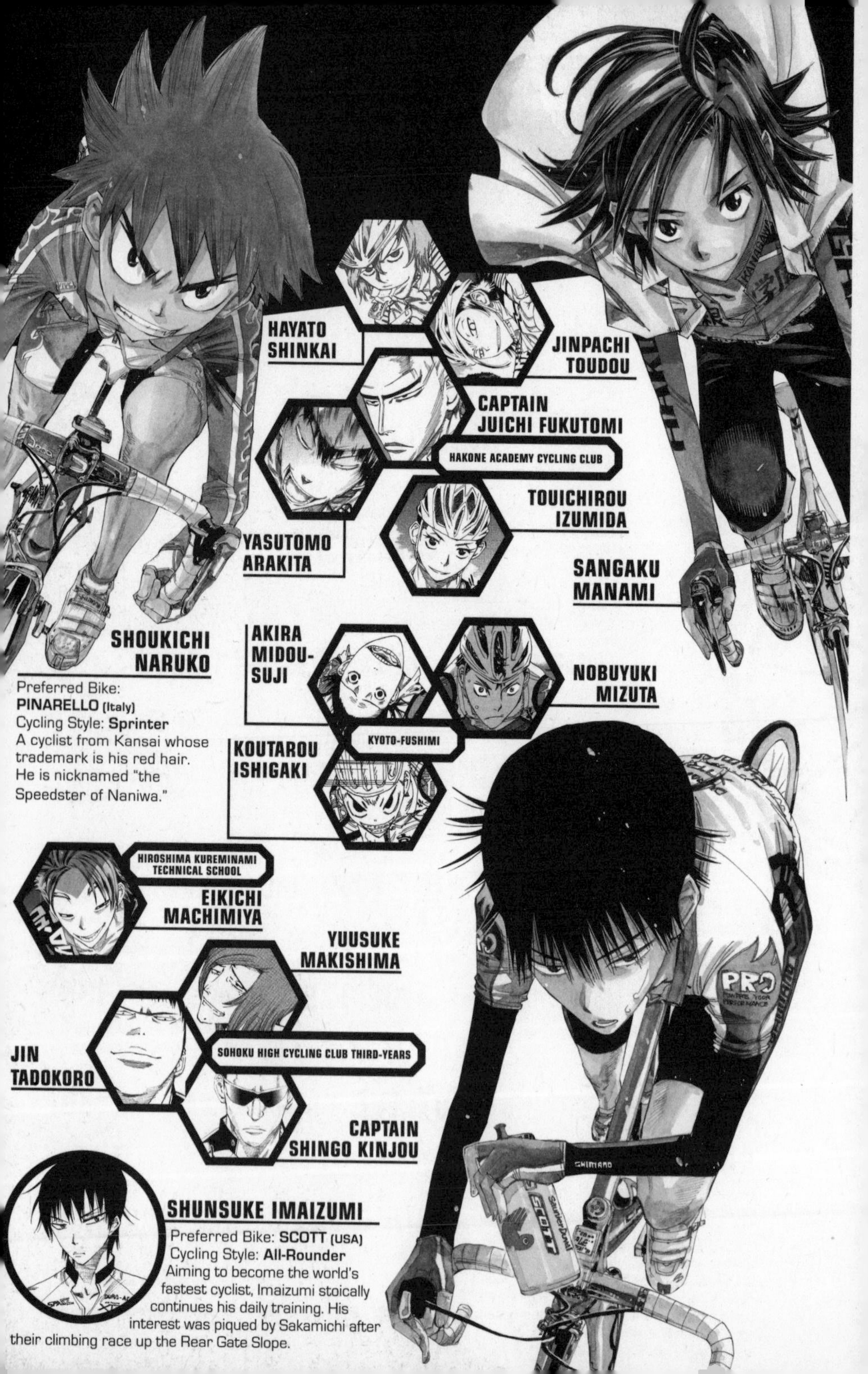
HAYATO
SHINKAI
JINPACHI
TOUDOU
CAPTAIN
JUICHI FUKUTOMI
HAKONE ACADEMY CYCLING CLUB
TOUICHIROU
IZUMIDA
YASUTOMO
ARAKITA
SANGAKU
MANAMI
AKIRA
MIDOU-
SUJI
NOBUYUKI
MIZUTA
KYOTO-FUSHIMI
KOUTAROU
ISHIGAKI
HIROSHIMA KUREMINAMI
TECHNICAL SCHOOL
EIKICHI
MACHIMIYA
YUUSUKE
MAKISHIMA
SOHOKU HIGH CYCLING CLUB THIRD-YEARS
JIN
TADOKORO
CAPTAIN
SHINGO KINJOU
PRO

SHOUKICHI NARUKO

Preferred Bike: **PINARELLO (Italy)**
Cycling Style: **Sprinter**
A cyclist from Kansai whose trademark is his red hair. He is nicknamed "the Speedster of Naniwa."

SHUNSUKE IMAIZUMI

Preferred Bike: **SCOTT (USA)**
Cycling Style: **All-Rounder**
Aiming to become the world's fastest cyclist, Imaizumi stoically continues his daily training. His interest was piqued by Sakamichi after their climbing race up the Rear Gate Slope.

VOL.11

YOWAMUSHI PEDAL
CONTENTS

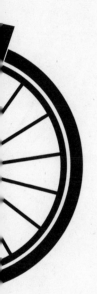

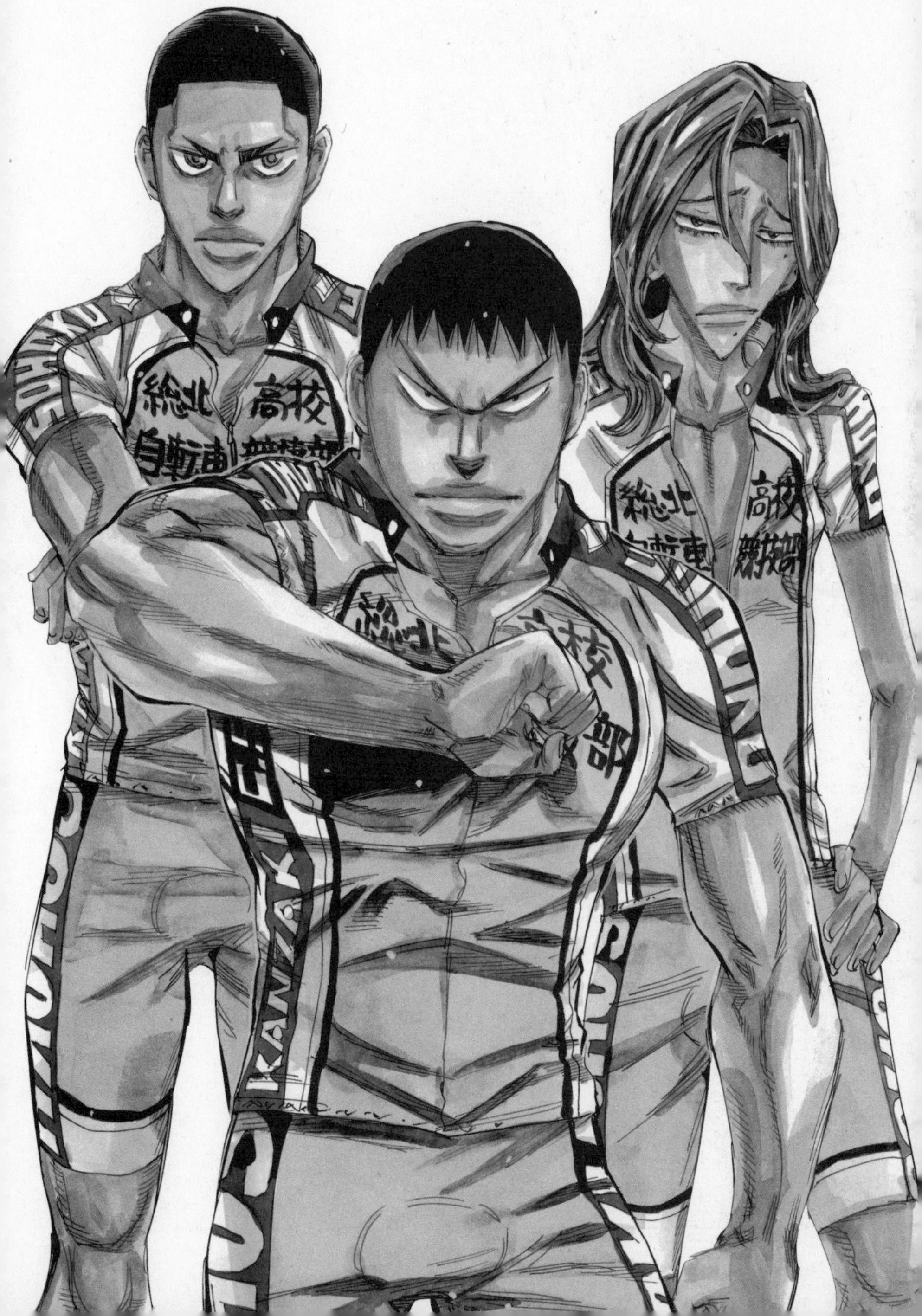
総北 高校
自転車 競技部
総北 高校
自転車 競技部

RIDE.173 GRUDGE-POWERED BOOST

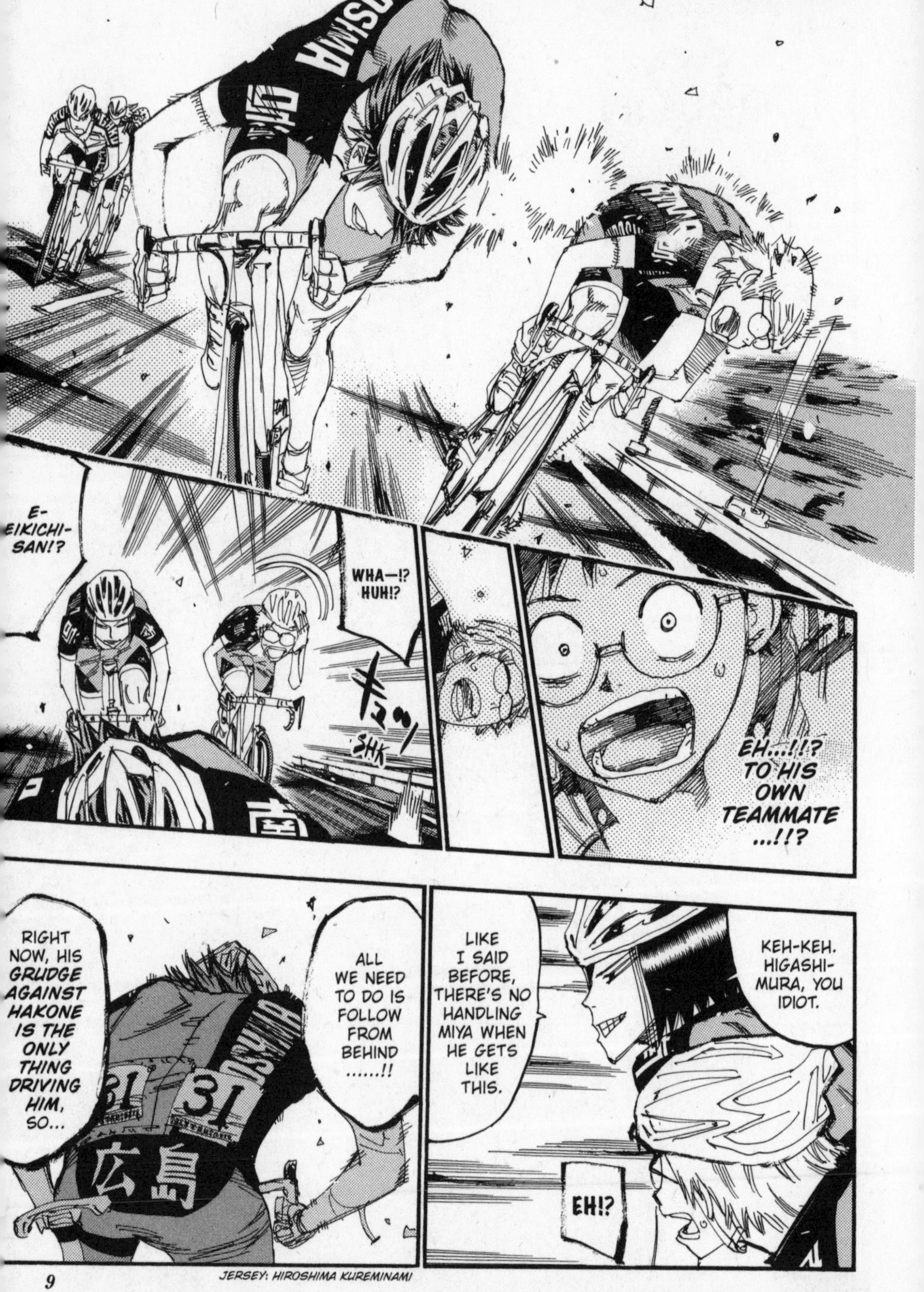
EH...!!? TO HIS OWN TEAMMATE ...!!?
WHA—!? HUH!?
SHK
E-EIKICHI-SAN!?
KEH-KEH. HIGASHI-MURA, YOU IDIOT.
LIKE I SAID BEFORE, THERE'S NO HANDLING MIYA WHEN HE GETS LIKE THIS.
EH!?
ALL WE NEED TO DO IS FOLLOW FROM BEHIND ......!!
RIGHT NOW, HIS GRUDGE AGAINST HAKONE IS THE ONLY THING DRIVING HIM, SO...

JERSEY: HIROSHIMA KUREMINAMI

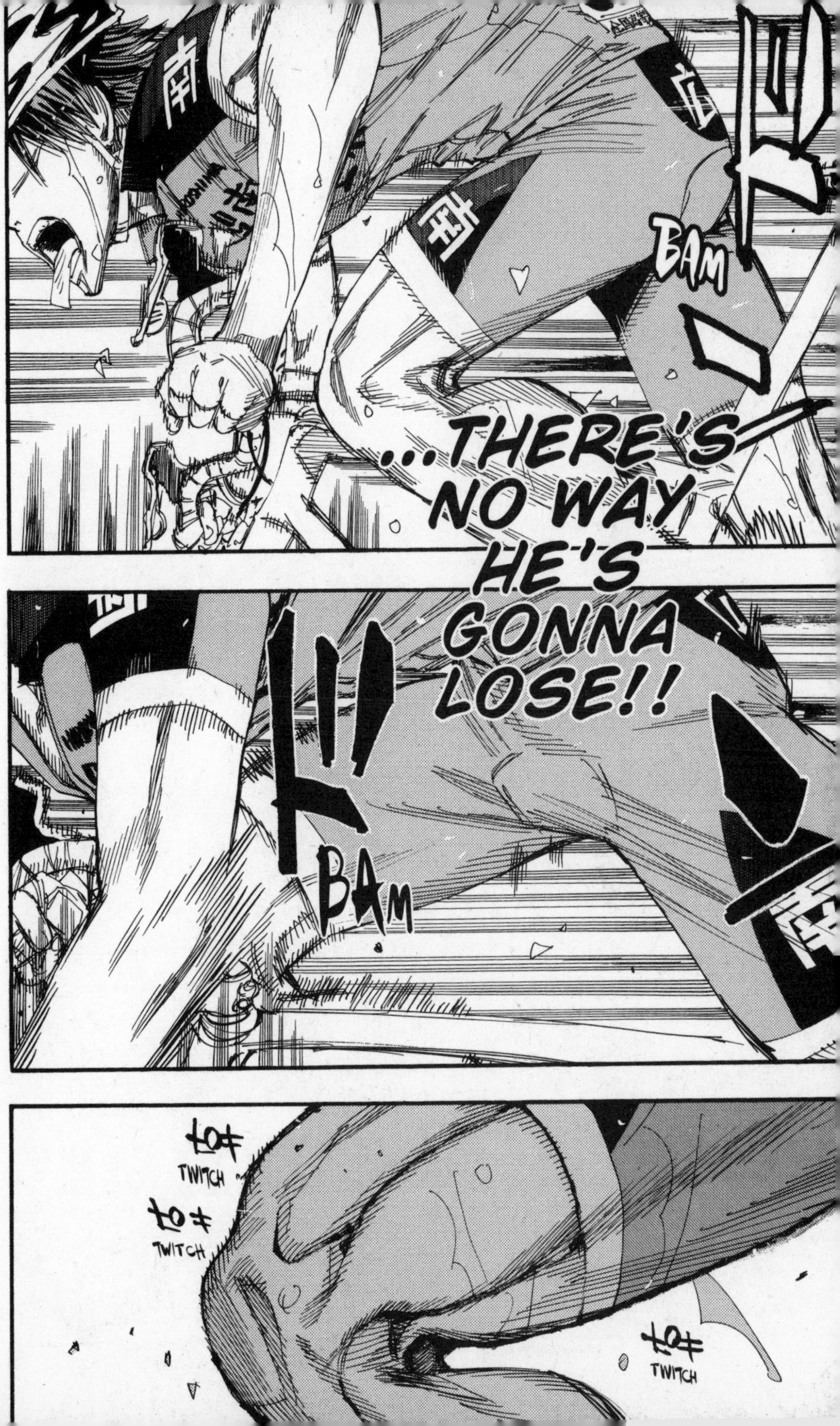
BAM
...THERE'S NO WAY HE'S GONNA LOSE!!
BAM
TWITCH
TWITCH
TWITCH

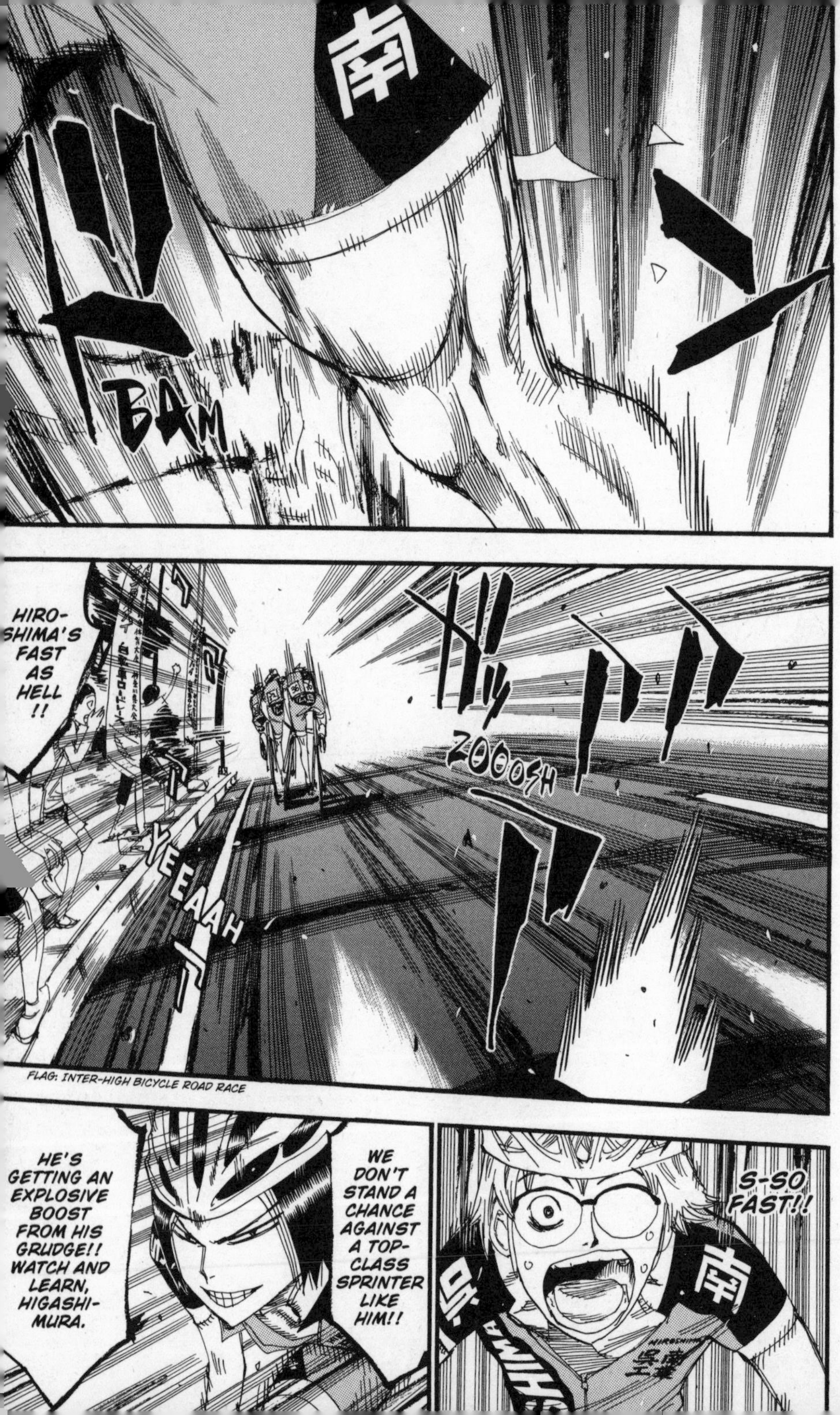
BAM
ZOOOSH
YEEAAH
HIRO-SHIMA'S FAST AS HELL!!
FLAG: INTER-HIGH BICYCLE ROAD RACE
S-SO FAST!!
WE DON'T STAND A CHANCE AGAINST A TOP-CLASS SPRINTER LIKE HIM!!
HE'S GETTING AN EXPLOSIVE BOOST FROM HIS GRUDGE!! WATCH AND LEARN, HIGASHI-MURA.

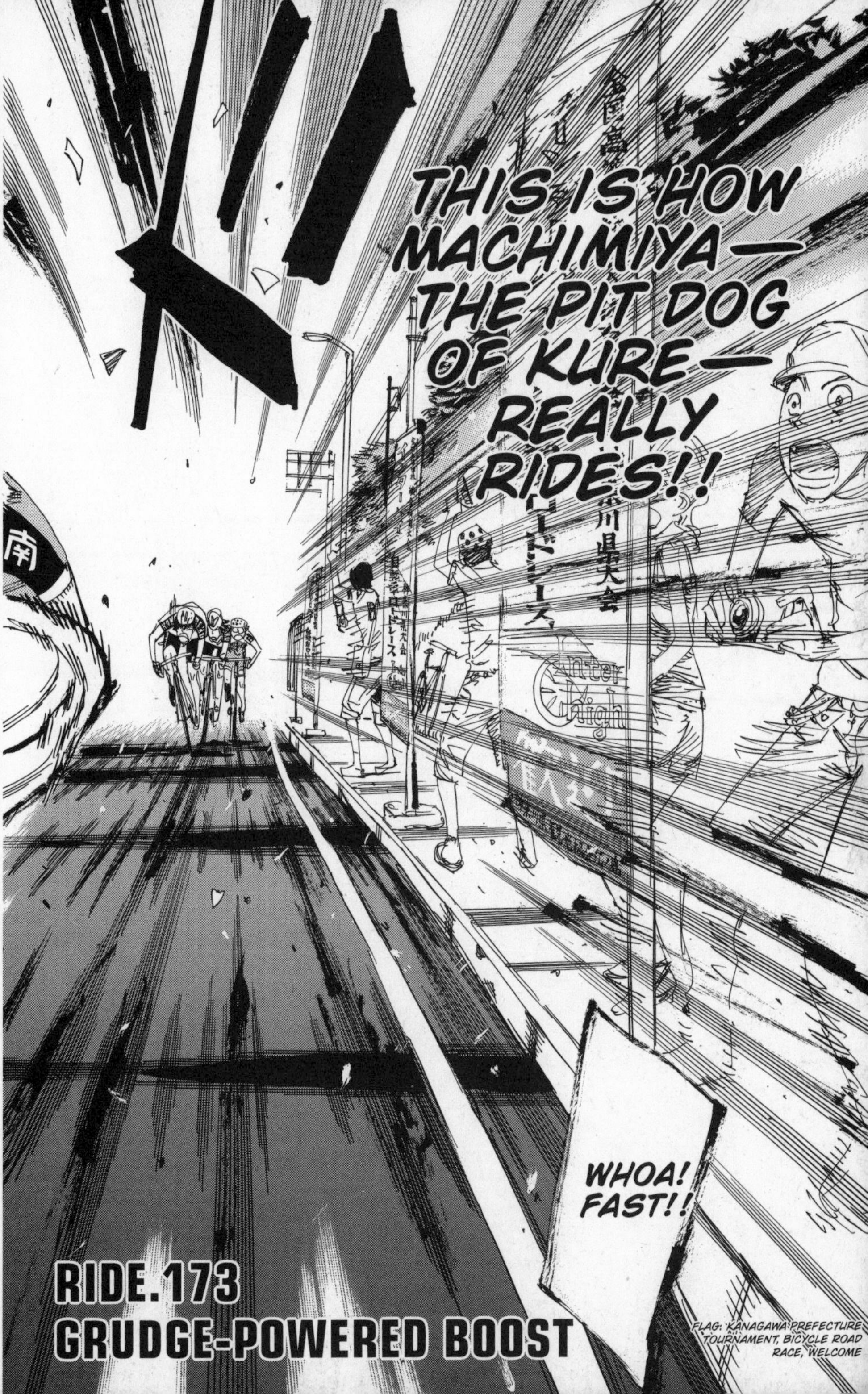
THIS IS HOW MACHIMIYA— THE PIT DOG OF KURE— REALLY RIDES!!
WHOA! FAST!!
RIDE.173
GRUDGE-POWERED BOOST
FLAG: KANAGAWA PREFECTURE TOURNAMENT, BICYCLE ROAD RACE, WELCOME

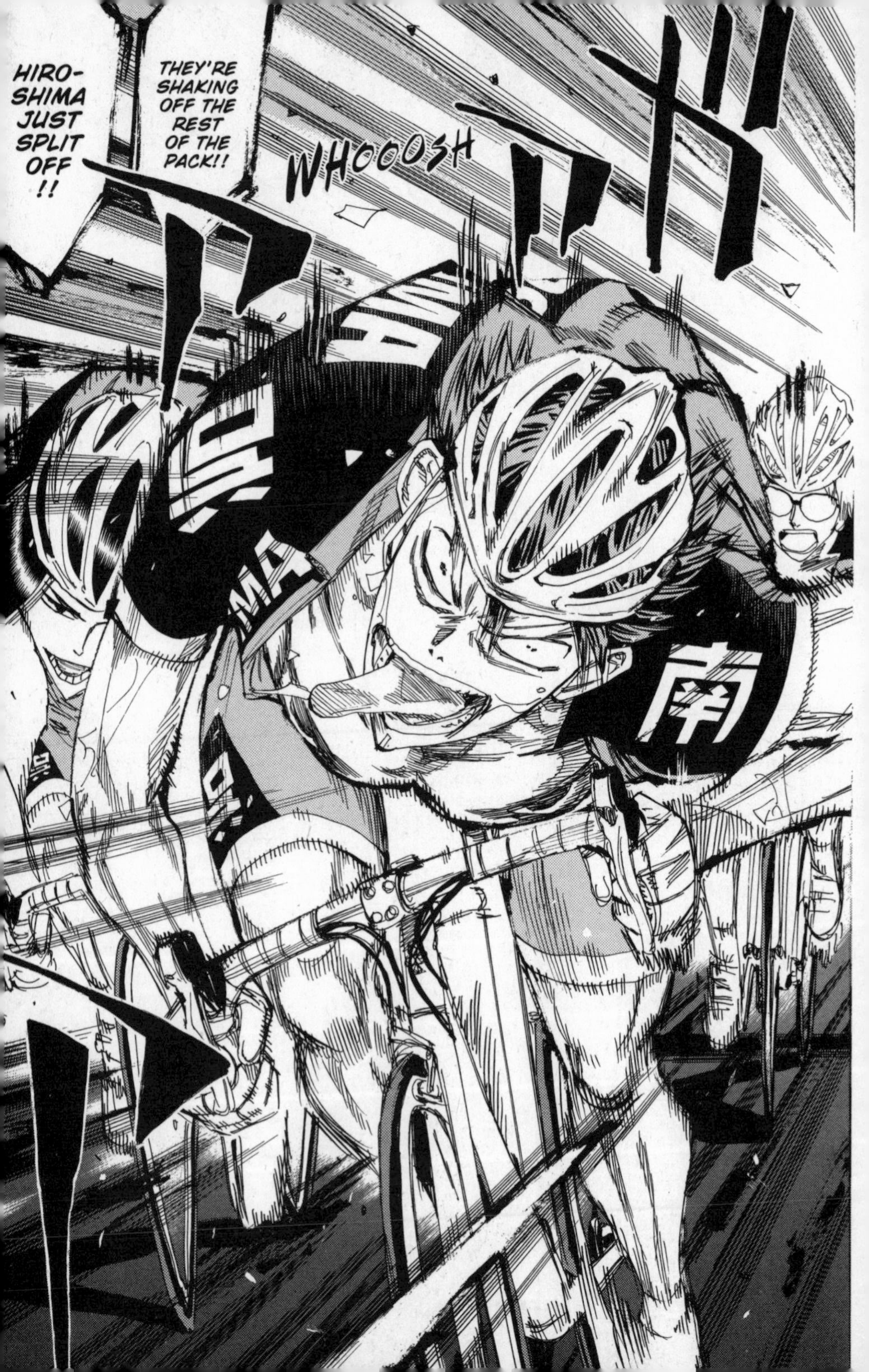
WHOOOSH
THEY'RE SHAKING OFF THE REST OF THE PACK!!
HIRO-SHIMA JUST SPLIT OFF!!

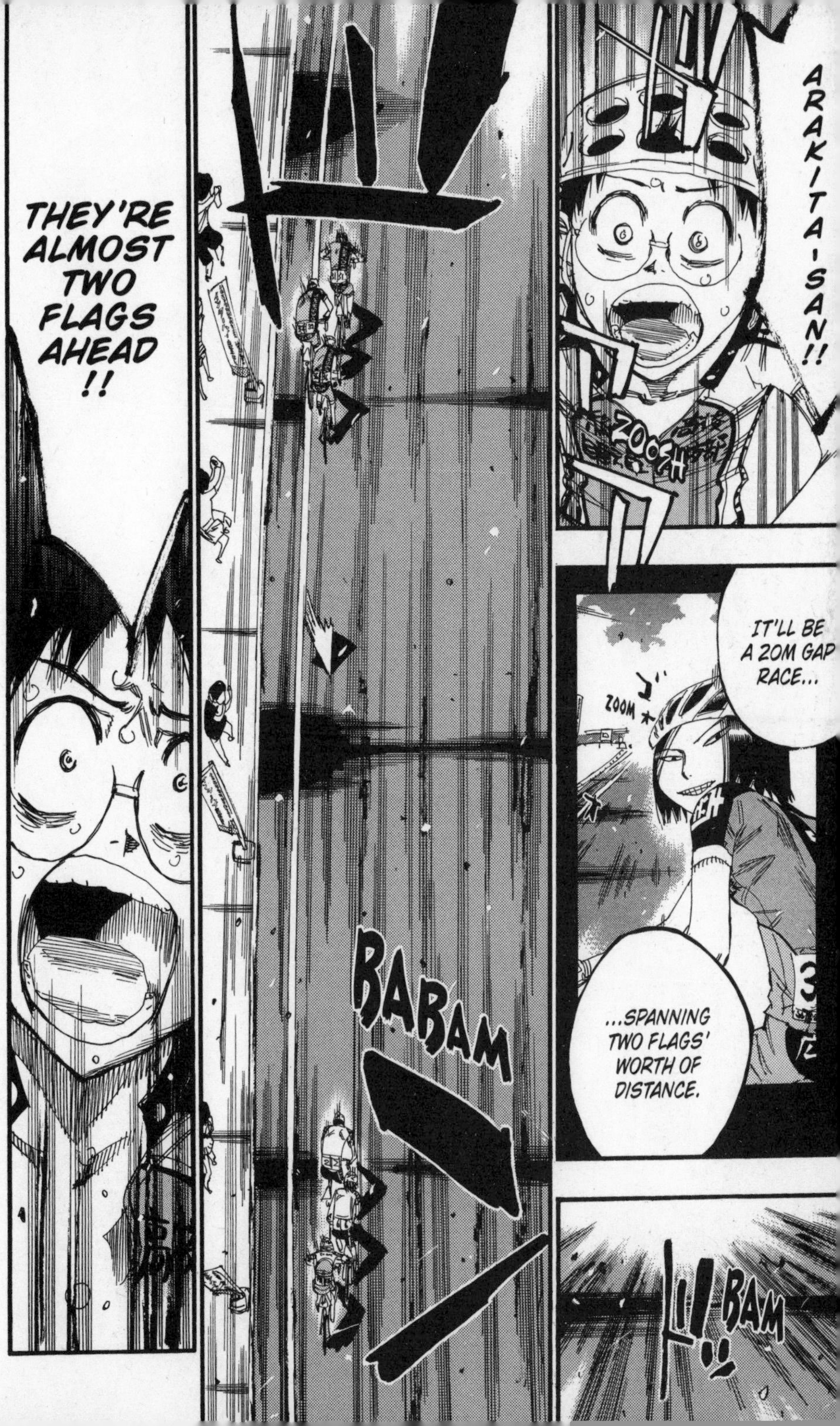
ARAKITA-SAN!!
ZOOSH
IT'LL BE A 20M GAP RACE...
ZOOM
...SPANNING TWO FLAGS' WORTH OF DISTANCE.
BAM
BABAM
THEY'RE ALMOST TWO FLAGS AHEAD!!

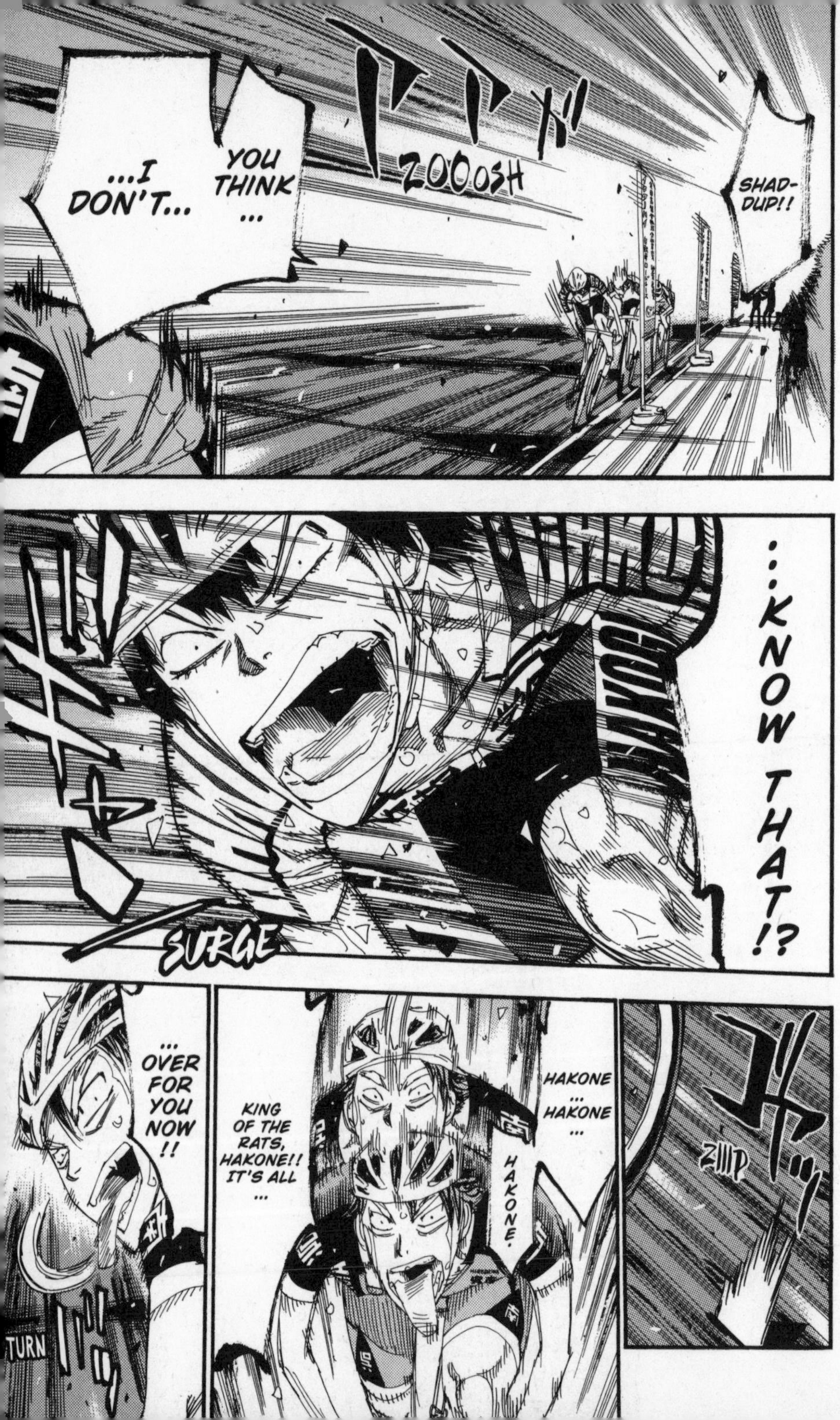
SHAD-DUP!!
ZOOOSH
YOU THINK ...
...I DON'T...
...KNOW THAT!?
SURGE
ZIIIP
HAKONE ... HAKONE ...
HAKONE.
KING OF THE RATS, HAKONE!! IT'S ALL ...
... OVER FOR YOU NOW!!
TURN

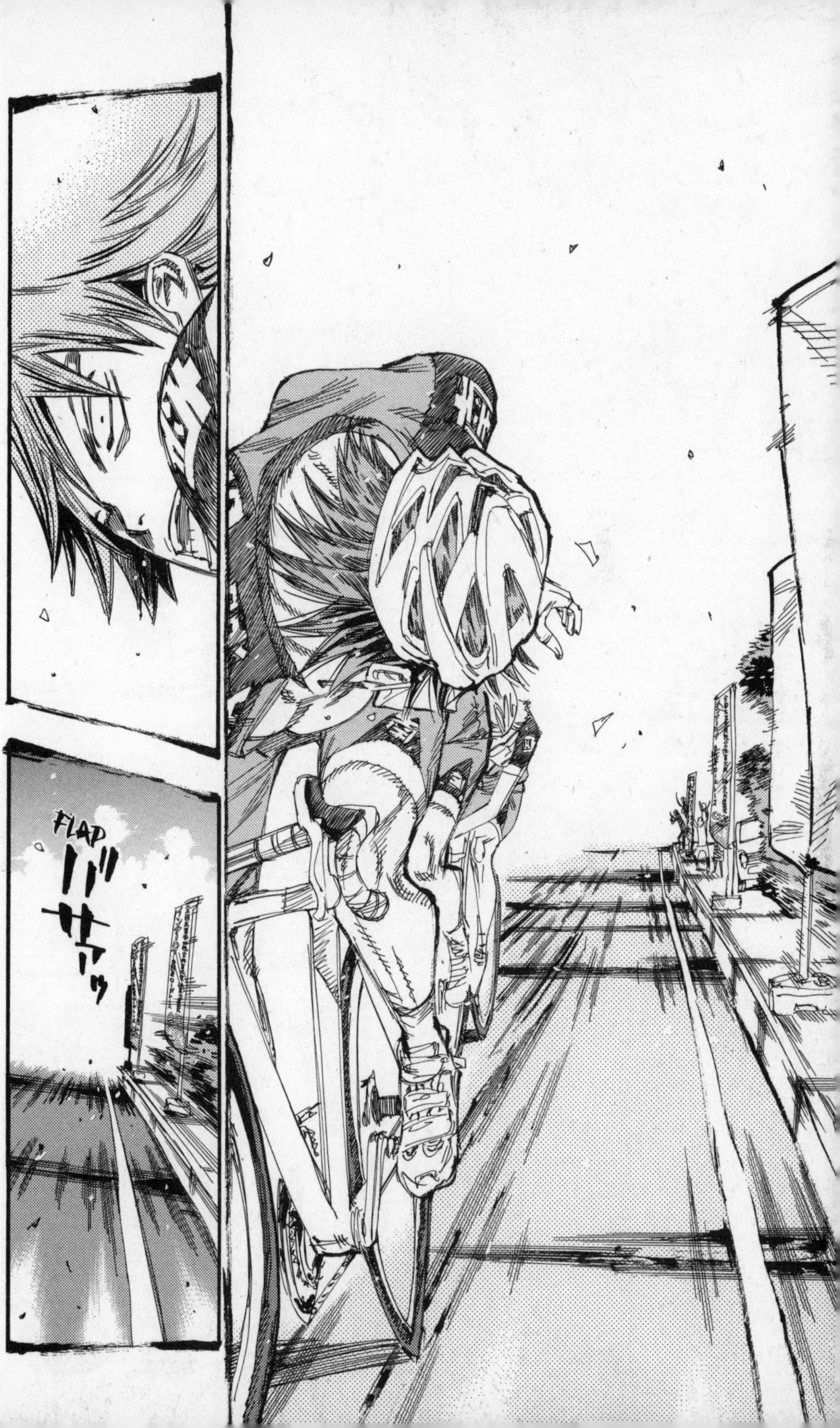
FLAP
バサァッ

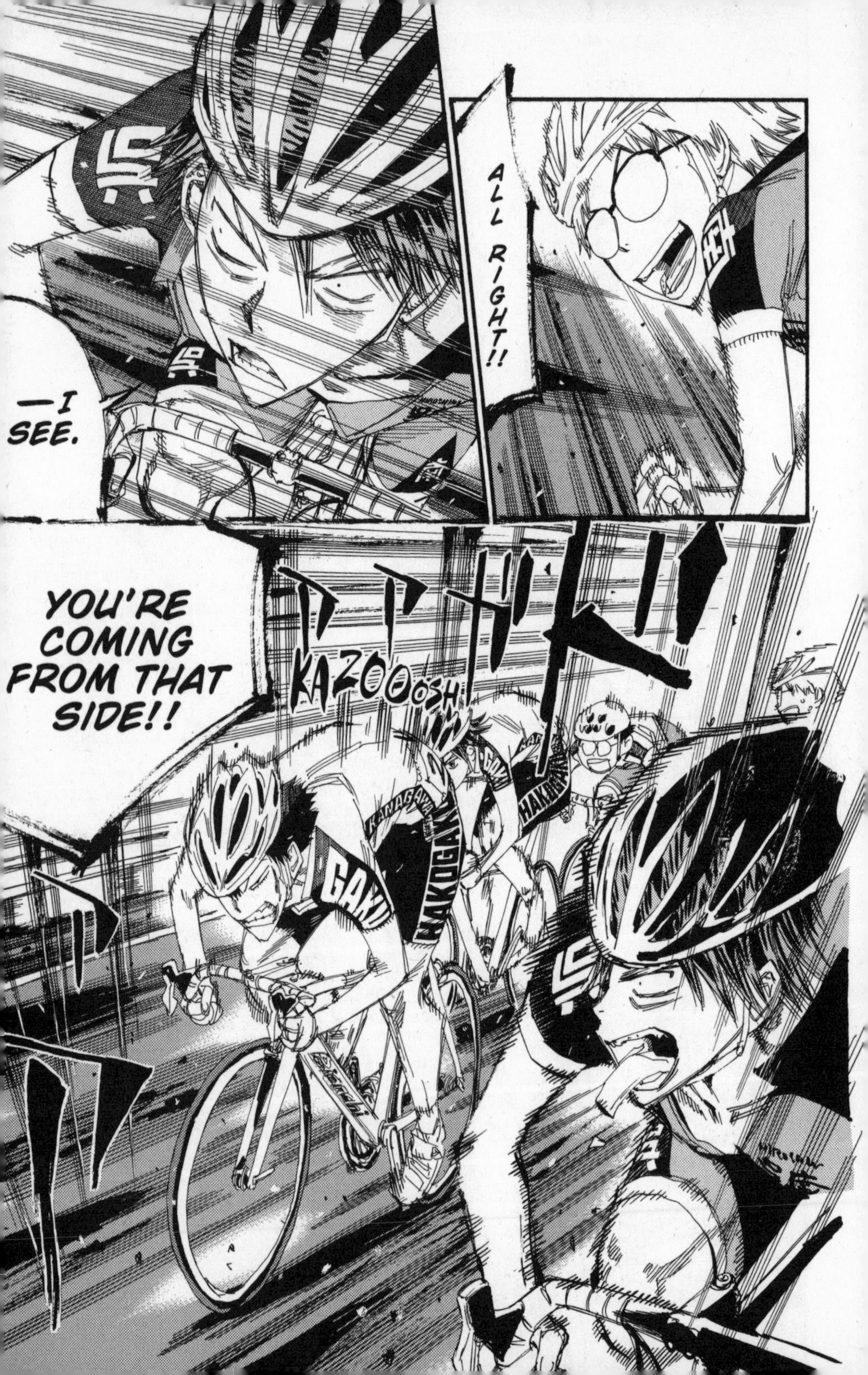
ALL RIGHT!!
—I SEE.
YOU'RE COMING FROM THAT SIDE!!
KAZOOOOSH

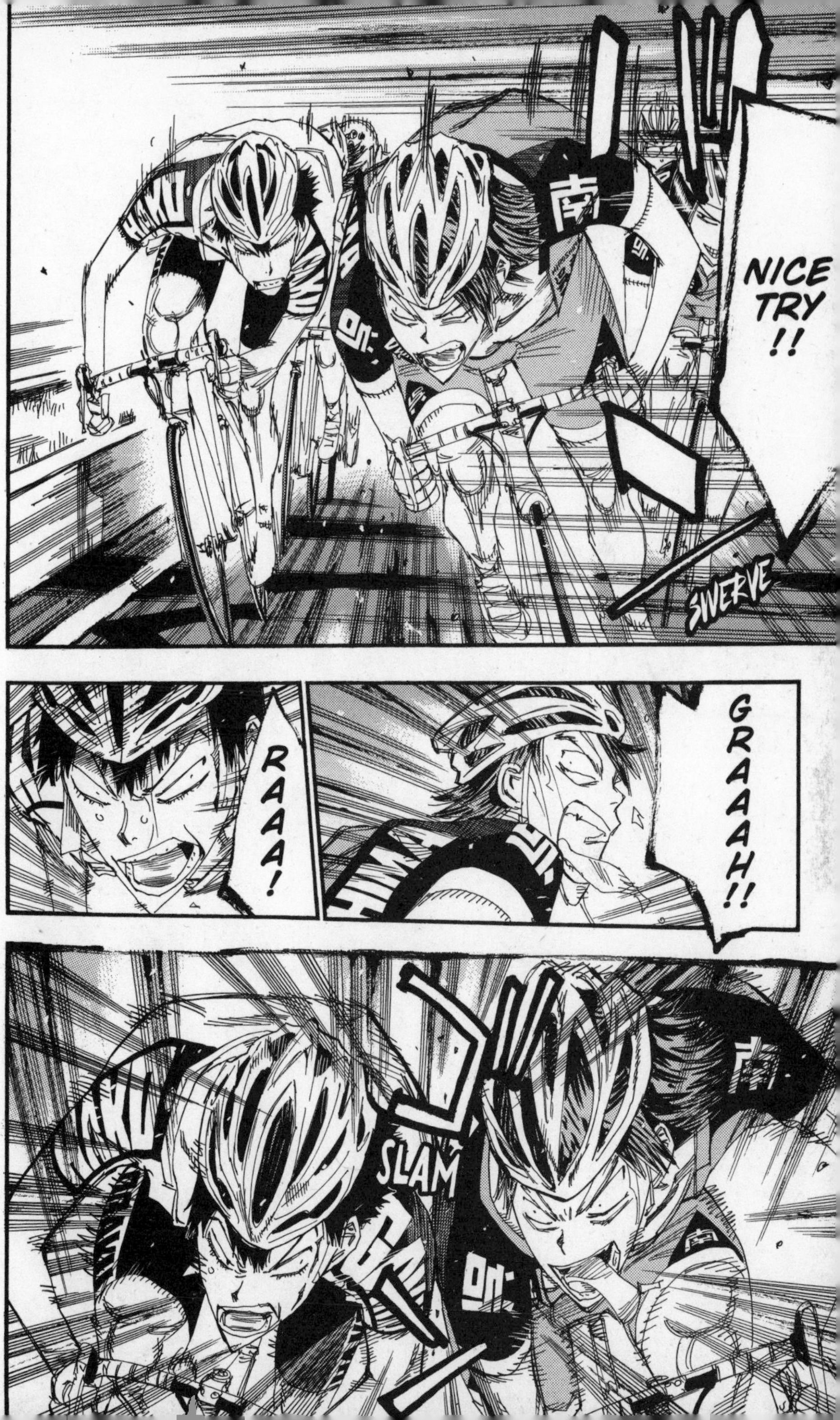
NICE TRY!!
SWERVE
GRAAAAH!!
RAAAA!
SLAM

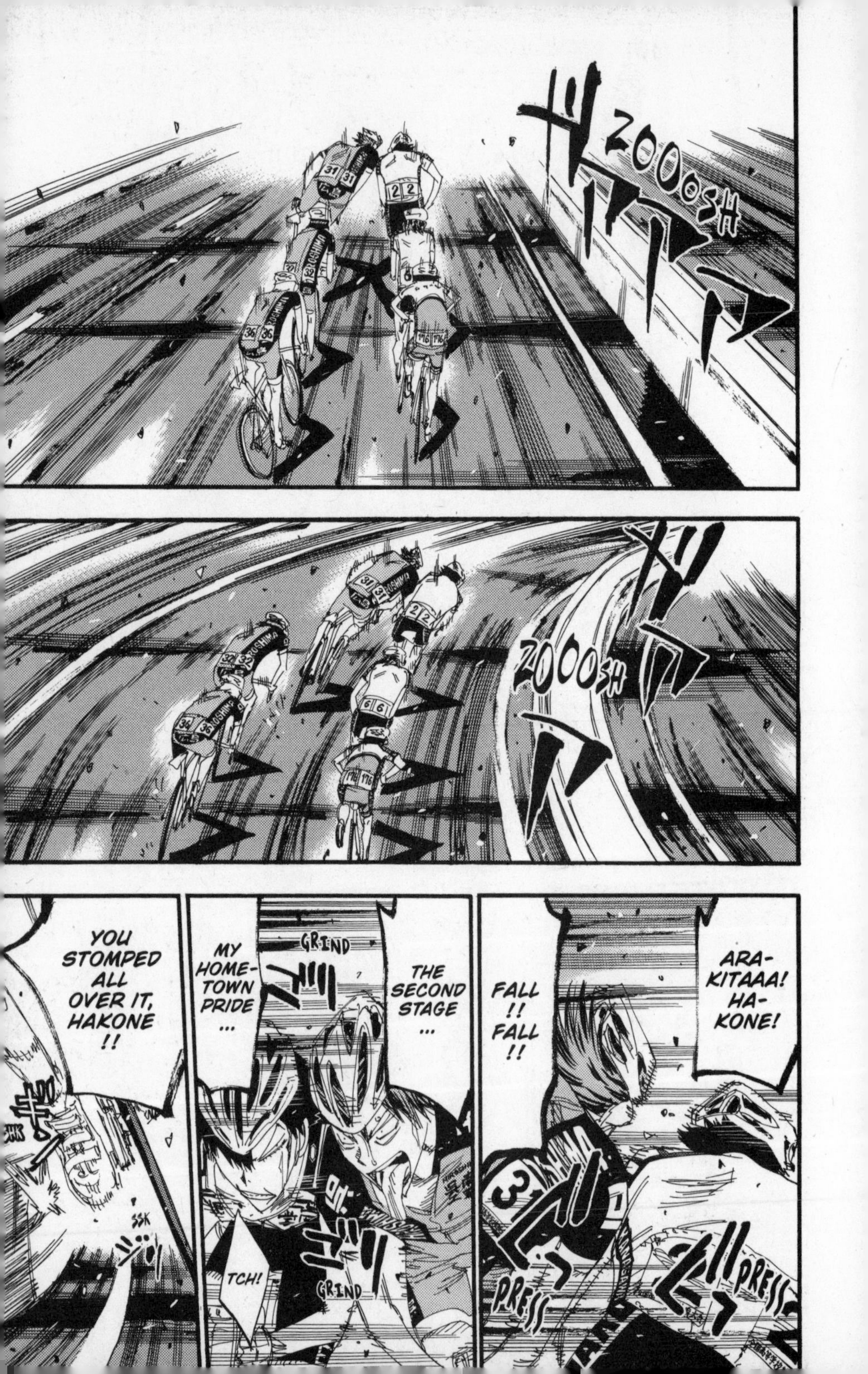
ZOOOSH
ZOOOSH
ARA-KITAAA! HA-KONE!
FALL!! FALL!!
PRESS
PRESS
THE SECOND STAGE...
MY HOME-TOWN PRIDE...
GRIND
GRIND
TCH!
YOU STOMPED ALL OVER IT, HAKONE!!
SSK

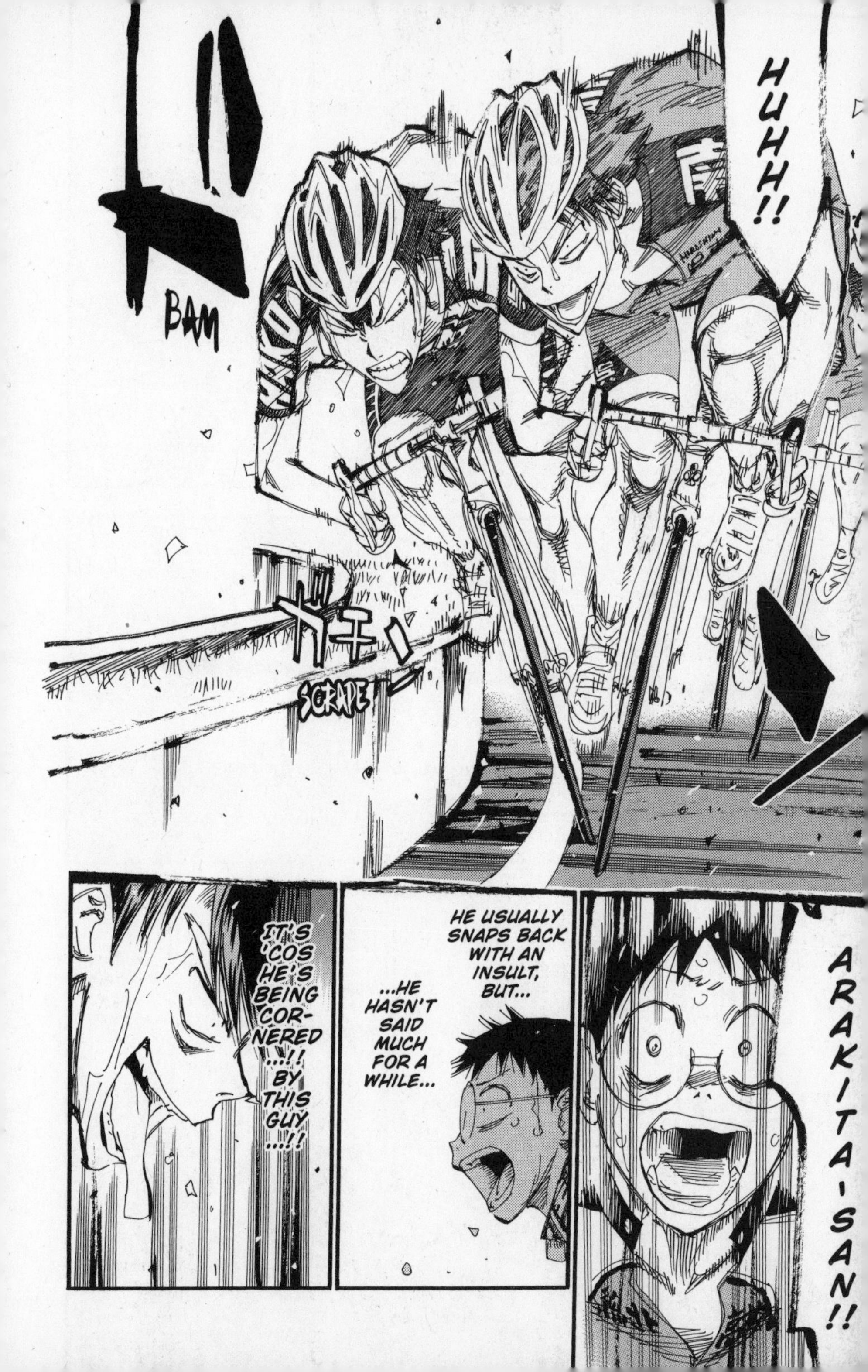
HUHHH!!
BAM
SCRAPE
ARAKITA-SAN!!
HE USUALLY SNAPS BACK WITH AN INSULT, BUT...
...HE HASN'T SAID MUCH FOR A WHILE...
IT'S 'COS HE'S BEING CORNERED...!! BY THIS GUY...!!

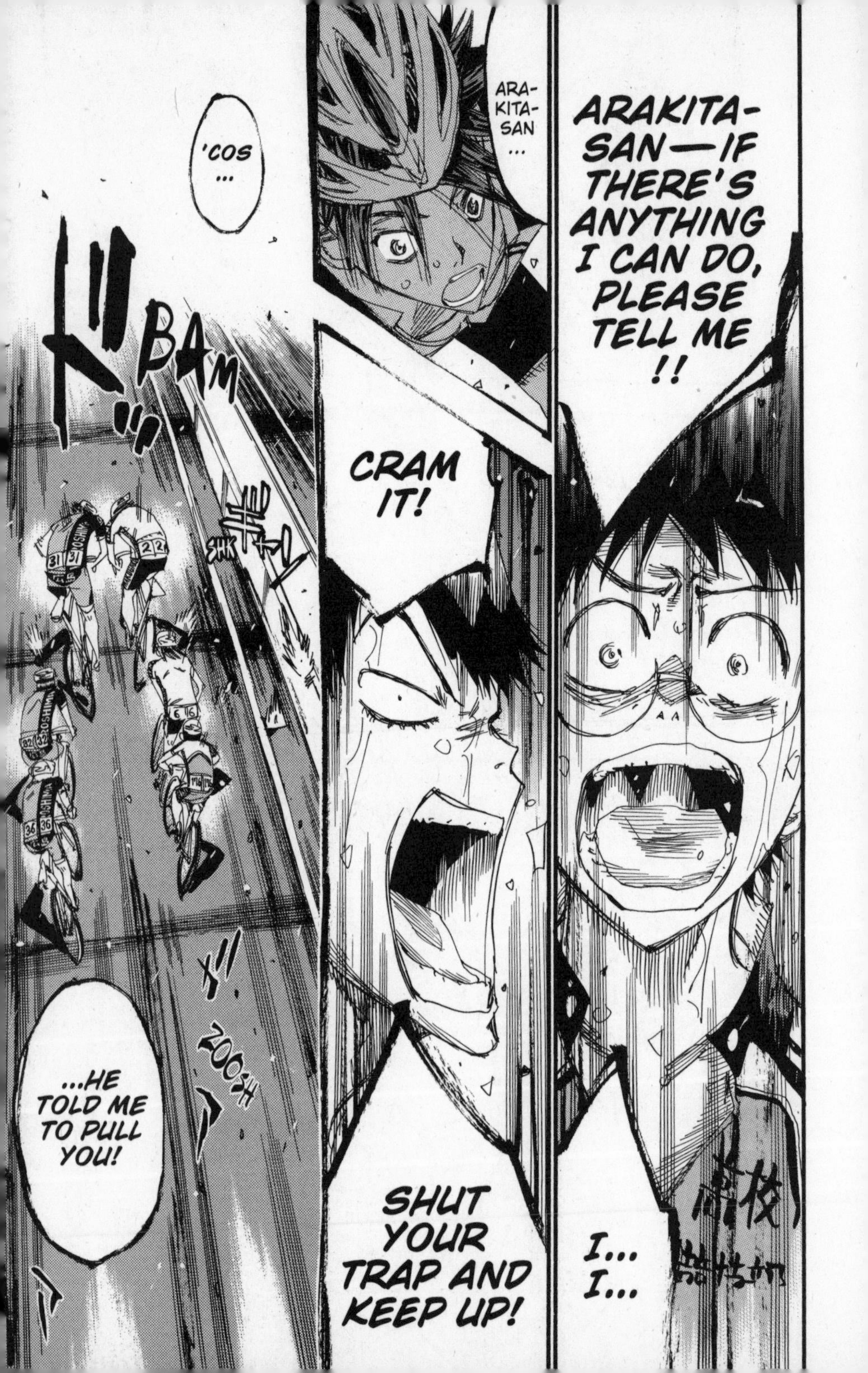
ARAKITA-SAN—IF THERE'S ANYTHING I CAN DO, PLEASE TELL ME!!
I... I...
ARA-KITA-SAN...
CRAM IT!
SHUT YOUR TRAP AND KEEP UP!
'COS...
BAM
SHK
ZOOSH
...HE TOLD ME TO PULL YOU!

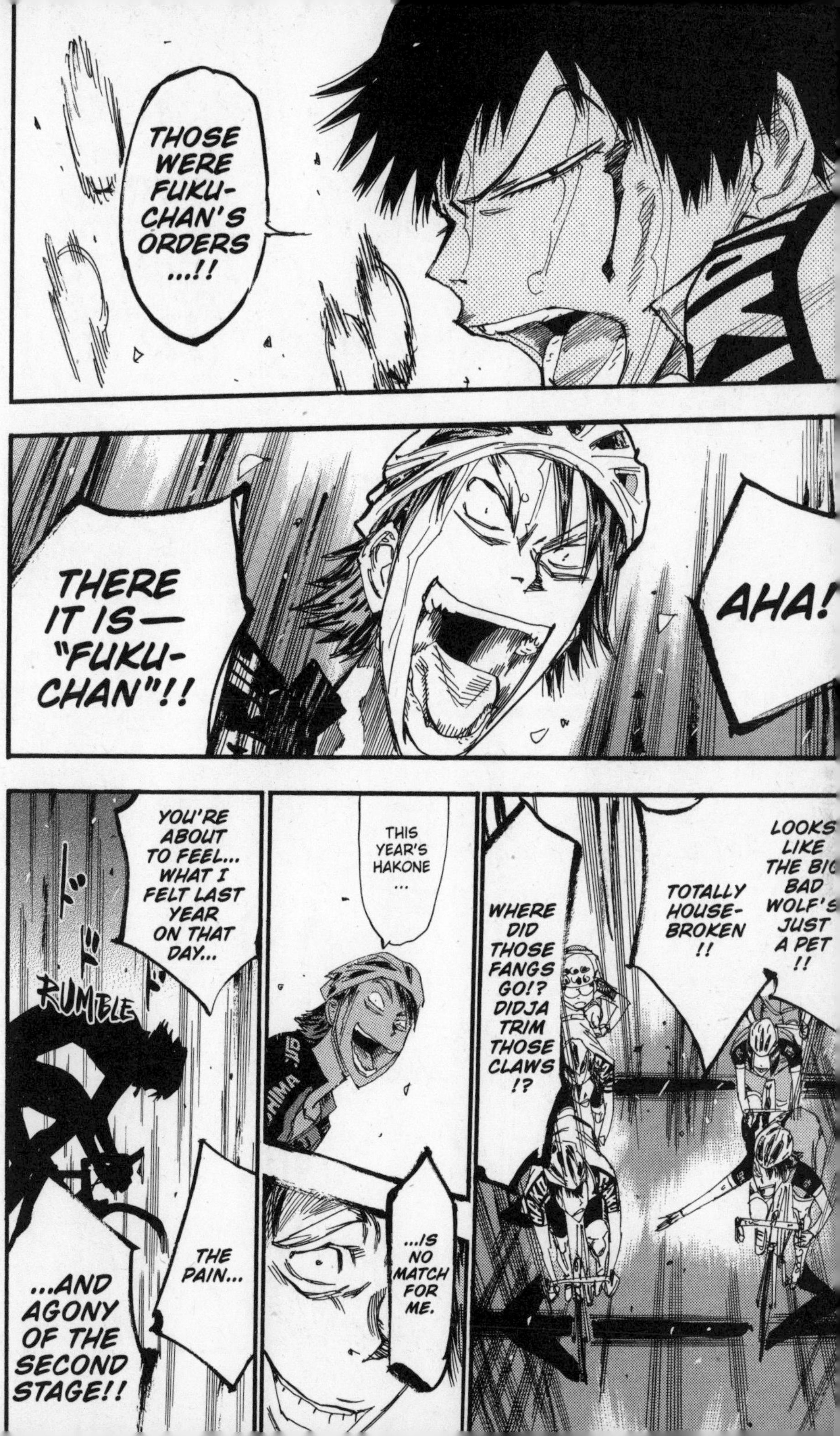
THOSE WERE FUKU-CHAN'S ORDERS ...!!
AHA!
THERE IT IS— "FUKU-CHAN"!!
LOOKS LIKE THE BIG BAD WOLF'S JUST A PET!!
TOTALLY HOUSE-BROKEN!!
WHERE DID THOSE FANGS GO!? DIDJA TRIM THOSE CLAWS!?
THIS YEAR'S HAKONE...
...IS NO MATCH FOR ME.
THE PAIN...
YOU'RE ABOUT TO FEEL... WHAT I FELT LAST YEAR ON THAT DAY...
ドド
RUMBLE
...AND AGONY OF THE SECOND STAGE!!

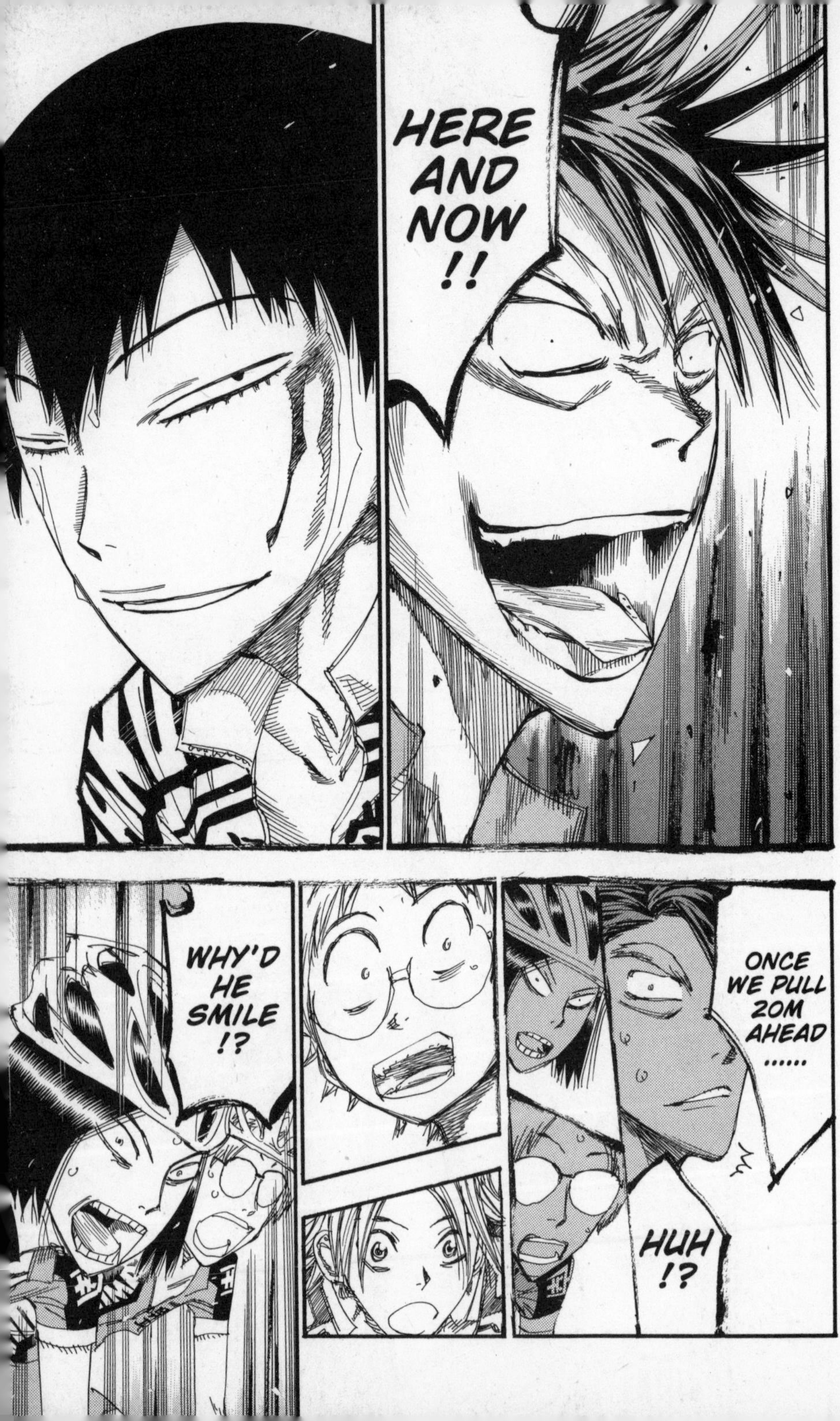
HERE AND NOW !!
ONCE WE PULL 20M AHEAD ......
HUH !?
WHY'D HE SMILE !?

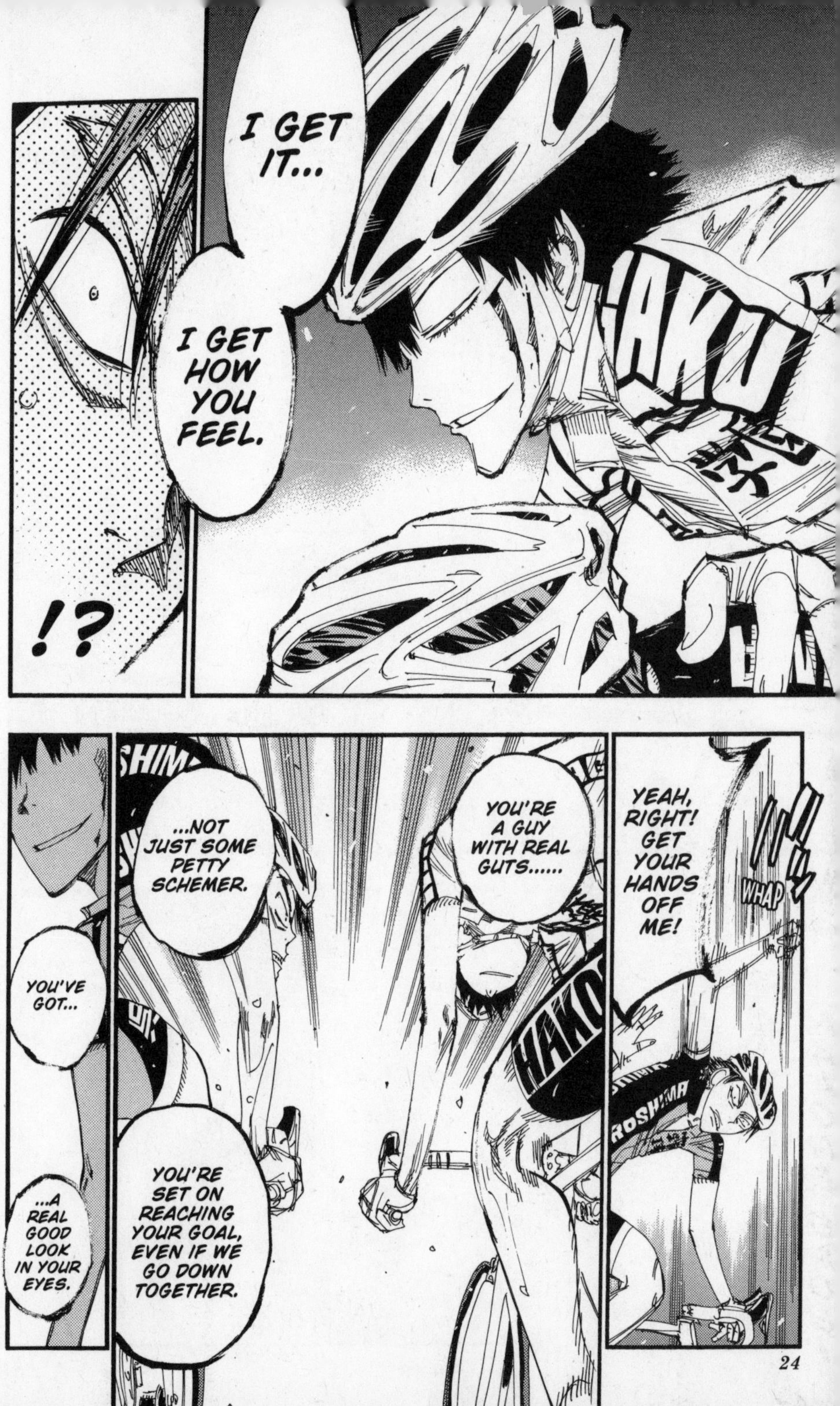
I GET IT...
I GET HOW YOU FEEL.
!?
YEAH, RIGHT! GET YOUR HANDS OFF ME!
WHAP
YOU'RE A GUY WITH REAL GUTS......
...NOT JUST SOME PETTY SCHEMER.
YOU'RE SET ON REACHING YOUR GOAL, EVEN IF WE GO DOWN TOGETHER.
YOU'VE GOT...
...A REAL GOOD LOOK IN YOUR EYES.

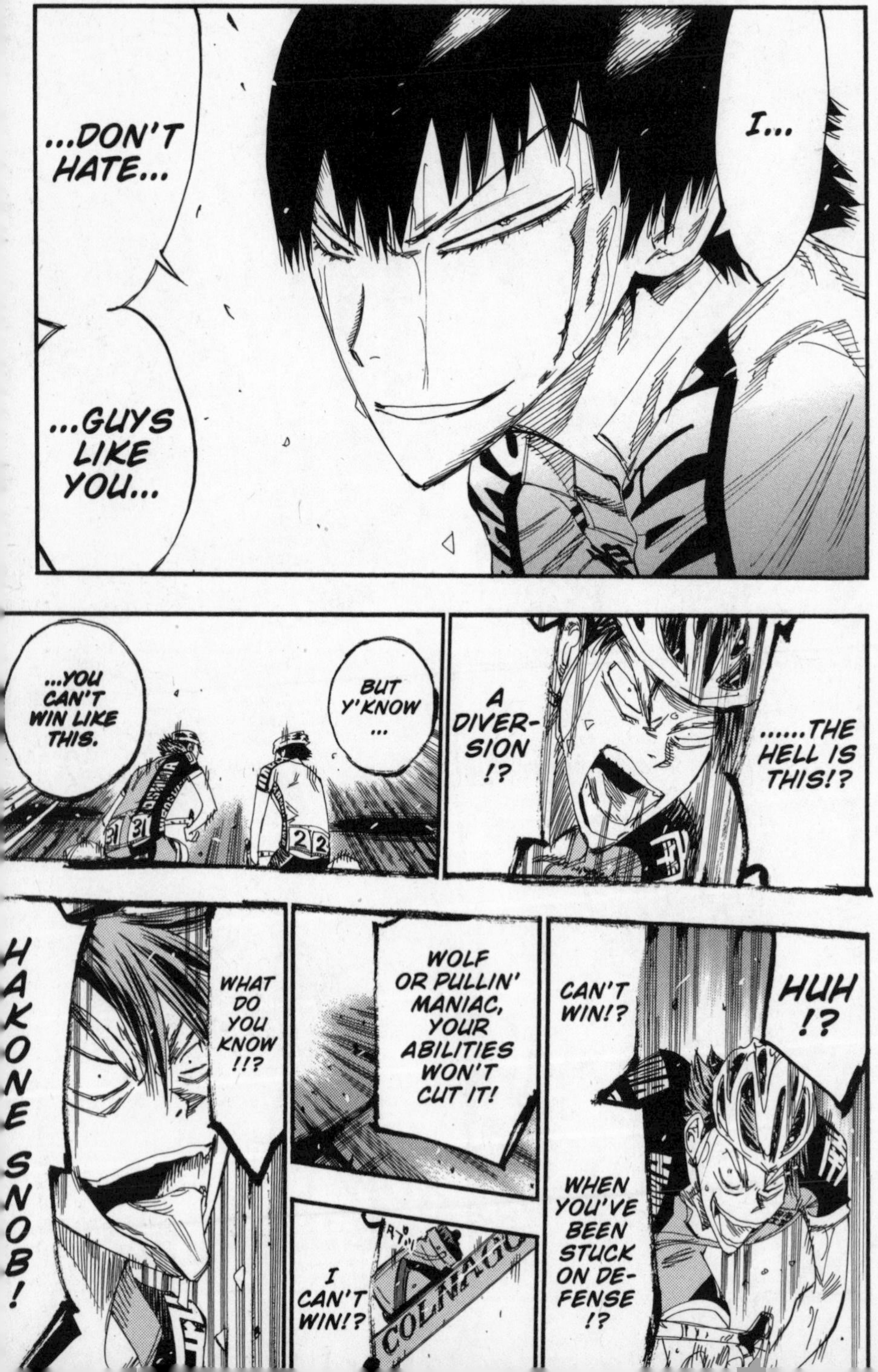
I...
...DON'T HATE...
...GUYS LIKE YOU...
......THE HELL IS THIS!?
A DIVERSION!?
BUT Y'KNOW...
...YOU CAN'T WIN LIKE THIS.
HUH!?
CAN'T WIN!?
WHEN YOU'VE BEEN STUCK ON DEFENSE!?
WOLF OR PULLIN' MANIAC, YOUR ABILITIES WON'T CUT IT!
I CAN'T WIN!?
COLNAGO
WHAT DO YOU KNOW!!?
HAKONE SNOB!

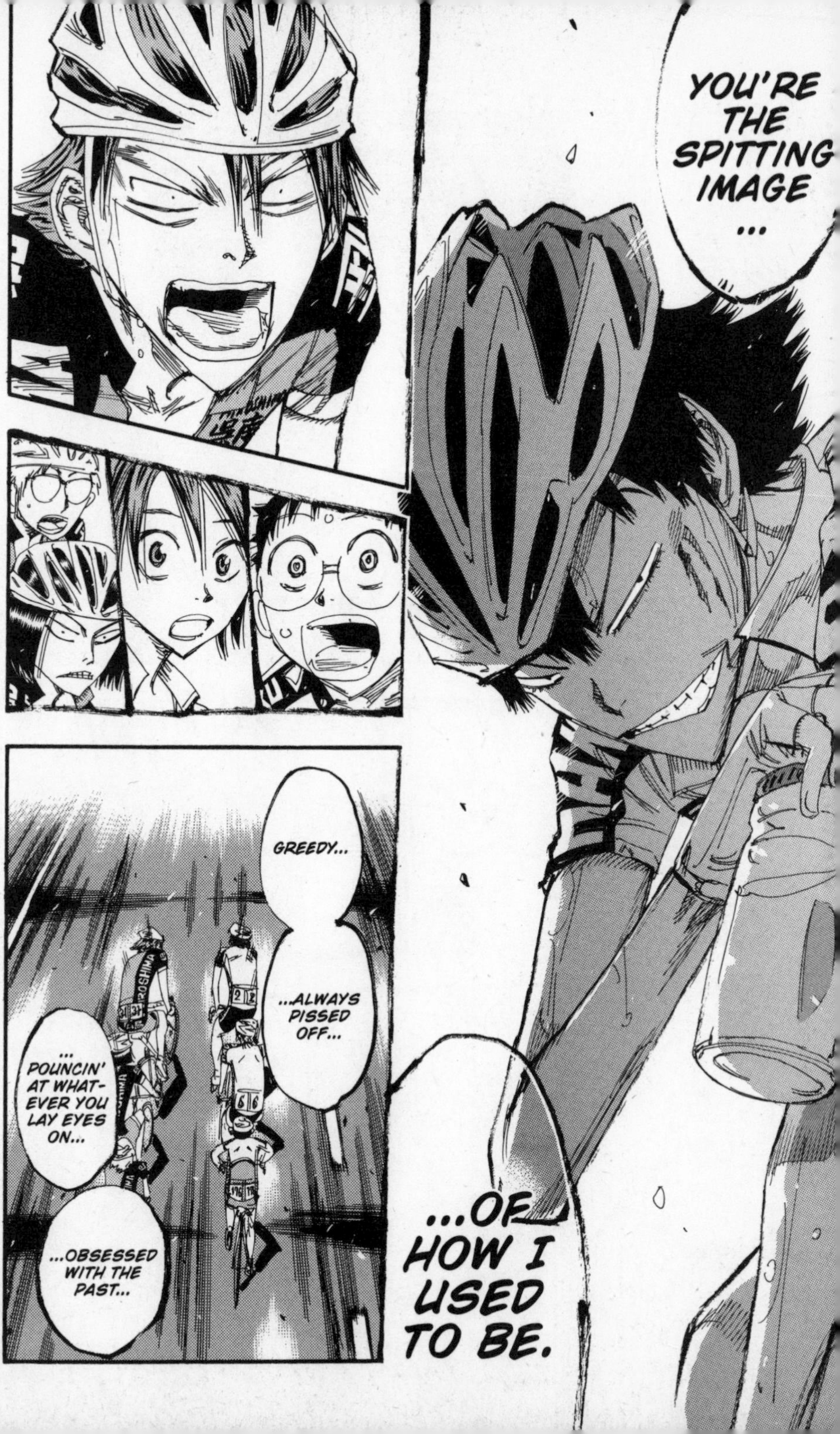
YOU'RE THE SPITTING IMAGE...
...OF HOW I USED TO BE.
GREEDY...
...ALWAYS PISSED OFF...
...POUNCIN' AT WHATEVER YOU LAY EYES ON...
...OBSESSED WITH THE PAST...

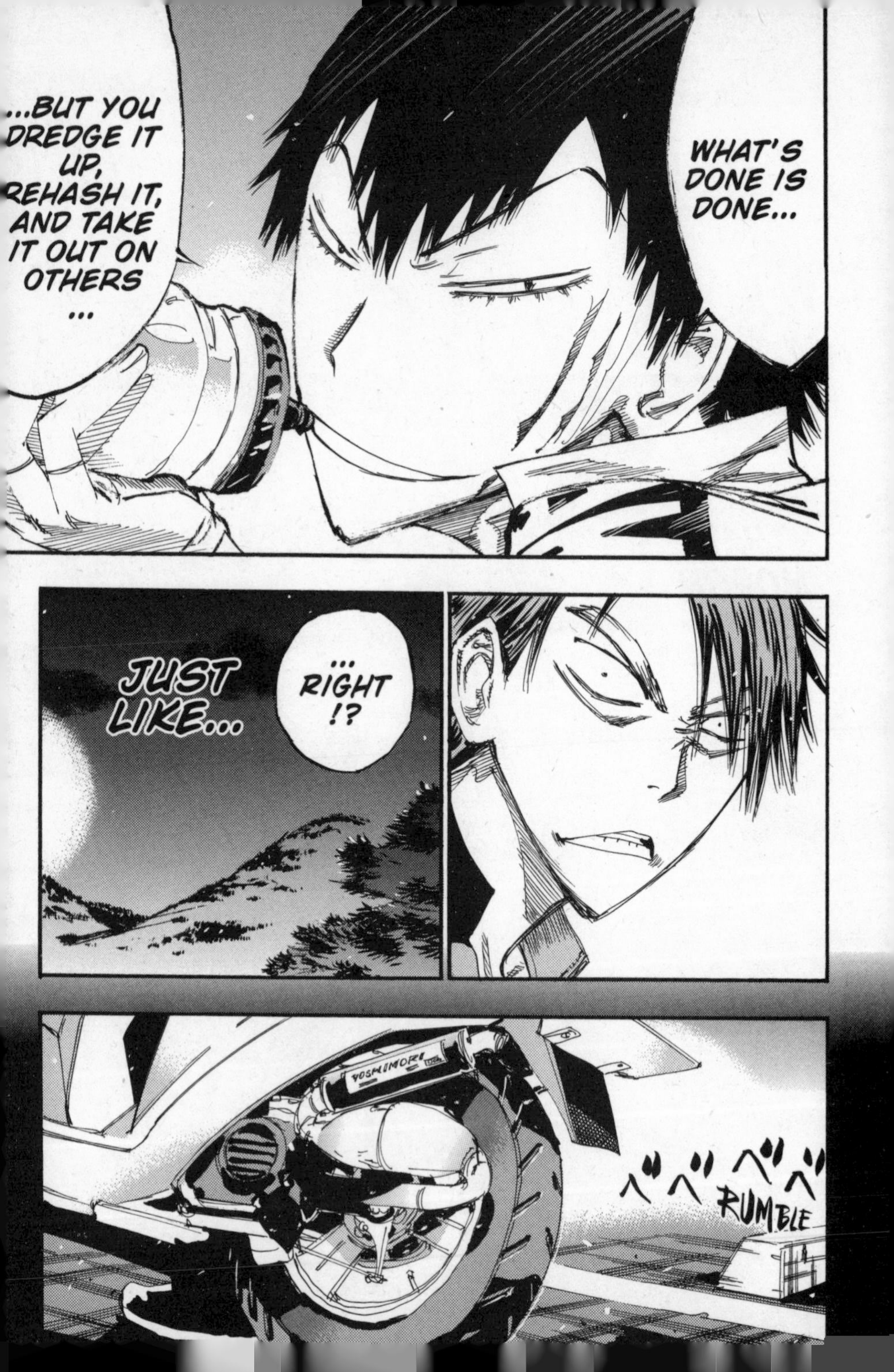
WHAT'S DONE IS DONE...
...BUT YOU DREDGE IT UP, REHASH IT, AND TAKE IT OUT ON OTHERS...
...RIGHT!?
JUST LIKE...
ベベベベ
RUMBLE

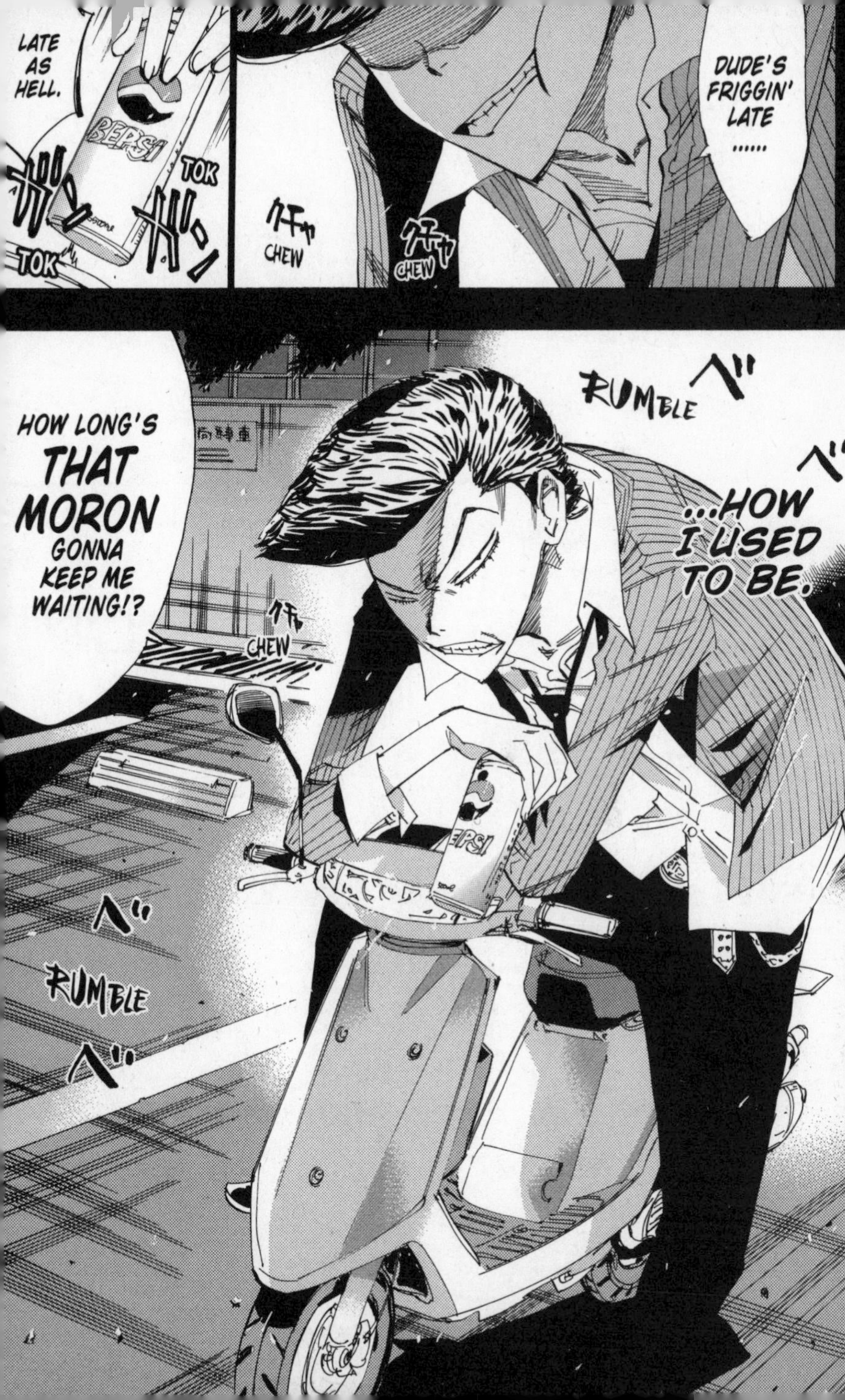
DUDE'S FRIGGIN' LATE ......
CHEW
CHEW
LATE AS HELL.
BEPSI
TOK
TOK
...HOW I USED TO BE.
RUMBLE
HOW LONG'S THAT MORON GONNA KEEP ME WAITING!?
CHEW
BEPSI
RUMBLE

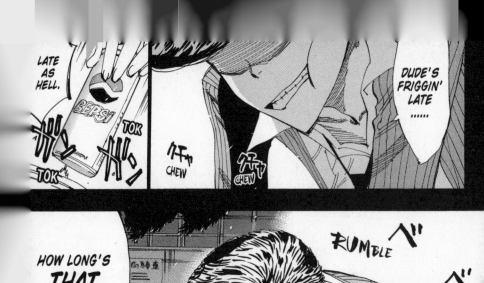

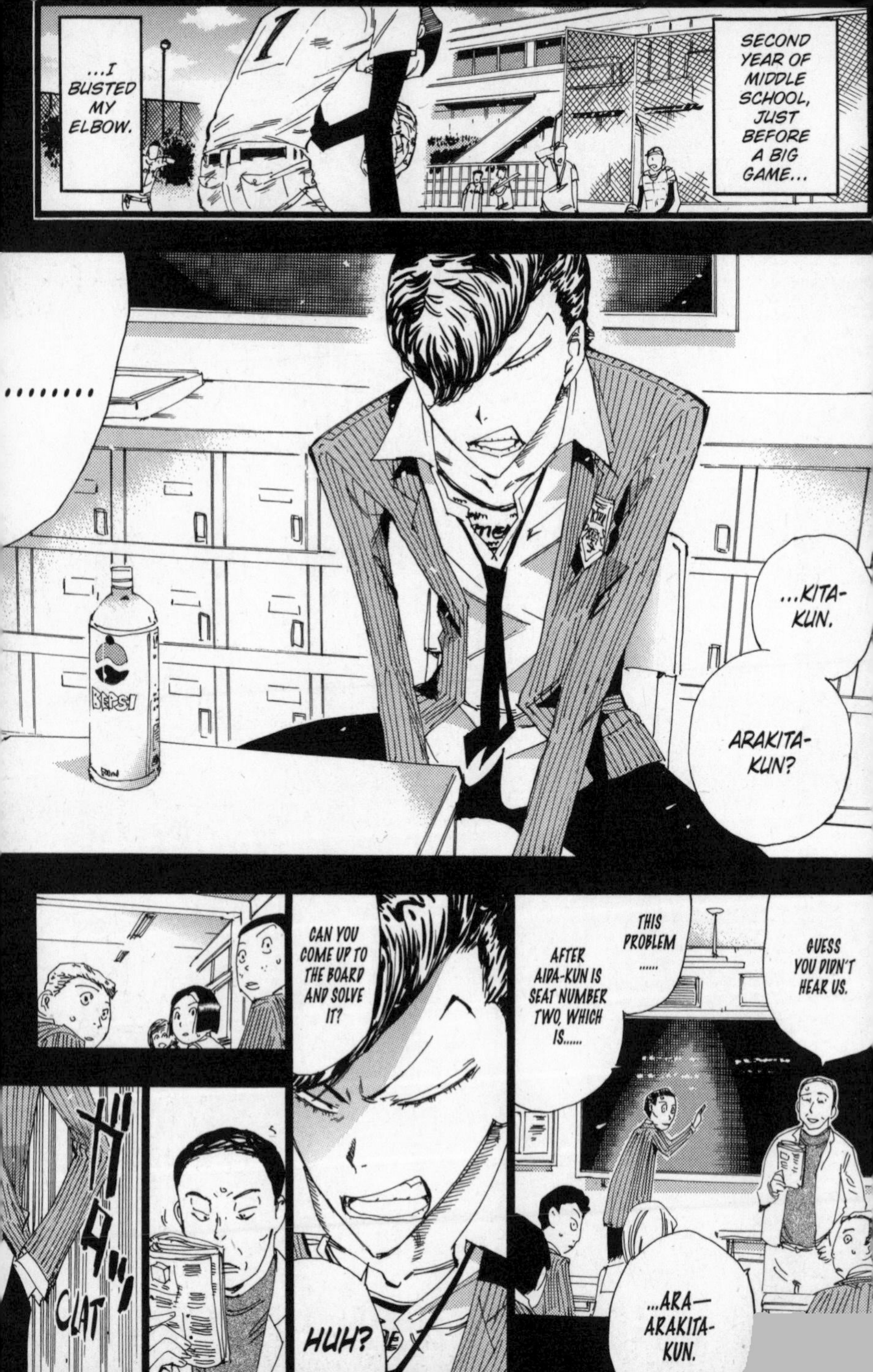
SECOND YEAR OF MIDDLE SCHOOL, JUST BEFORE A BIG GAME...
...I BUSTED MY ELBOW.
...KITA-KUN.
ARAKITA-KUN?
....
GUESS YOU DIDN'T HEAR US.
THIS PROBLEM ......
AFTER AIDA-KUN IS SEAT NUMBER TWO, WHICH IS......
...ARA— ARAKITA-KUN.
CAN YOU COME UP TO THE BOARD AND SOLVE IT?
HUH?
CLAT

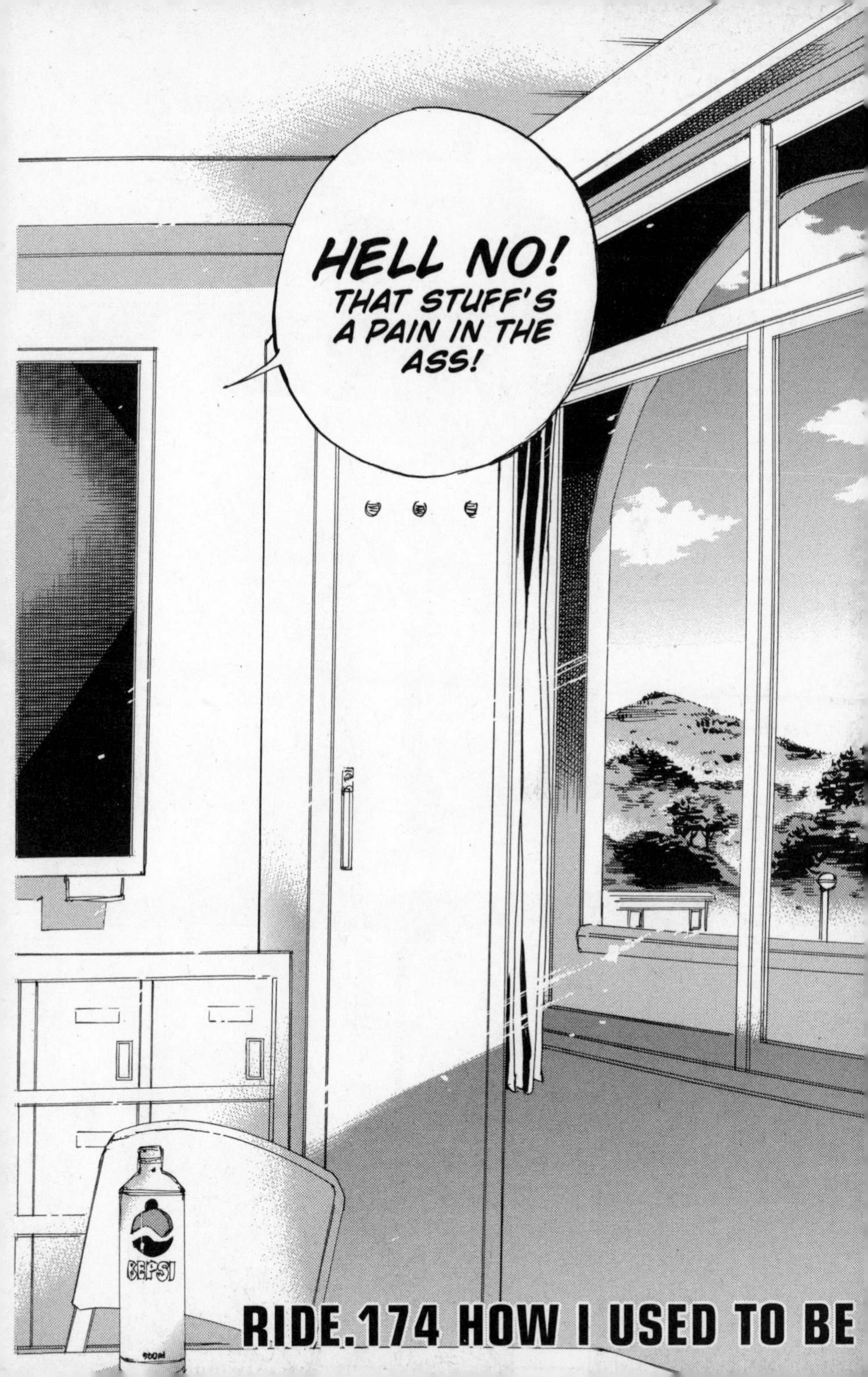
HELL NO! THAT STUFF'S A PAIN IN THE ASS!
BEPSI
RIDE.174 HOW I USED TO BE

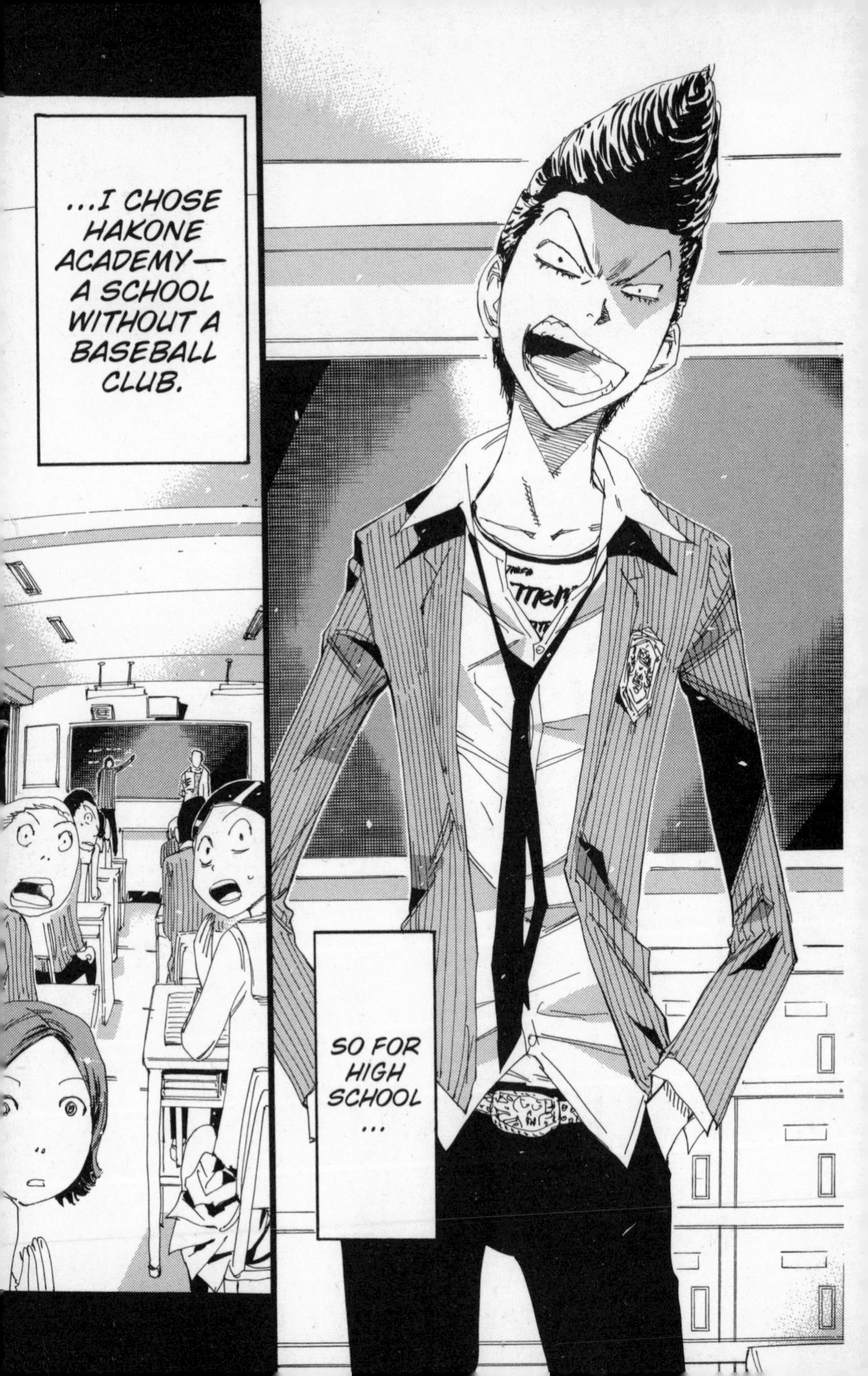
SO FOR HIGH SCHOOL ...
...I CHOSE HAKONE ACADEMY— A SCHOOL WITHOUT A BASEBALL CLUB.

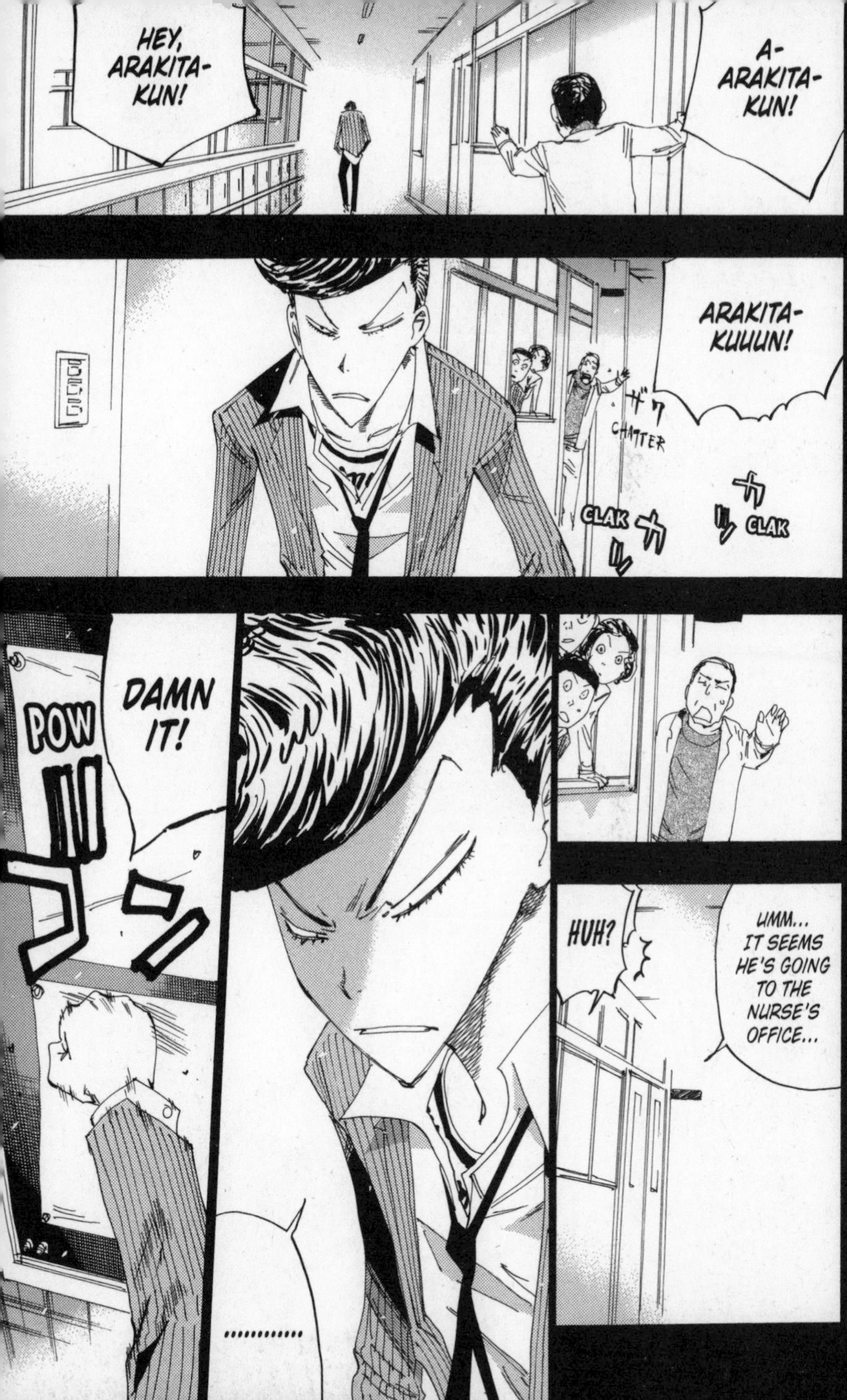
A-ARAKITA-KUN!
HEY, ARAKITA-KUN!
ARAKITA-KUUUN!
CHATTER
CLAK
CLAK
UMM... IT SEEMS HE'S GOING TO THE NURSE'S OFFICE...
HUH?
....
DAMN IT!
POW

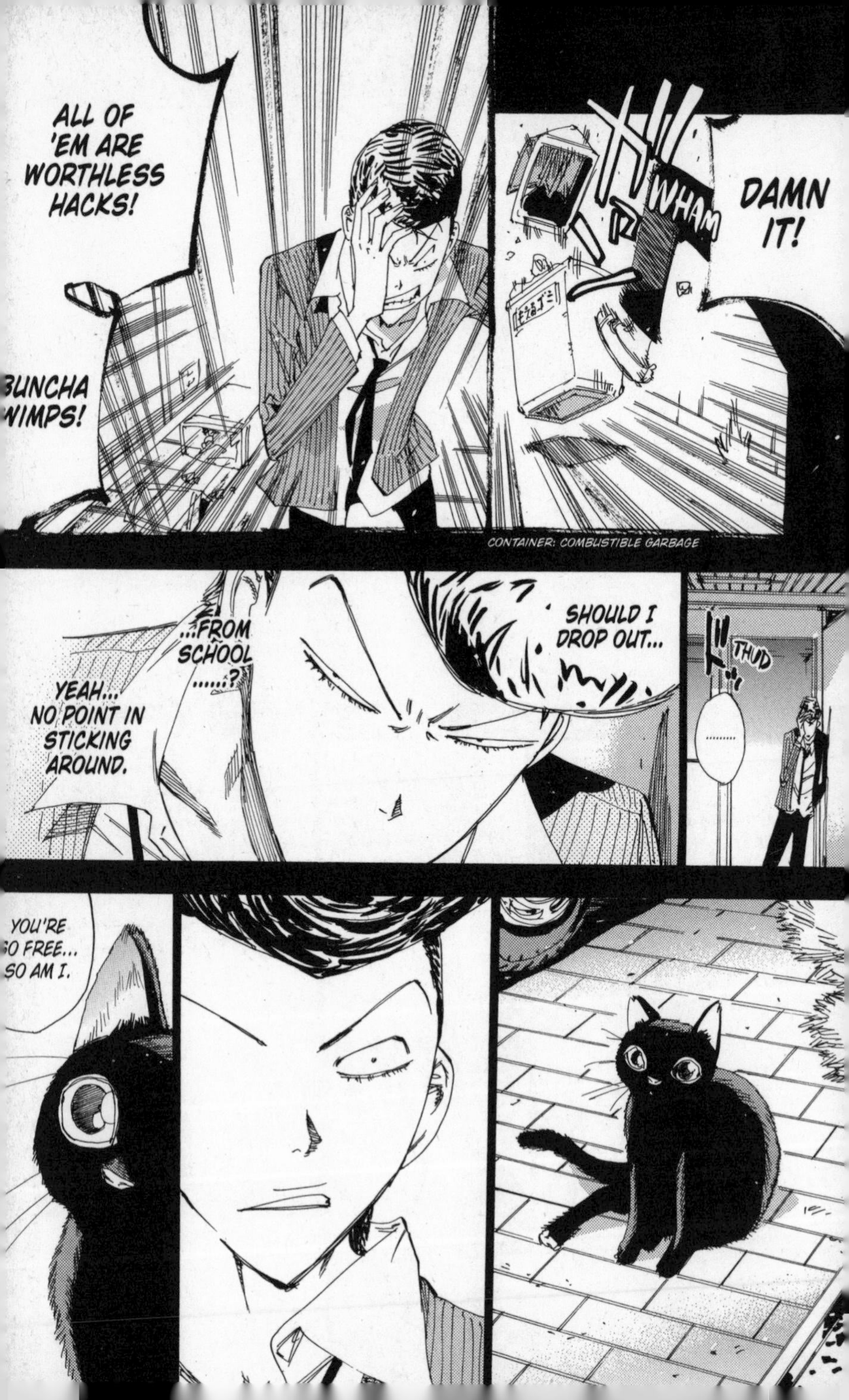
DAMN IT!
WHAM
CONTAINER: COMBUSTIBLE GARBAGE
ALL OF 'EM ARE WORTHLESS HACKS!
BUNCHA WIMPS!
THUD
....
SHOULD I DROP OUT...
...FROM SCHOOL ......?
YEAH... NO POINT IN STICKING AROUND.
YOU'RE SO FREE... SO AM I.

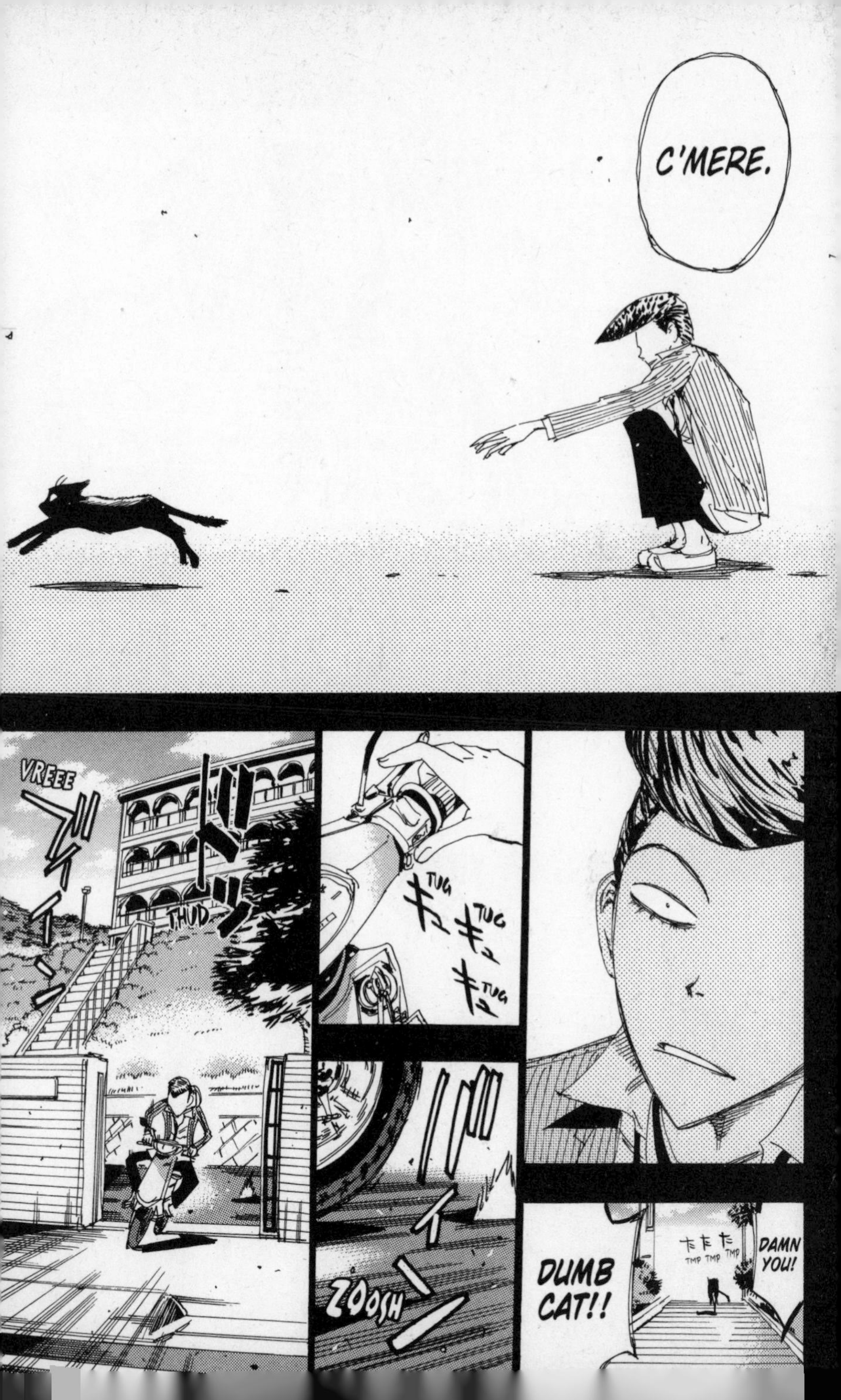
C'MERE.
DAMN YOU!
たたた
TMP TMP TMP
DUMB CAT!!
TUG
TUG
TUG
ZOOSH
VREEE
THUD

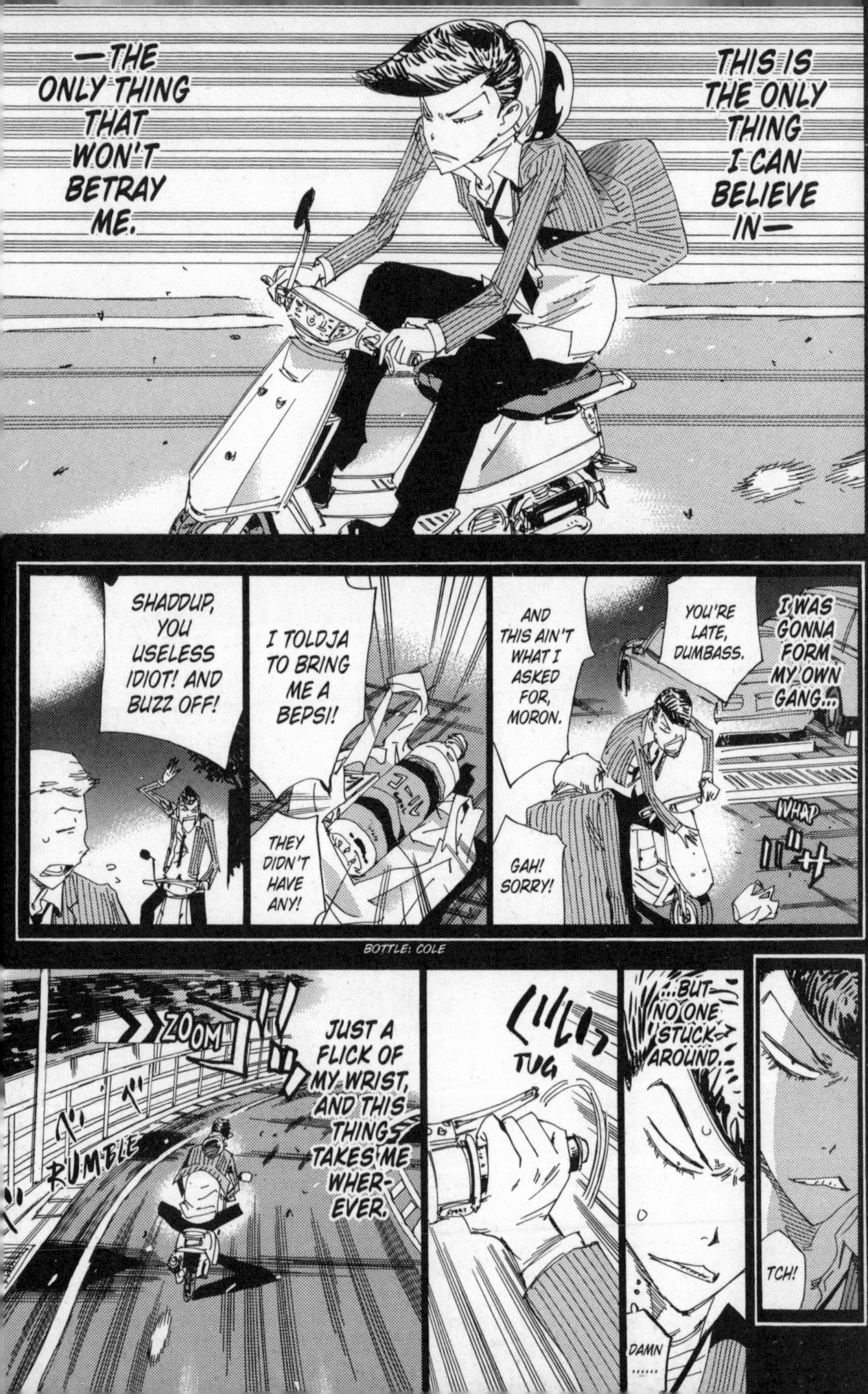
THIS IS THE ONLY THING I CAN BELIEVE IN—
—THE ONLY THING THAT WON'T BETRAY ME.
I WAS GONNA FORM MY OWN GANG...
YOU'RE LATE, DUMBASS.
AND THIS AIN'T WHAT I ASKED FOR, MORON.
WHAP
GAH! SORRY!
I TOLDJA TO BRING ME A BEPSI!
THEY DIDN'T HAVE ANY!
SHADDUP, YOU USELESS IDIOT! AND BUZZ OFF!
BOTTLE: COLE
TCH!
...BUT NO ONE STUCK AROUND.
DAMN ......
TUG
JUST A FLICK OF MY WRIST, AND THIS THINGS TAKES ME WHER-EVER.
ZOOM
RUMBLE

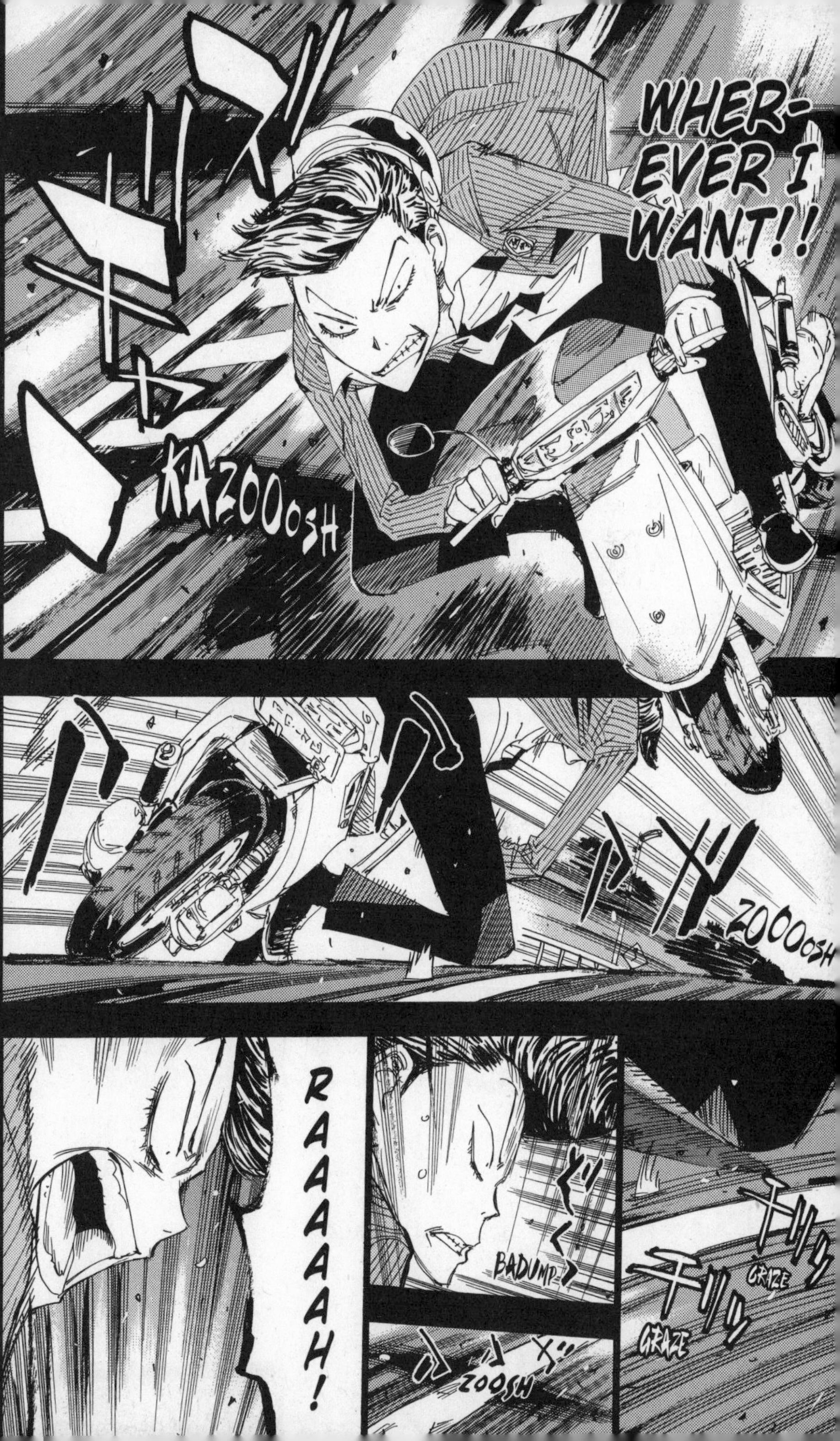
WHER-EVER I WANT!!
KAZOOOSH
ZOOOOSH
GRAZE
GRAZE
BADUMP
ZOOSH
RAAAAAAH!

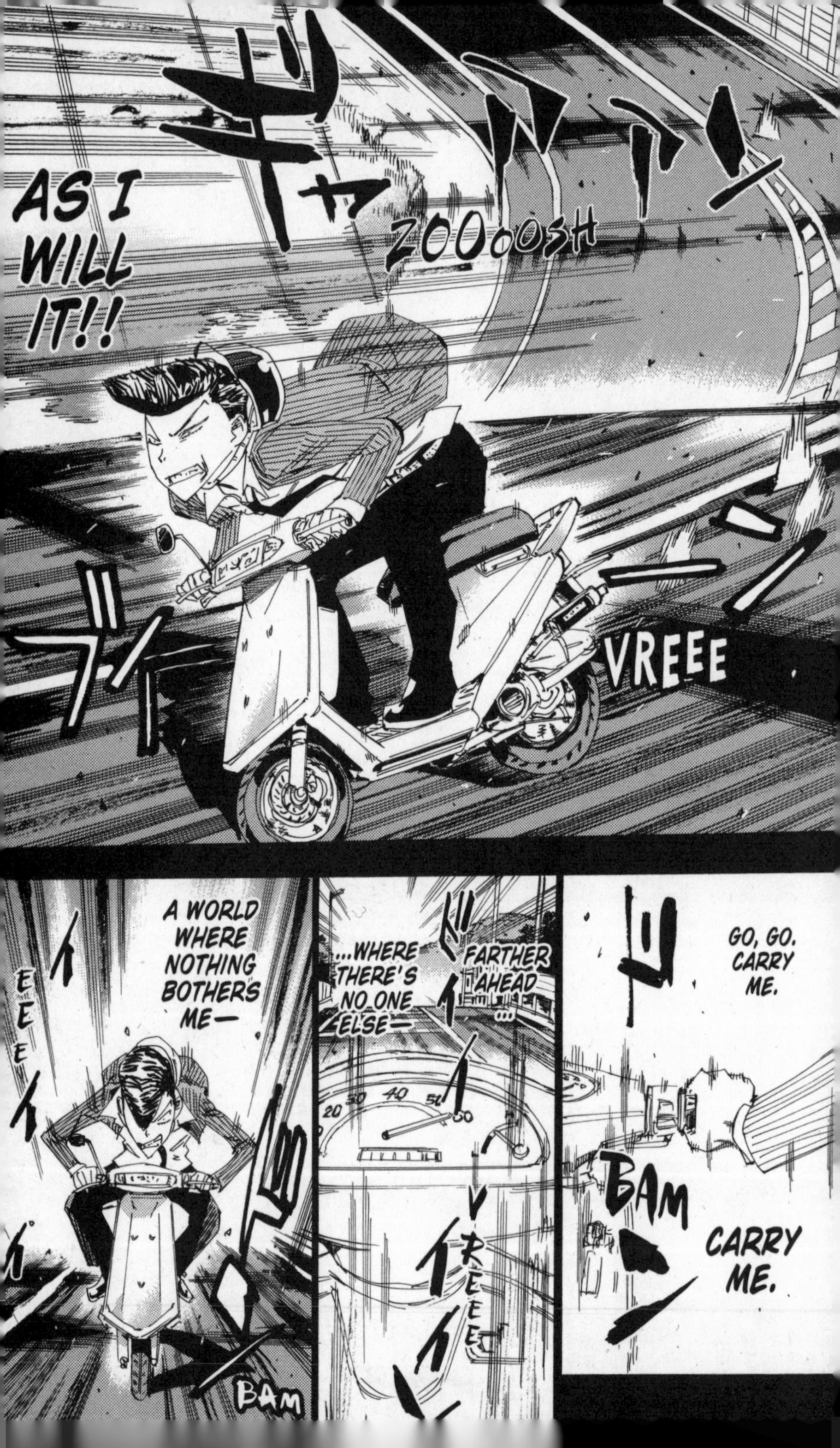
ZOOoooSH
AS I WILL IT!!
VREEE
GO, GO. CARRY ME.
BAM
CARRY ME.
FARTHER AHEAD...
...WHERE THERE'S NO ONE ELSE—
VREEE
A WORLD WHERE NOTHING BOTHERS ME—
EEEE
BAM

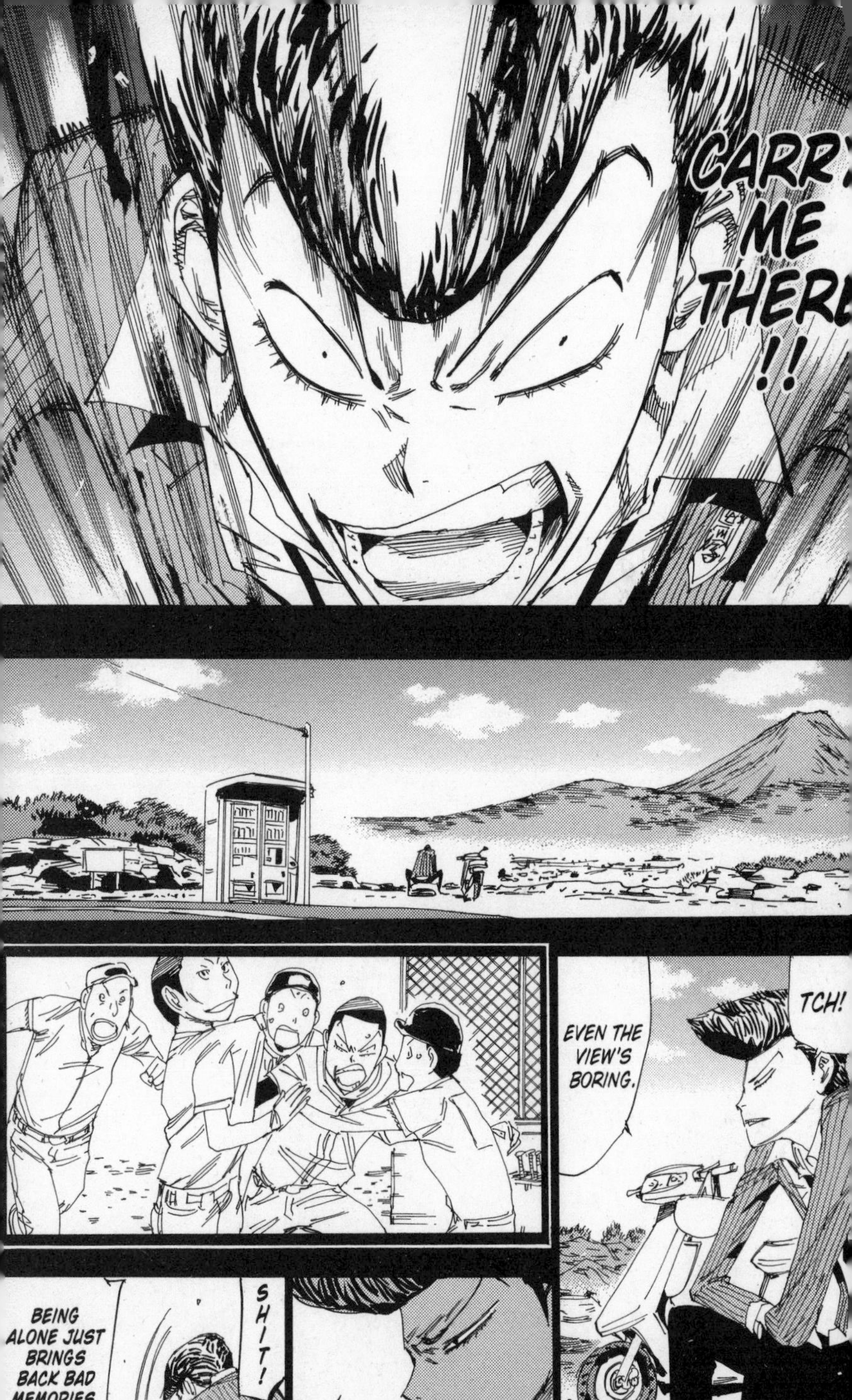
CARR
ME
THERE
!!
TCH!
EVEN THE VIEW'S BORING.
IRK
SHIT!
BEING ALONE JUST BRINGS BACK BAD MEMORIES.

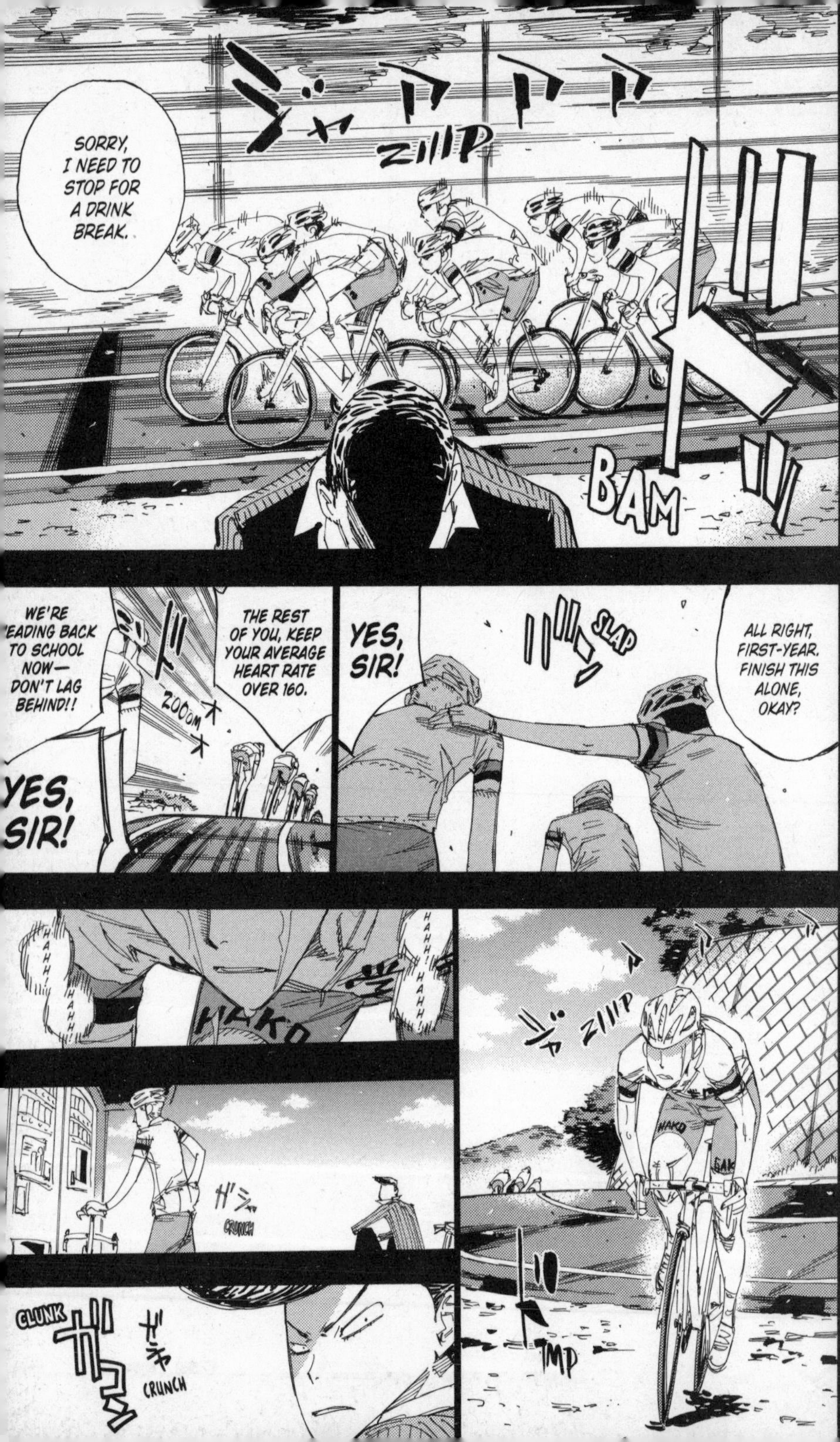
SORRY, I NEED TO STOP FOR A DRINK BREAK.
ZIIIP
BAM
ALL RIGHT, FIRST-YEAR. FINISH THIS ALONE, OKAY?
SLAP
YES, SIR!
THE REST OF YOU, KEEP YOUR AVERAGE HEART RATE OVER 160.
WE'RE EADING BACK TO SCHOOL NOW— DON'T LAG BEHIND!!
ZOOOM
YES, SIR!
ZIIIP
TMP
HAHH! HAHH!
HAHH! HAHH!
HAKO
CRUNCH
CLUNK
CRUNCH

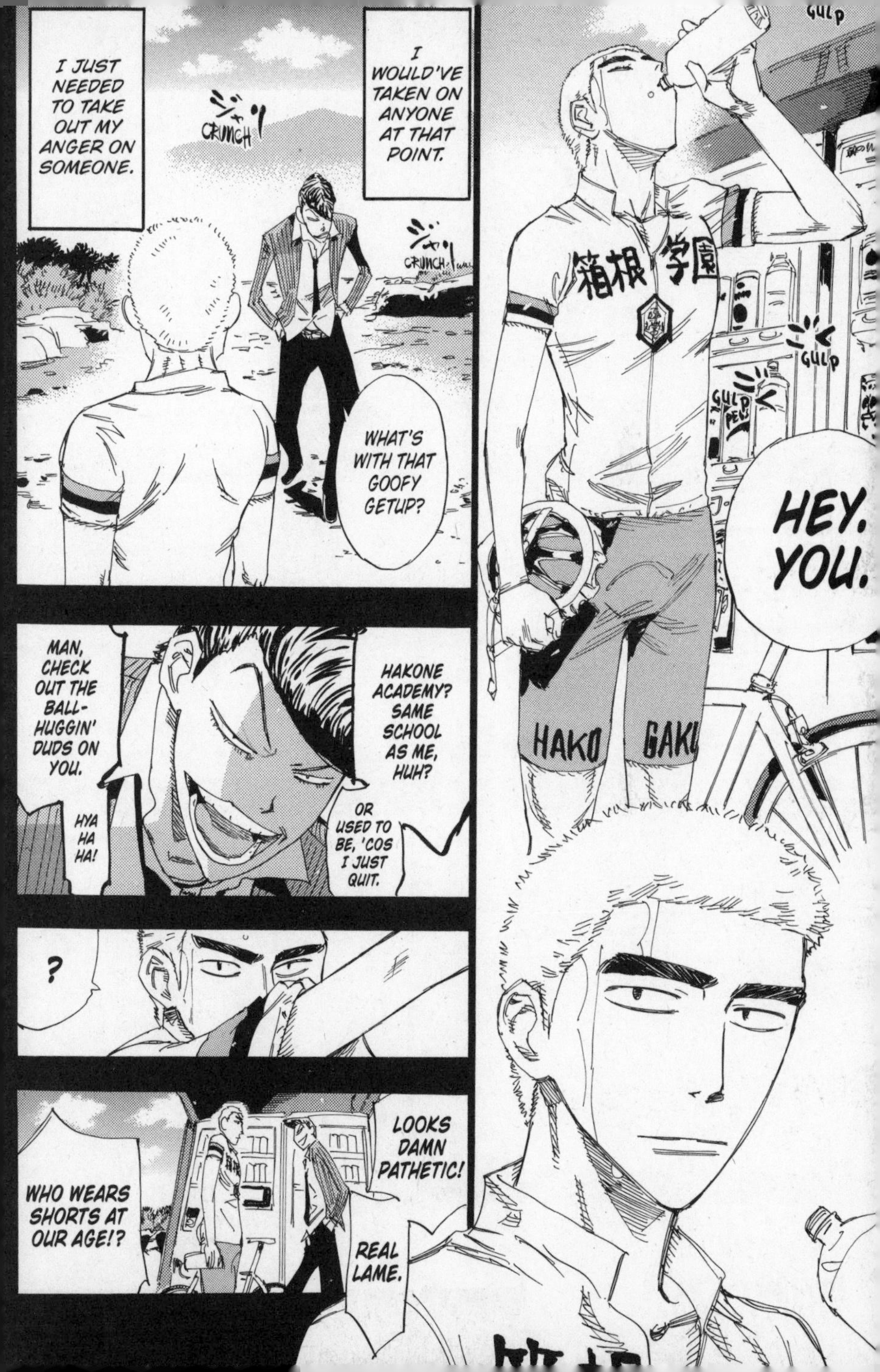
GULP
箱根学園
GULP
GULP
HEY. YOU.
HAKO GAKU
I WOULD'VE TAKEN ON ANYONE AT THAT POINT.
I JUST NEEDED TO TAKE OUT MY ANGER ON SOMEONE.
CRUNCH
CRUNCH
WHAT'S WITH THAT GOOFY GETUP?
HAKONE ACADEMY? SAME SCHOOL AS ME, HUH?
MAN, CHECK OUT THE BALL-HUGGIN' DUDS ON YOU.
OR USED TO BE, 'COS I JUST QUIT.
HYA HA HA!
?
LOOKS DAMN PATHETIC!
WHO WEARS SHORTS AT OUR AGE!?
REAL LAME.

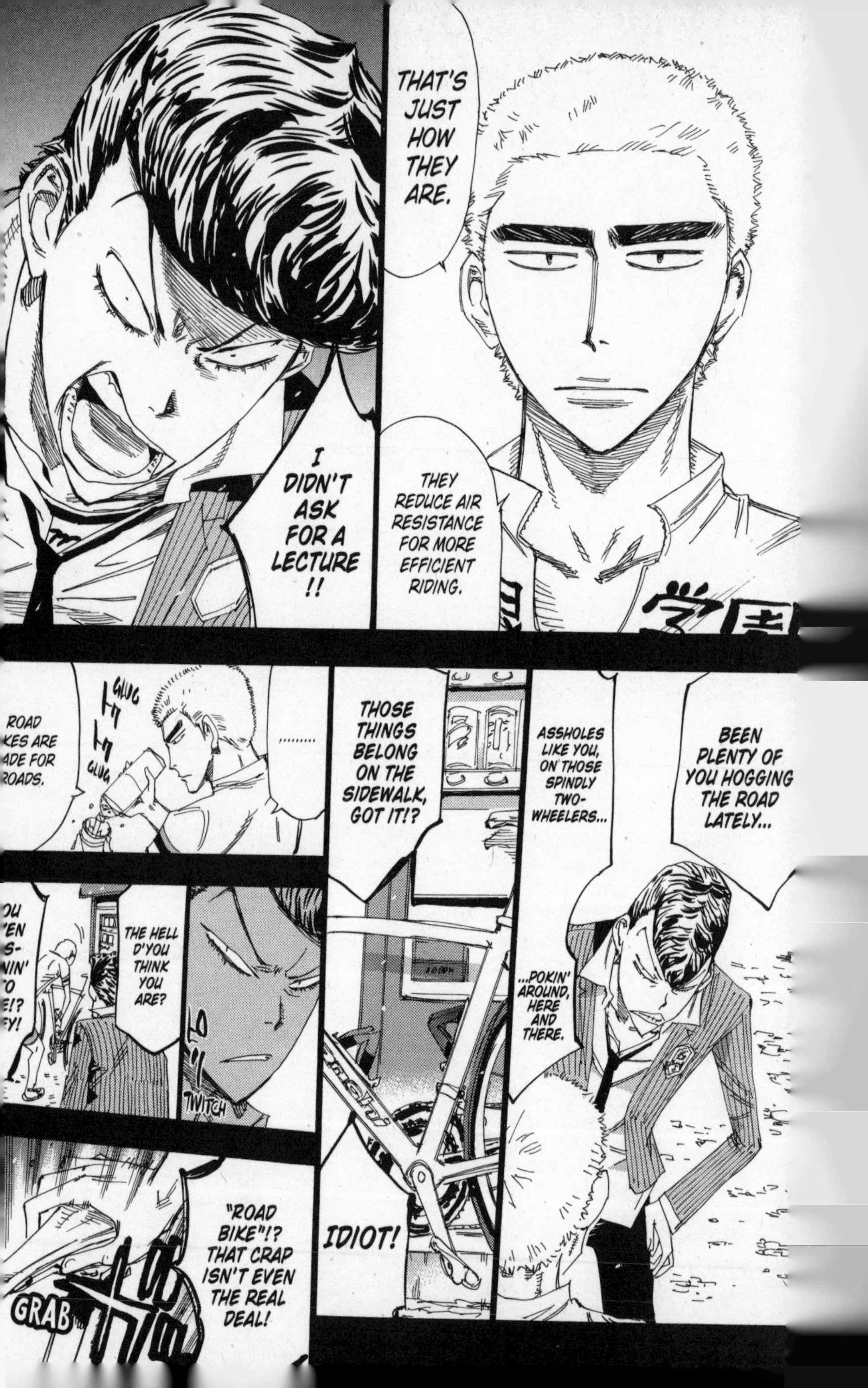
THAT'S JUST HOW THEY ARE.
THEY REDUCE AIR RESISTANCE FOR MORE EFFICIENT RIDING.
I DIDN'T ASK FOR A LECTURE!!
BEEN PLENTY OF YOU HOGGING THE ROAD LATELY...
ASSHOLES LIKE YOU, ON THOSE SPINDLY TWO-WHEELERS...
...POKIN' AROUND, HERE AND THERE.
THOSE THINGS BELONG ON THE SIDEWALK, GOT IT!?
IDIOT!
....
GLUG
GLUG
ROAD KES ARE ADE FOR ROADS.
THE HELL D'YOU THINK YOU ARE?
TWITCH
"ROAD BIKE"!? THAT CRAP ISN'T EVEN THE REAL DEAL!
GRAB

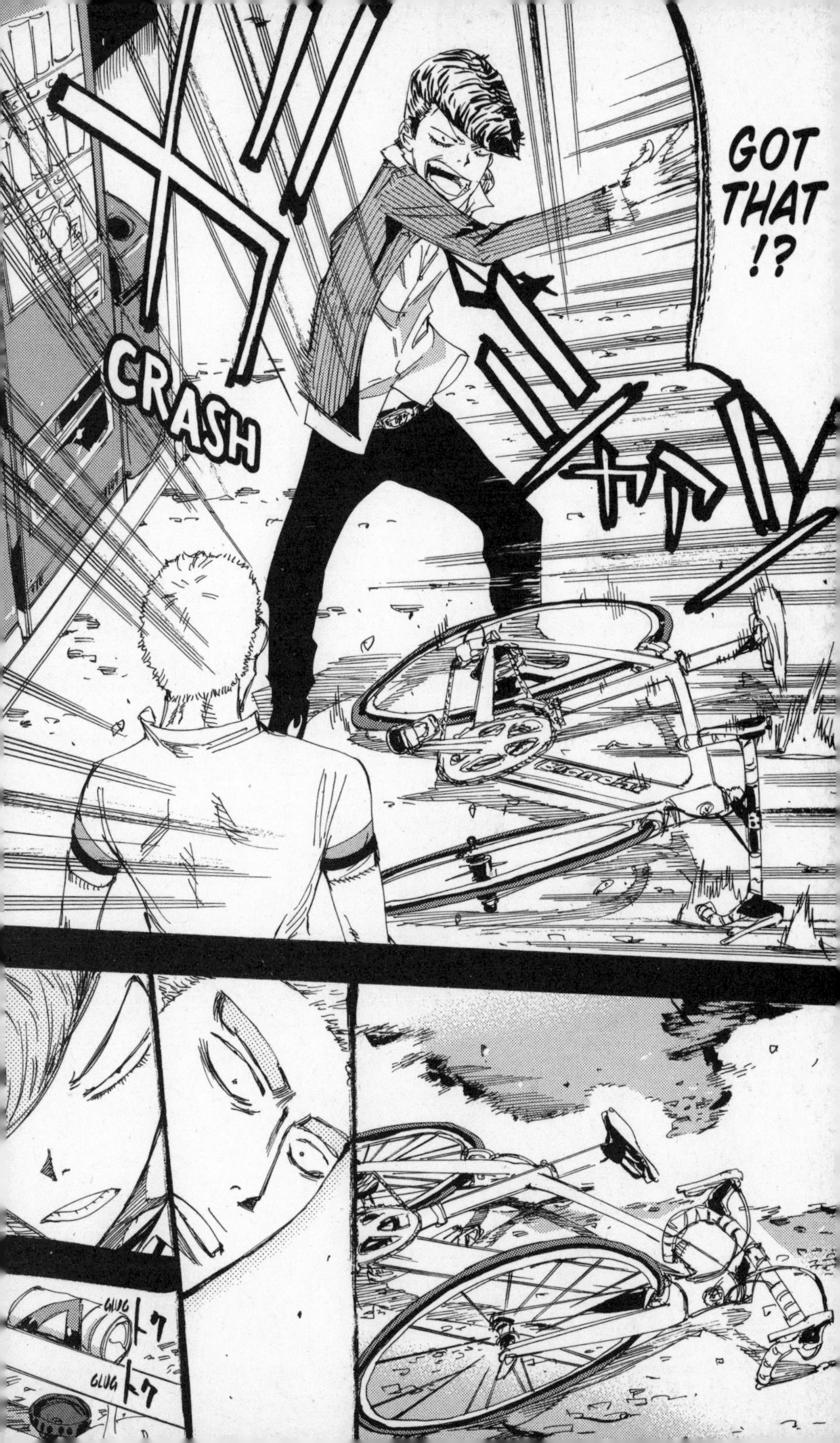
GOT THAT!?
CRASH
GLUG
GLUG

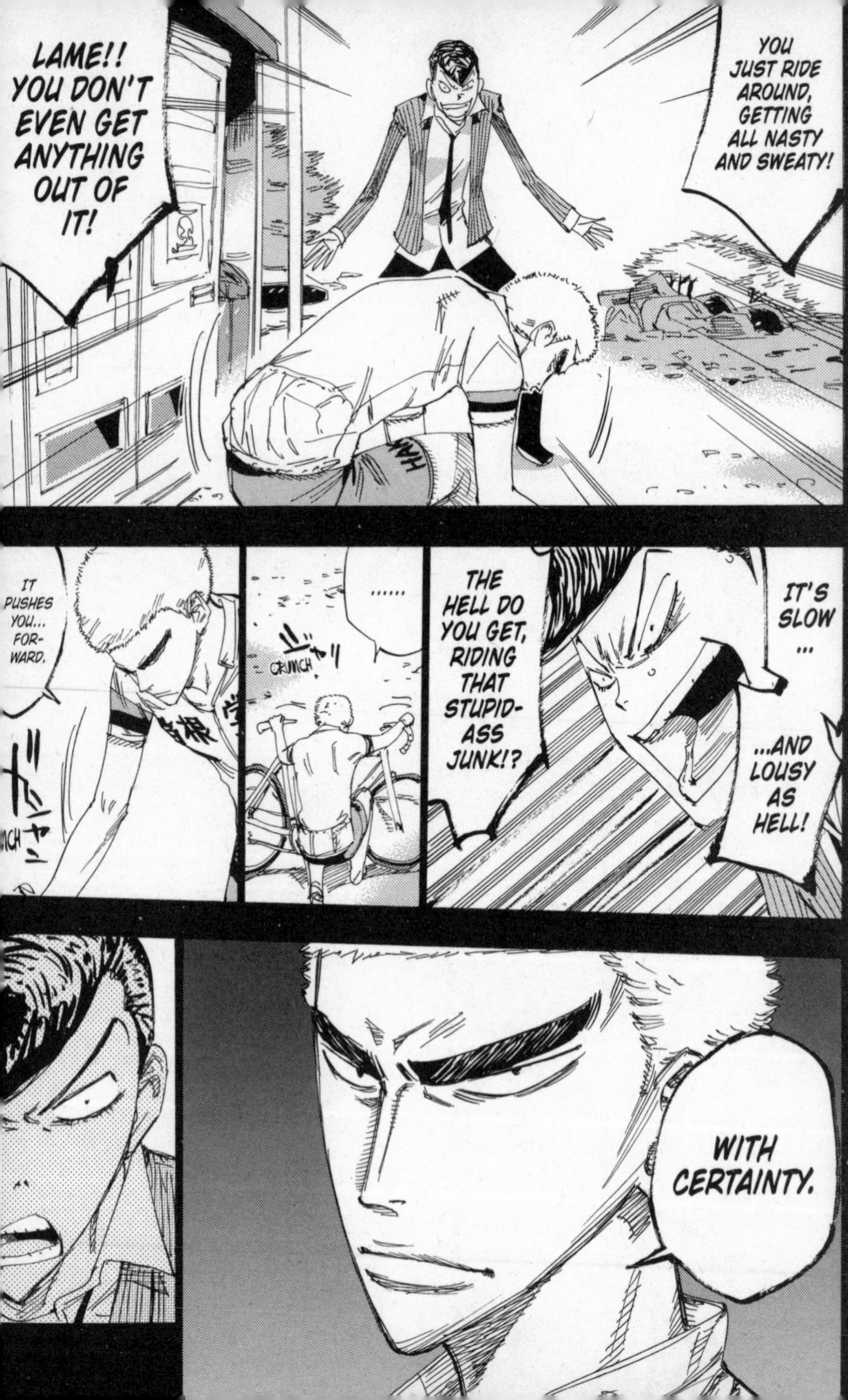
YOU JUST RIDE AROUND, GETTING ALL NASTY AND SWEATY!
LAME!! YOU DON'T EVEN GET ANYTHING OUT OF IT!
IT'S SLOW ...
...AND LOUSY AS HELL!
THE HELL DO YOU GET, RIDING THAT STUPID-ASS JUNK!?
......
CRUNCH
IT PUSHES YOU... FOR-WARD.
WITH CERTAINTY.

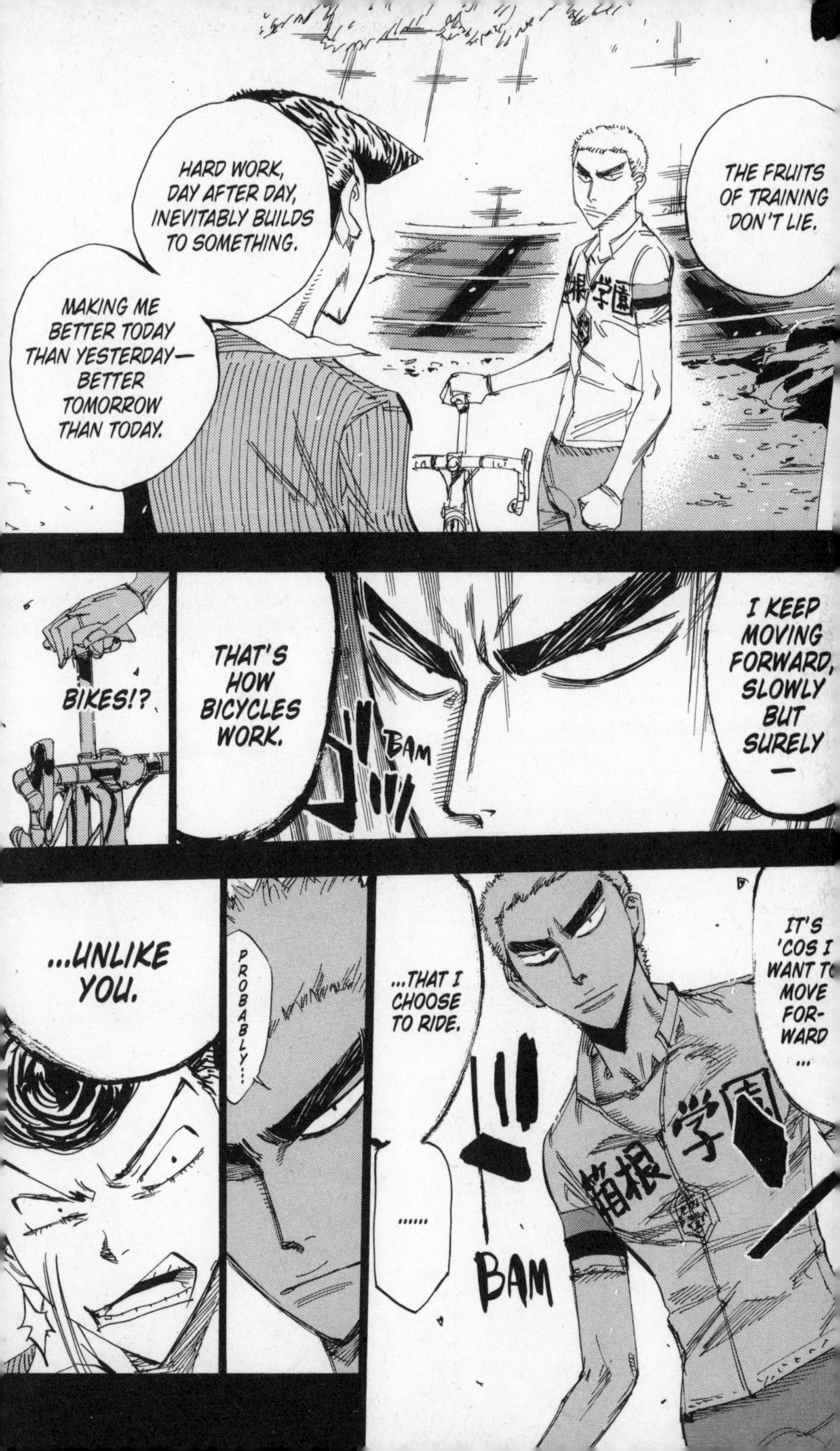
THE FRUITS OF TRAINING DON'T LIE.
HARD WORK, DAY AFTER DAY, INEVITABLY BUILDS TO SOMETHING.
MAKING ME BETTER TODAY THAN YESTERDAY— BETTER TOMORROW THAN TODAY.
I KEEP MOVING FORWARD, SLOWLY BUT SURELY —
BAM
THAT'S HOW BICYCLES WORK.
BIKES!?
IT'S 'COS I WANT T MOVE FOR-WARD ...
箱根学園
BAM
...THAT I CHOOSE TO RIDE.
......
PROBABLY...
...UNLIKE YOU.

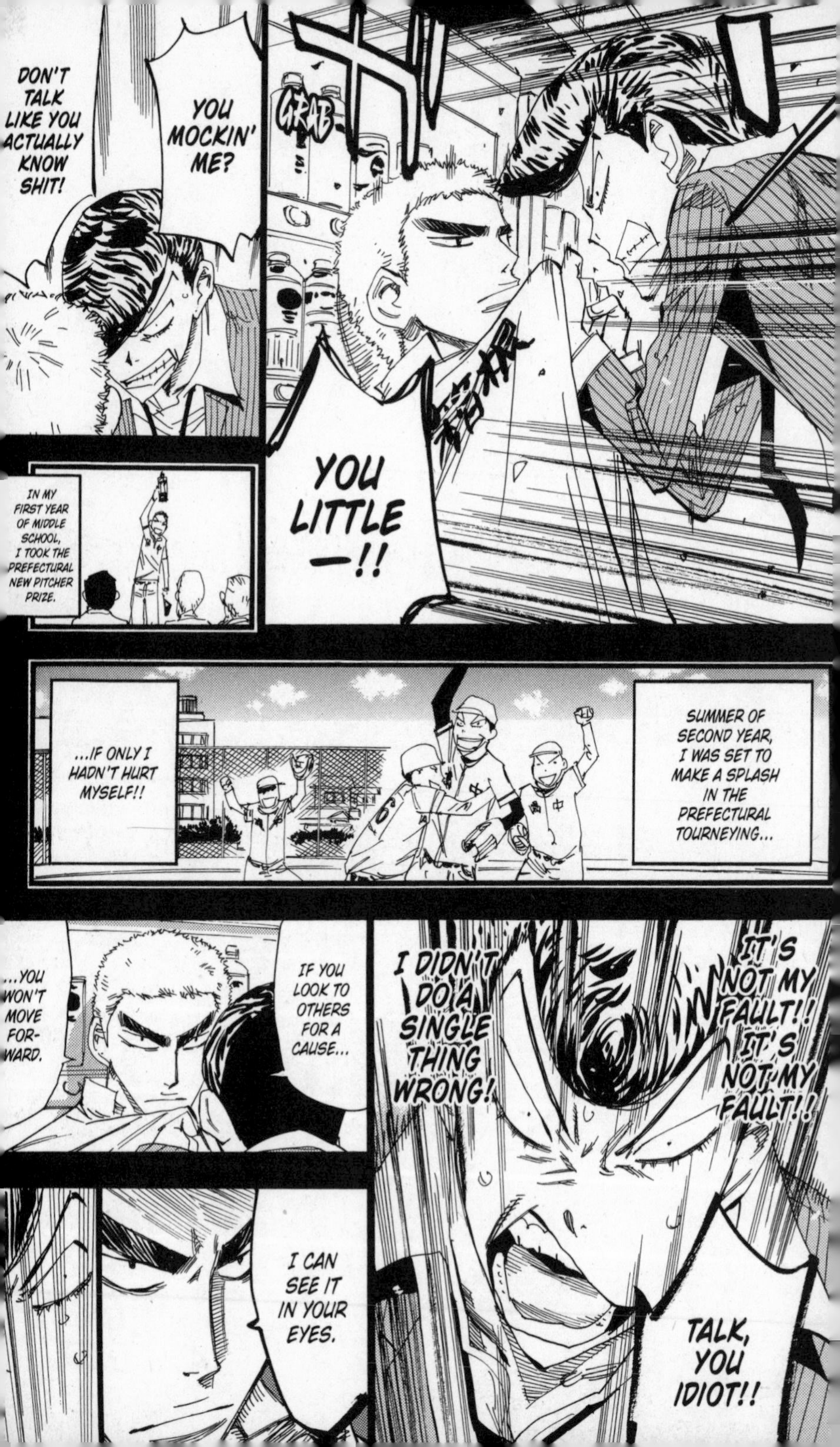
GRAB
YOU LITTLE—!!
YOU MOCKIN' ME?
DON'T TALK LIKE YOU ACTUALLY KNOW SHIT!
IN MY FIRST YEAR OF MIDDLE SCHOOL, I TOOK THE PREFECTURAL NEW PITCHER PRIZE.
SUMMER OF SECOND YEAR, I WAS SET TO MAKE A SPLASH IN THE PREFECTURAL TOURNEYING...
...IF ONLY I HADN'T HURT MYSELF!!
IT'S NOT MY FAULT!! IT'S NOT MY FAULT!!
I DIDN'T DO A SINGLE THING WRONG!
TALK, YOU IDIOT!!
IF YOU LOOK TO OTHERS FOR A CAUSE...
...YOU WON'T MOVE FORWARD.
I CAN SEE IT IN YOUR EYES.

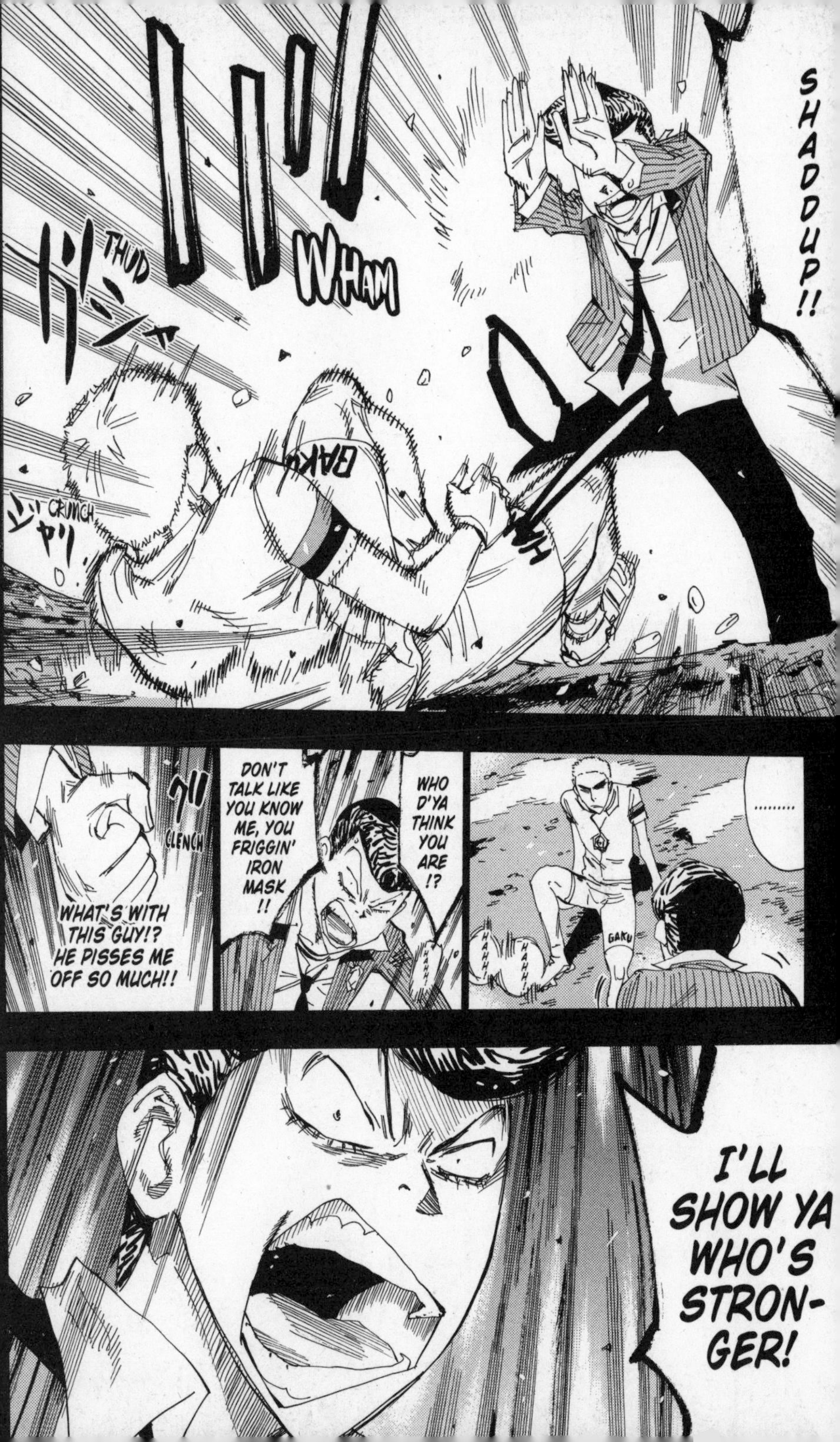
SHADDUP!!
WHAM
THUD
CRUNCH
GAKU
....
WHO D'YA THINK YOU ARE!?
DON'T TALK LIKE YOU KNOW ME, YOU FRIGGIN' IRON MASK!!
HAHH
HAHH
GAKU
CLENCH
WHAT'S WITH THIS GUY!? HE PISSES ME OFF SO MUCH!!
I'LL SHOW YA WHO'S STRON-GER!

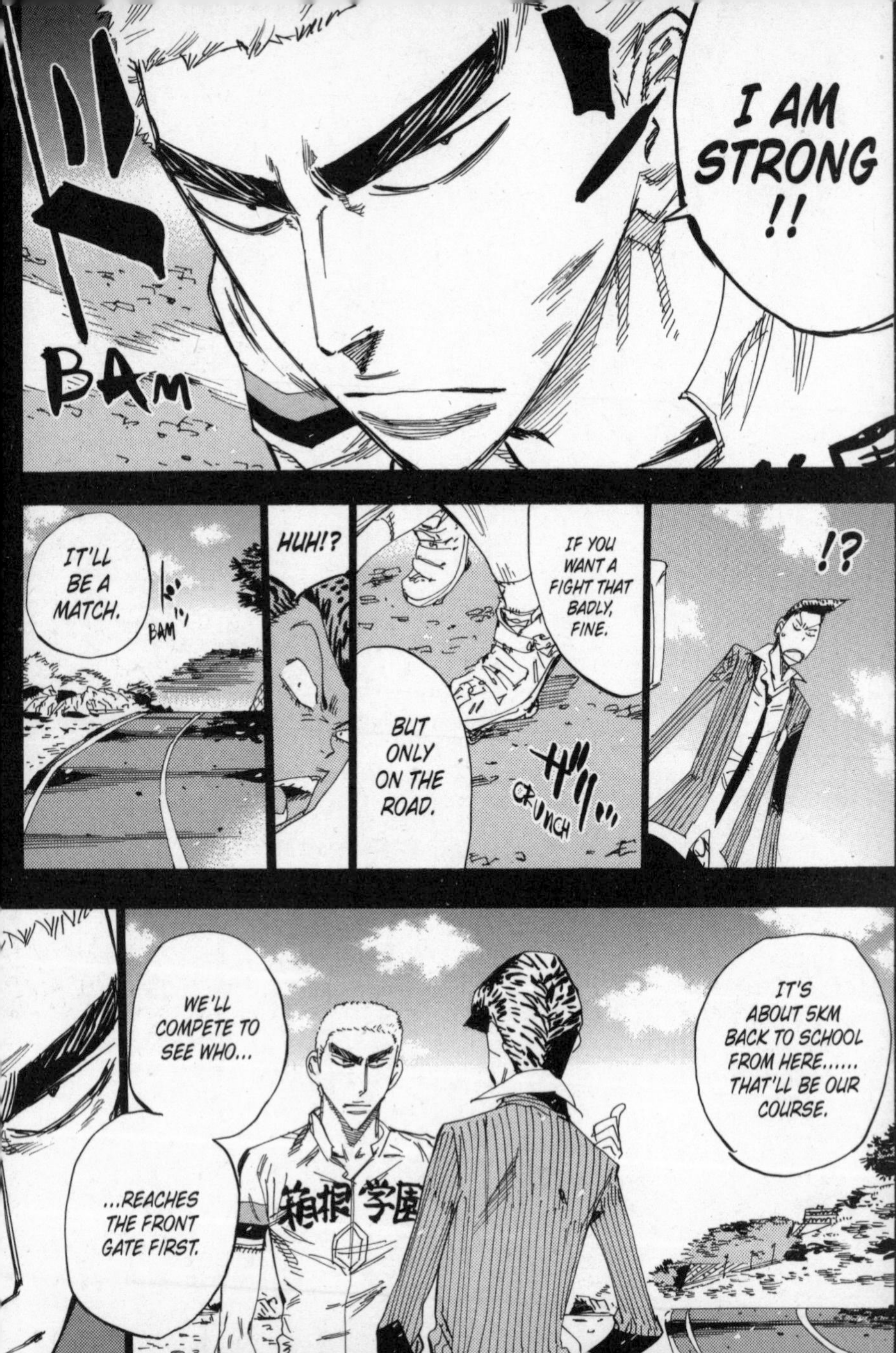
I AM STRONG !!
BAM
!?
IF YOU WANT A FIGHT THAT BADLY, FINE.
BUT ONLY ON THE ROAD.
CRUNCH
HUH!?
IT'LL BE A MATCH.
BAM
IT'S ABOUT 5KM BACK TO SCHOOL FROM HERE...... THAT'LL BE OUR COURSE.
WE'LL COMPETE TO SEE WHO...
箱根学園
...REACHES THE FRONT GATE FIRST.

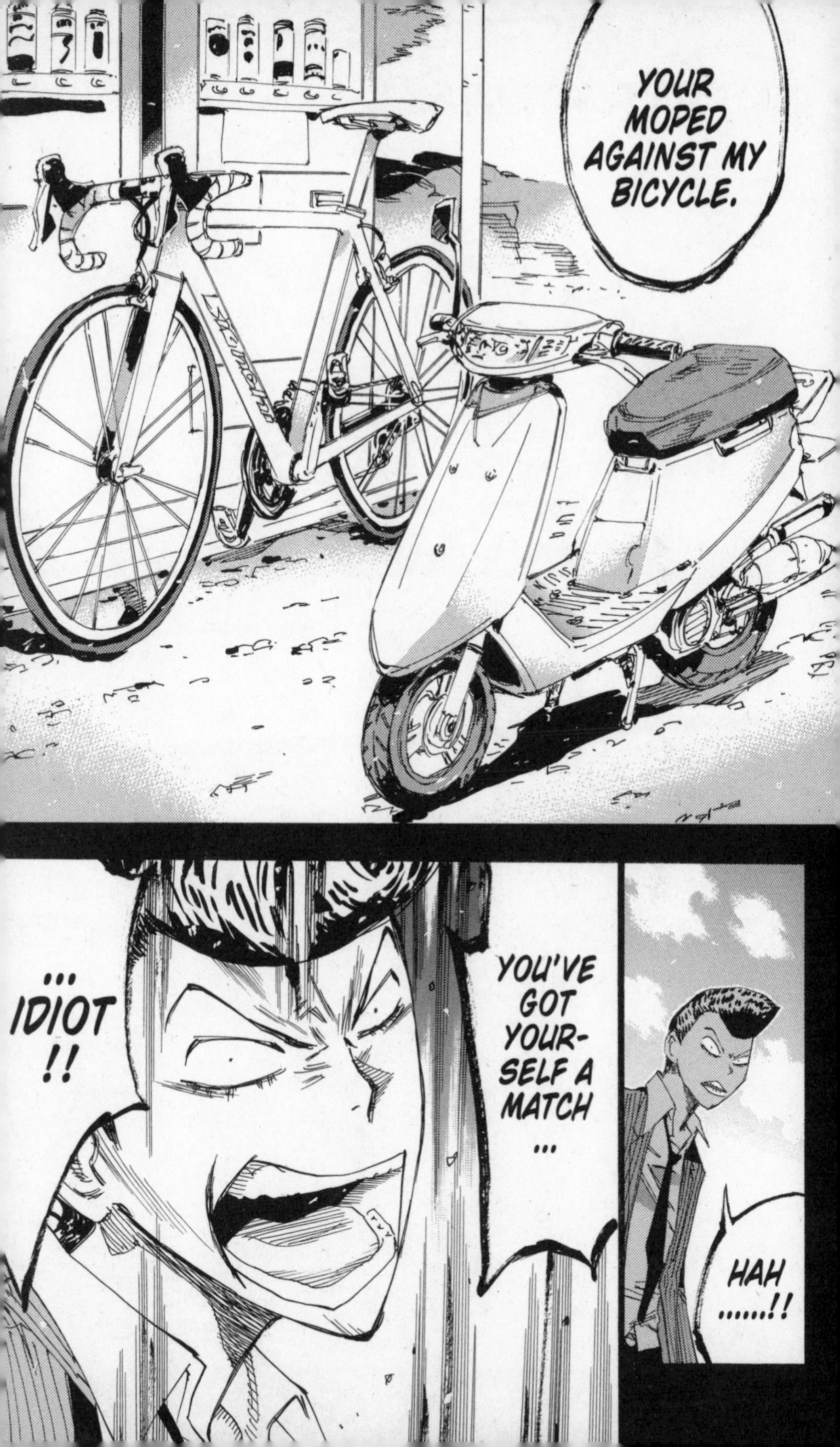
YOUR MOPED AGAINST MY BICYCLE.
HAH ......!!
YOU'VE GOT YOUR-SELF A MATCH ...
... IDIOT !!

RIDE.175 FORWARD

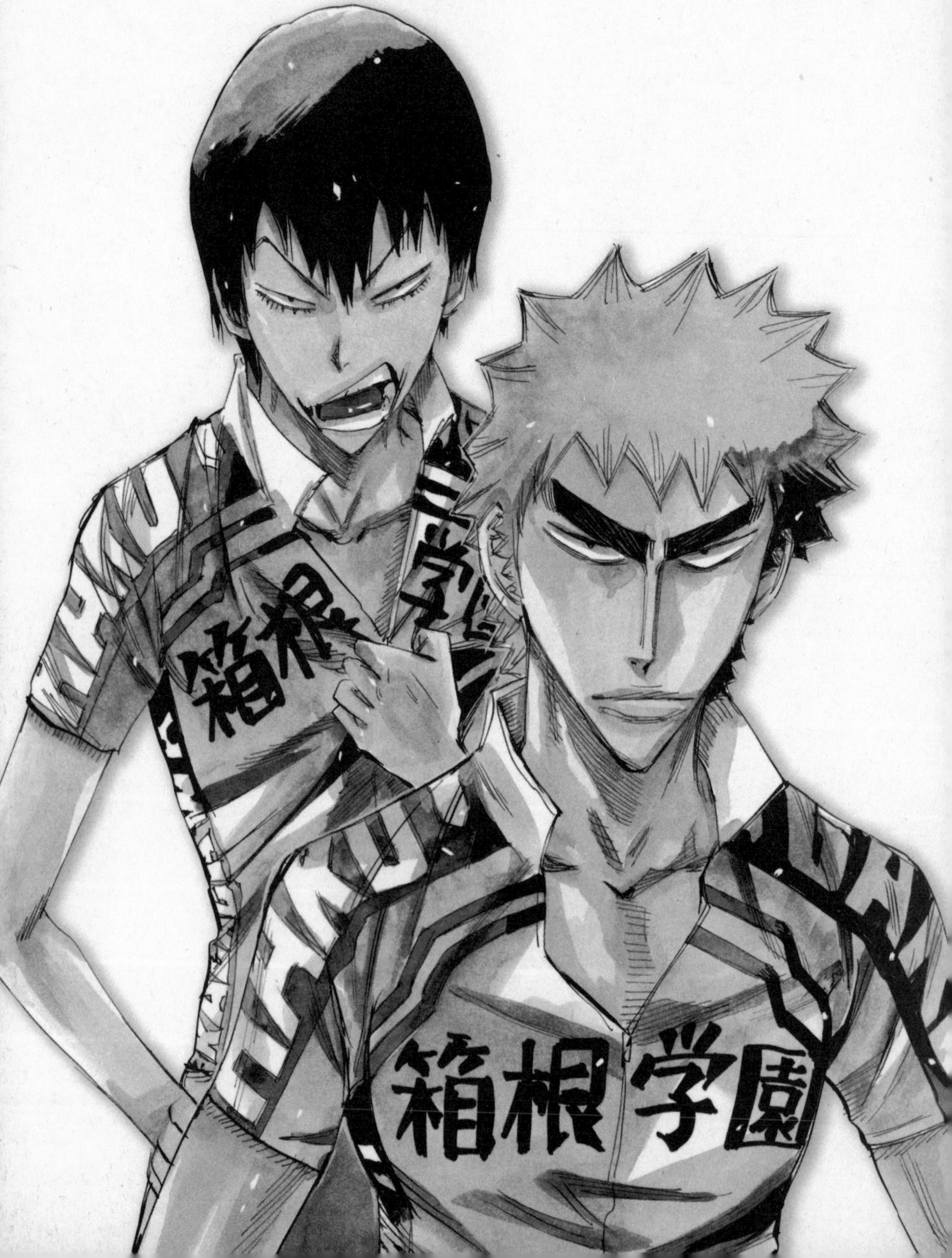
箱根学園

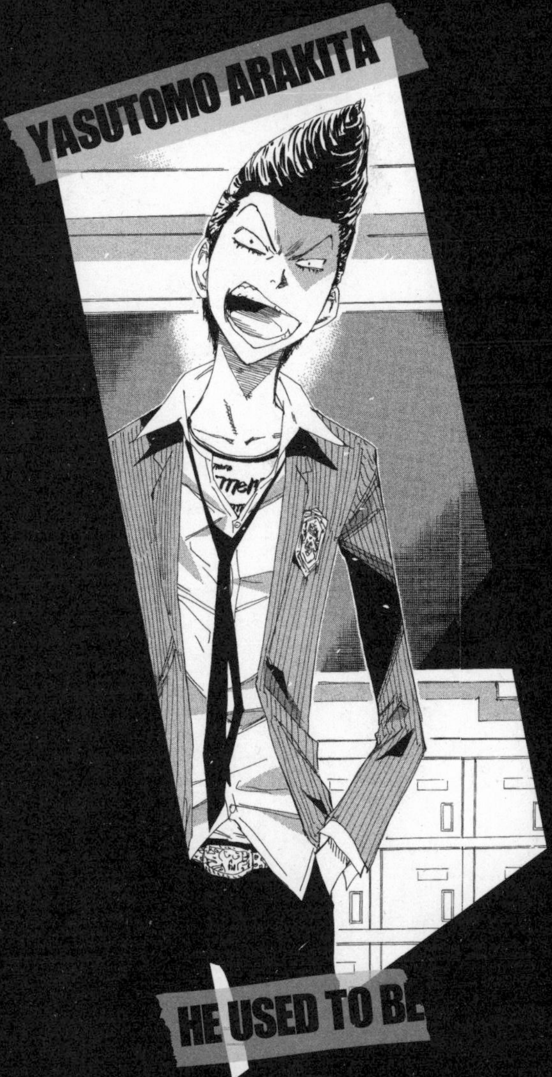
YASUTOMO ARAKITA
HE USED TO BE

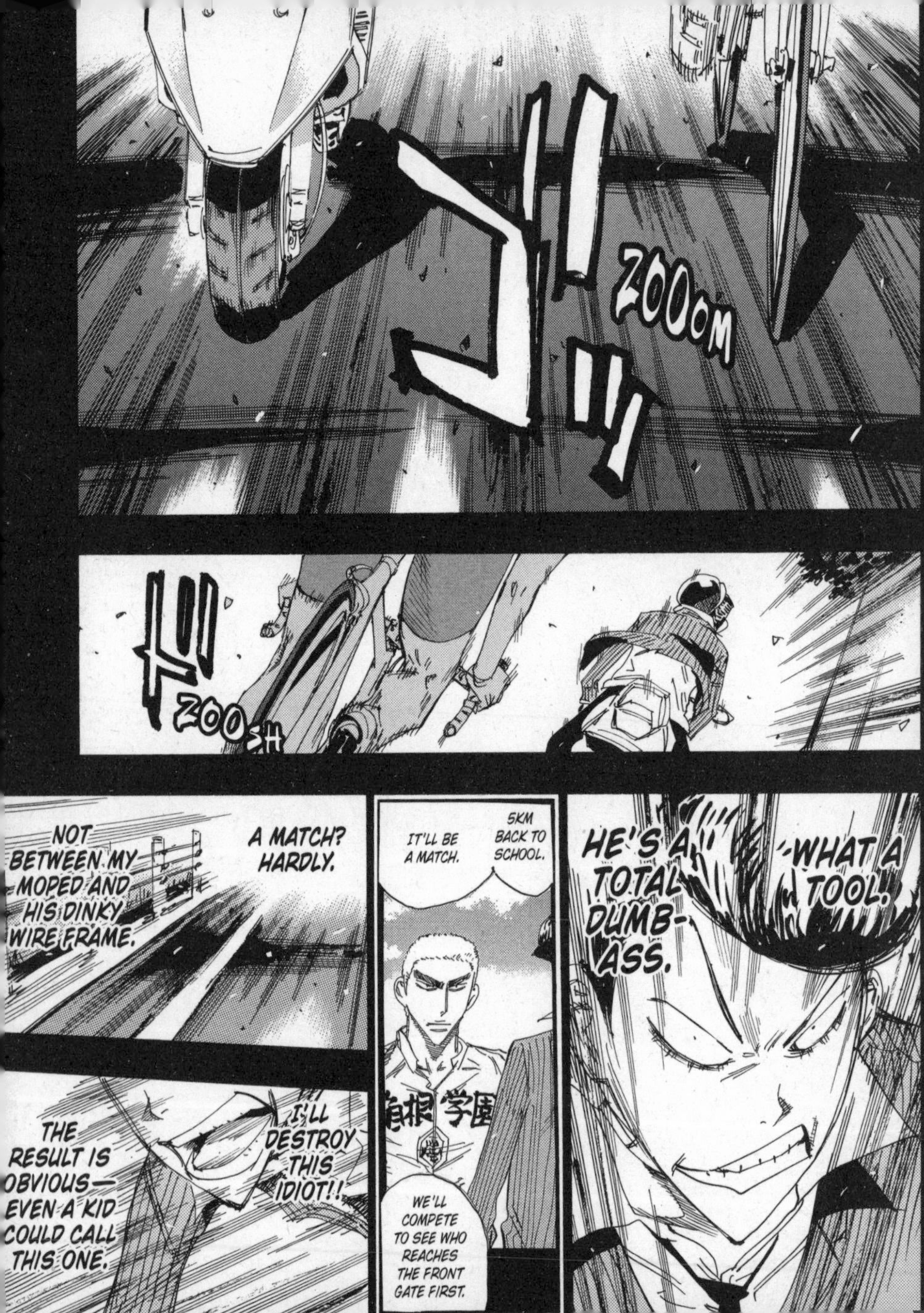
ZOOOM
ZOOSH
WHAT A TOOL.
HE'S A TOTAL DUMB-ASS.
5KM BACK TO SCHOOL.
IT'LL BE A MATCH.
WE'LL COMPETE TO SEE WHO REACHES THE FRONT GATE FIRST.
A MATCH? HARDLY.
NOT BETWEEN MY MOPED AND HIS DINKY WIRE FRAME.
I'LL DESTROY THIS IDIOT!!
THE RESULT IS OBVIOUS—EVEN A KID COULD CALL THIS ONE.

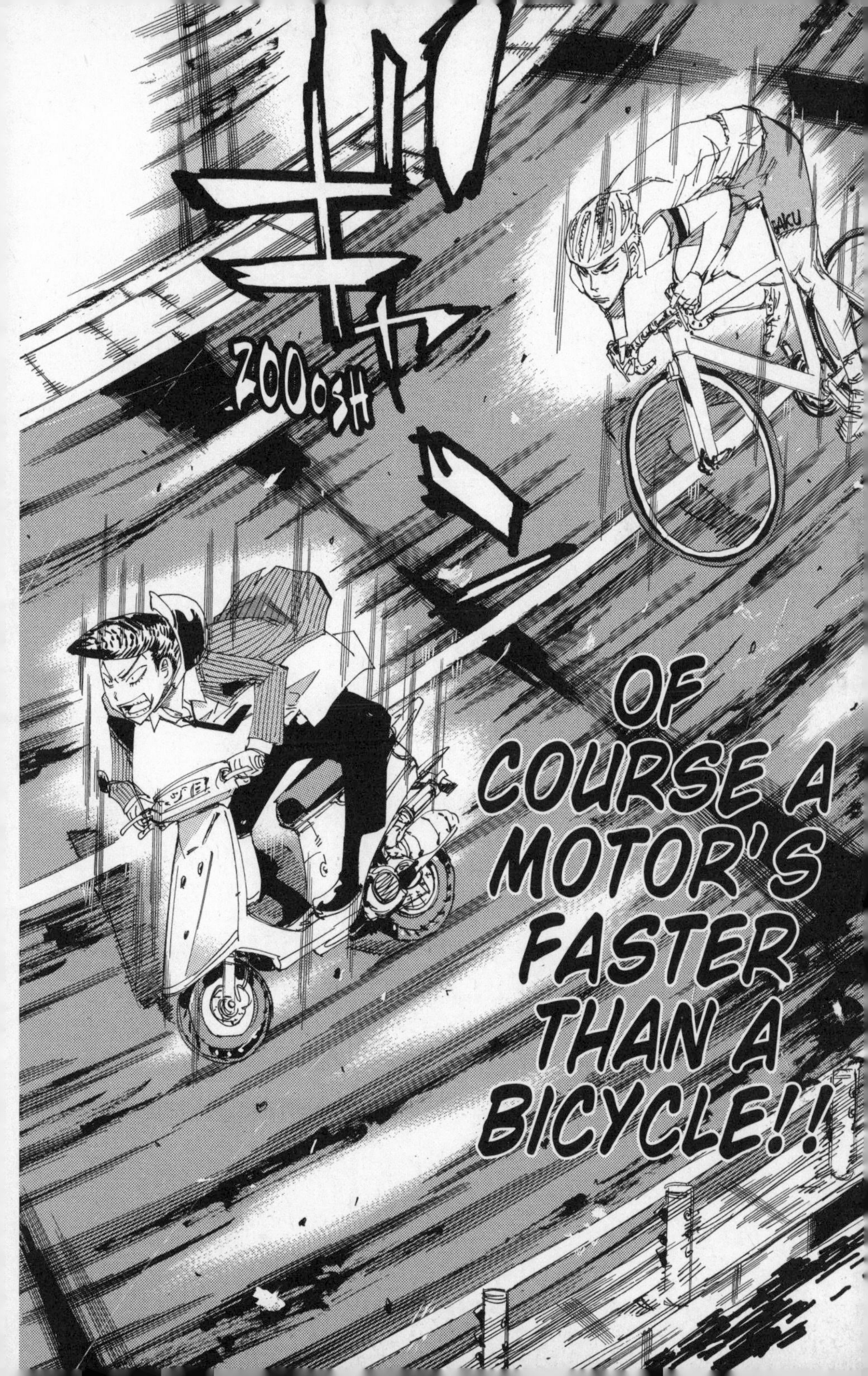
ZOOOSH
OF COURSE A MOTOR'S FASTER THAN A BICYCLE!!

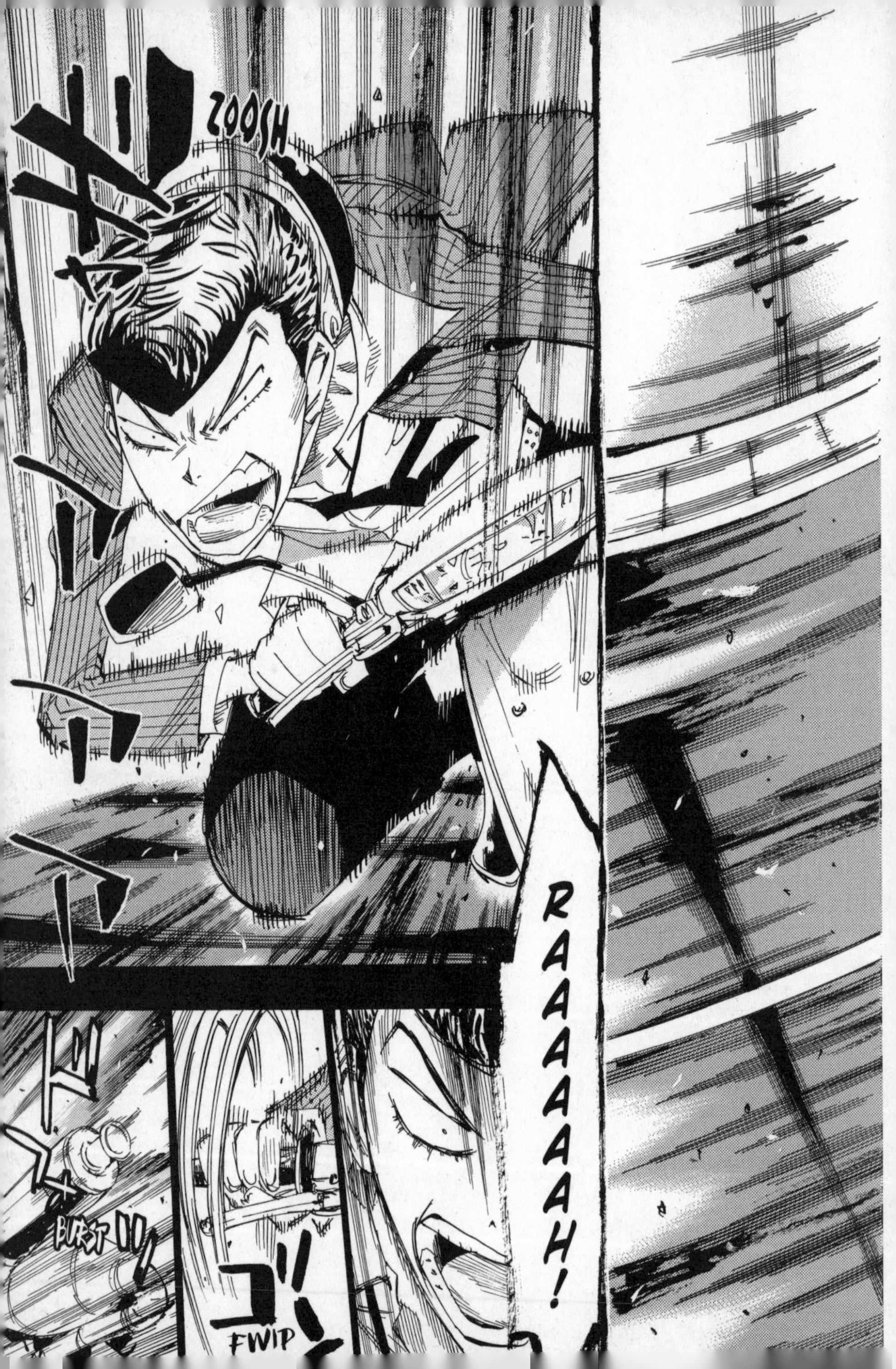
ZOOSH
RAAAAAAAH!
FWIP
BURST

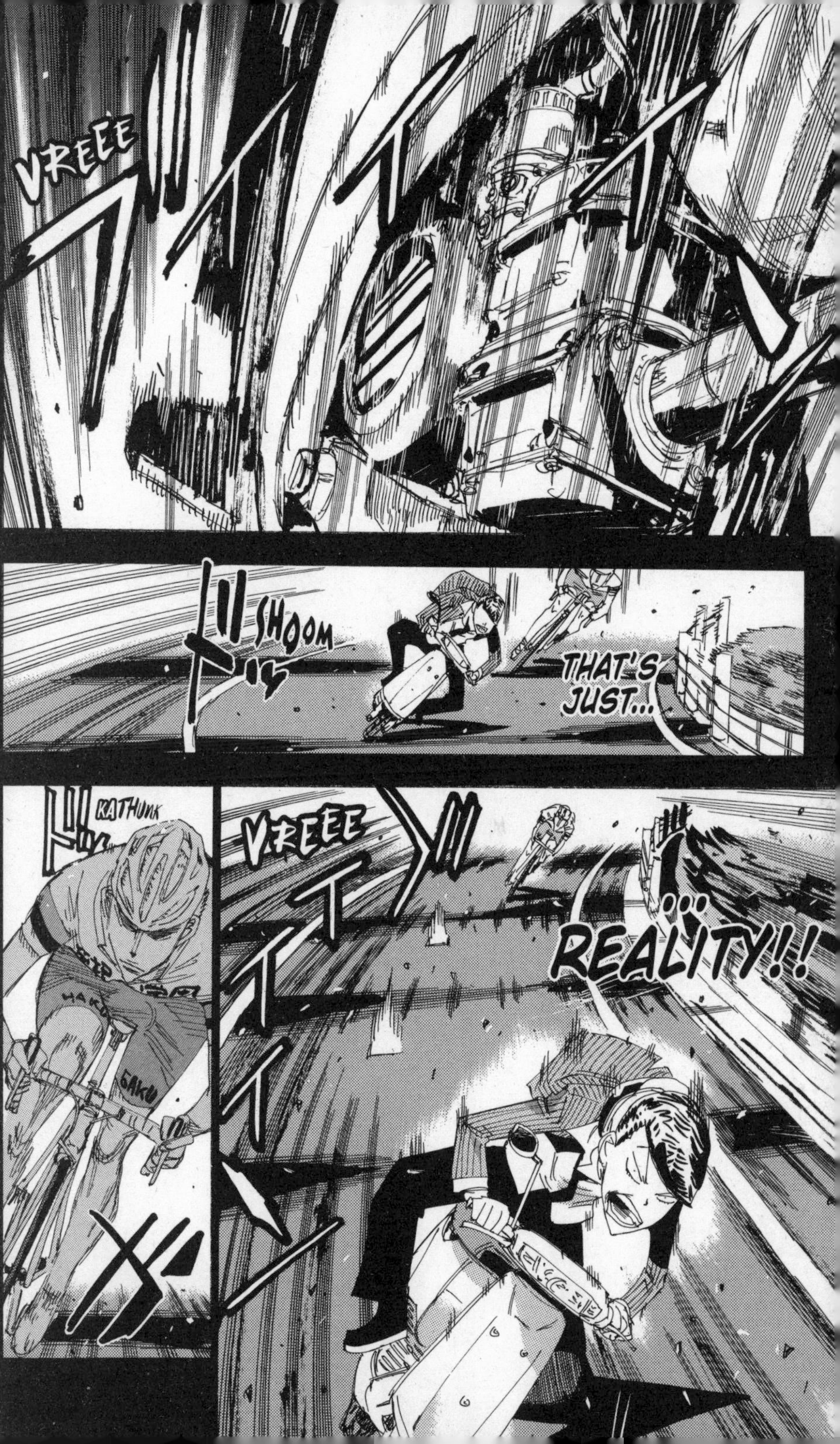
VREEE
THAT'S JUST...
SHOOM
VREEE
...REALITY!!
KATHUNK

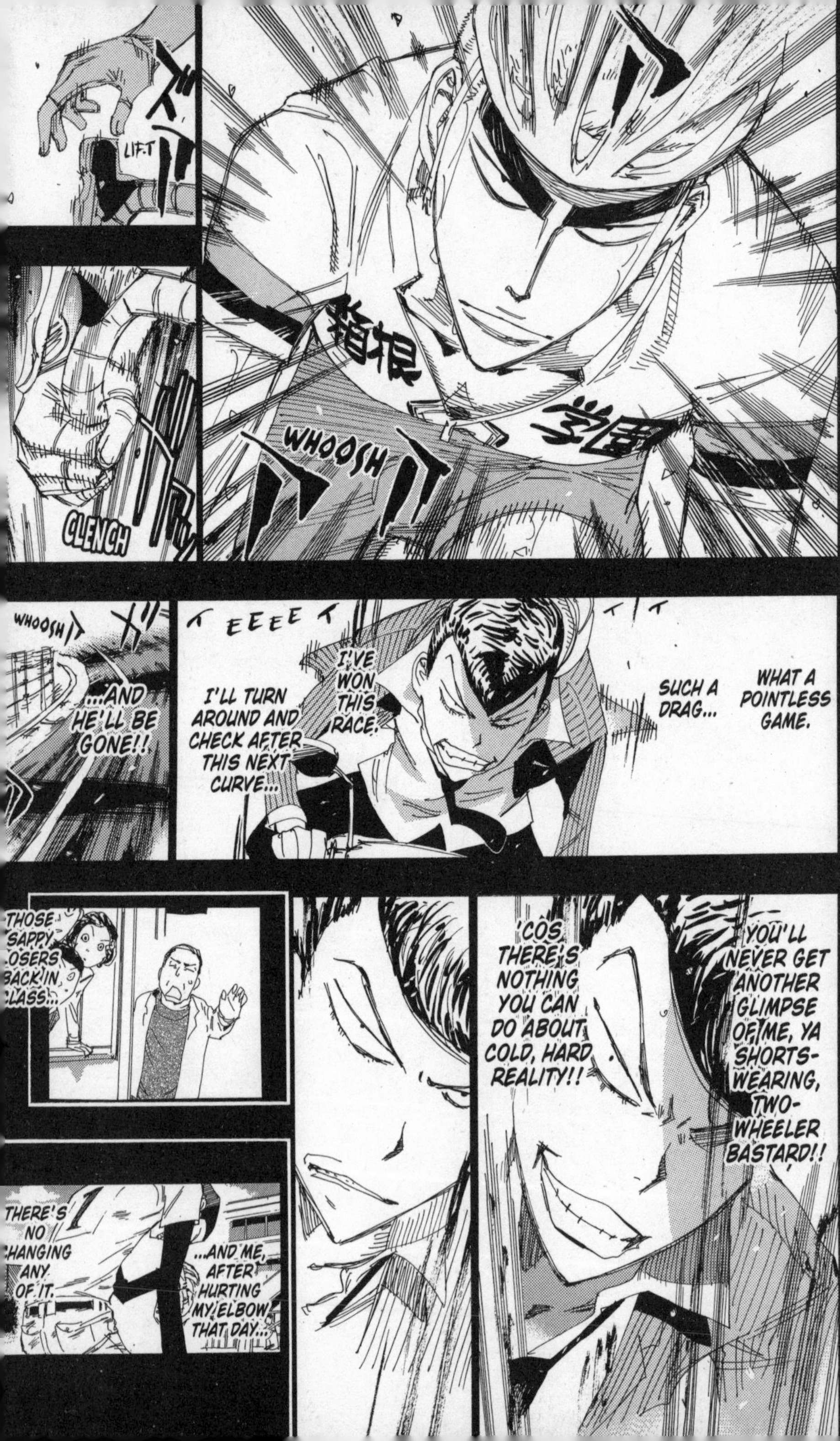
WHOOSH
箱根
学園
LIFT
CLENCH
EEEE
WHAT A POINTLESS GAME.
SUCH A DRAG...
I'VE WON THIS RACE.
I'LL TURN AROUND AND CHECK AFTER THIS NEXT CURVE...
WHOOSH
...AND HE'LL BE GONE!!
YOU'LL NEVER GET ANOTHER GLIMPSE OF ME, YA SHORTS-WEARING, TWO-WHEELER BASTARD!!
'COS THERE'S NOTHING YOU CAN DO ABOUT COLD, HARD REALITY!!
THOSE SAPPY LOSERS BACK IN CLASS...
...AND ME, AFTER HURTING MY ELBOW THAT DAY...
THERE'S NO CHANGING ANY OF IT.

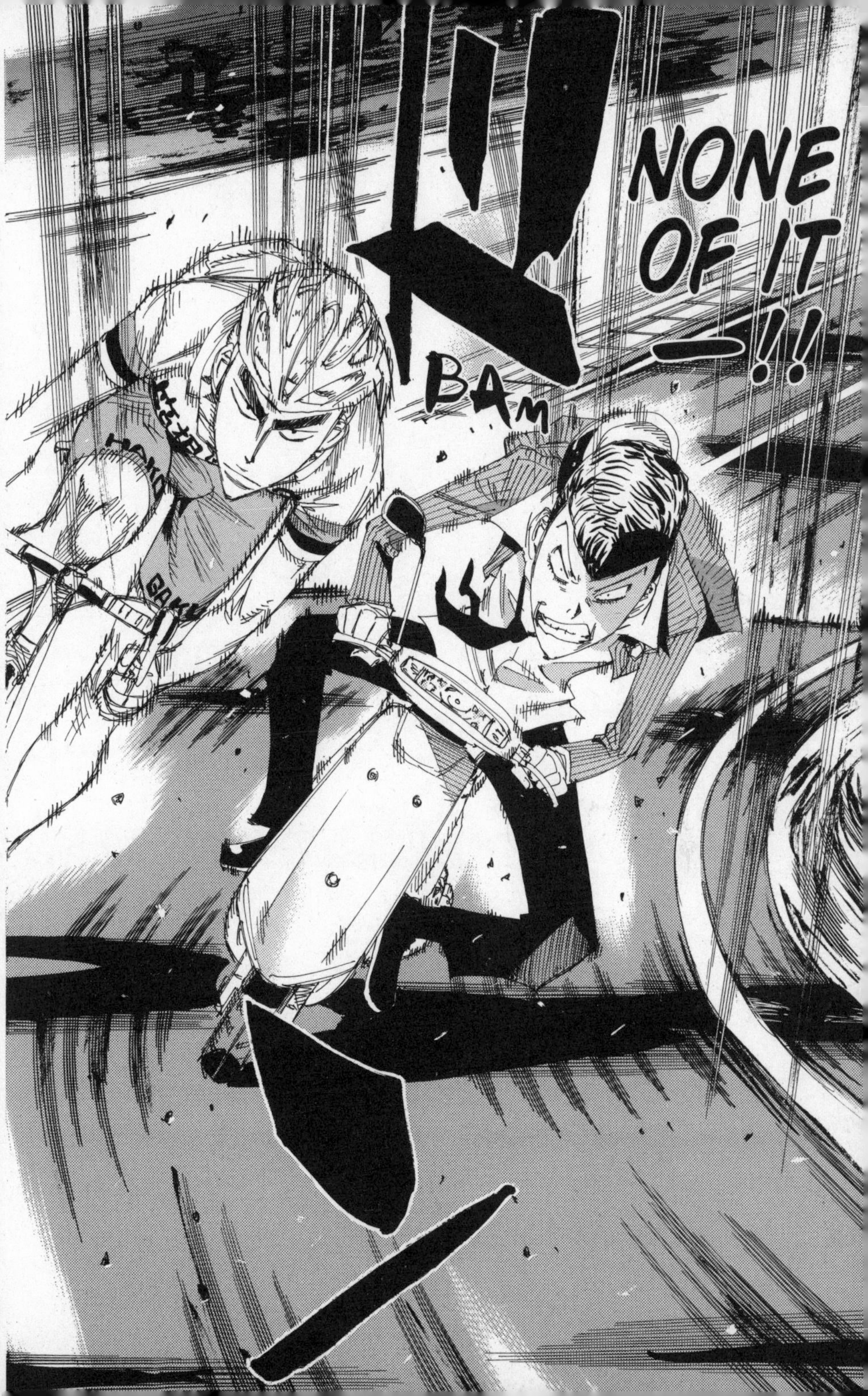
NONE OF IT—!!
BAM

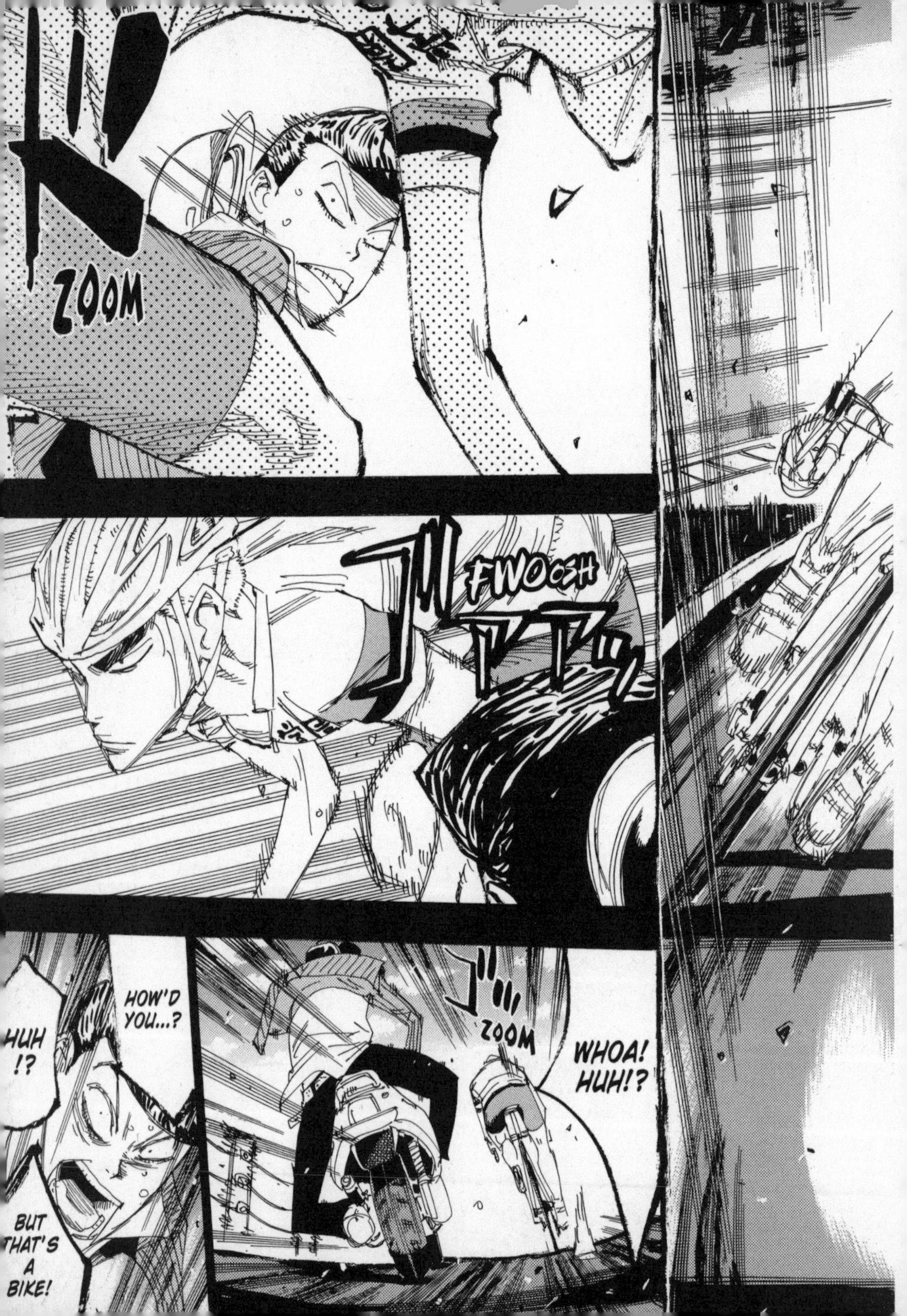
ZOOM
FWOOSH
ZOOM
WHOA! HUH!?
HOW'D YOU...?
HUH!?
BUT THAT'S A BIKE!

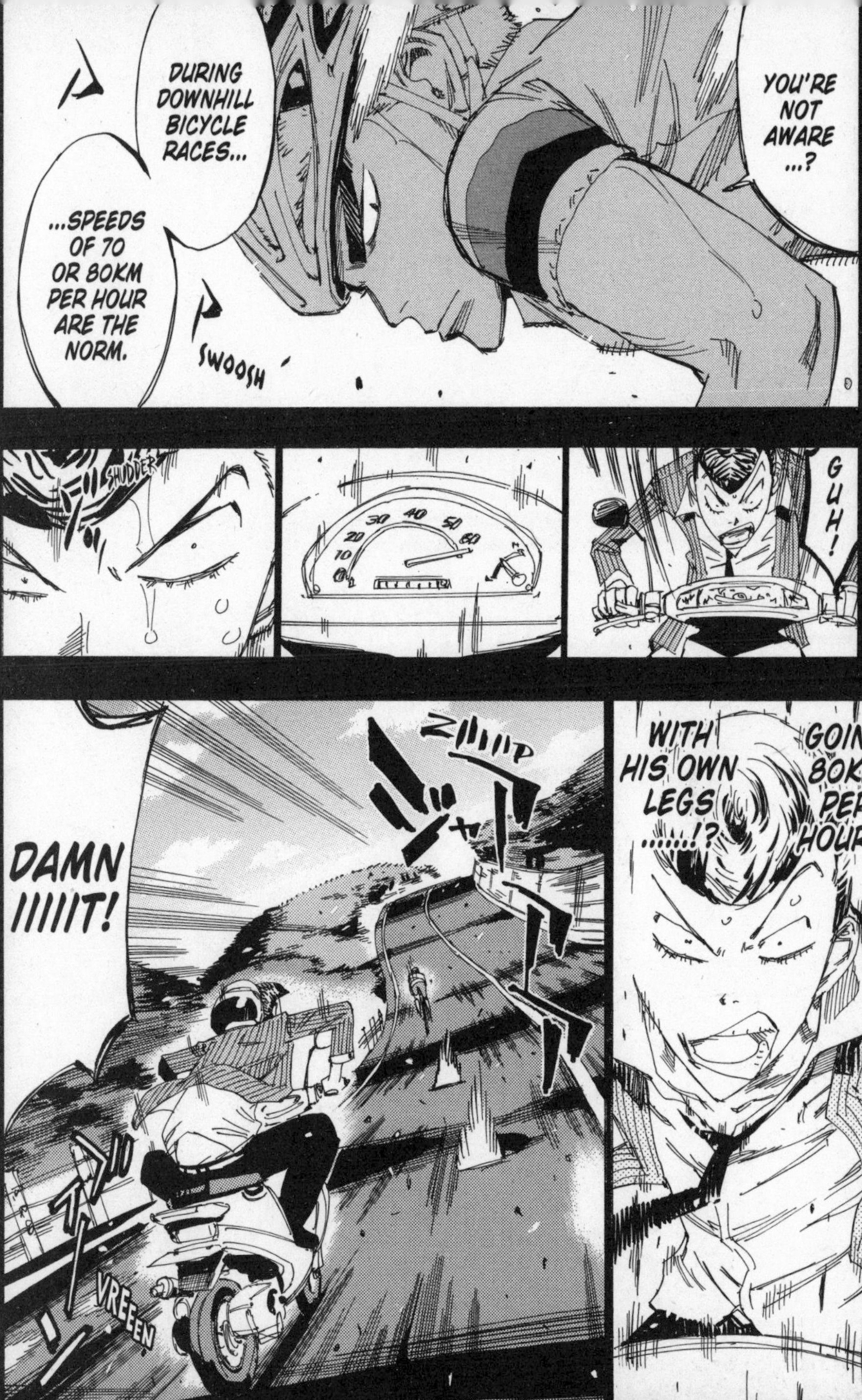
YOU'RE NOT AWARE ...?
DURING DOWNHILL BICYCLE RACES...
...SPEEDS OF 70 OR 80KM PER HOUR ARE THE NORM.
SWOOSH
GUH!
SHUDDER
GOING 80KM PER HOUR...
WITH HIS OWN LEGS ......!?
ZIIIIP
DAMN IIIIIT!
VREEEN

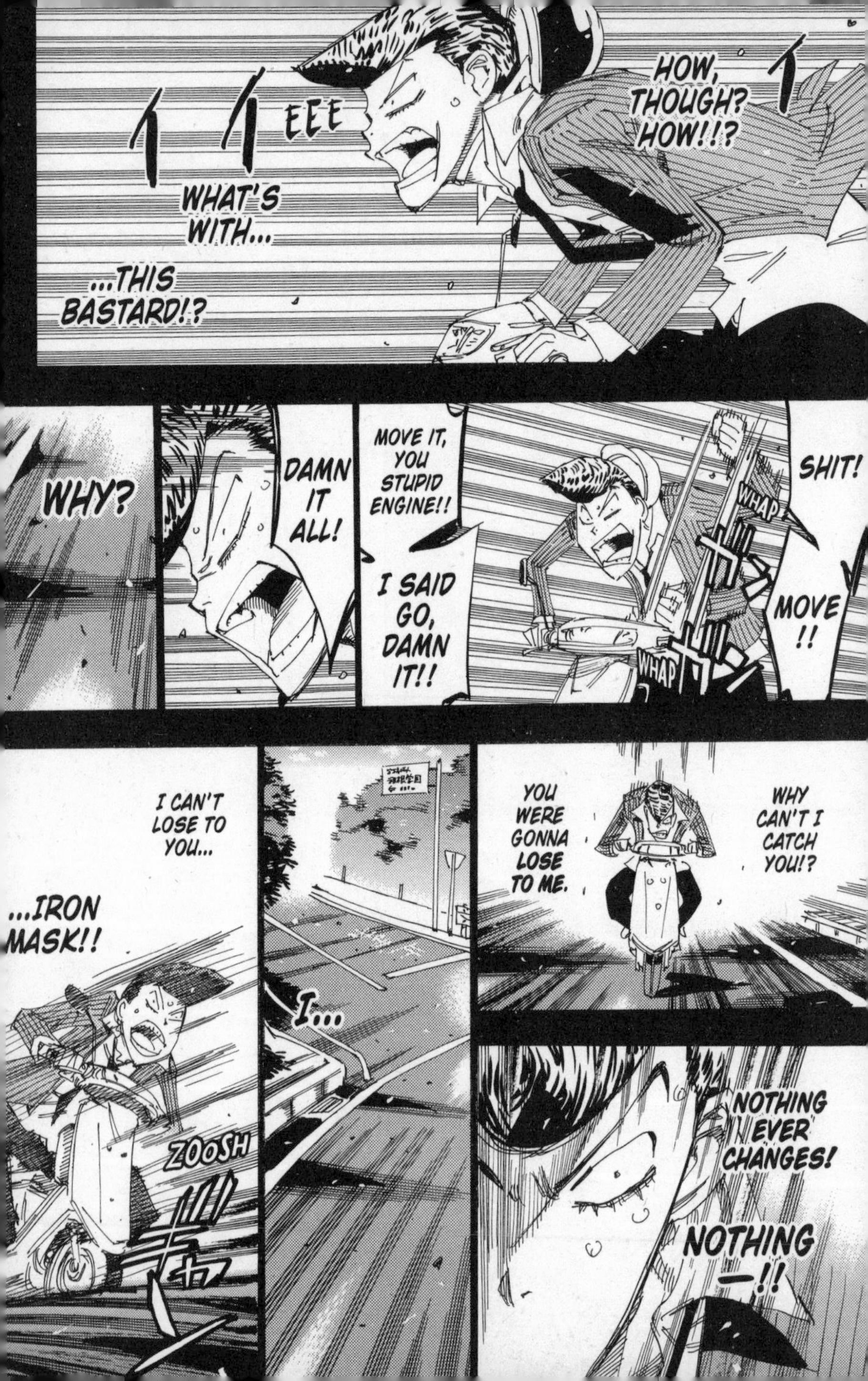
HOW, THOUGH? HOW!!?
EEE
WHAT'S WITH...
...THIS BASTARD!?
SHIT!
WHAP
MOVE!!
WHAP
MOVE IT, YOU STUPID ENGINE!!
I SAID GO, DAMN IT!!
DAMN IT ALL!
WHY?
WHY CAN'T I CATCH YOU!?
YOU WERE GONNA LOSE TO ME.
NOTHING EVER CHANGES!
NOTHING—!!
I...
I CAN'T LOSE TO YOU...
...IRON MASK!!
ZOOSH

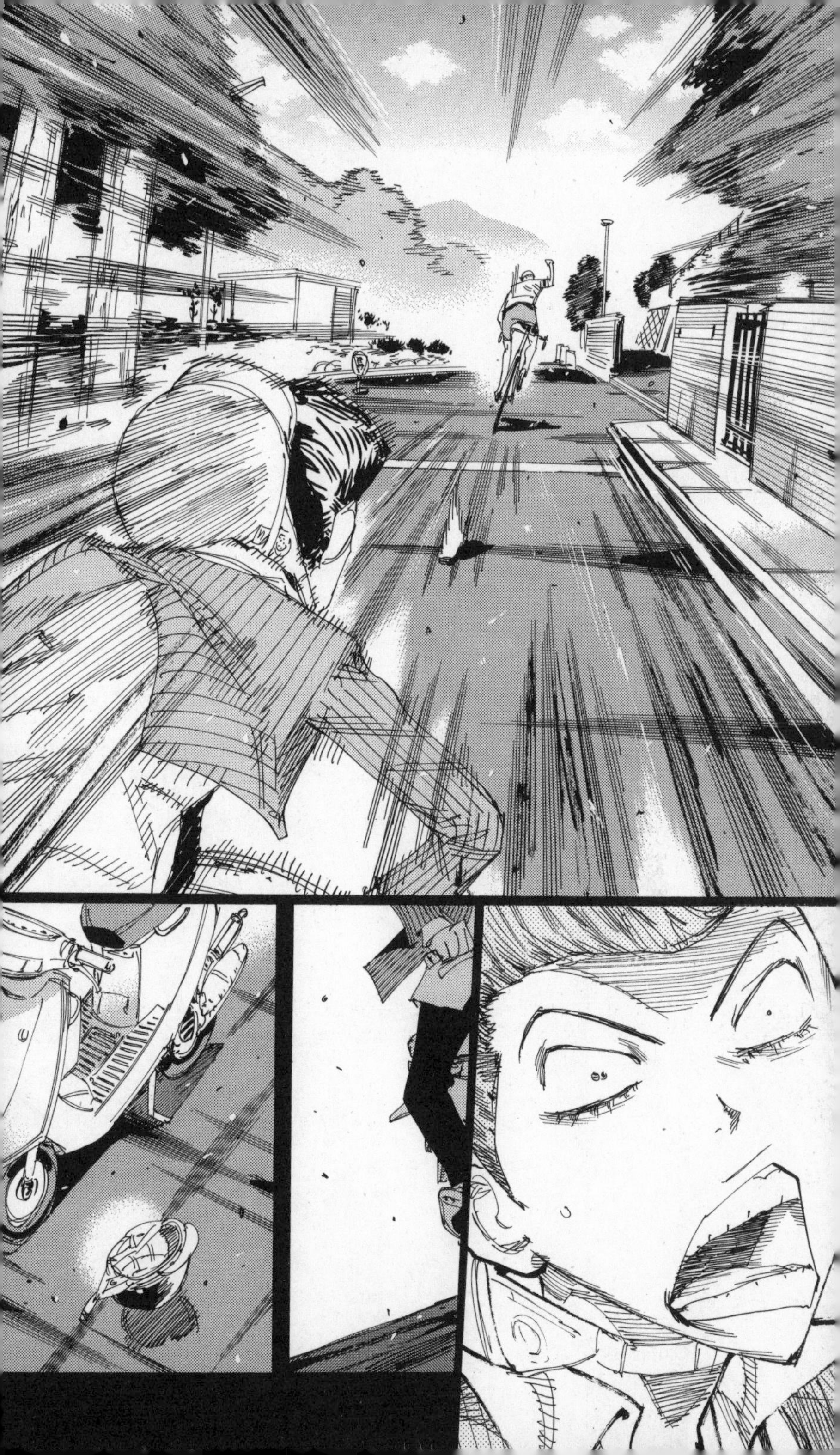

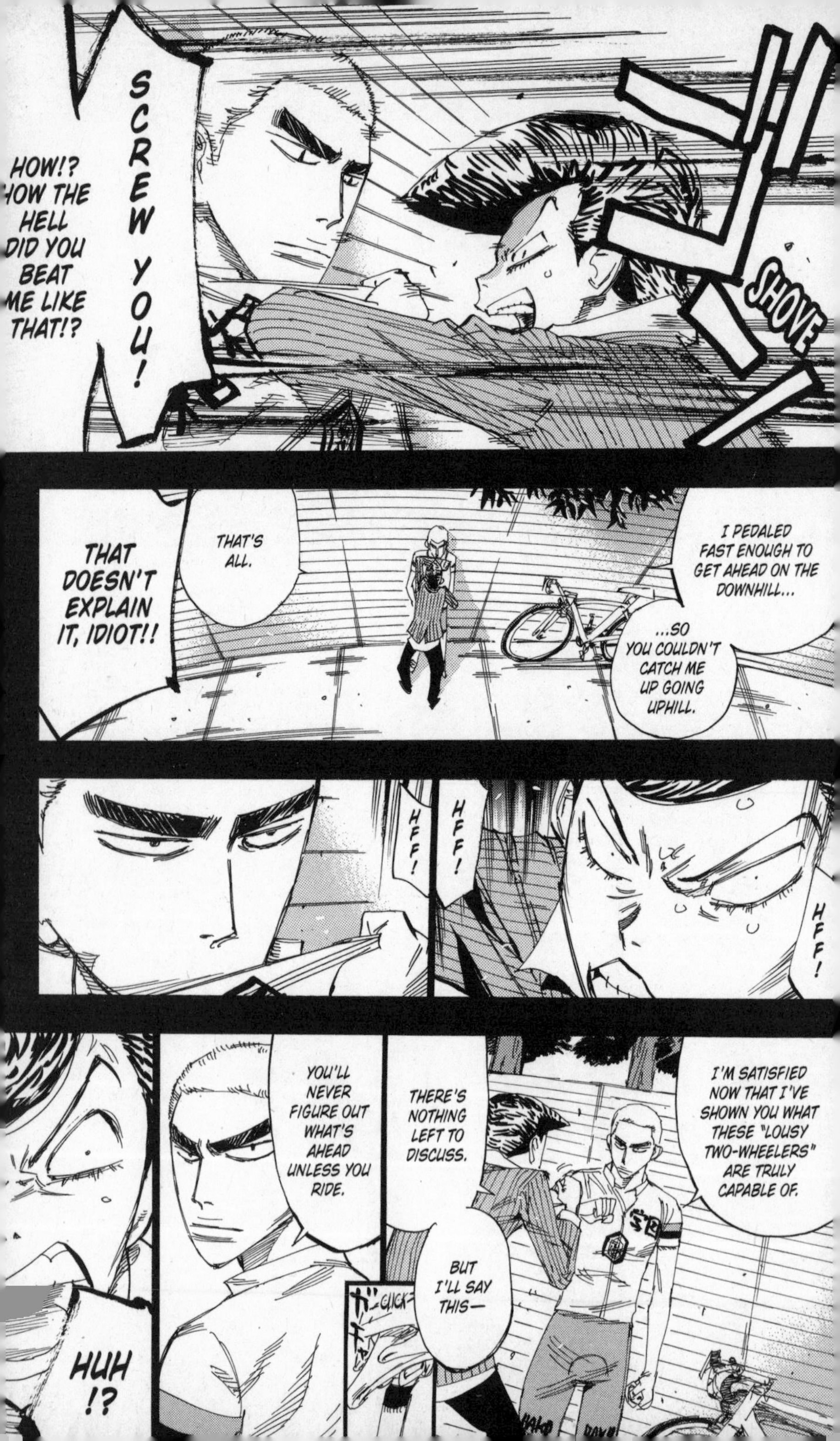
SHOVE
SCREW YOU!
HOW!? HOW THE HELL DID YOU BEAT ME LIKE THAT!?
I PEDALED FAST ENOUGH TO GET AHEAD ON THE DOWNHILL...
...SO YOU COULDN'T CATCH ME UP GOING UPHILL.
THAT'S ALL.
THAT DOESN'T EXPLAIN IT, IDIOT!!
HFF!
HFF!
HFF!
I'M SATISFIED NOW THAT I'VE SHOWN YOU WHAT THESE "LOUSY TWO-WHEELERS" ARE TRULY CAPABLE OF.
THERE'S NOTHING LEFT TO DISCUSS.
BUT I'LL SAY THIS—
YOU'LL NEVER FIGURE OUT WHAT'S AHEAD UNLESS YOU RIDE.
CLICK
HUH!?

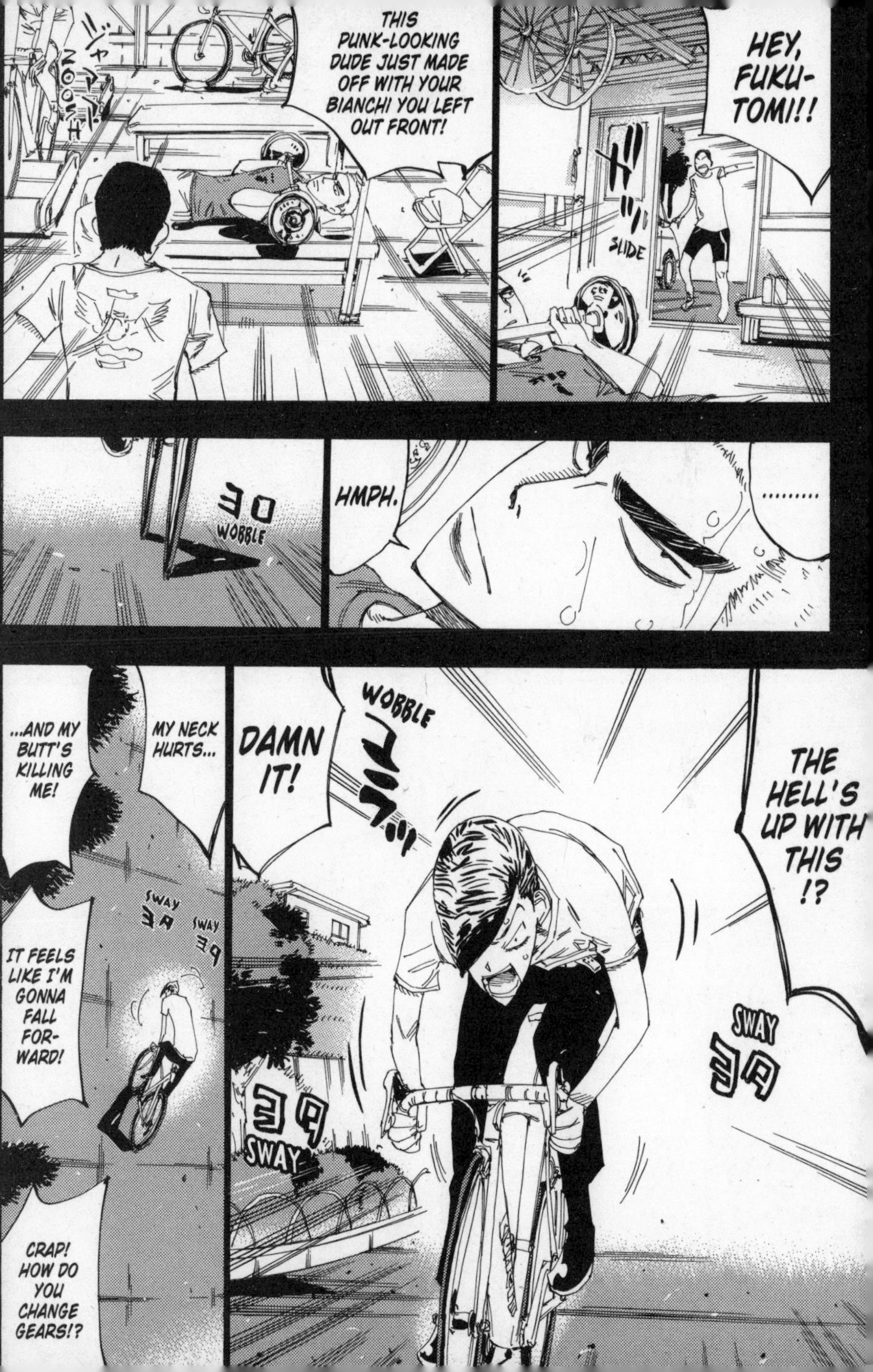
HEY, FUKU-TOMI!!
SLIDE
THIS PUNK-LOOKING DUDE JUST MADE OFF WITH YOUR BIANCHI YOU LEFT OUT FRONT!
ZOOSH
....
HMPH.
WOBBLE
THE HELL'S UP WITH THIS!?
WOBBLE
DAMN IT!
SWAY
SWAY
MY NECK HURTS...
...AND MY BUTT'S KILLING ME!
SWAY
SWAY
IT FEELS LIKE I'M GONNA FALL FOR-WARD!
CRAP! HOW DO YOU CHANGE GEARS!?

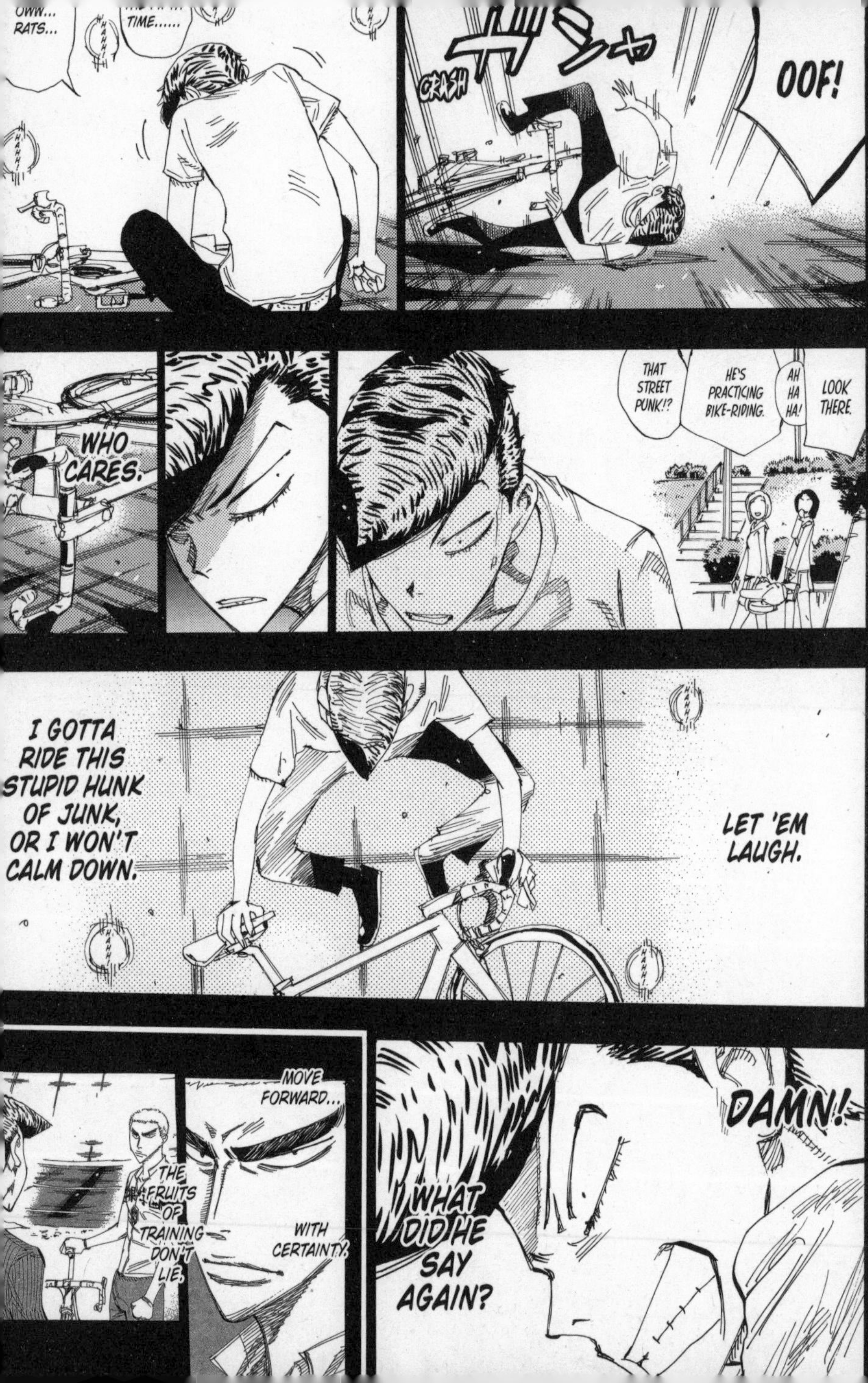
CRASH
OOF!
OWW... RATS...
TIME......
LOOK THERE.
AH HA HA!
HE'S PRACTICING BIKE-RIDING.
THAT STREET PUNK!?
WHO CARES.
LET 'EM LAUGH.
I GOTTA RIDE THIS STUPID HUNK OF JUNK, OR I WON'T CALM DOWN.
DAMN!
WHAT DID HE SAY AGAIN?
MOVE FORWARD...
WITH CERTAINTY.
THE FRUITS OF TRAINING DON'T LIE.

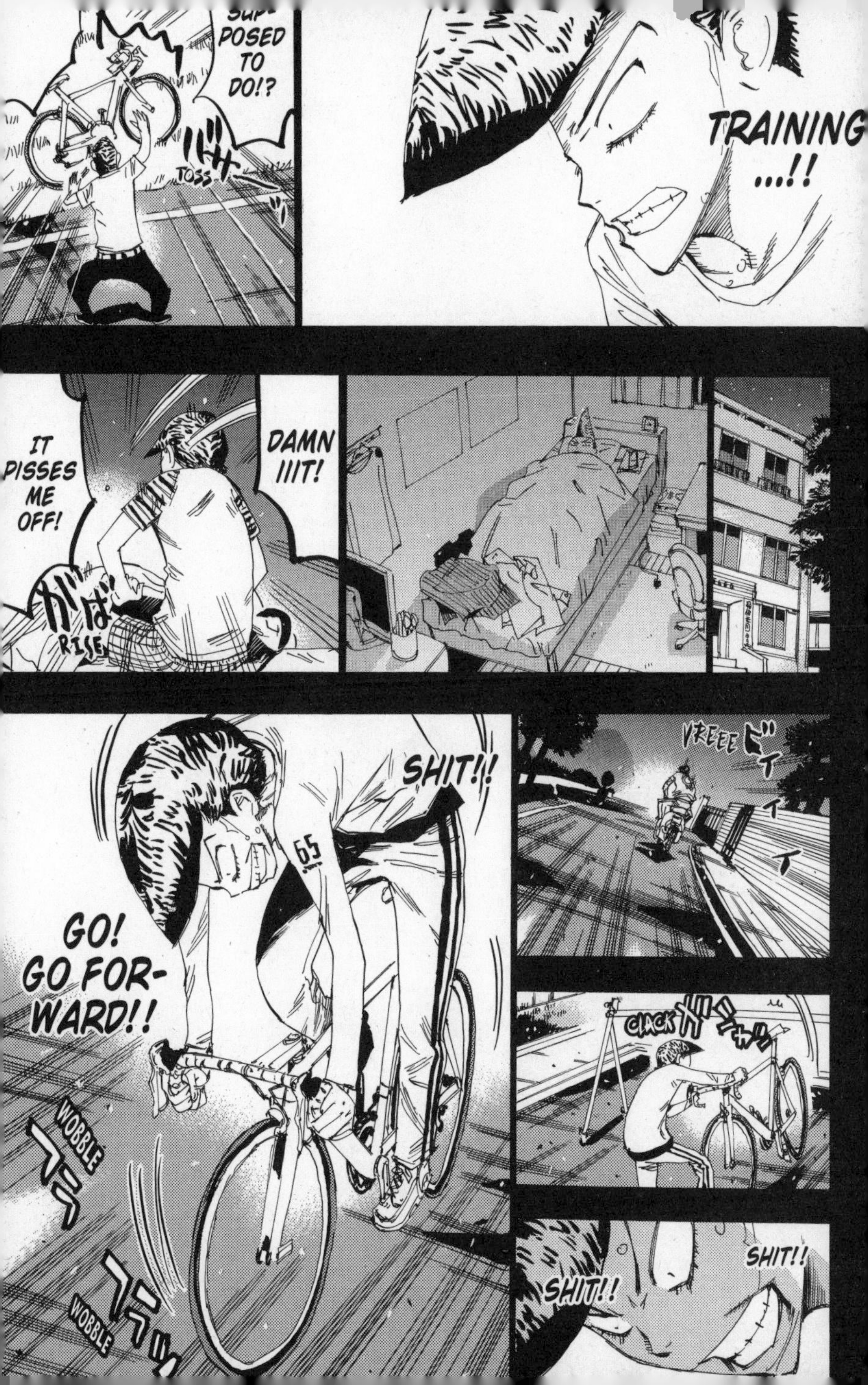
TRAINING ...!!
SUP-POSED TO DO!?
TOSS
DAMN IIIT!
IT PISSES ME OFF!
RISE
VREEE
CLACK
SHIT!!
SHIT!!
SHIT!!
GO! GO FOR-WARD!!
WOBBLE
WOBBLE

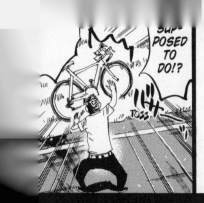

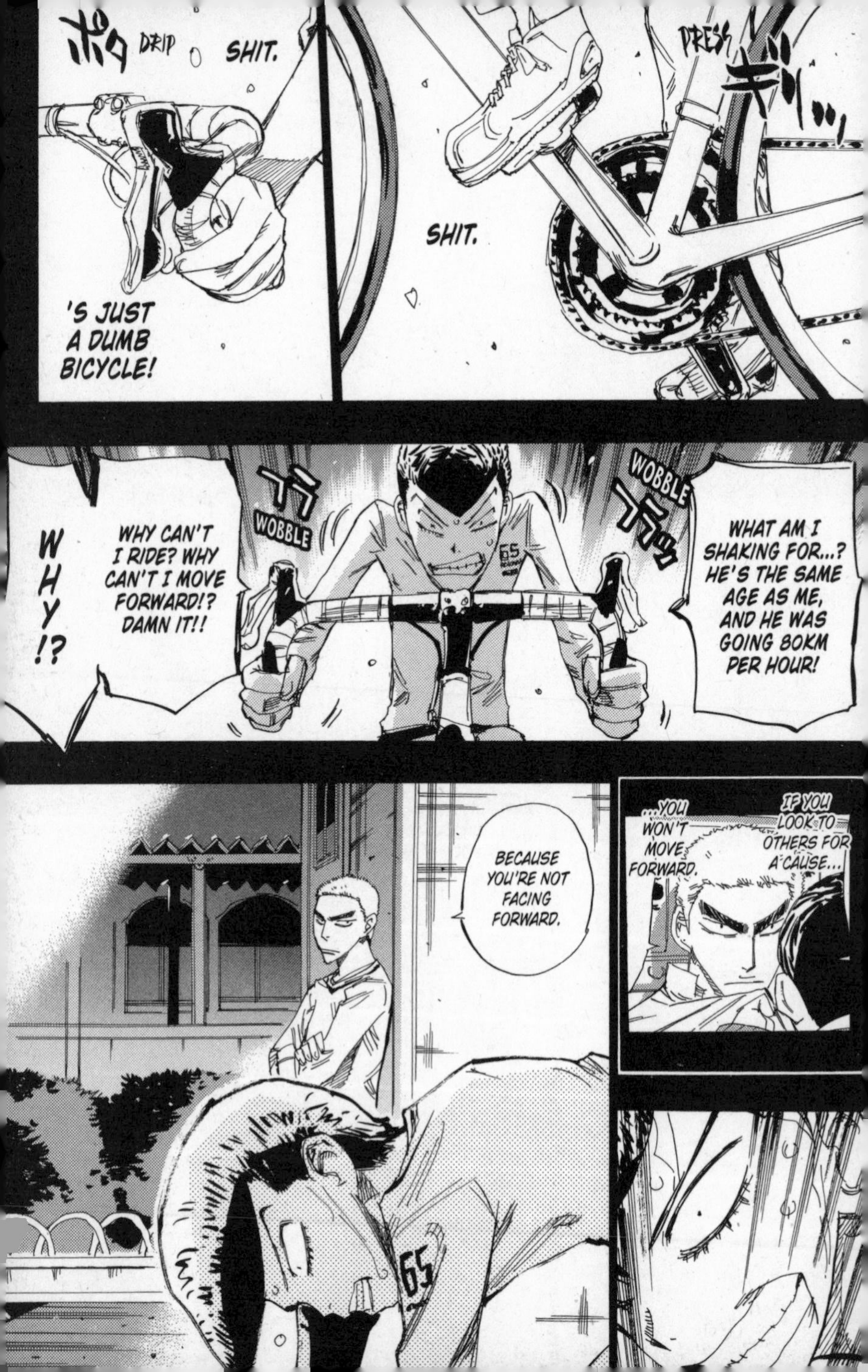
PRESS
ギリ…
SHIT.
ポタ DRIP
SHIT.
'S JUST A DUMB BICYCLE!
フラッ WOBBLE
WHAT AM I SHAKING FOR...? HE'S THE SAME AGE AS ME, AND HE WAS GOING 80KM PER HOUR!
フラ WOBBLE
WHY CAN'T I RIDE? WHY CAN'T I MOVE FORWARD!? DAMN IT!!
WHY!?
IF YOU LOOK TO OTHERS FOR A CAUSE...
...YOU WON'T MOVE FORWARD.
BECAUSE YOU'RE NOT FACING FORWARD.

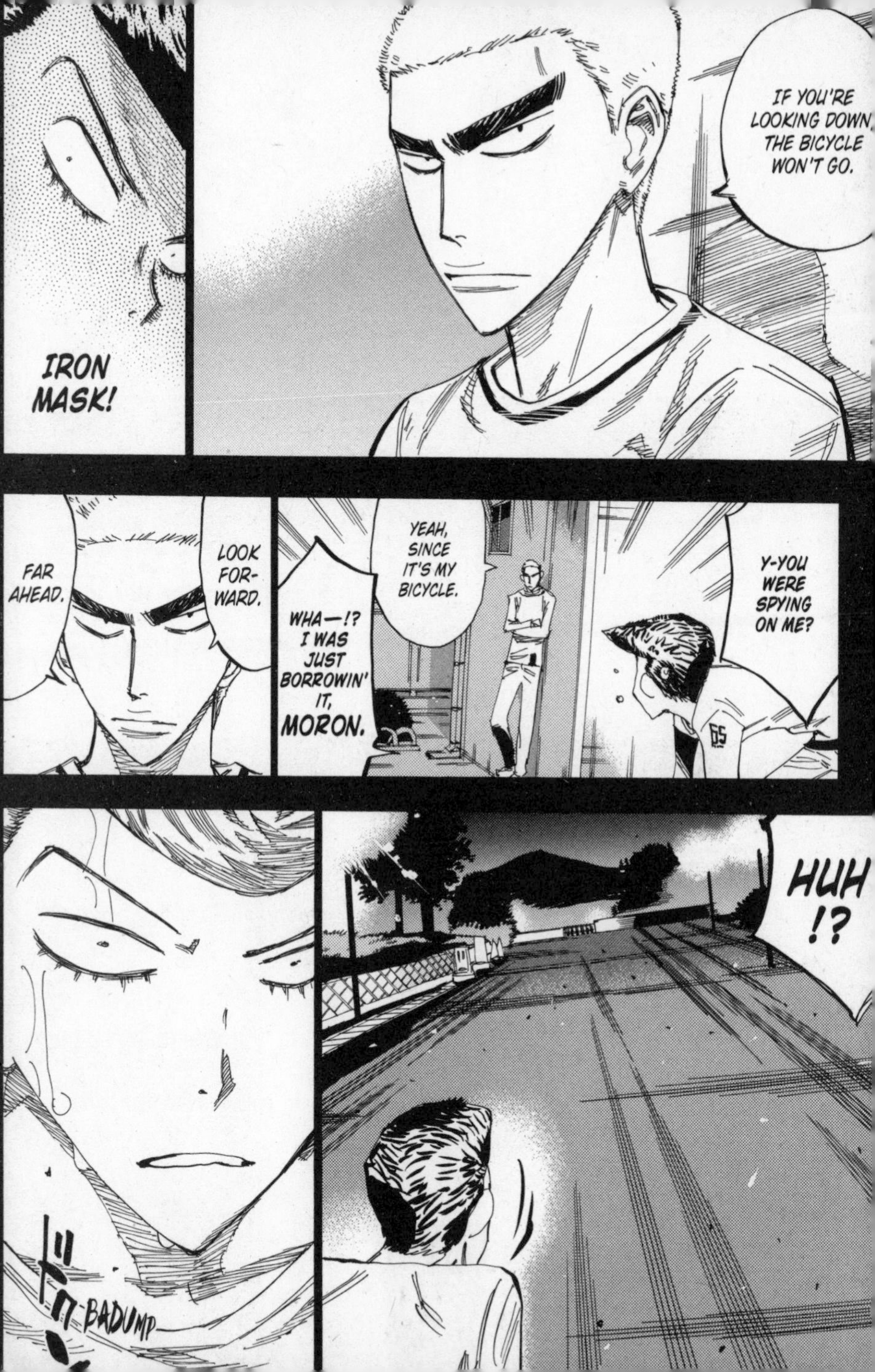
IF YOU'RE LOOKING DOWN, THE BICYCLE WON'T GO.
IRON MASK!
Y-YOU WERE SPYING ON ME?
YEAH, SINCE IT'S MY BICYCLE.
WHA—!? I WAS JUST BORROWIN' IT, MORON.
LOOK FOR-WARD.
FAR AHEAD.
HUH !?
BADUMP

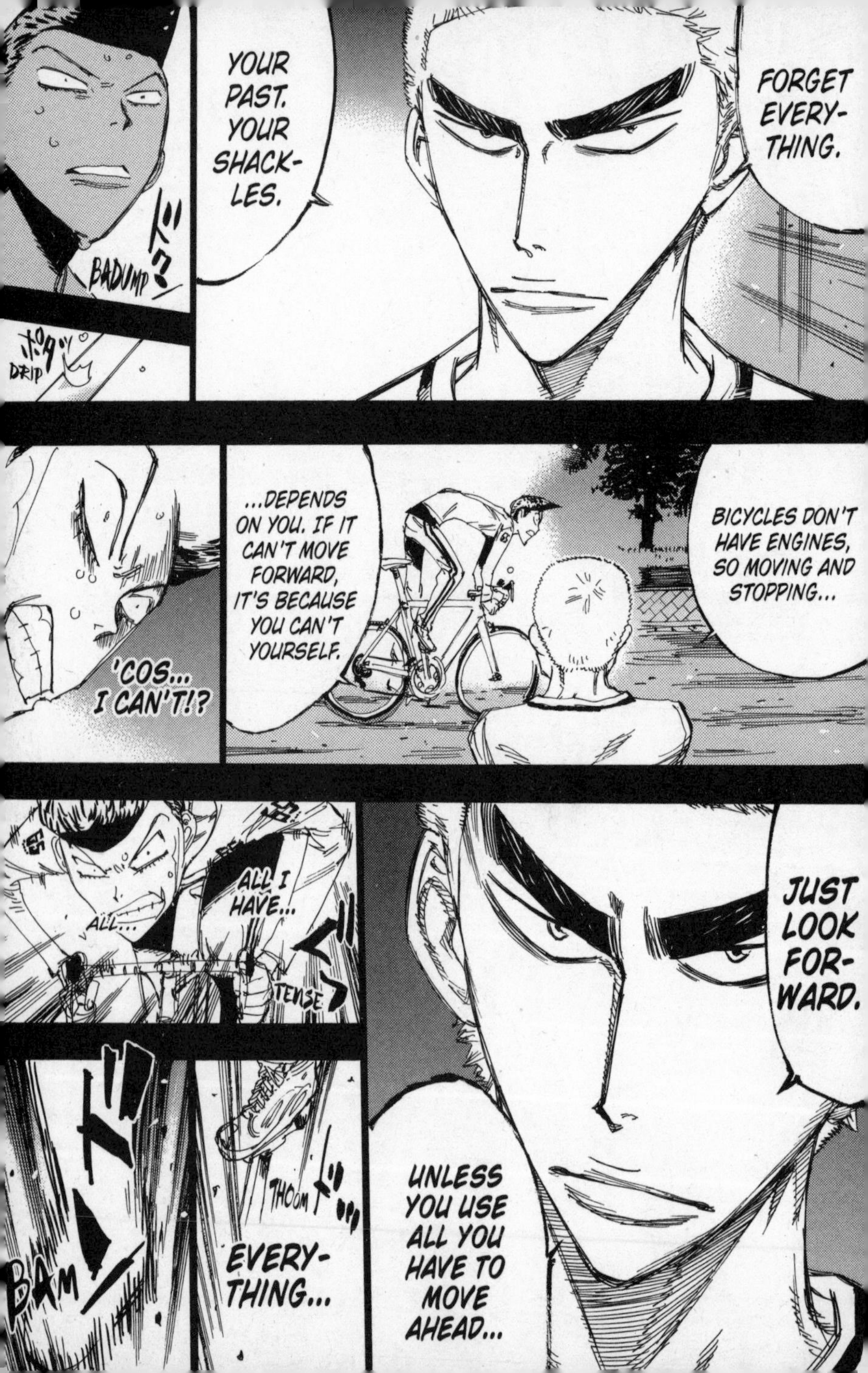
FORGET EVERY-THING.
YOUR PAST. YOUR SHACK-LES.
BADUMP
DRIP
BICYCLES DON'T HAVE ENGINES, SO MOVING AND STOPPING...
...DEPENDS ON YOU. IF IT CAN'T MOVE FORWARD, IT'S BECAUSE YOU CAN'T YOURSELF.
'COS... I CAN'T!?
JUST LOOK FOR-WARD.
UNLESS YOU USE ALL YOU HAVE TO MOVE AHEAD...
ALL I HAVE...
ALL...
TENSE
EVERY-THING...
THOOM
BAM

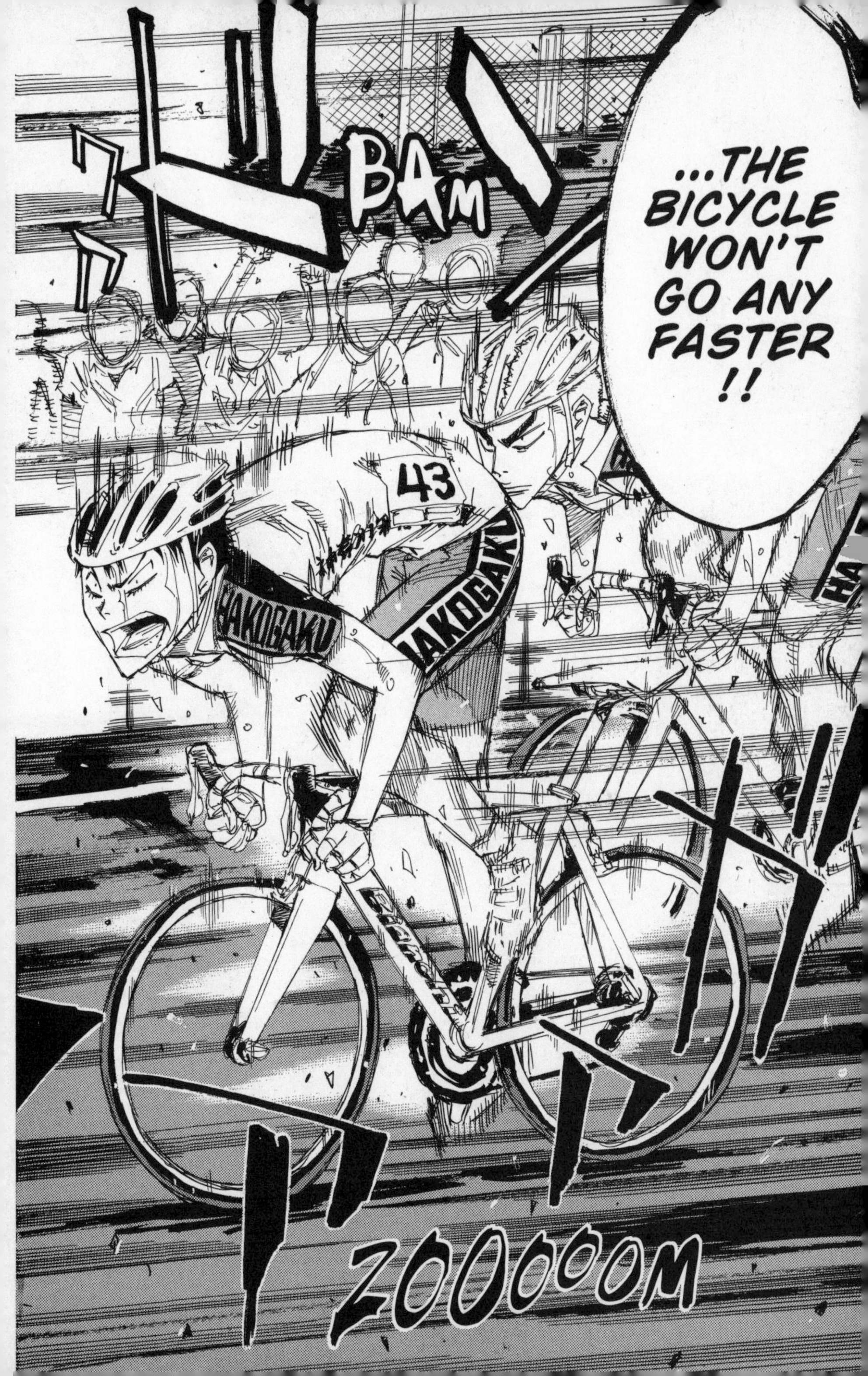

BAM
...THE BICYCLE WON'T GO ANY FASTER !!
43
HAKOGAKU
HAKOGAKU
ZOOOOOM

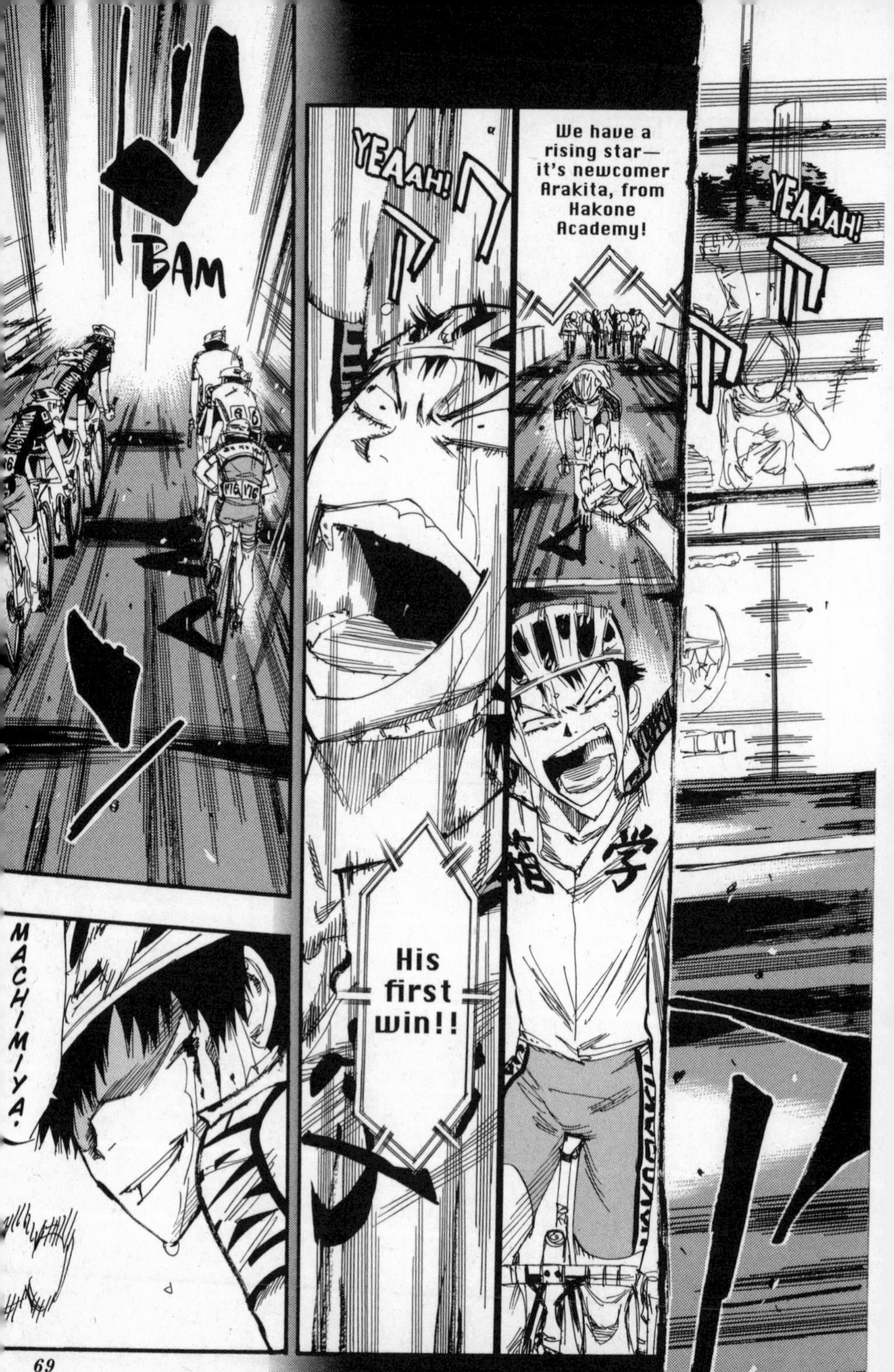
YEAAAH!
We have a rising star—it's newcomer Arakita, from Hakone Academy!
YEAAH!
His first win!!
BAM
MACHIMIYA.

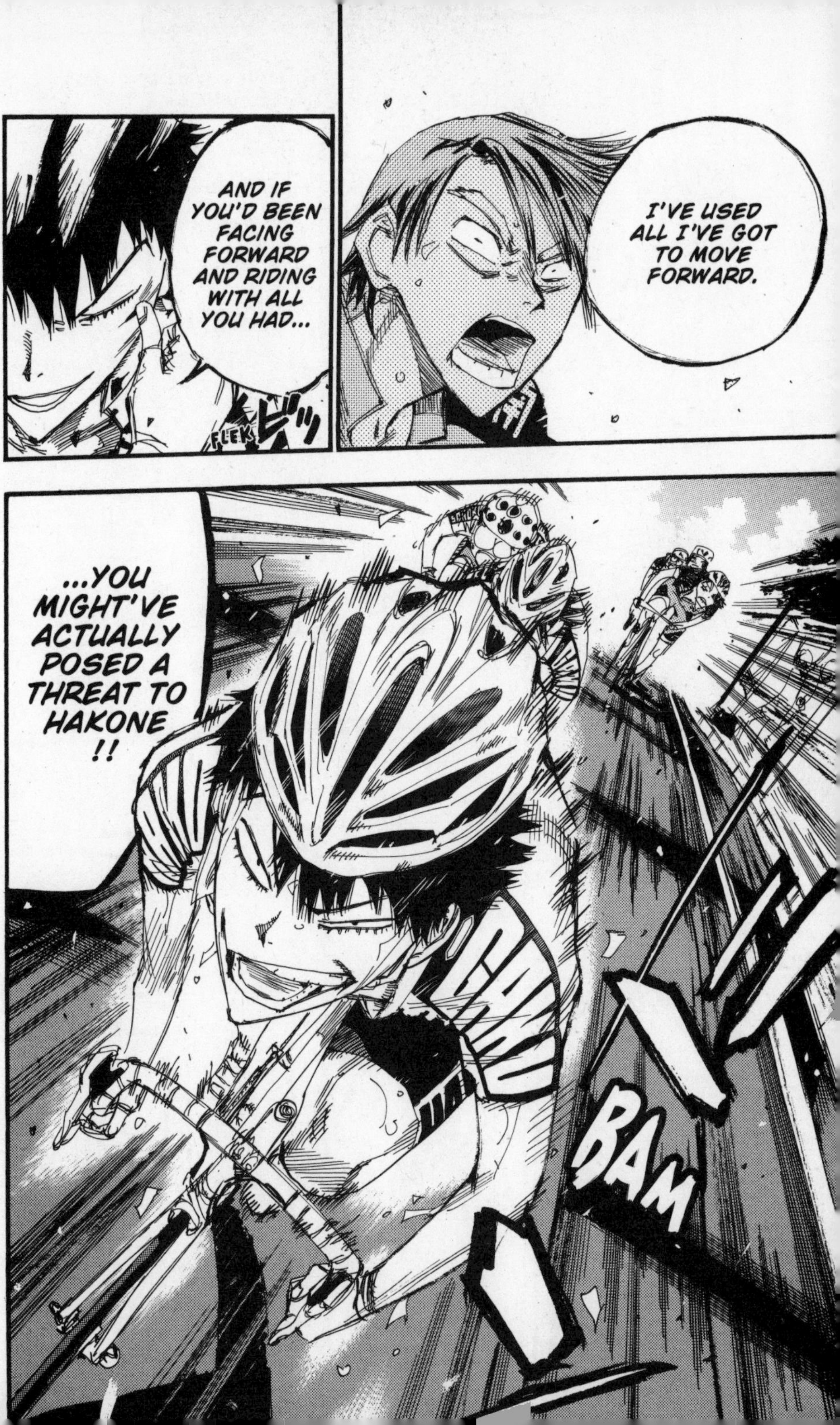
I'VE USED ALL I'VE GOT TO MOVE FORWARD.
AND IF YOU'D BEEN FACING FORWARD AND RIDING WITH ALL YOU HAD...
FLEK
ビッ
...YOU MIGHT'VE ACTUALLY POSED A THREAT TO HAKONE !!
BAM

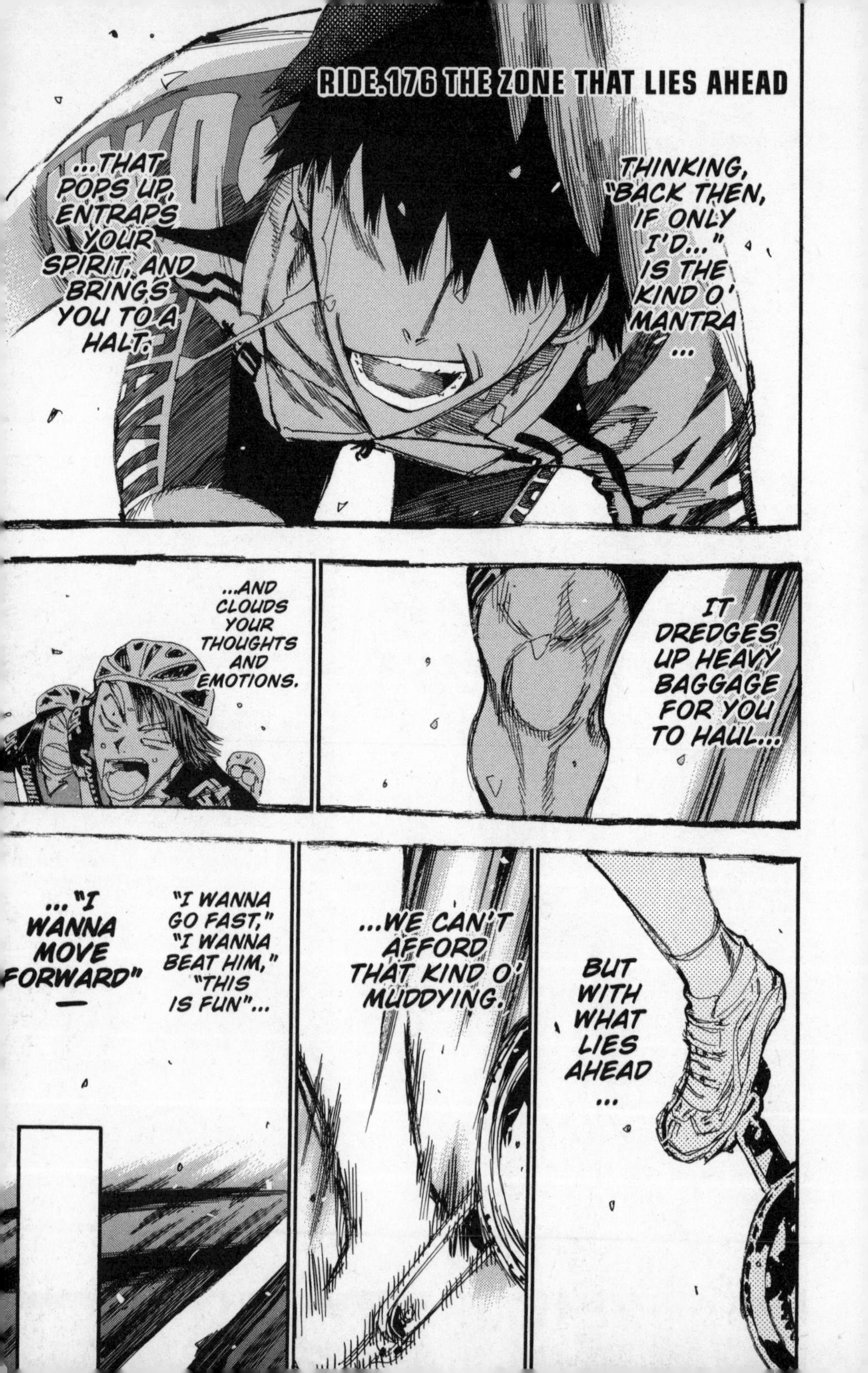
RIDE.176 THE ZONE THAT LIES AHEAD
THINKING, "BACK THEN, IF ONLY I'D..." IS THE KIND O' MANTRA...
...THAT POPS UP, ENTRAPS YOUR SPIRIT, AND BRINGS YOU TO A HALT.
IT DREDGES UP HEAVY BAGGAGE FOR YOU TO HAUL...
...AND CLOUDS YOUR THOUGHTS AND EMOTIONS.
BUT WITH WHAT LIES AHEAD...
...WE CAN'T AFFORD THAT KIND O' MUDDYING.
"I WANNA GO FAST," "I WANNA BEAT HIM," "THIS IS FUN"...
..."I WANNA MOVE FORWARD"—

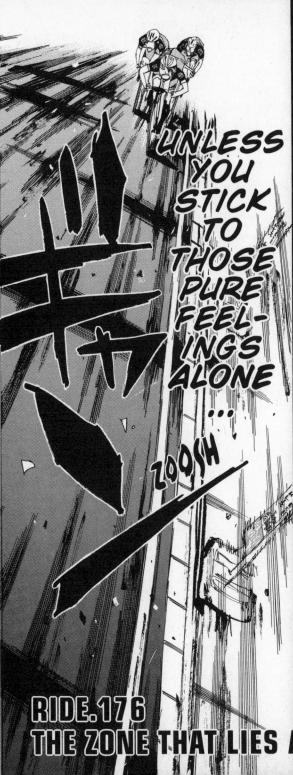

UNLESS YOU STICK TO THOSE PURE FEELINGS ALONE...

ZOOSH

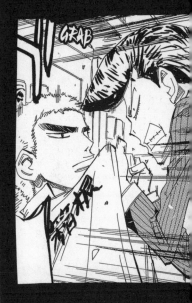

GRAB

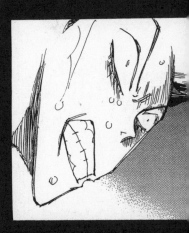

RIDE.176
THE ZONE THAT LIES AHEAD

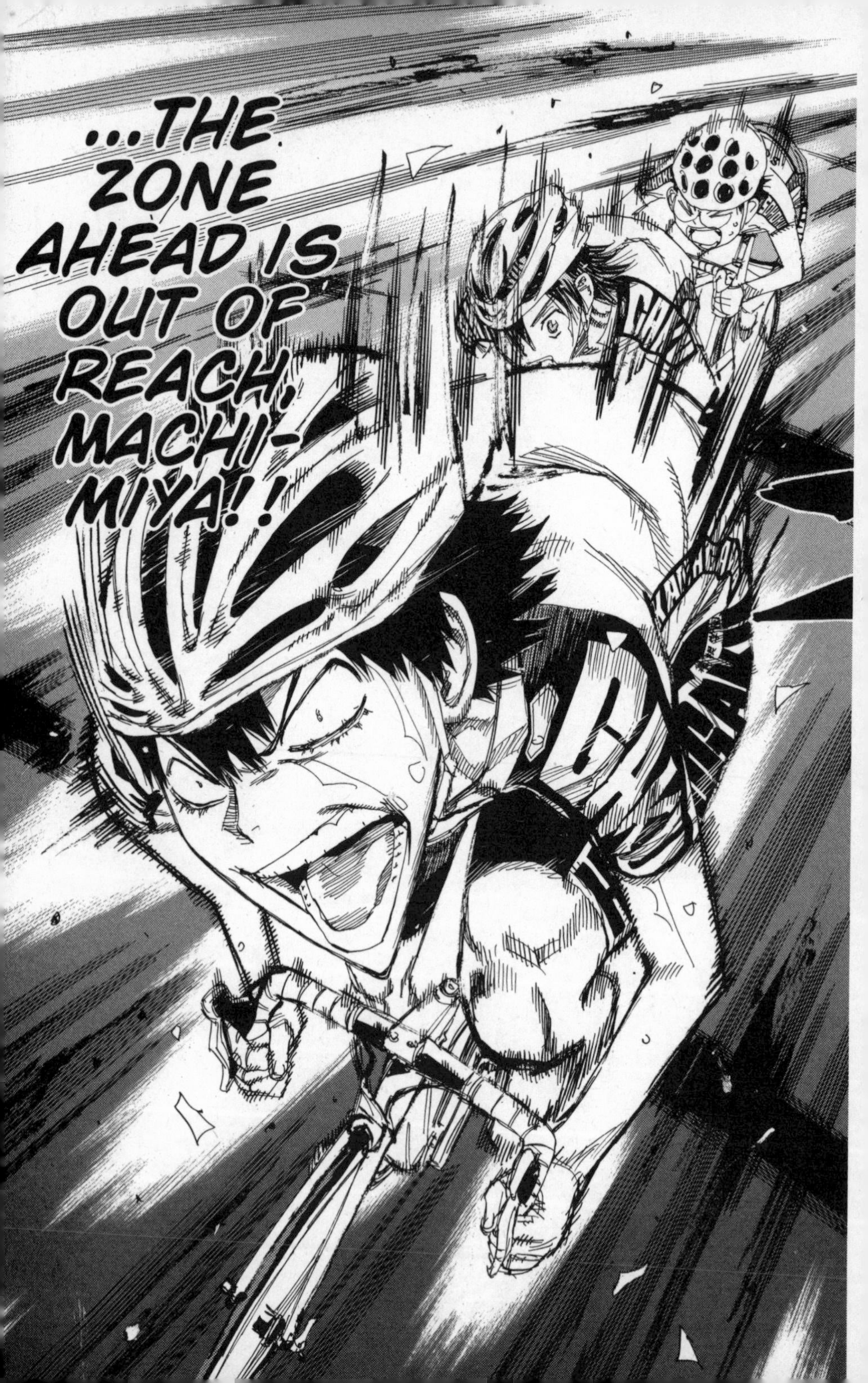
...THE ZONE AHEAD IS OUT OF REACH, MACHI-MIYA!!

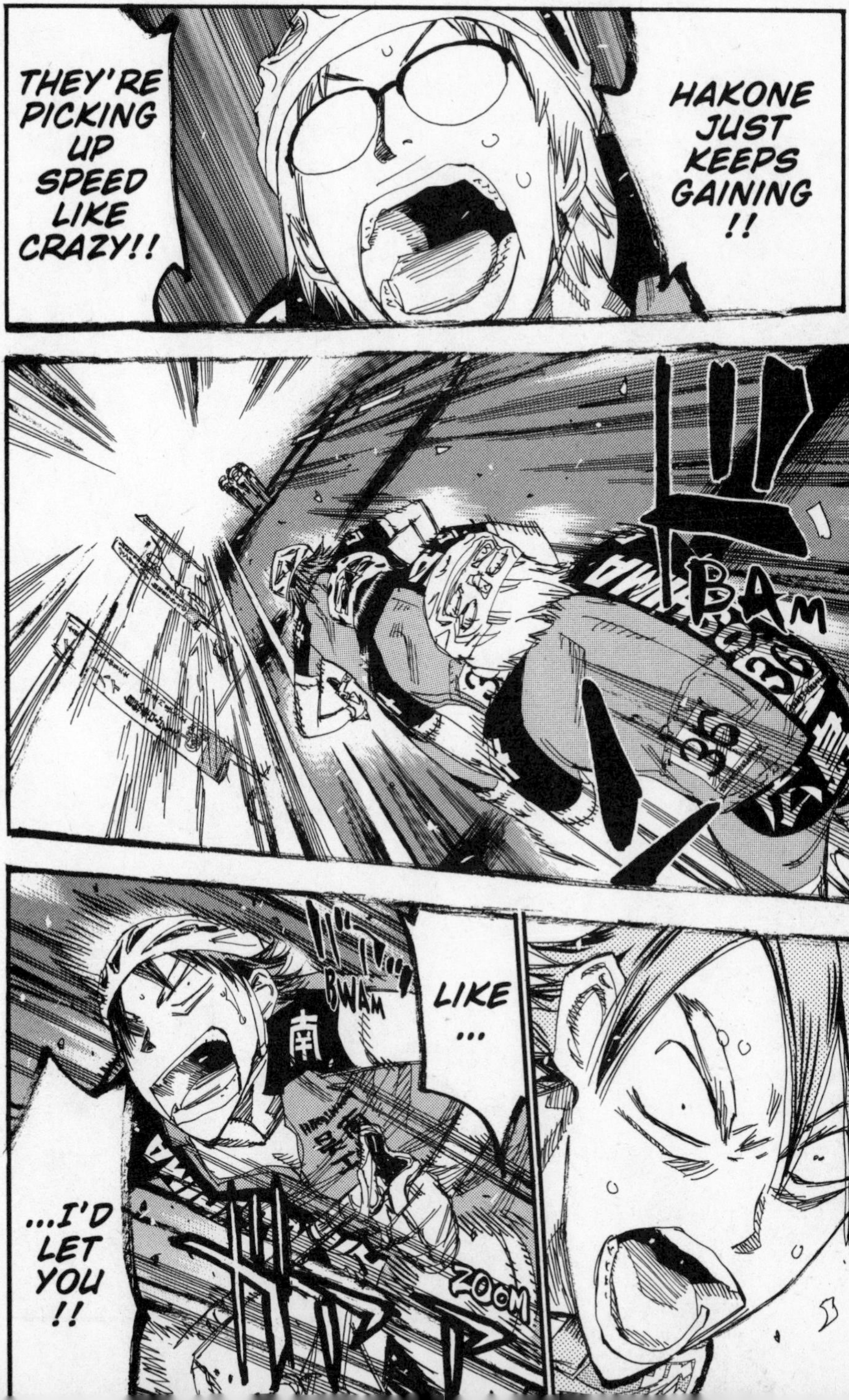
HAKONE JUST KEEPS GAINING!!
THEY'RE PICKING UP SPEED LIKE CRAZY!!
BAM
BWAM
LIKE...
...I'D LET YOU!!
ZOOM

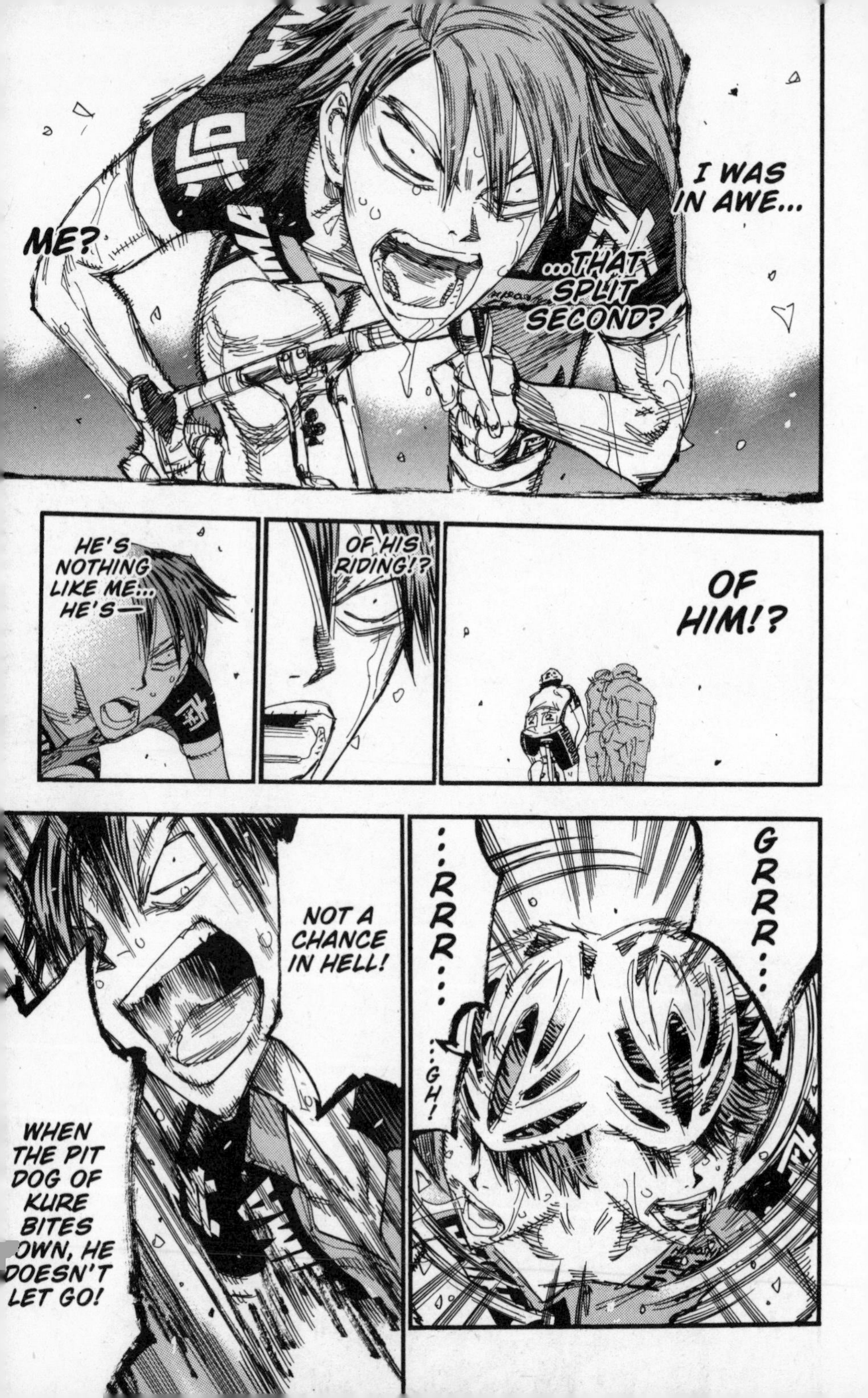
I WAS IN AWE...
...THAT SPLIT SECOND?
ME?
OF HIM!?
OF HIS RIDING!?
HE'S NOTHING LIKE ME... HE'S—
GRRR...
...RRR...
...GH!
NOT A CHANCE IN HELL!
WHEN THE PIT DOG OF KURE BITES OWN, HE DOESN'T LET GO!

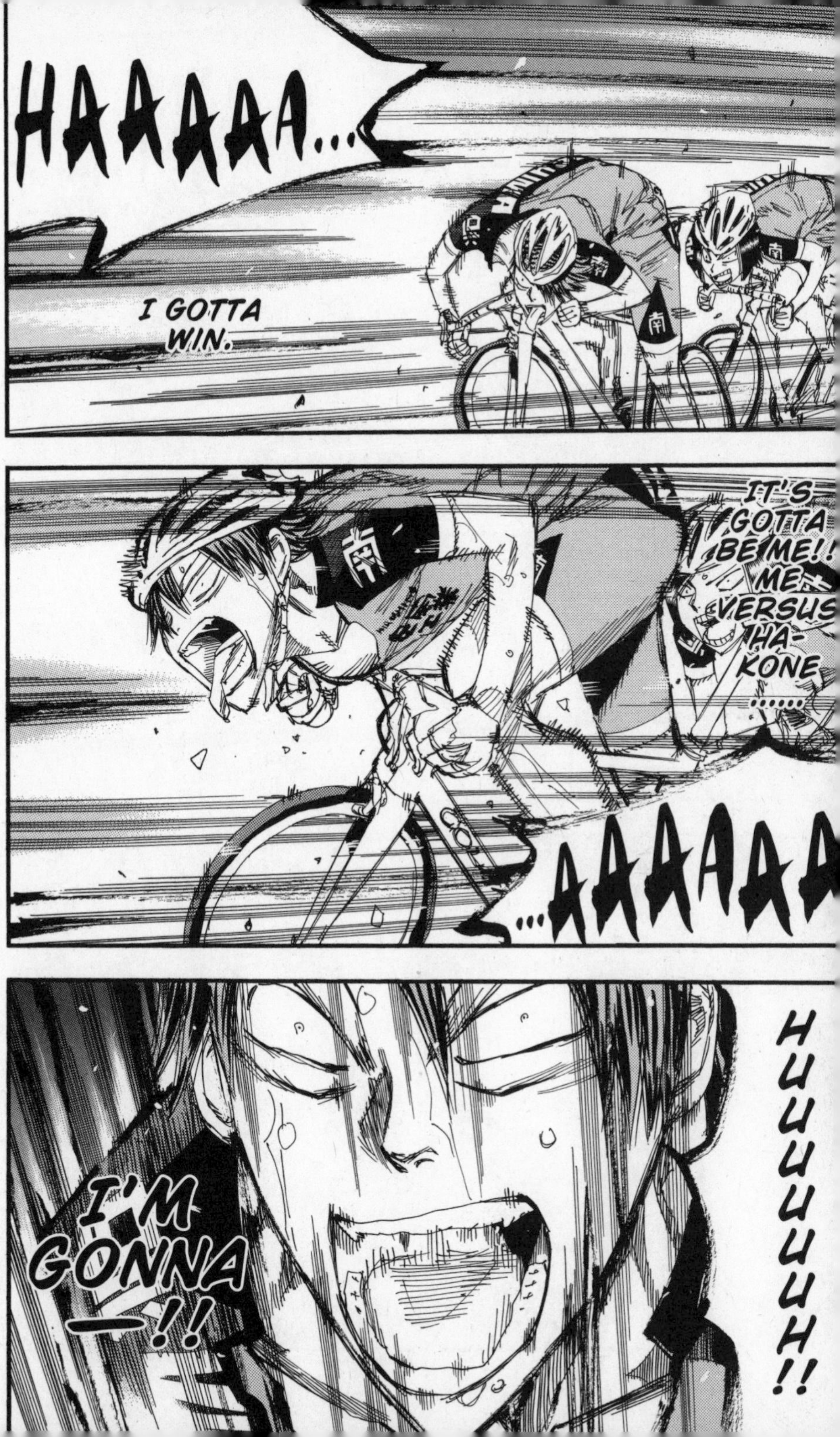
HAAAAA...
I GOTTA WIN.
IT'S GOTTA BE ME!! ME VERSUS HAKONE......
...AAAAA
HUUUUUUUH!!
I'M GONNA—!!

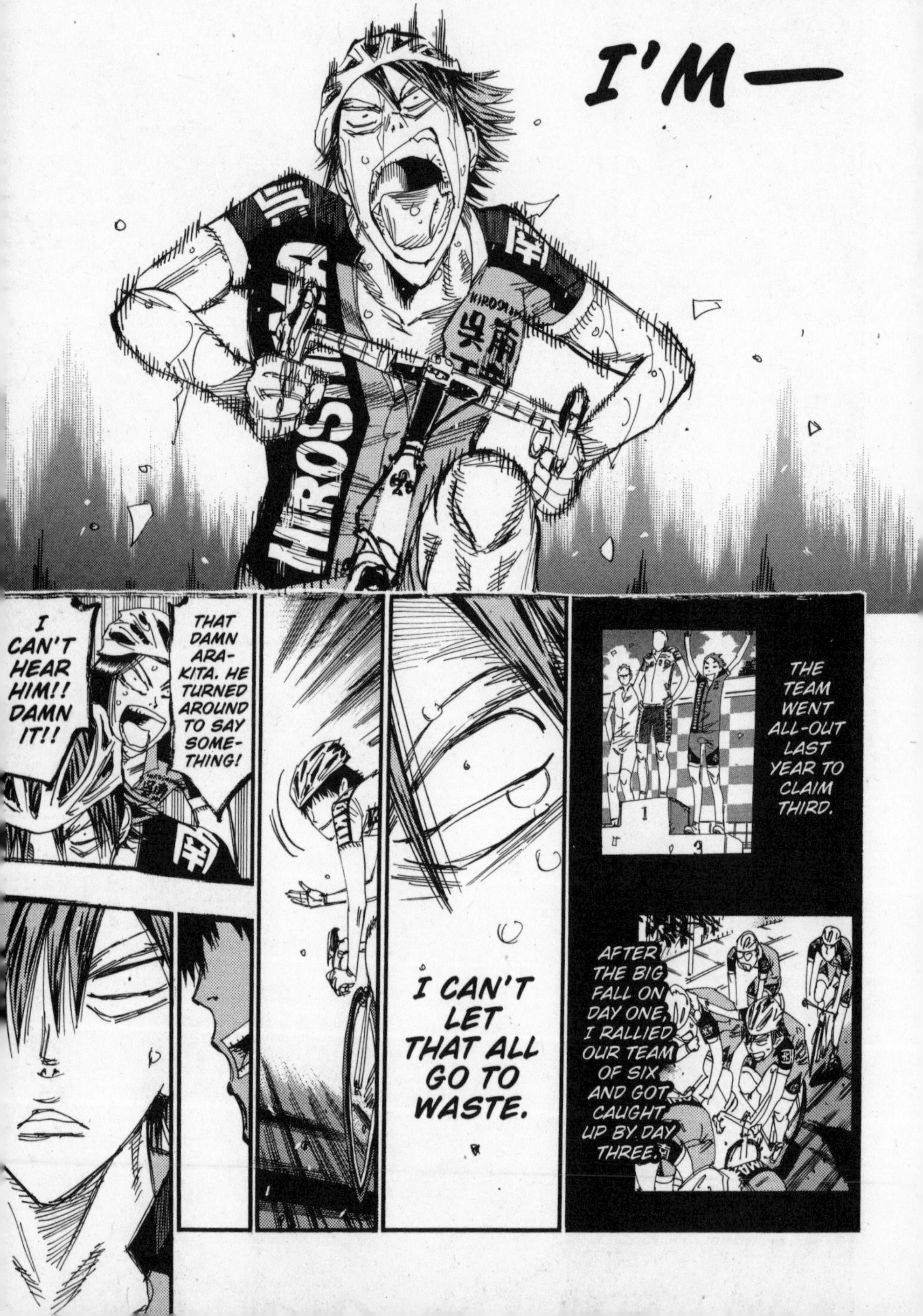
I'M—
THE TEAM WENT ALL-OUT LAST YEAR TO CLAIM THIRD.
AFTER THE BIG FALL ON DAY ONE, I RALLIED OUR TEAM OF SIX AND GOT CAUGHT UP BY DAY THREE.
I CAN'T LET THAT ALL GO TO WASTE.
THAT DAMN ARAKITA. HE TURNED AROUND TO SAY SOMETHING!
I CAN'T HEAR HIM!! DAMN IT!!

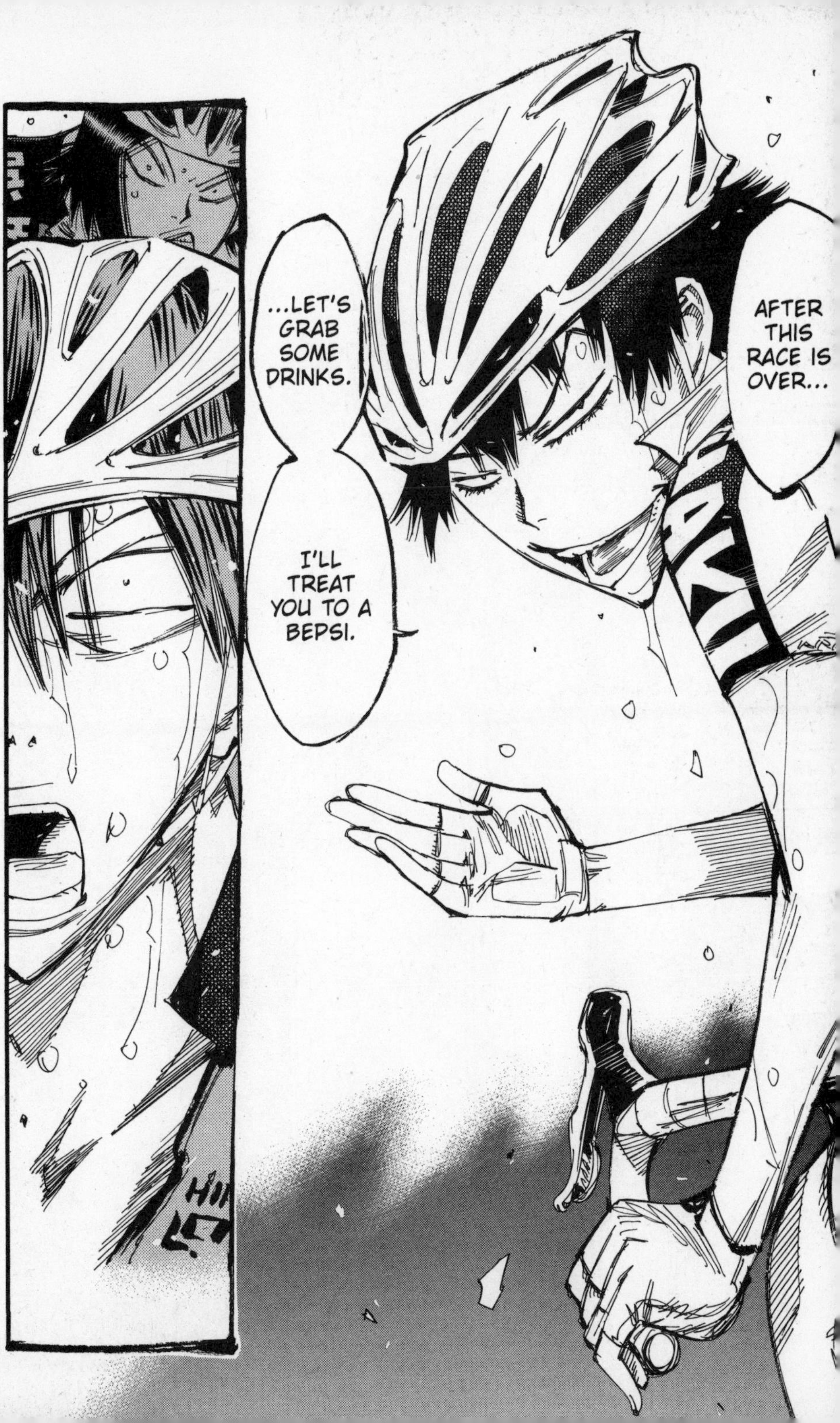
AFTER THIS RACE IS OVER...
...LET'S GRAB SOME DRINKS.
I'LL TREAT YOU TO A BEPSI.

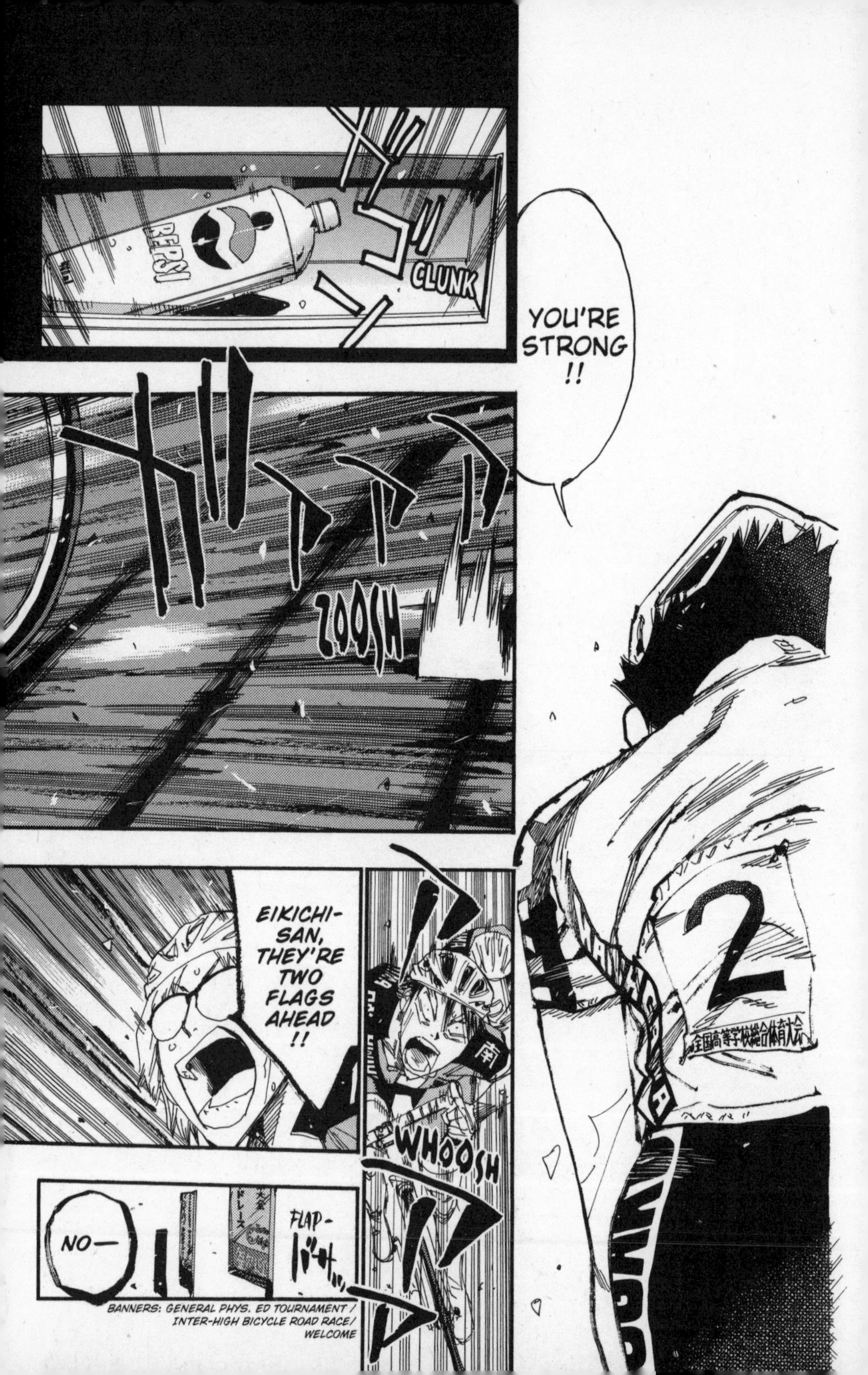
YOU'RE STRONG!!
CLUNK
ZOOSH
WHOOSH
EIKICHI-SAN, THEY'RE TWO FLAGS AHEAD!!
FLAP-
NO—
BANNERS: GENERAL PHYS. ED TOURNAMENT / INTER-HIGH BICYCLE ROAD RACE/ WELCOME

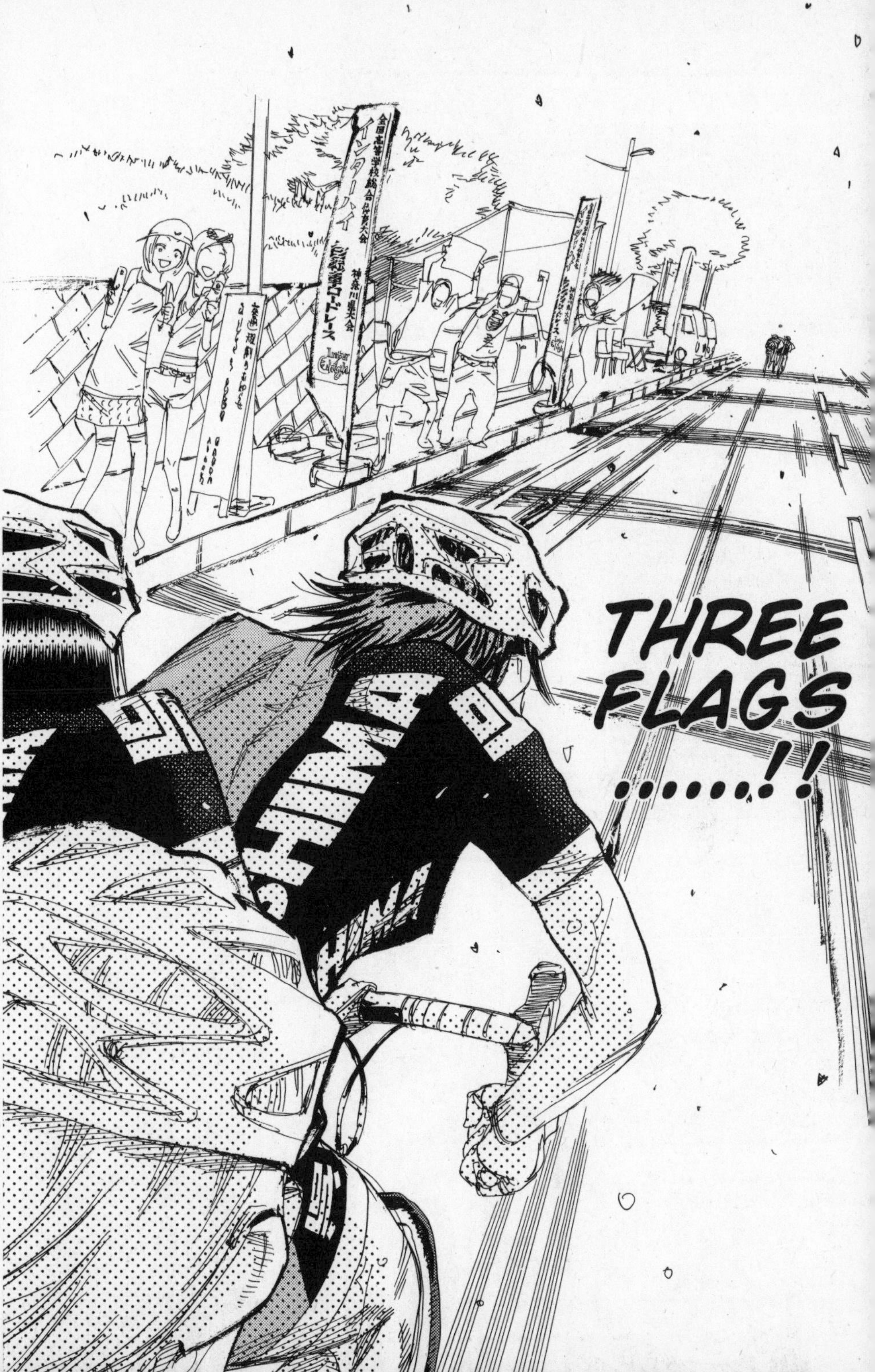
THREE FLAGS ......!!

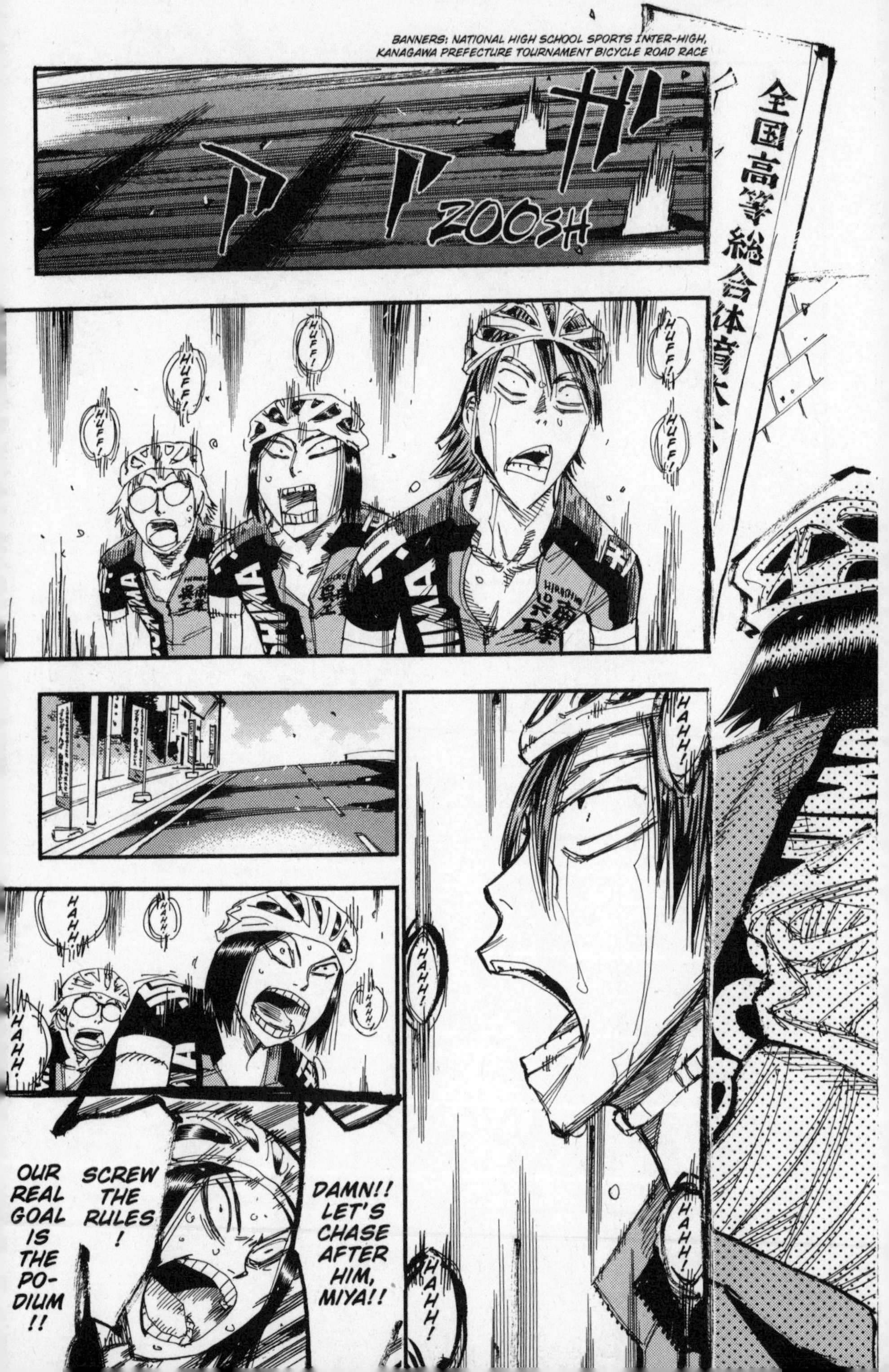
BANNERS: NATIONAL HIGH SCHOOL SPORTS INTER-HIGH, KANAGAWA PREFECTURE TOURNAMENT BICYCLE ROAD RACE
全国高等総合体育
ガアア
ZOOSH
HUFF!
HUFF!
HUFF!
HUFF!
HUFF!
HAHH!
HAHH!
HAHH!
HAHH!
HAHH!
HAHH!
HAHH!
HAHH!
DAMN!! LET'S CHASE AFTER HIM, MIYA!!
SCREW THE RULES!
OUR REAL GOAL IS THE PO-DIUM!!

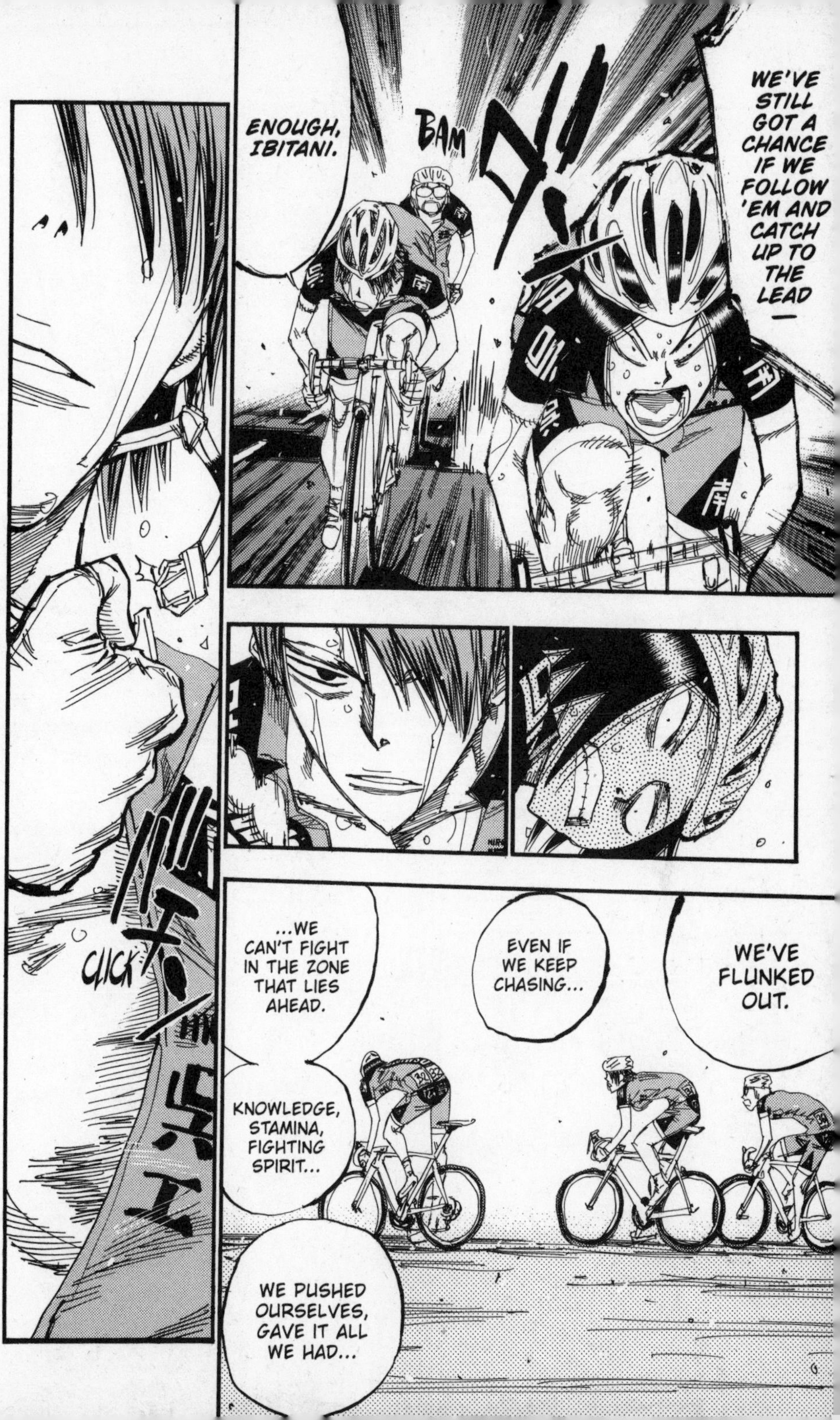
WE'VE STILL GOT A CHANCE IF WE FOLLOW 'EM AND CATCH UP TO THE LEAD—
BAM
ENOUGH, IBITANI.
WE'VE FLUNKED OUT.
EVEN IF WE KEEP CHASING...
...WE CAN'T FIGHT IN THE ZONE THAT LIES AHEAD.
KNOWLEDGE, STAMINA, FIGHTING SPIRIT...
WE PUSHED OURSELVES, GAVE IT ALL WE HAD...
CLICK

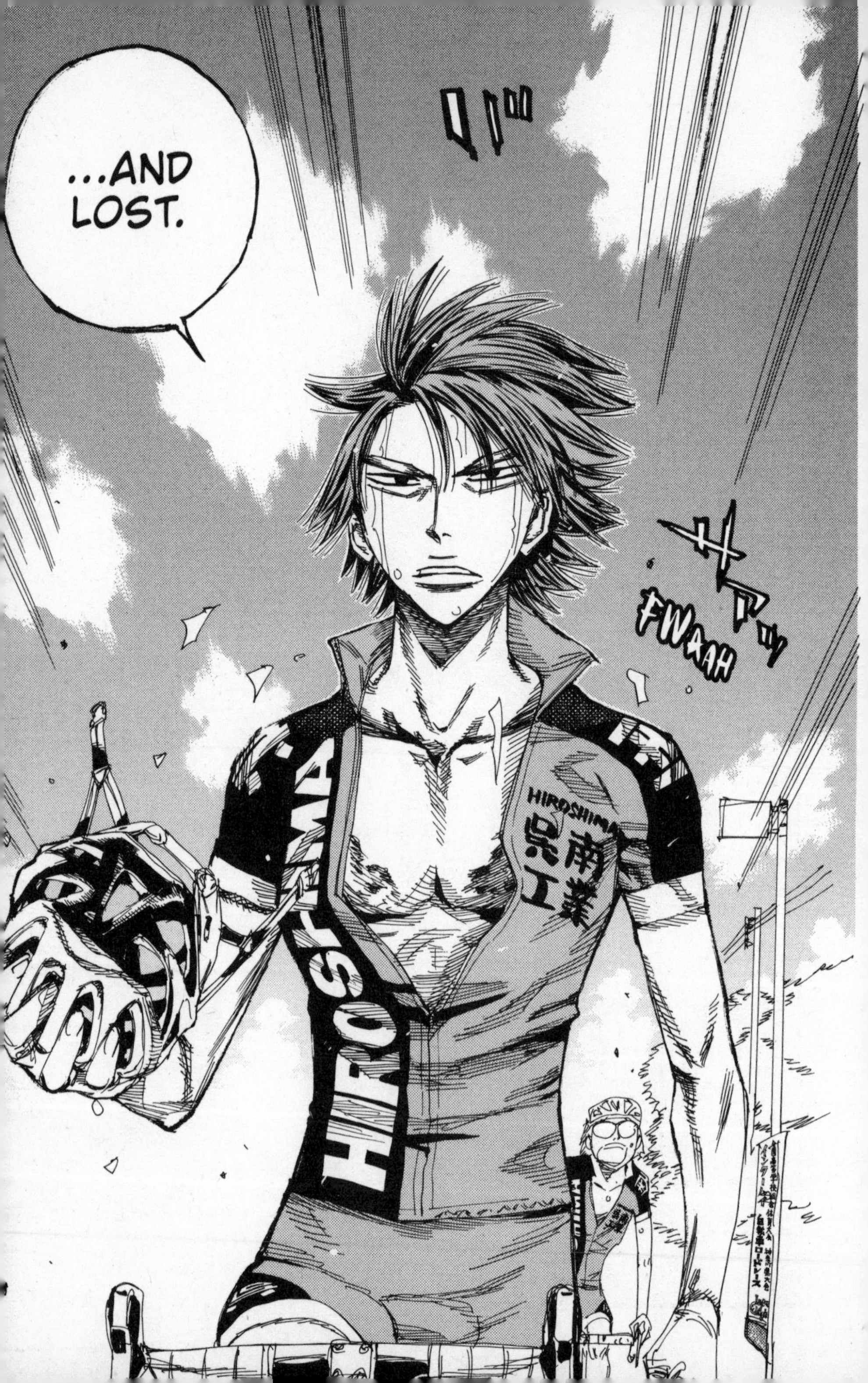
...AND LOST.
FWAAH
HIROSHIMA
HIROSHIMA
呉南工業

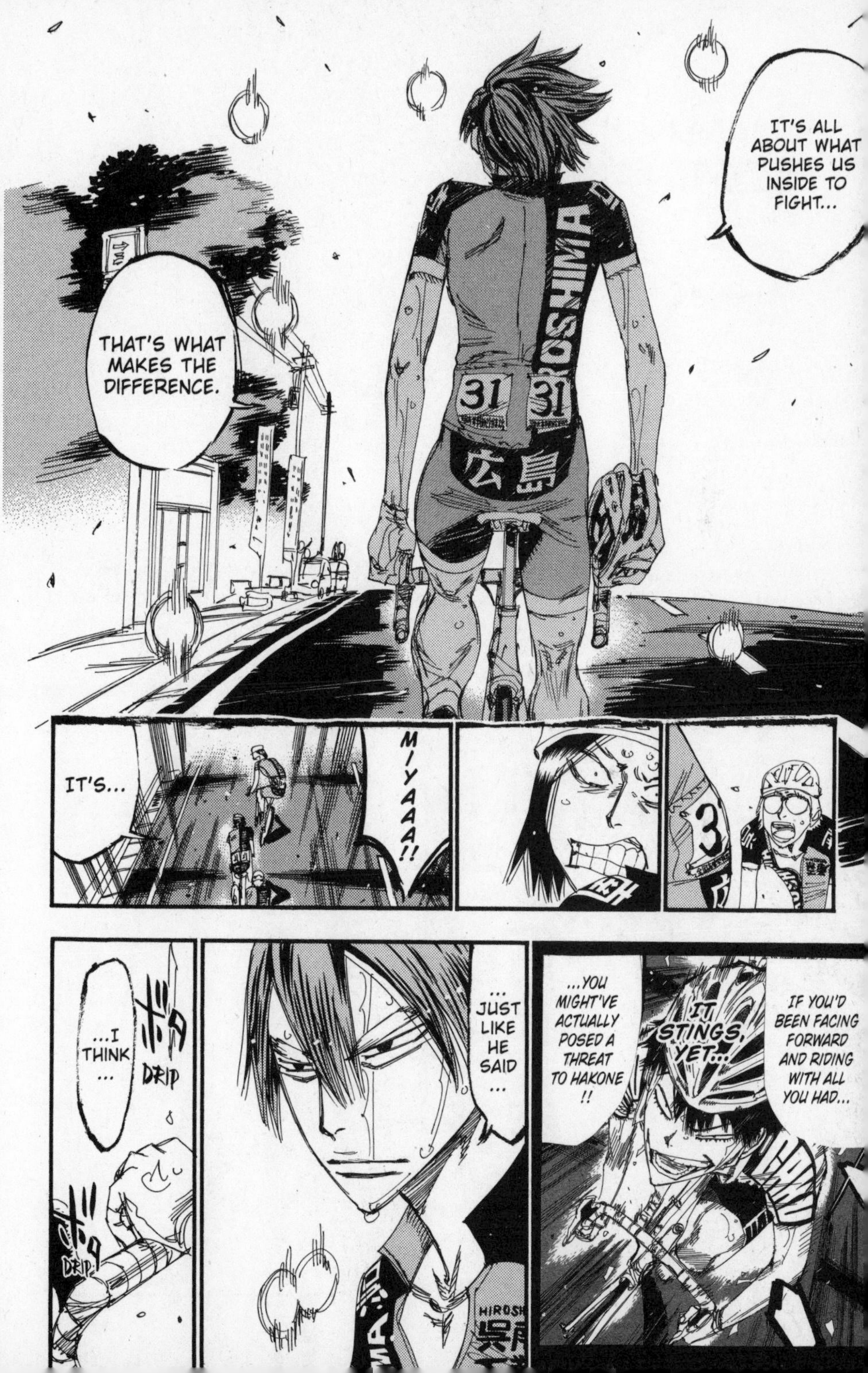
IT'S ALL ABOUT WHAT PUSHES US INSIDE TO FIGHT...
THAT'S WHAT MAKES THE DIFFERENCE.
MIYAAAA!!
IT'S...
IF YOU'D BEEN FACING FORWARD AND RIDING WITH ALL YOU HAD...
IT STINGS, YET...
...YOU MIGHT'VE ACTUALLY POSED A THREAT TO HAKONE!!
...JUST LIKE HE SAID...
DRIP
...I THINK...
DRIP

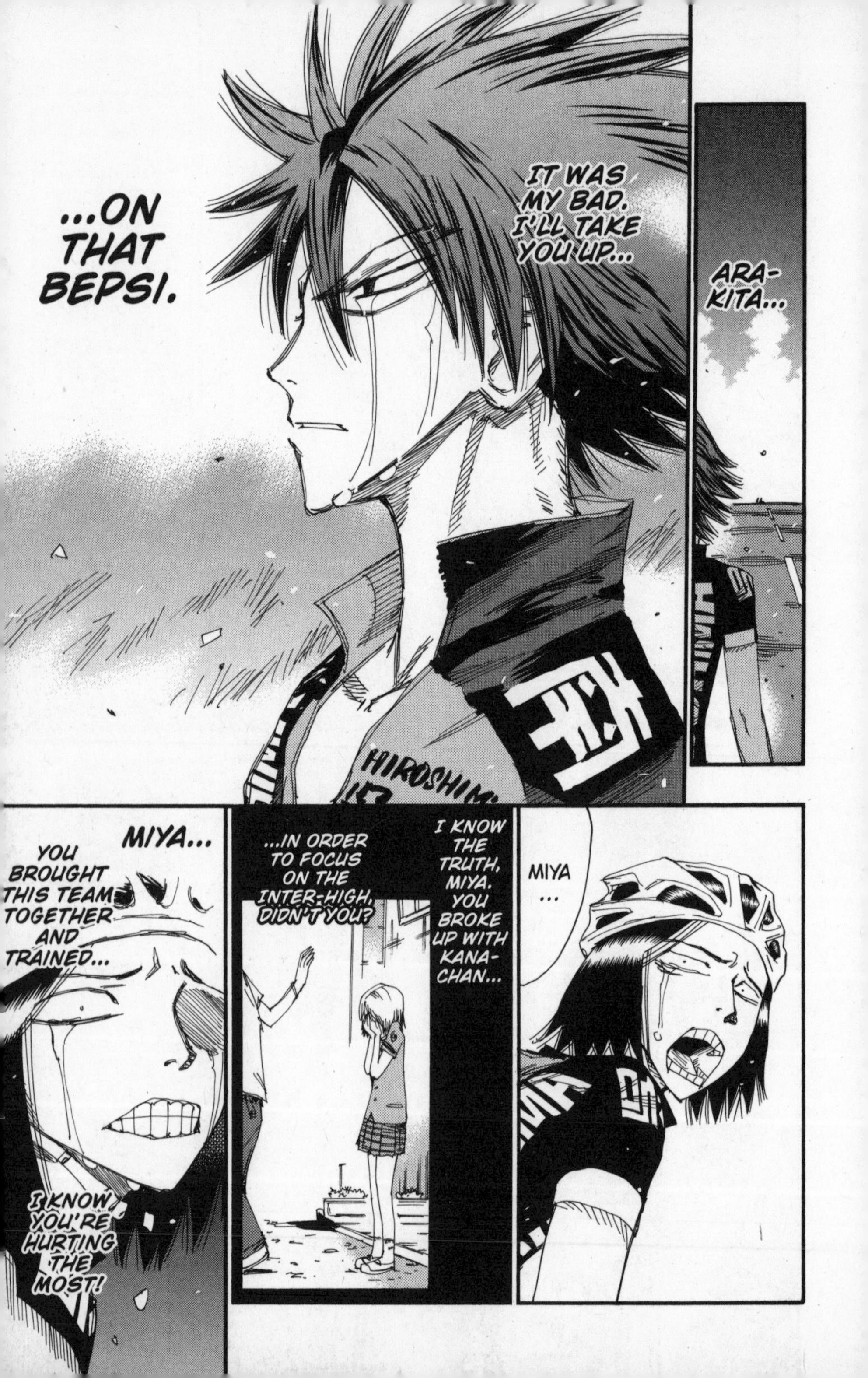
ARA-KITA...
IT WAS MY BAD. I'LL TAKE YOU UP...
...ON THAT BEPSI.
HIROSHIMA
MIYA ...
I KNOW THE TRUTH, MIYA. YOU BROKE UP WITH KANA-CHAN...
...IN ORDER TO FOCUS ON THE INTER-HIGH, DIDN'T YOU?
MIYA...
YOU BROUGHT THIS TEAM TOGETHER AND TRAINED...
I KNOW YOU'RE HURTING THE MOST!

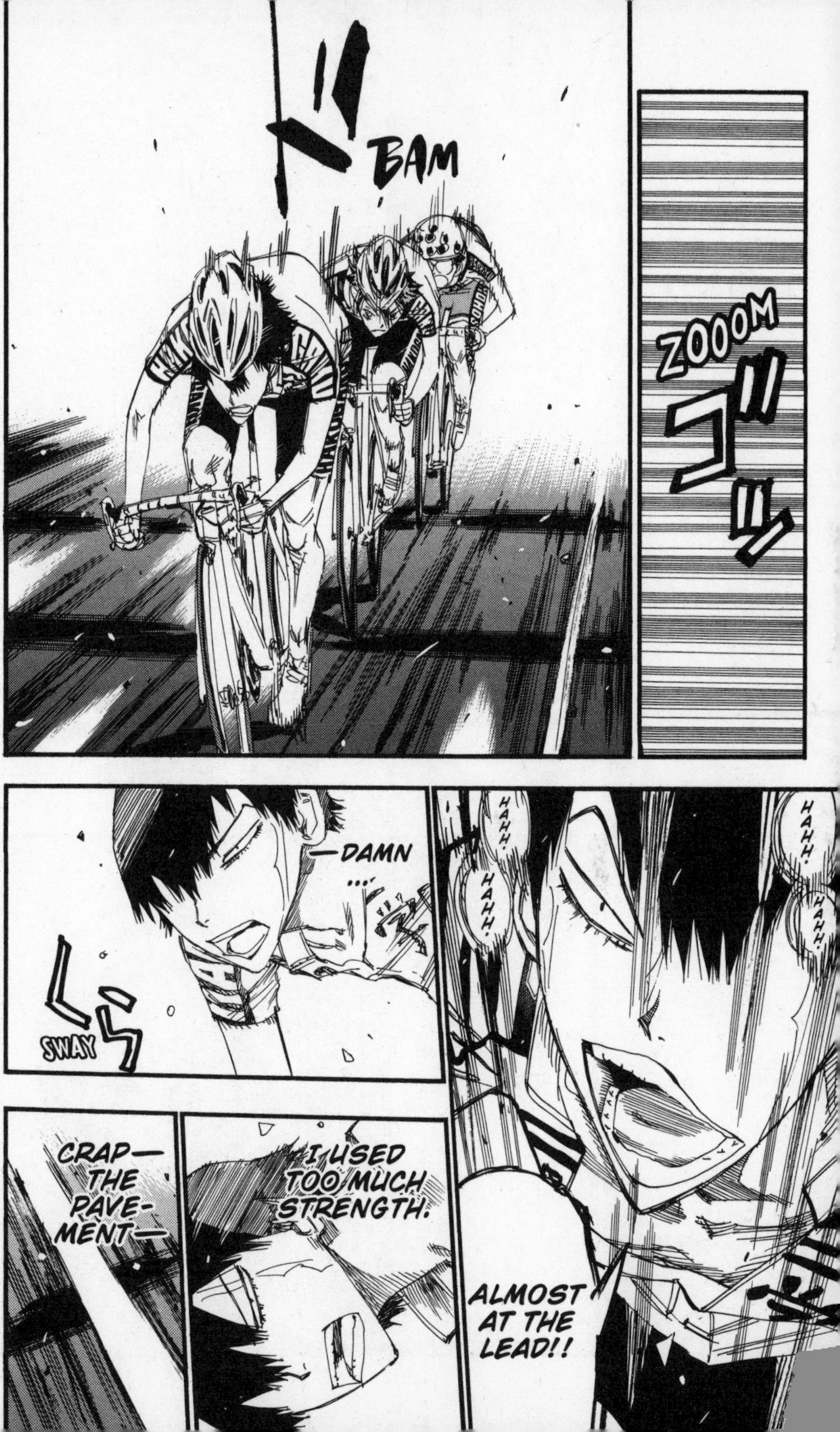
ZOOOM
BAM
HAHH.
HAHH.
HAHH.
HAHH.
ALMOST AT THE LEAD!!
—DAMN ...
SWAY
I USED TOO MUCH STRENGTH.
CRAP—THE PAVEMENT—

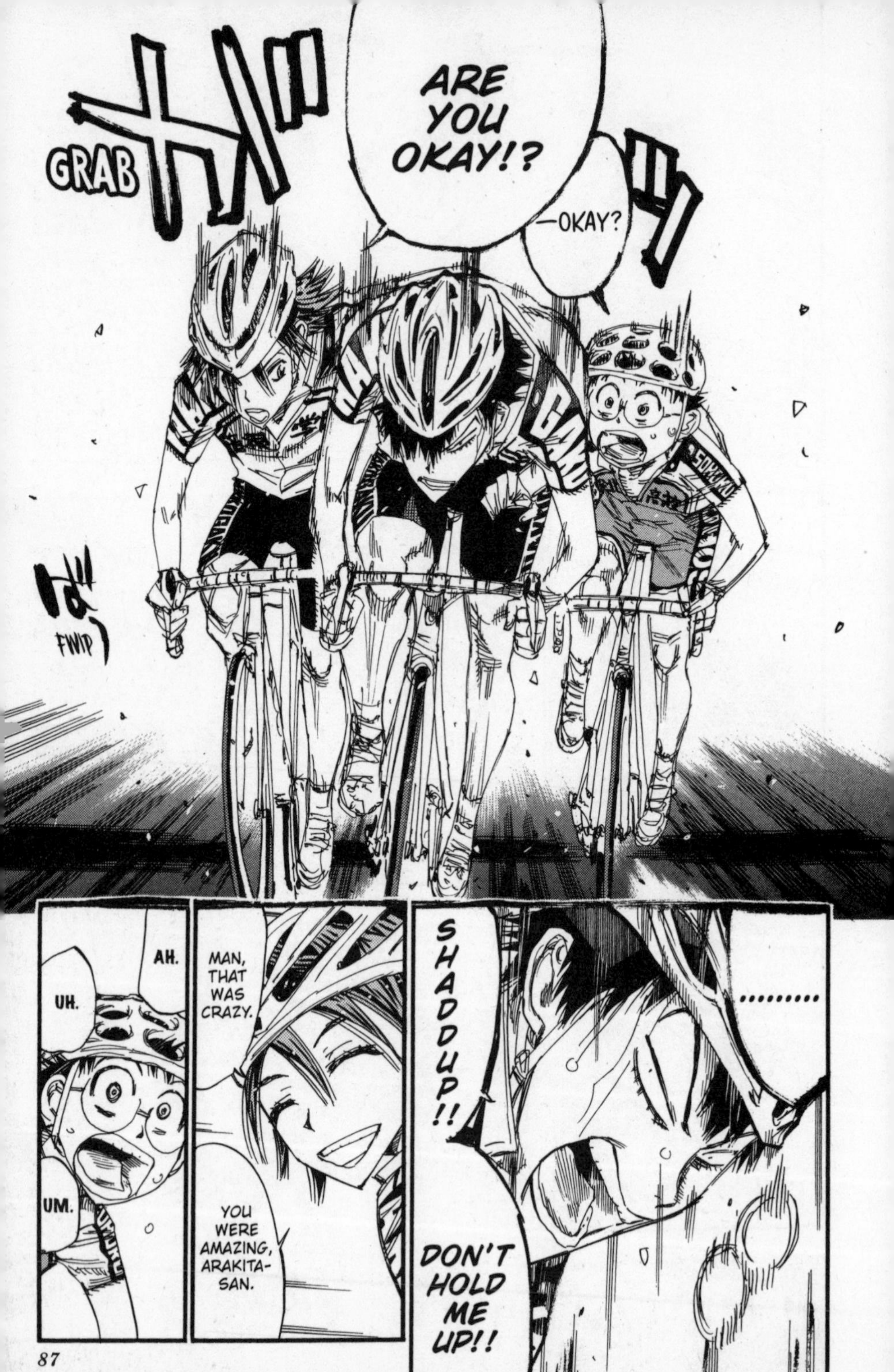
ARE YOU OKAY!?
—OKAY?
GRAB
FWIP
....
SHADDUP!!
DON'T HOLD ME UP!!
MAN, THAT WAS CRAZY.
YOU WERE AMAZING, ARAKITA-SAN.
AH.
UH.
UM.

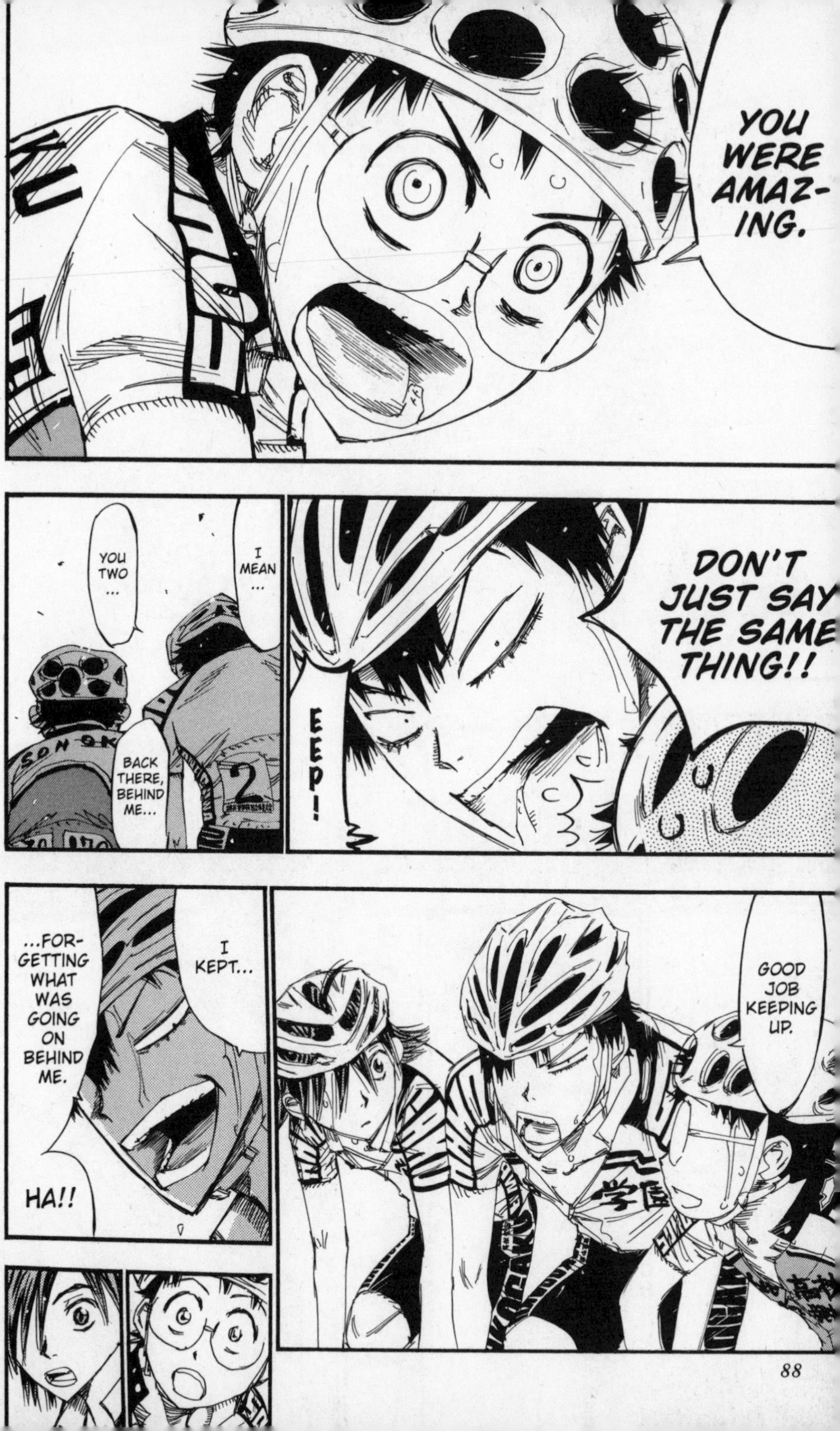
YOU WERE AMAZ-ING.
DON'T JUST SAY THE SAME THING!!
EEP!
I MEAN ...
YOU TWO ...
BACK THERE, BEHIND ME...
GOOD JOB KEEPING UP.
I KEPT...
...FOR-GETTING WHAT WAS GOING ON BEHIND ME.
HA!!

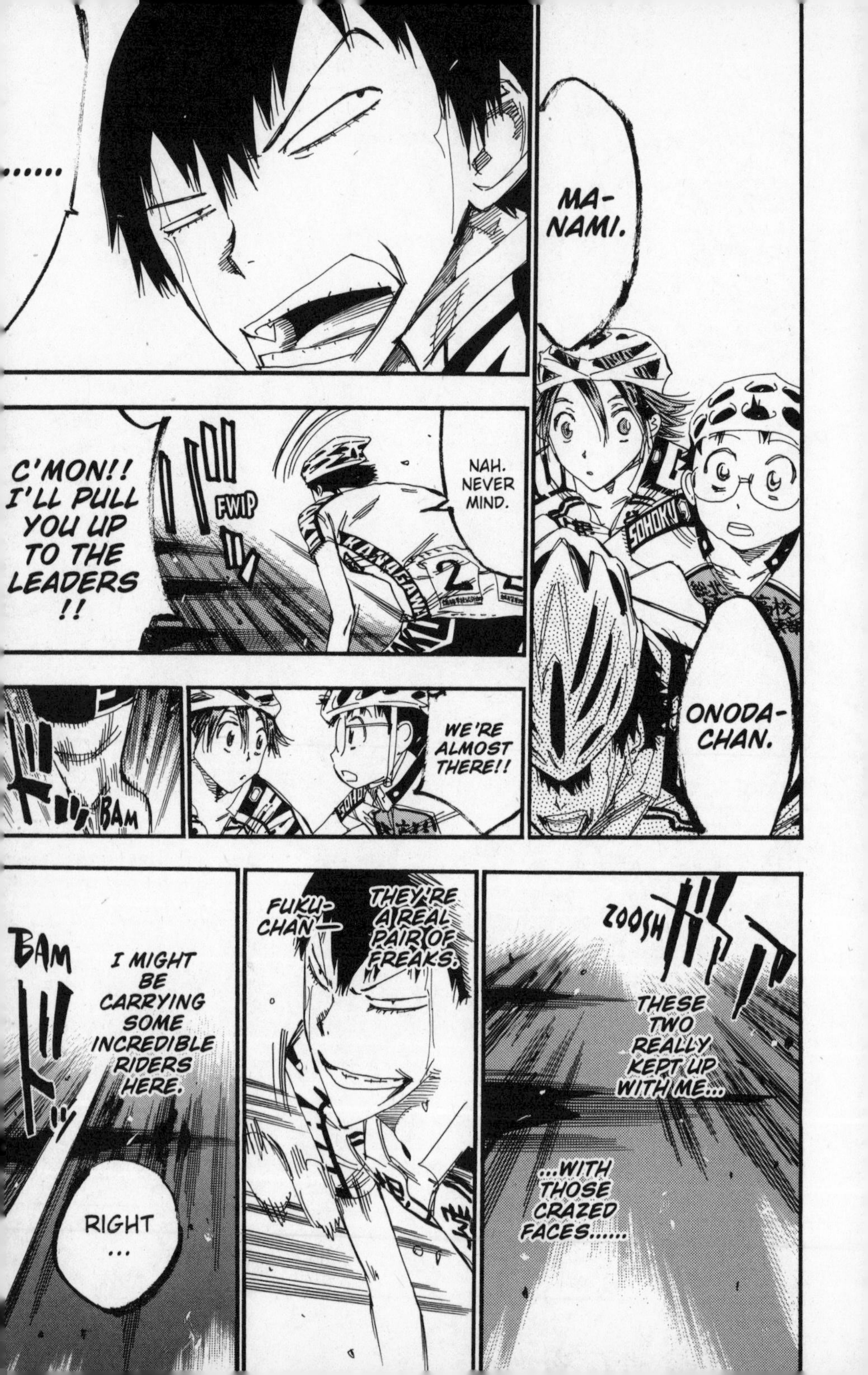
MA-NAMI.
ONODA-CHAN.
......
NAH. NEVER MIND.
FWIP
C'MON!! I'LL PULL YOU UP TO THE LEADERS!!
WE'RE ALMOST THERE!!
BAM
ZOOSH
THESE TWO REALLY KEPT UP WITH ME...
...WITH THOSE CRAZED FACES......
THEY'RE A REAL PAIR OF FREAKS.
FUKU-CHAN—
BAM
I MIGHT BE CARRYING SOME INCREDIBLE RIDERS HERE.
RIGHT ...

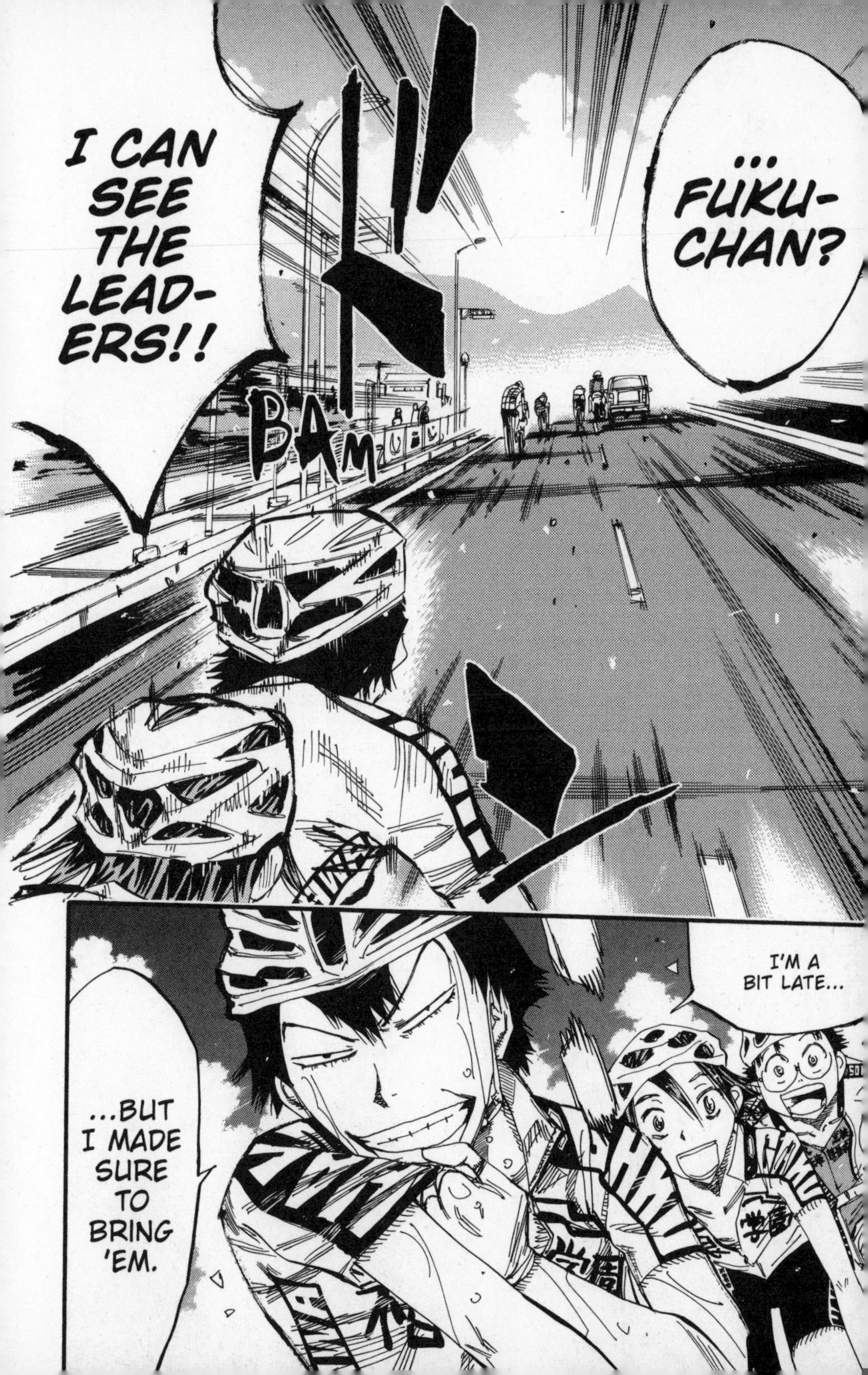
...FÜKU-CHAN?
I CAN SEE THE LEADERS!!
BAM
I'M A BIT LATE...
...BUT I MADE SURE TO BRING 'EM.

RIDE.177 TEAMS REUNITED

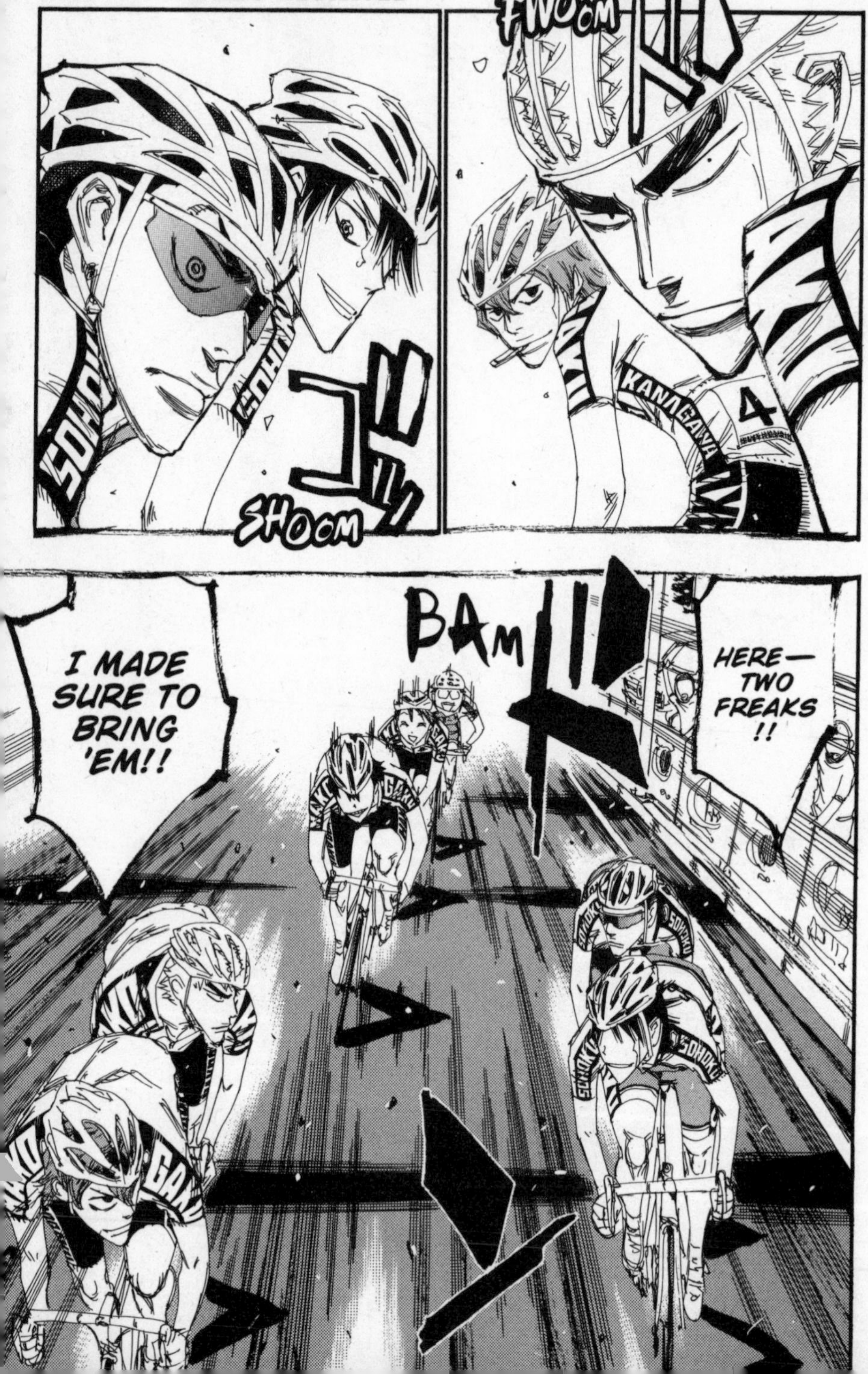
FWOOM
KANAGAWA
4
SOHOKU
SHOOM
HERE—TWO FREAKS!!
BAM
I MADE SURE TO BRING 'EM!!

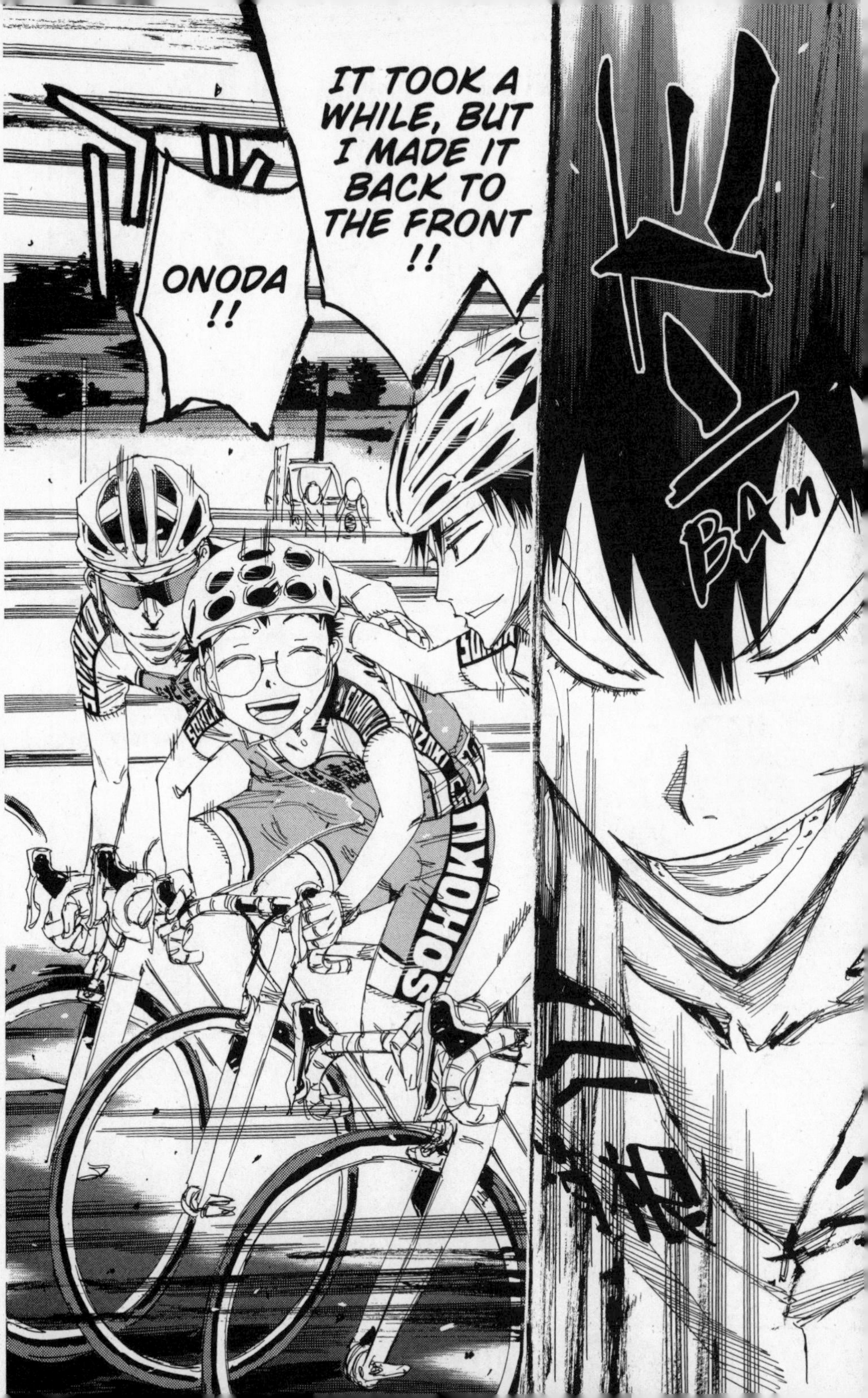
BAM
IT TOOK A WHILE, BUT I MADE IT BACK TO THE FRONT !!
ONODA !!

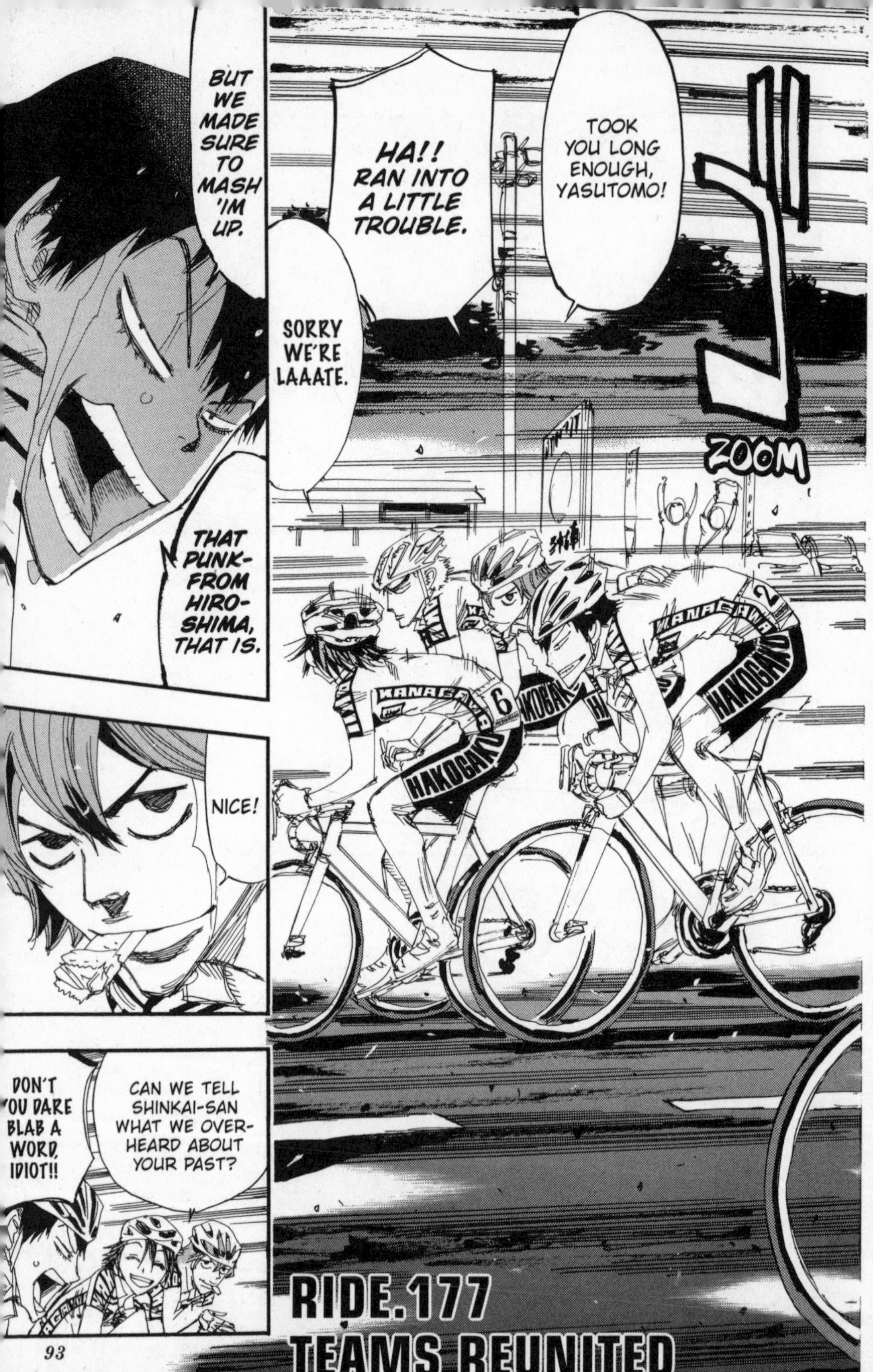
TOOK YOU LONG ENOUGH, YASUTOMO!
ZOOM
HA!! RAN INTO A LITTLE TROUBLE.
SORRY WE'RE LAAATE.
BUT WE MADE SURE TO MASH 'IM UP.
THAT PUNK-FROM HIROSHIMA, THAT IS.
NICE!
CAN WE TELL SHINKAI-SAN WHAT WE OVER-HEARD ABOUT YOUR PAST?
DON'T YOU DARE BLAB A WORD, IDIOT!!

RIDE.177 TEAMS REUNITED

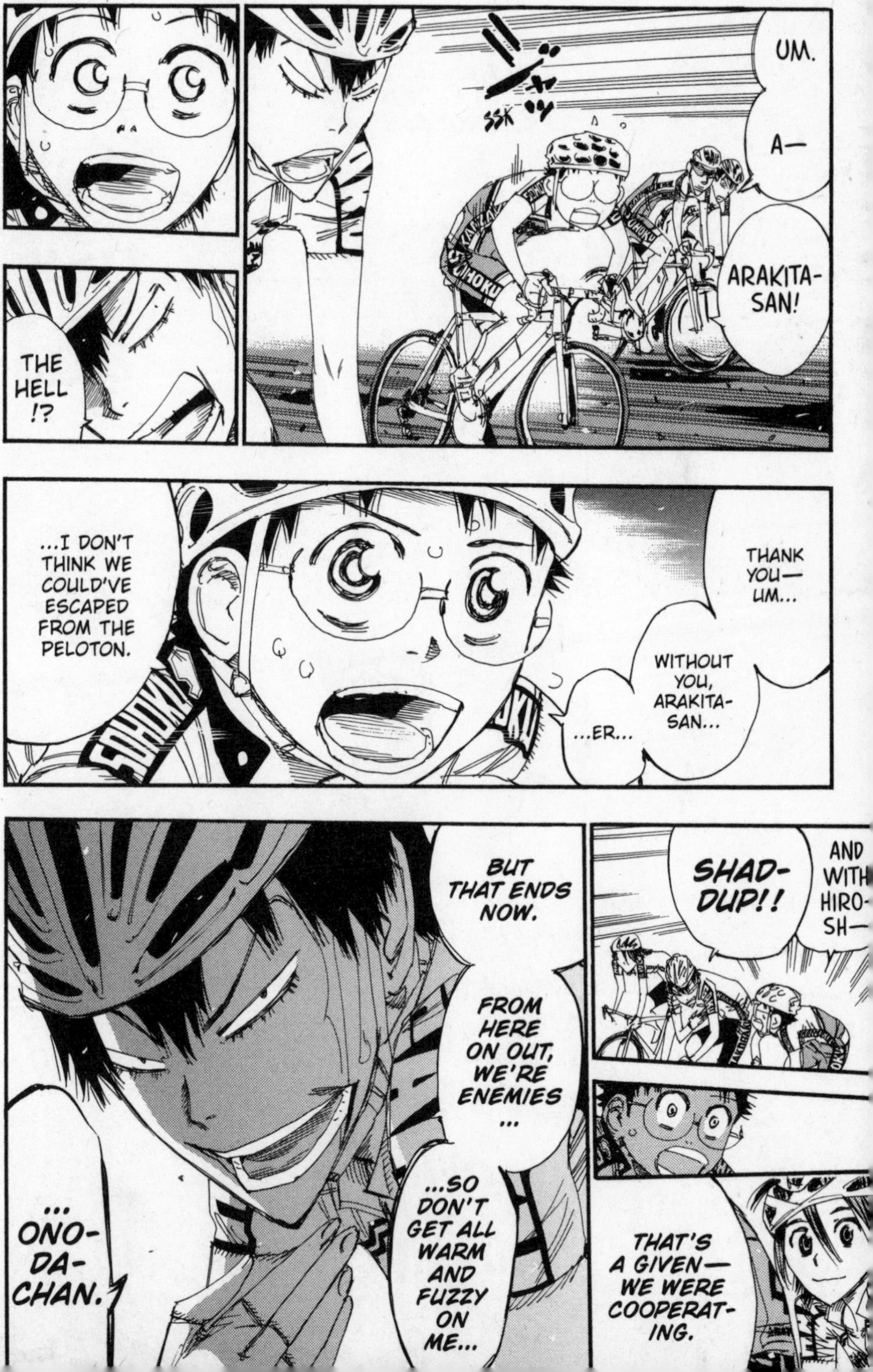
SSK
UM.
A—
ARAKITA-SAN!
THE HELL !?
THANK YOU— UM...
WITHOUT YOU, ARAKITA-SAN...
...ER...
...I DON'T THINK WE COULD'VE ESCAPED FROM THE PELOTON.
AND WITH HIRO-SH—
SHAD-DUP!!
THAT'S A GIVEN— WE WERE COOPERATING.
BUT THAT ENDS NOW.
FROM HERE ON OUT, WE'RE ENEMIES...
...SO DON'T GET ALL WARM AND FUZZY ON ME...
...ONODA-CHAN.

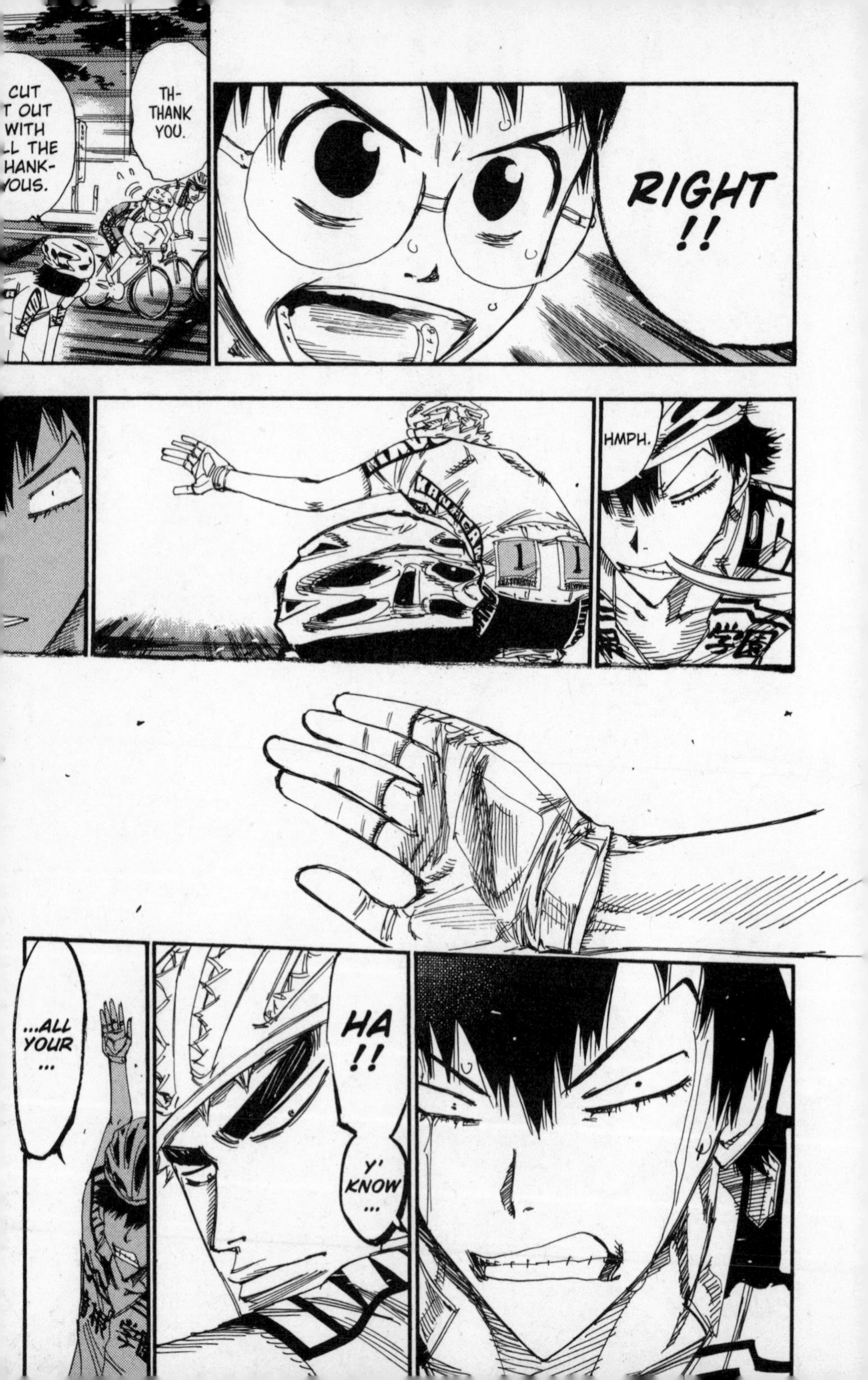
RIGHT !!
TH-THANK YOU.
CUT T OUT WITH LL THE HANK-YOUS.
HMPH.
HA !!
Y' KNOW ...
...ALL YOUR ...

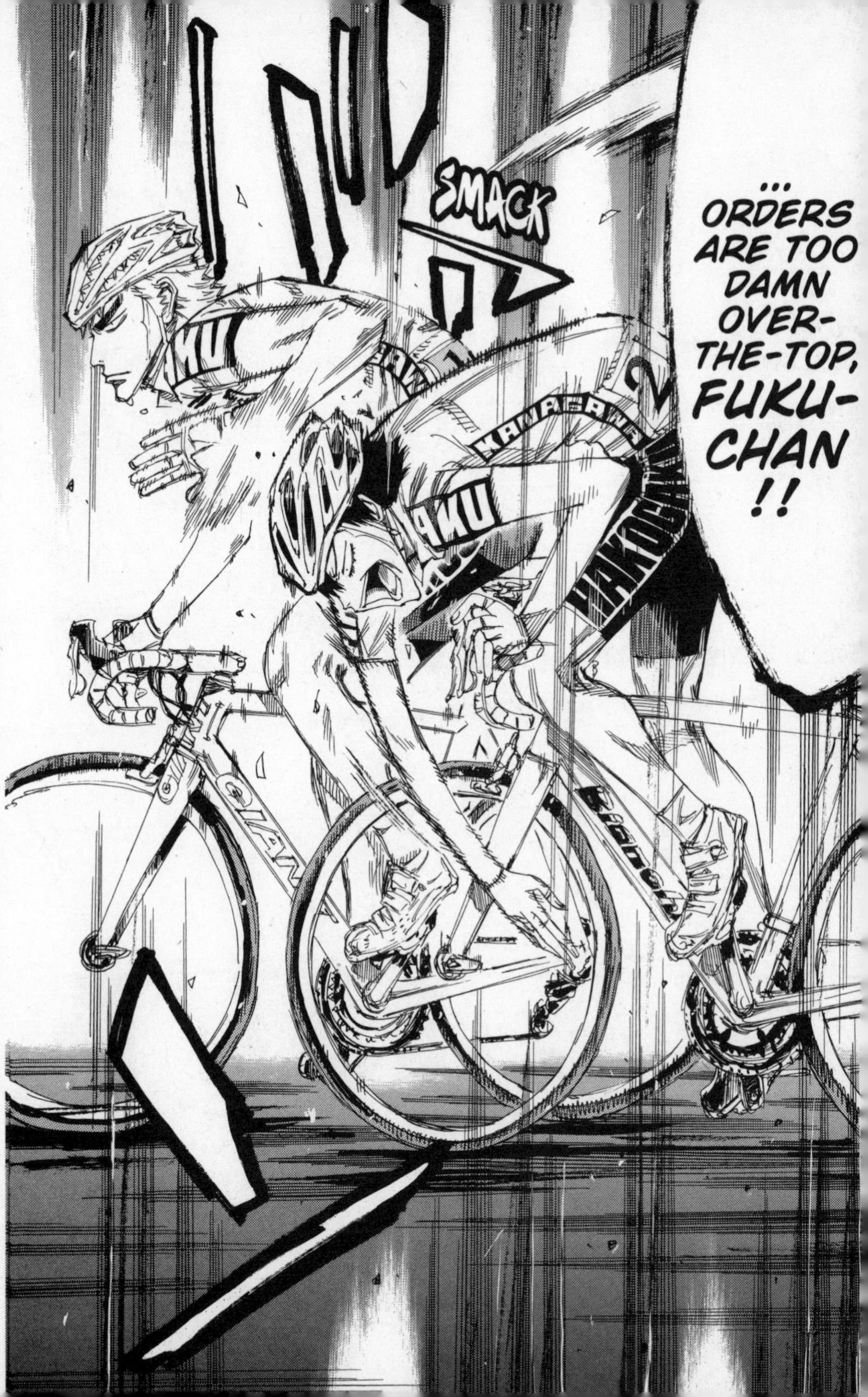
...ORDERS ARE TOO DAMN OVER-THE-TOP, FUKU-CHAN!!
SMACK

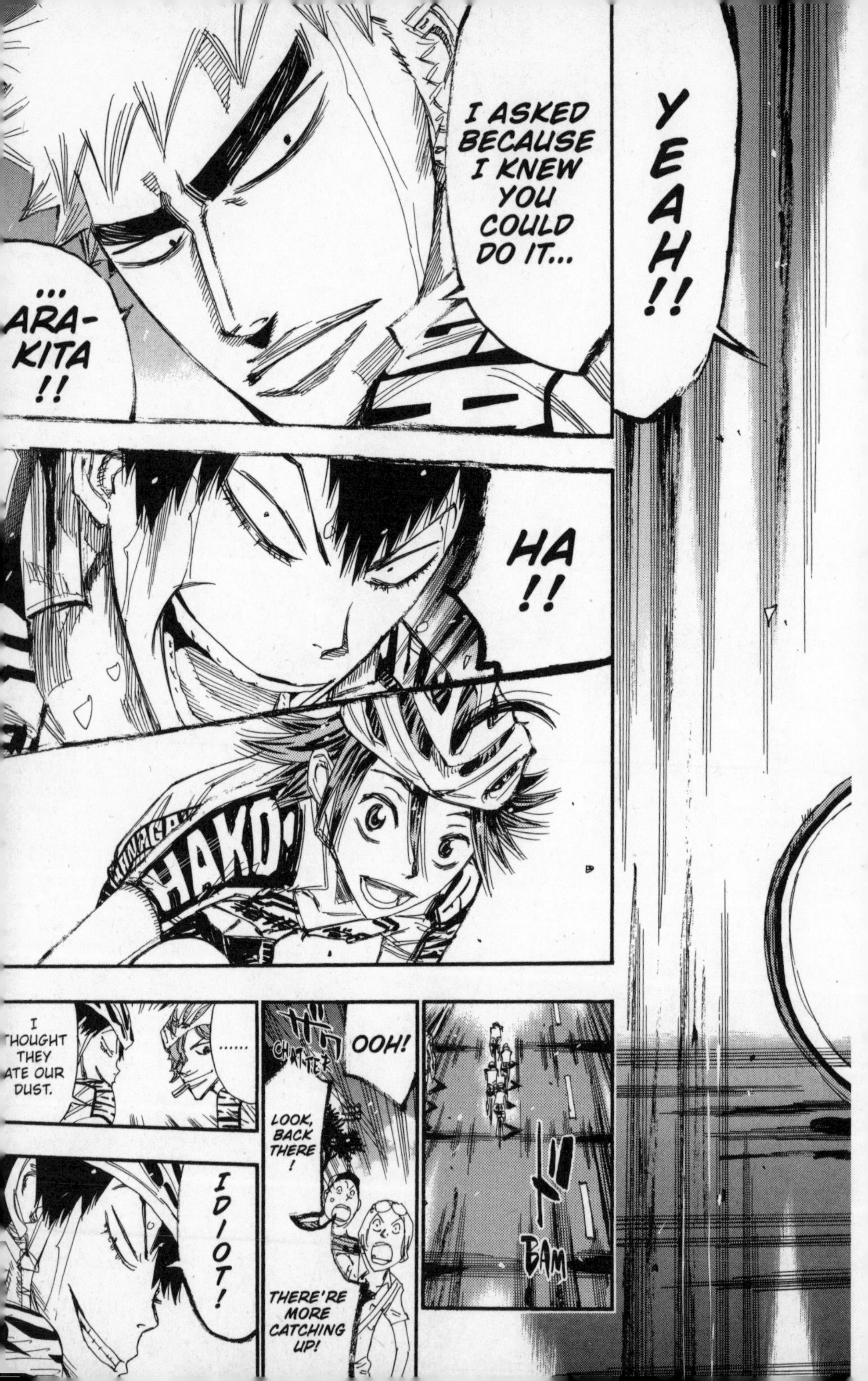
YEAH!!
I ASKED BECAUSE I KNEW YOU COULD DO IT...
...ARA-KITA!!
HA!!
BAM
OOH!
CHATTER
LOOK, BACK THERE!
THERE'RE MORE CATCHING UP!
......
I THOUGHT THEY ATE OUR DUST.
IDIOT!

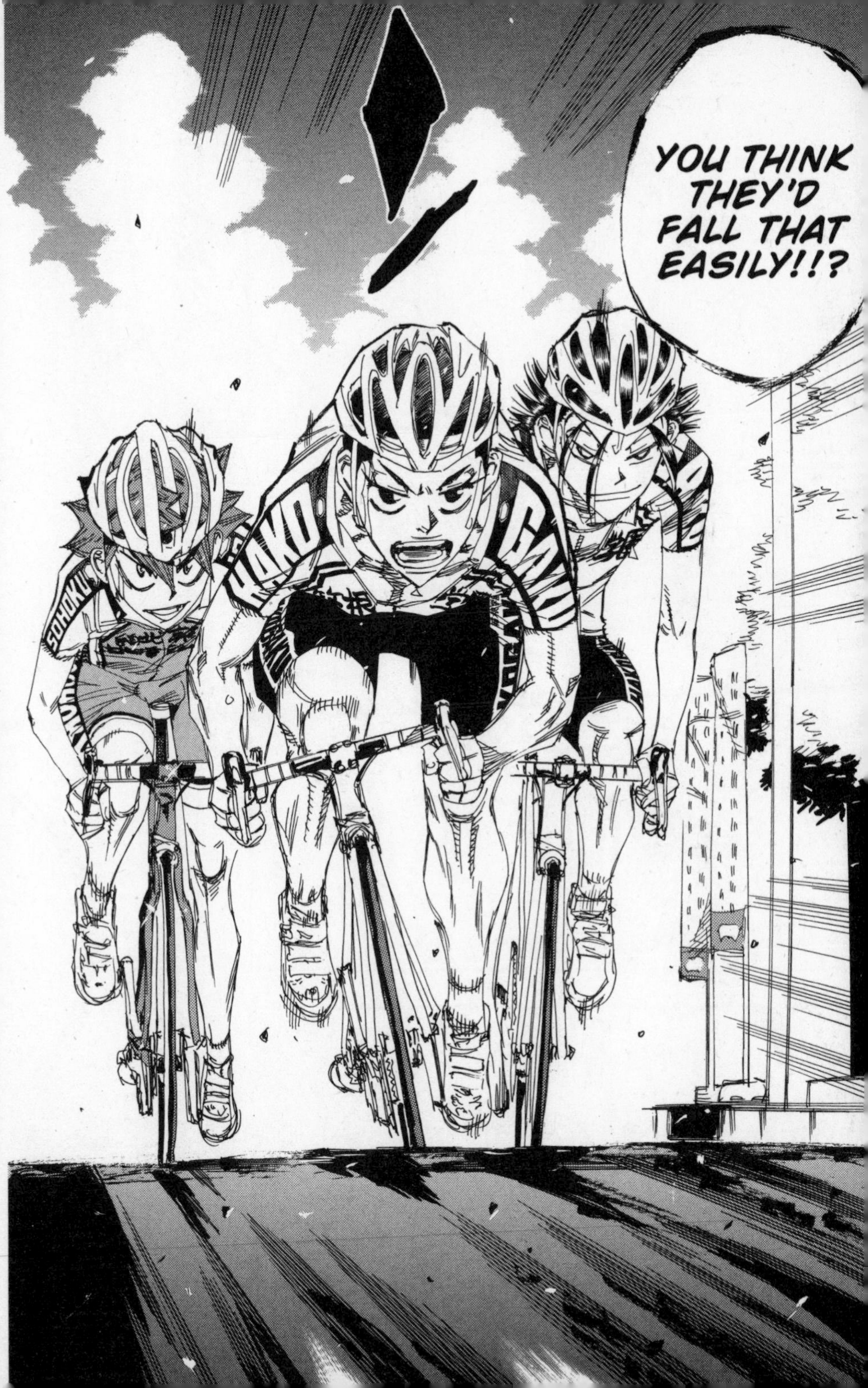
YOU THINK THEY'D FALL THAT EASILY!!?

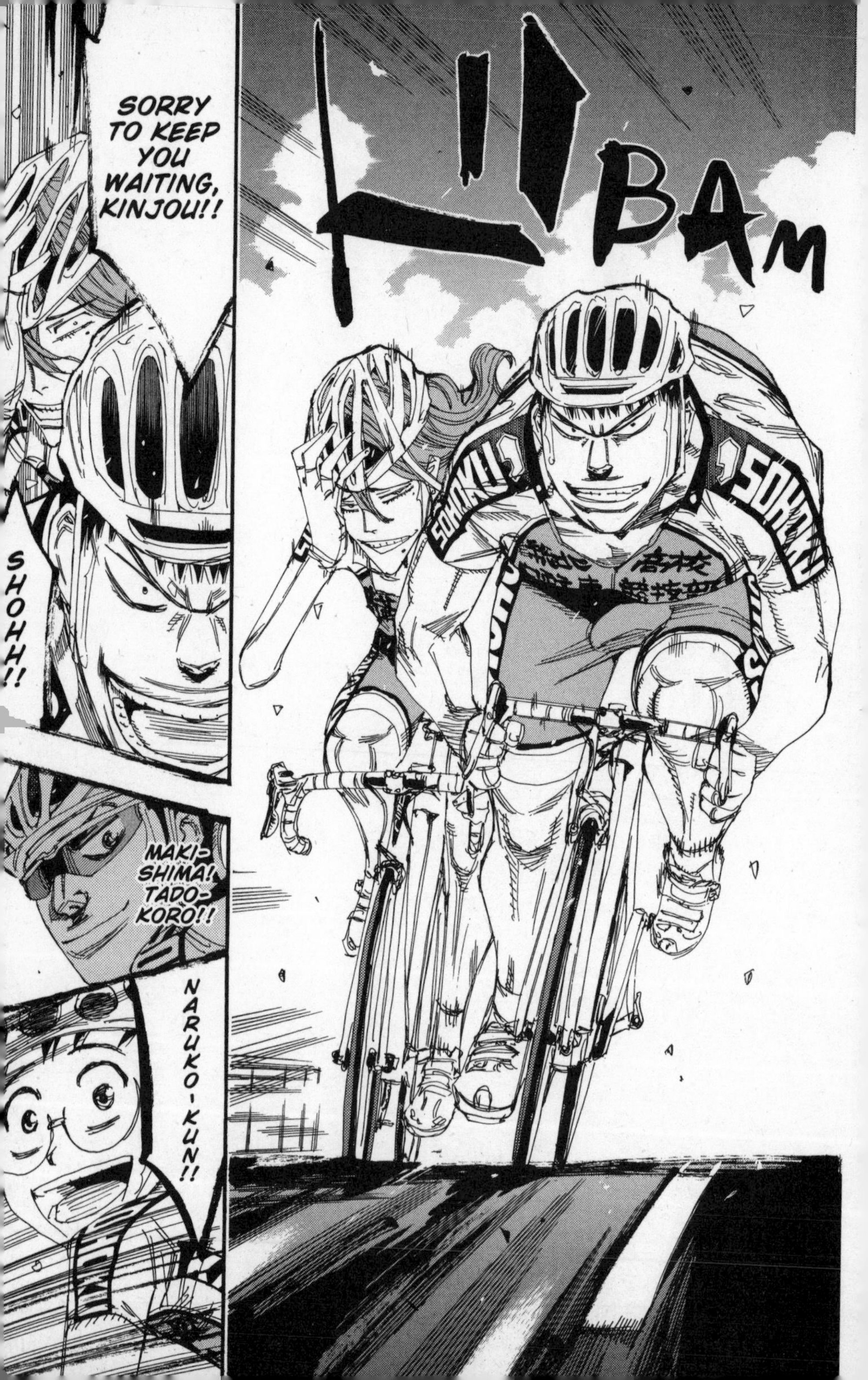
BAM
SORRY TO KEEP YOU WAITING, KINJOU!!
SHOHHH!!
MAKI-SHIMA! TADO-KORO!!
NARUKO-KUN!!

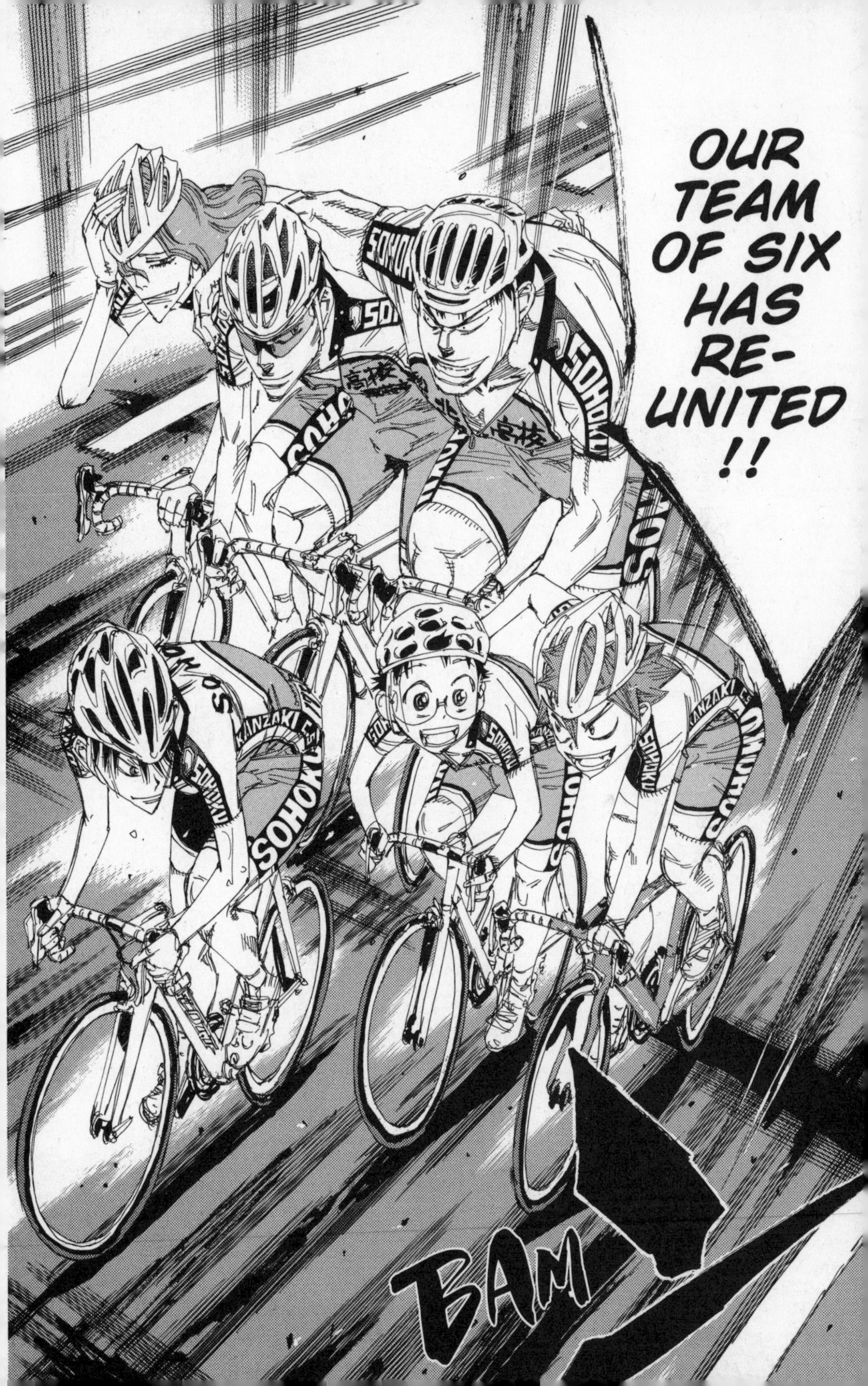
OUR TEAM OF SIX HAS RE-UNITED!!
BAM

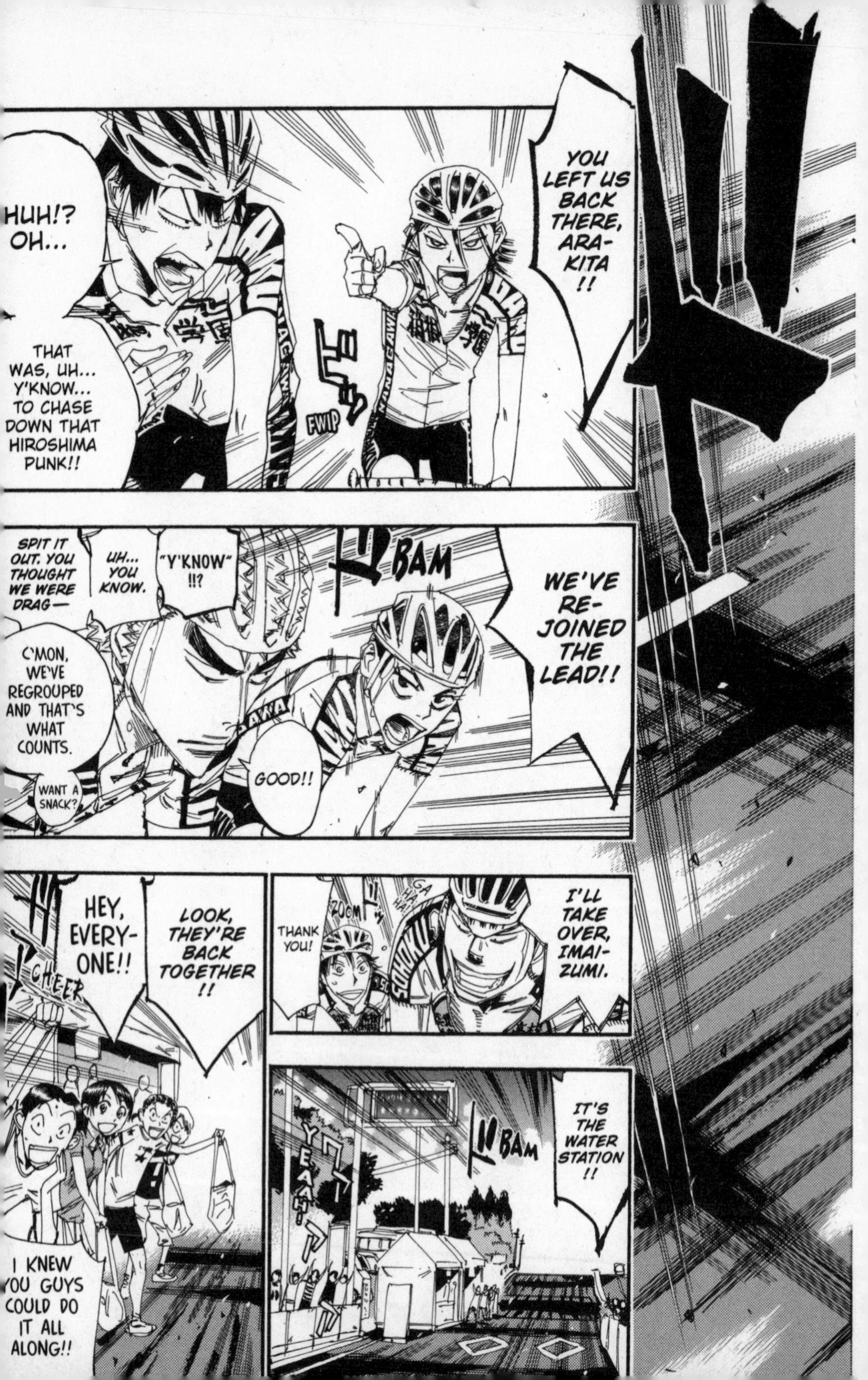
YOU LEFT US BACK THERE, ARAKITA!!
FWIP
HUH!? OH...
THAT WAS, UH... Y'KNOW... TO CHASE DOWN THAT HIROSHIMA PUNK!!
BAM
WE'VE REJOINED THE LEAD!!
GOOD!!
"Y'KNOW" !!?
UH... YOU KNOW.
SPIT IT OUT. YOU THOUGHT WE WERE DRAG—
C'MON, WE'VE REGROUPED AND THAT'S WHAT COUNTS.
WANT A SNACK?
I'LL TAKE OVER, IMAIZUMI.
GA HA HA!
ZOOM
THANK YOU!
BAM
IT'S THE WATER STATION!!
YEAAH!
LOOK, THEY'RE BACK TOGETHER!!
HEY, EVERYONE!!
CHEER
I KNEW YOU GUYS COULD DO IT ALL ALONG!!

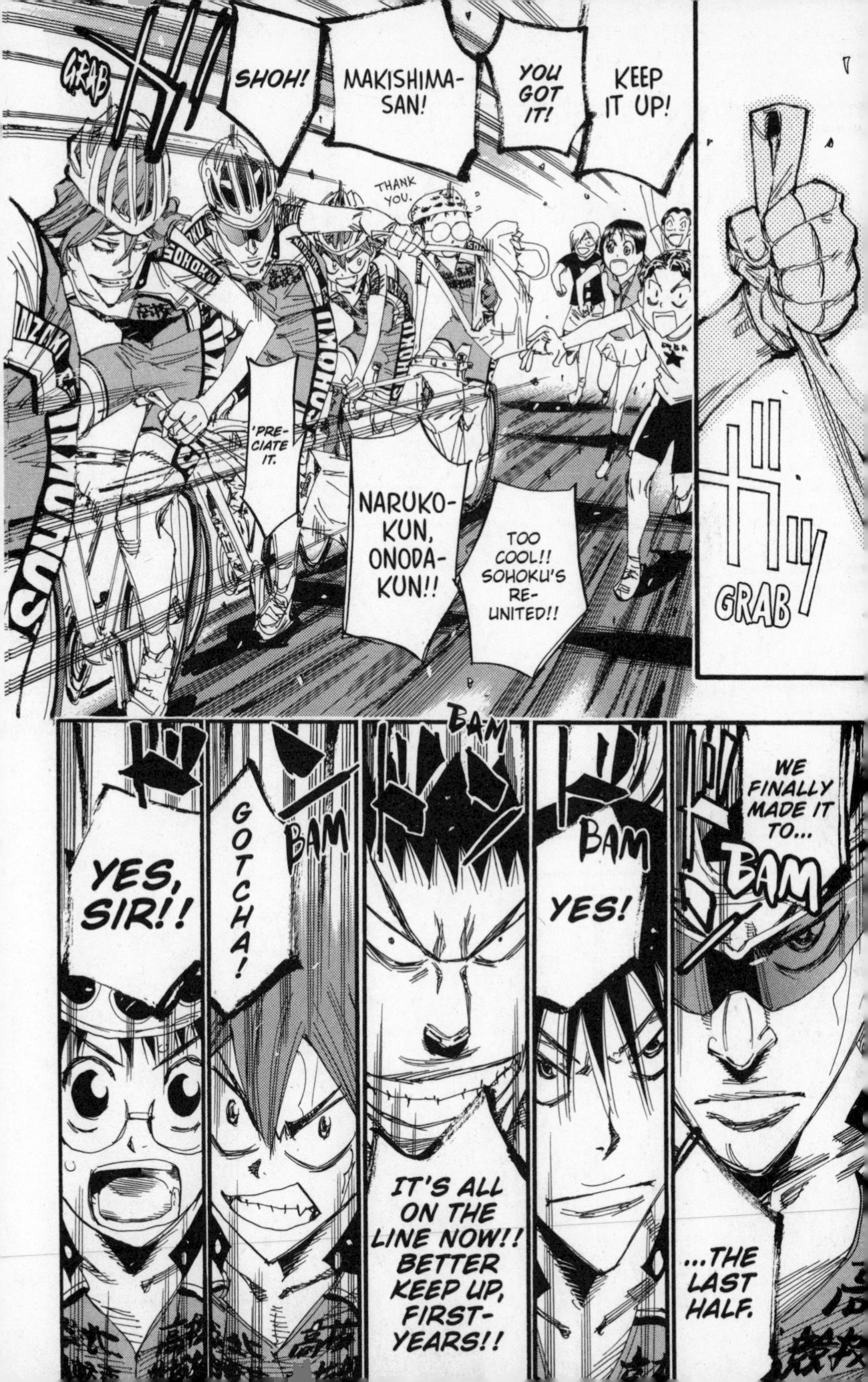
GRAB
KEEP IT UP!
YOU GOT IT!
MAKISHIMA-SAN!
SHOH!
GRAB
THANK YOU.
TOO COOL!! SOHOKU'S RE-UNITED!!
NARUKO-KUN, ONODA-KUN!!
'PRE-CIATE IT.
WE FINALLY MADE IT TO...
BAM
...THE LAST HALF.
BAM
YES!
BAM
IT'S ALL ON THE LINE NOW!! BETTER KEEP UP, FIRST-YEARS!!
BAM
GOTCHA!
YES, SIR!!

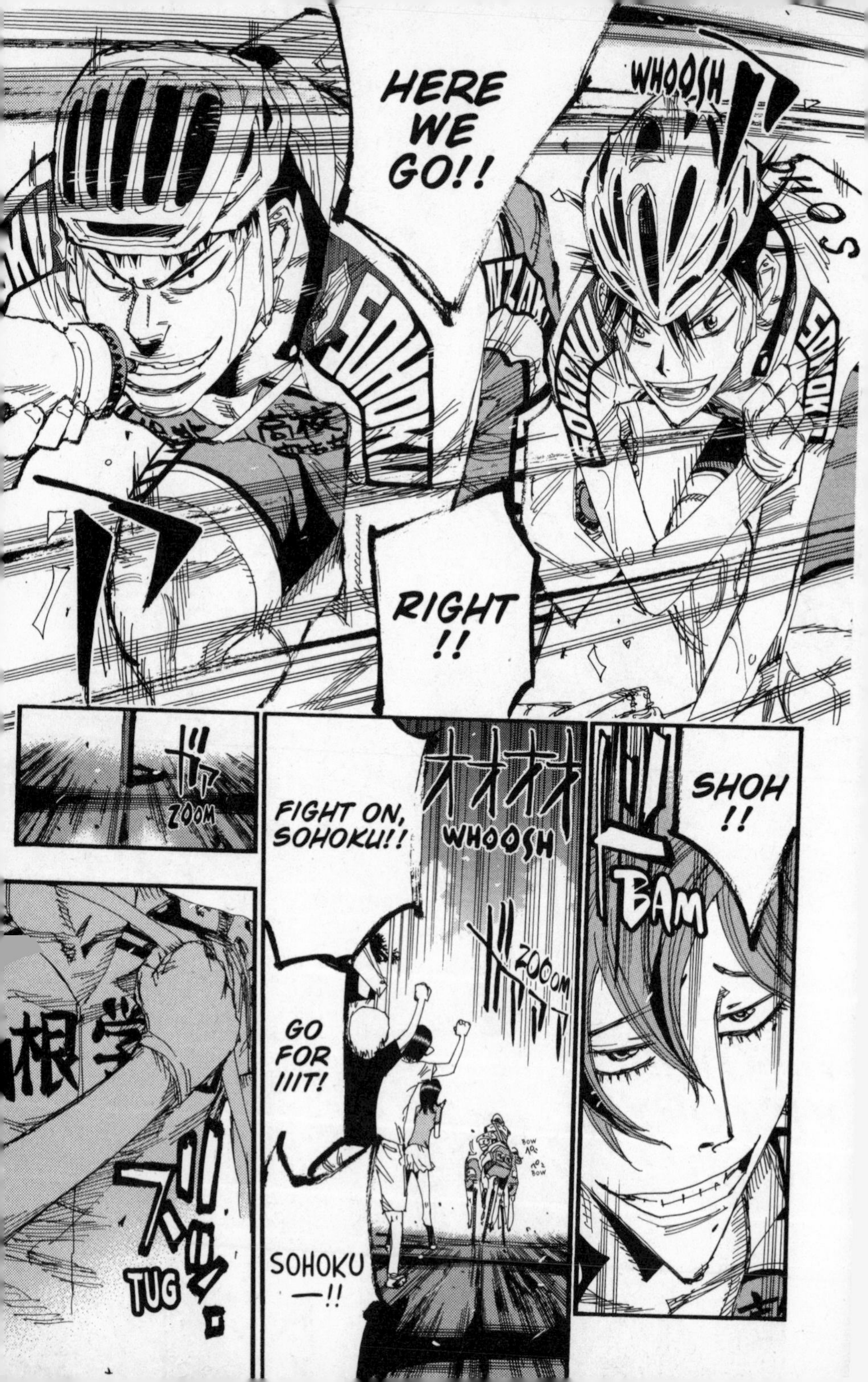
WHOOSH
HERE WE GO!!
RIGHT!!
SHOH!!
BAM
オオオオ
WHOOSH
FIGHT ON, SOHOKU!!
ZOOOM
GO FOR IIIT!
SOHOKU—!!
ZOOM
TUG

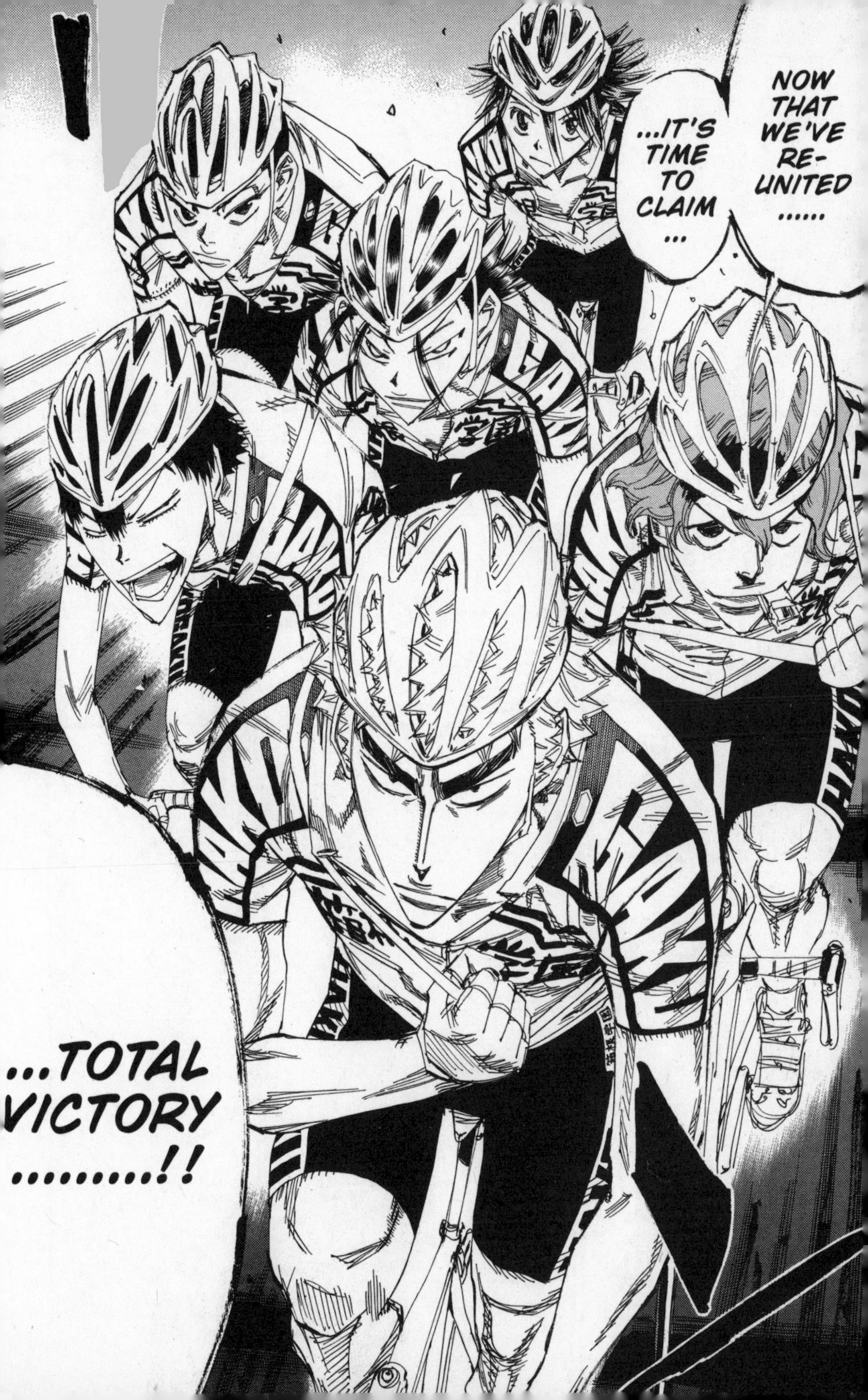
NOW THAT WE'VE RE-UNITED ......
...IT'S TIME TO CLAIM ...
...TOTAL VICTORY ....!!

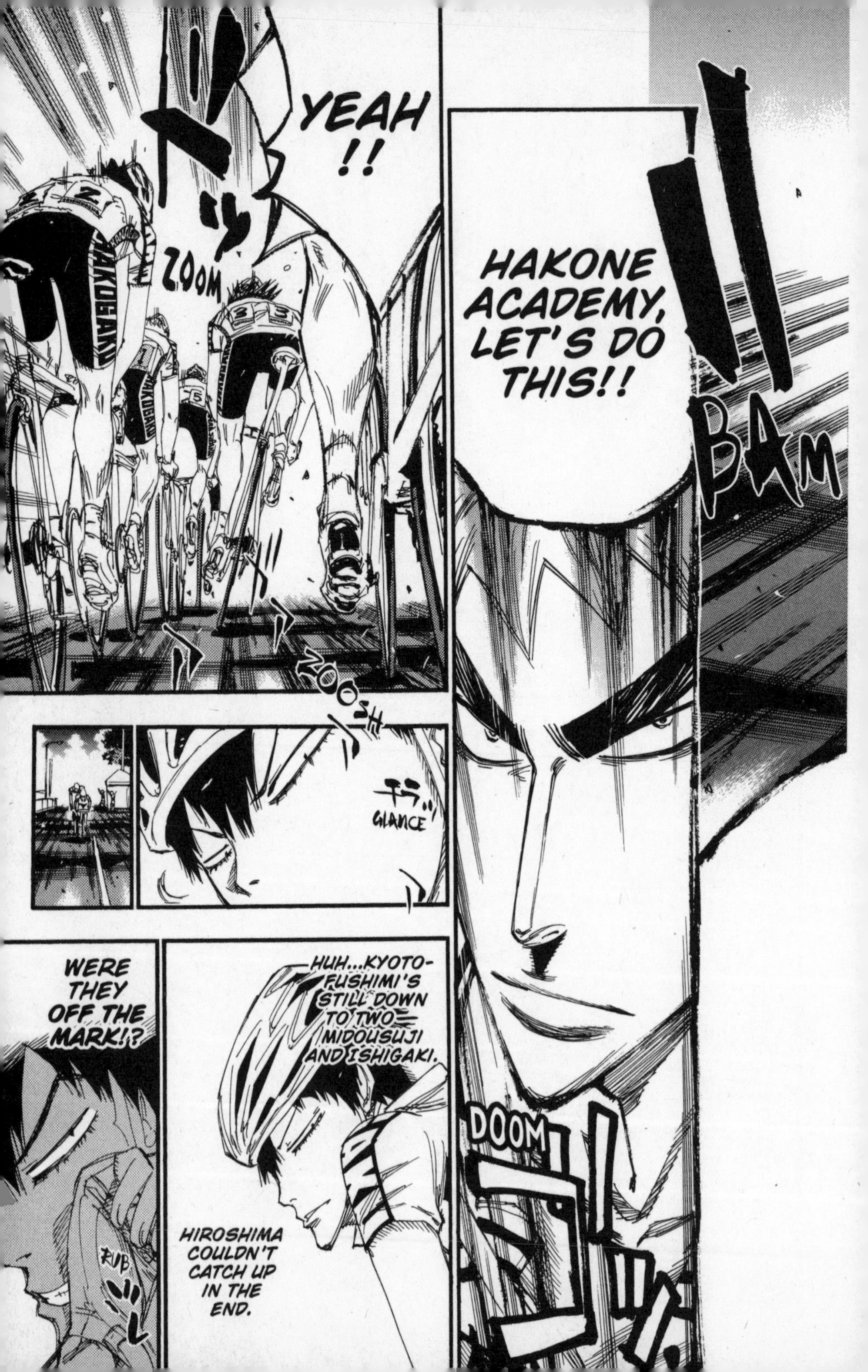
HAKONE ACADEMY, LET'S DO THIS!!
BAM
DOOM
YEAH!!
ZOOM
ZOOSH
GLANCE
HUH...KYOTO-FUSHIMI'S STILL DOWN TO TWO—MIDOUSUJI AND ISHIGAKI.
HIROSHIMA COULDN'T CATCH UP IN THE END.
WERE THEY OFF THE MARK!?
RUB

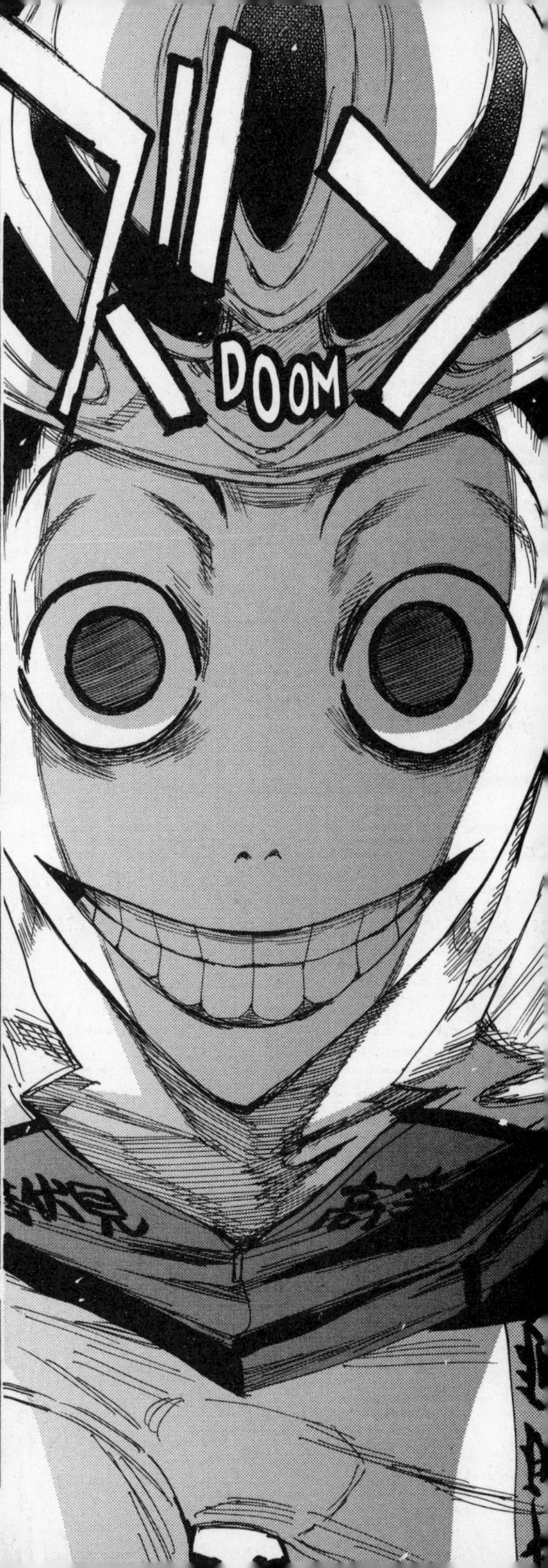
DOOM

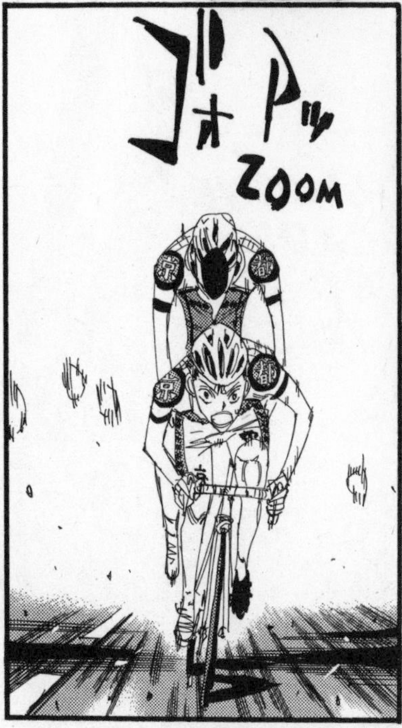
ZOOM

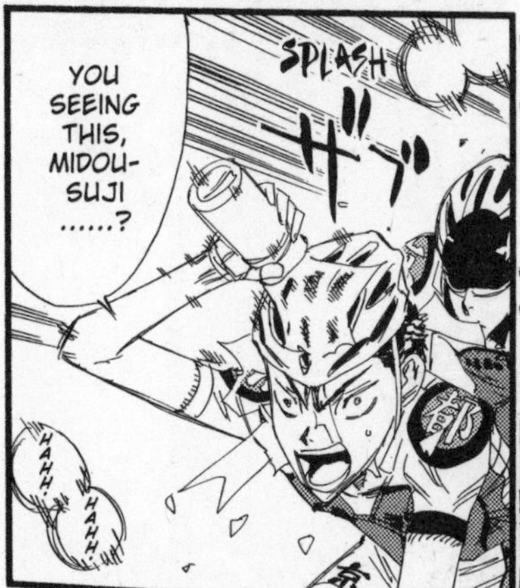
YOU SEEING THIS, MIDOU-SUJI ......?
SPLASH
HAHH
HAHH

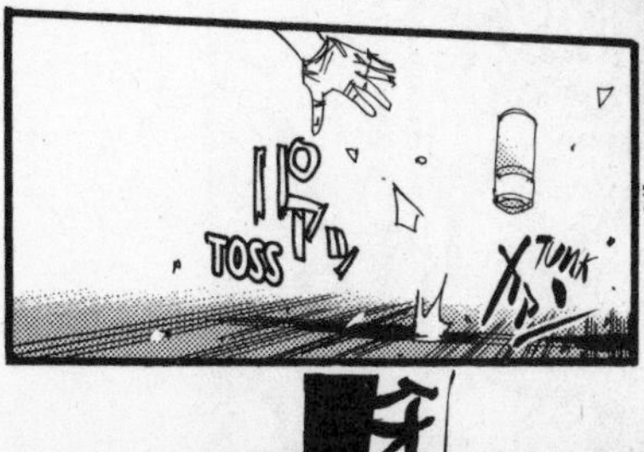
TOSS
TUNK

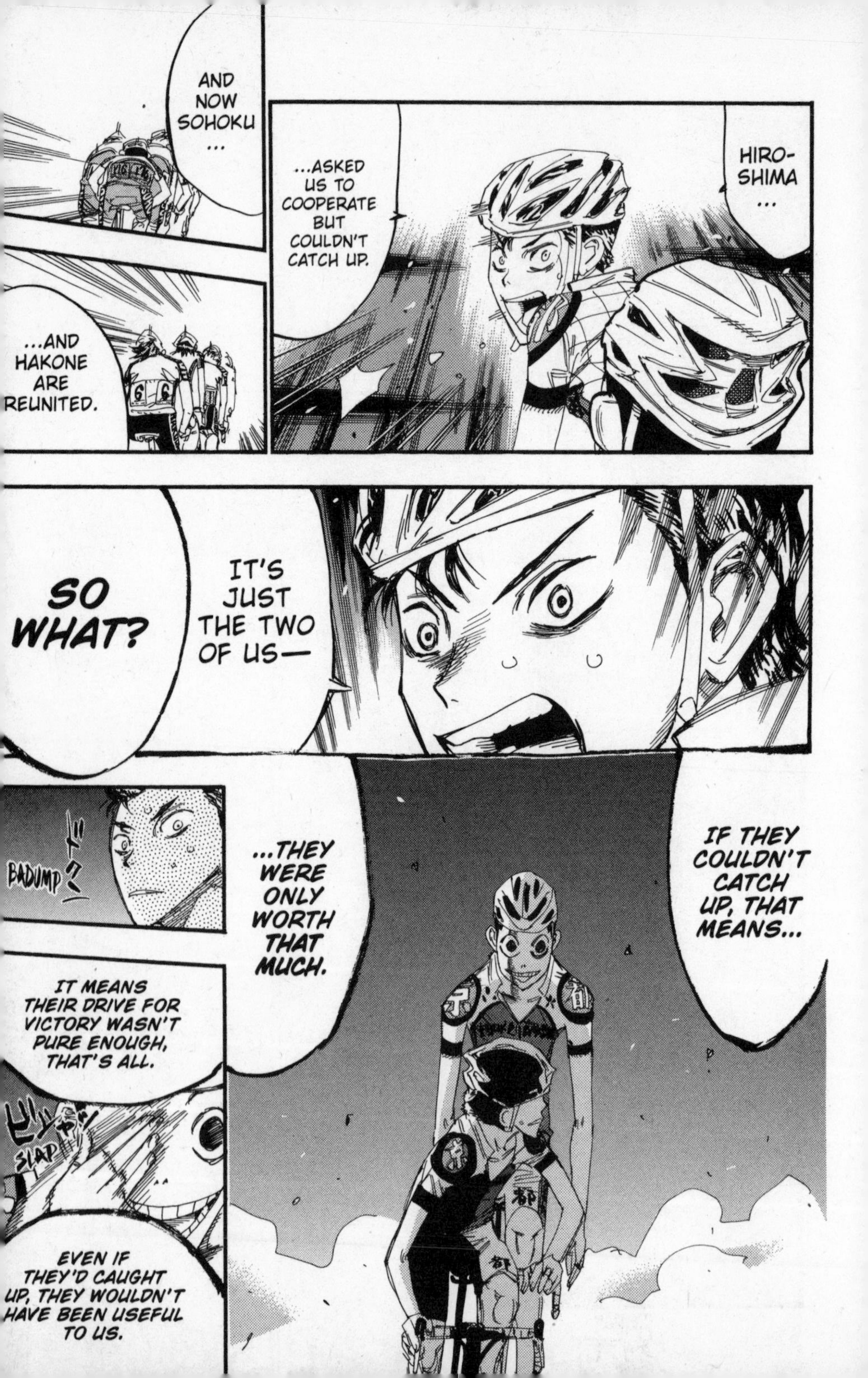
HIRO-SHIMA...
...ASKED US TO COOPERATE BUT COULDN'T CATCH UP.
AND NOW SOHOKU...
...AND HAKONE ARE REUNITED.
IT'S JUST THE TWO OF US—
SO WHAT?
IF THEY COULDN'T CATCH UP, THAT MEANS...
...THEY WERE ONLY WORTH THAT MUCH.
BADUMP
IT MEANS THEIR DRIVE FOR VICTORY WASN'T PURE ENOUGH, THAT'S ALL.
SLAP
EVEN IF THEY'D CAUGHT UP, THEY WOULDN'T HAVE BEEN USEFUL TO US.

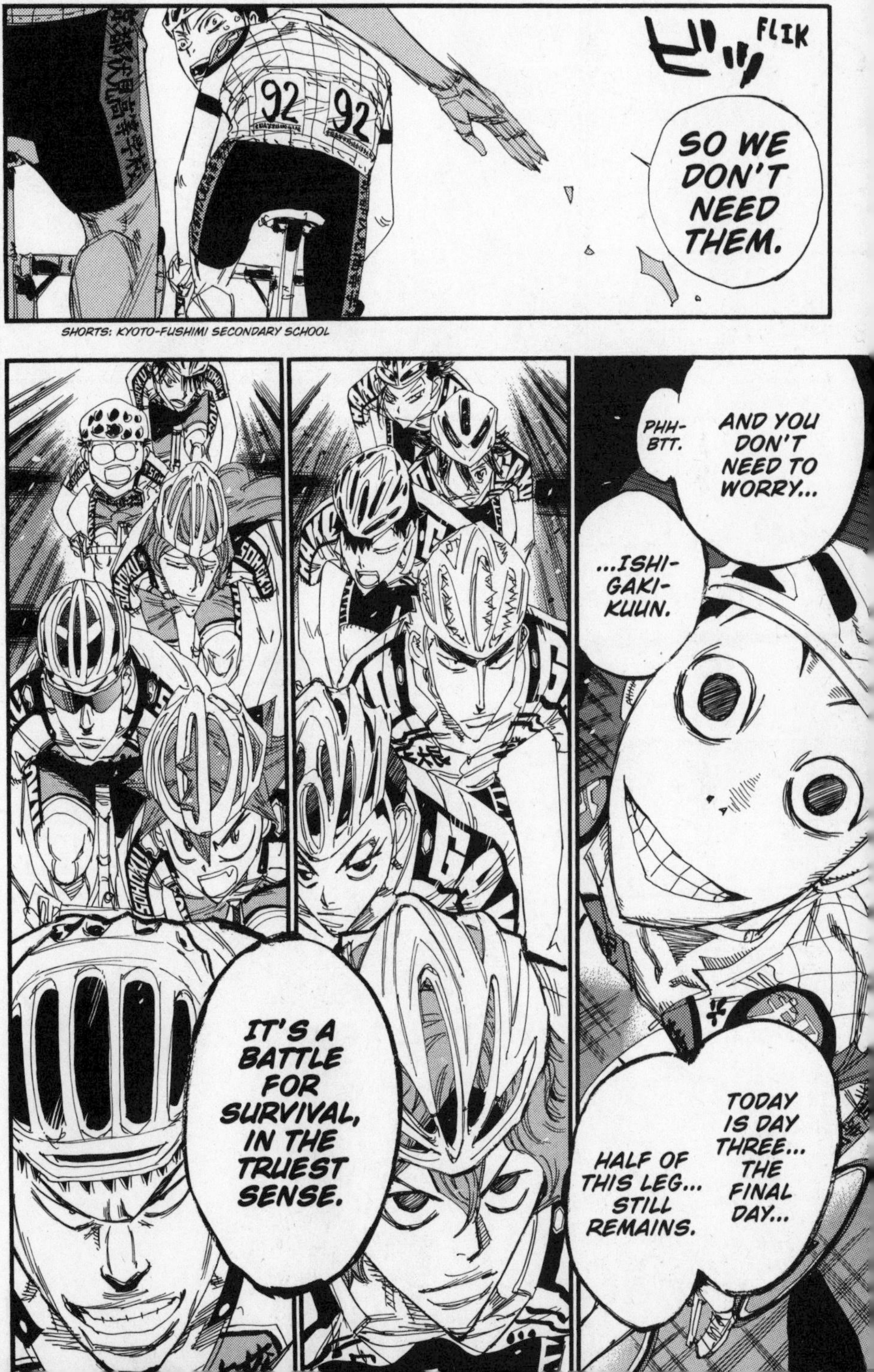
FLIK
SO WE DON'T NEED THEM.
SHORTS: KYOTO-FUSHIMI SECONDARY SCHOOL
AND YOU DON'T NEED TO WORRY...
PHH-BTT.
...ISHI-GAKI-KUUN.
TODAY IS DAY THREE... THE FINAL DAY...
HALF OF THIS LEG... STILL REMAINS.
IT'S A BATTLE FOR SURVIVAL, IN THE TRUEST SENSE.

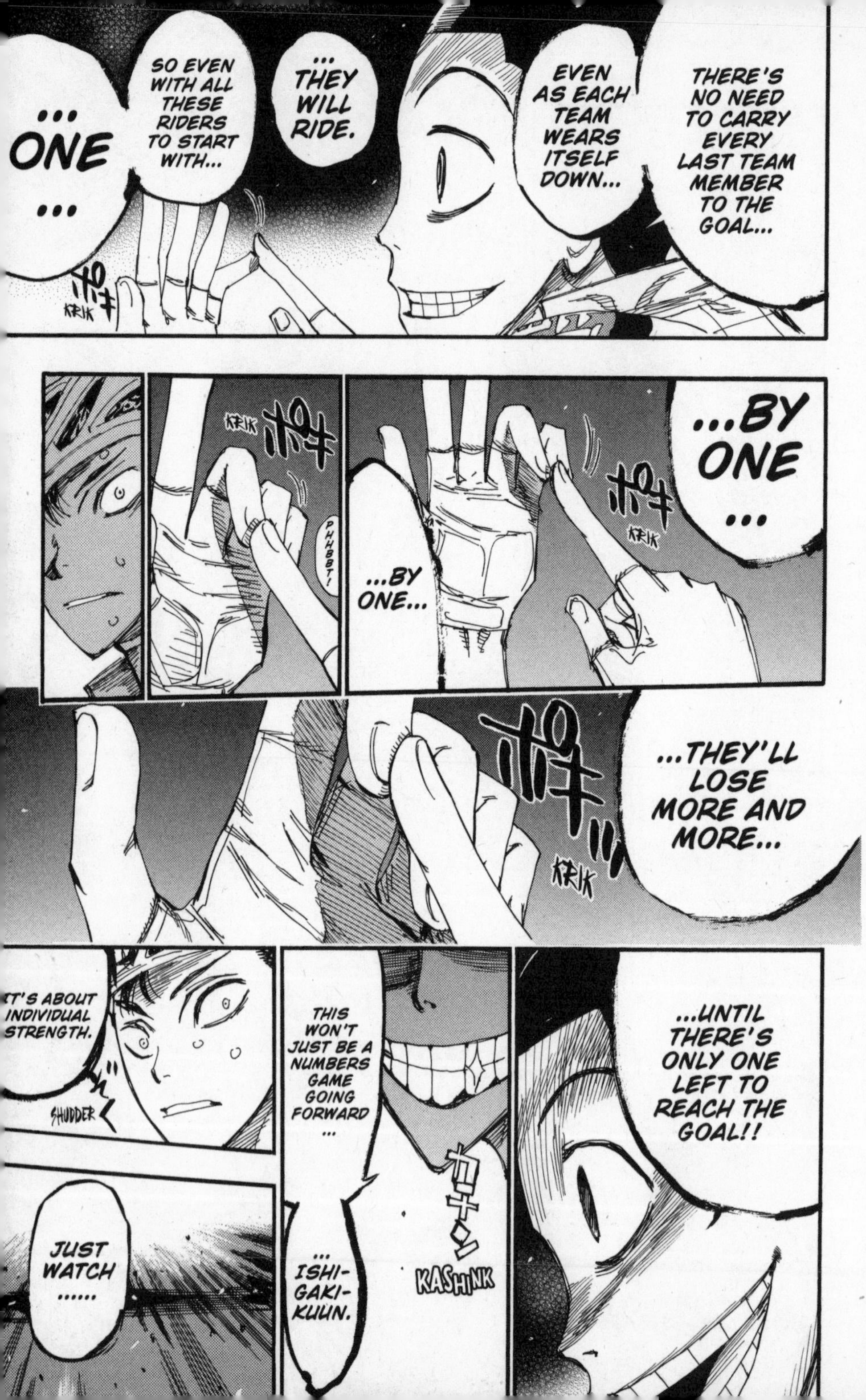
THERE'S NO NEED TO CARRY EVERY LAST TEAM MEMBER TO THE GOAL...
EVEN AS EACH TEAM WEARS ITSELF DOWN...
...THEY WILL RIDE.
SO EVEN WITH ALL THESE RIDERS TO START WITH...
...ONE...
ポキ
KRIK
...BY ONE...
ポキ
KRIK
...BY ONE...
ポキ
KRIK
PHHBBT!
...THEY'LL LOSE MORE AND MORE...
ポキッ
KRIK
...UNTIL THERE'S ONLY ONE LEFT TO REACH THE GOAL!!
THIS WON'T JUST BE A NUMBERS GAME GOING FORWARD...
KASHINK
...ISHI-GAKI-KUUN.
T'S ABOUT INDIVIDUAL STRENGTH.
SHUDDER
JUST WATCH......

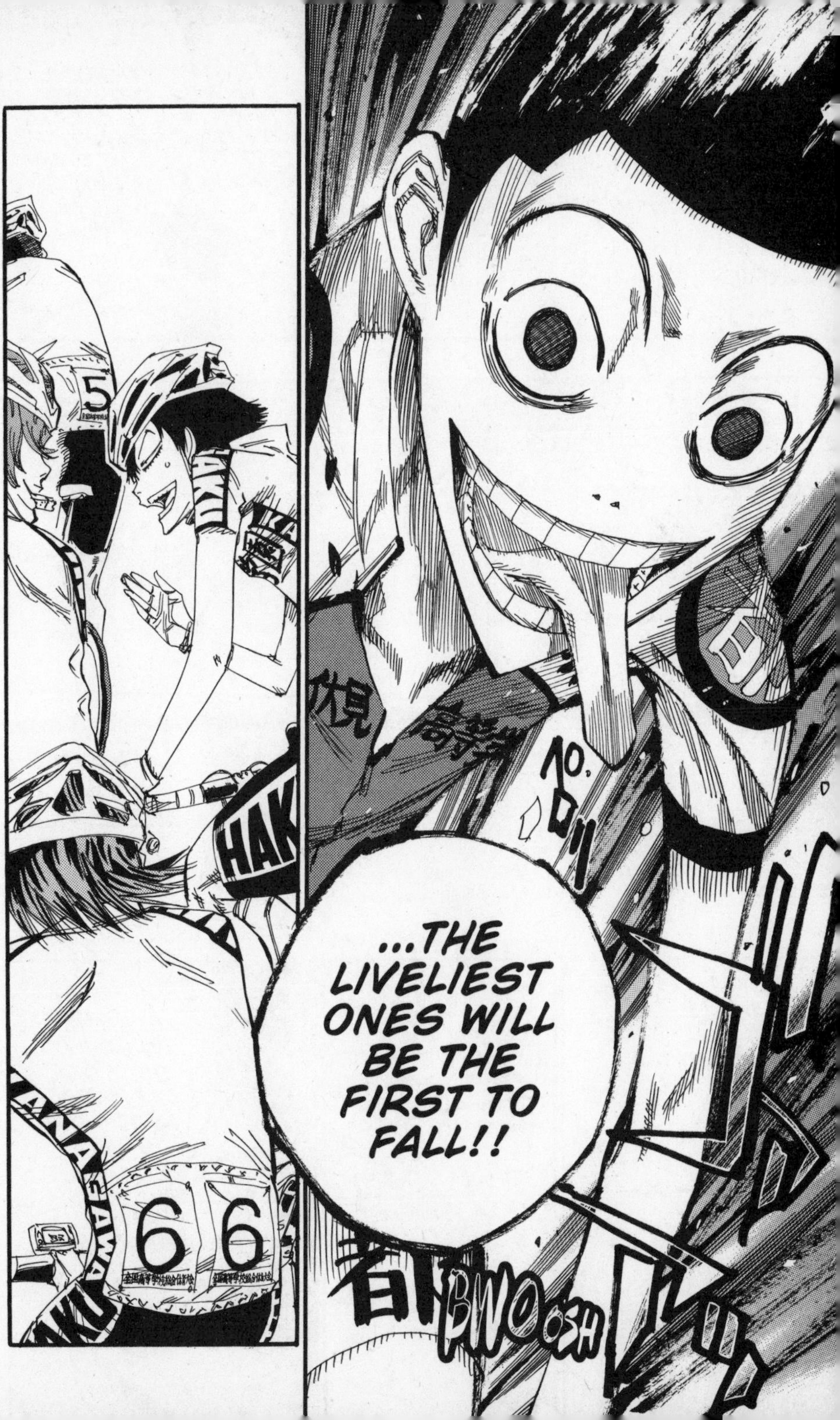
...THE LIVELIEST ONES WILL BE THE FIRST TO FALL!!
BWOOSH

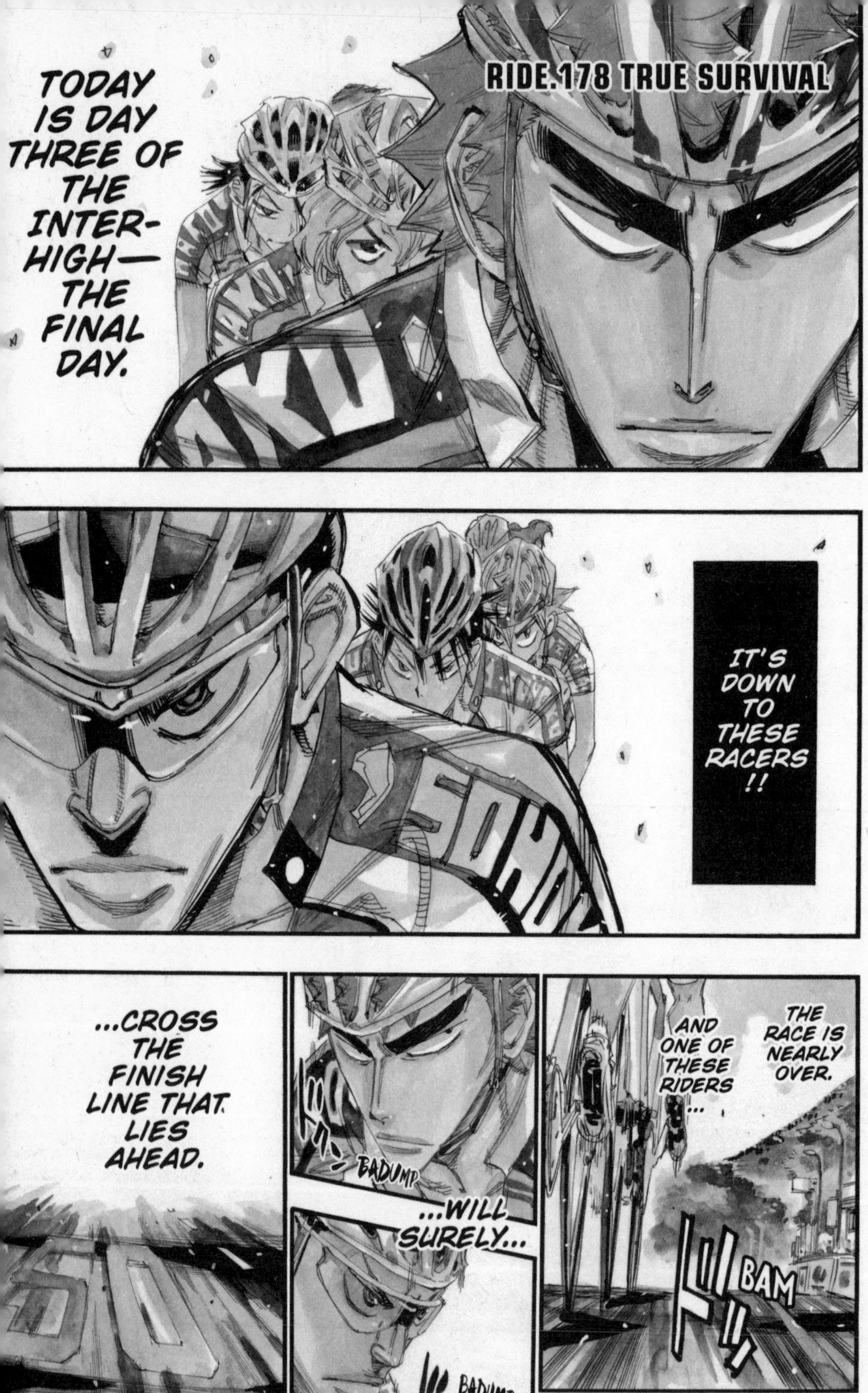
RIDE.178 TRUE SURVIVAL
TODAY IS DAY THREE OF THE INTER-HIGH—THE FINAL DAY.
IT'S DOWN TO THESE RACERS!!
THE RACE IS NEARLY OVER.
AND ONE OF THESE RIDERS...
BAM
BADUMP
...WILL SURELY...
BADUMP
...CROSS THE FINISH LINE THAT LIES AHEAD.

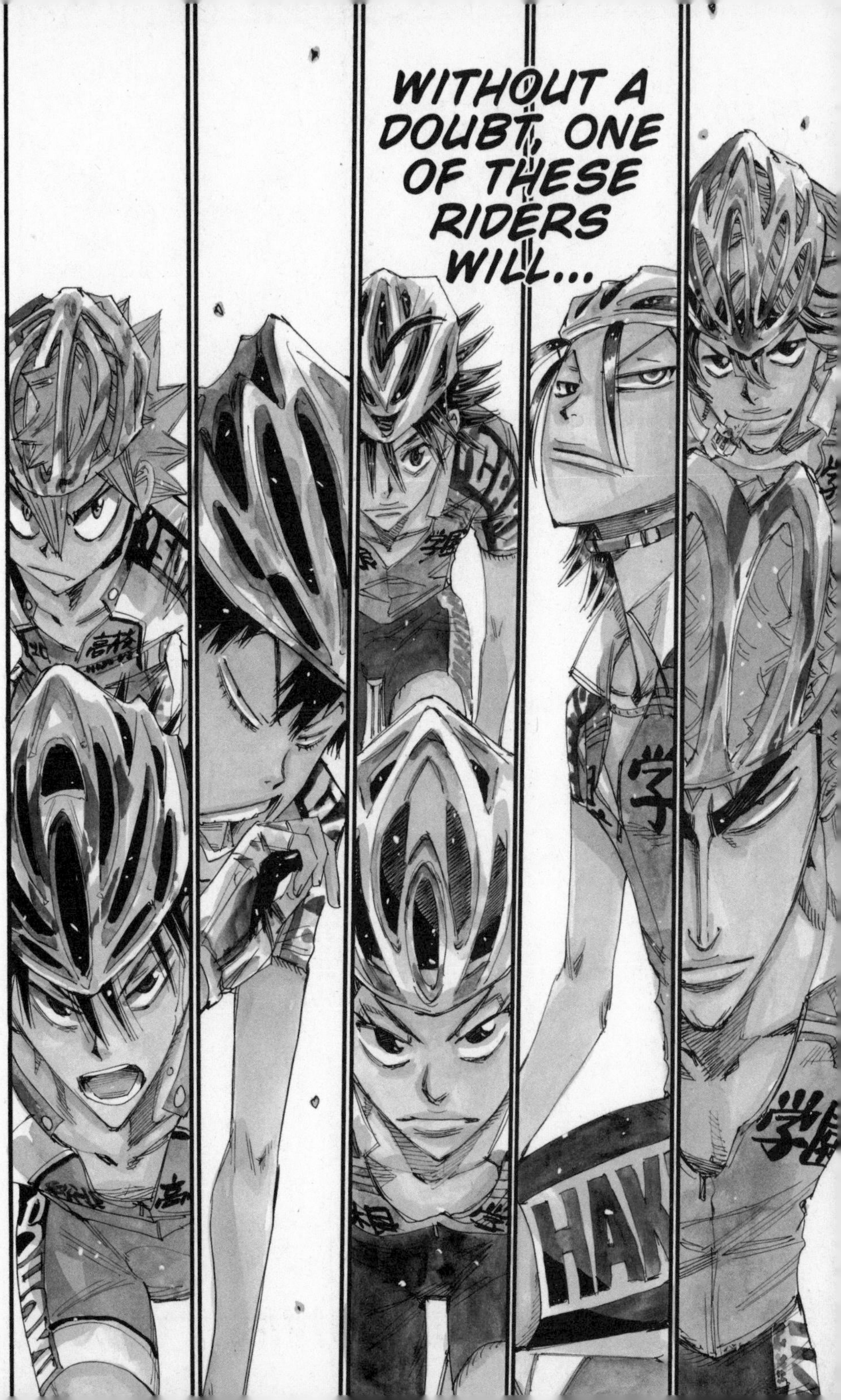
WITHOUT A DOUBT, ONE OF THESE RIDERS WILL...

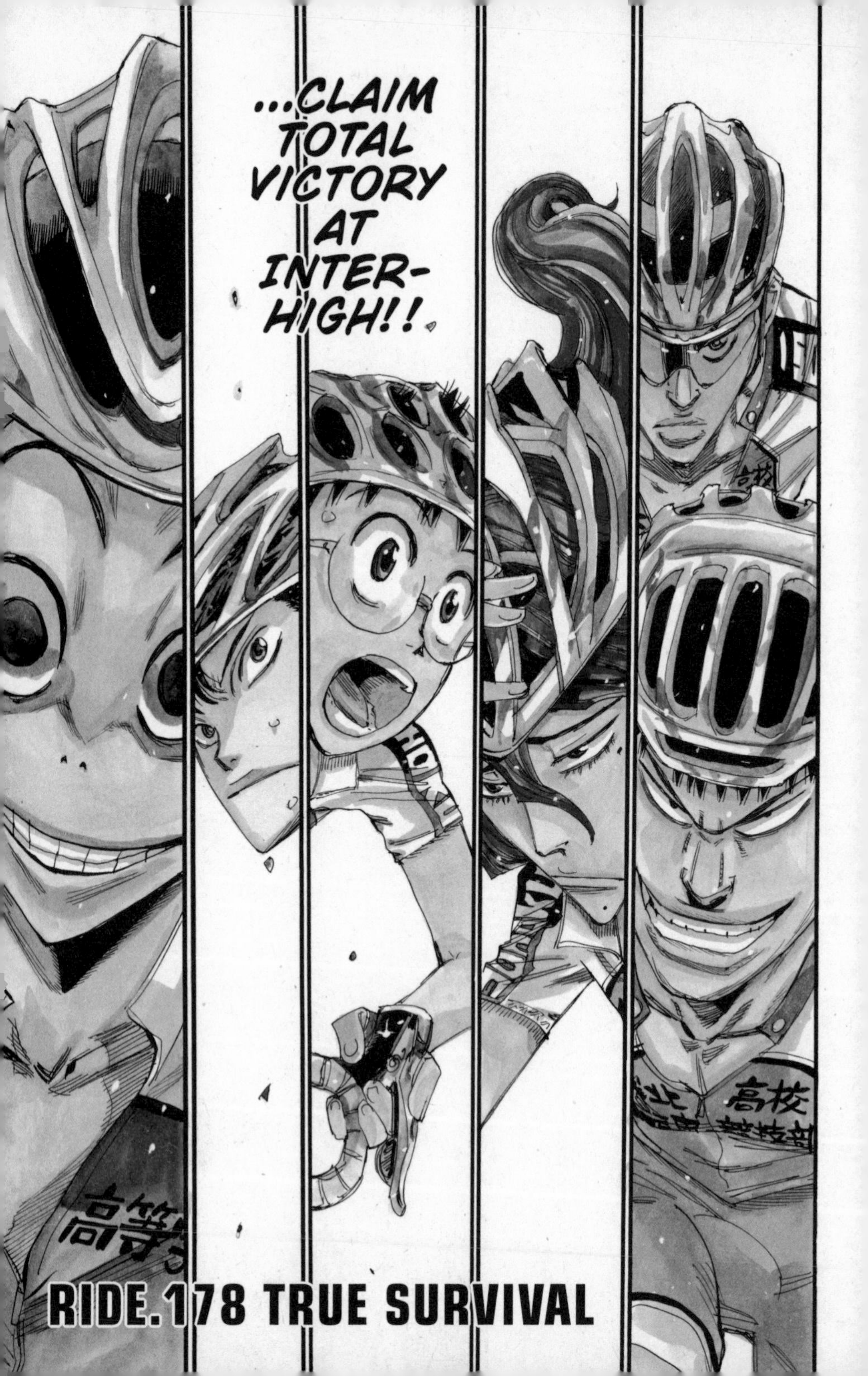
...CLAIM TOTAL VICTORY AT INTER-HIGH!!
RIDE.178 TRUE SURVIVAL

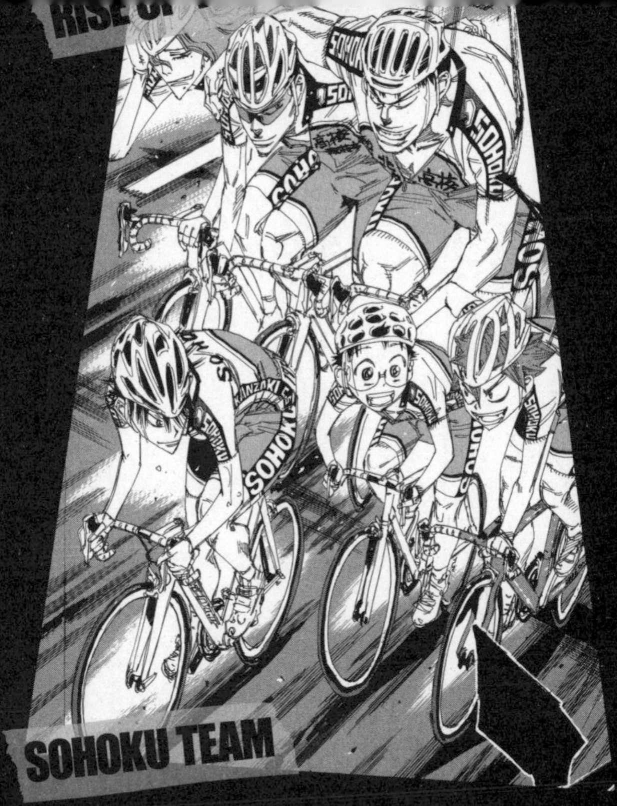
SOHOKU TEAM

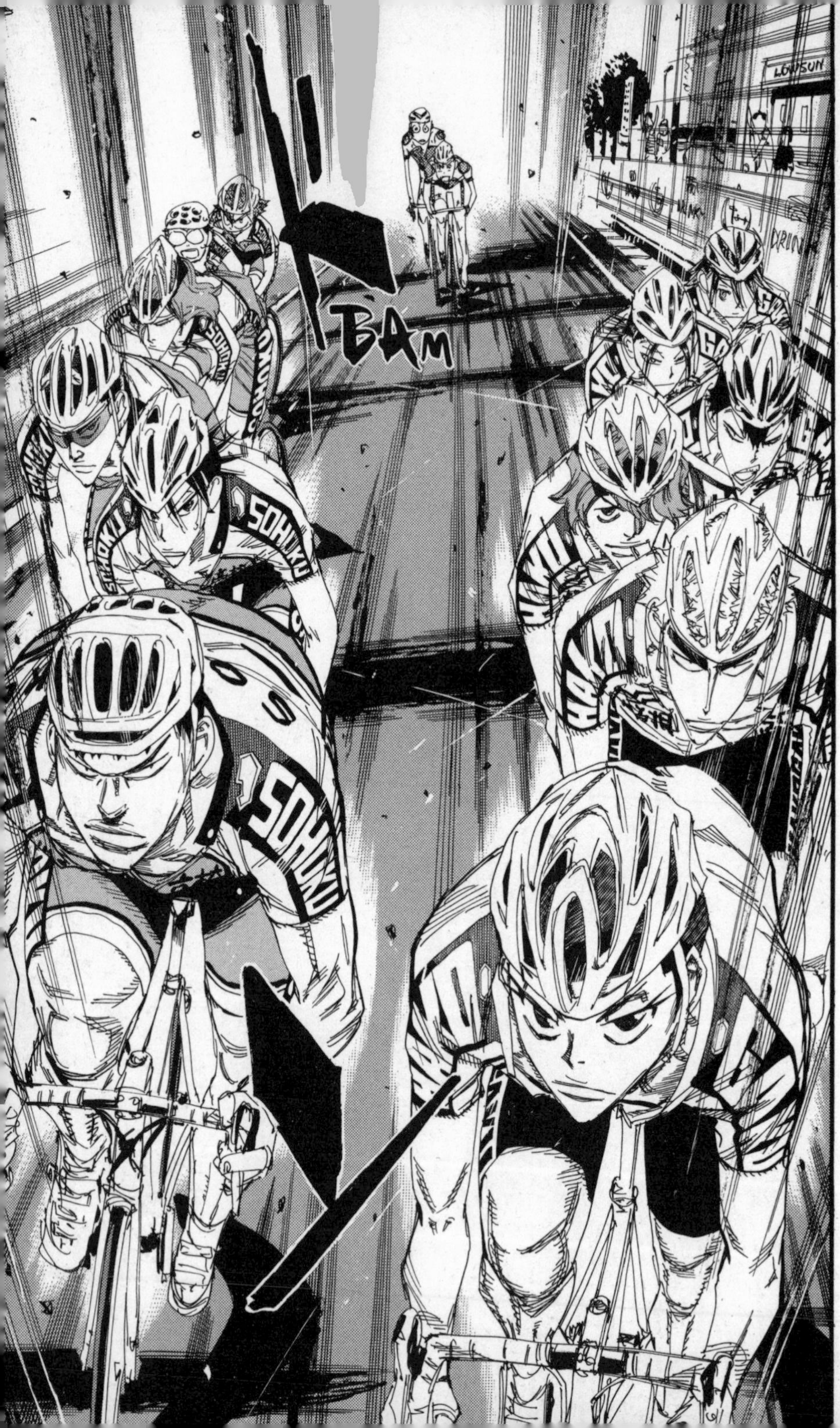
BAM
LOWSUN

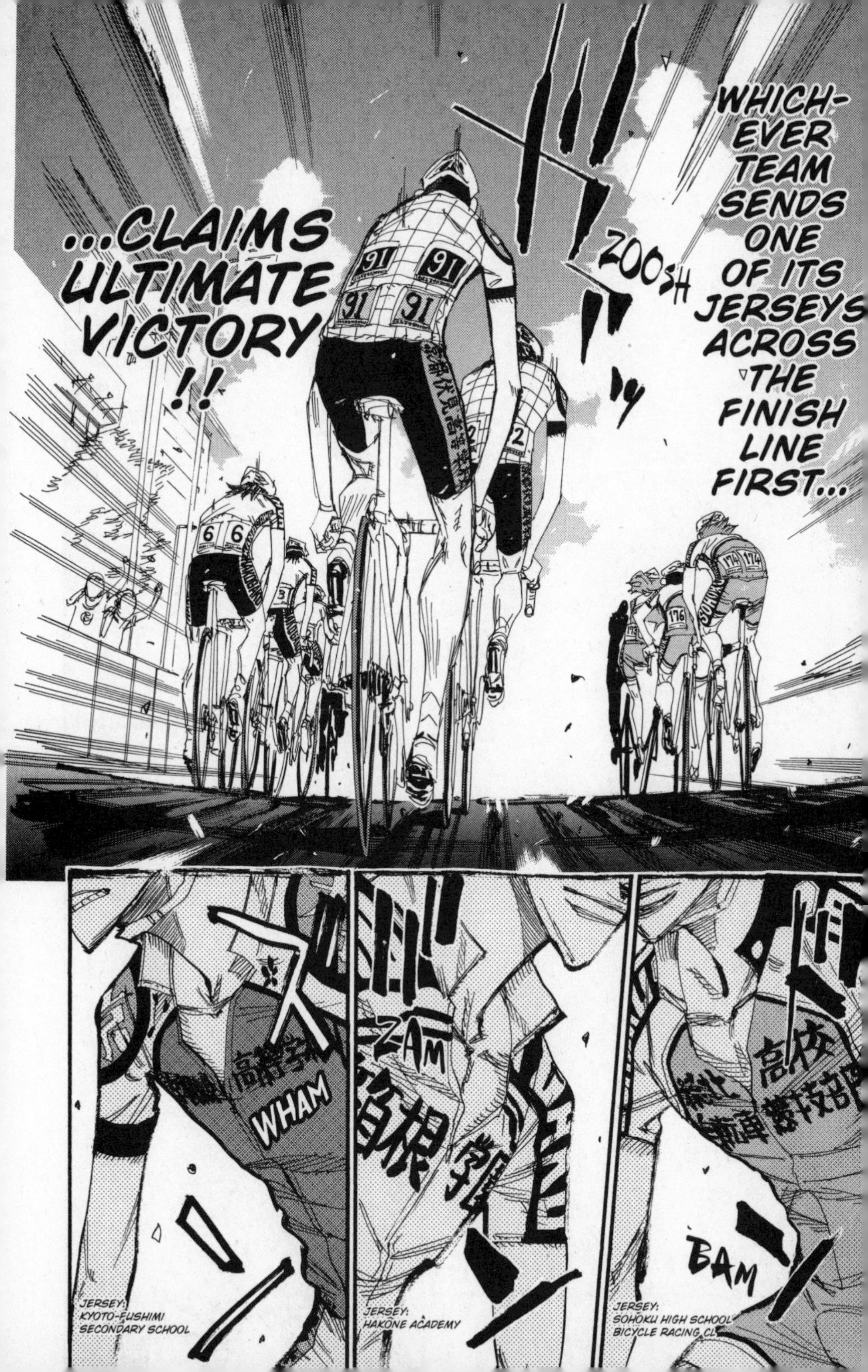
WHICH-EVER TEAM SENDS ONE OF ITS JERSEYS ACROSS THE FINISH LINE FIRST...
ZOOSH
...CLAIMS ULTIMATE VICTORY!!
BAM
JERSEY: SOHOKU HIGH SCHOOL BICYCLE RACING CL
ZAM
JERSEY: HAKONE ACADEMY
WHAM
JERSEY: KYOTO-FUSHIMI SECONDARY SCHOOL

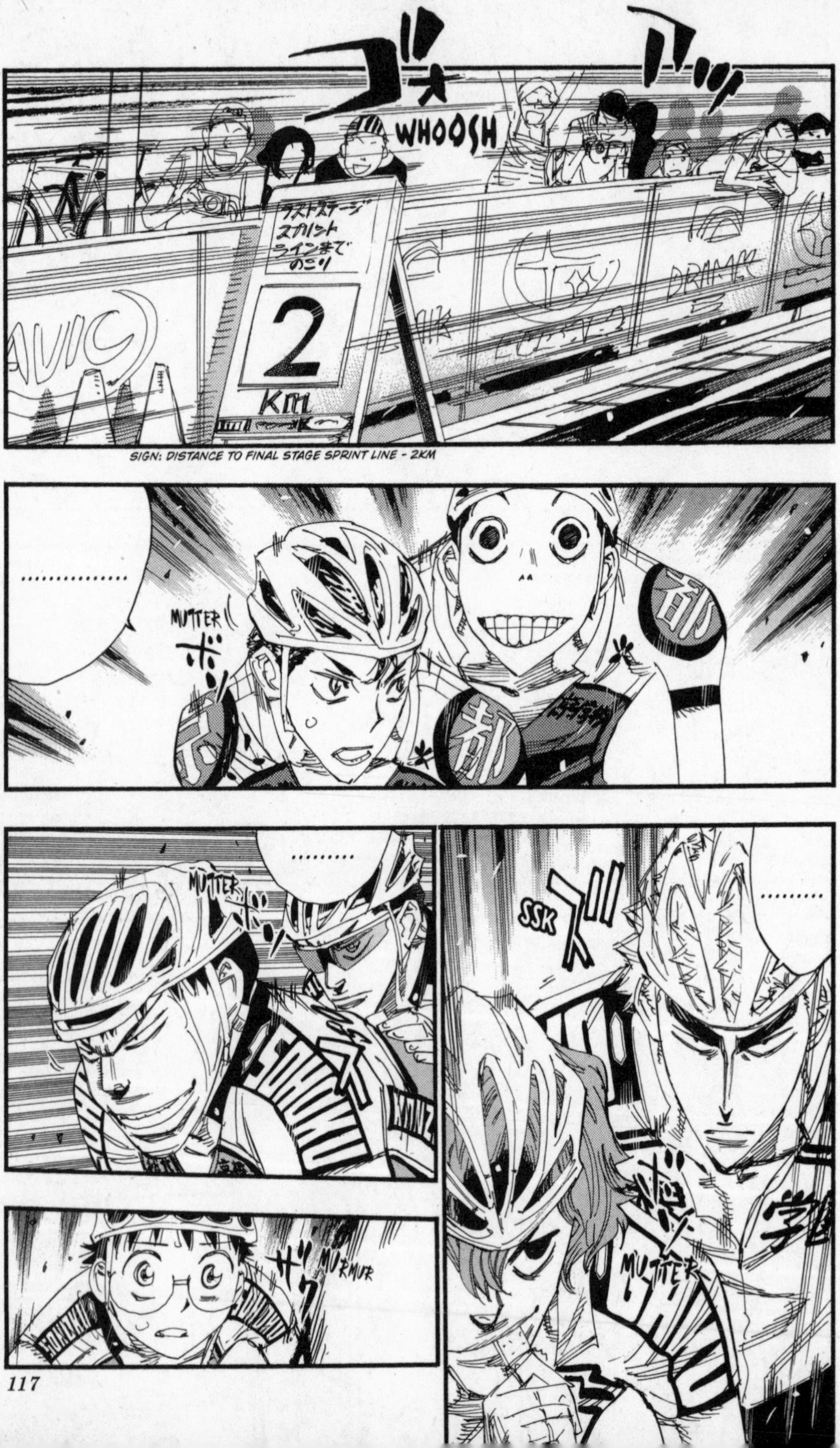

WHOOSH
ラストステージ
スプリント
ラインまで
のこり
2
Km
SIGN: DISTANCE TO FINAL STAGE SPRINT LINE - 2KM
....
MUTTER
....
SSK
MUTTER
....
MUTTER
MURMUR

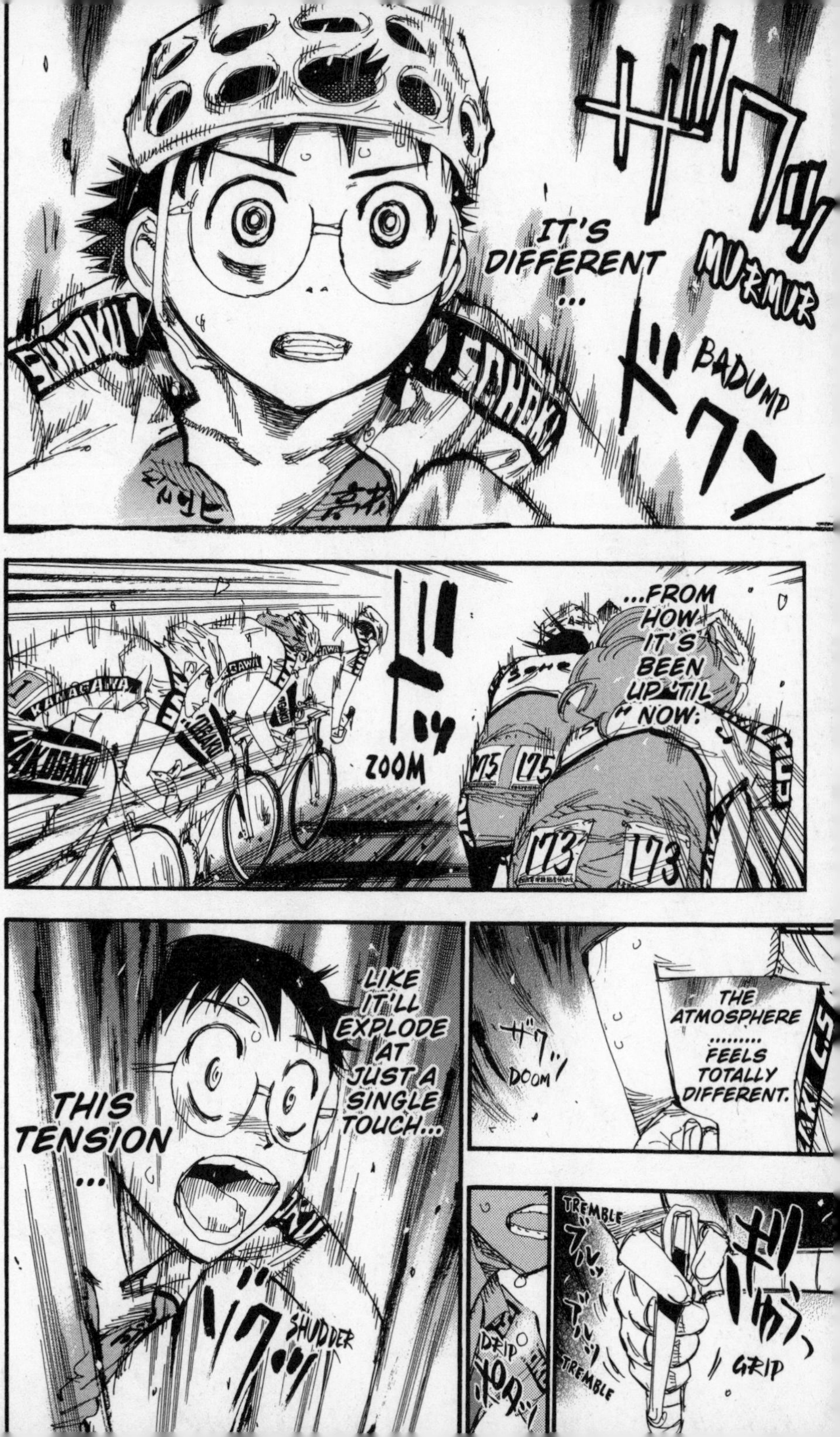
MURMUR
IT'S DIFFERENT ...
BADUMP
...FROM HOW IT'S BEEN UP 'TIL NOW.
ZOOM
THE ATMOSPHERE .... FEELS TOTALLY DIFFERENT.
DOOM
GRIP
TREMBLE
TREMBLE
DRIP
LIKE IT'LL EXPLODE AT JUST A SINGLE TOUCH...
THIS TENSION ...
SHUDDER

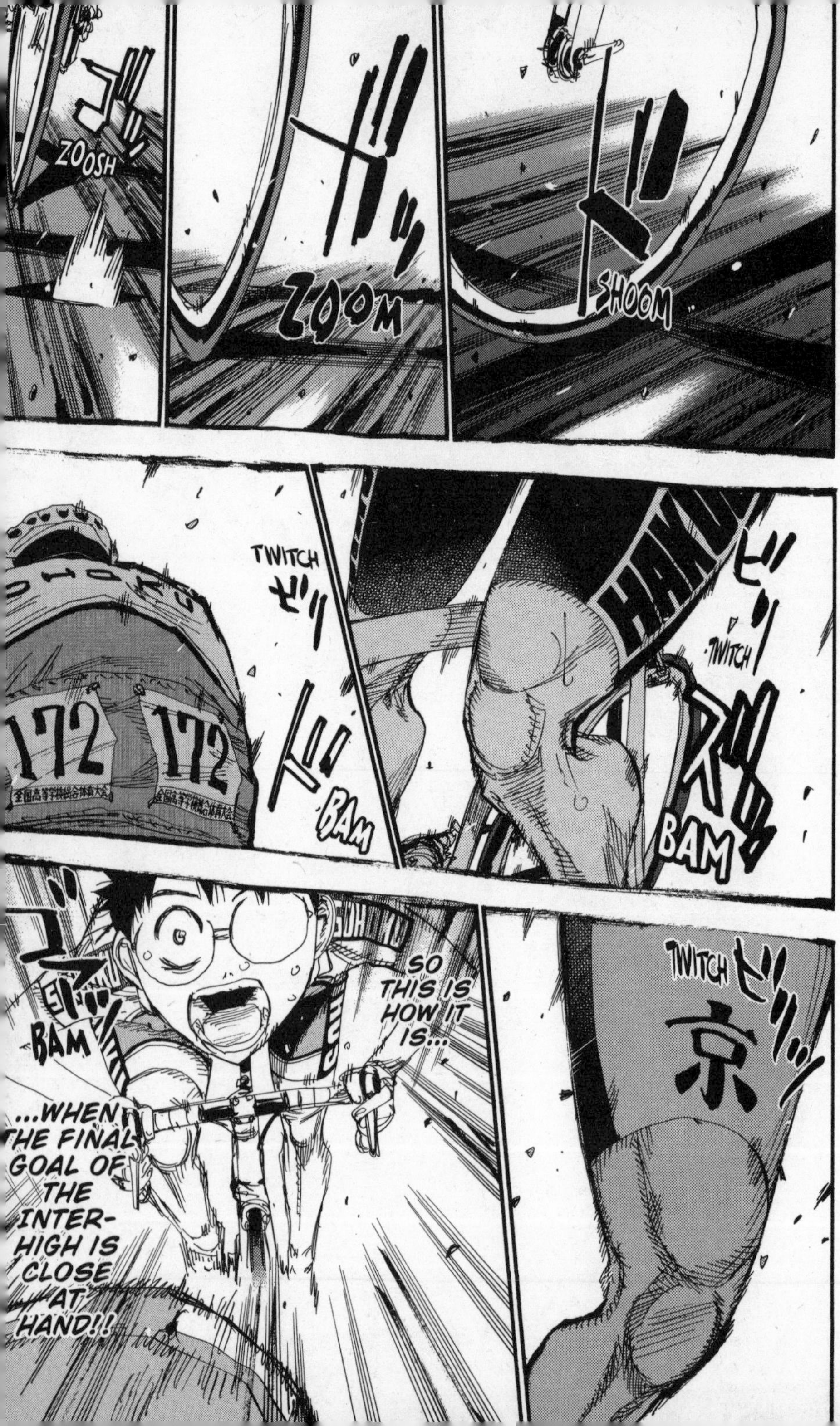
SHOOM
ZOOM
ZOOSH
TWITCH
BAM
TWITCH
172
172
BAM
TWITCH
京
SO THIS IS HOW IT IS...
...WHEN THE FINAL GOAL OF THE INTER-HIGH IS CLOSE AT HAND!!
BAM

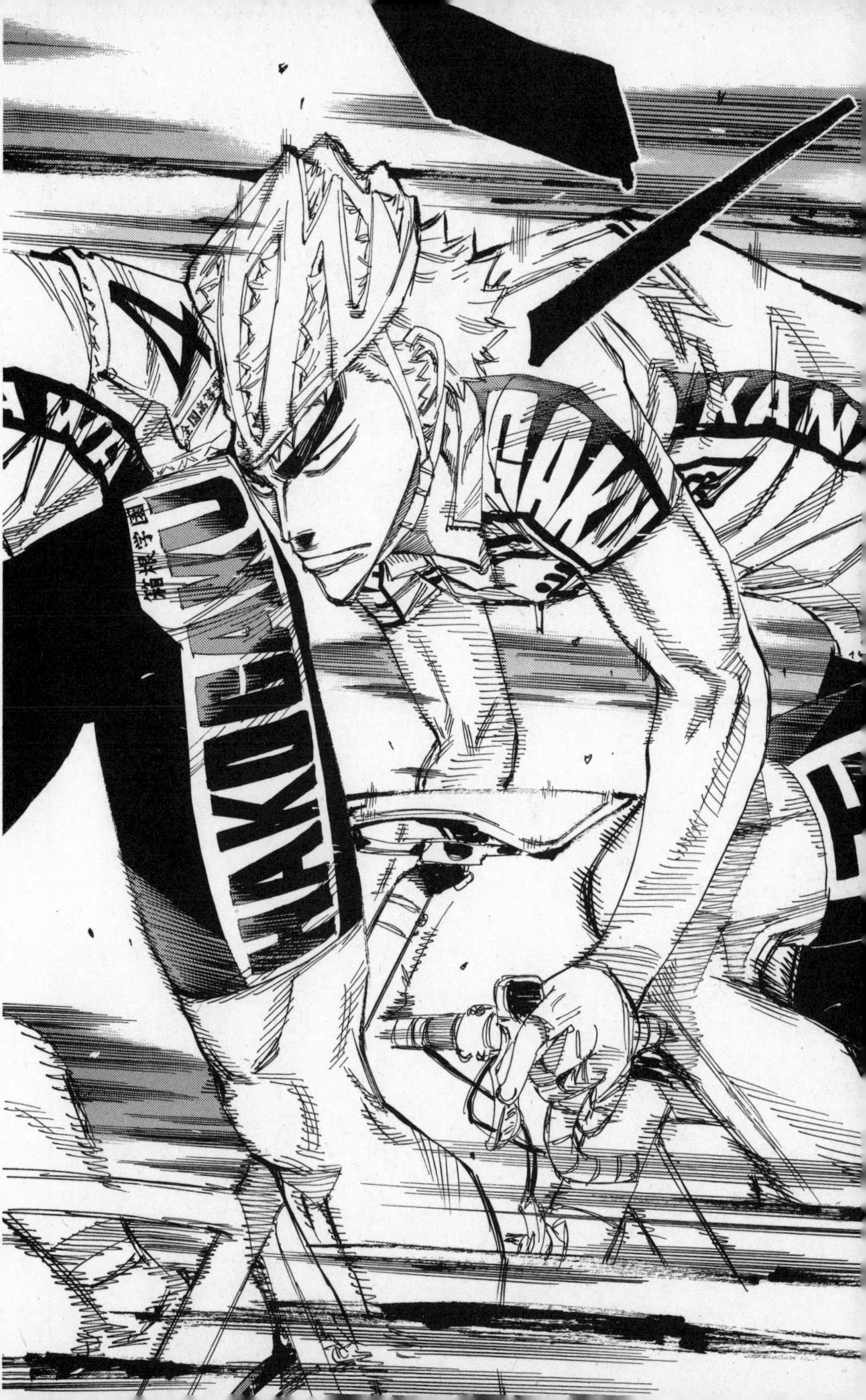
箱根学園
HAKOGAKU

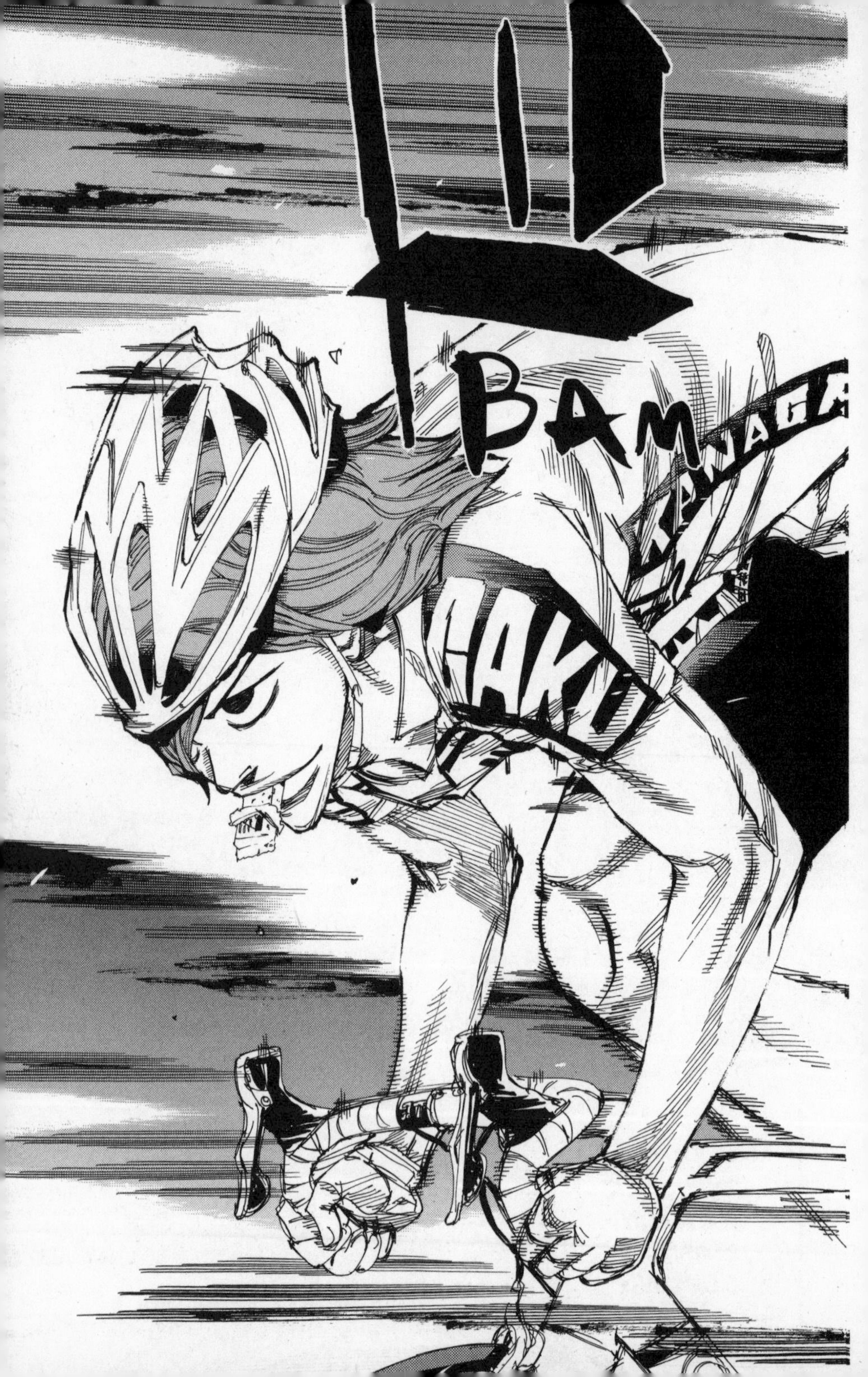
BAM

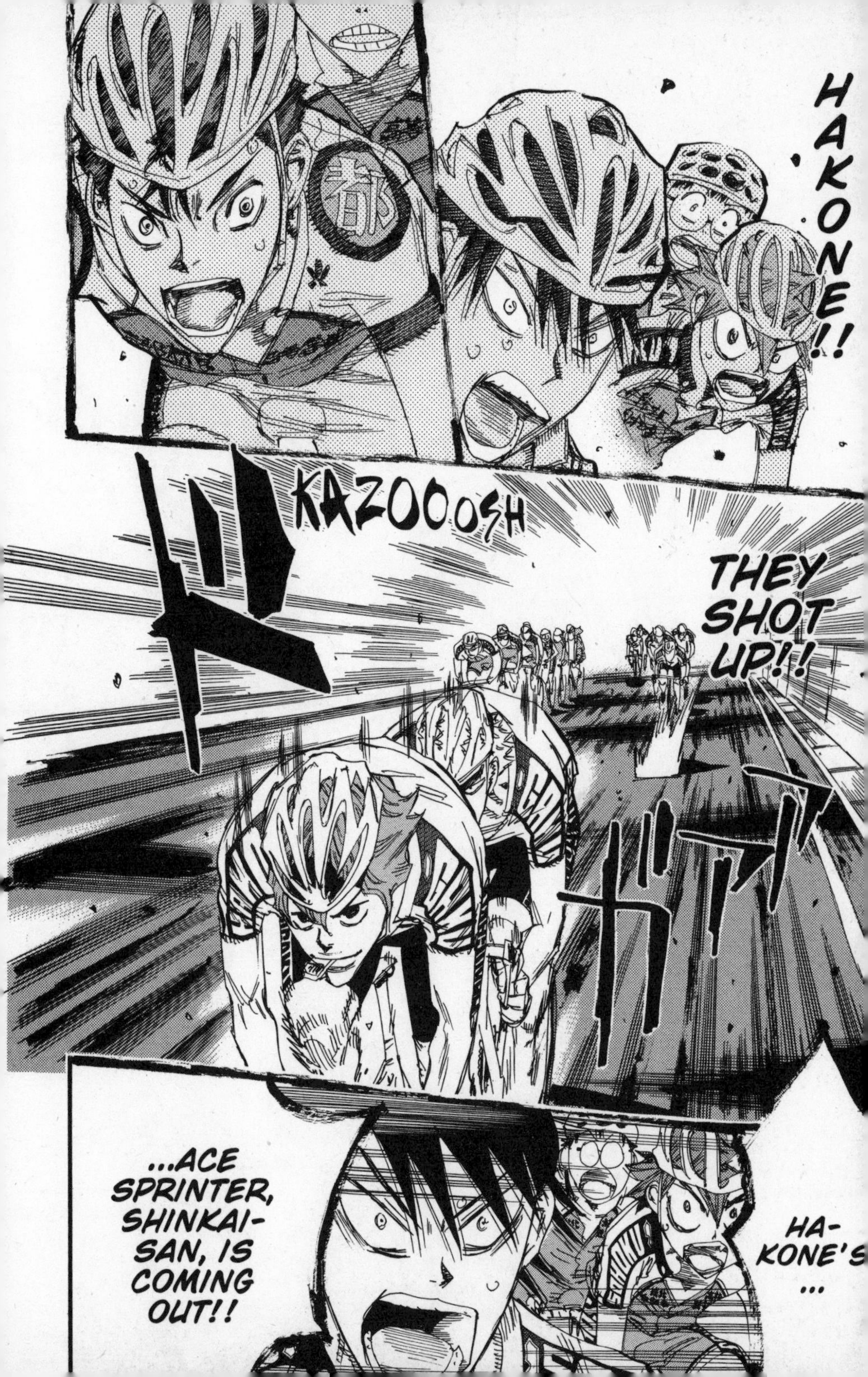
HAKONE!!
KAZOOOSH
THEY SHOT UP!!
HA-KONE'S ...
...ACE SPRINTER, SHINKAI-SAN, IS COMING OUT!!

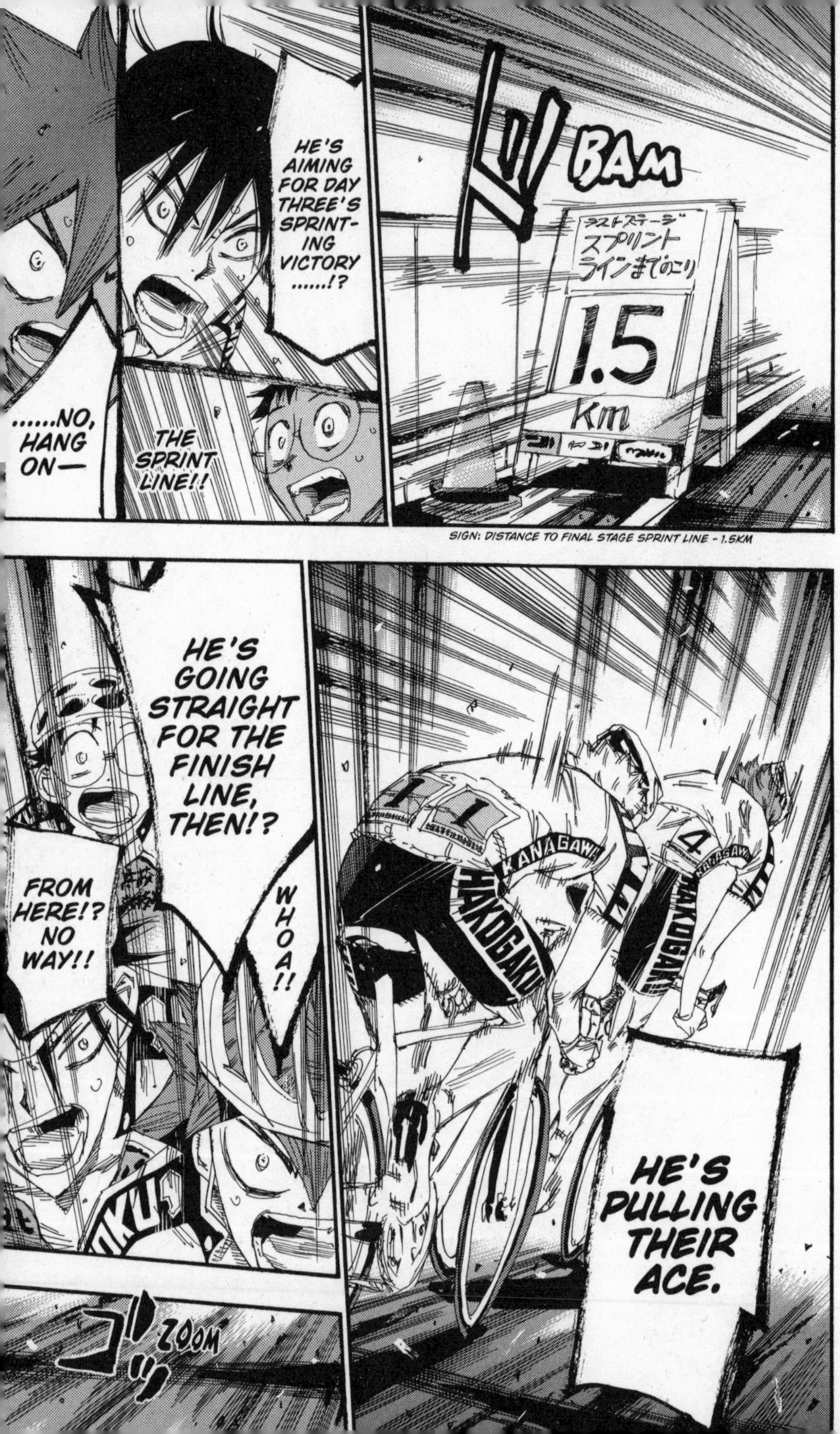
BAM
ラストステージ
スプリント
ラインまでのこり
1.5
Km
HE'S AIMING FOR DAY THREE'S SPRINTING VICTORY ......!?
THE SPRINT LINE!!
......NO, HANG ON—
SIGN: DISTANCE TO FINAL STAGE SPRINT LINE - 1.5KM
HE'S PULLING THEIR ACE.
WHOA!!
HE'S GOING STRAIGHT FOR THE FINISH LINE, THEN!?
FROM HERE!? NO WAY!!
ZOOM

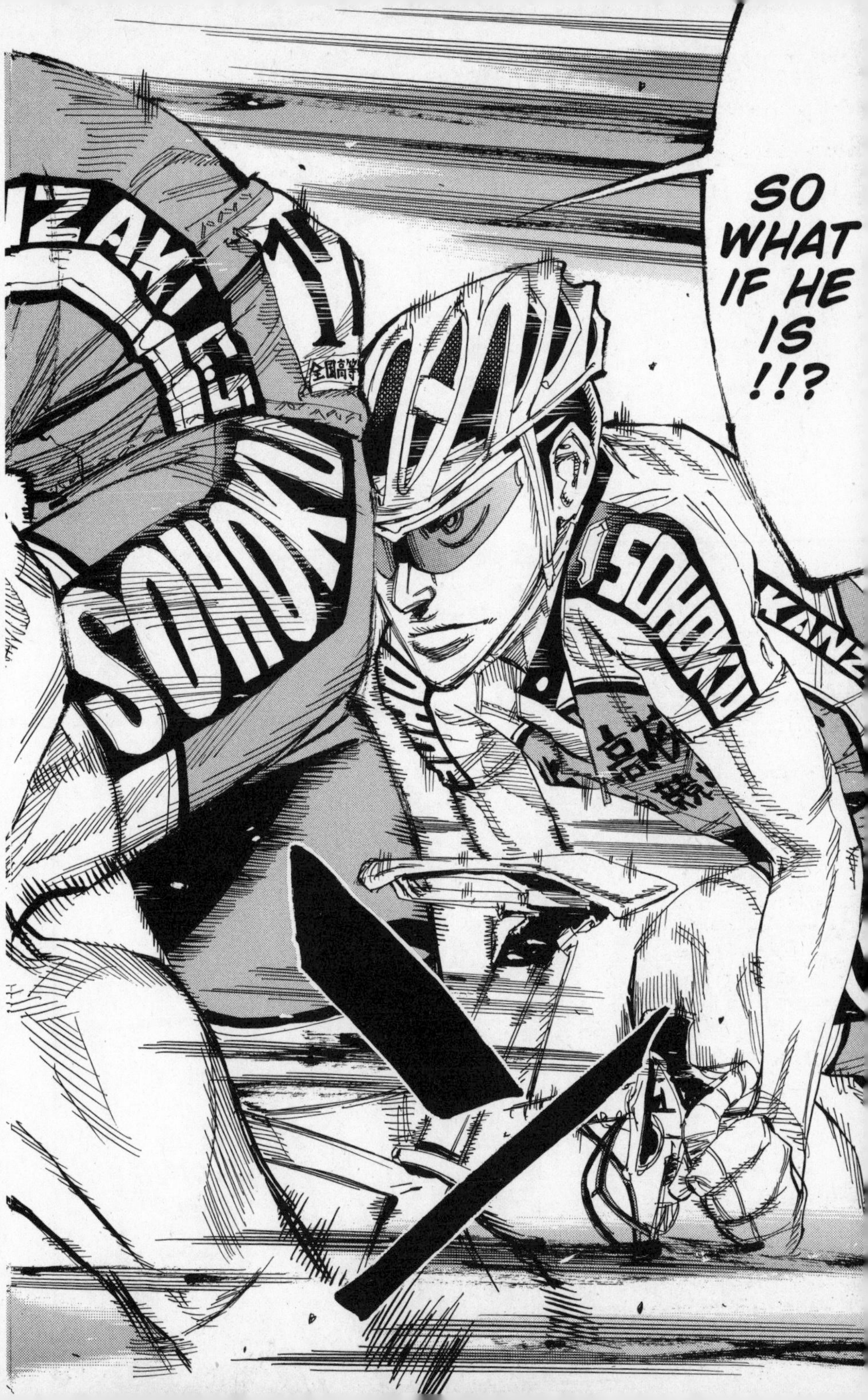
SO WHAT IF HE IS !!?

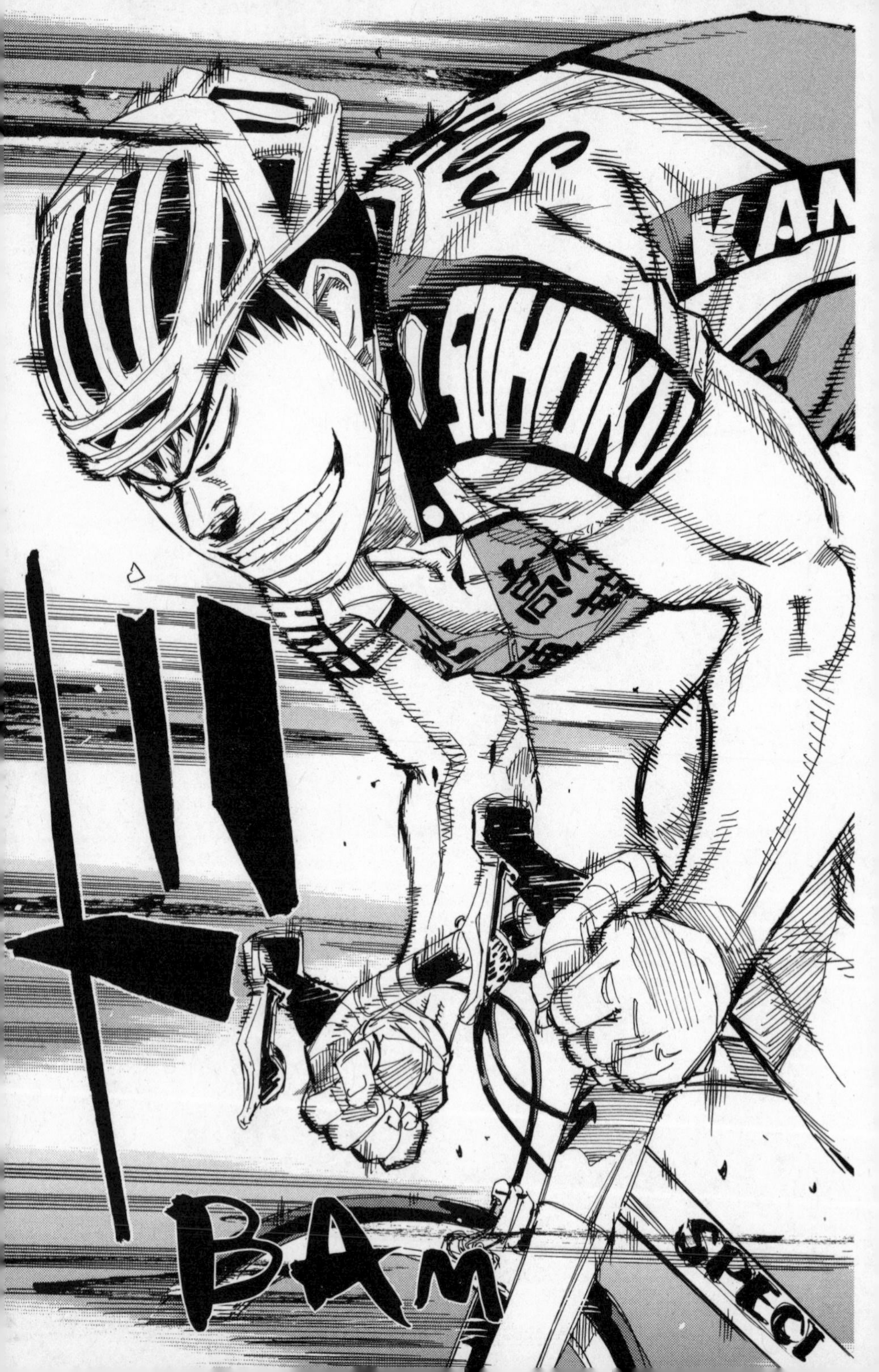
SOHOKU
BAM

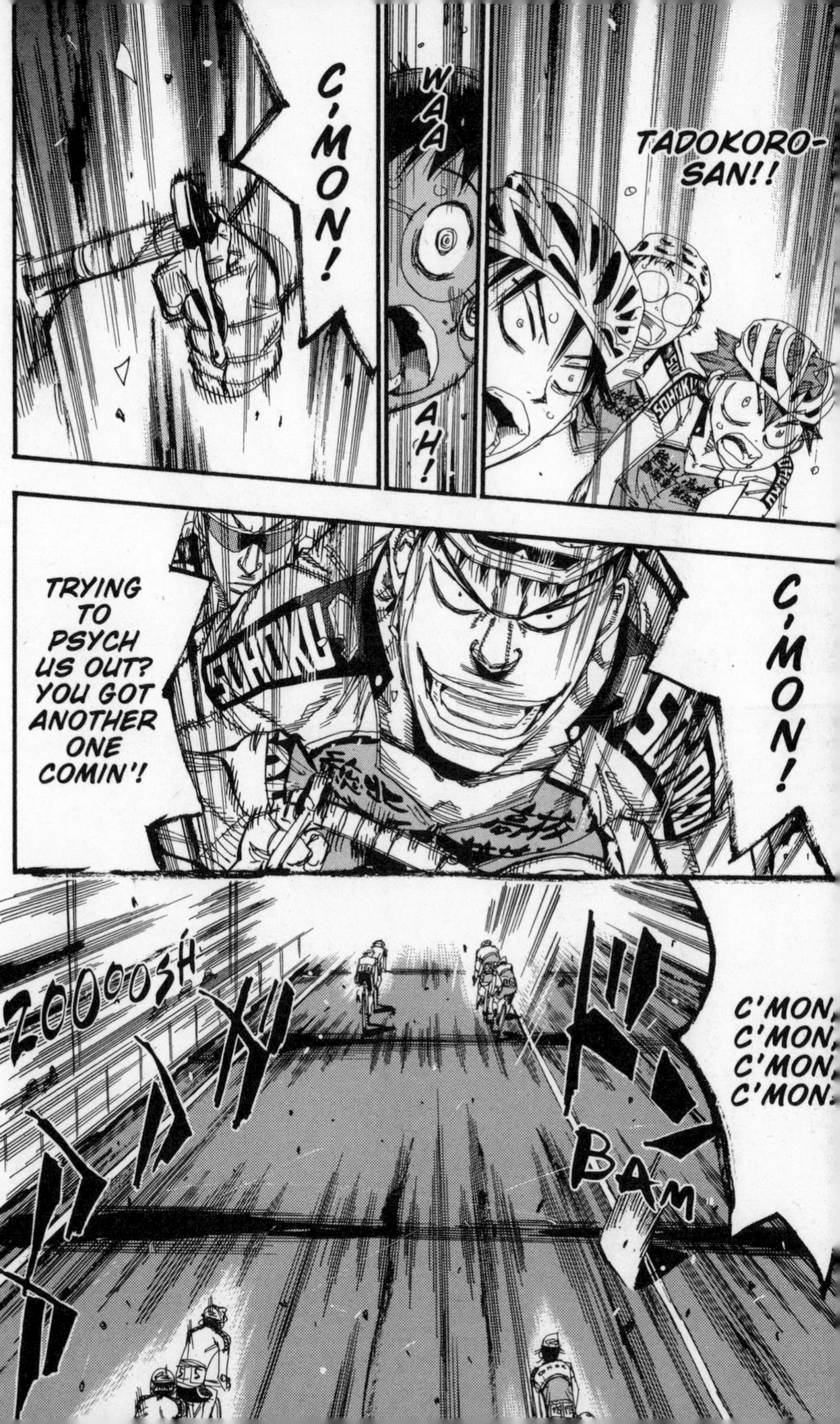
TADOKORO-SAN!!
WAAAAH!
C'MON!
C'MON!
TRYING TO PSYCH US OUT? YOU GOT ANOTHER ONE COMIN'!
C'MON, C'MON, C'MON, C'MON.
BAM
ZOOOOSH

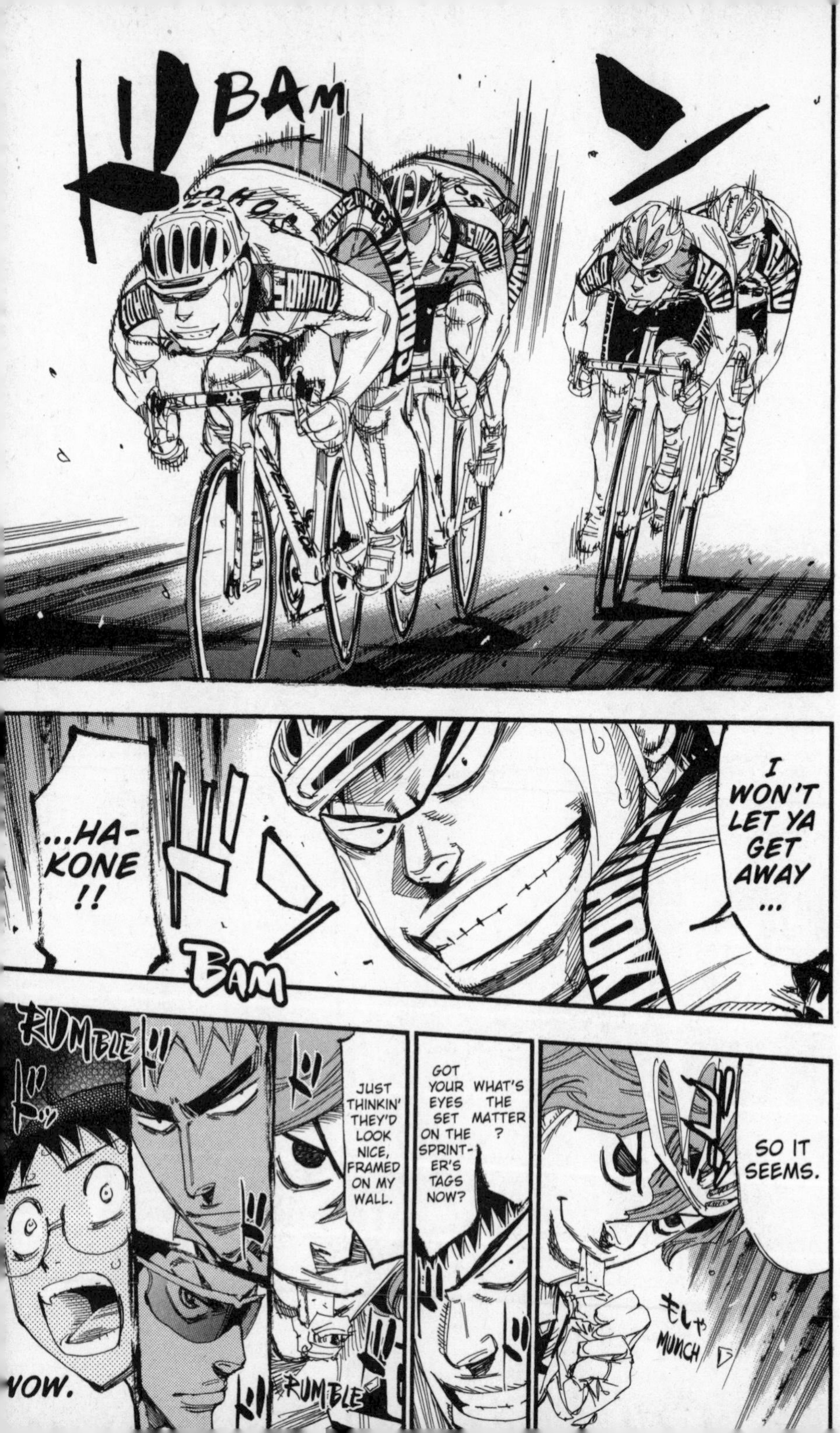
BAM
I WON'T LET YA GET AWAY...
...HA-KONE!!
BAM
SO IT SEEMS.
もしゃ
MUNCH
WHAT'S THE MATTER?
GOT YOUR EYES SET ON THE SPRINTER'S TAGS NOW?
JUST THINKIN' THEY'D LOOK NICE, FRAMED ON MY WALL.
RUMBLE
RUMBLE!!
NOW.

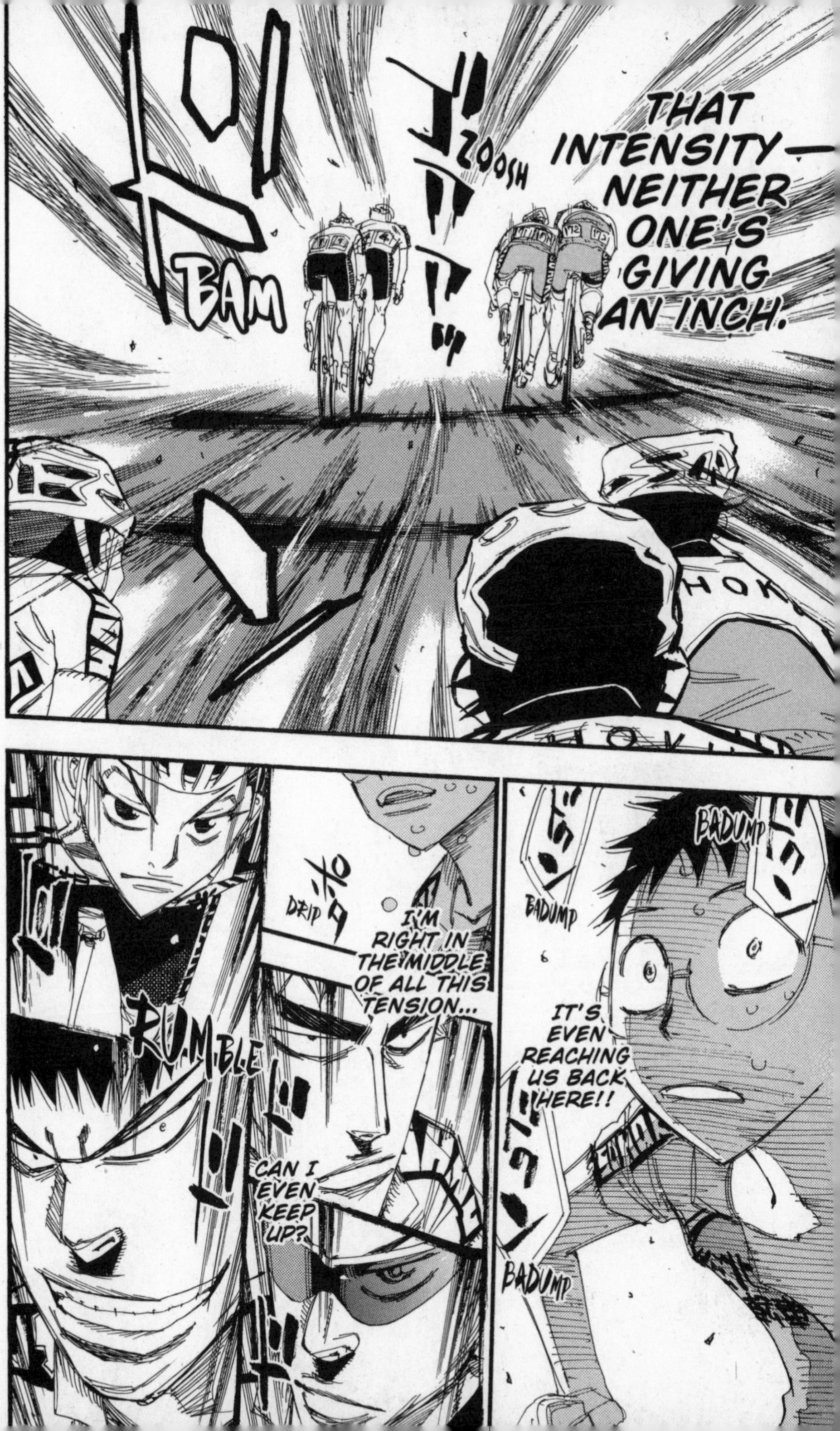
THAT INTENSITY— NEITHER ONE'S GIVING AN INCH.
ZOOSH
BAM
BADUMP
BADUMP
IT'S EVEN REACHING US BACK HERE!!
BADUMP
DRIP
I'M RIGHT IN THE MIDDLE OF ALL THIS TENSION...
CAN I EVEN KEEP UP?
RUMBLE

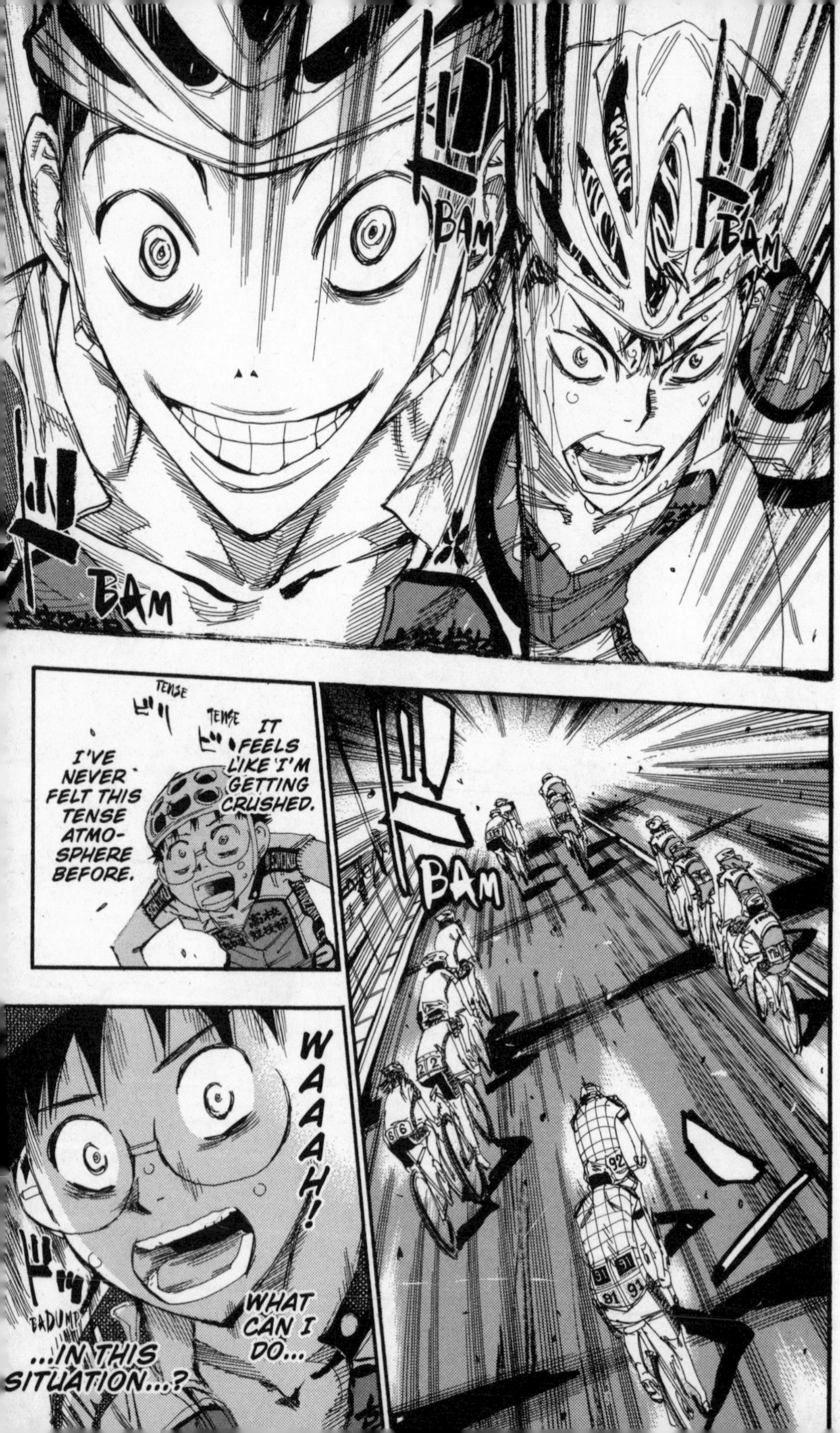
BAM
BAM
BAM
BAM
TENSE
TENSE
IT FEELS LIKE I'M GETTING CRUSHED.
I'VE NEVER FELT THIS TENSE ATMOSPHERE BEFORE.
WAAAAH!
WHAT CAN I DO...
BADUMP
...IN THIS SITUATION...?

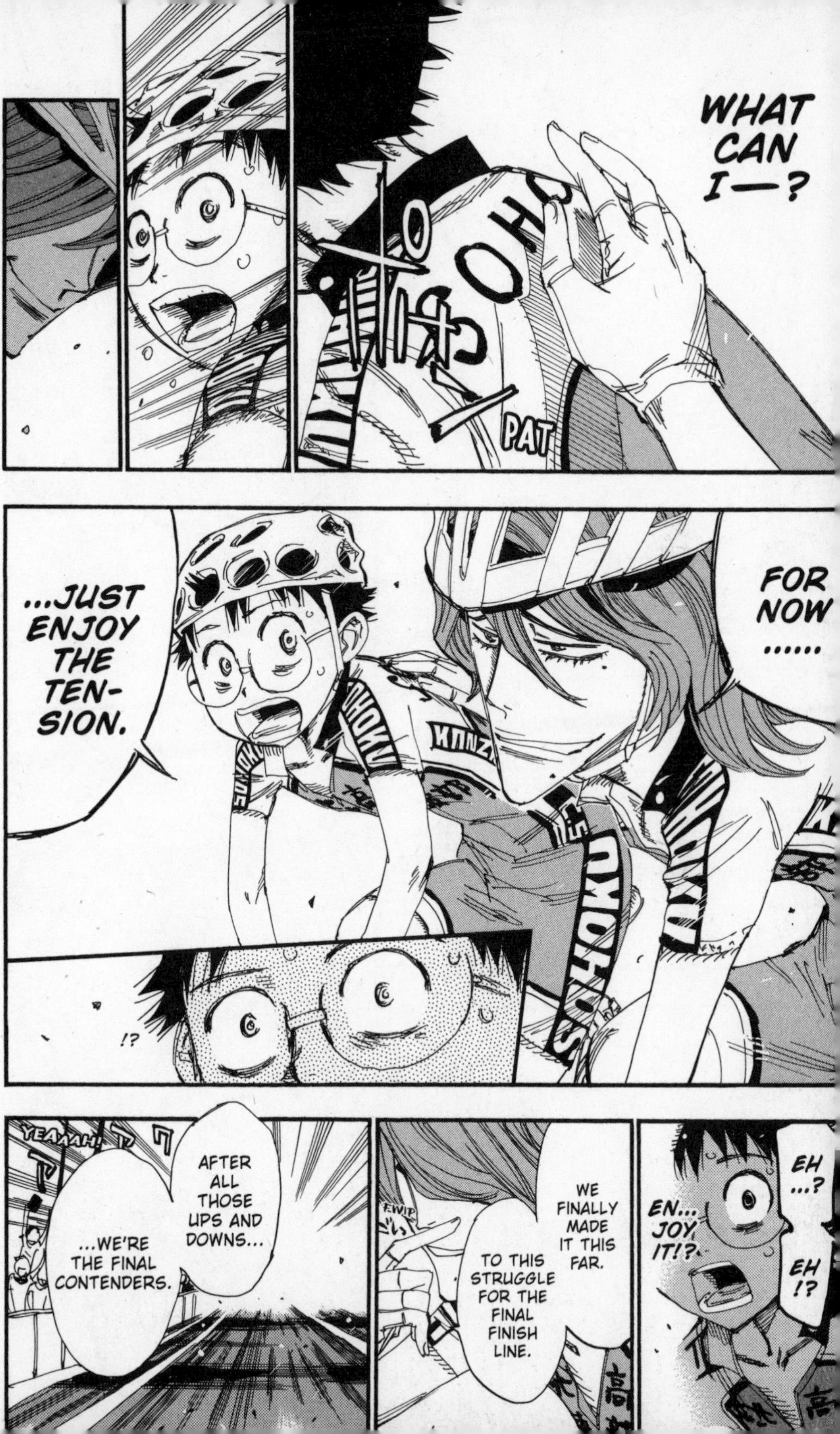
WHAT CAN I—?
PAT
FOR NOW ......
...JUST ENJOY THE TEN-SION.
!?
EH ...?
EN... JOY IT!?
EH !?
WE FINALLY MADE IT THIS FAR.
TO THIS STRUGGLE FOR THE FINAL FINISH LINE.
FWIP
AFTER ALL THOSE UPS AND DOWNS...
...WE'RE THE FINAL CONTENDERS.
YEAAAH!

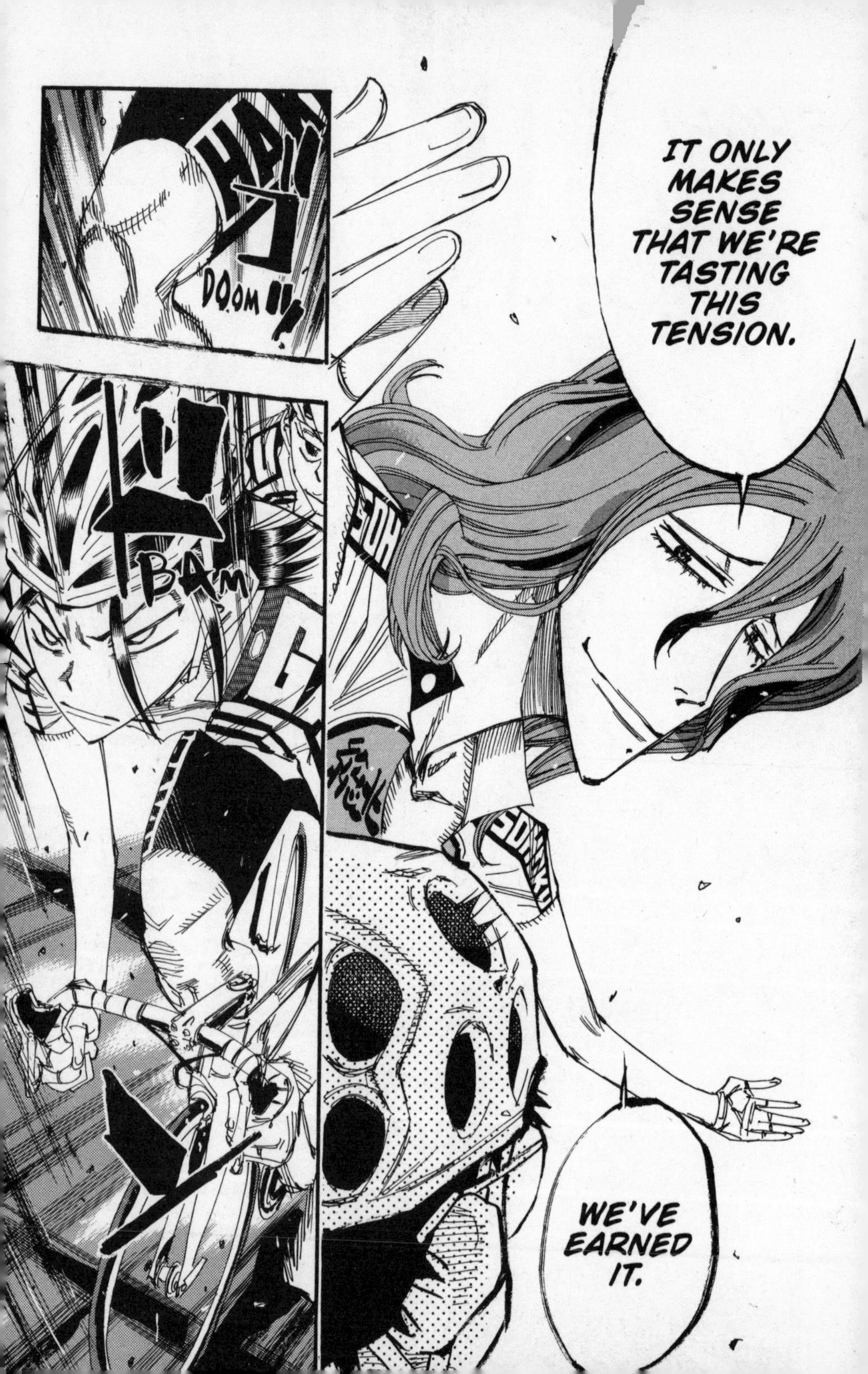
IT ONLY MAKES SENSE THAT WE'RE TASTING THIS TENSION.
WE'VE EARNED IT.
DOOM
BAM

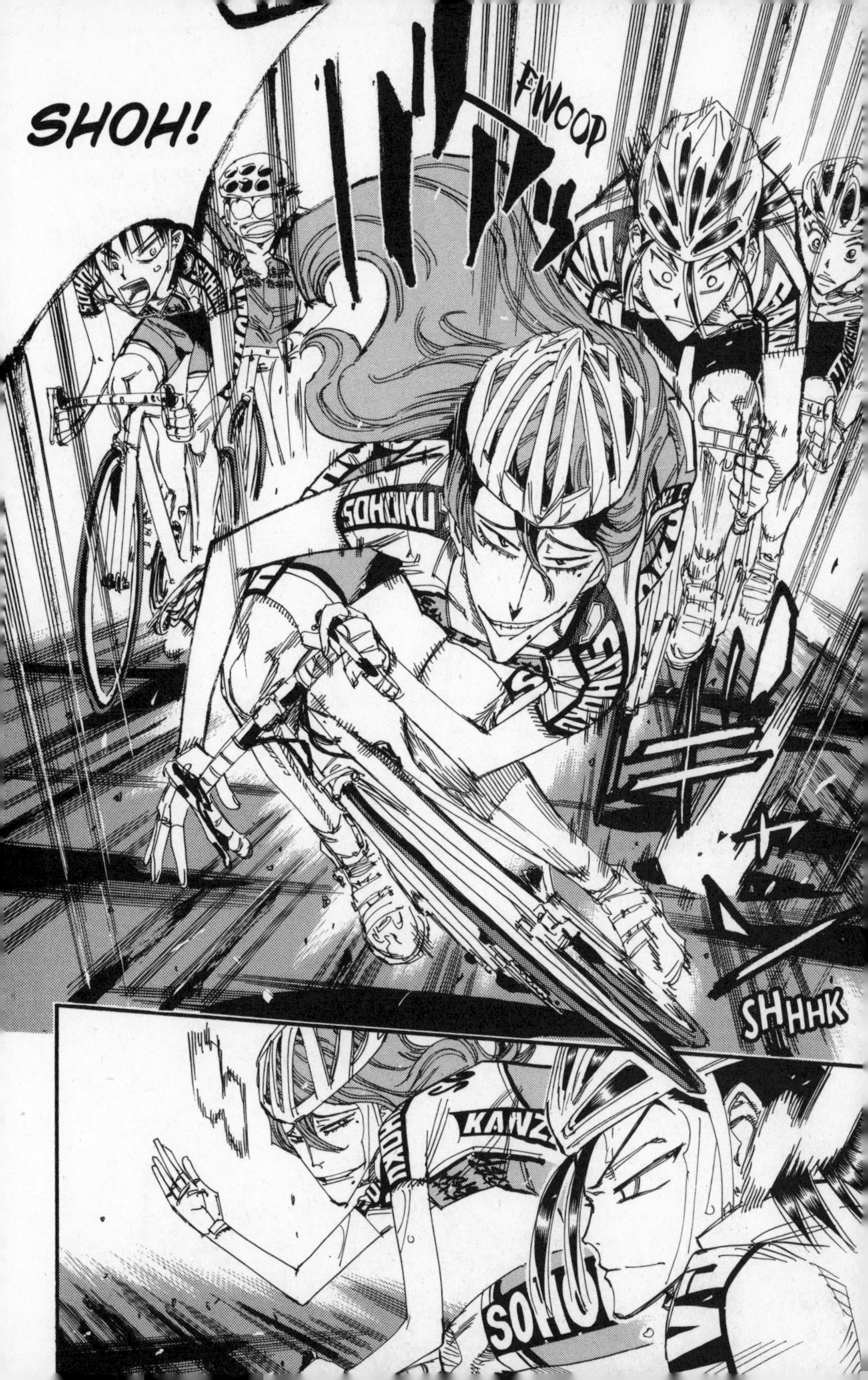
FWOOP
SHOH!
SHHHK

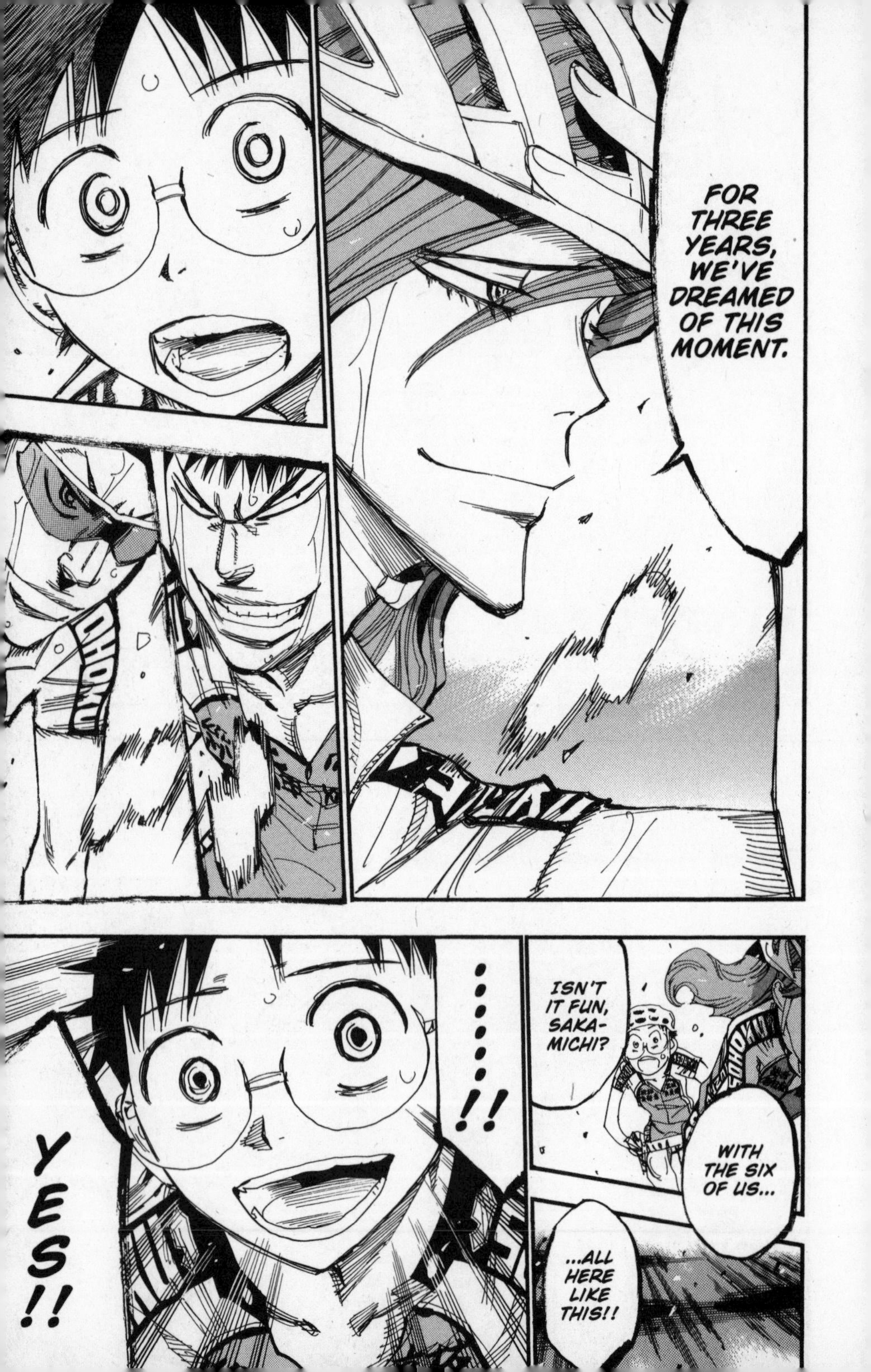
FOR THREE YEARS, WE'VE DREAMED OF THIS MOMENT.
ISN'T IT FUN, SAKAMICHI?
WITH THE SIX OF US...
...ALL HERE LIKE THIS!!
......!!
YES!!

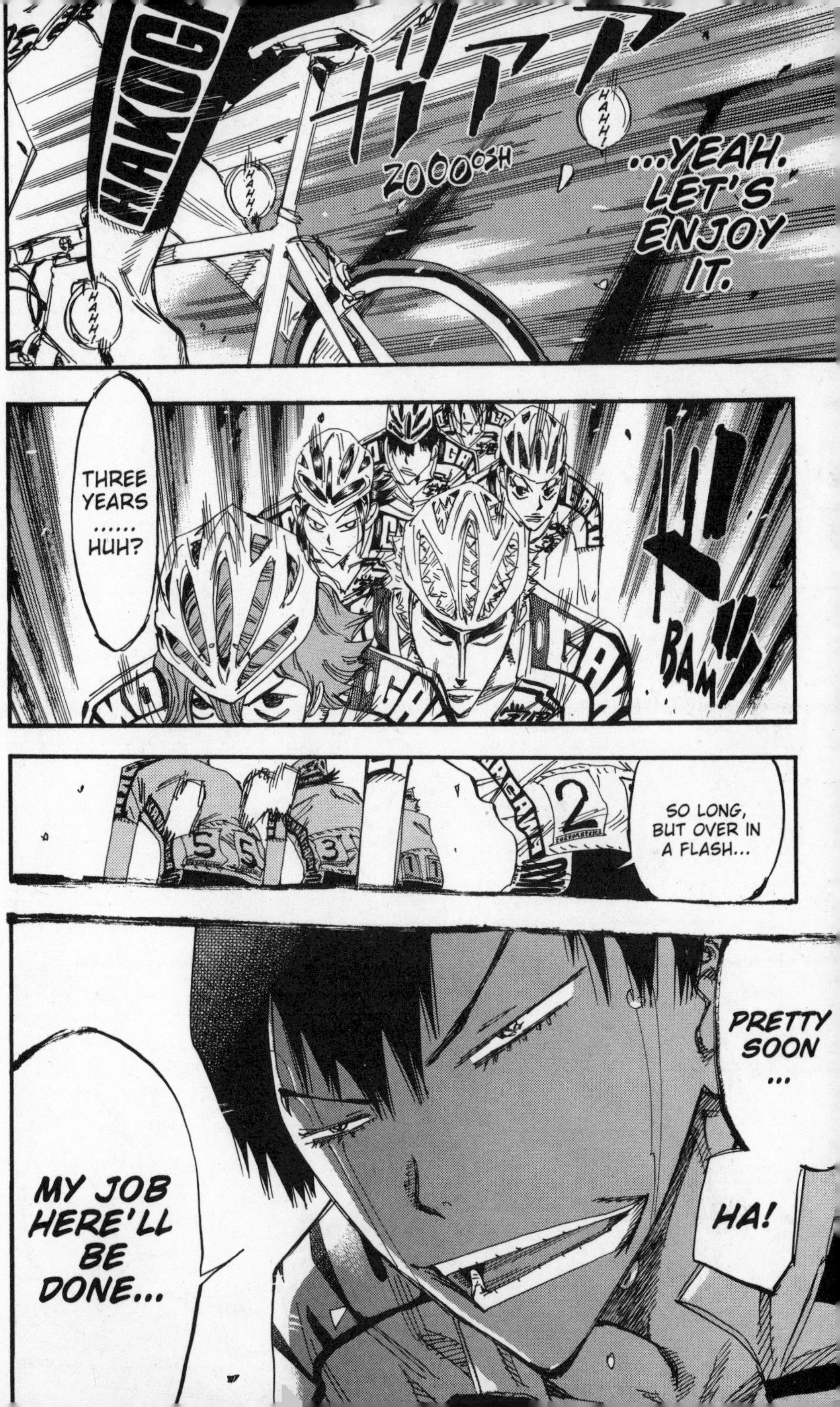
...YEAH. LET'S ENJOY IT.
HAHH!
ZOOOOSH
HAHH!
HAHH!
BAM
THREE YEARS ...... HUH?
SO LONG, BUT OVER IN A FLASH...
PRETTY SOON ...
HA!
MY JOB HERE'LL BE DONE...

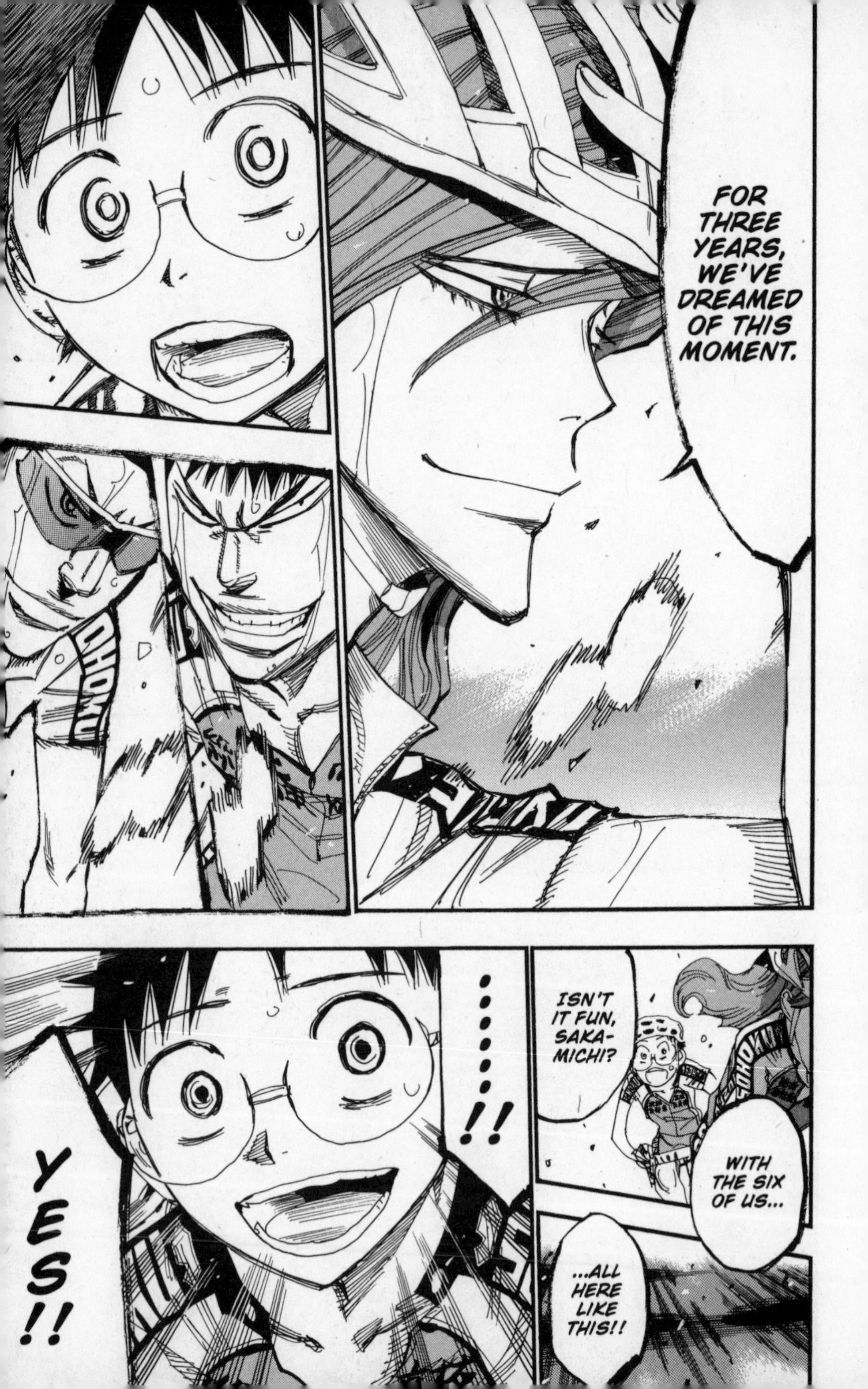
FOR THREE YEARS, WE'VE DREAMED OF THIS MOMENT.
ISN'T IT FUN, SAKAMICHI?
WITH THE SIX OF US...
...ALL HERE LIKE THIS!!
......!!
YES!!

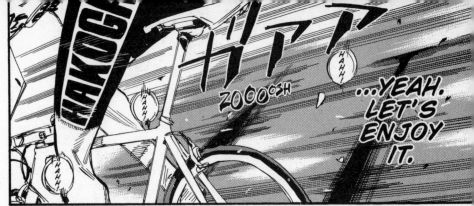

...YEAH. LET'S ENJOY IT.

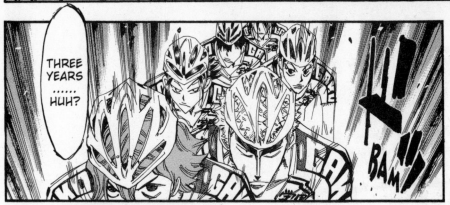

THREE YEARS ...... HUH?

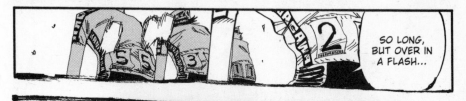

SO LONG, BUT OVER IN A FLASH...

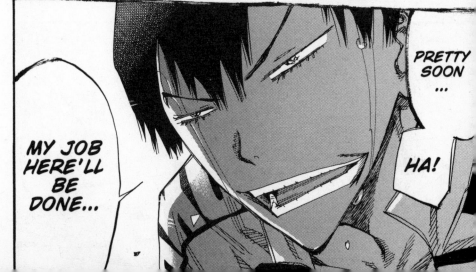

PRETTY SOON...

HA!

MY JOB HERE'LL BE DONE...

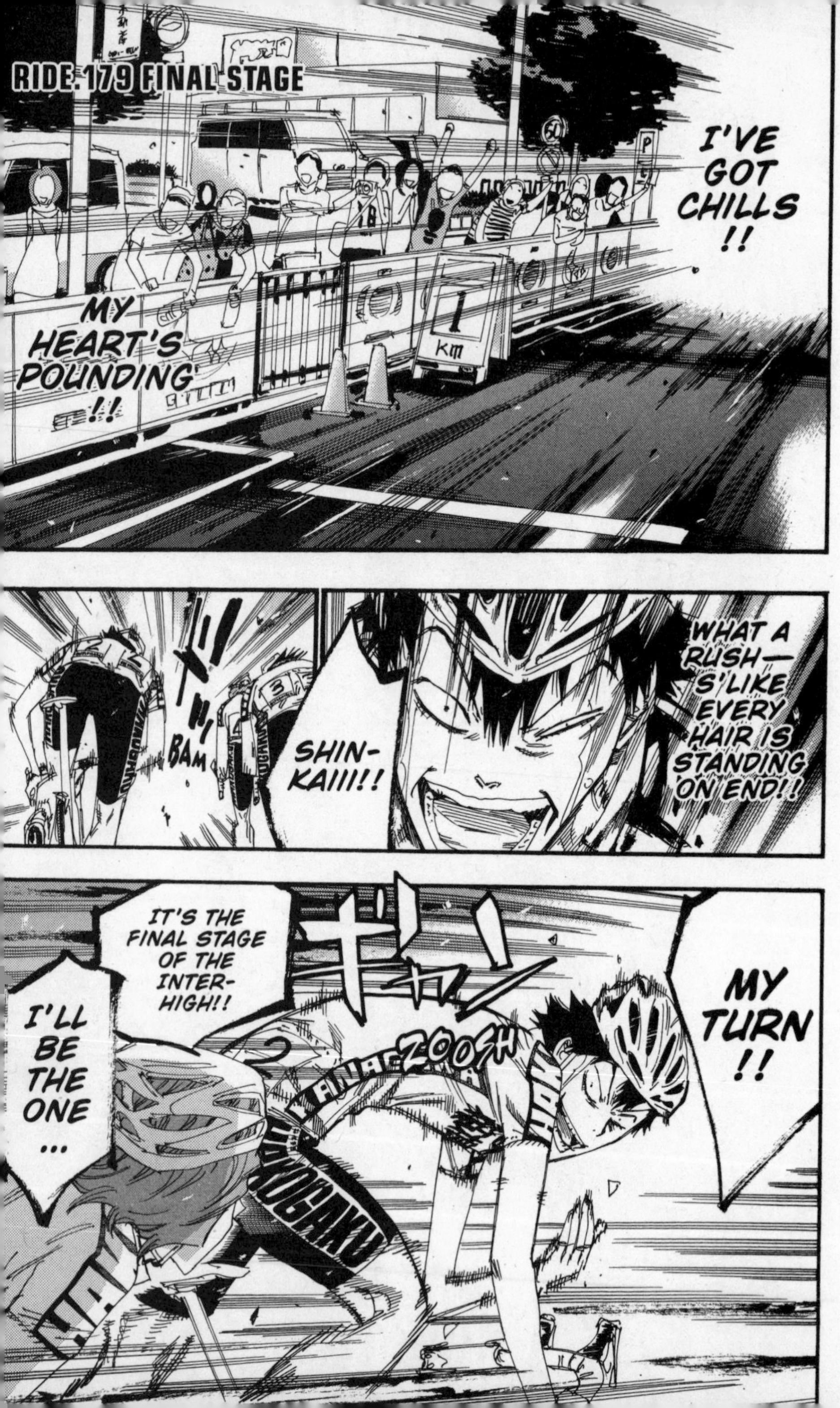
RIDE.179 FINAL STAGE
I'VE GOT CHILLS!!
MY HEART'S POUNDING!!
WHAT A RUSH—S'LIKE EVERY HAIR IS STANDING ON END!!
SHIN-KAIII!!
BAM
MY TURN!!
IT'S THE FINAL STAGE OF THE INTER-HIGH!!
ZOOSH
I'LL BE THE ONE...

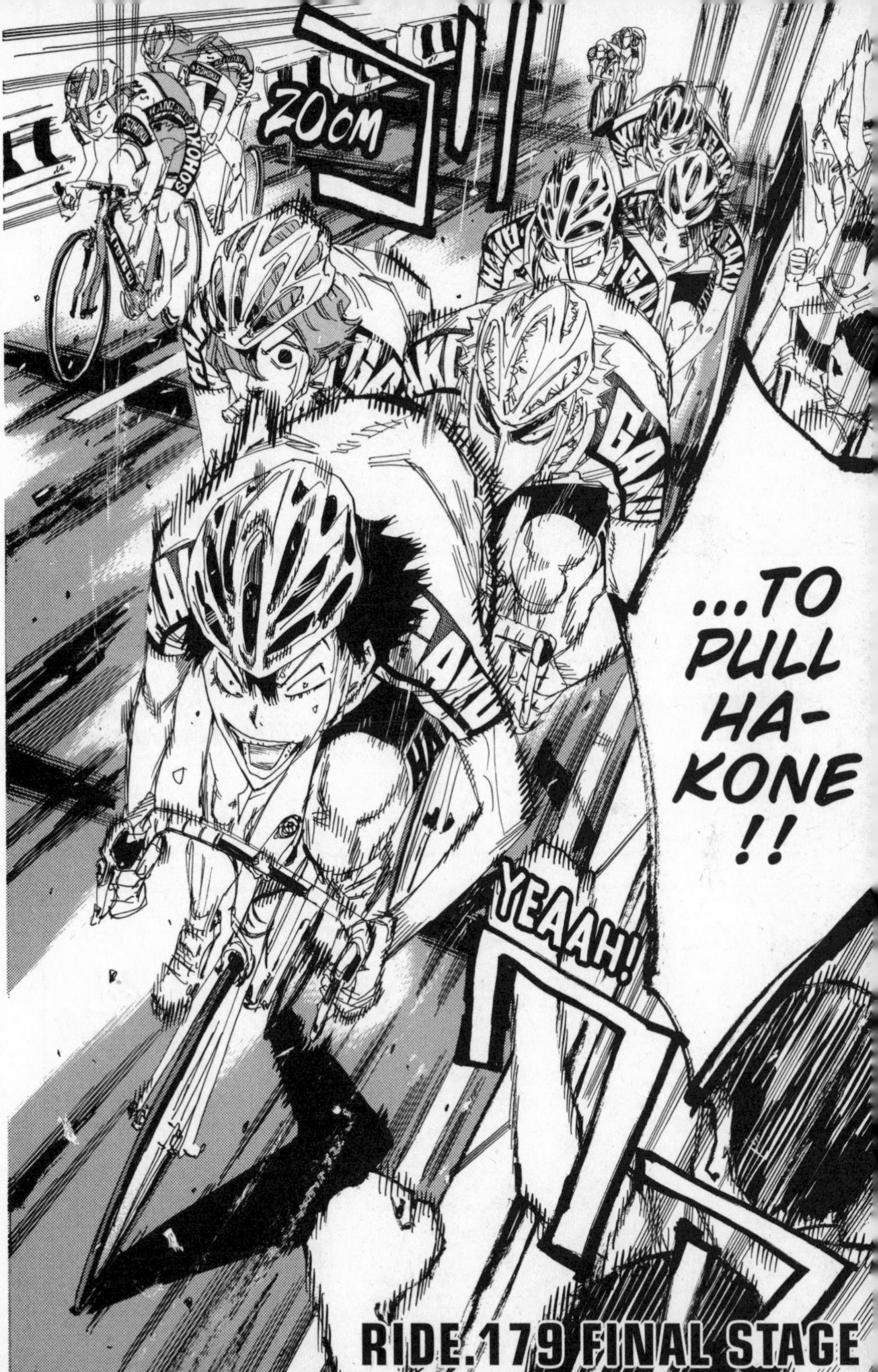
ZOOM
...TO PULL HA-KONE!!
YEAAAH!

RIDE.179 FINAL STAGE

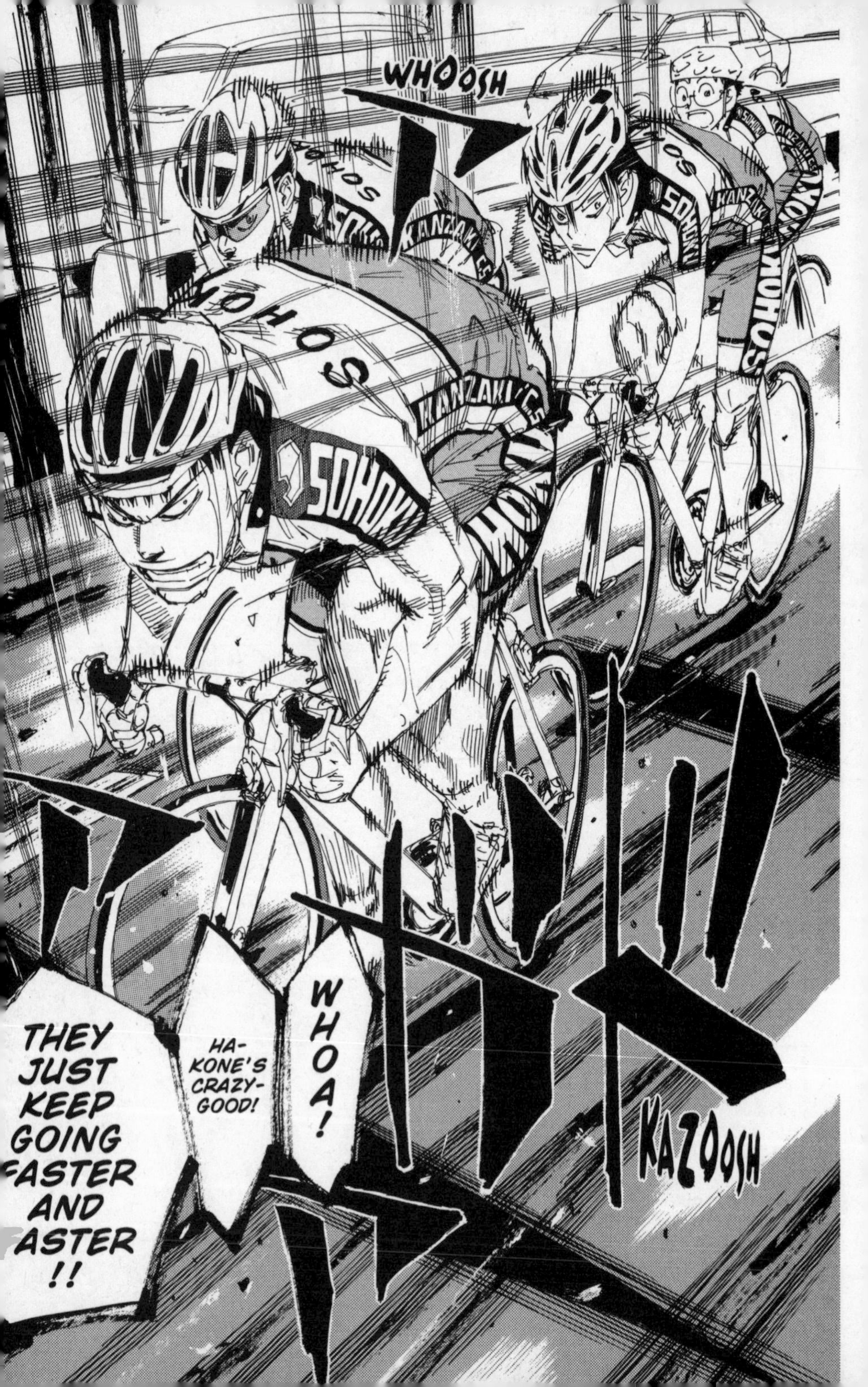
WHOOSH
KAZOOSH
WHOA!
HA-KONE'S CRAZY-GOOD!
THEY JUST KEEP GOING FASTER AND FASTER!!

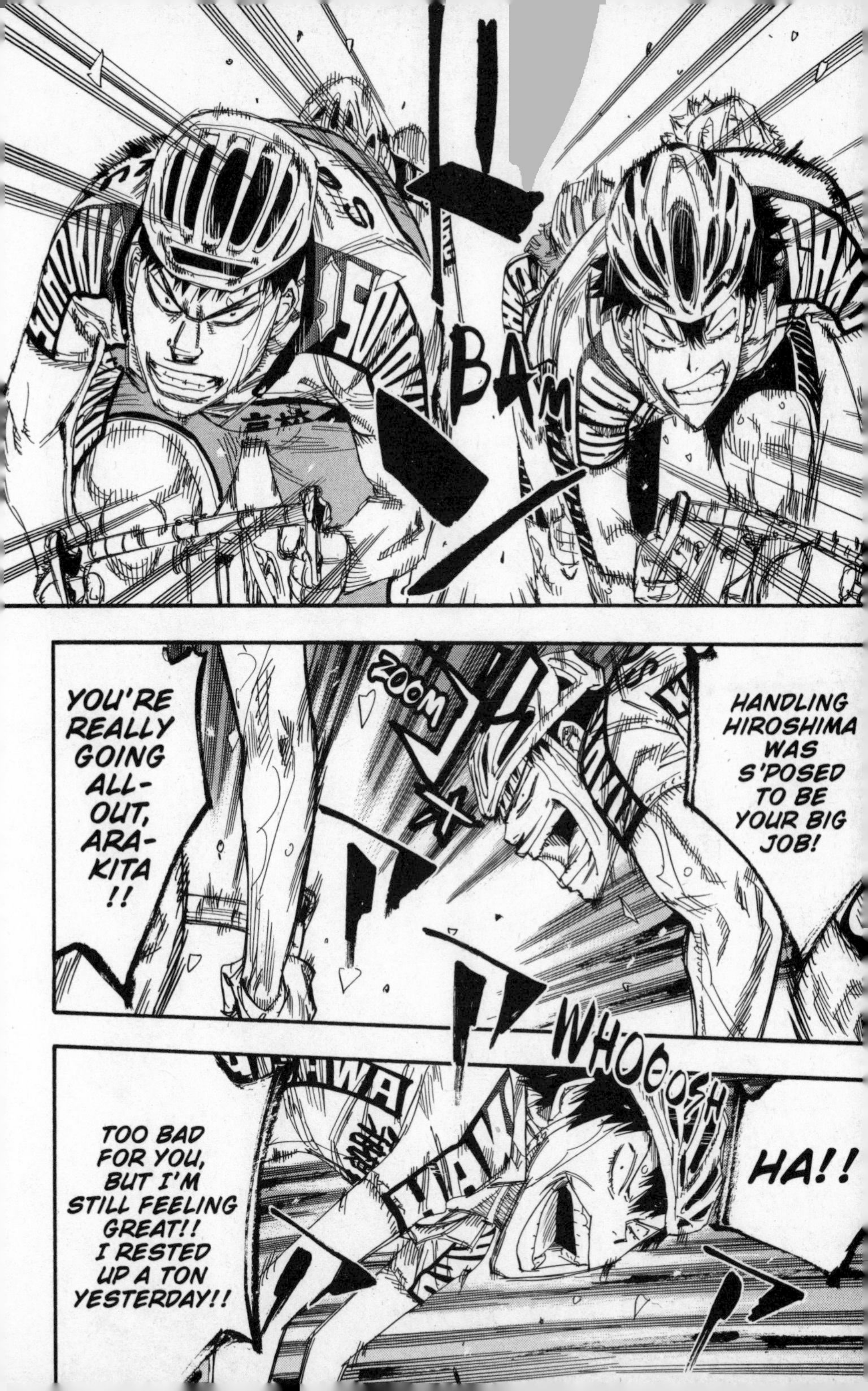
BAM
HANDLING HIROSHIMA WAS S'POSED TO BE YOUR BIG JOB!
ZOOM
YOU'RE REALLY GOING ALL-OUT, ARA-KITA!!
WHOOOSH
HA!!
TOO BAD FOR YOU, BUT I'M STILL FEELING GREAT!! I RESTED UP A TON YESTERDAY!!

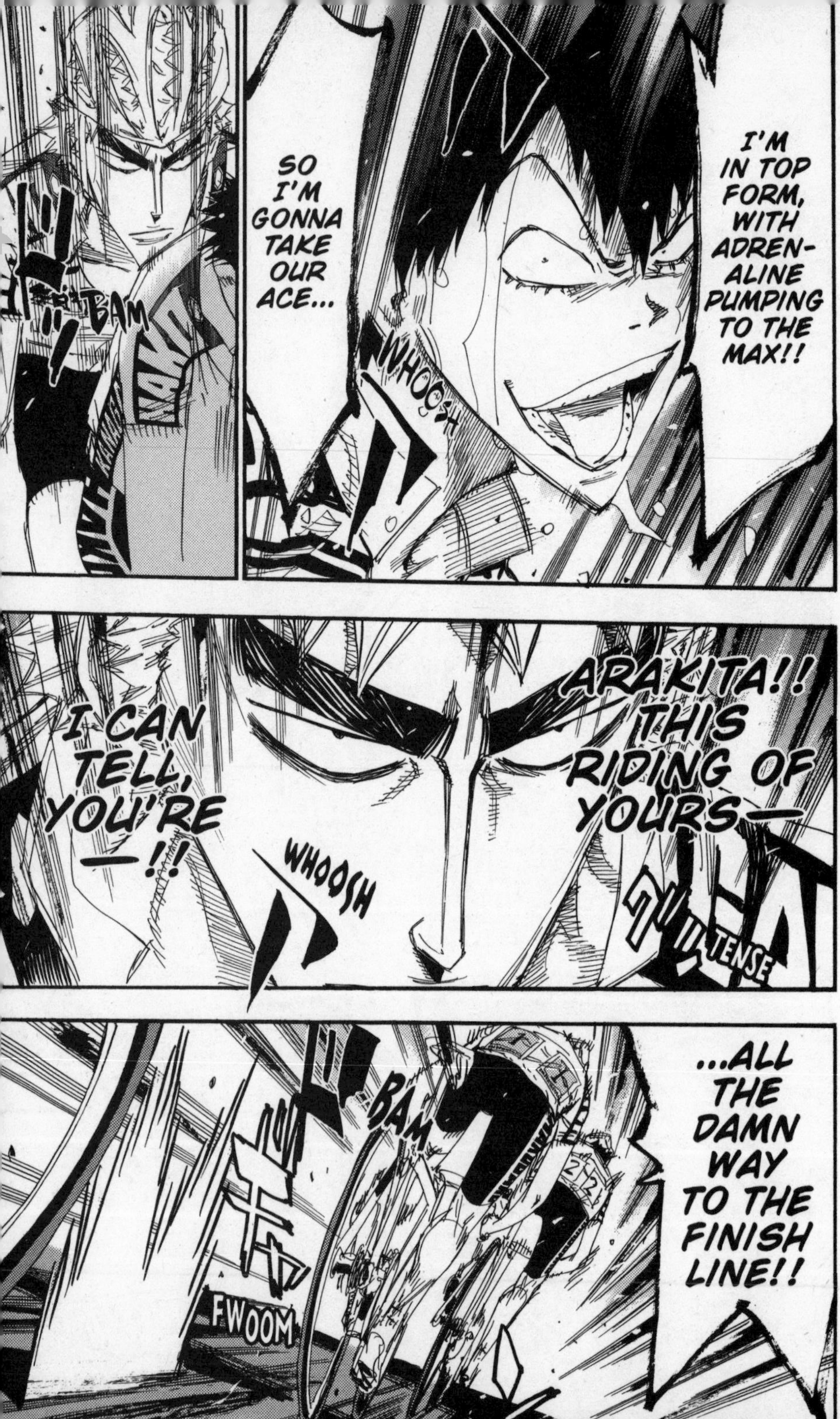
I'M IN TOP FORM, WITH ADREN-ALINE PUMPING TO THE MAX!!
SO I'M GONNA TAKE OUR ACE...
WHOOSH
BAM
ARAKITA!! THIS RIDING OF YOURS—
I CAN TELL, YOU'RE —!!
WHOOSH
TENSE
...ALL THE DAMN WAY TO THE FINISH LINE!!
BAM
FWOOM

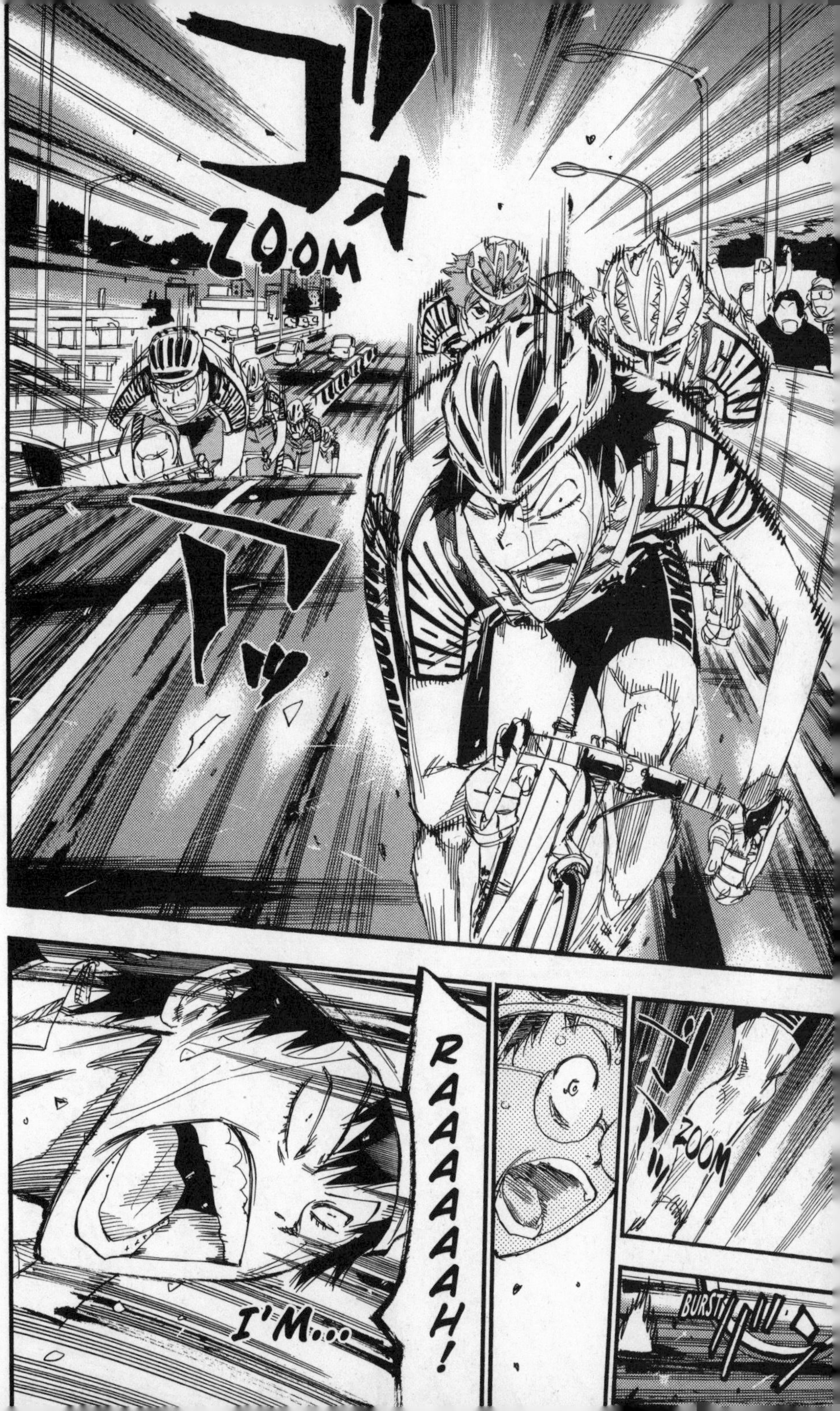
ZOOM
ZOOM
BURST
RAAAAAAAAH!
I'M...

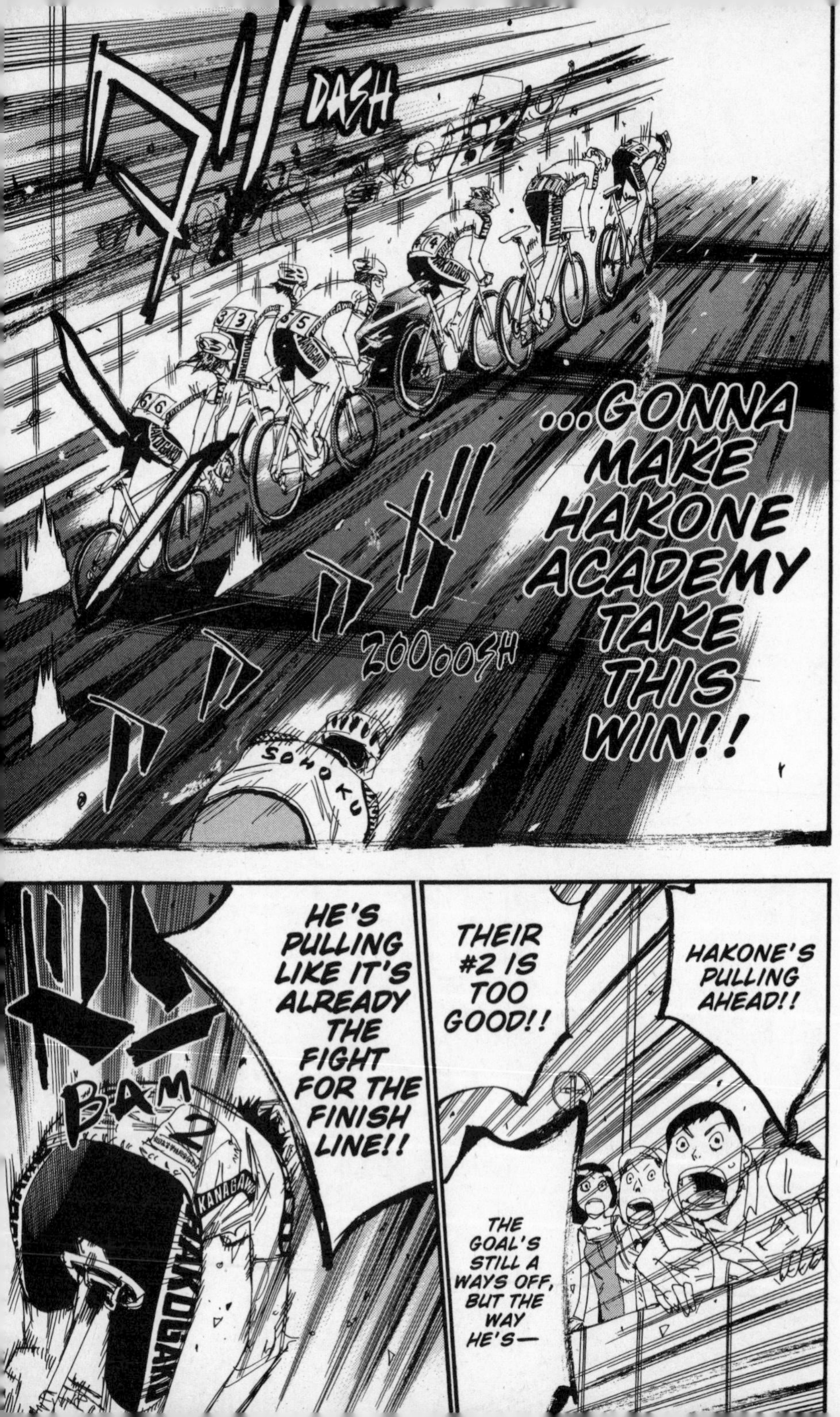
DASH
...GONNA MAKE HAKONE ACADEMY TAKE THIS WIN!!
ZOOOOOSH
HAKONE'S PULLING AHEAD!!
THEIR #2 IS TOO GOOD!!
THE GOAL'S STILL A WAYS OFF, BUT THE WAY HE'S—
HE'S PULLING LIKE IT'S ALREADY THE FIGHT FOR THE FINISH LINE!!
BAM

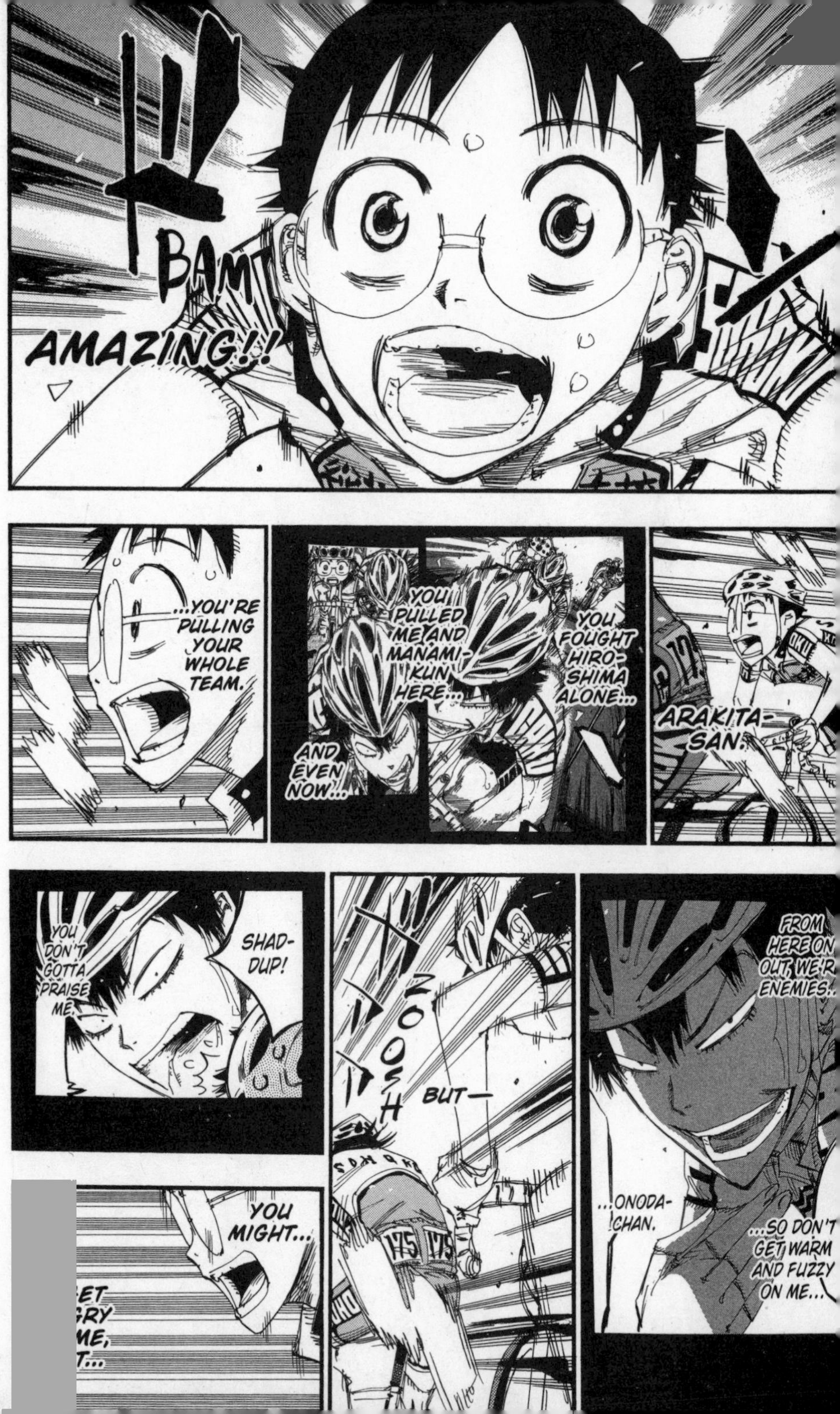
BAMT
AMAZING!!
ARAKITA-SAN.
YOU FOUGHT HIROSHIMA ALONE...
YOU PULLED ME AND MANAMI-KUN HERE...
AND EVEN NOW...
...YOU'RE PULLING YOUR WHOLE TEAM.
FROM HERE ON OUT, WE'R ENEMIES...
...ONODA-CHAN.
...SO DON'T GET WARM AND FUZZY ON ME...
ZOOSH
BUT—
SHAD-DUP!
YOU DON'T GOTTA PRAISE ME.
YOU MIGHT...

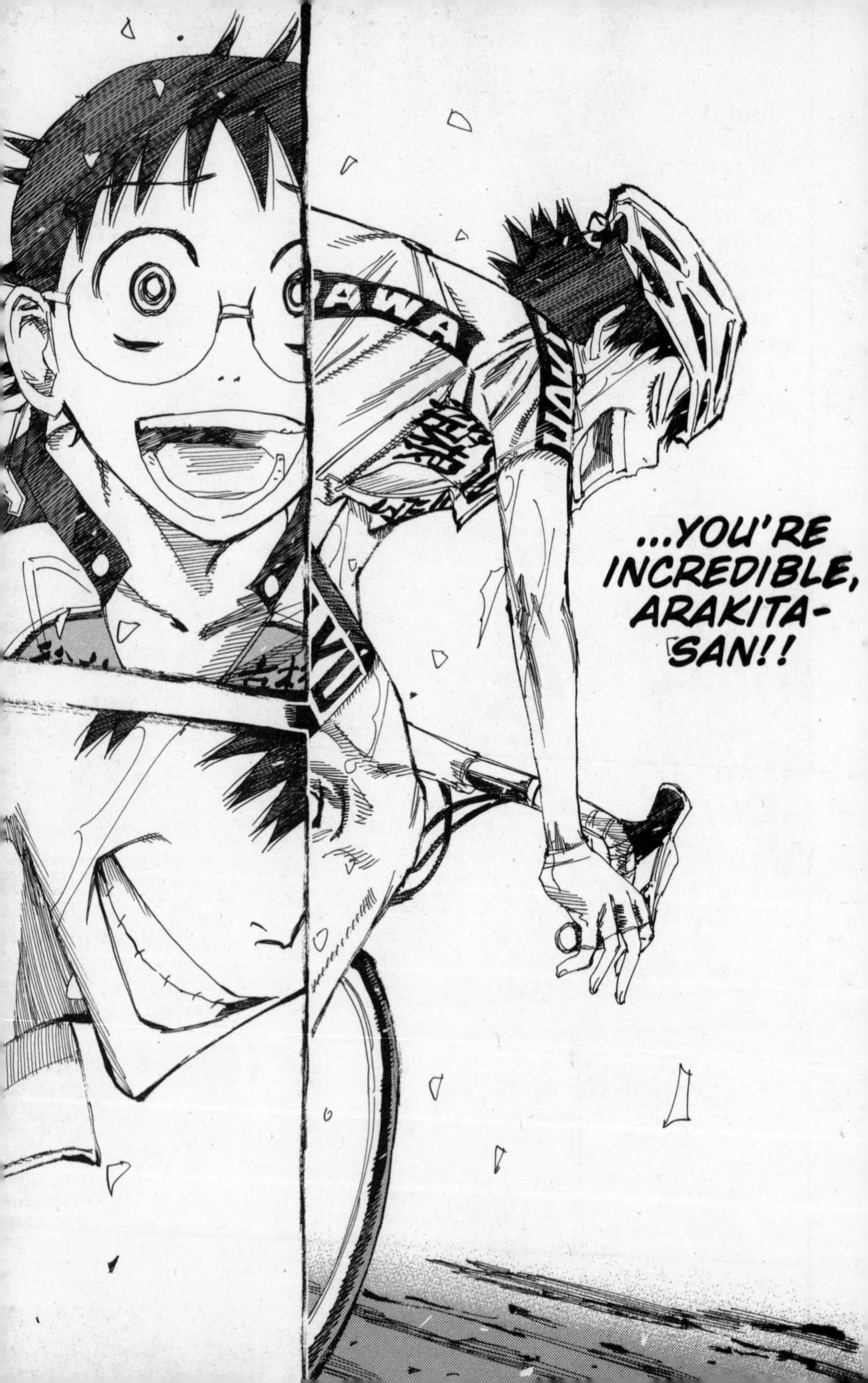
...YOU'RE INCREDIBLE, ARAKITA-SAN!!

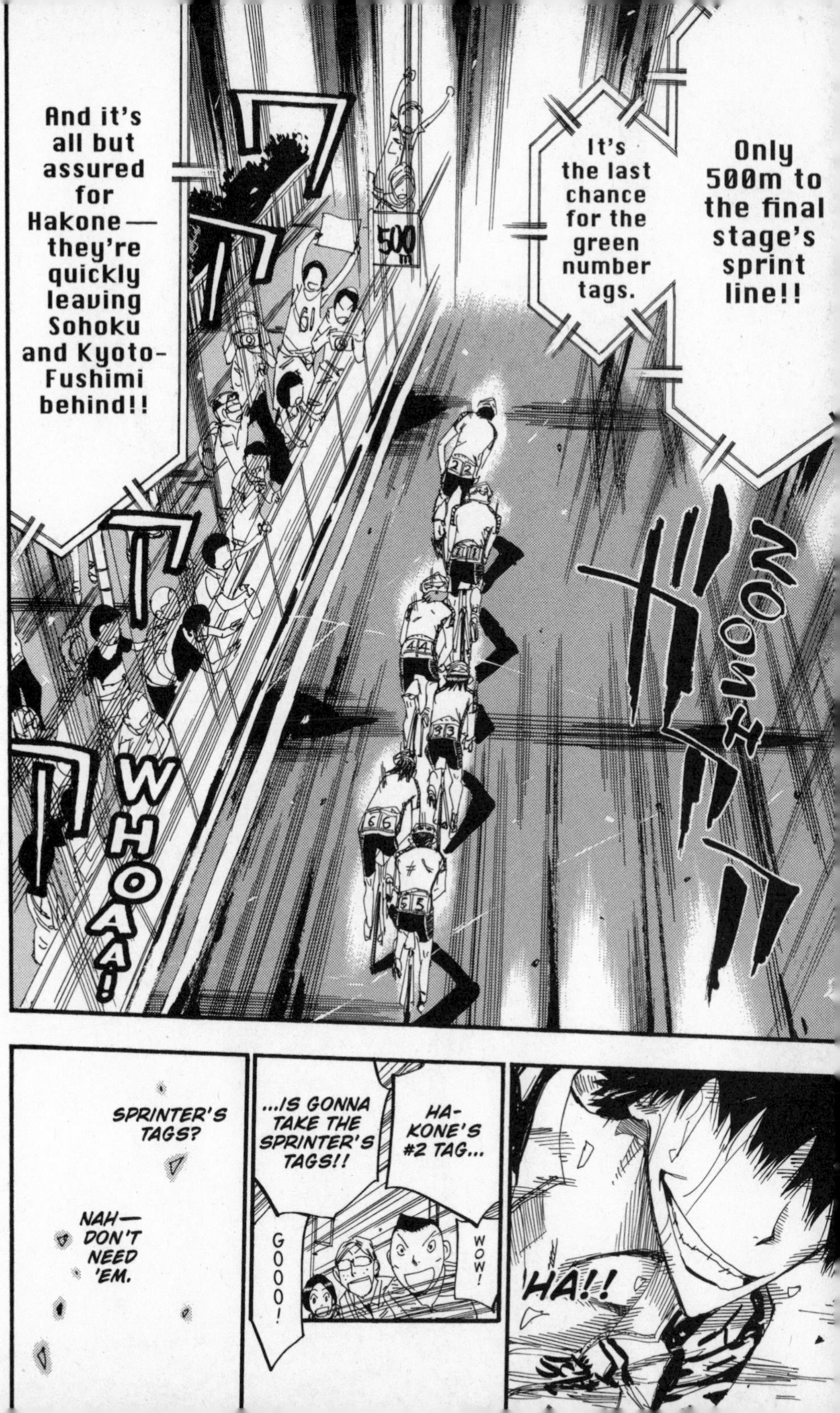
Only 500m to the final stage's sprint line!!
It's the last chance for the green number tags.
And it's all but assured for Hakone—they're quickly leaving Sohoku and Kyoto-Fushimi behind!!
500 m
ZOOSH
WHOAA!
HA!!
HA-KONE'S #2 TAG...
...IS GONNA TAKE THE SPRINTER'S TAGS!!
WOW!
GOOOO!
SPRINTER'S TAGS?
NAH—DON'T NEED 'EM.

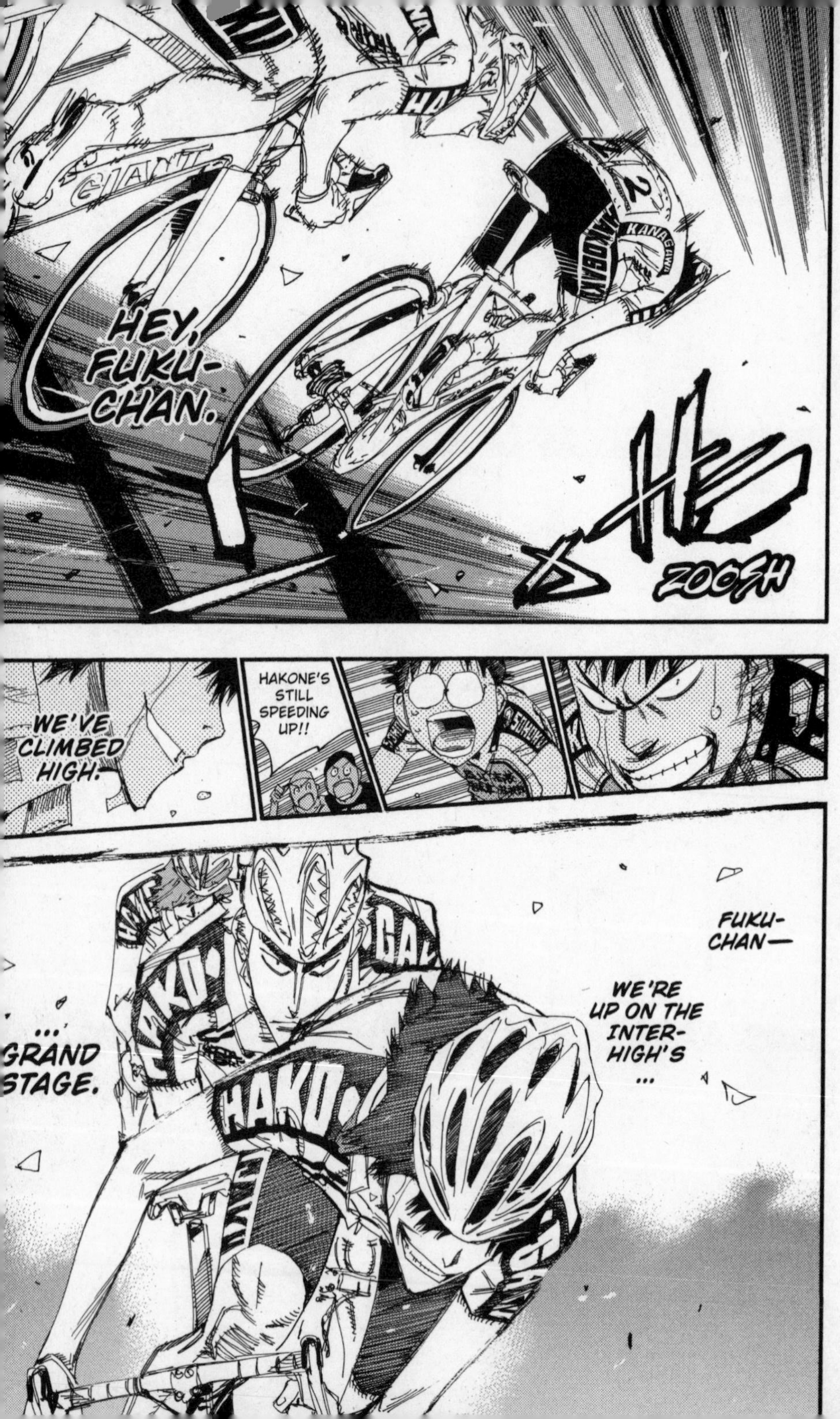
HEY, FUKU-CHAN.
ZOOSH
HAKONE'S STILL SPEEDING UP!!
WE'VE CLIMBED HIGH.
FUKU-CHAN—
WE'RE UP ON THE INTER-HIGH'S ...
... GRAND STAGE.

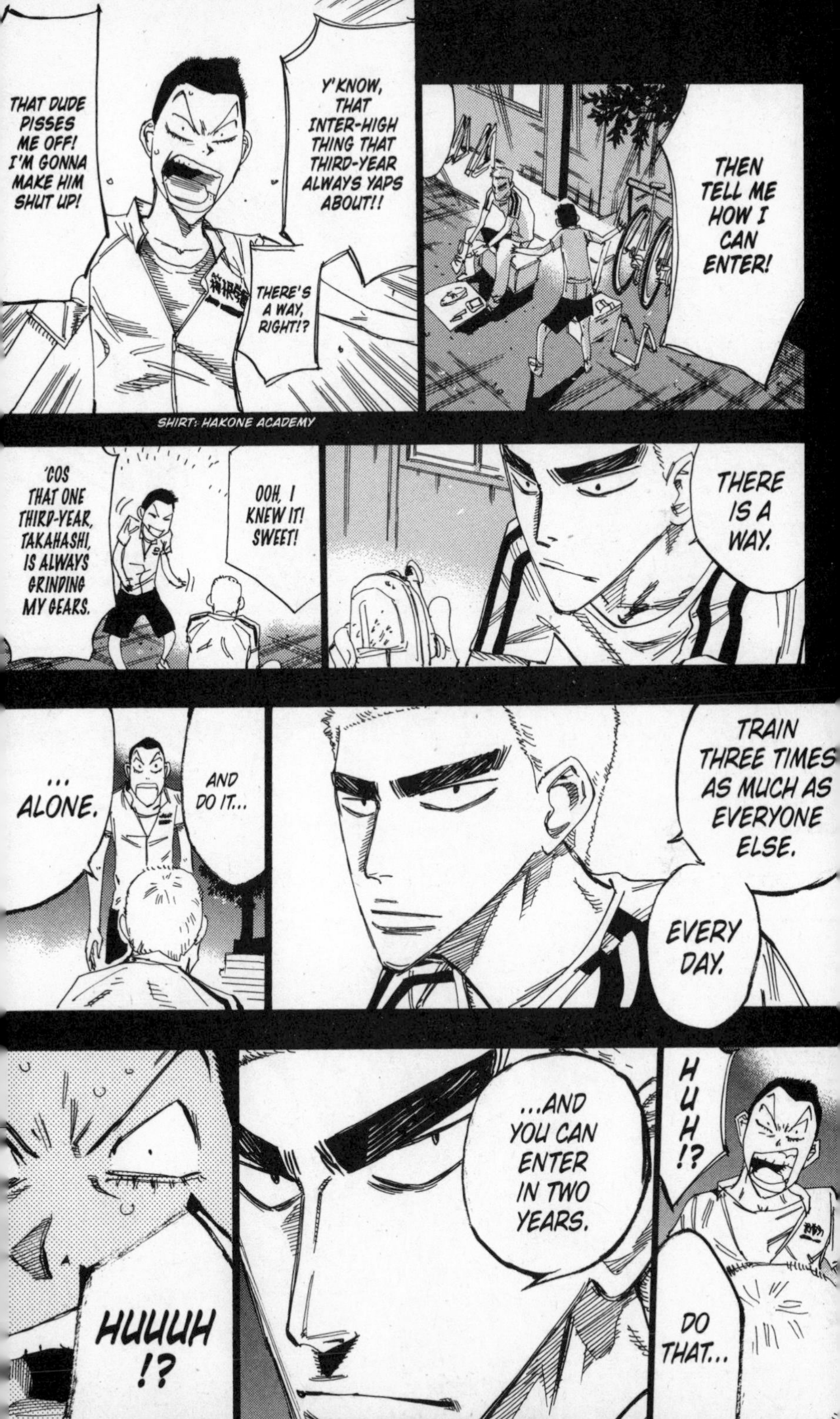
THEN TELL ME HOW I CAN ENTER!
Y'KNOW, THAT INTER-HIGH THING THAT THIRD-YEAR ALWAYS YAPS ABOUT!!
THERE'S A WAY, RIGHT!?
THAT DUDE PISSES ME OFF! I'M GONNA MAKE HIM SHUT UP!
SHIRT: HAKONE ACADEMY
THERE IS A WAY.
OOH, I KNEW IT! SWEET!
'COS THAT ONE THIRD-YEAR, TAKAHASHI, IS ALWAYS GRINDING MY GEARS.
TRAIN THREE TIMES AS MUCH AS EVERYONE ELSE.
EVERY DAY.
AND DO IT...
... ALONE.
HUH!?
DO THAT...
...AND YOU CAN ENTER IN TWO YEARS.
HUUUH!?

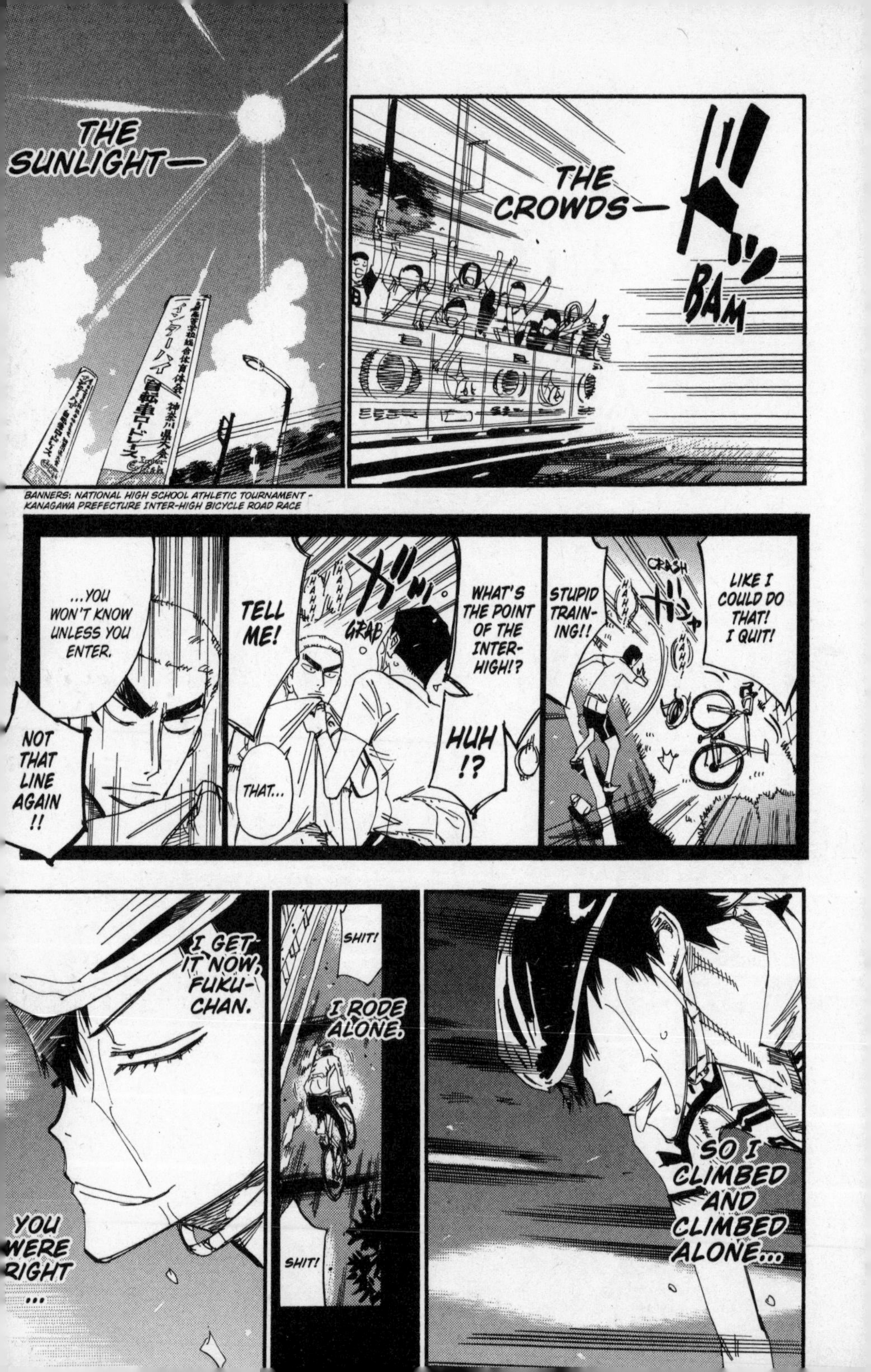
THE CROWDS—
BAM
THE SUNLIGHT—
BANNERS: NATIONAL HIGH SCHOOL ATHLETIC TOURNAMENT - KANAGAWA PREFECTURE INTER-HIGH BICYCLE ROAD RACE
LIKE I COULD DO THAT! I QUIT!
CRASH
HAHH!
HAHH!
STUPID TRAIN-ING!!
WHAT'S THE POINT OF THE INTER-HIGH!?
GRAB
HAHH!
HAHH!
TELL ME!
HUH!?
THAT...
...YOU WON'T KNOW UNLESS YOU ENTER.
NOT THAT LINE AGAIN!!
SO I CLIMBED AND CLIMBED ALONE...
SHIT!
I RODE ALONE.
SHIT!
I GET IT NOW, FUKU-CHAN.
YOU WERE RIGHT...

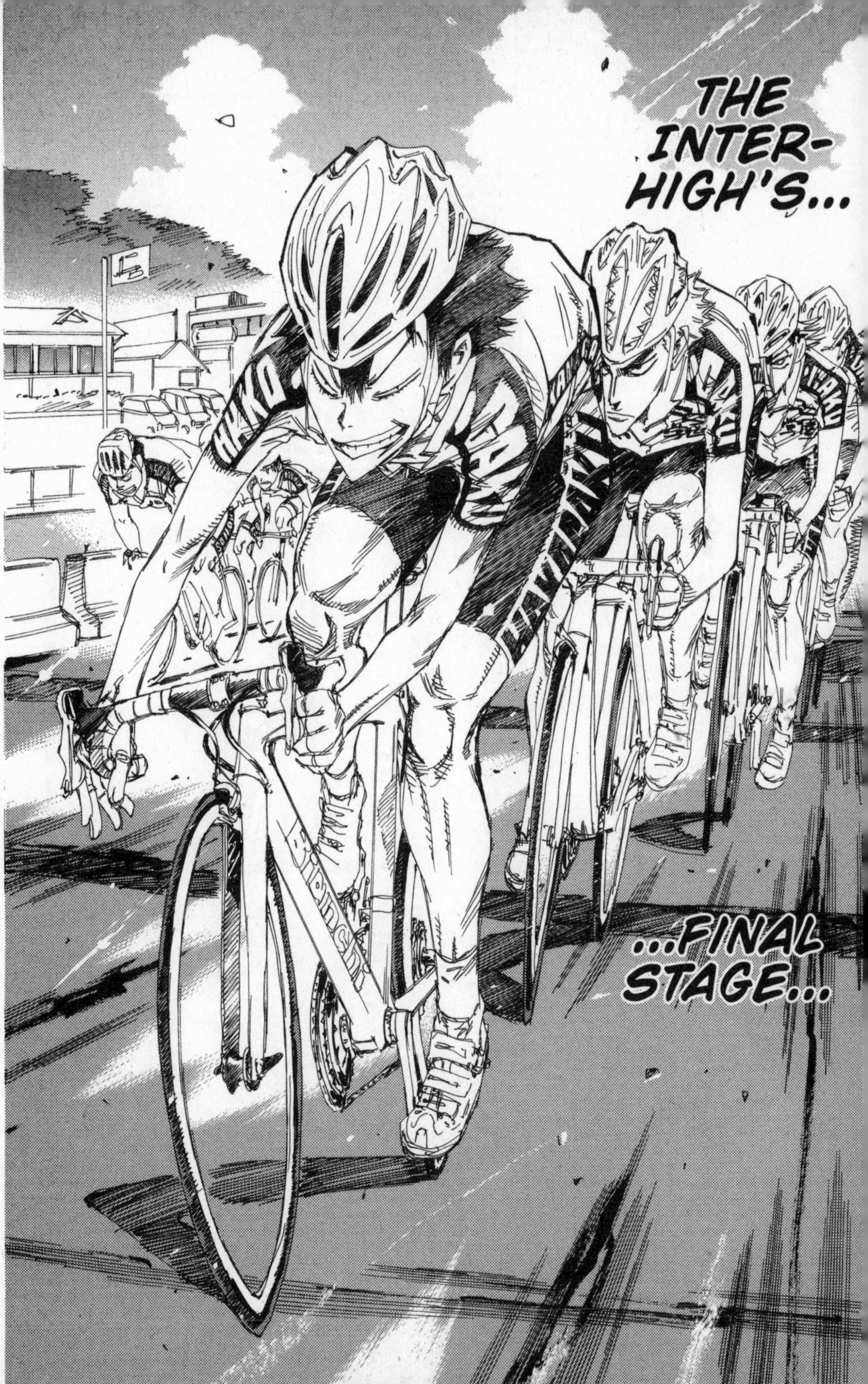
THE INTER-HIGH'S...
...FINAL STAGE...

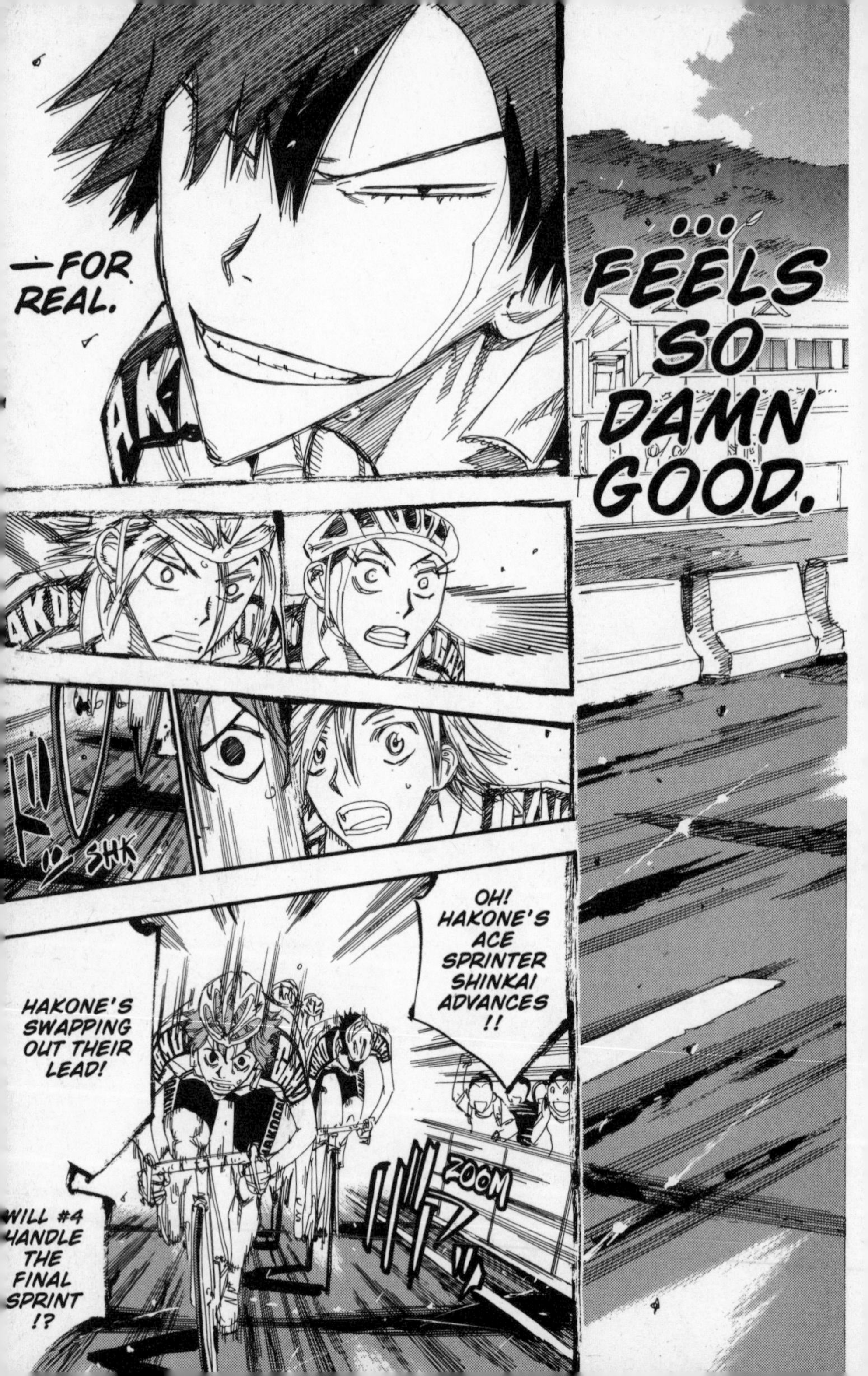
...FEELS SO DAMN GOOD.
—FOR REAL.
SHK
OH! HAKONE'S ACE SPRINTER SHINKAI ADVANCES!!
HAKONE'S SWAPPING OUT THEIR LEAD!
ZOOM
WILL #4 HANDLE THE FINAL SPRINT!?

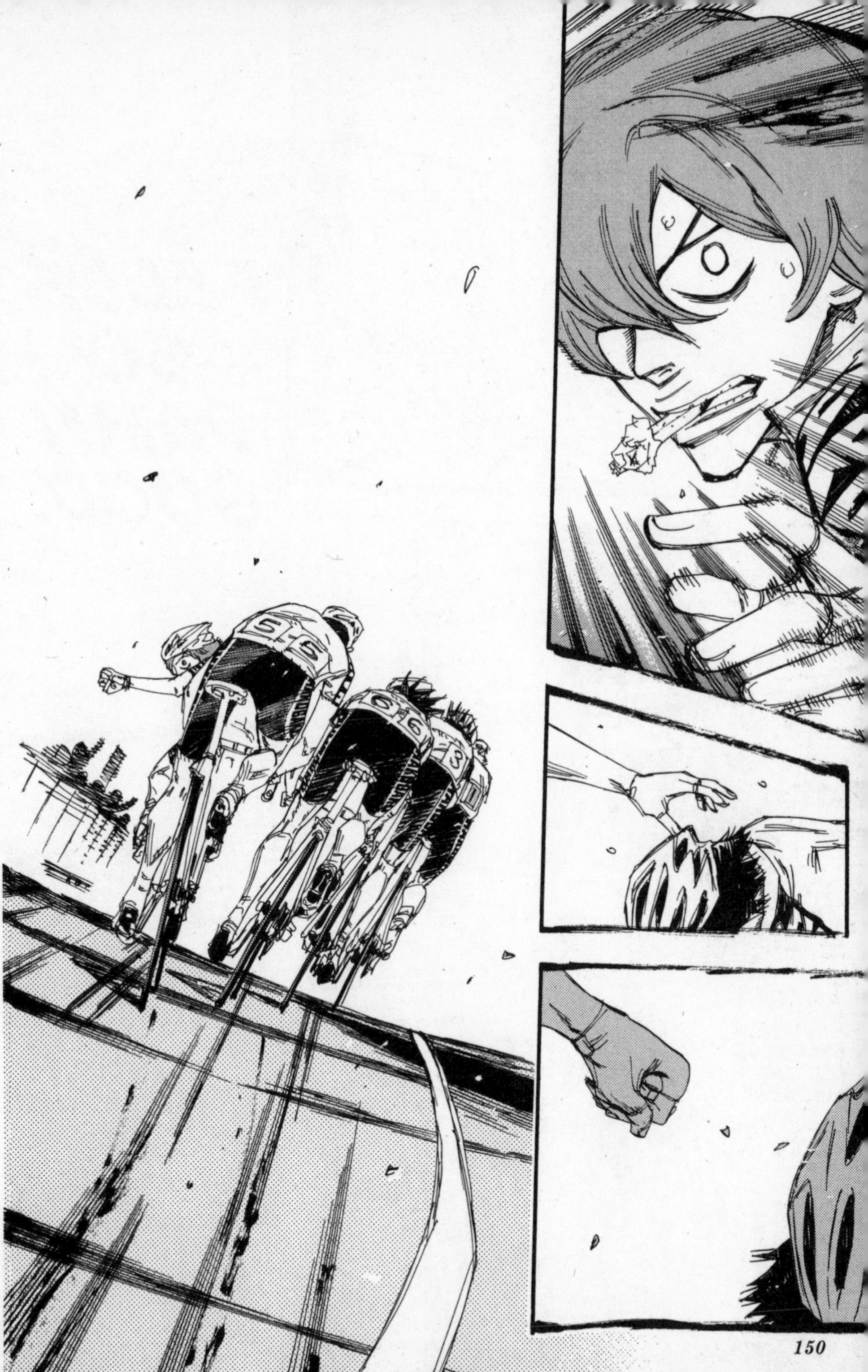

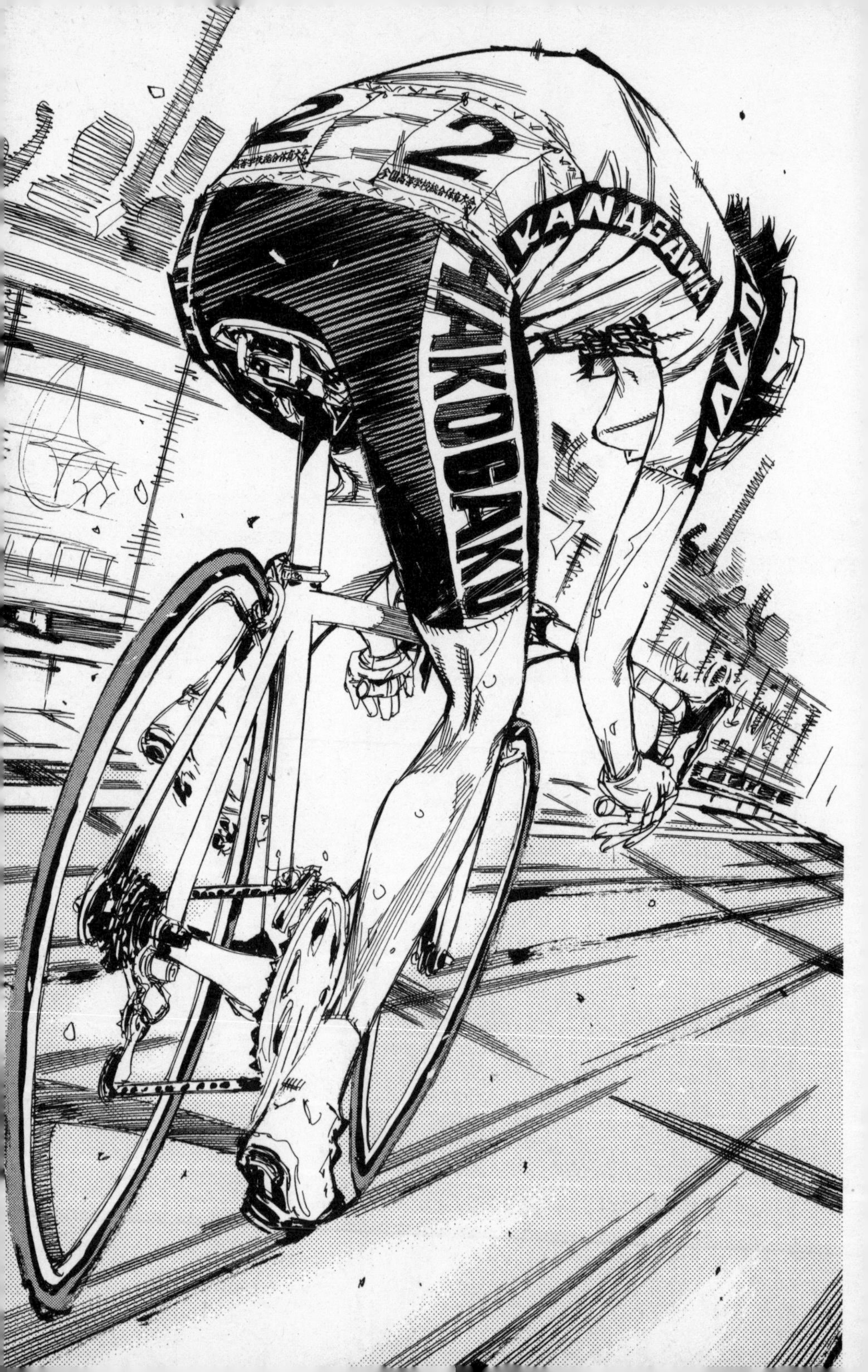
2
KANAGAWA
HAKOGAKU

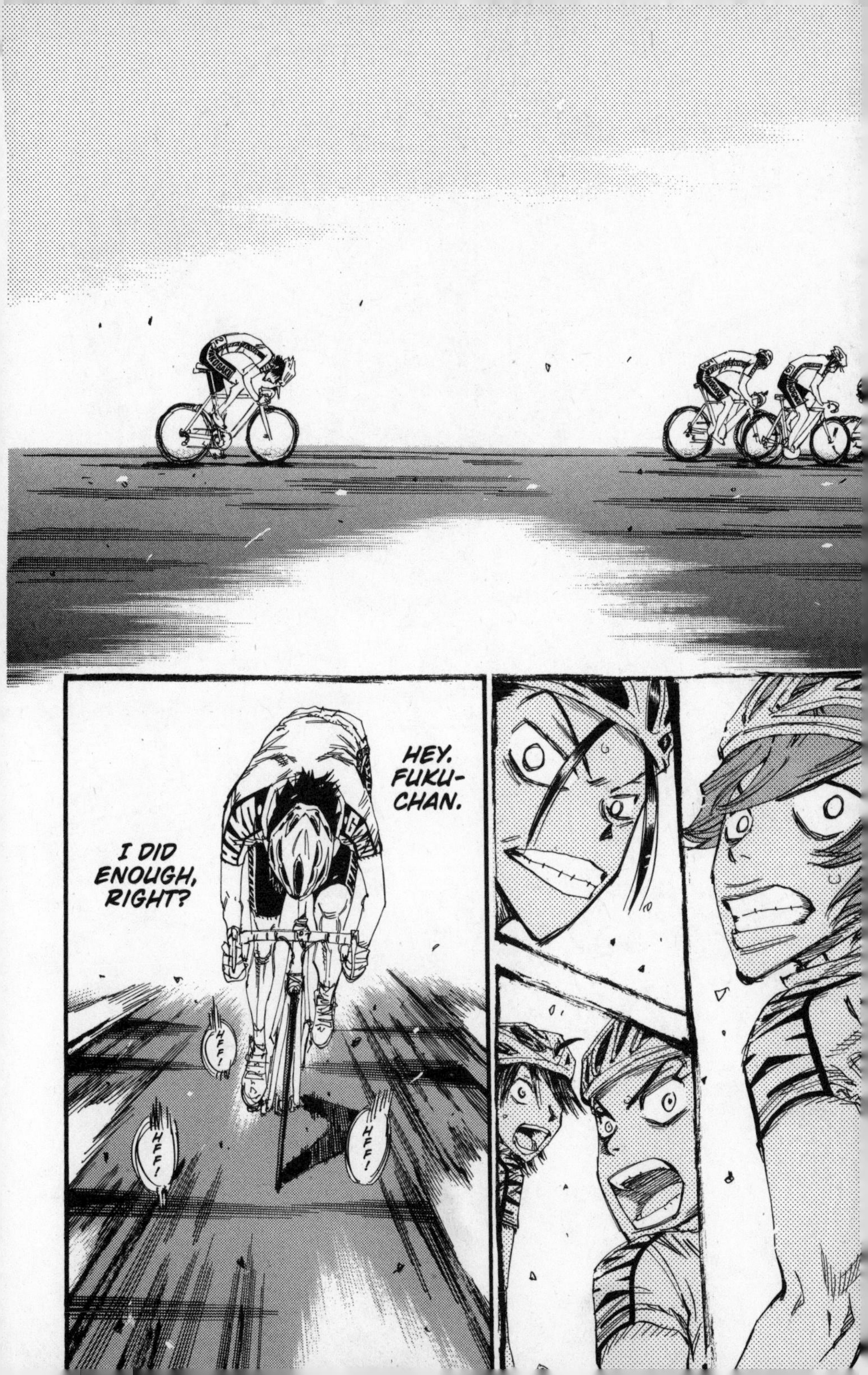
HEY. FUKU-CHAN.
I DID ENOUGH, RIGHT?
HFF!
HFF!
HFF!

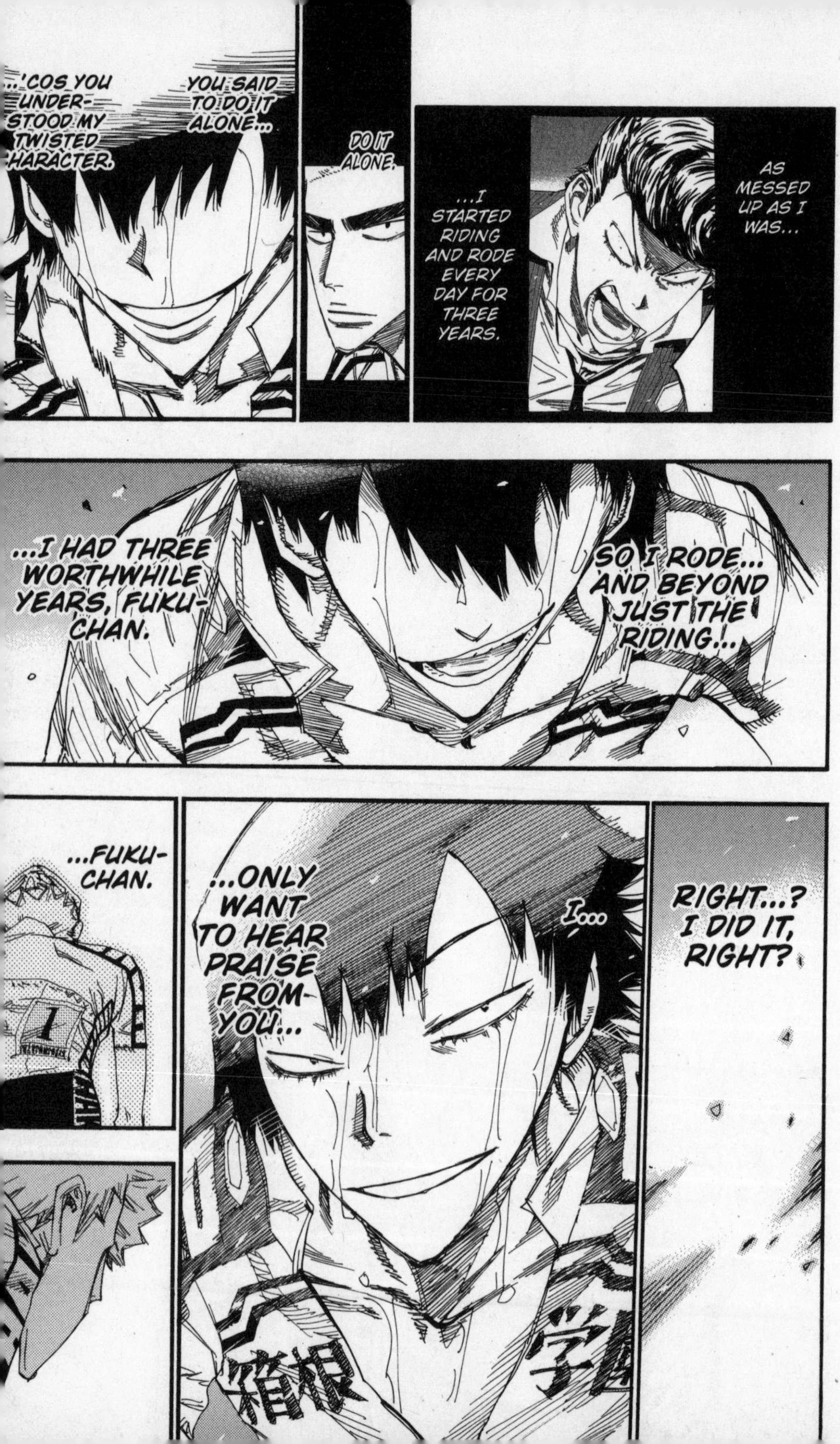
AS MESSED UP AS I WAS...
...I STARTED RIDING AND RODE EVERY DAY FOR THREE YEARS.
DO IT ALONE.
YOU SAID TO DO IT ALONE...
...'COS YOU UNDER-STOOD MY TWISTED HARACTER.
SO I RODE... AND BEYOND JUST THE RIDING...!
...I HAD THREE WORTHWHILE YEARS, FUKU-CHAN.
RIGHT...? I DID IT, RIGHT?
I...
...ONLY WANT TO HEAR PRAISE FROM YOU...
...FUKU-CHAN.

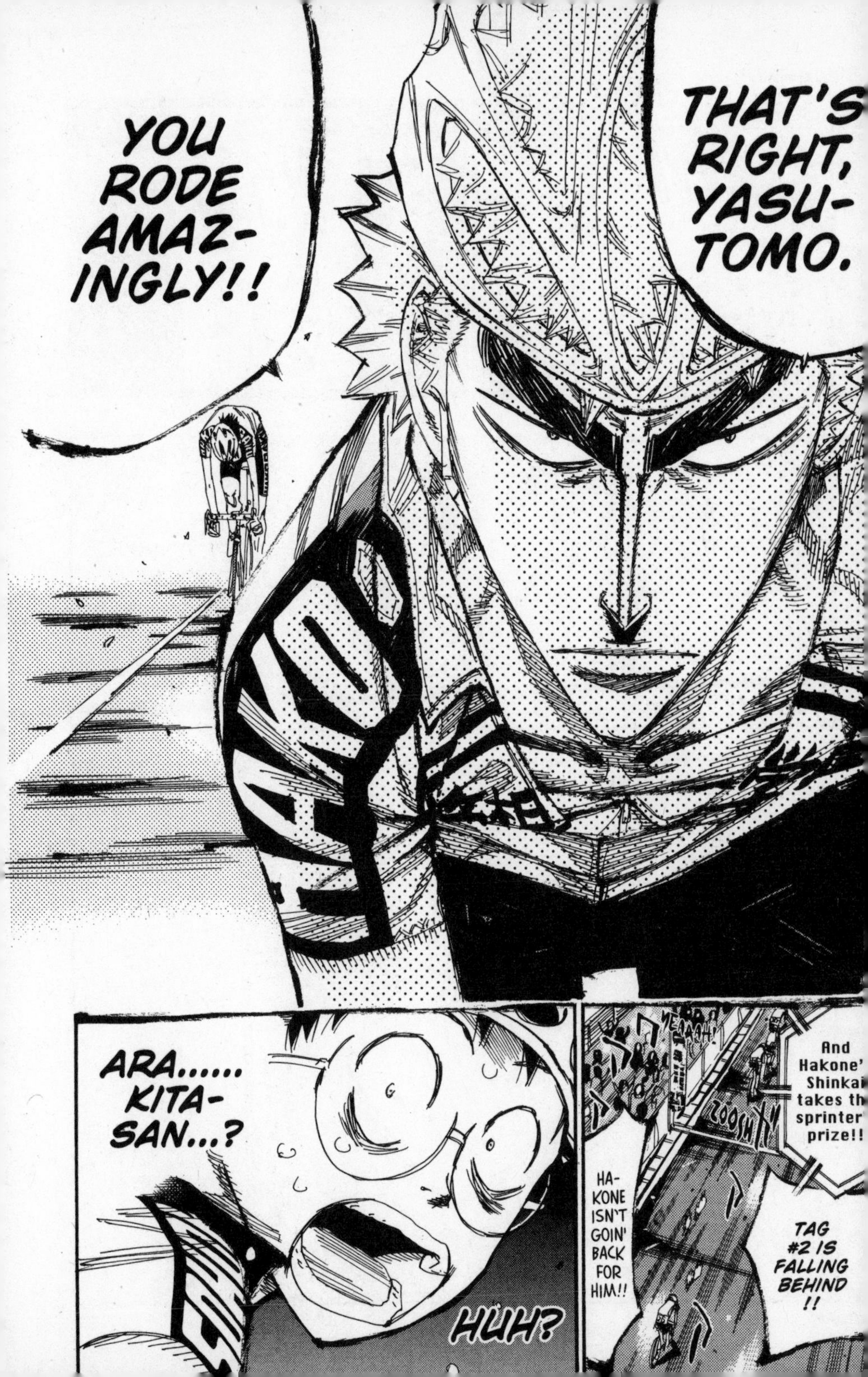
THAT'S RIGHT, YASU-TOMO.
YOU RODE AMAZ-INGLY!!
And Hakone' Shinkai takes th sprinter' prize!!
YEAAAH!
ZOOSH
HA-KONE ISN'T GOIN' BACK FOR HIM!!
TAG #2 IS FALLING BEHIND !!
ARA...... KITA-SAN...?
HUH?

RIDE.180 A SINGLE JERSEY

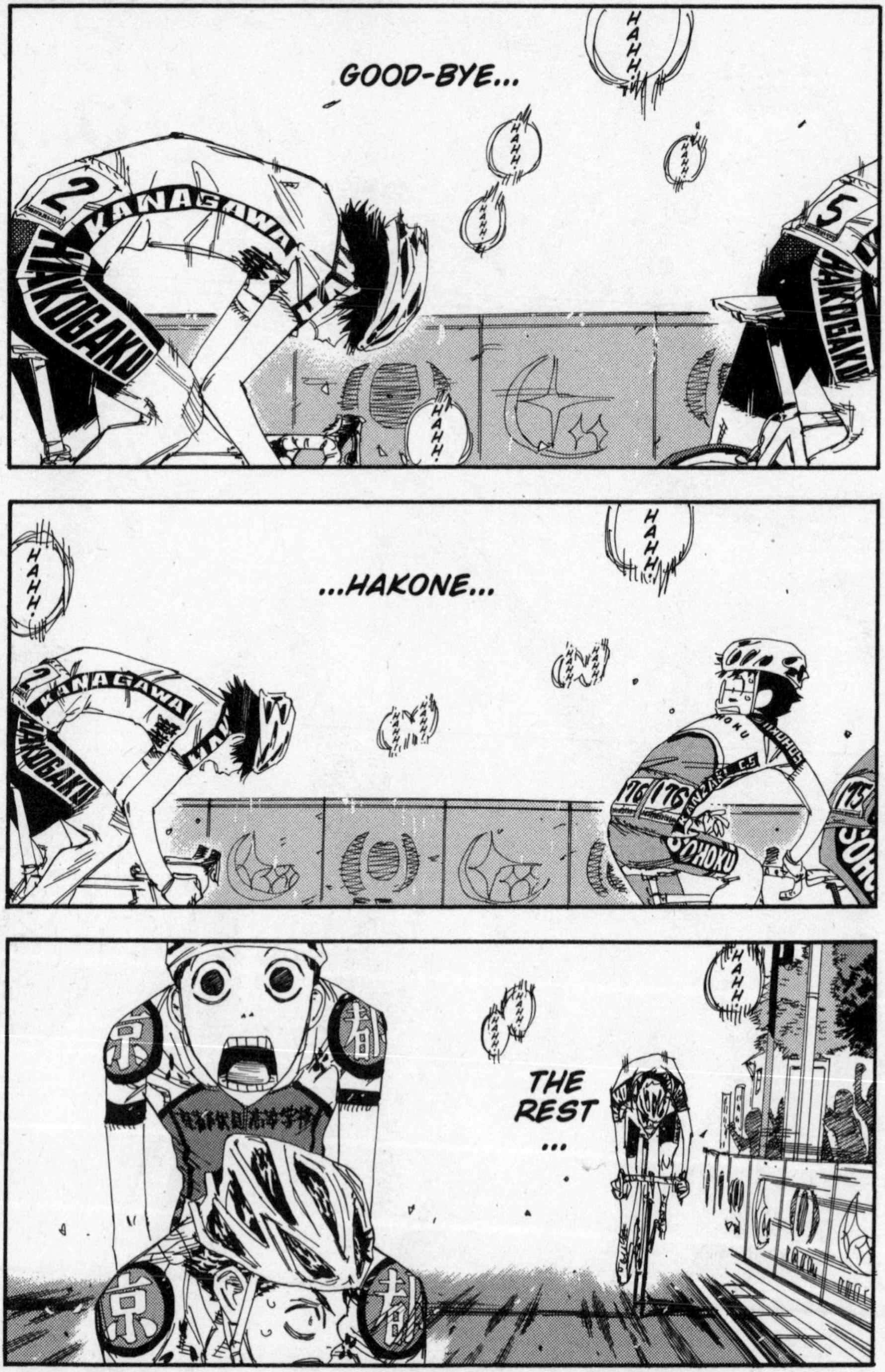
HAHH!
GOOD-BYE...
HAHH!
HAHH!
HAHH!
HAHH!
KANAGAWA
HAKOGAKU
HAKOGAKU
HAHH!
...HAKONE...
HAHH!
KANAGAWA
HAKOGAKU
SOHOKU
HAHH!
THE REST
...

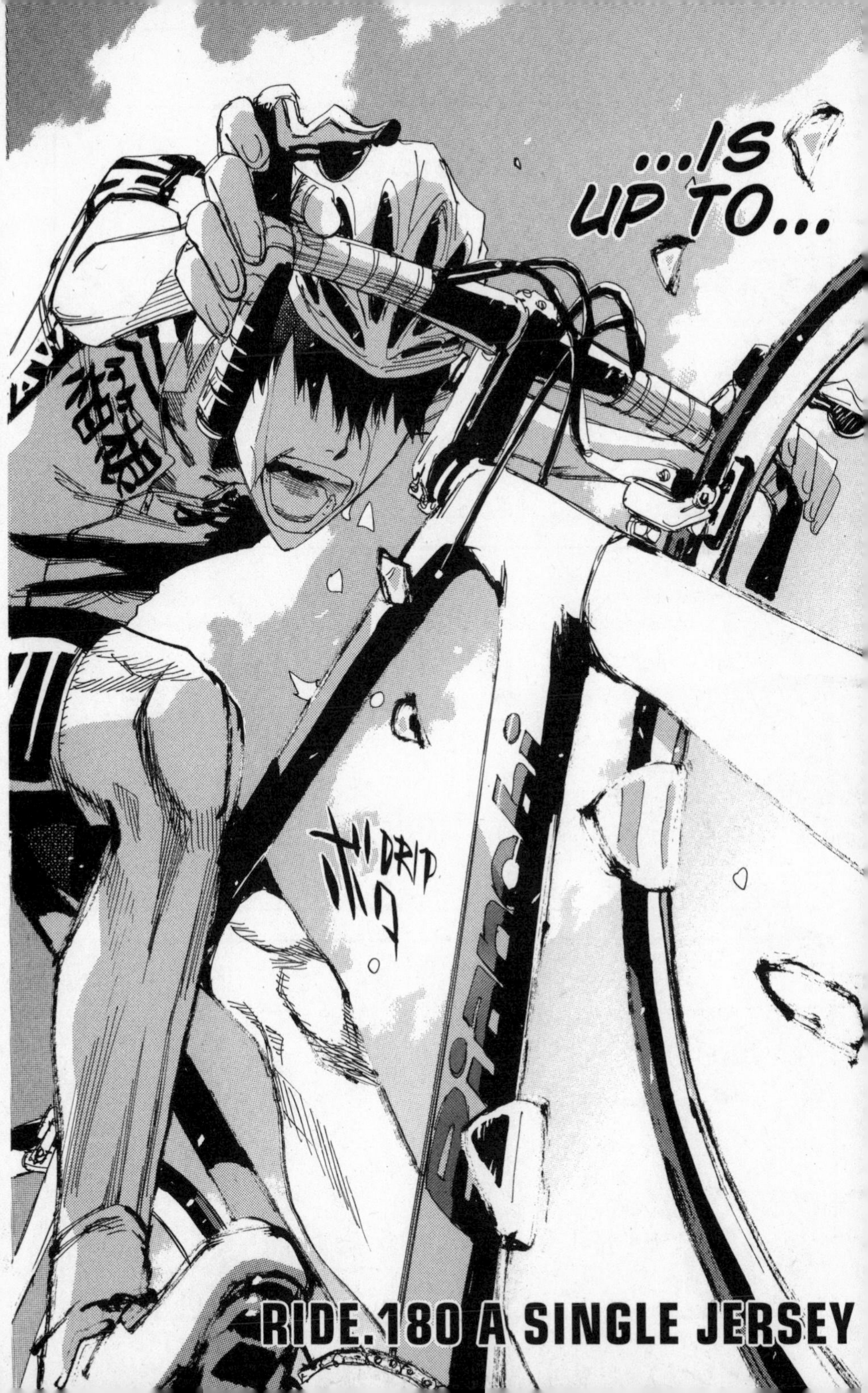
...IS UP TO...
DRIP
RIDE.180 A SINGLE JERSEY

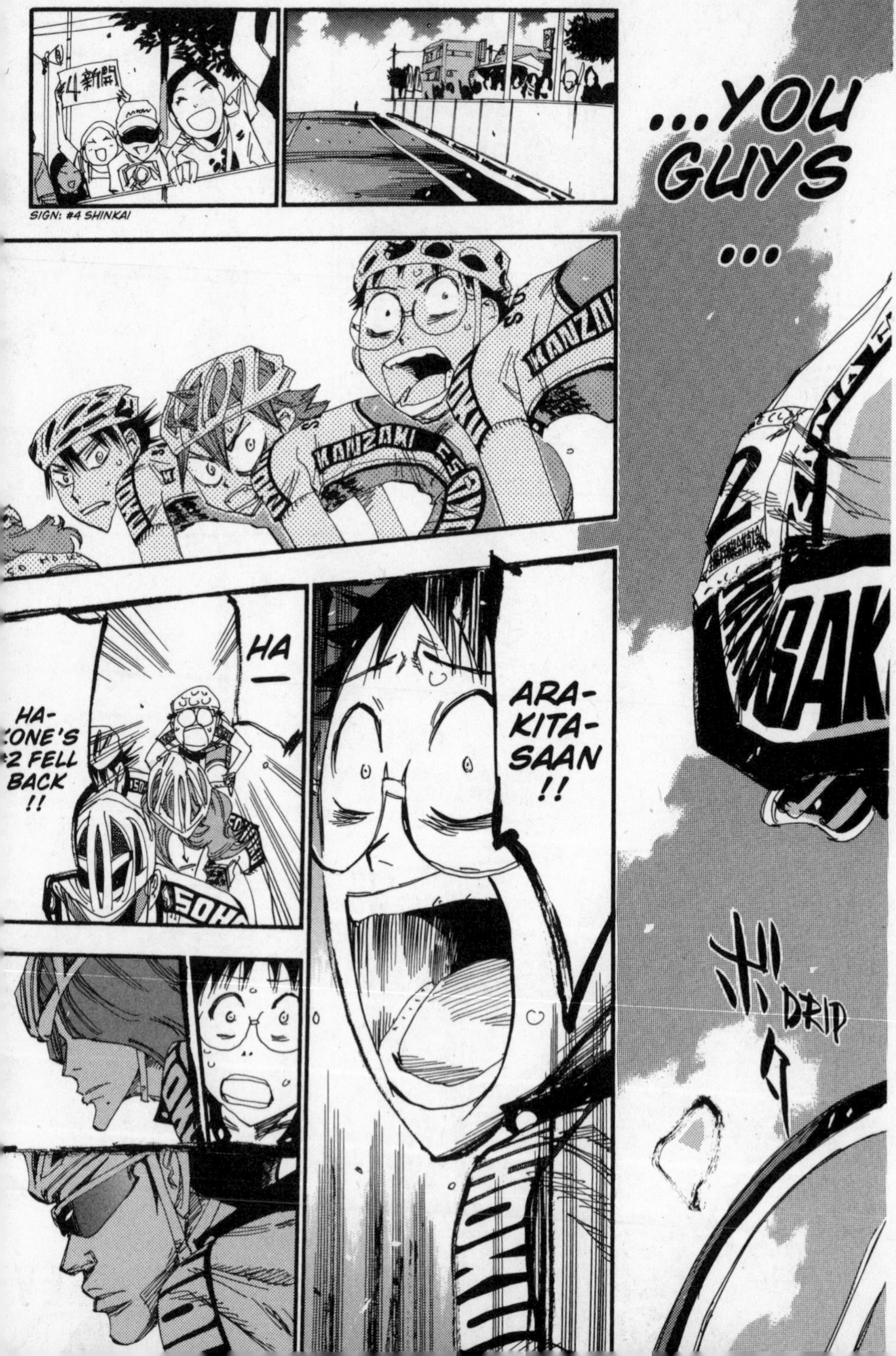
...YOU GUYS ...
DRIP
SIGN: #4 SHINKAI
ARA-KITA-SAAN!!
HA—
HA-KONE'S #2 FELL BACK!!

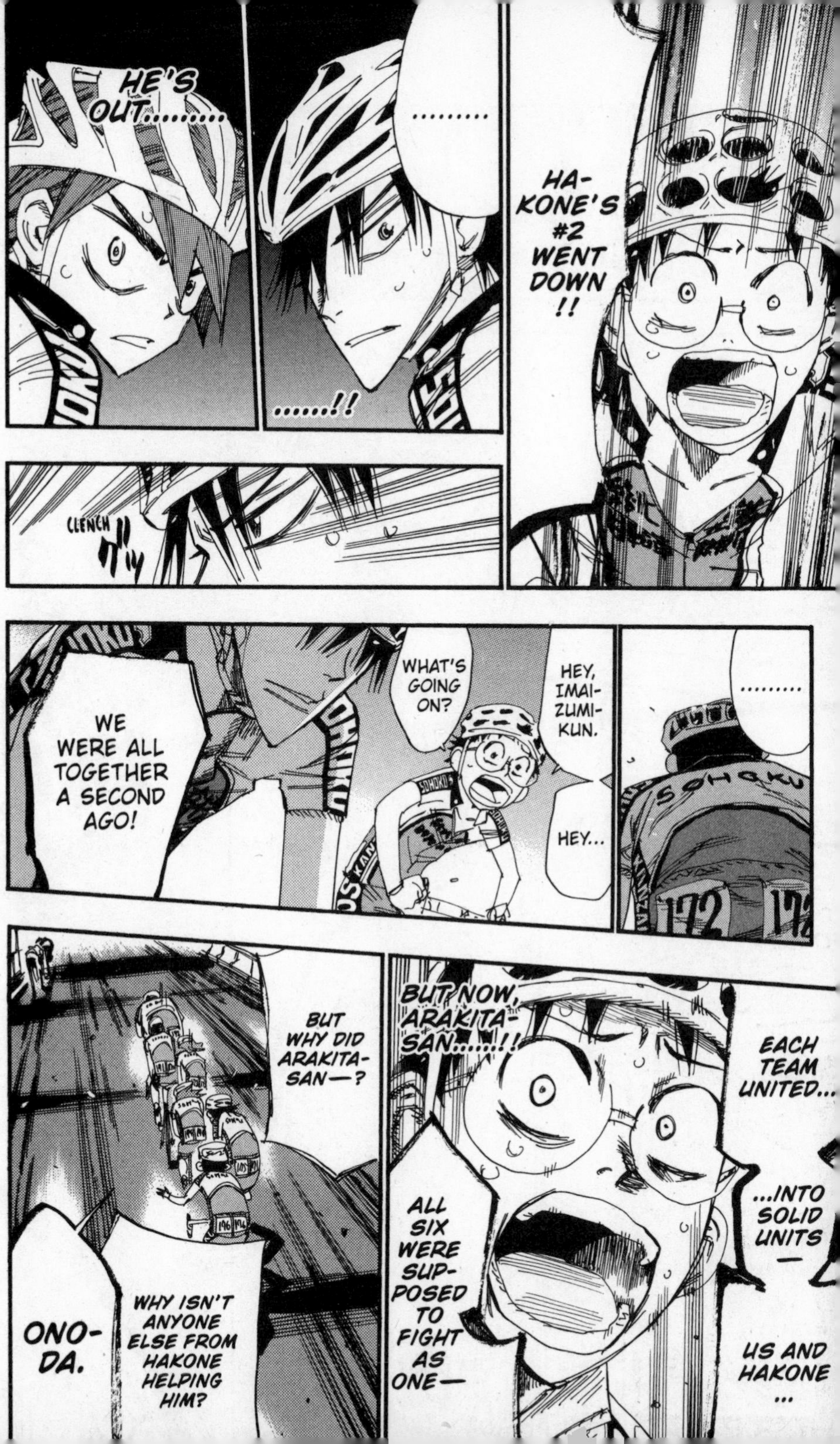

HAKONE'S #2 WENT DOWN!!
....
......!!
HE'S OUT........
CLENCH
....
HEY, IMAIZUMI-KUN.
WHAT'S GOING ON?
HEY...
WE WERE ALL TOGETHER A SECOND AGO!
EACH TEAM UNITED...
...INTO SOLID UNITS—
US AND HAKONE...
ALL SIX WERE SUPPOSED TO FIGHT AS ONE—
BUT NOW, ARAKITA-SAN......!!
BUT WHY DID ARAKITA-SAN—?
WHY ISN'T ANYONE ELSE FROM HAKONE HELPING HIM?
ONODA.

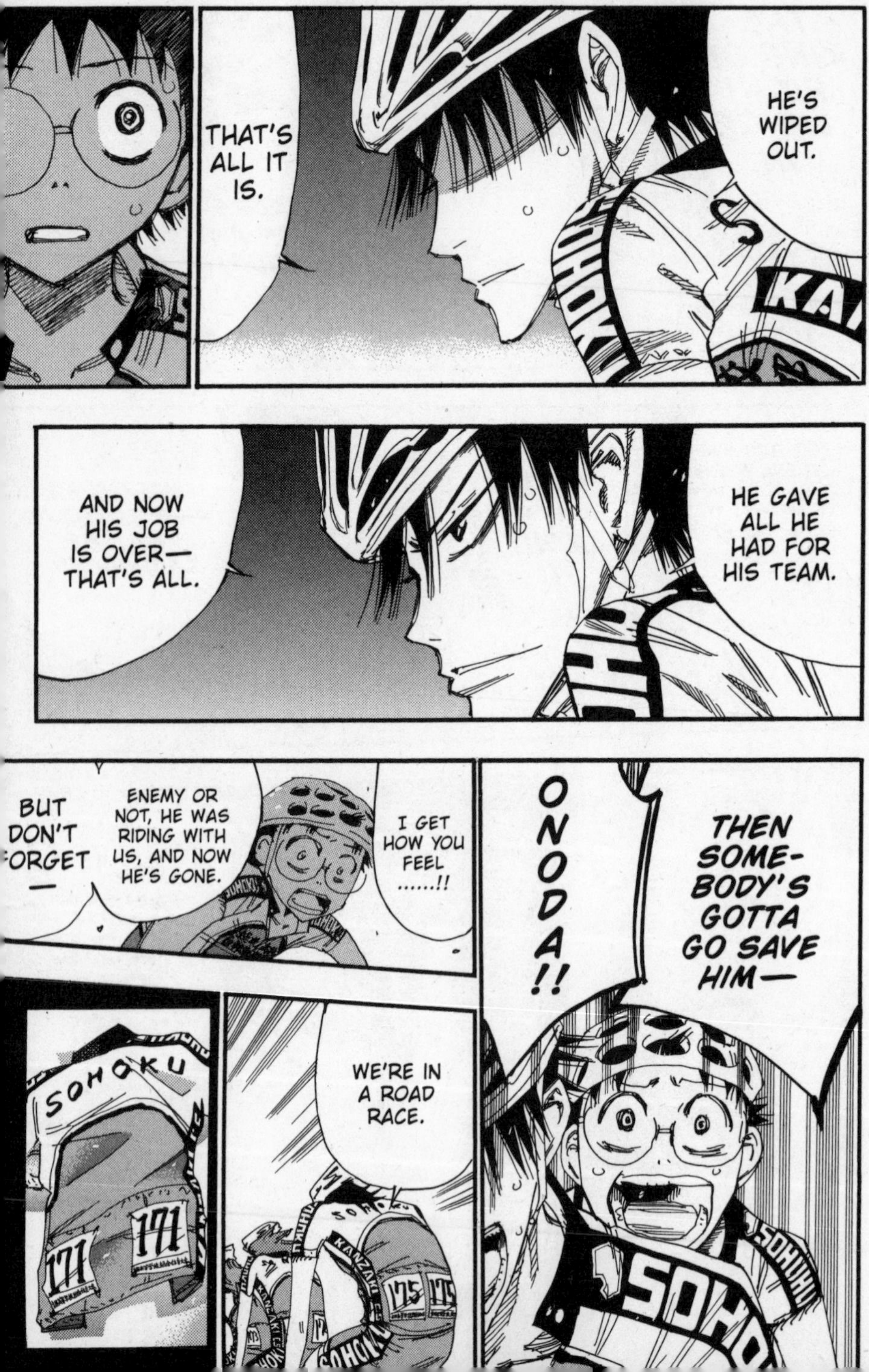
HE'S WIPED OUT.
THAT'S ALL IT IS.
HE GAVE ALL HE HAD FOR HIS TEAM.
AND NOW HIS JOB IS OVER— THAT'S ALL.
THEN SOMEBODY'S GOTTA GO SAVE HIM—
ONODA!!
I GET HOW YOU FEEL ......!!
ENEMY OR NOT, HE WAS RIDING WITH US, AND NOW HE'S GONE.
BUT DON'T FORGET —
WE'RE IN A ROAD RACE.

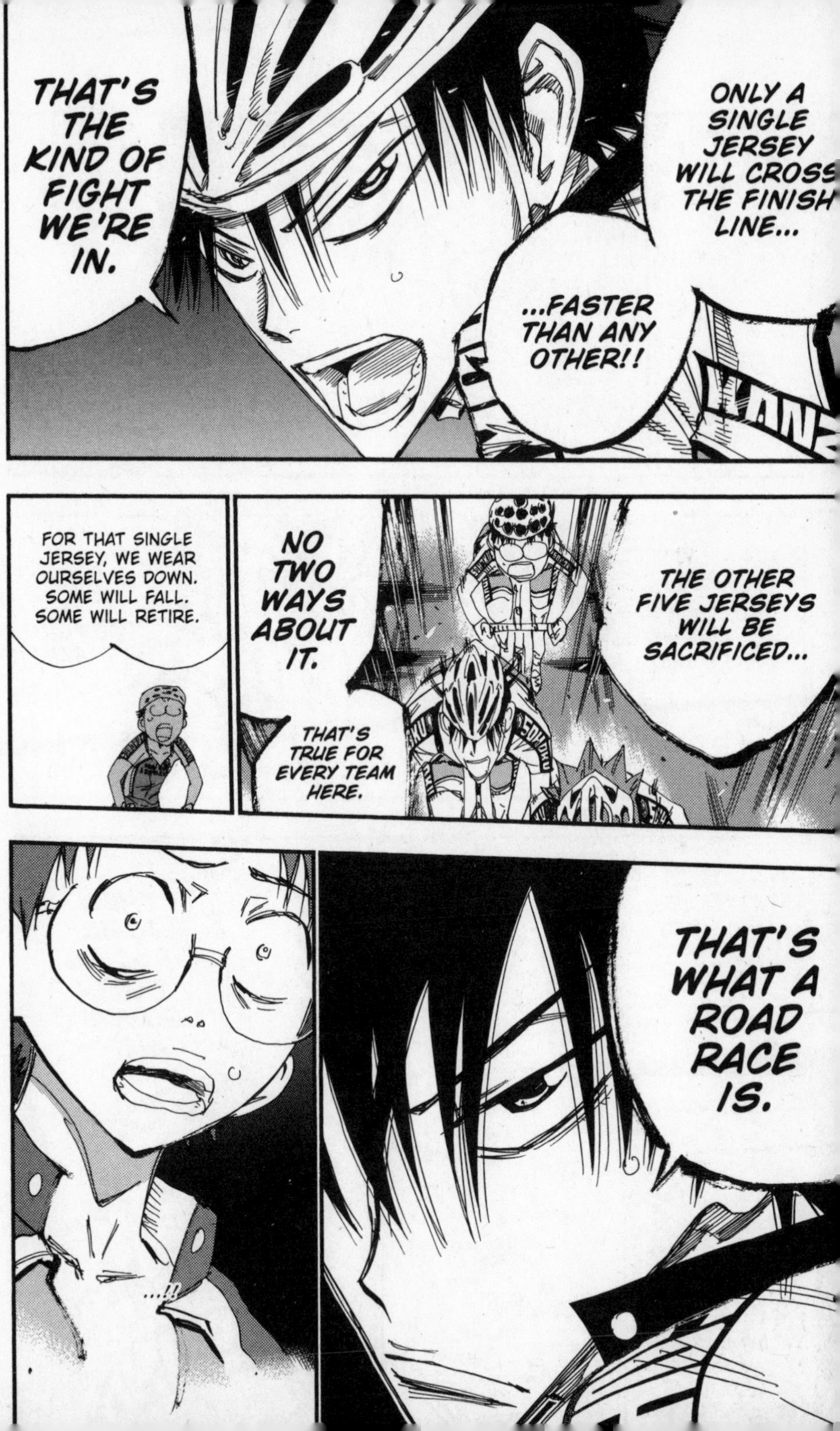
ONLY A SINGLE JERSEY WILL CROSS THE FINISH LINE...
...FASTER THAN ANY OTHER!!
THAT'S THE KIND OF FIGHT WE'RE IN.
THE OTHER FIVE JERSEYS WILL BE SACRIFICED...
NO TWO WAYS ABOUT IT.
THAT'S TRUE FOR EVERY TEAM HERE.
FOR THAT SINGLE JERSEY, WE WEAR OURSELVES DOWN. SOME WILL FALL. SOME WILL RETIRE.
THAT'S WHAT A ROAD RACE IS.
...!!

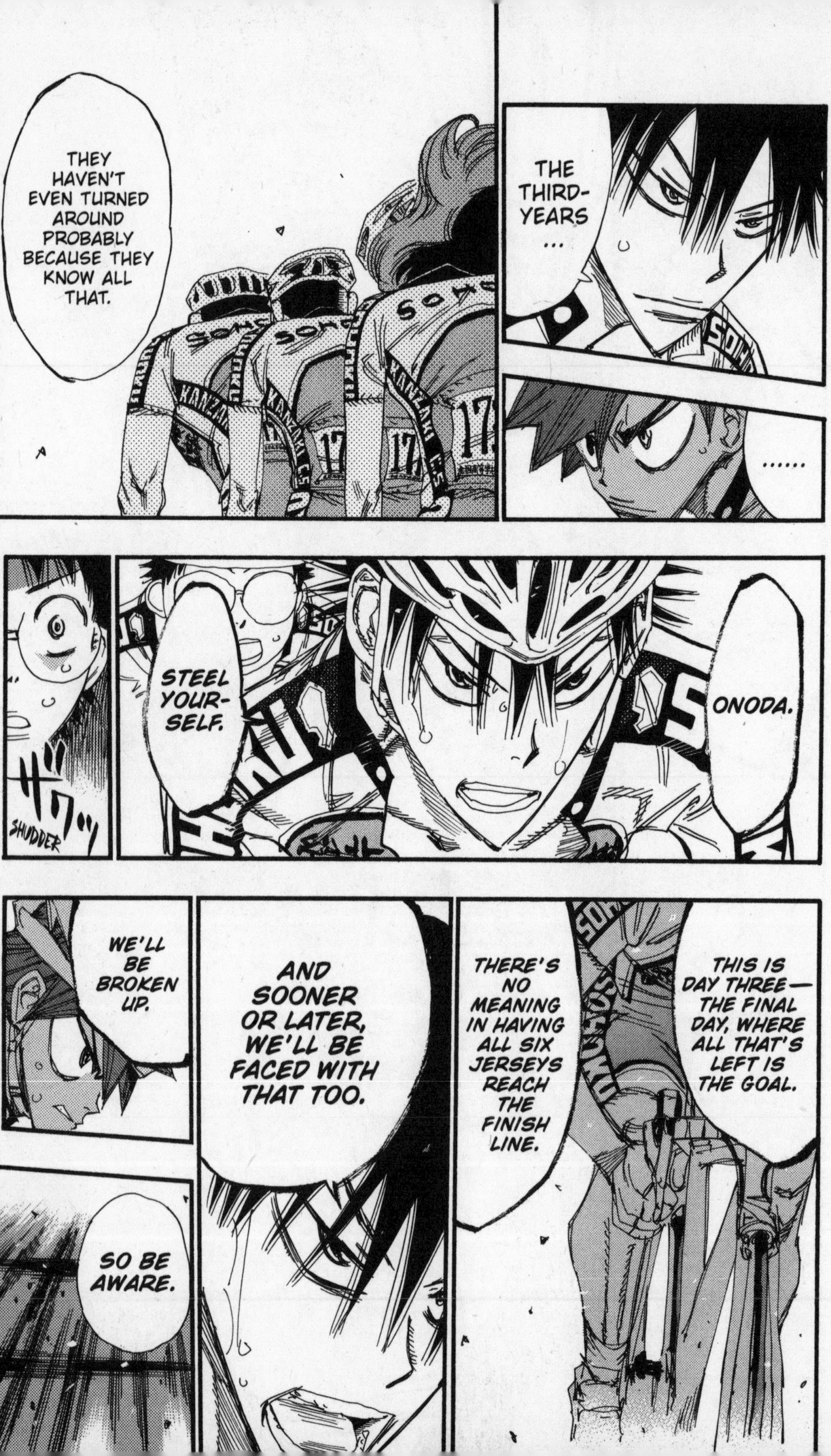
THE THIRD-YEARS ...
......
THEY HAVEN'T EVEN TURNED AROUND PROBABLY BECAUSE THEY KNOW ALL THAT.
SONODA.
STEEL YOURSELF.
SHUDDER
THIS IS DAY THREE—THE FINAL DAY, WHERE ALL THAT'S LEFT IS THE GOAL.
THERE'S NO MEANING IN HAVING ALL SIX JERSEYS REACH THE FINISH LINE.
AND SOONER OR LATER, WE'LL BE FACED WITH THAT TOO.
WE'LL BE BROKEN UP.
SO BE AWARE.

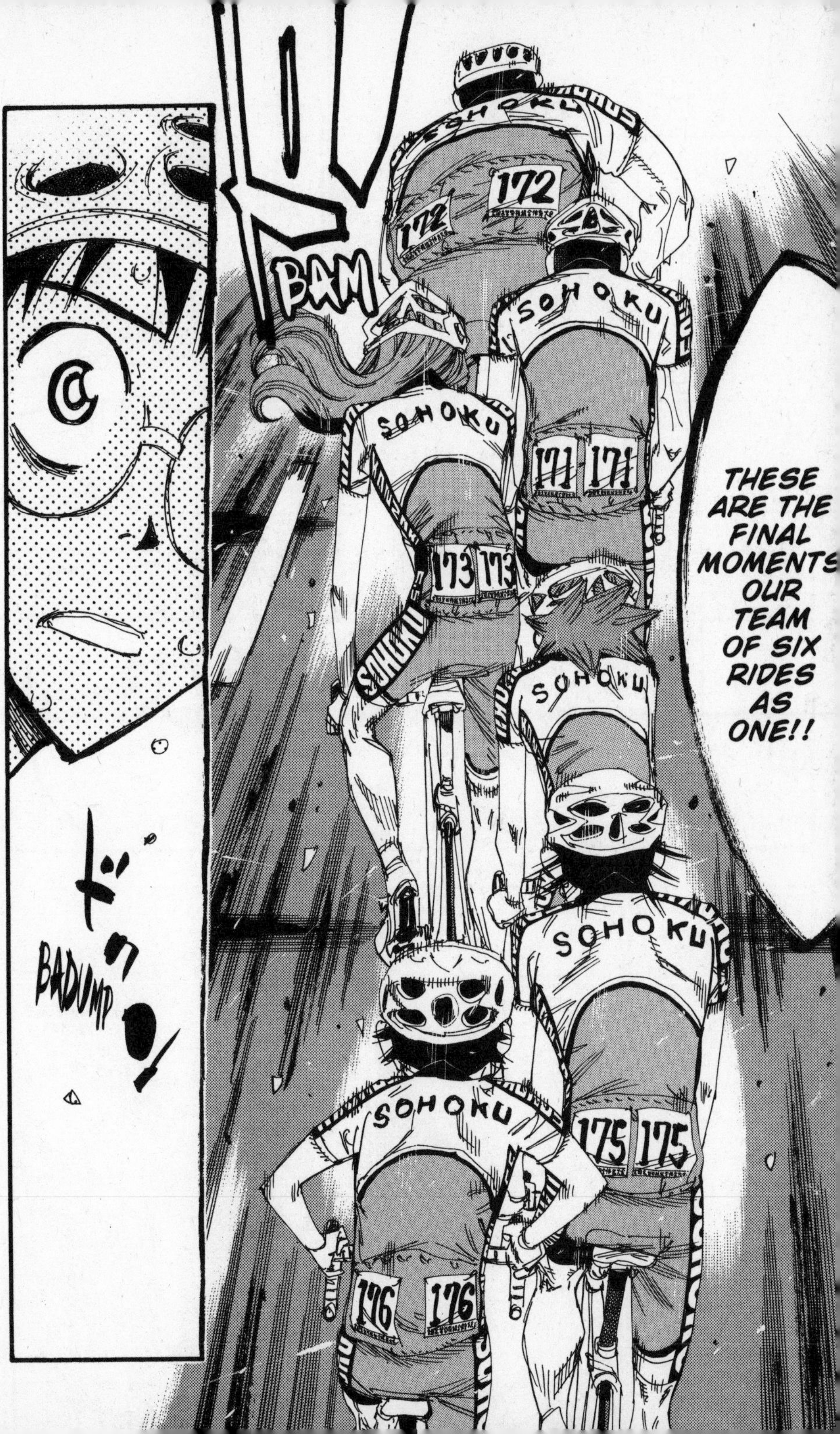
BAM
THESE ARE THE FINAL MOMENTS OUR TEAM OF SIX RIDES AS ONE!!
BADUMP

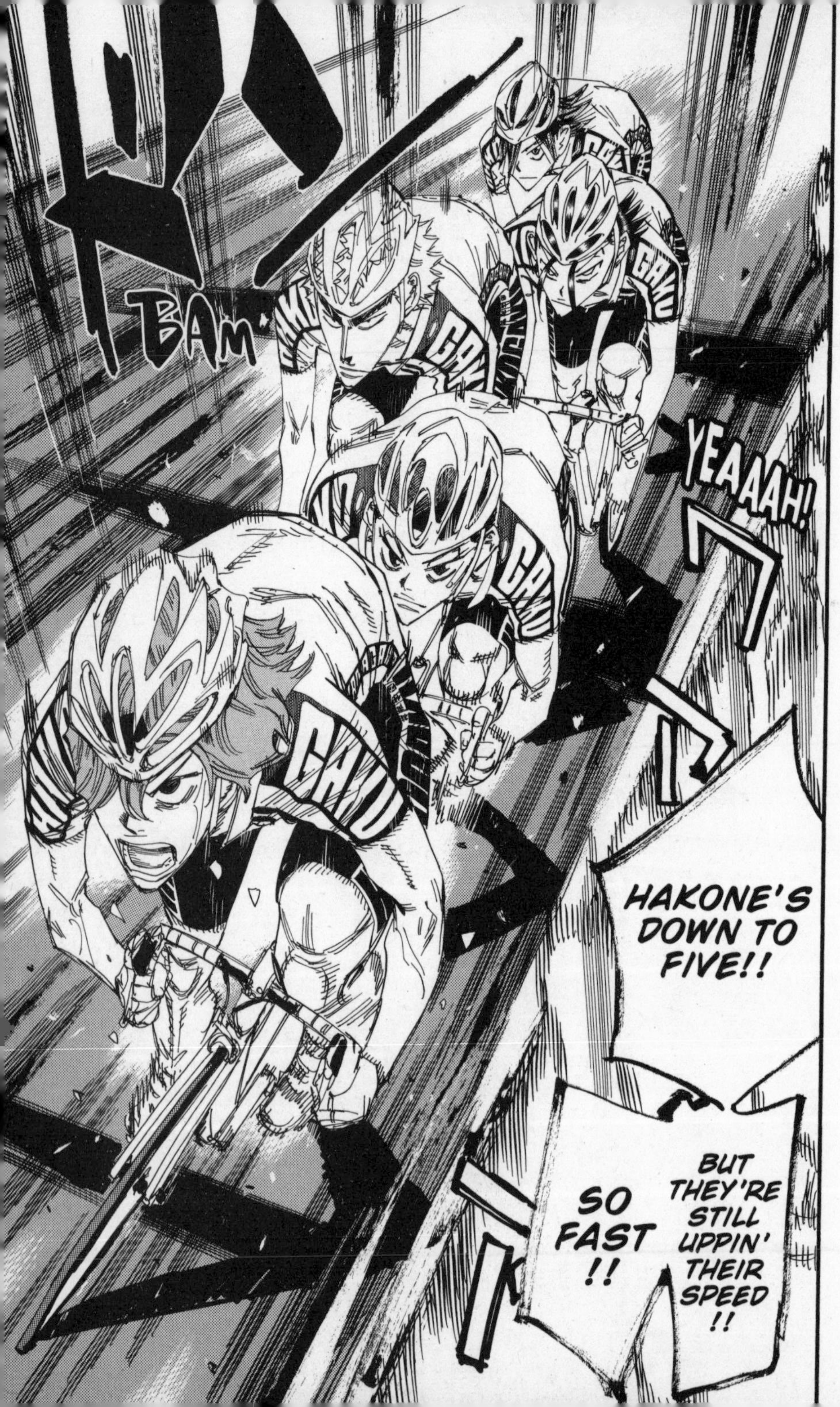
YEAAAH!
HAKONE'S DOWN TO FIVE!!
BUT THEY'RE STILL UPPIN' THEIR SPEED!!
SO FAST!!
BAM

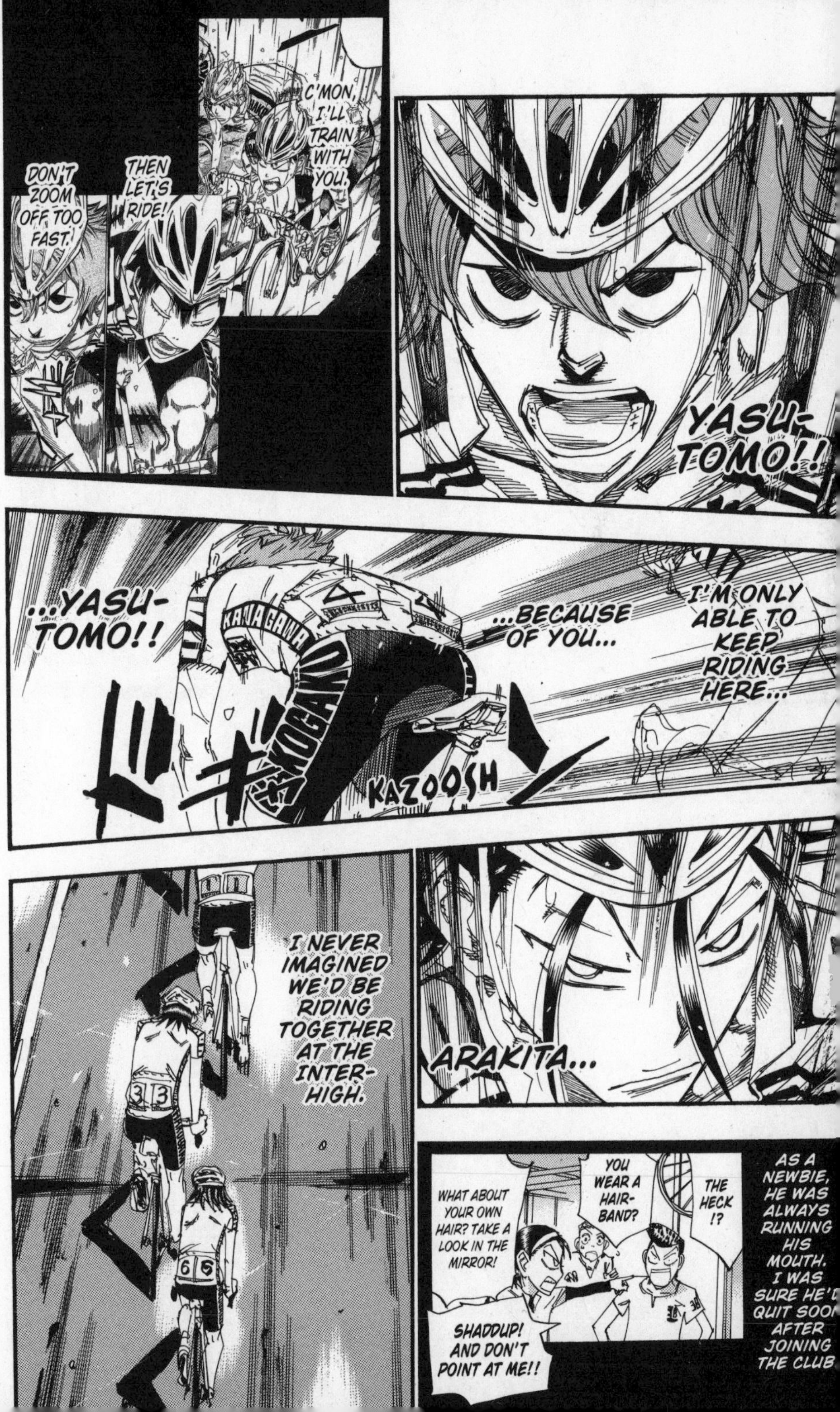
YASU-TOMO!!
C'MON, I'LL TRAIN WITH YOU.
THEN LET'S RIDE!
DON'T ZOOM OFF TOO FAST.
I'M ONLY ABLE TO KEEP RIDING HERE...
...BECAUSE OF YOU...
...YASU-TOMO!!
KAZOOSH
ARAKITA...
AS A NEWBIE, HE WAS ALWAYS RUNNING HIS MOUTH. I WAS SURE HE'D QUIT SOON AFTER JOINING THE CLUB
THE HECK !?
YOU WEAR A HAIR-BAND?
WHAT ABOUT YOUR OWN HAIR? TAKE A LOOK IN THE MIRROR!
SHADDUP! AND DON'T POINT AT ME!!
I NEVER IMAGINED WE'D BE RIDING TOGETHER AT THE INTER-HIGH.

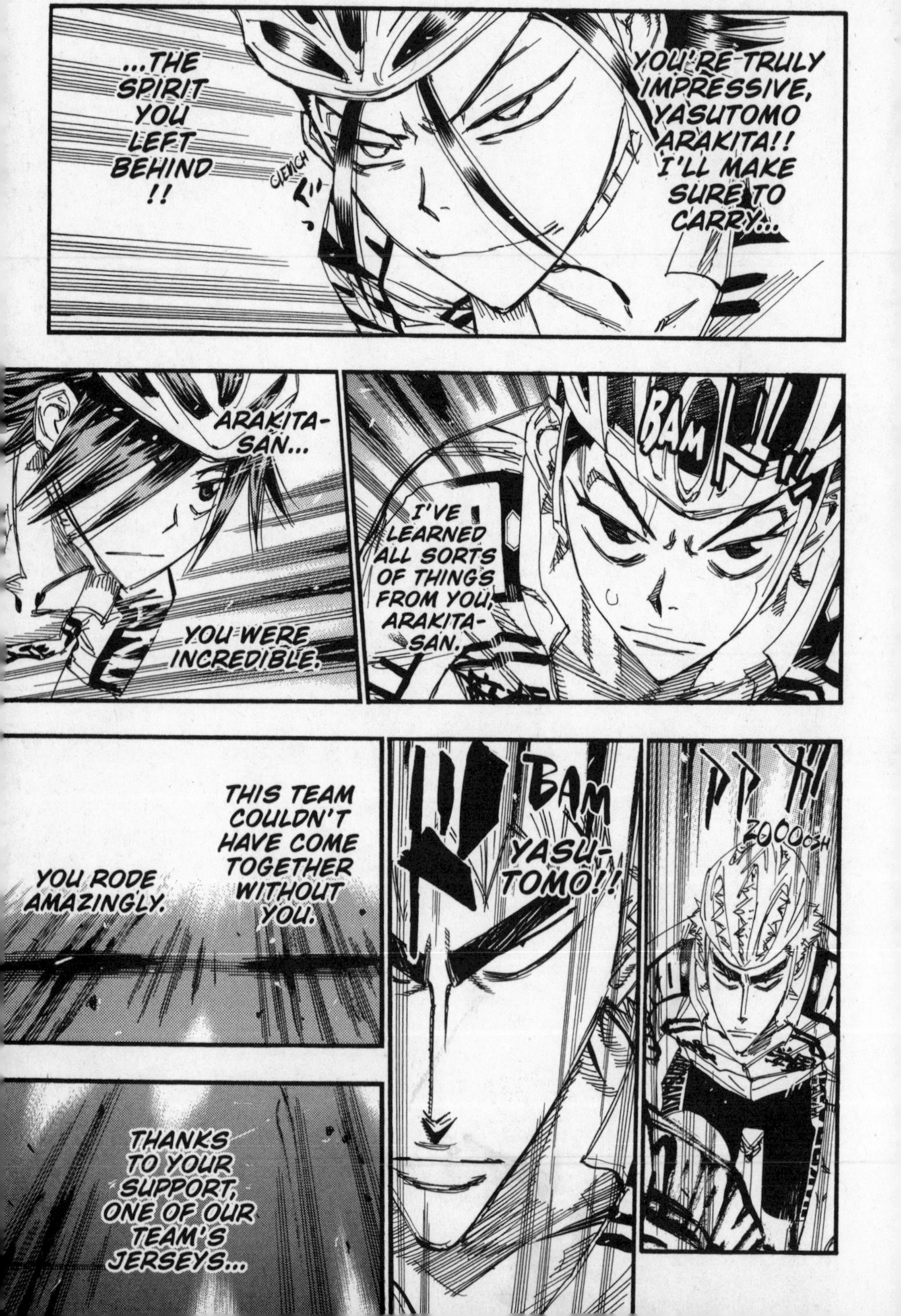
YOU'RE TRULY IMPRESSIVE, YASUTOMO ARAKITA!! I'LL MAKE SURE TO CARRY...
CLENCH
...THE SPIRIT YOU LEFT BEHIND!!
BAM
I'VE LEARNED ALL SORTS OF THINGS FROM YOU, ARAKITA-SAN.
ARAKITA-SAN...
YOU WERE INCREDIBLE.
ZOOOOSH
BAM
YASU-TOMO!!
THIS TEAM COULDN'T HAVE COME TOGETHER WITHOUT YOU.
YOU RODE AMAZINGLY.
THANKS TO YOUR SUPPORT, ONE OF OUR TEAM'S JERSEYS...

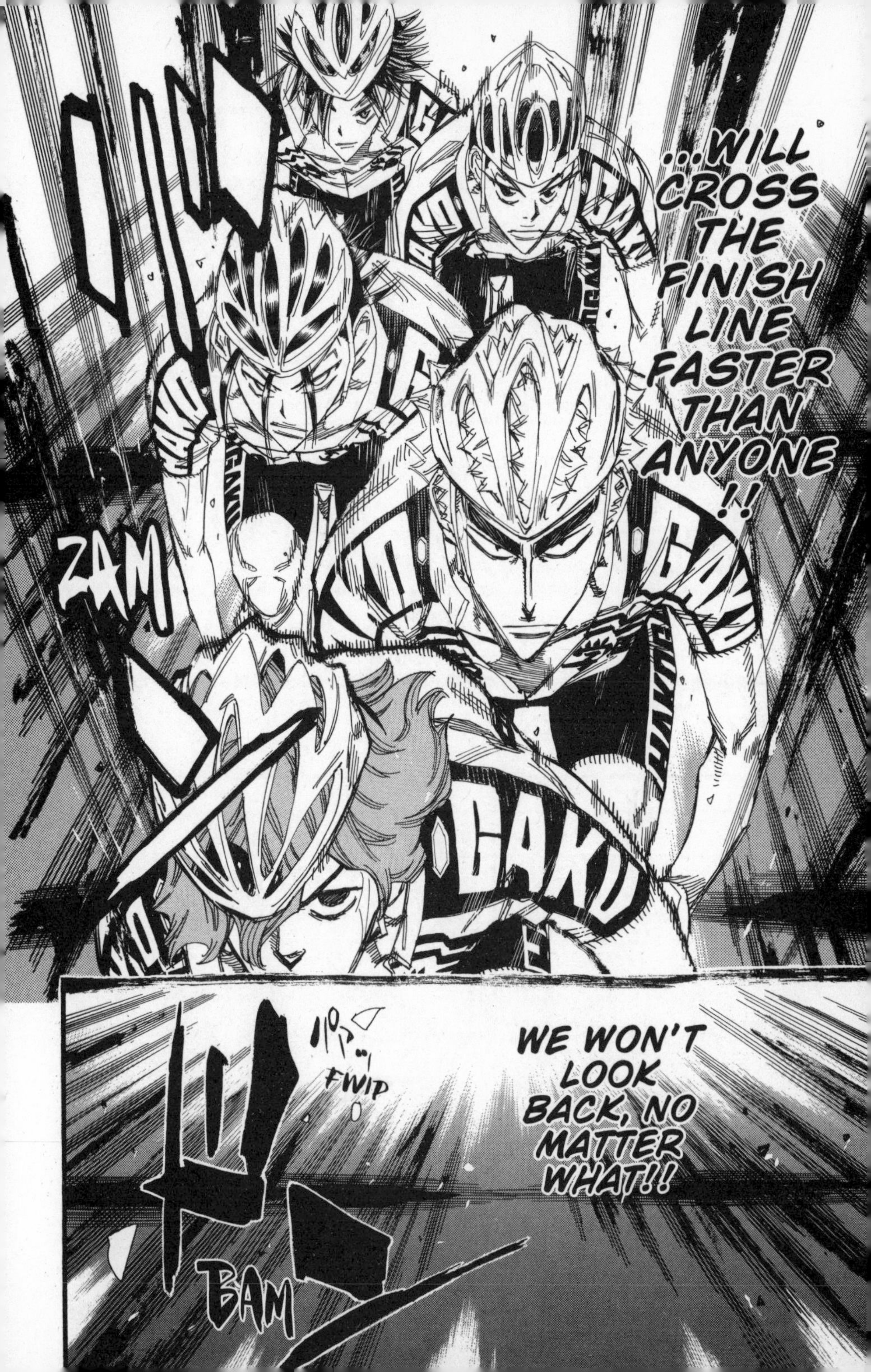
...WILL CROSS THE FINISH LINE FASTER THAN ANYONE!!
ZAM
WE WON'T LOOK BACK, NO MATTER WHAT!!
FWIP
BAM

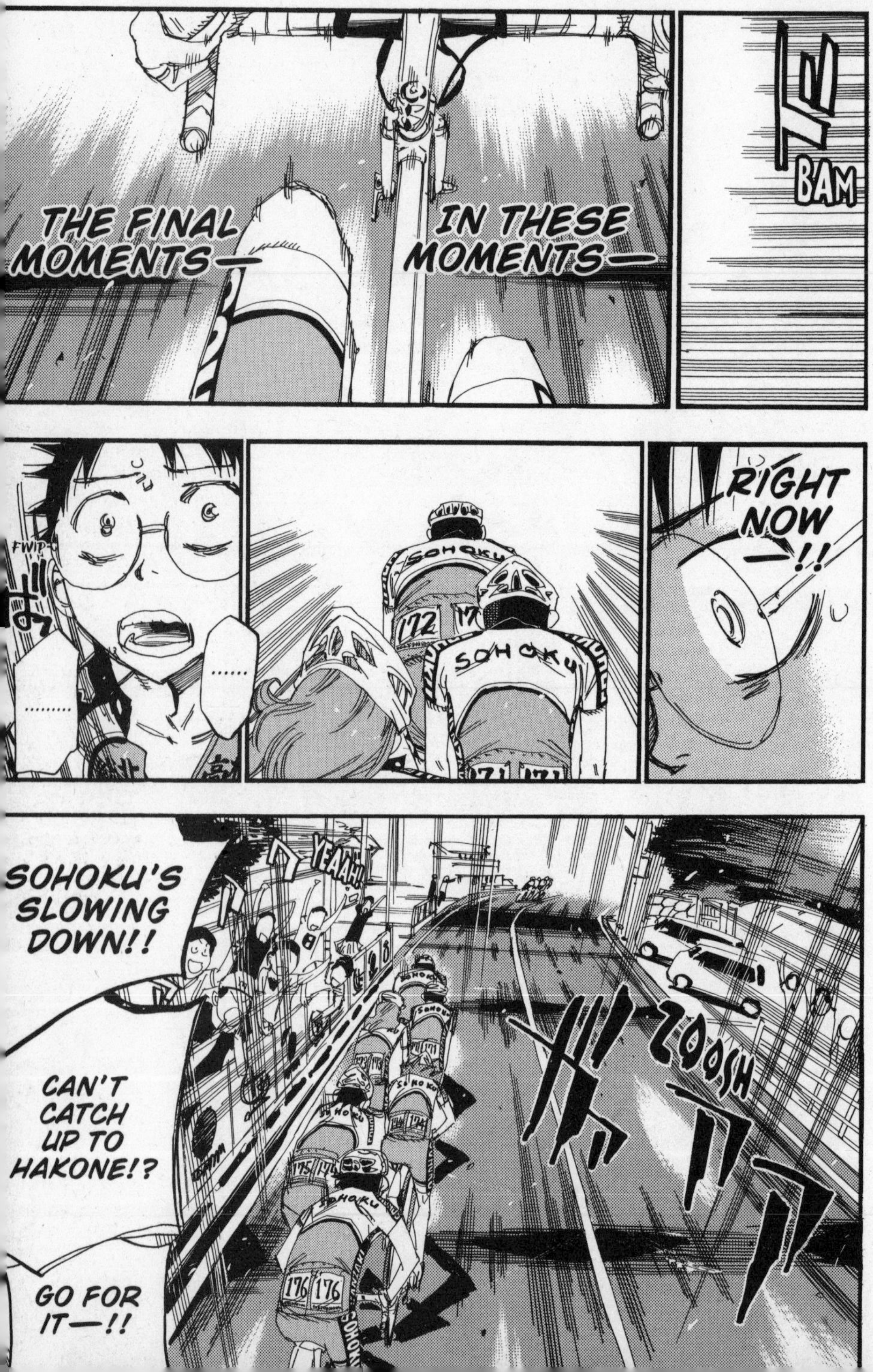
BAM
IN THESE MOMENTS—
THE FINAL MOMENTS—
RIGHT NOW—!!
......
....
FWIP
ZOOSH
YEAAH!
SOHOKU'S SLOWING DOWN!!
CAN'T CATCH UP TO HAKONE!?
GO FOR IT—!!

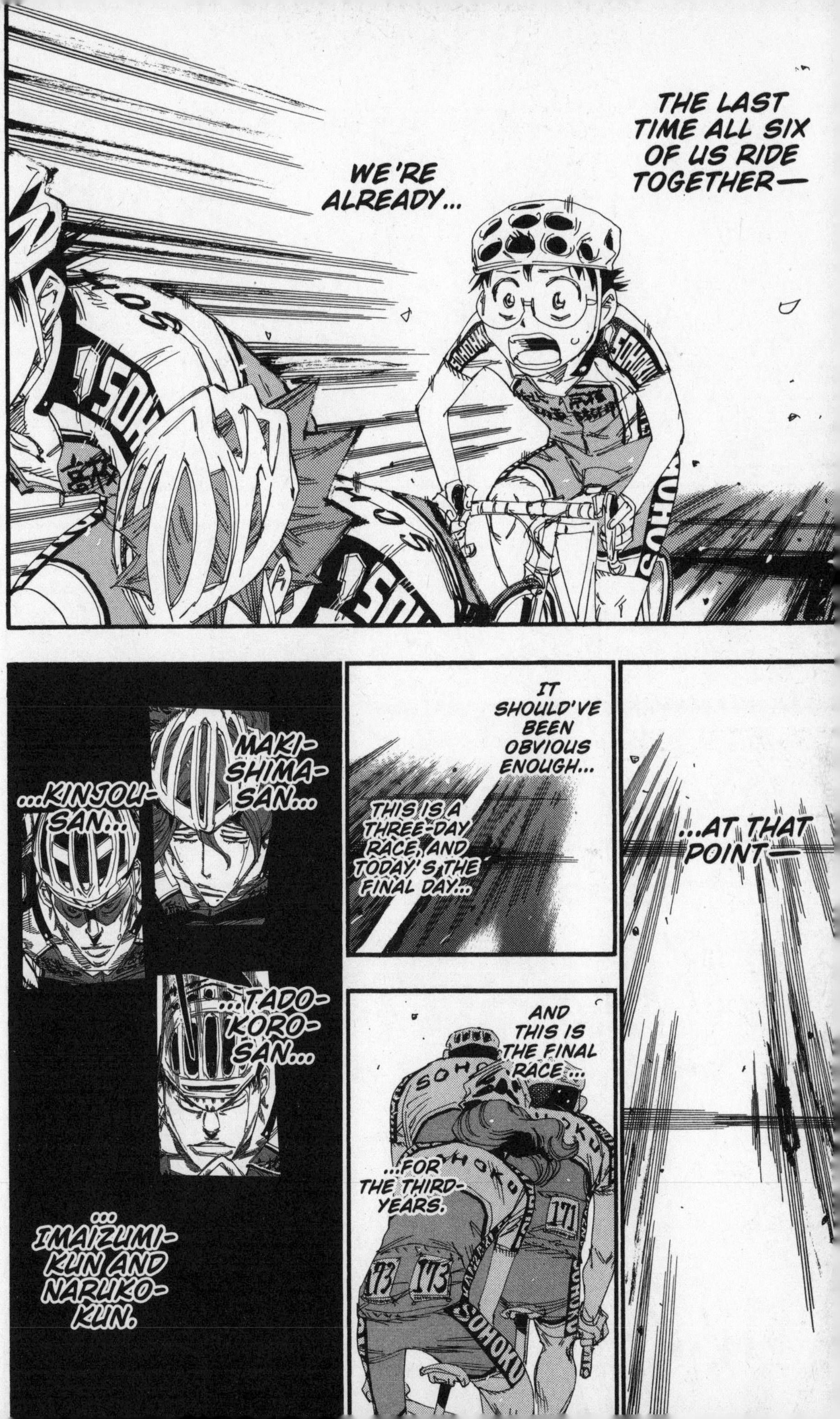
THE LAST TIME ALL SIX OF US RIDE TOGETHER—
WE'RE ALREADY...
...AT THAT POINT—
IT SHOULD'VE BEEN OBVIOUS ENOUGH...
THIS IS A THREE-DAY RACE, AND TODAY'S THE FINAL DAY...
AND THIS IS THE FINAL RACE...
...FOR THE THIRD-YEARS.
MAKI-SHIMA-SAN...
...KINJOU-SAN...
...TADO-KORO-SAN...
...IMAIZUMI-KUN AND NARUKO-KUN.

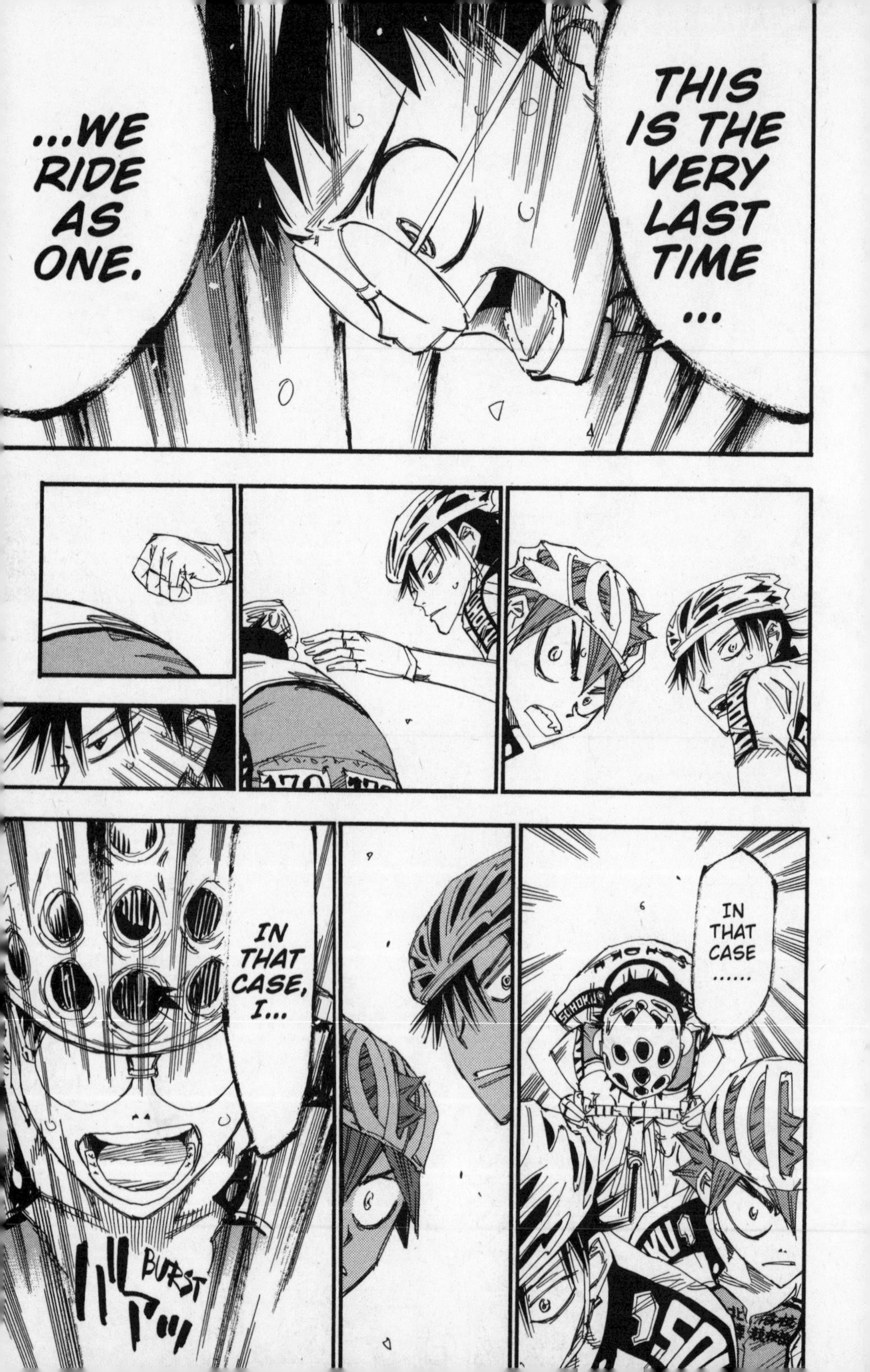
THIS IS THE VERY LAST TIME...
...WE RIDE AS ONE.
IN THAT CASE......
IN THAT CASE, I...
BURST

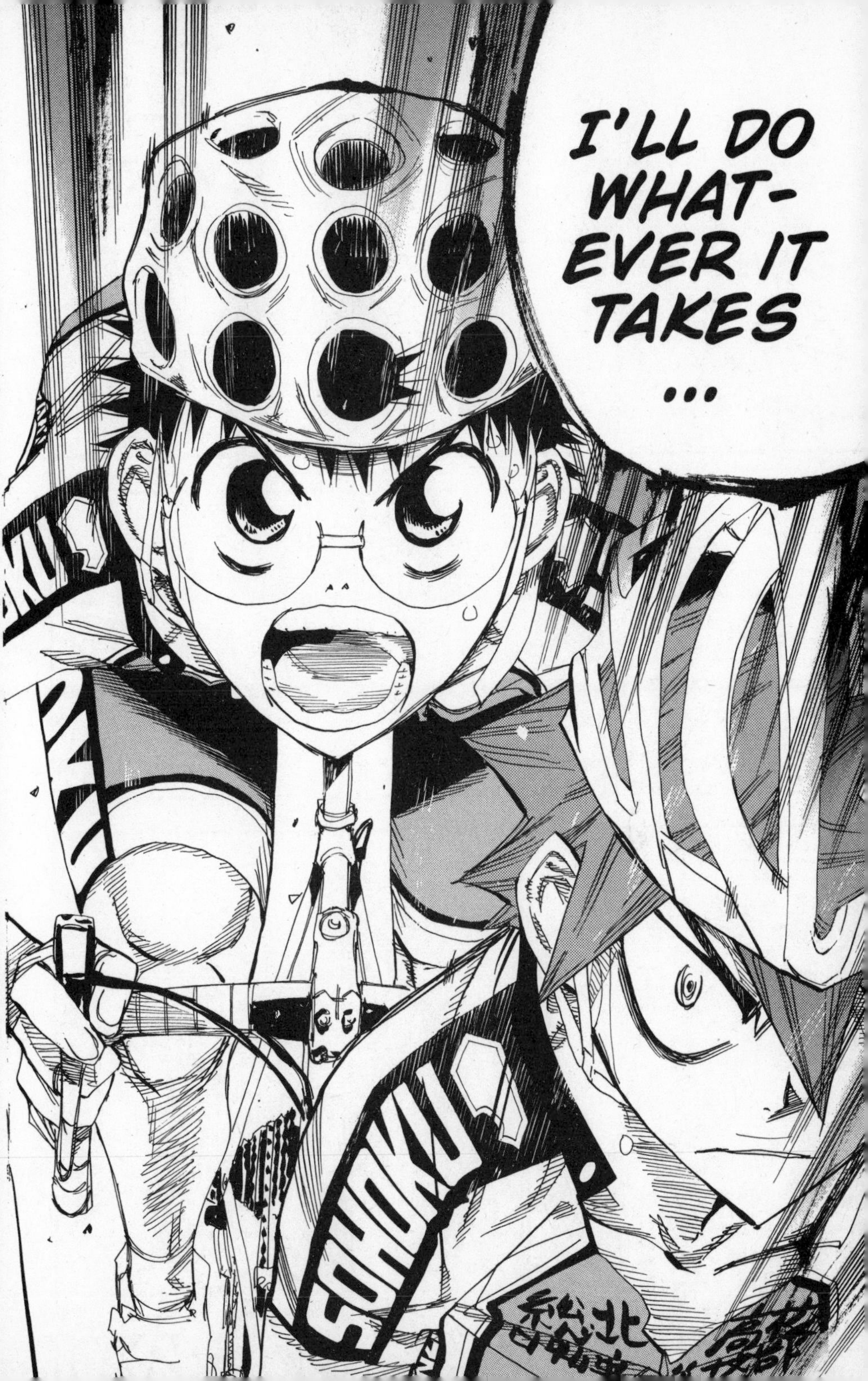
I'LL DO WHAT-EVER IT TAKES ...
SOHOKU

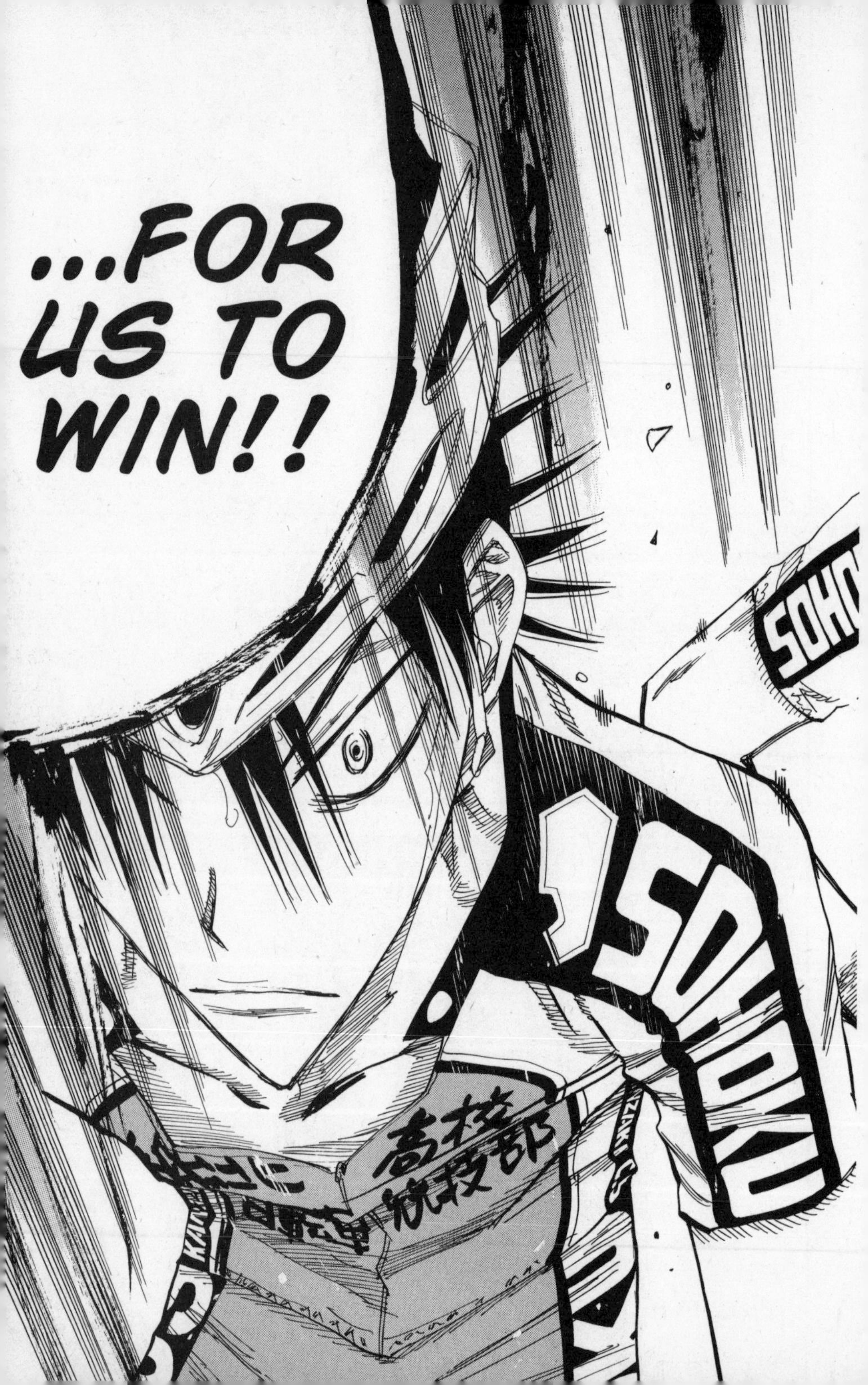
...FOR US TO WIN!!

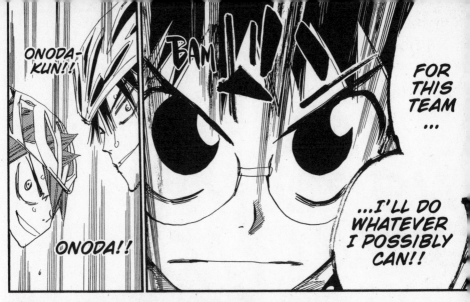

ONODA-KUN!!

BAM

ONODA!!

FOR THIS TEAM...

...I'LL DO WHATEVER I POSSIBLY CAN!!

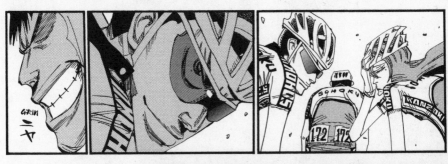

GRIN

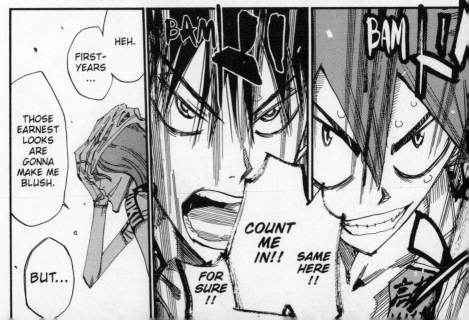

HEH. FIRST-YEARS...

THOSE EARNEST LOOKS ARE GONNA MAKE ME BLUSH.

BUT...

BAM

BAM

COUNT ME IN!!

FOR SURE!!

SAME HERE!!

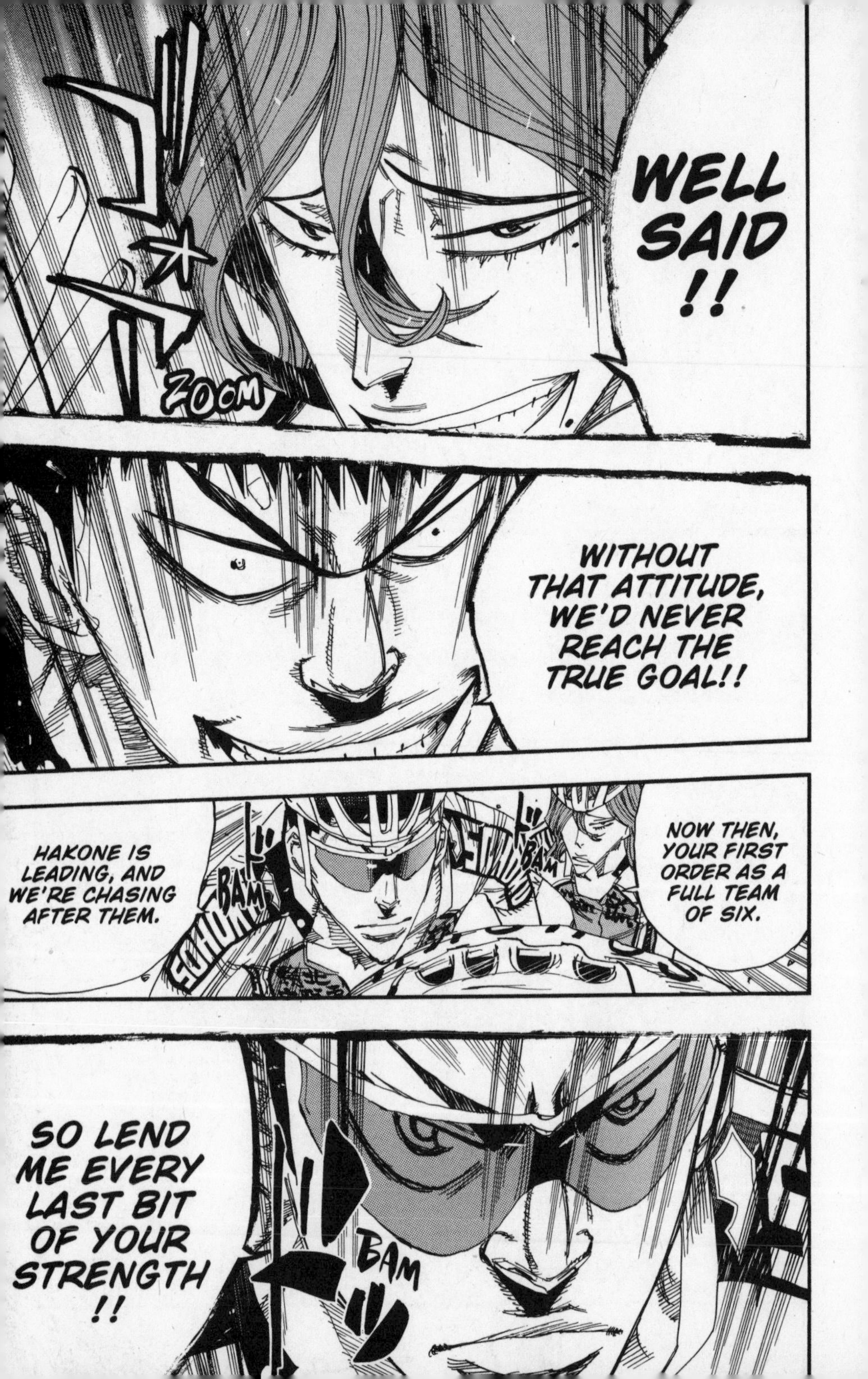
WELL SAID!!
ZOOM
WITHOUT THAT ATTITUDE, WE'D NEVER REACH THE TRUE GOAL!!
NOW THEN, YOUR FIRST ORDER AS A FULL TEAM OF SIX.
BAM
BAM
HAKONE IS LEADING, AND WE'RE CHASING AFTER THEM.
SO LEND ME EVERY LAST BIT OF YOUR STRENGTH!!
BAM

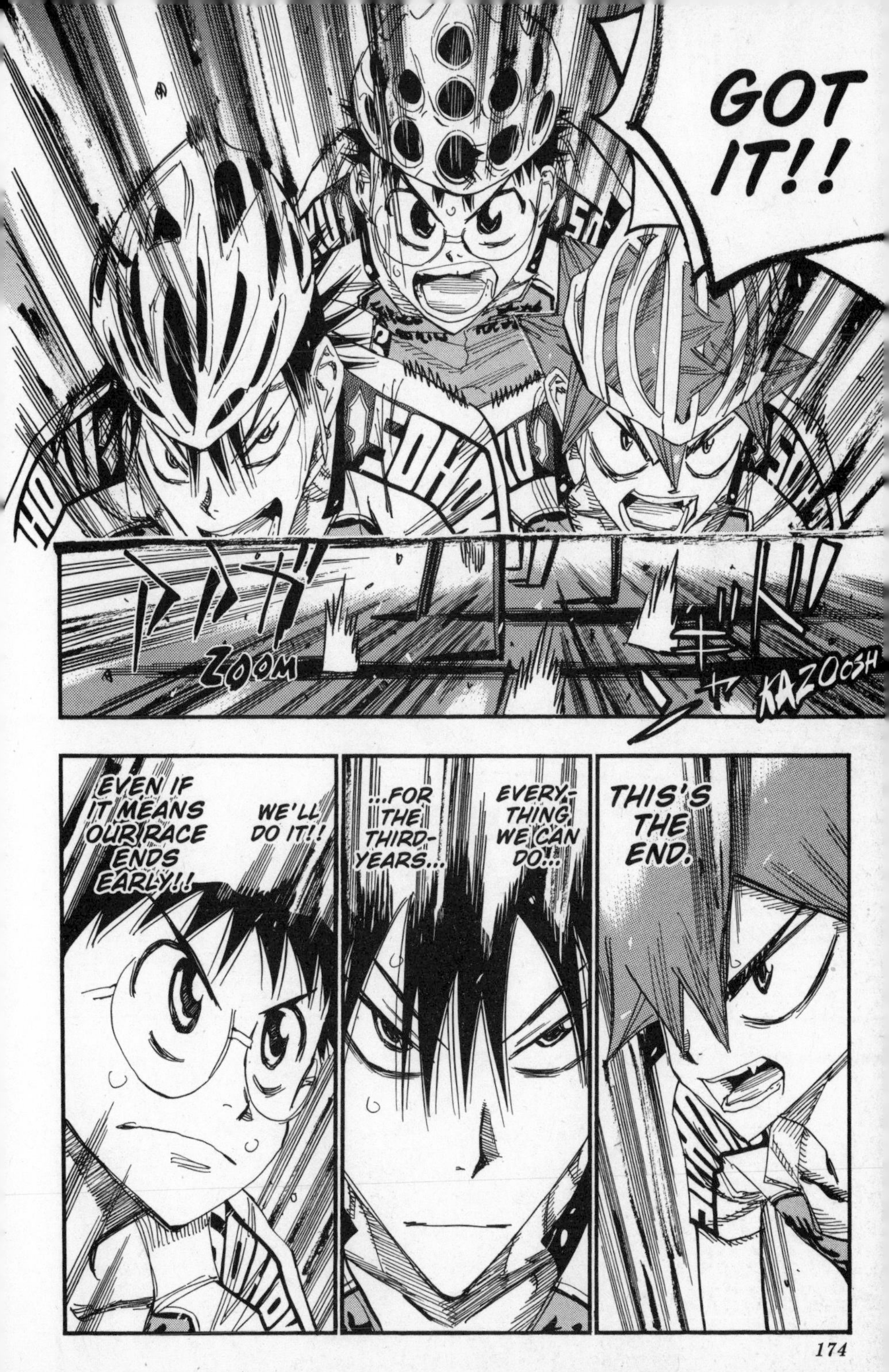
GOT IT!!
KAZOOSH
ZOOM
THIS'S THE END.
EVERY-THING WE CAN DO...
...FOR THE THIRD-YEARS...
WE'LL DO IT!!
EVEN IF IT MEANS OUR RACE ENDS EARLY!!

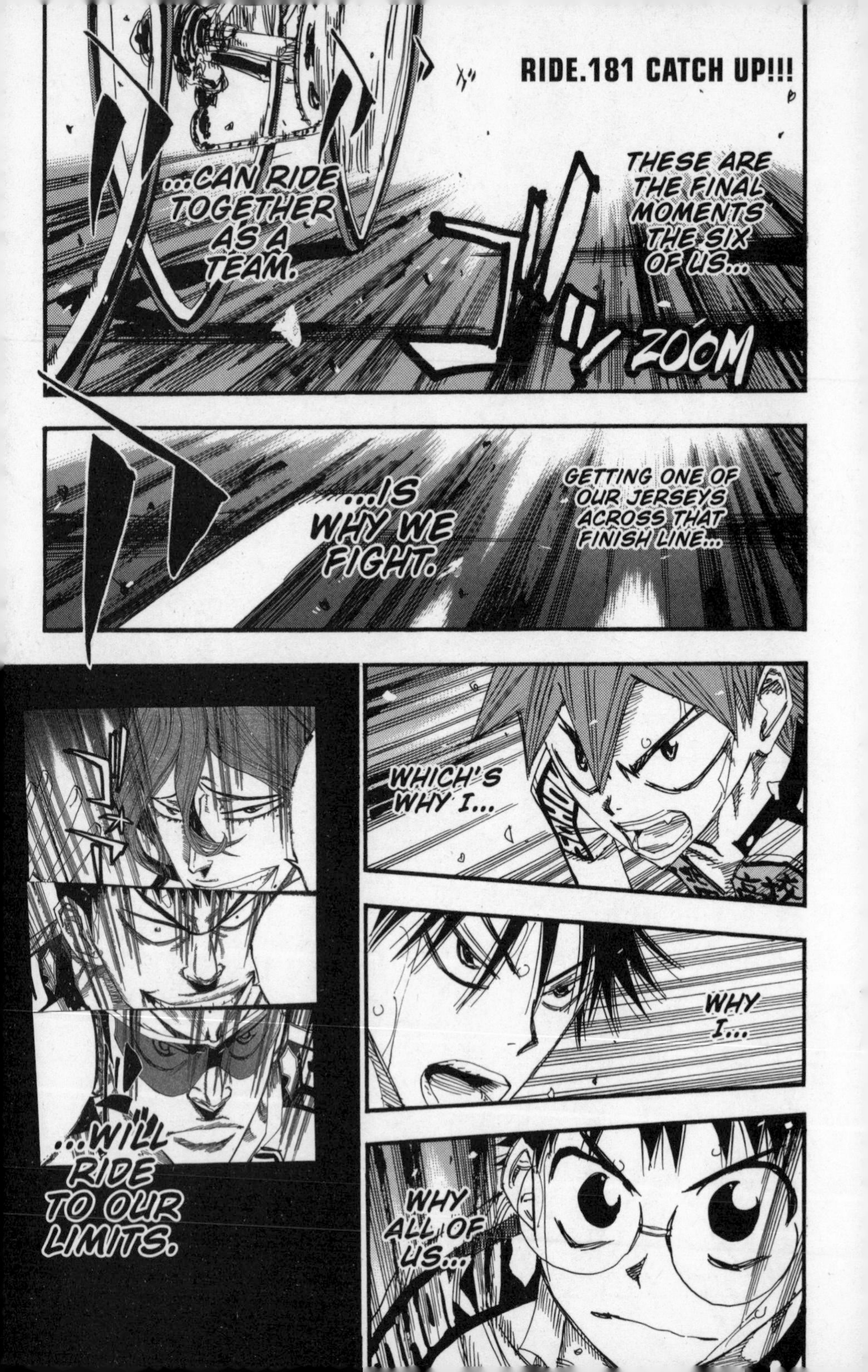
RIDE.181 CATCH UP!!!
THESE ARE THE FINAL MOMENTS THE SIX OF US...
...CAN RIDE TOGETHER AS A TEAM.
ZOOM
GETTING ONE OF OUR JERSEYS ACROSS THAT FINISH LINE...
...IS WHY WE FIGHT.
WHICH'S WHY I...
WHY I...
WHY ALL OF US...
...WILL RIDE TO OUR LIMITS.

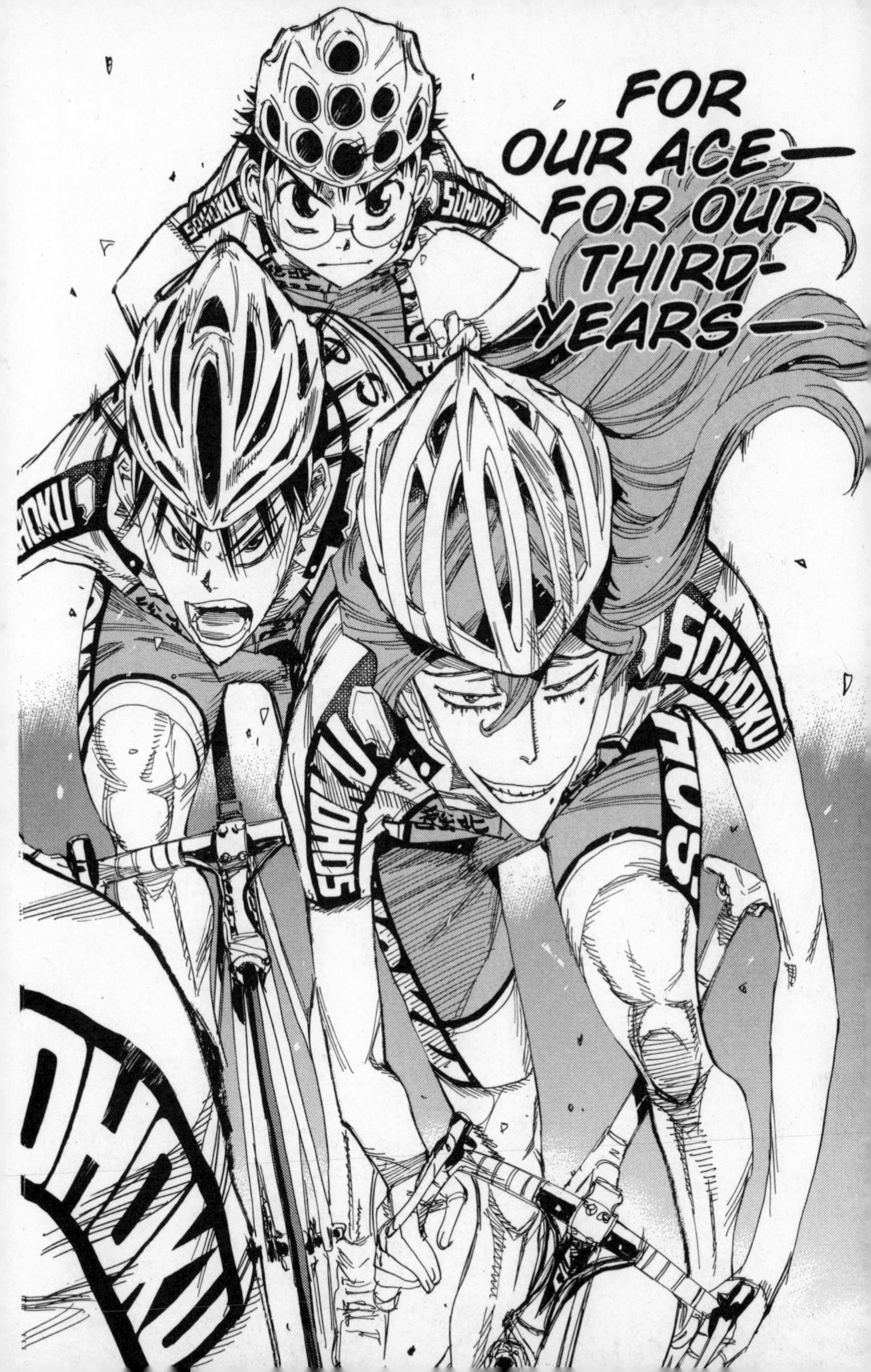
FOR OUR ACE—
FOR OUR THIRD-YEARS—

RIDE.181 CATCH UP!!!

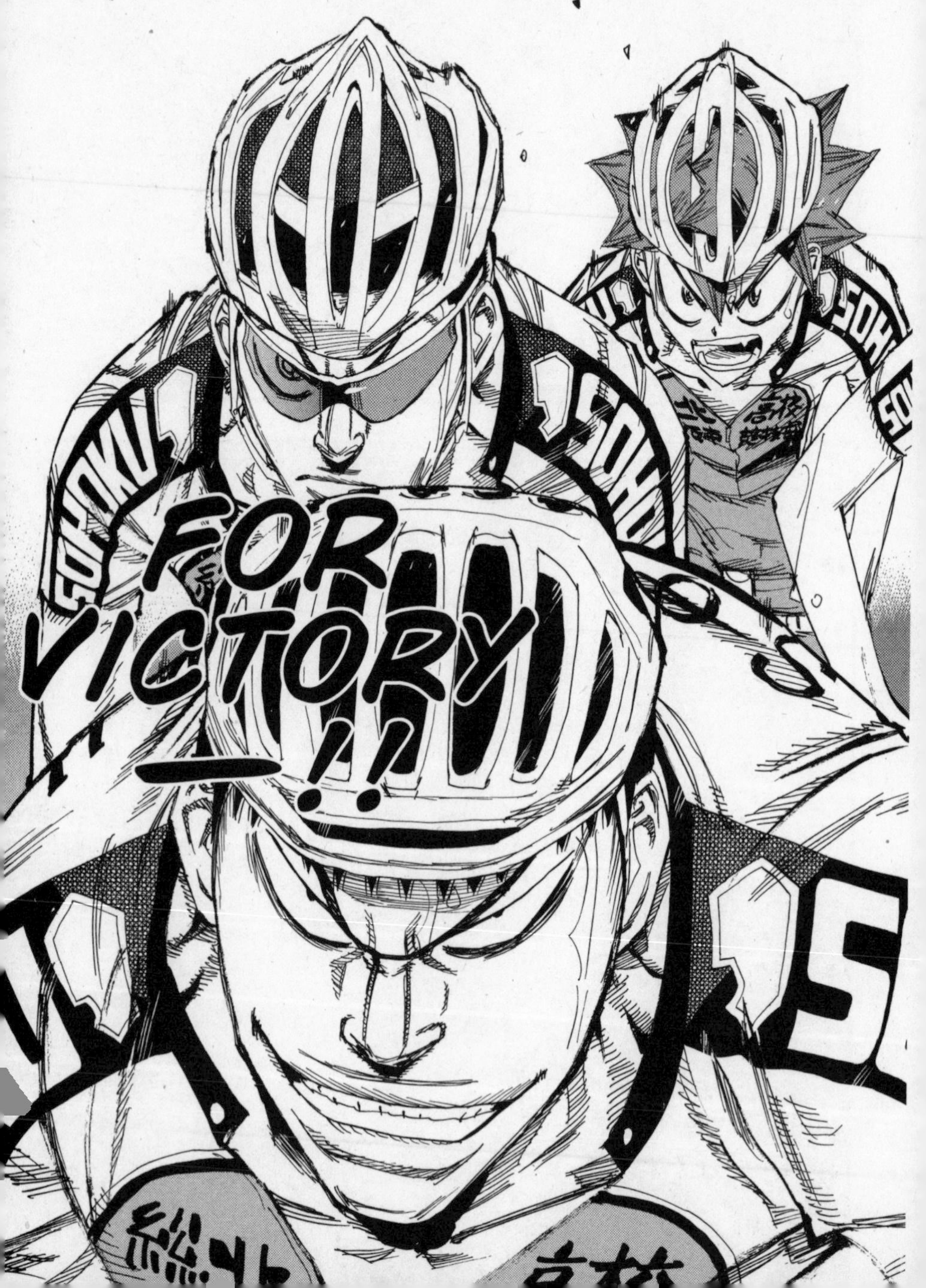
FOR VICTORY—!!

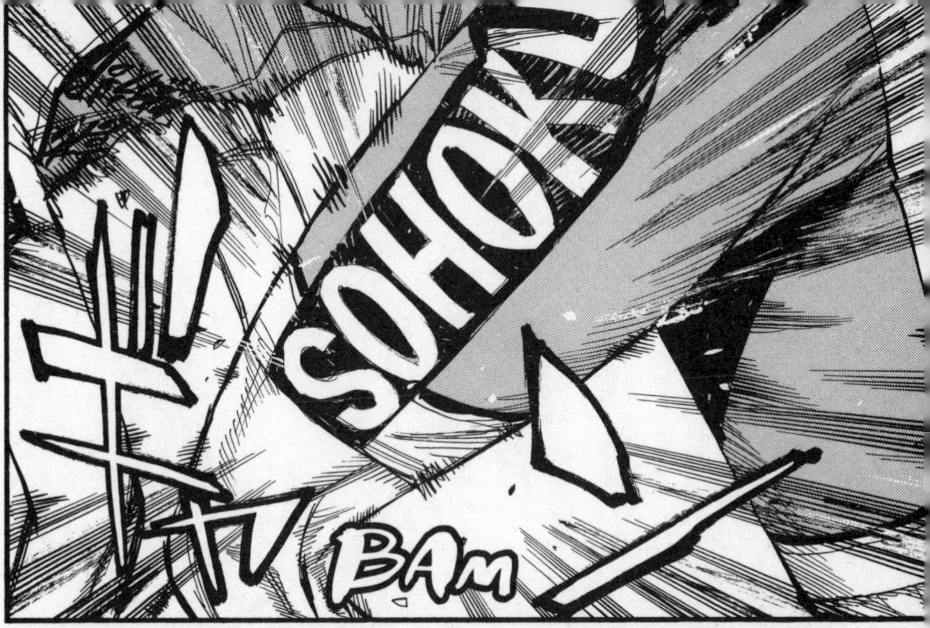
SOHOK
BAM
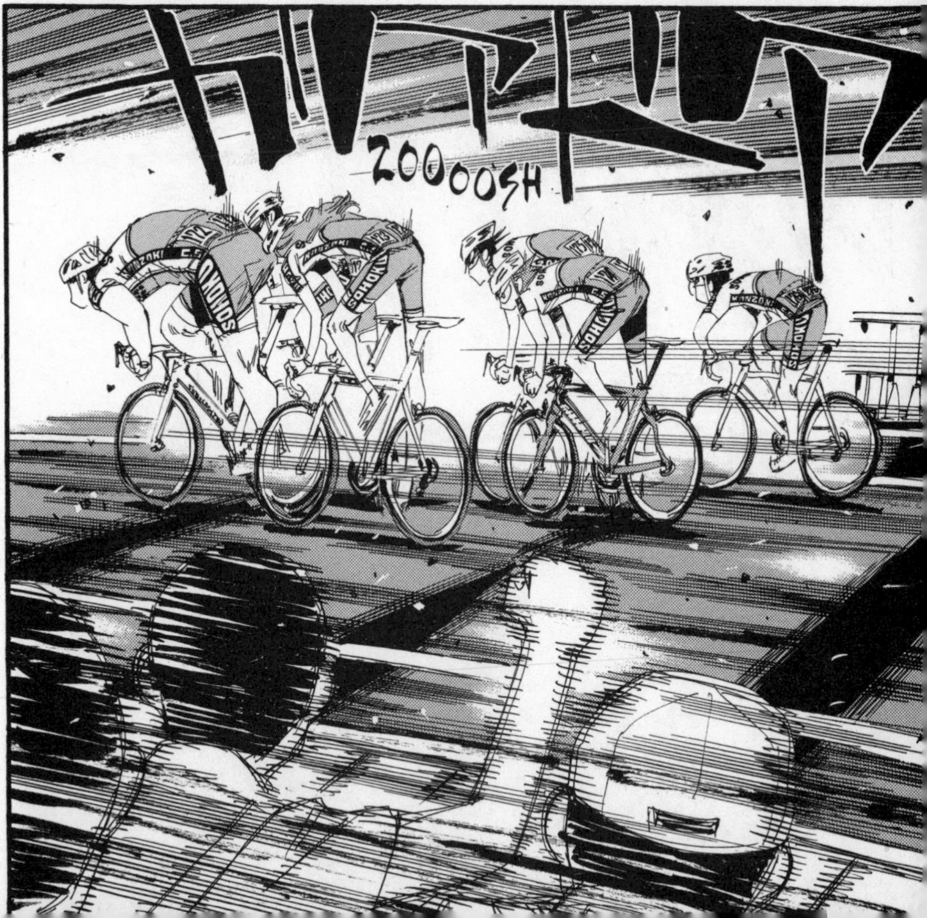
ZOOOOSH

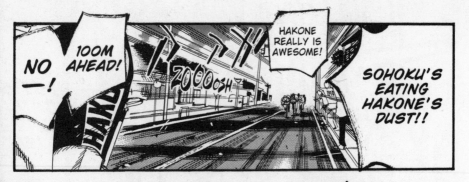

NO—! 100M AHEAD!

HAKONE REALLY IS AWESOME!

SOHOKU'S EATING HAKONE'S DUST!!

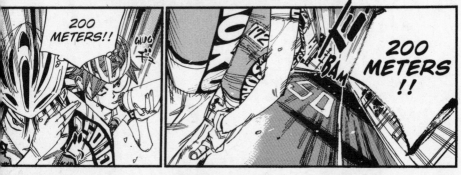

200 METERS!!

GHUG

BAM

200 METERS!!

CHAK

FLEK

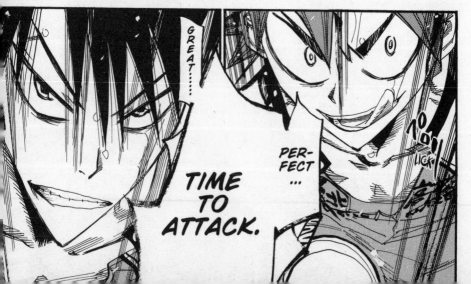

GREAT.....

TIME TO ATTACK.

PER-FECT...

LICK

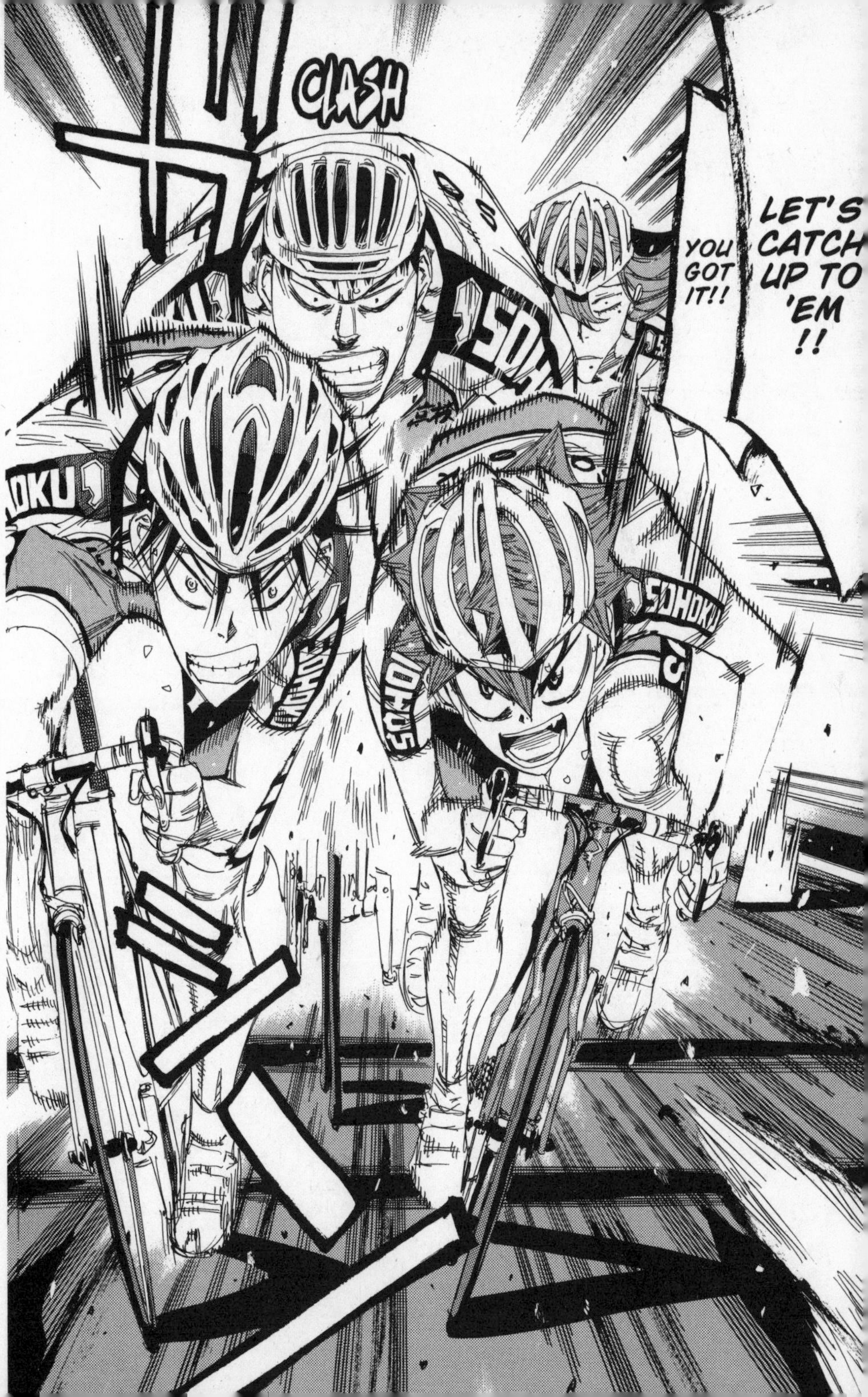
LET'S CATCH UP TO 'EM!!
YOU GOT IT!!
CLASH

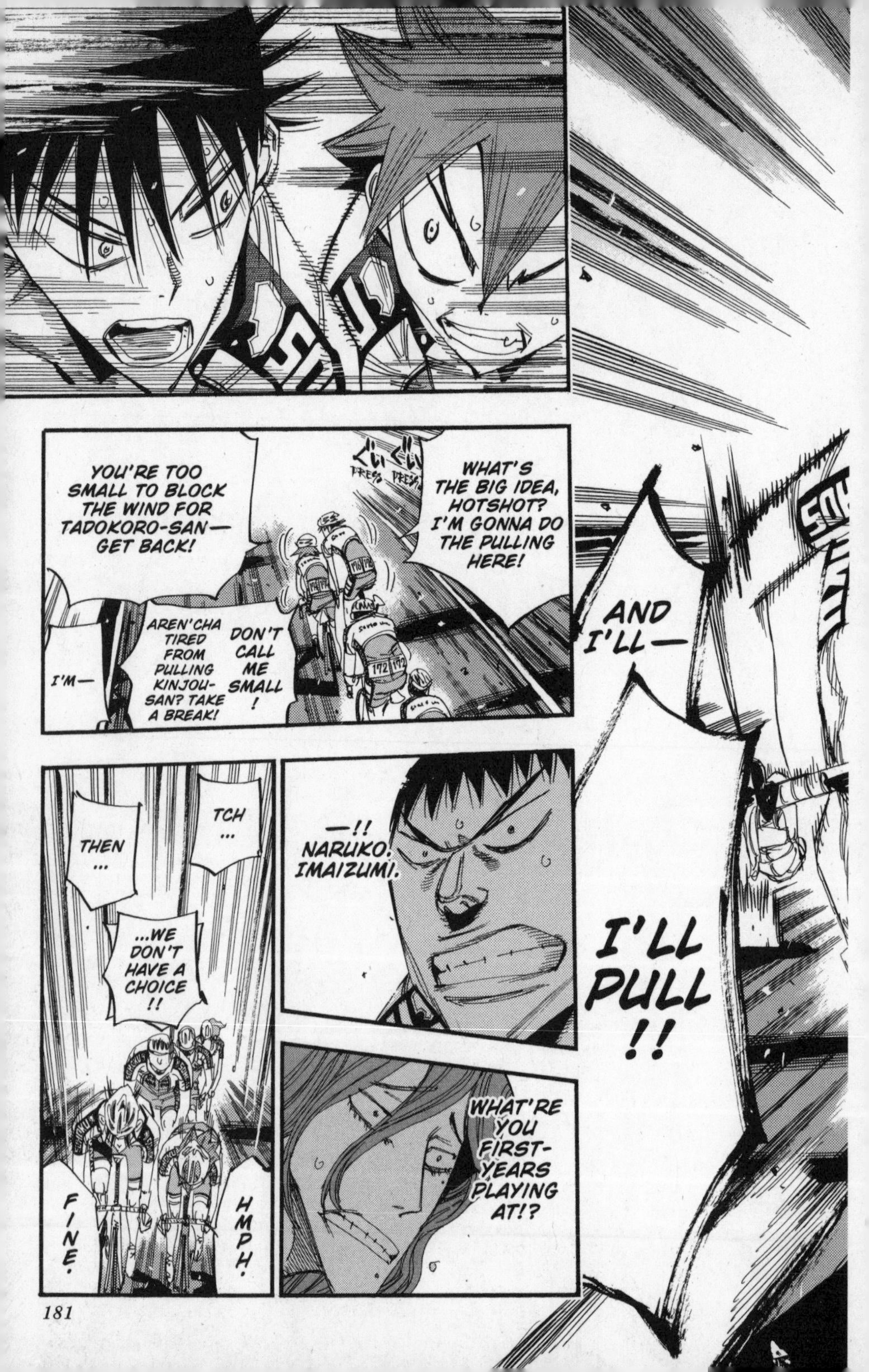
AND I'LL—
I'LL PULL!!
WHAT'S THE BIG IDEA, HOTSHOT? I'M GONNA DO THE PULLING HERE!
PRESS PRESS
YOU'RE TOO SMALL TO BLOCK THE WIND FOR TADOKORO-SAN—GET BACK!
DON'T CALL ME SMALL!
AREN'CHA TIRED FROM PULLING KINJOU-SAN? TAKE A BREAK!
I'M—
—!! NARUKO. IMAIZUMI.
WHAT'RE YOU FIRST-YEARS PLAYING AT!?
TCH...
THEN...
...WE DON'T HAVE A CHOICE!!
HMPH.
FINE.

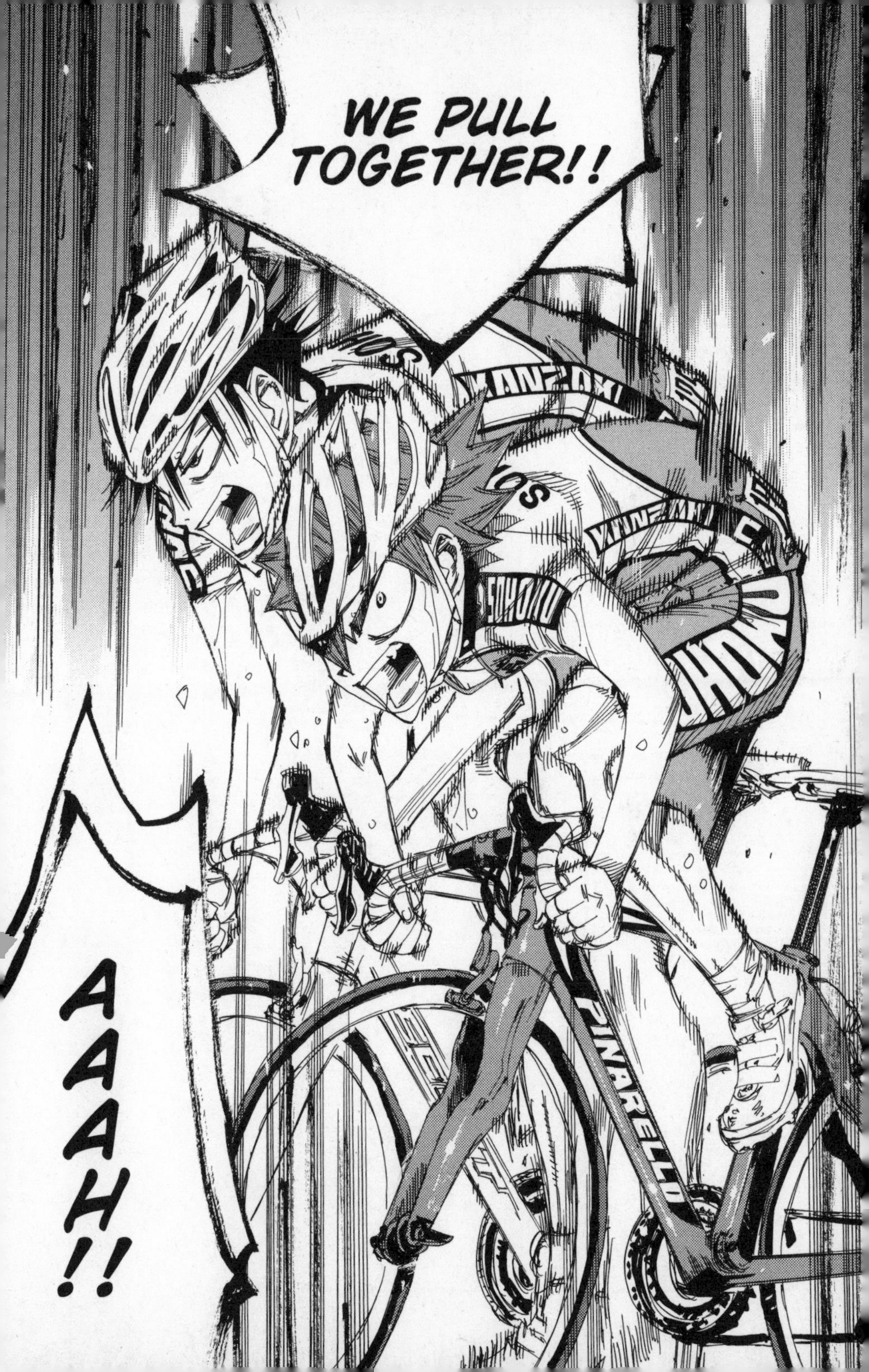
WE PULL TOGETHER!!
AAAAH!!
PINARELLO

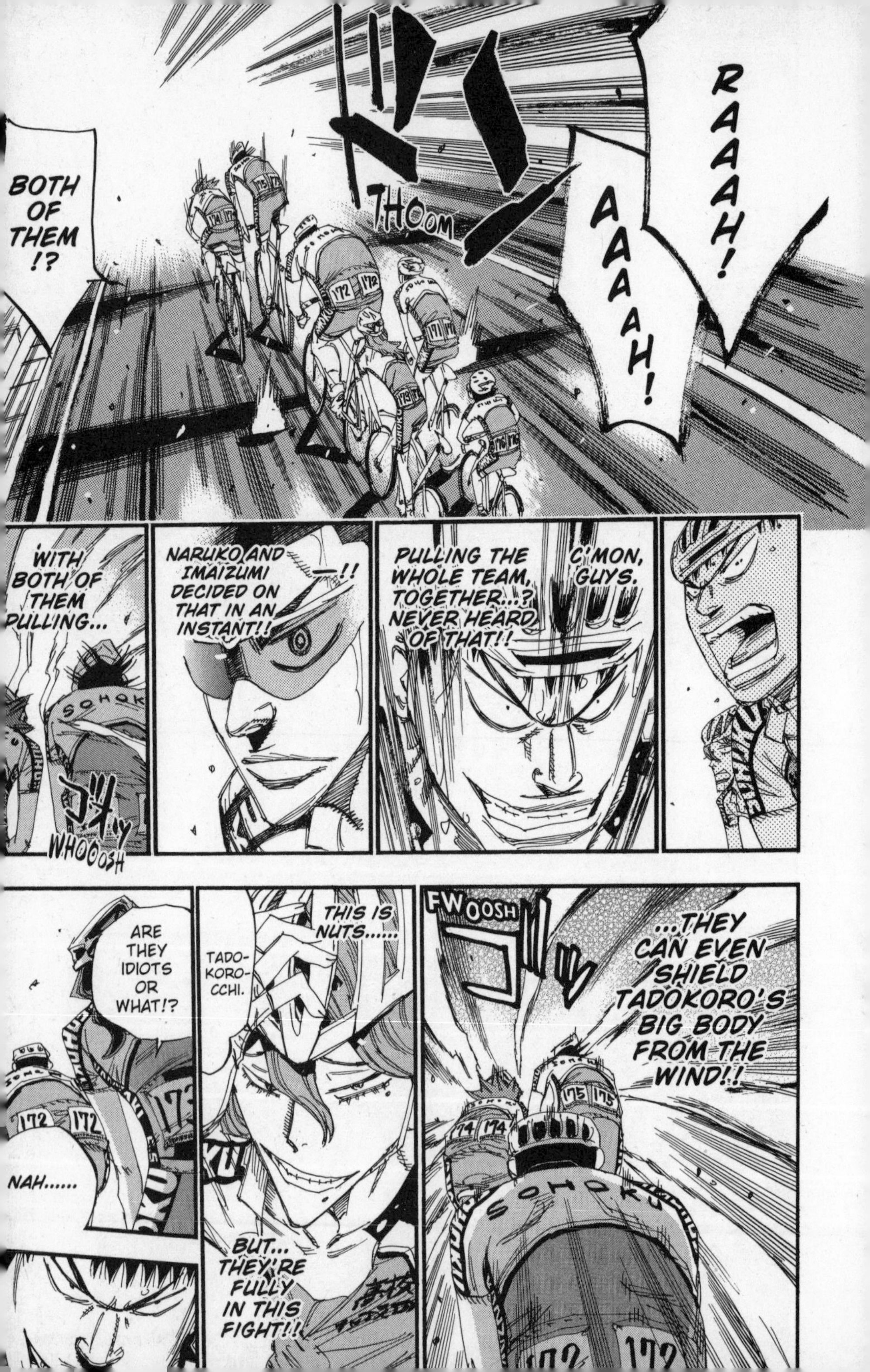
RAAAH!
AAAAH!
THOOM
BOTH OF THEM !?
C'MON, GUYS.
PULLING THE WHOLE TEAM, TOGETHER...? NEVER HEARD OF THAT!!
—!!
NARUKO AND IMAIZUMI DECIDED ON THAT IN AN INSTANT!!
WITH BOTH OF THEM PULLING...
WHOOOSH
FWOOSH
...THEY CAN EVEN SHIELD TADOKORO'S BIG BODY FROM THE WIND!!
THIS IS NUTS......
TADOKOROCCHI.
BUT... THEY'RE FULLY IN THIS FIGHT!!
ARE THEY IDIOTS OR WHAT!?
NAH......

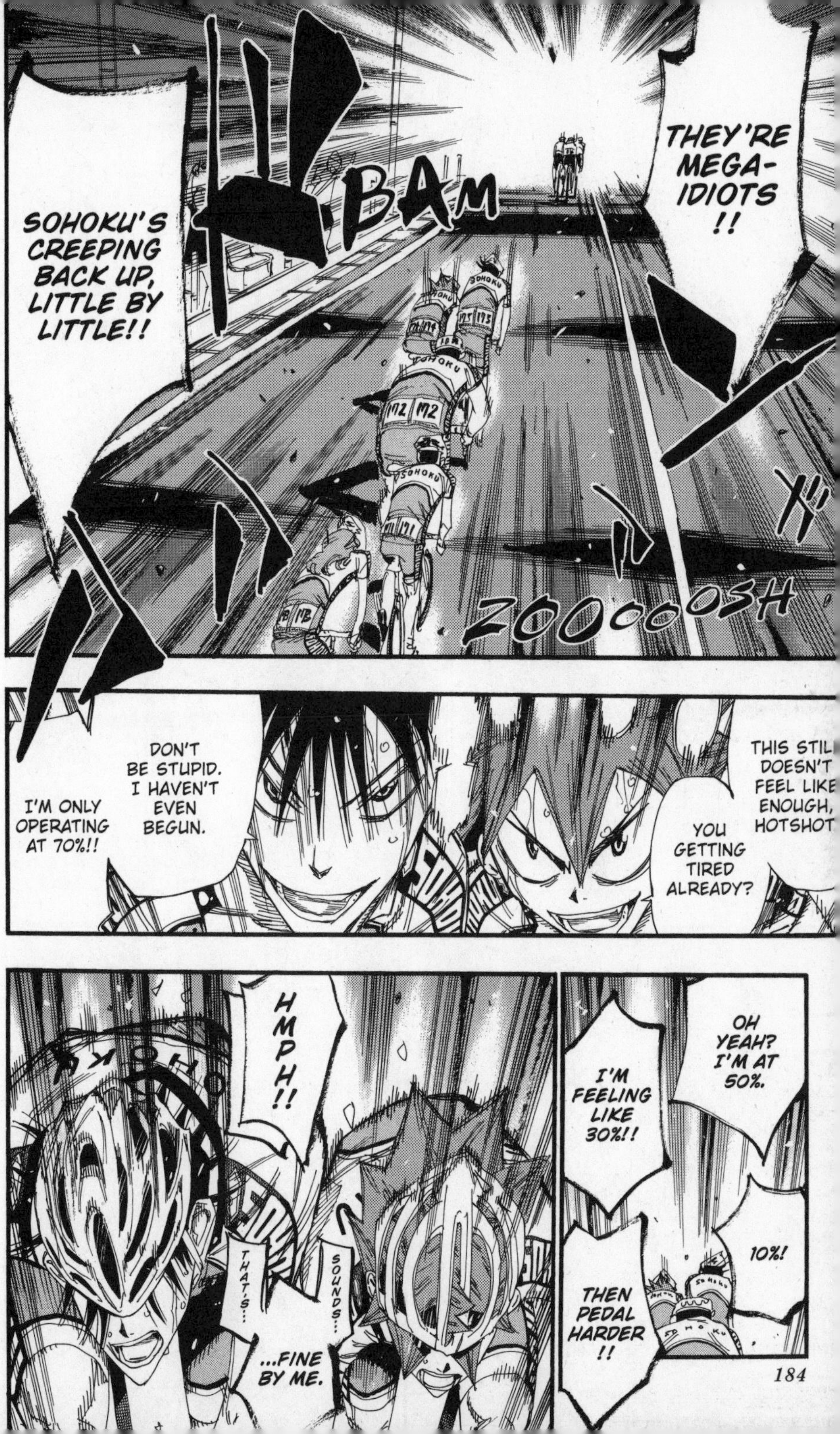
THEY'RE MEGA-IDIOTS!!
BAM
SOHOKU'S CREEPING BACK UP, LITTLE BY LITTLE!!
ZOOOOOOSH
THIS STIL DOESN'T FEEL LIKE ENOUGH, HOTSHOT
YOU GETTING TIRED ALREADY?
DON'T BE STUPID. I HAVEN'T EVEN BEGUN.
I'M ONLY OPERATING AT 70%!!
OH YEAH? I'M AT 50%.
I'M FEELING LIKE 30%!!
10%!
THEN PEDAL HARDER!!
HMPH!!
SOUNDS...
THAT'S...
...FINE BY ME.

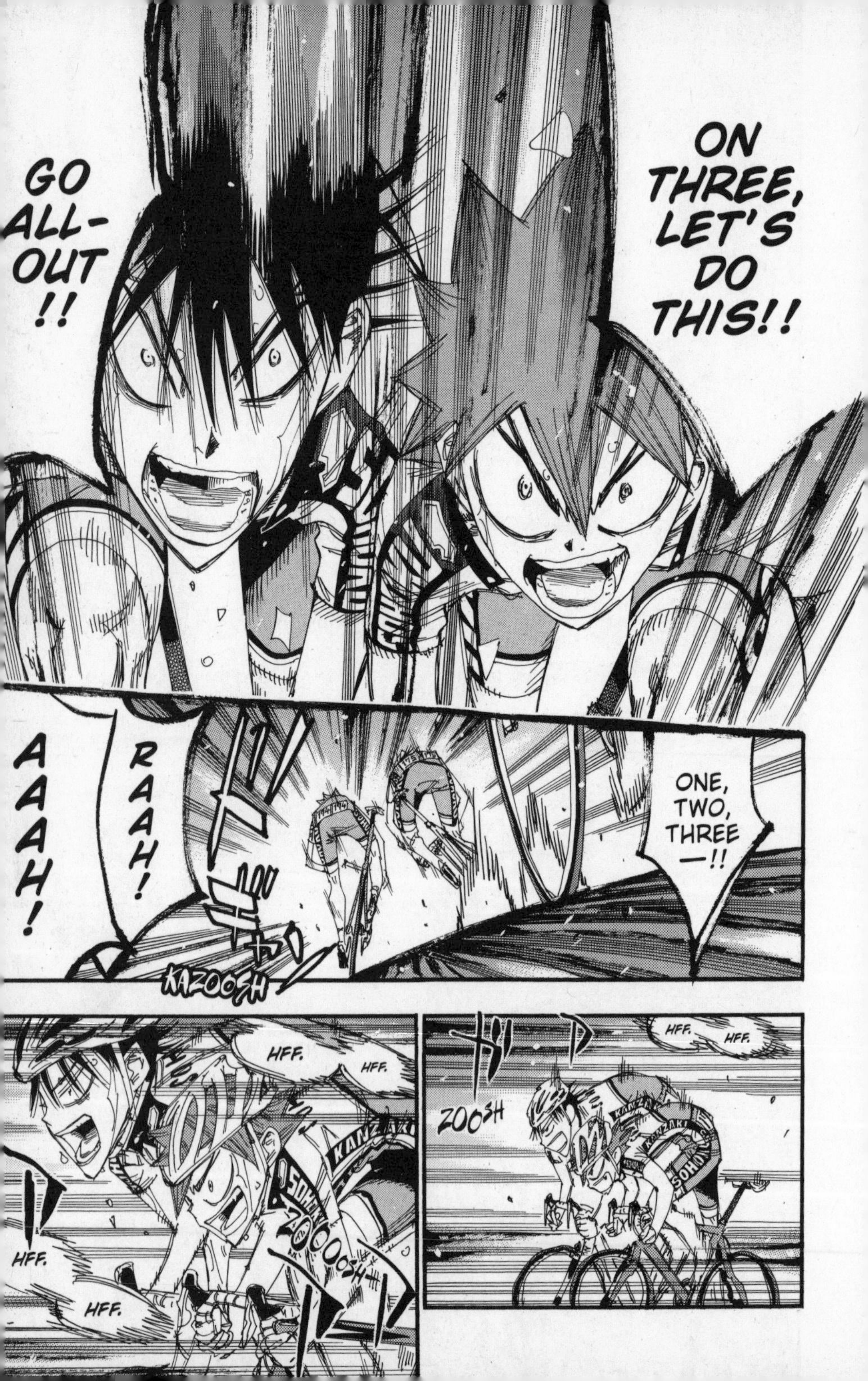
ON THREE, LET'S DO THIS!!
GO ALL-OUT!!
ONE, TWO, THREE—!!
RAAH!
AAAAH!
KAZOOSH
HFF.
HFF.
ZOOSH
HFF.
HFF.
ZOOOOSH
HFF.
HFF.

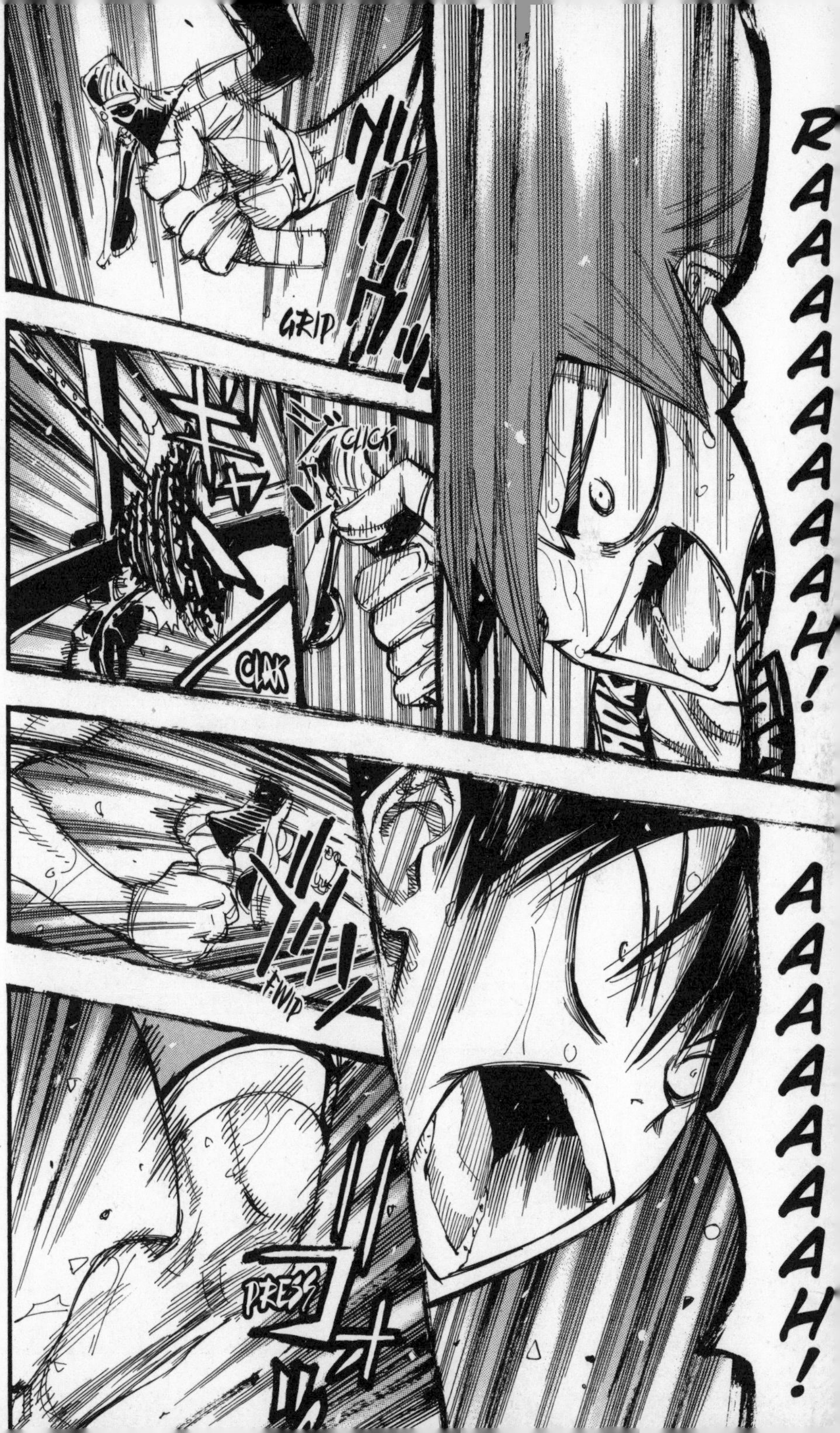
RAAAAAAAAH!
GRIP
CLICK
CLAK
AAAAAAAAAAH!
FWIP
PRESS

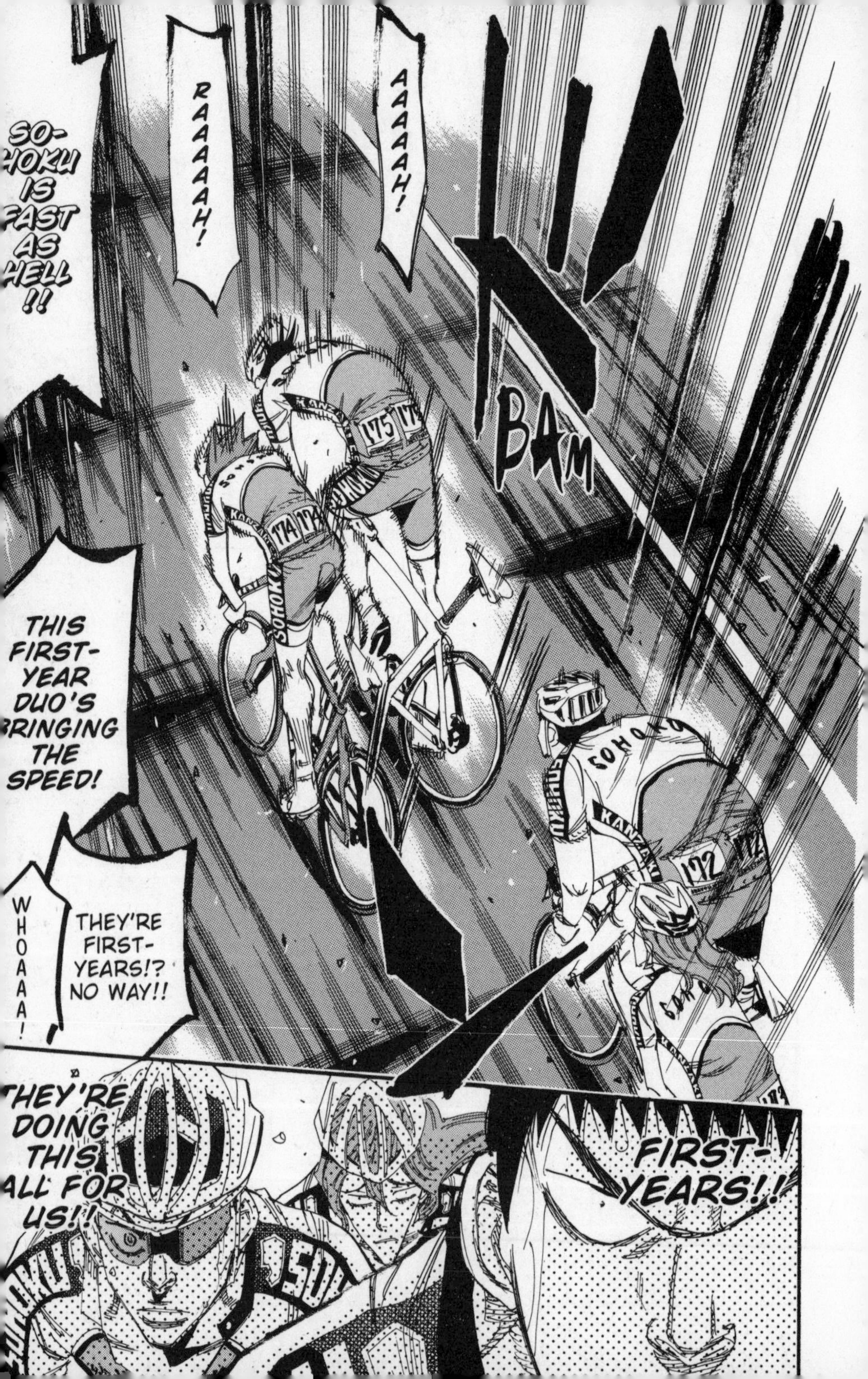
AAAAAAH!
RAAAAAAH!
BAM
SO-HOKU IS FAST AS HELL!!
THIS FIRST-YEAR DUO'S BRINGING THE SPEED!
THEY'RE FIRST-YEARS!? NO WAY!!
WHOAAAA!
FIRST-YEARS!!
THEY'RE DOING THIS ALL FOR US!!

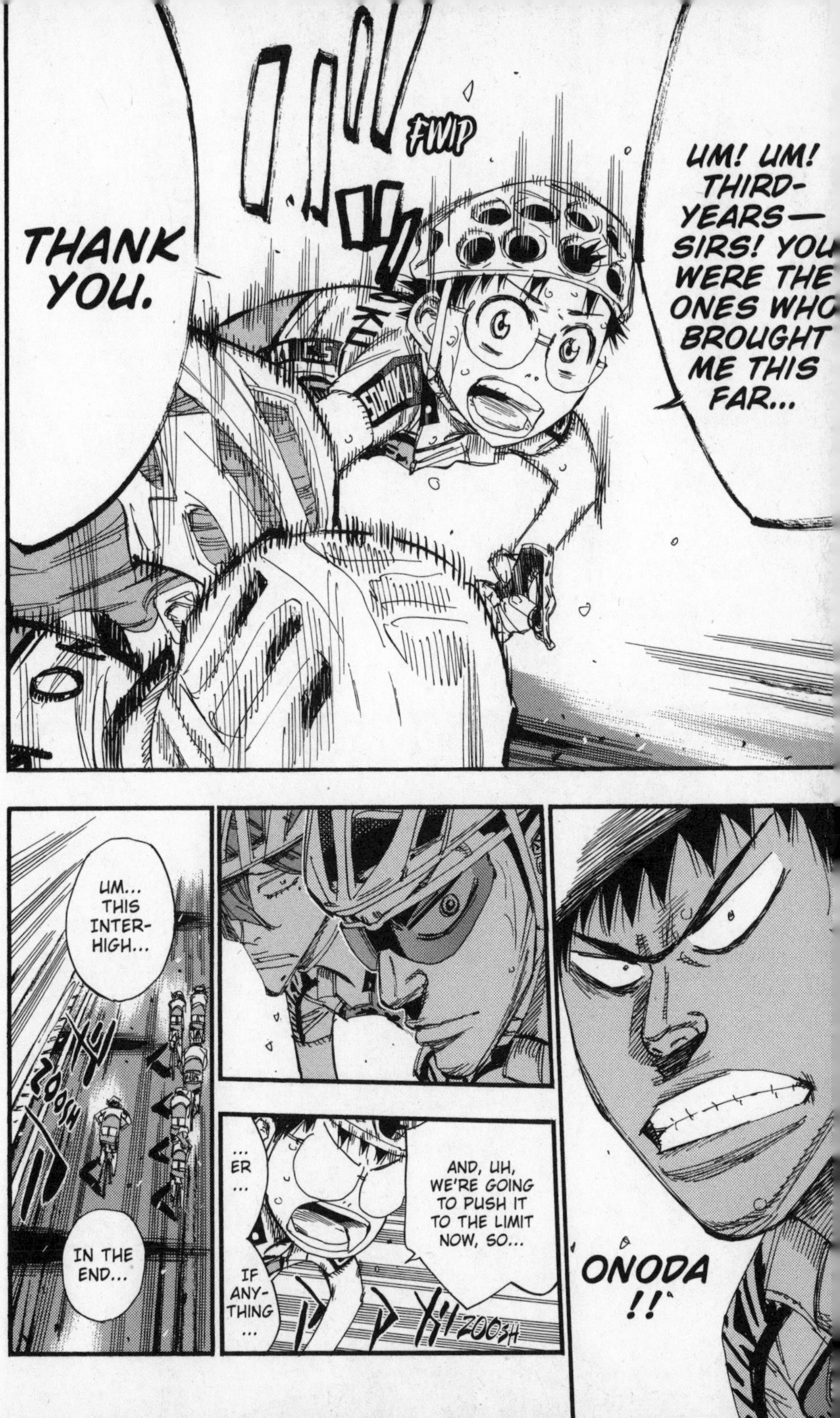
UM! UM! THIRD-YEARS—SIRS! YOU WERE THE ONES WHO BROUGHT ME THIS FAR...
FWIP
THANK YOU.
ONODA!!
AND, UH, WE'RE GOING TO PUSH IT TO THE LIMIT NOW, SO...
...ER...
IF ANYTHING...
ZOOSH
UM... THIS INTER-HIGH...
ZOOSH
IN THE END...

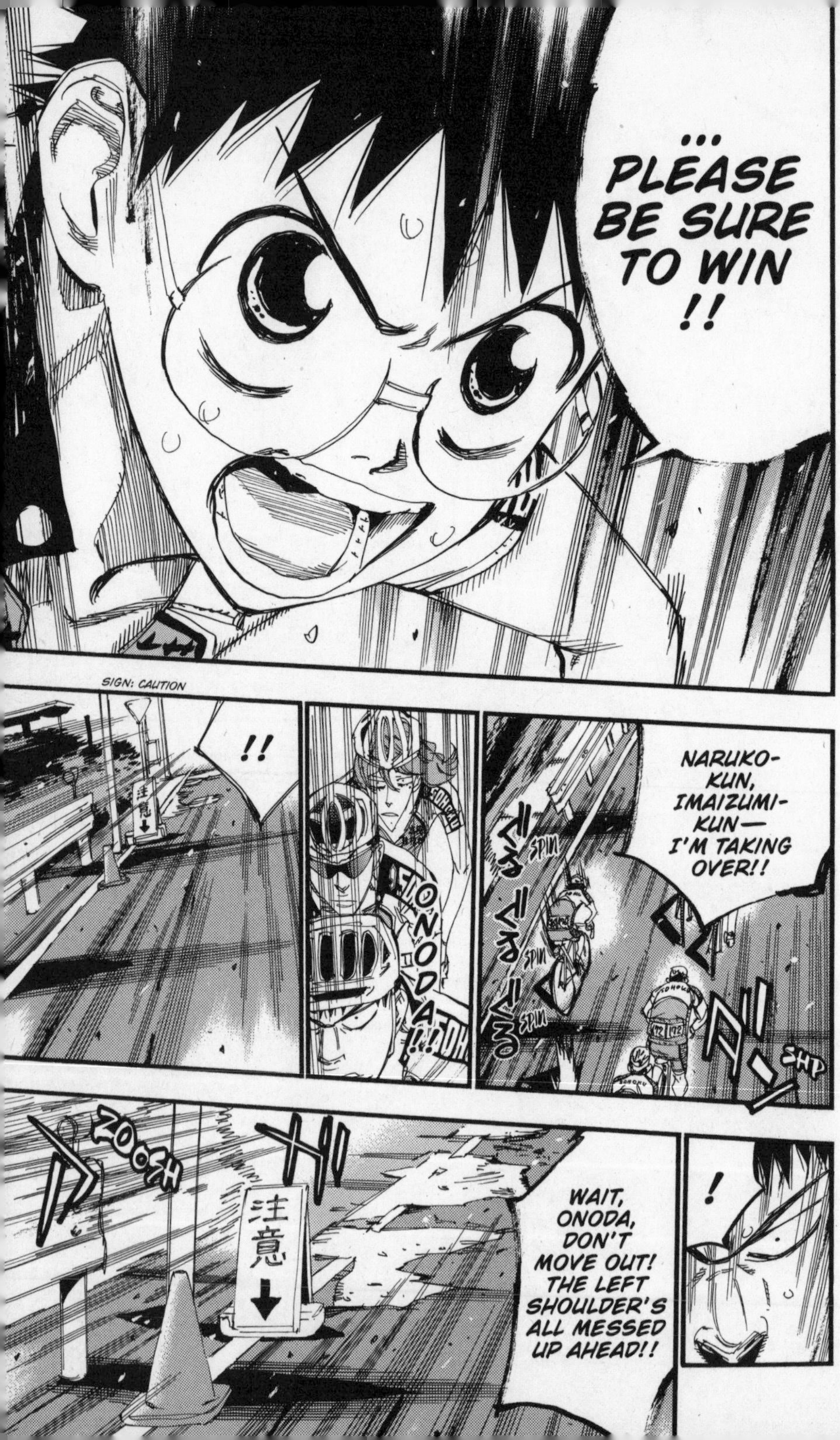
...PLEASE BE SURE TO WIN!!
NARUKO-KUN, IMAIZUMI-KUN— I'M TAKING OVER!!
SPIN
SPIN
SPIN
SHP
ONODA!!
!!
SIGN: CAUTION
注意
!
WAIT, ONODA, DON'T MOVE OUT! THE LEFT SHOULDER'S ALL MESSED UP AHEAD!!
ZOOSH
注意

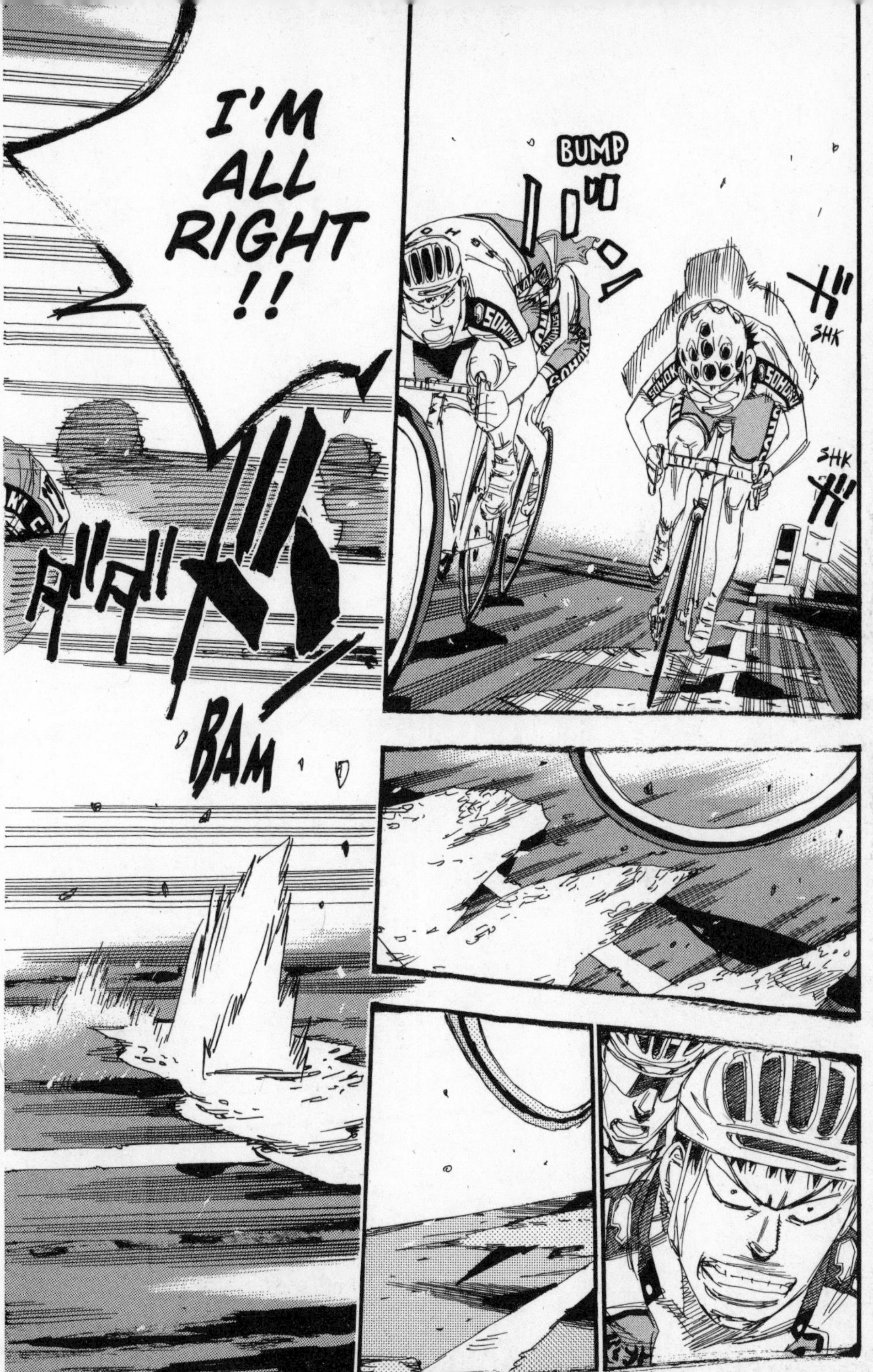
BUMP
SHK
SHK
I'M ALL RIGHT!!
BAM

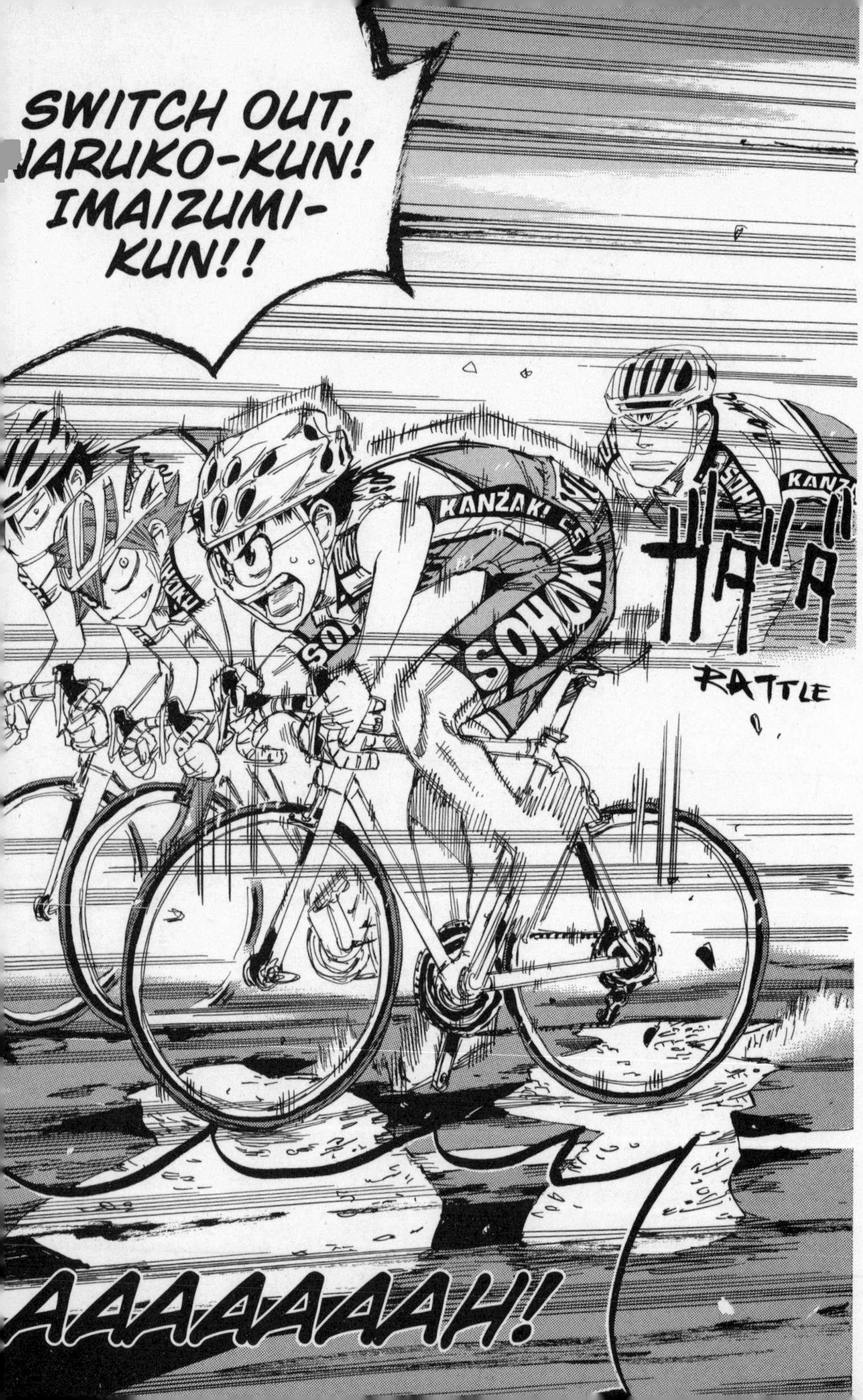
SWITCH OUT, NARUKO-KUN! IMAIZUMI-KUN!!
HA HA
RATTLE
AAAAAAAH!

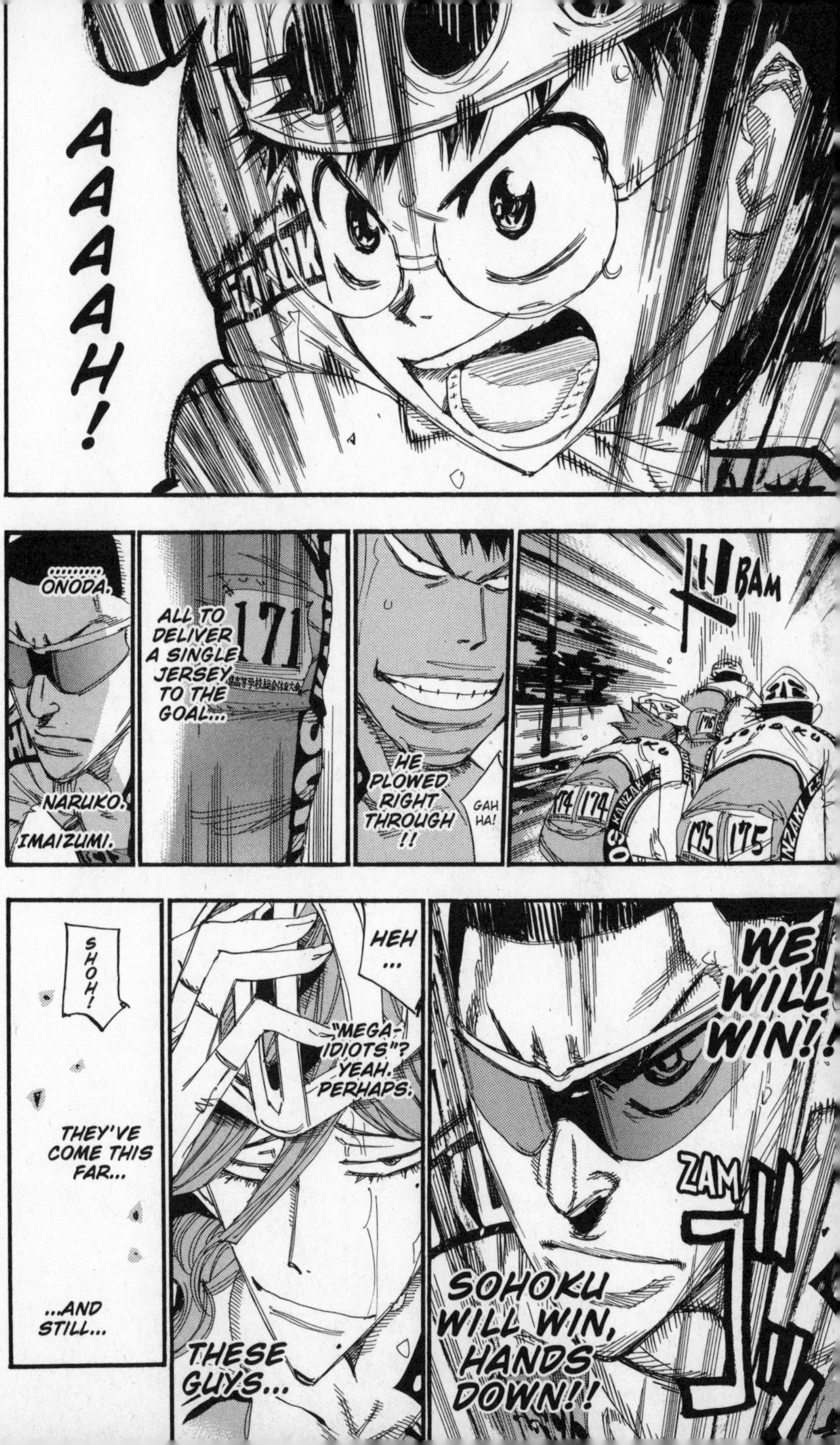
AAAAAH!
BAM
GAH HA!
HE PLOWED RIGHT THROUGH!!
ALL TO DELIVER A SINGLE JERSEY TO THE GOAL...
....
ONODA.
NARUKO.
IMAIZUMI.
WE WILL WIN!!
ZAM
SOHOKU WILL WIN, HANDS DOWN!!
HEH...
"MEGA-IDIOTS"? YEAH. PERHAPS.
THESE GUYS...
SHOH!
THEY'VE COME THIS FAR...
...AND STILL...

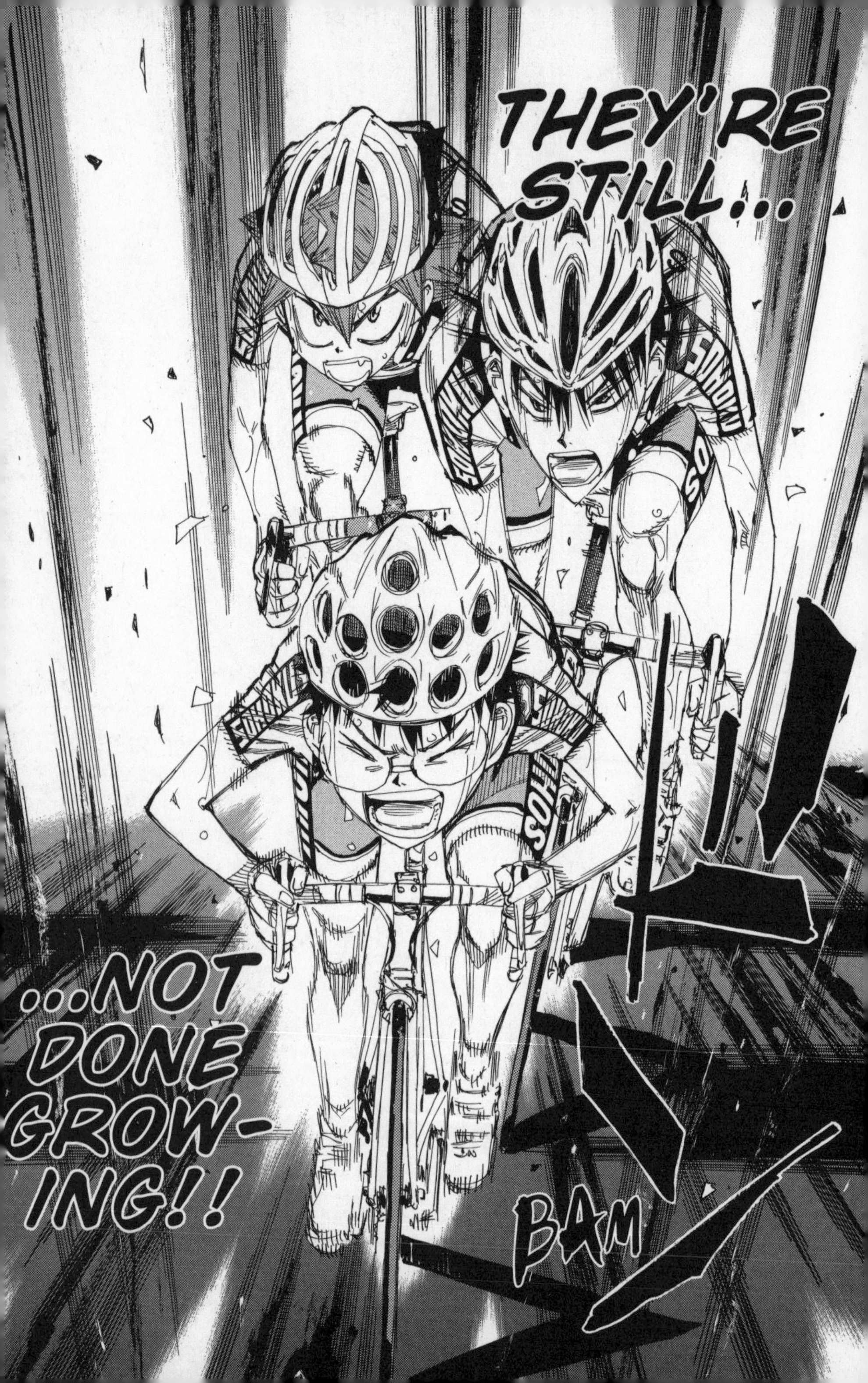
THEY'RE STILL...
...NOT DONE GROWING!!
BAM

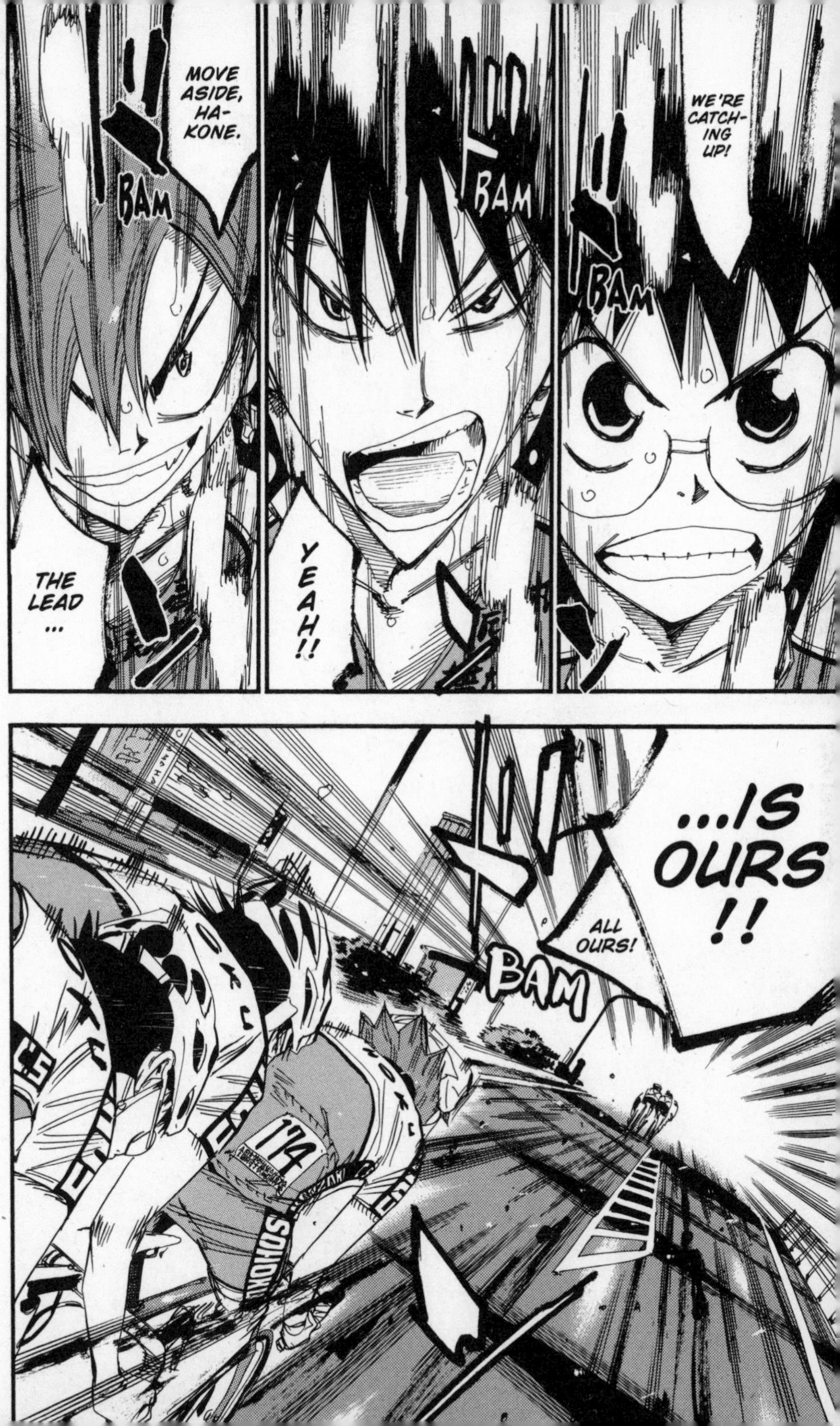
WE'RE CATCHING UP!
BAM
BAM
YEAH!!
MOVE ASIDE, HAKONE.
BAM
THE LEAD ...
...IS OURS!!
ALL OURS!
BAM

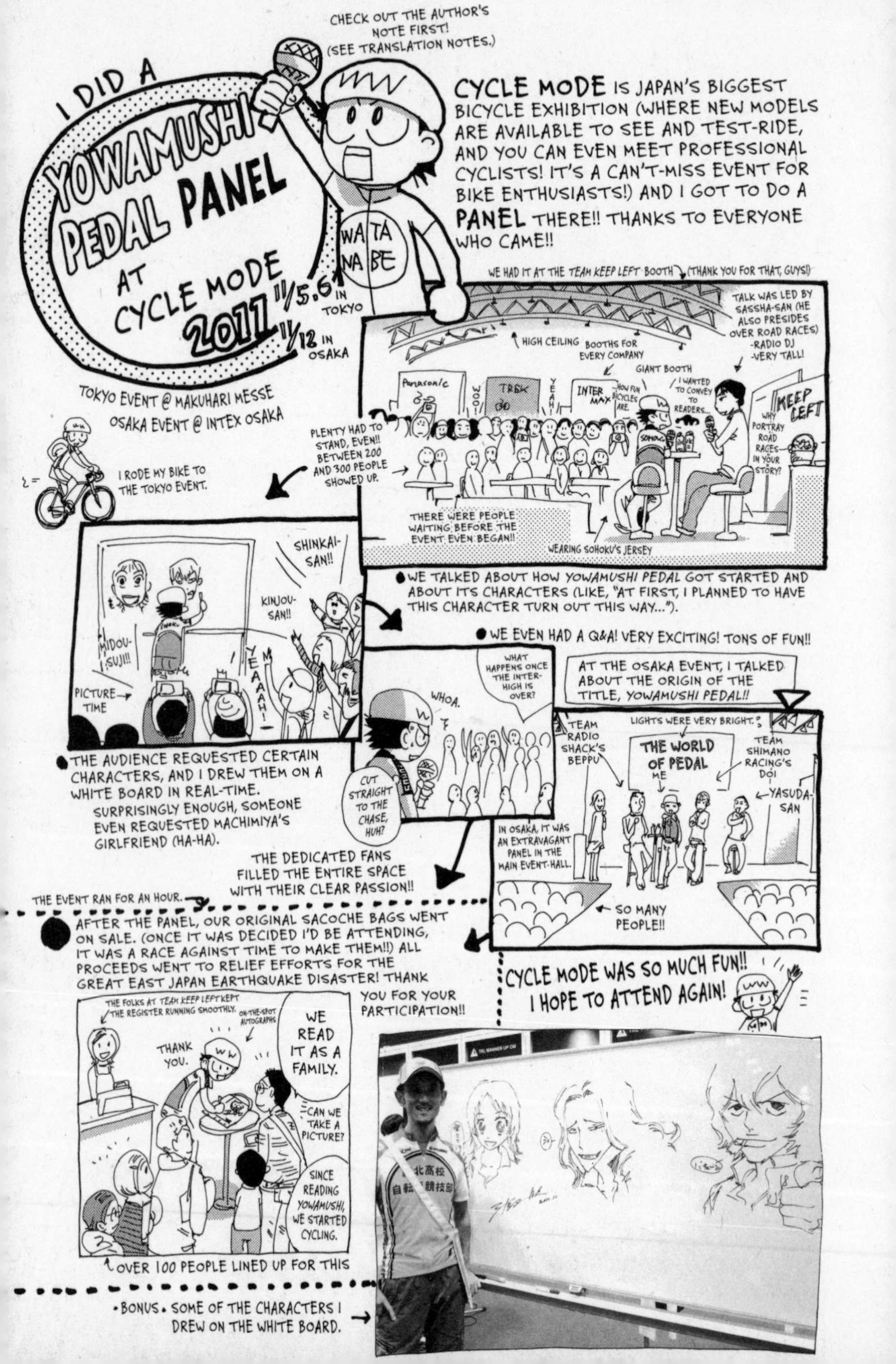

CHECK OUT THE AUTHOR'S NOTE FIRST! (SEE TRANSLATION NOTES.)
I DID A YOWAMUSHI PEDAL PANEL AT CYCLE MODE 2011 11/5.6 IN TOKYO 11/12 IN OSAKA
WATANABE
CYCLE MODE IS JAPAN'S BIGGEST BICYCLE EXHIBITION (WHERE NEW MODELS ARE AVAILABLE TO SEE AND TEST-RIDE, AND YOU CAN EVEN MEET PROFESSIONAL CYCLISTS! IT'S A CAN'T-MISS EVENT FOR BIKE ENTHUSIASTS!) AND I GOT TO DO A PANEL THERE!! THANKS TO EVERYONE WHO CAME!!
TOKYO EVENT @ MAKUHARI MESSE
OSAKA EVENT @ INTEX OSAKA
I RODE MY BIKE TO THE TOKYO EVENT.
WE HAD IT AT THE TEAM KEEP LEFT BOOTH (THANK YOU FOR THAT, GUYS!)
HIGH CEILING
BOOTHS FOR EVERY COMPANY
GIANT BOOTH
TALK WAS LED BY SASSHA-SAN (HE ALSO PRESIDES OVER ROAD RACES) -RADIO DJ -VERY TALL!
Panasonic
TREK
INTER MAX
WOO!
YEAH!
HOW FUN BICYCLES ARE.
I WANTED TO CONVEY TO READERS...
KEEP LEFT
WHY PORTRAY ROAD RACES IN YOUR STORY?
PLENTY HAD TO STAND, EVEN!! BETWEEN 200 AND 300 PEOPLE SHOWED UP.
THERE WERE PEOPLE WAITING BEFORE THE EVENT EVEN BEGAN!!
WEARING SOHOKU'S JERSEY
WE TALKED ABOUT HOW YOWAMUSHI PEDAL GOT STARTED AND ABOUT ITS CHARACTERS (LIKE, "AT FIRST, I PLANNED TO HAVE THIS CHARACTER TURN OUT THIS WAY...").
SHINKAI-SAN!!
KINJOU-SAN!!
MIDOU-SUJI!!!
YEAAAAH!
PICTURE TIME
THE AUDIENCE REQUESTED CERTAIN CHARACTERS, AND I DREW THEM ON A WHITE BOARD IN REAL-TIME.
SURPRISINGLY ENOUGH, SOMEONE EVEN REQUESTED MACHIMIYA'S GIRLFRIEND (HA-HA).
WE EVEN HAD A Q&A! VERY EXCITING! TONS OF FUN!!
WHAT HAPPENS ONCE THE INTER-HIGH IS OVER?
WHOA.
CUT STRAIGHT TO THE CHASE, HUH?
THE DEDICATED FANS FILLED THE ENTIRE SPACE WITH THEIR CLEAR PASSION!!
AT THE OSAKA EVENT, I TALKED ABOUT THE ORIGIN OF THE TITLE, YOWAMUSHI PEDAL!!
LIGHTS WERE VERY BRIGHT.
TEAM RADIO SHACK'S BEPPU
THE WORLD OF PEDAL
ME
TEAM SHIMANO RACING'S DOI
YASUDA-SAN
IN OSAKA, IT WAS AN EXTRAVAGANT PANEL IN THE MAIN EVENT-HALL.
SO MANY PEOPLE!!
THE EVENT RAN FOR AN HOUR.
AFTER THE PANEL, OUR ORIGINAL SACOCHE BAGS WENT ON SALE. (ONCE IT WAS DECIDED I'D BE ATTENDING, IT WAS A RACE AGAINST TIME TO MAKE THEM!!) ALL PROCEEDS WENT TO RELIEF EFFORTS FOR THE GREAT EAST JAPAN EARTHQUAKE DISASTER! THANK YOU FOR YOUR PARTICIPATION!!
THE FOLKS AT TEAM KEEP LEFT KEPT THE REGISTER RUNNING SMOOTHLY.
ON-THE-SPOT AUTOGRAPHS
THANK YOU.
WE READ IT AS A FAMILY.
CAN WE TAKE A PICTURE?
SINCE READING YOWAMUSHI, WE STARTED CYCLING.
OVER 100 PEOPLE LINED UP FOR THIS
CYCLE MODE WAS SO MUCH FUN!! I HOPE TO ATTEND AGAIN!
•BONUS• SOME OF THE CHARACTERS I DREW ON THE WHITE BOARD.

YOWAMUSHI PEDAL

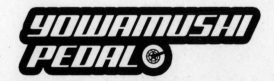

RIDE.182 CULLING

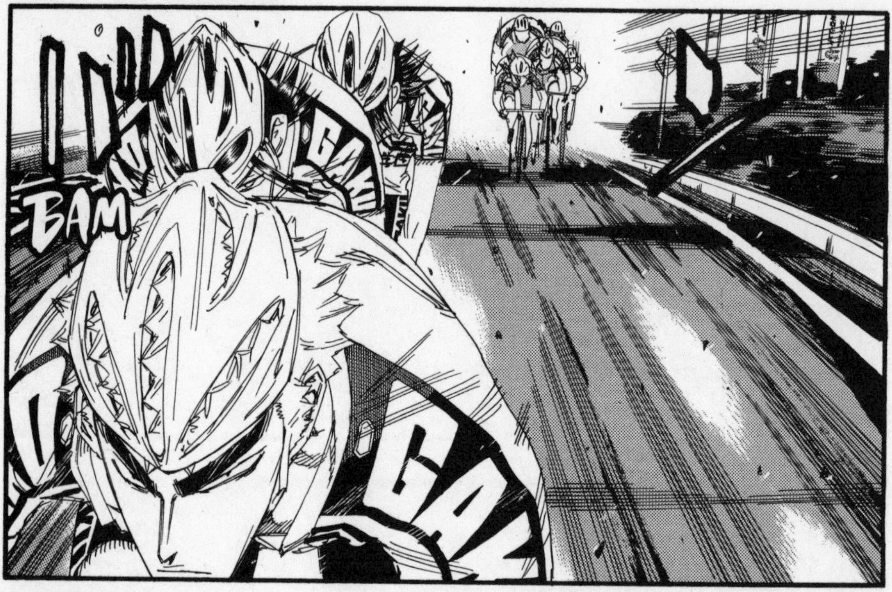
DDDD
BAM
D

SIGN: 28KM TO GOAL

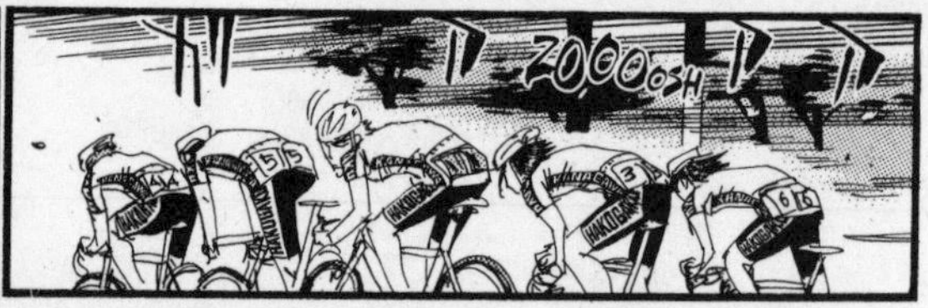
ZOOOOSH

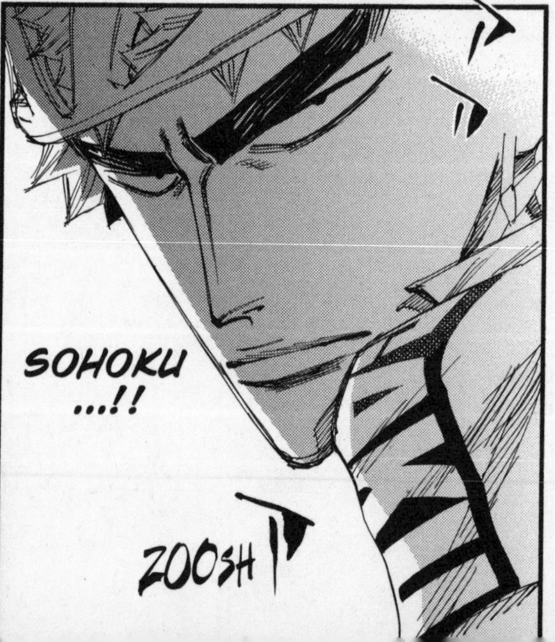
SOHOKU ...!!
ZOOSH

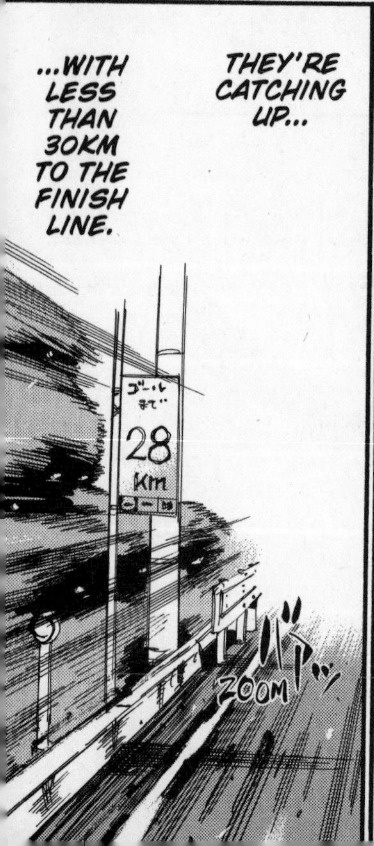
THEY'RE CATCHING UP...
...WITH LESS THAN 30KM TO THE FINISH LINE.
28 Km
ZOOM

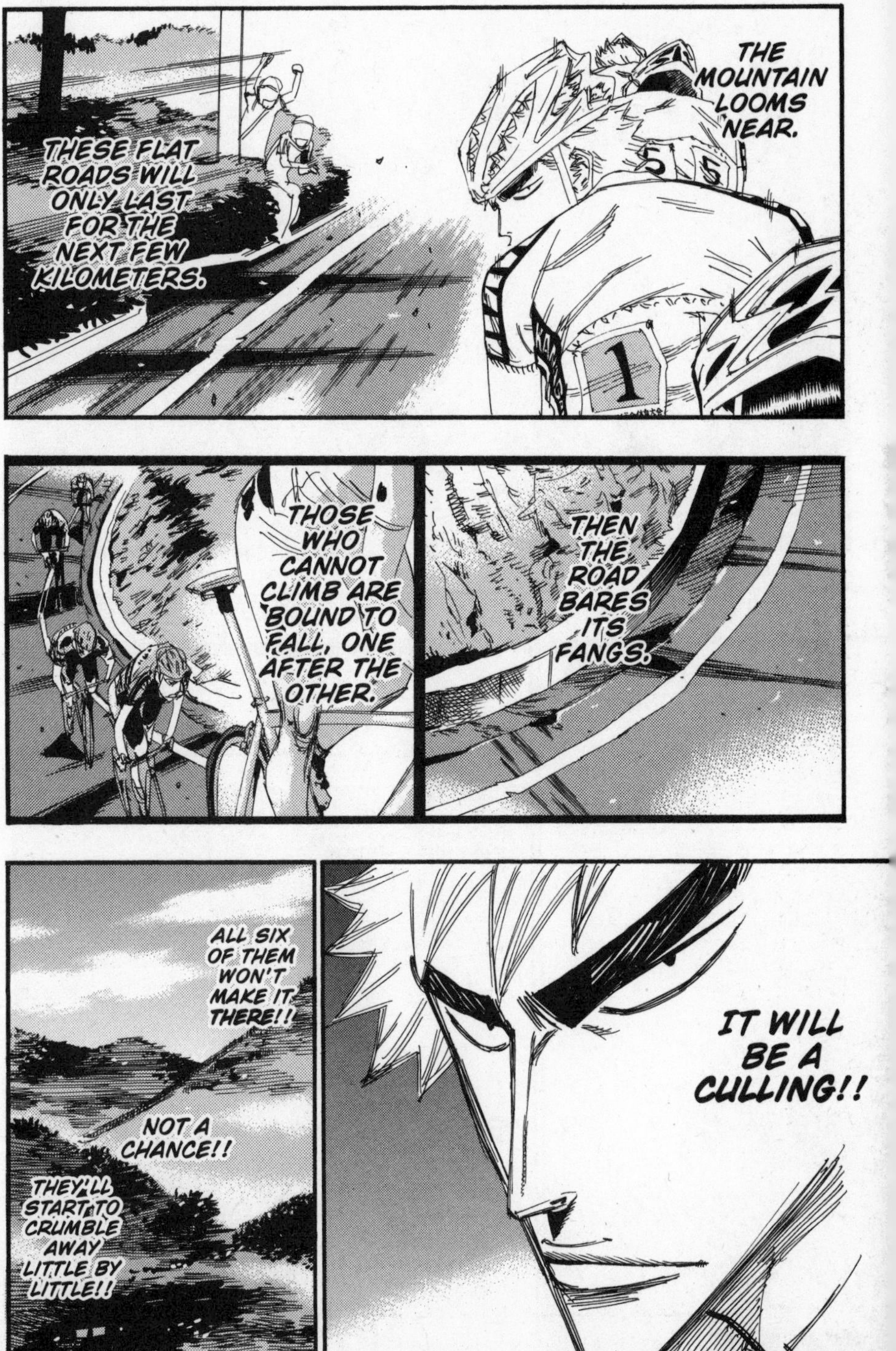
THE MOUNTAIN LOOMS NEAR.
THESE FLAT ROADS WILL ONLY LAST FOR THE NEXT FEW KILOMETERS.
THEN THE ROAD BARES ITS FANGS.
THOSE WHO CANNOT CLIMB ARE BOUND TO FALL, ONE AFTER THE OTHER.
IT WILL BE A CULLING!!
ALL SIX OF THEM WON'T MAKE IT THERE!!
NOT A CHANCE!!
THEY'LL START TO CRUMBLE AWAY LITTLE BY LITTLE!!

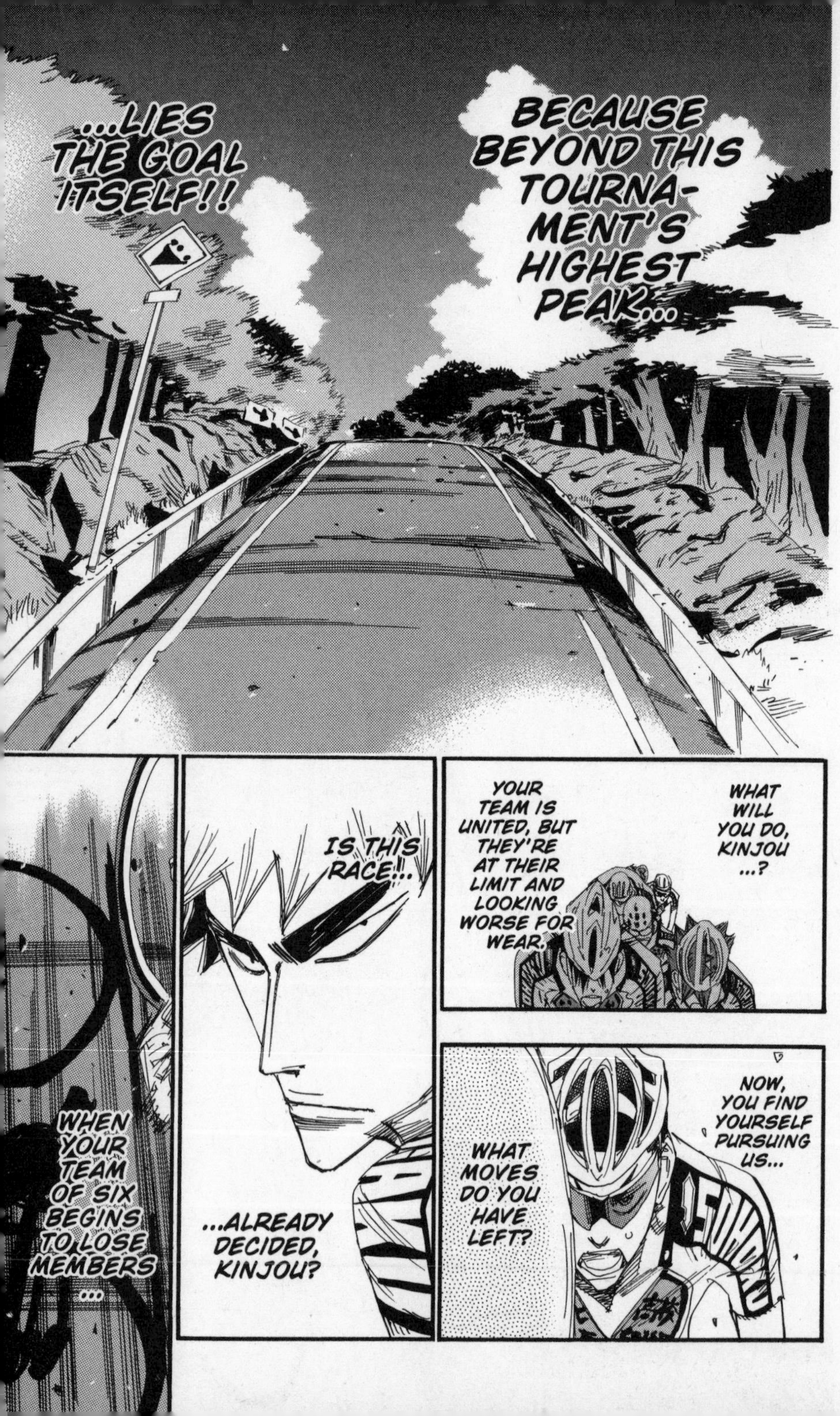
BECAUSE BEYOND THIS TOURNA-MENT'S HIGHEST PEAK...
...LIES THE GOAL ITSELF!!
WHAT WILL YOU DO, KINJOU ...?
YOUR TEAM IS UNITED, BUT THEY'RE AT THEIR LIMIT AND LOOKING WORSE FOR WEAR.
NOW, YOU FIND YOURSELF PURSUING US...
WHAT MOVES DO YOU HAVE LEFT?
IS THIS RACE...
...ALREADY DECIDED, KINJOU?
WHEN YOUR TEAM OF SIX BEGINS TO LOSE MEMBERS...

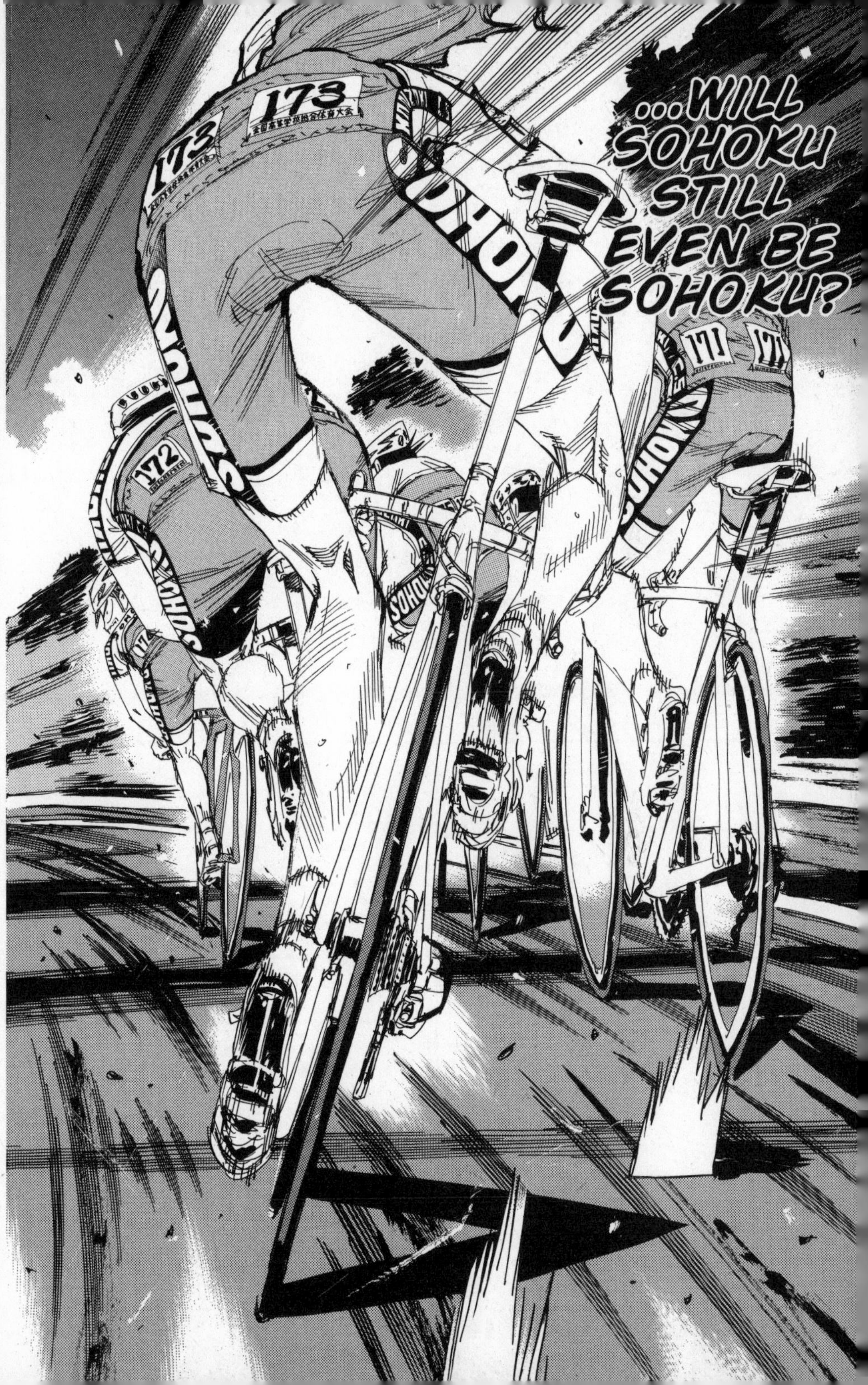
...WILL SOHOKU STILL EVEN BE SOHOKU?

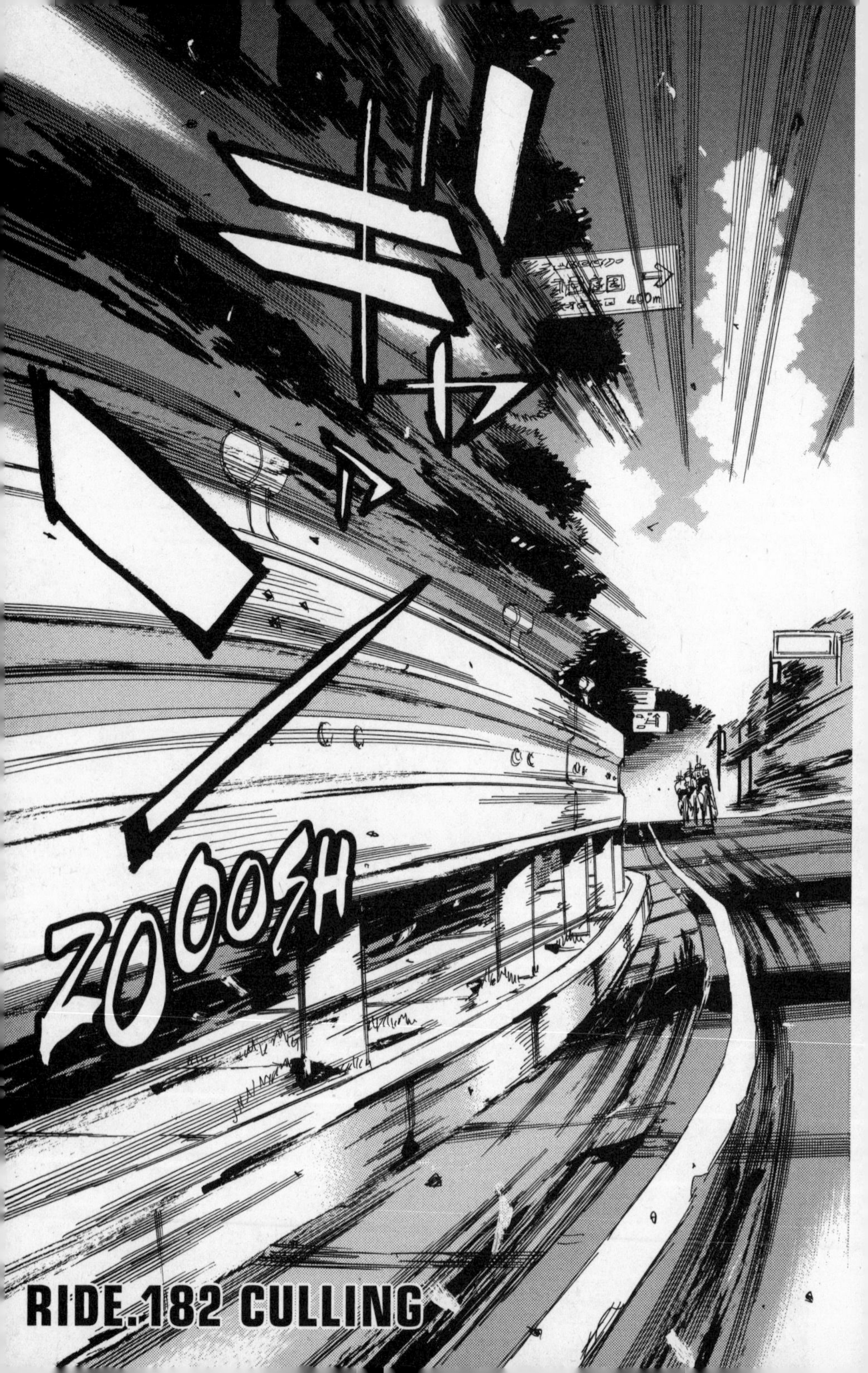
ZOOOSH

RIDE.182 CULLING

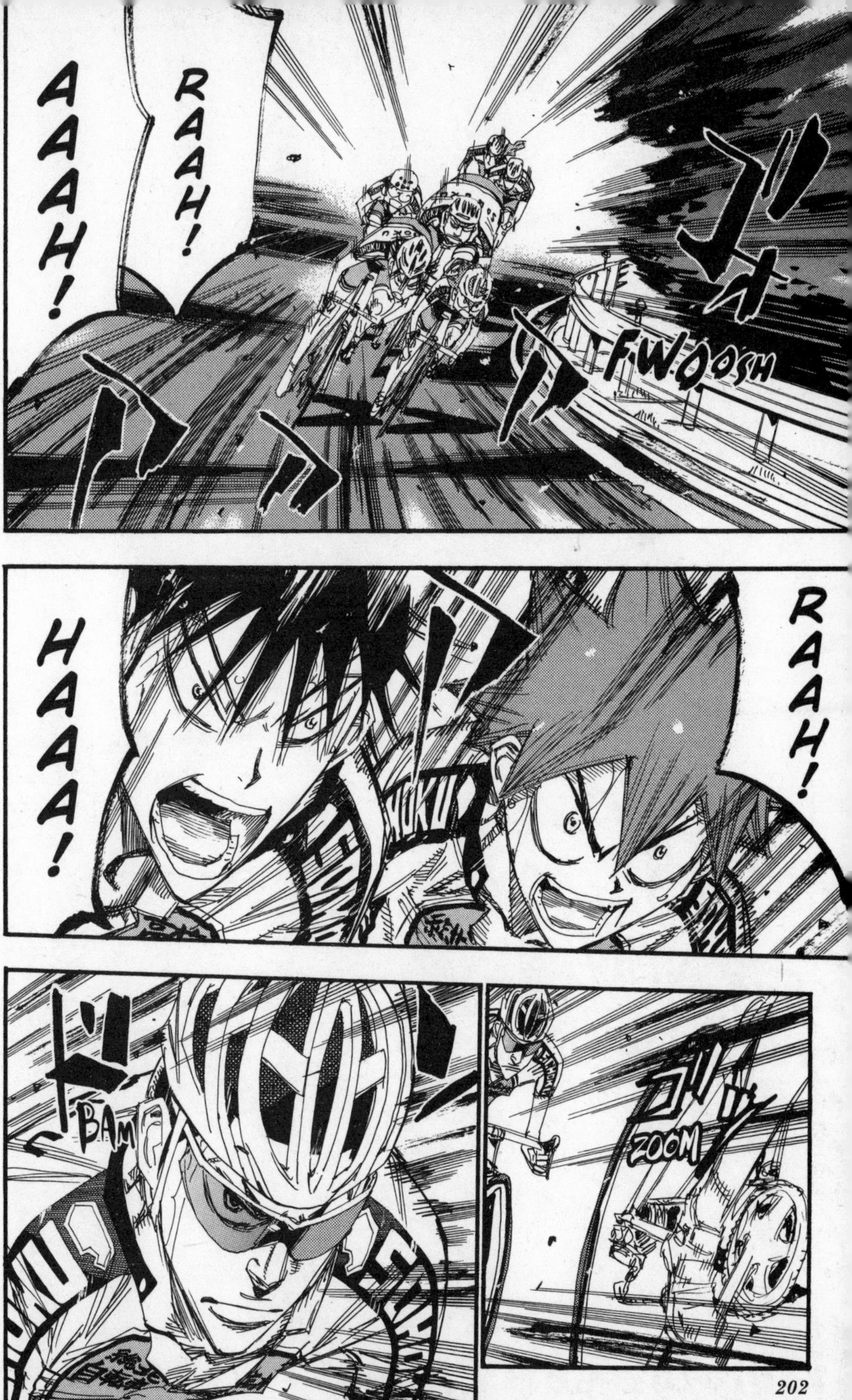
RAAH!
AAAAH!
FWOOSH
RAAAH!
HAAAA!
ZOOM
BAM

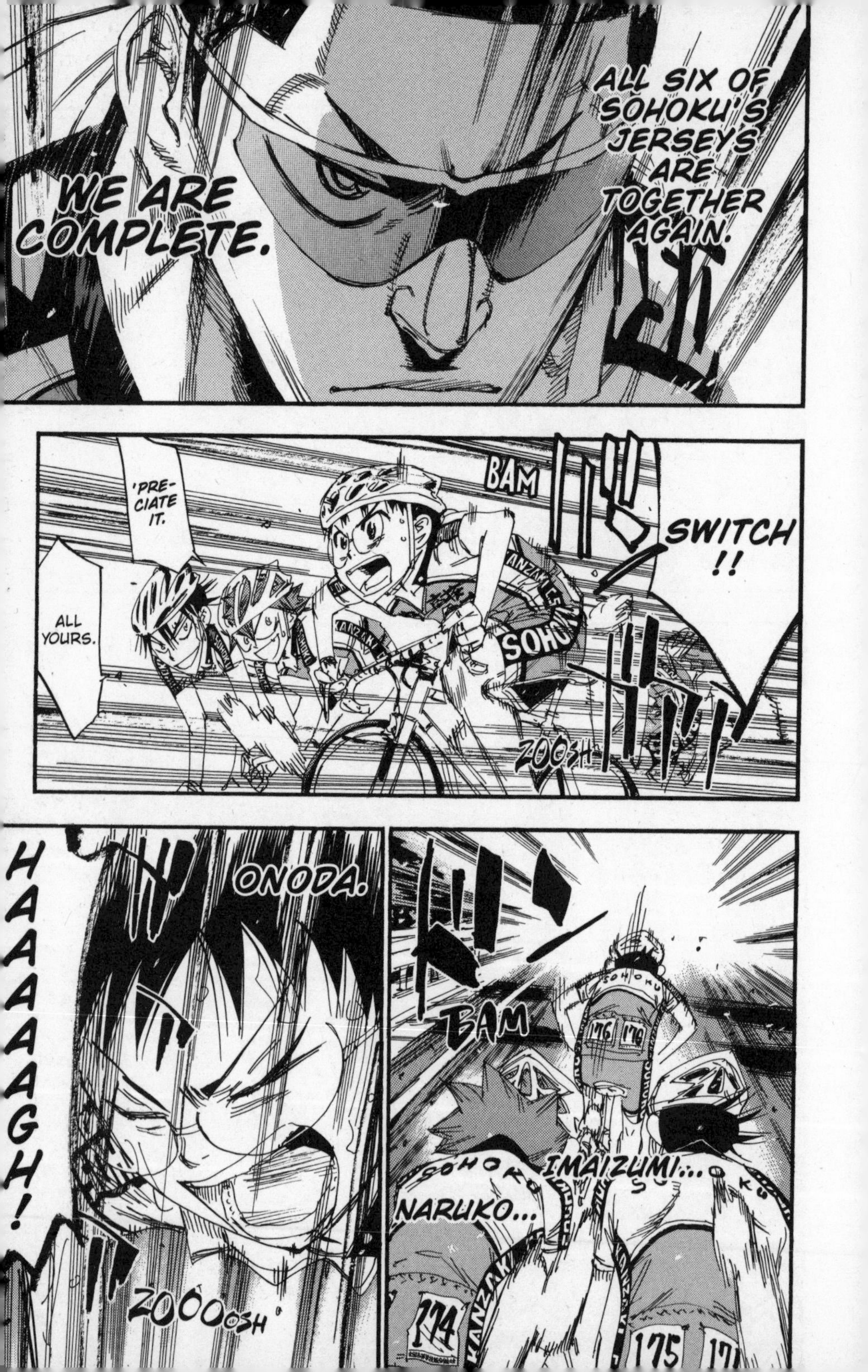
ALL SIX OF SOHOKU'S JERSEYS ARE TOGETHER AGAIN.
WE ARE COMPLETE.
BAM
SWITCH!!
'PRE-CIATE IT.
ALL YOURS.
ZOOSH
BAM
IMAIZUMI...
NARUKO...
ONODA.
HAAAAAAAGH!
ZOOOOSH

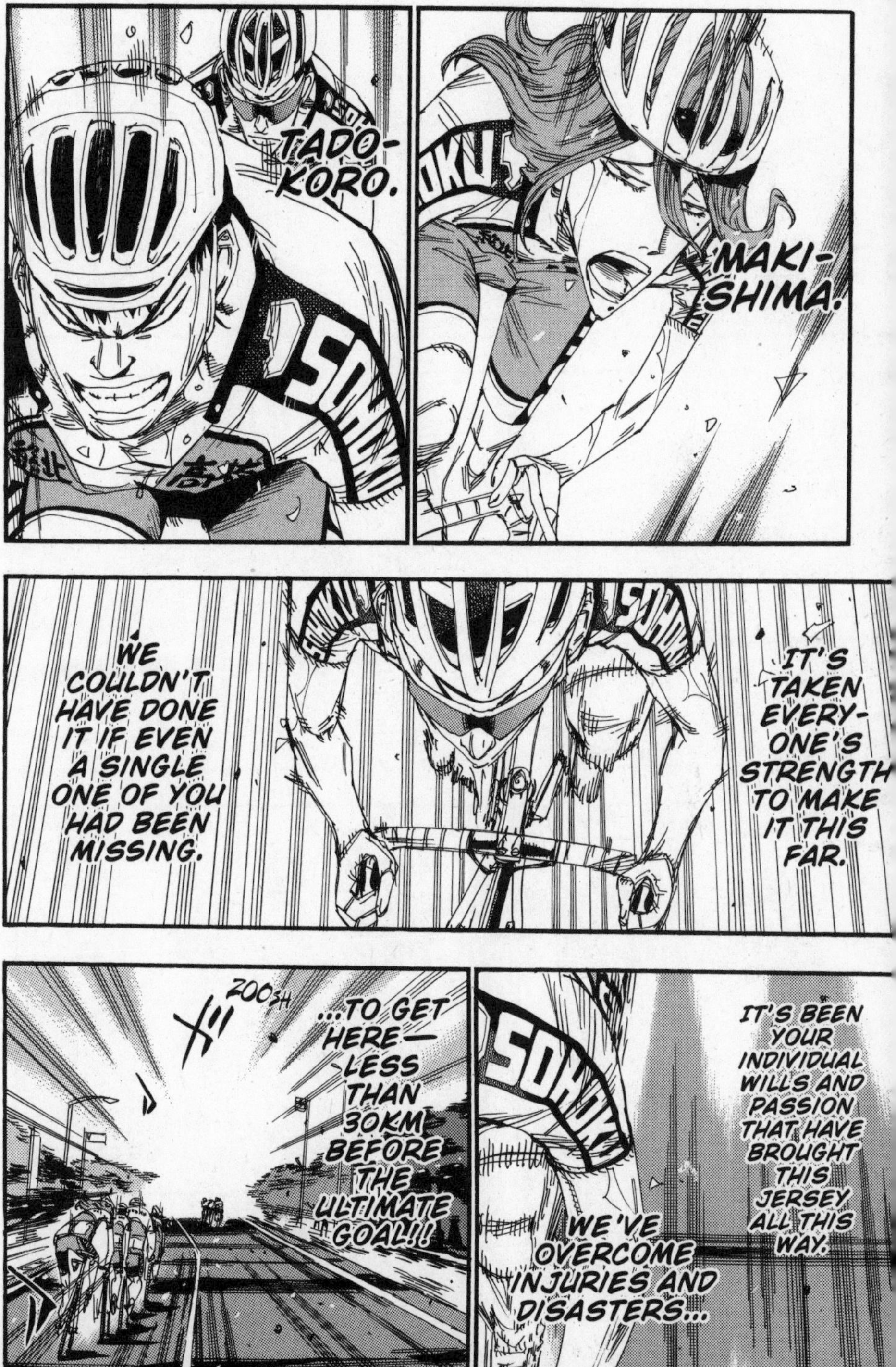
MAKI-SHIMA.
TADO-KORO.
IT'S TAKEN EVERY-ONE'S STRENGTH TO MAKE IT THIS FAR.
WE COULDN'T HAVE DONE IT IF EVEN A SINGLE ONE OF YOU HAD BEEN MISSING.
IT'S BEEN YOUR INDIVIDUAL WILLS AND PASSION THAT HAVE BROUGHT THIS JERSEY ALL THIS WAY.
WE'VE OVERCOME INJURIES AND DISASTERS...
ZOOSH
...TO GET HERE—LESS THAN 30KM BEFORE THE ULTIMATE GOAL!!

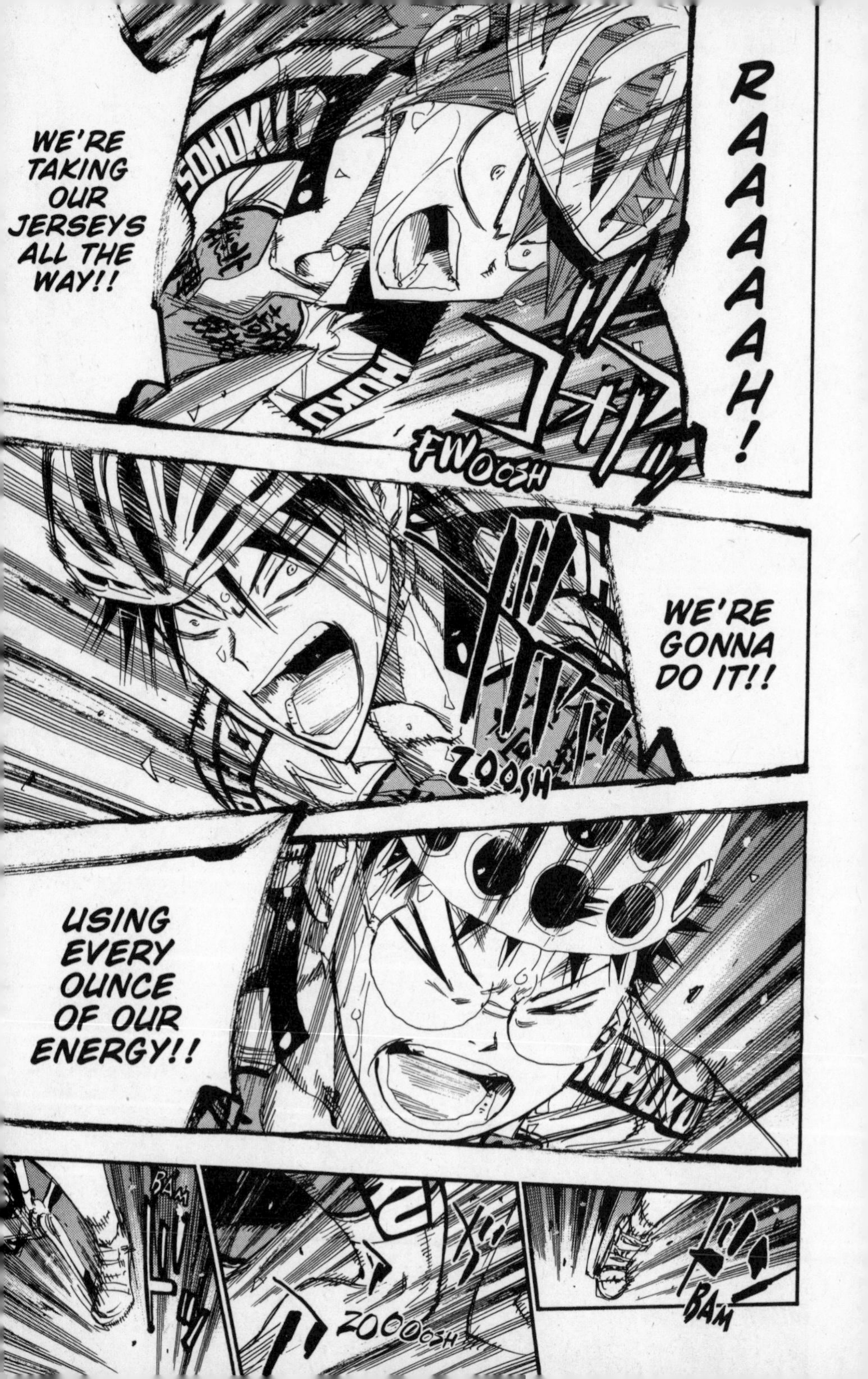
RAAAAAH!
WE'RE TAKING OUR JERSEYS ALL THE WAY!!
FWOOSH
WE'RE GONNA DO IT!!
ZOOSH
USING EVERY OUNCE OF OUR ENERGY!!
BAM
ZOOOOOSH
BAM

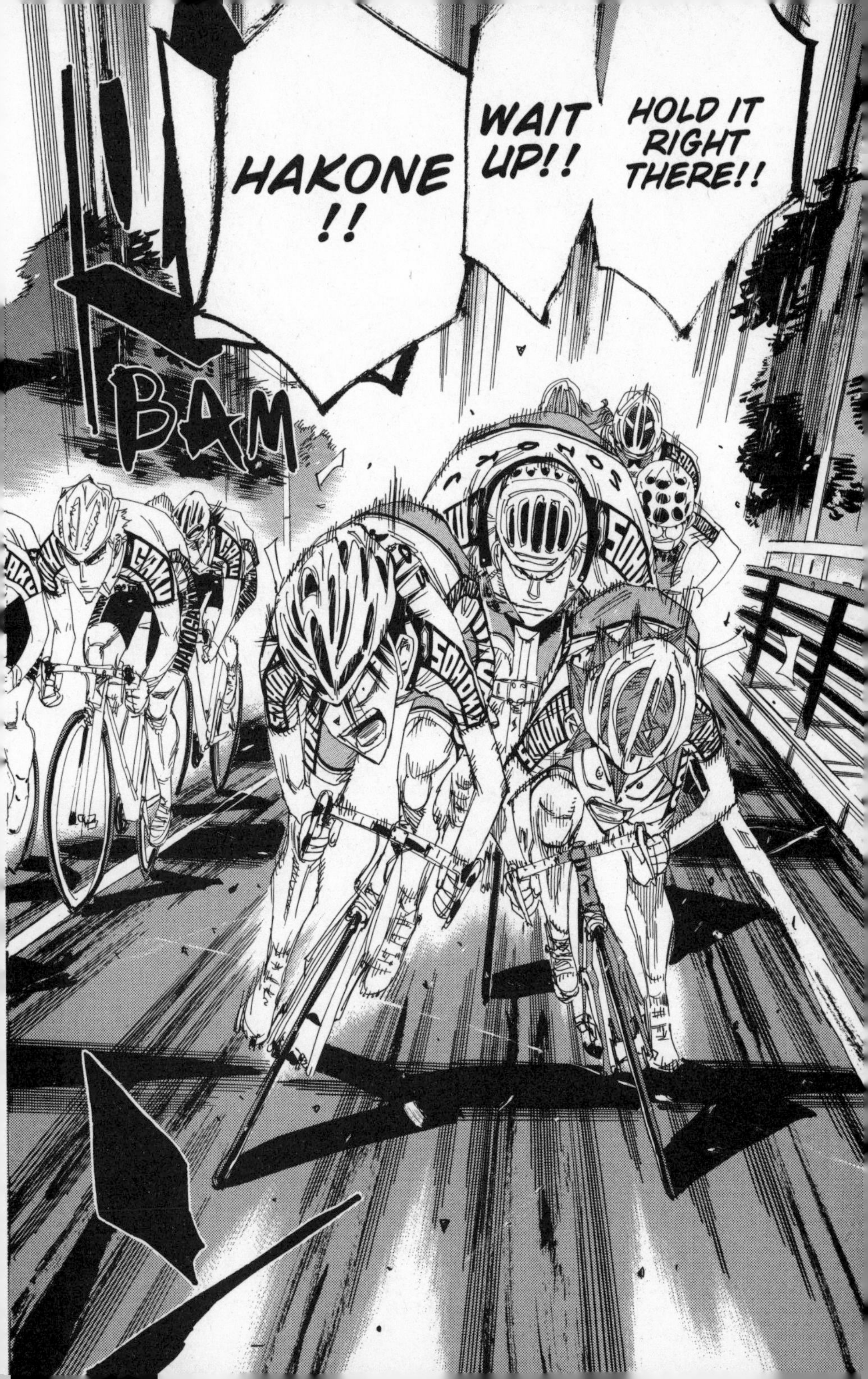
HOLD IT RIGHT THERE!!
WAIT UP!!
HAKONE !!
BAM

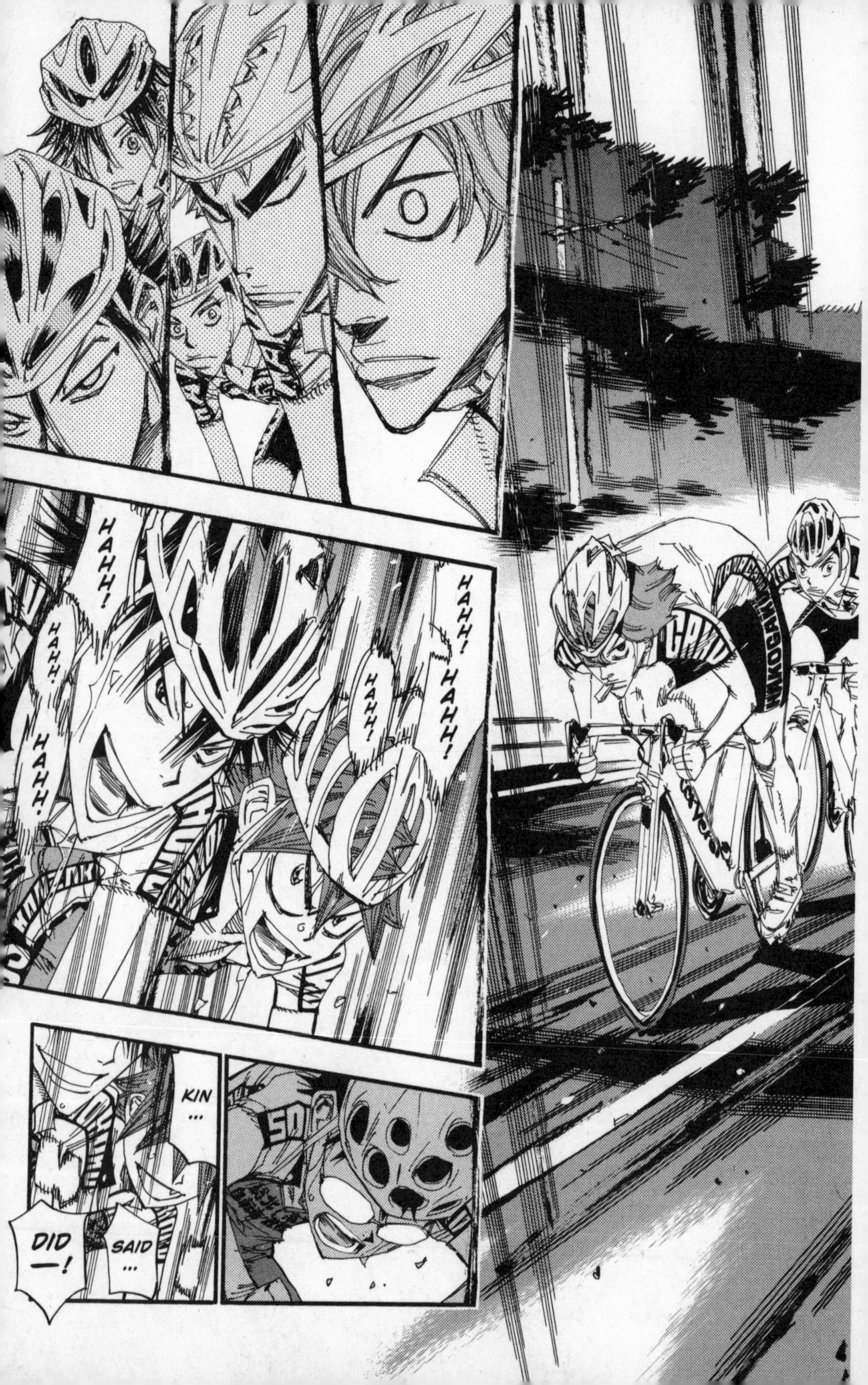
HAHH! HAHH!
HAHH!
HAHH!
HAHH!
HAHH!
KIN ...
SAID ...
DID —!

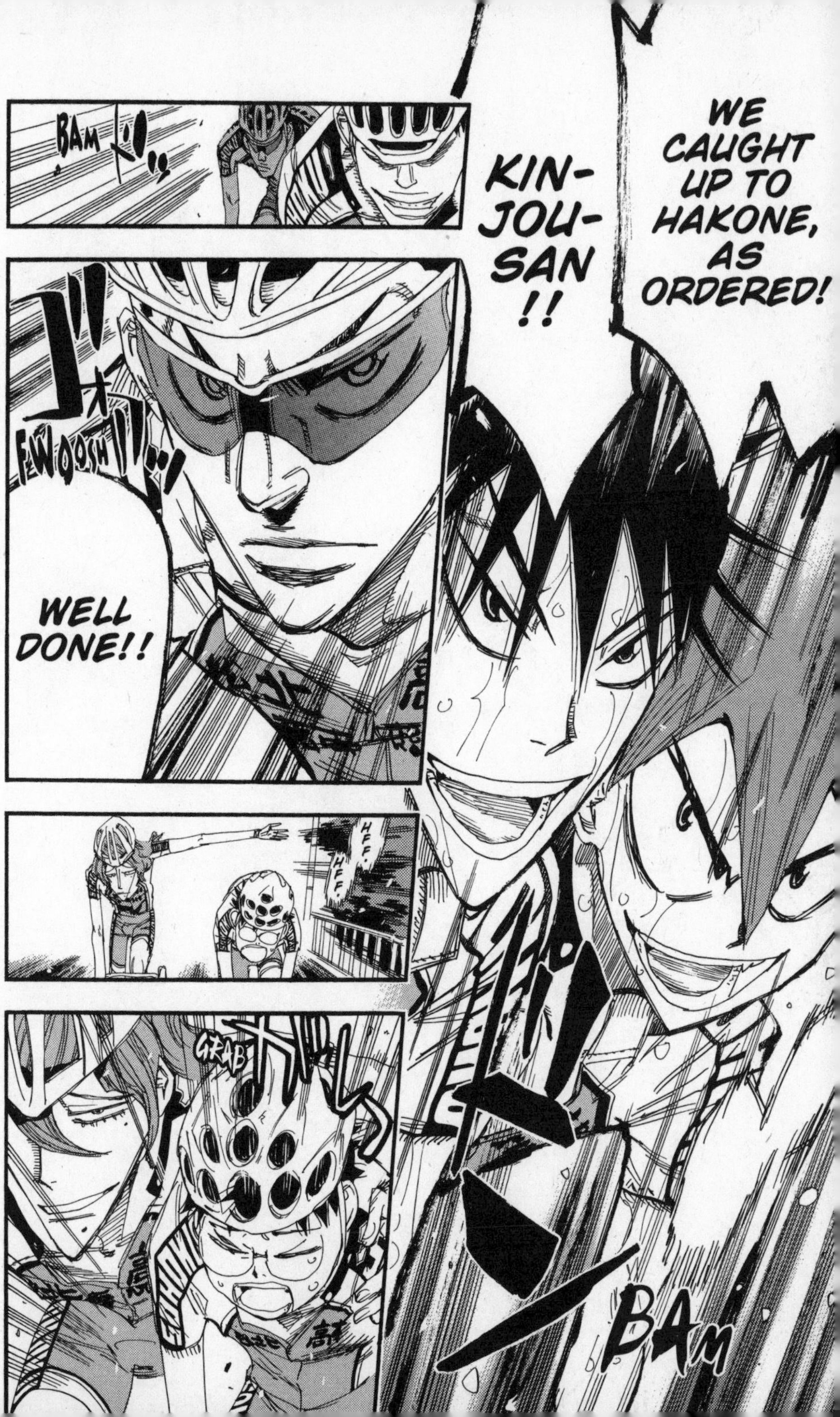
WE CAUGHT UP TO HAKONE, AS ORDERED!
KIN-JOU-SAN!!
BAM
BAM
FWOOSH
WELL DONE!!
HFF. HFF.
GRAB

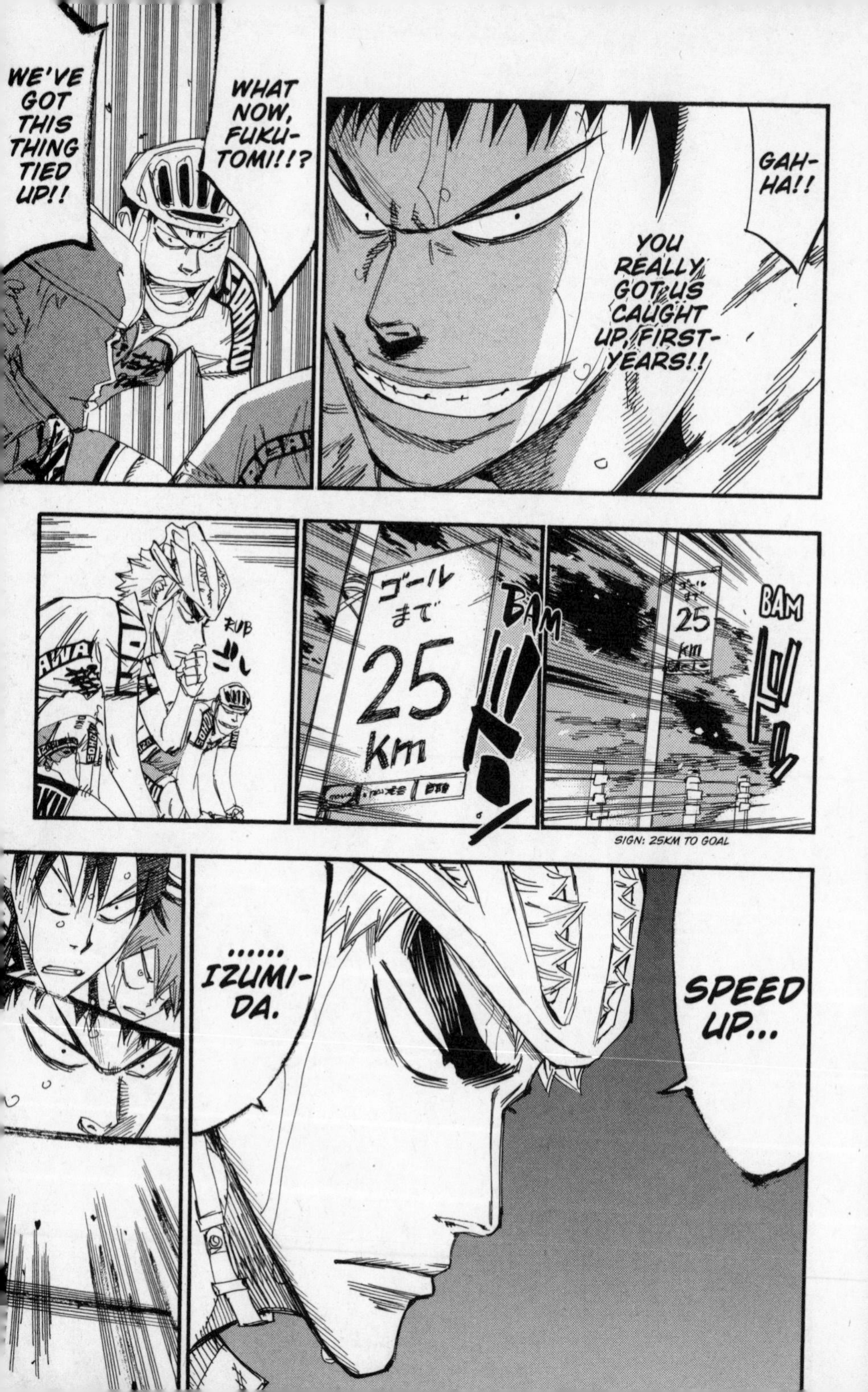
GAH-HA!!
YOU REALLY GOT US CAUGHT UP, FIRST-YEARS!!
WHAT NOW, FUKUTOMI!!?
WE'VE GOT THIS THING TIED UP!!
BAM
ゴールまで 25 km
ゴールまで 25 km
BAM
RUB
ごし
SIGN: 25KM TO GOAL
SPEED UP...
......IZUMIDA.

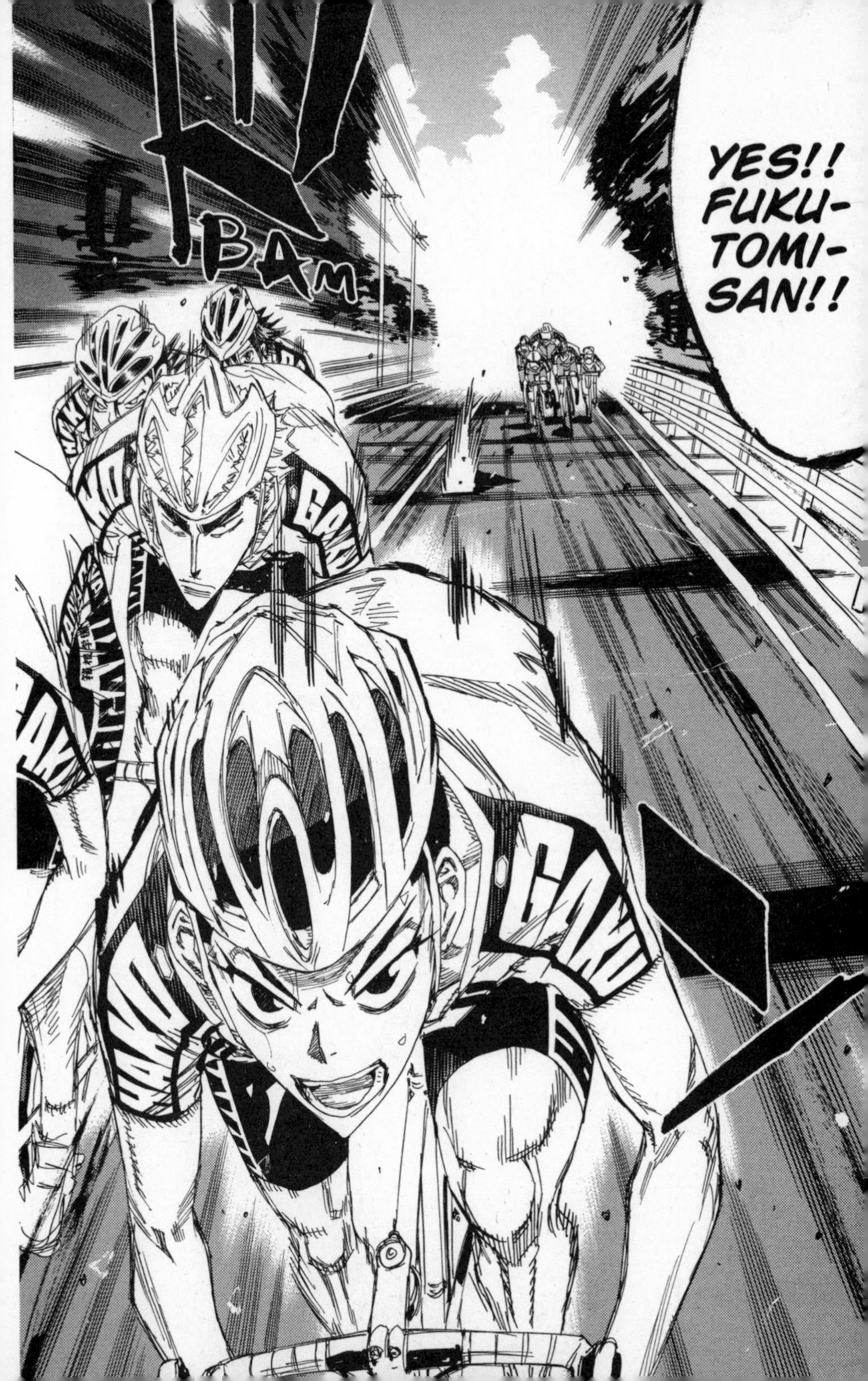
YES!! FUKU-TOMI-SAN!!
BAM

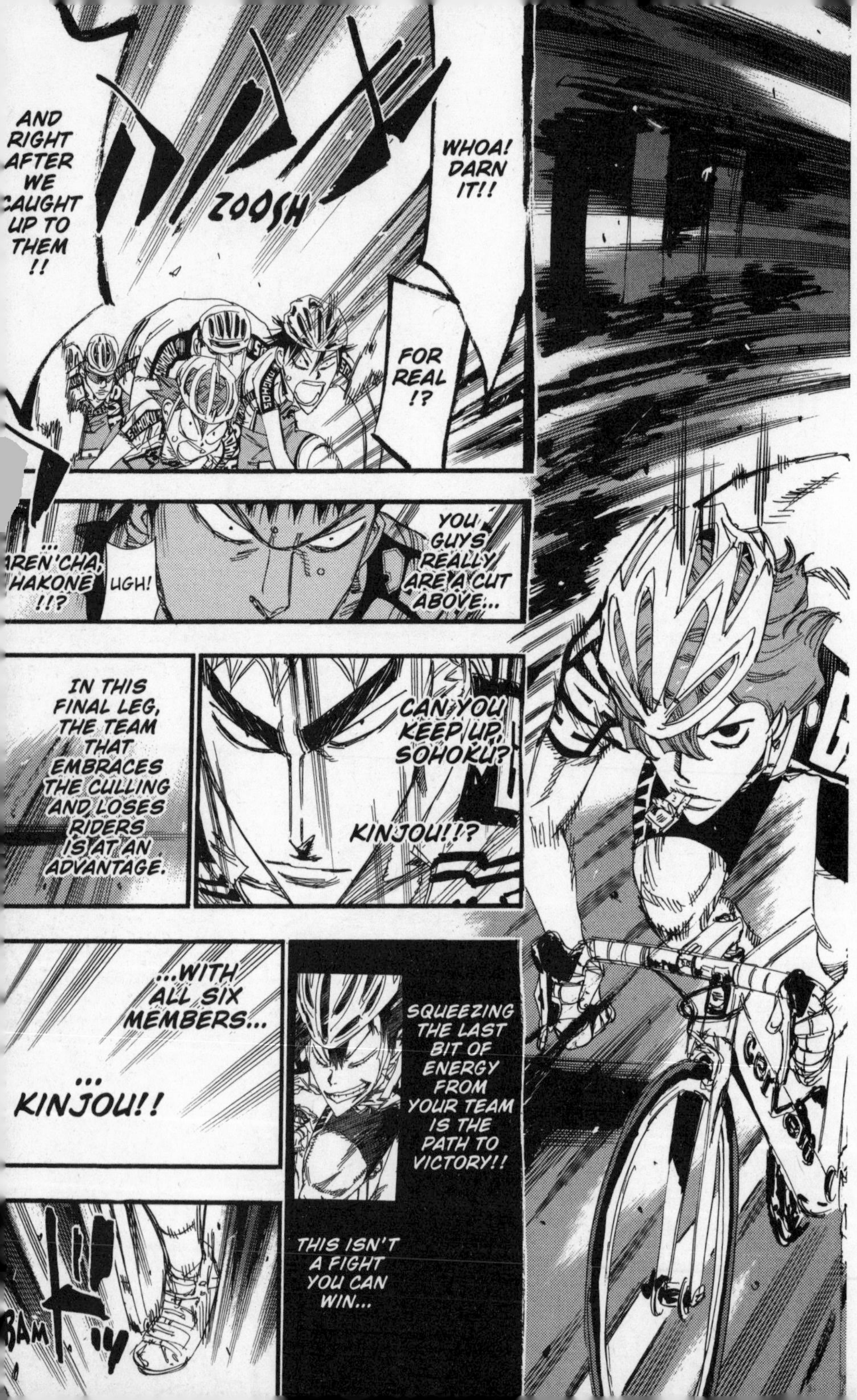
WHOA! DARN IT!!
ZOOSH
FOR REAL!?
AND RIGHT AFTER WE CAUGHT UP TO THEM!!
YOU GUYS REALLY ARE A CUT ABOVE...
UGH!
...AREN'CHA, HAKONE!!?
CAN YOU KEEP UP, SOHOKU?
KINJOU!!?
IN THIS FINAL LEG, THE TEAM THAT EMBRACES THE CULLING AND LOSES RIDERS IS AT AN ADVANTAGE.
SQUEEZING THE LAST BIT OF ENERGY FROM YOUR TEAM IS THE PATH TO VICTORY!!
THIS ISN'T A FIGHT YOU CAN WIN...
...WITH ALL SIX MEMBERS...
...KINJOU!!
BAM

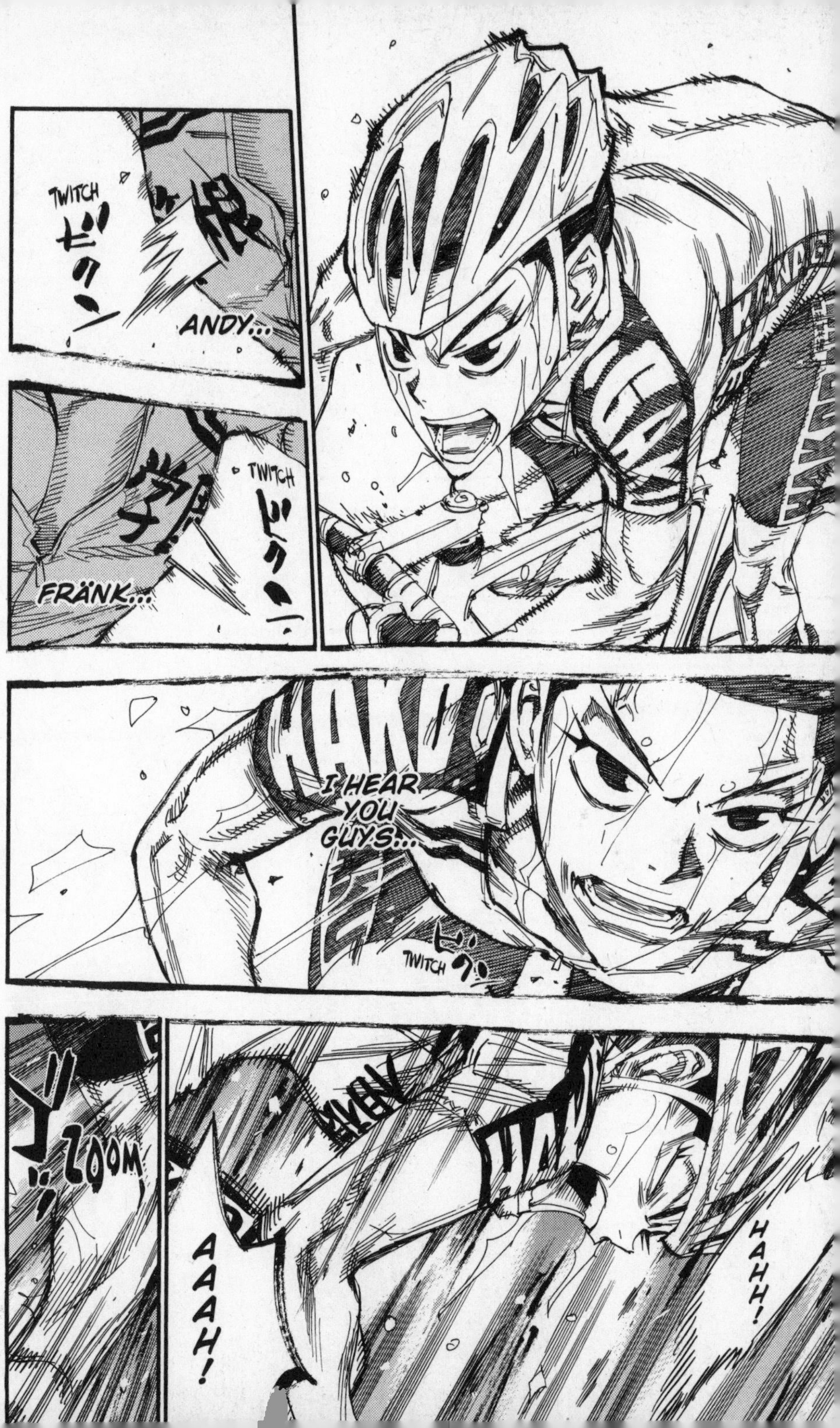
TWITCH
ANDY...
TWITCH
FRÄNK...
I HEAR YOU GUYS...
TWITCH
HAHH!
AAAAH!
ZOOM

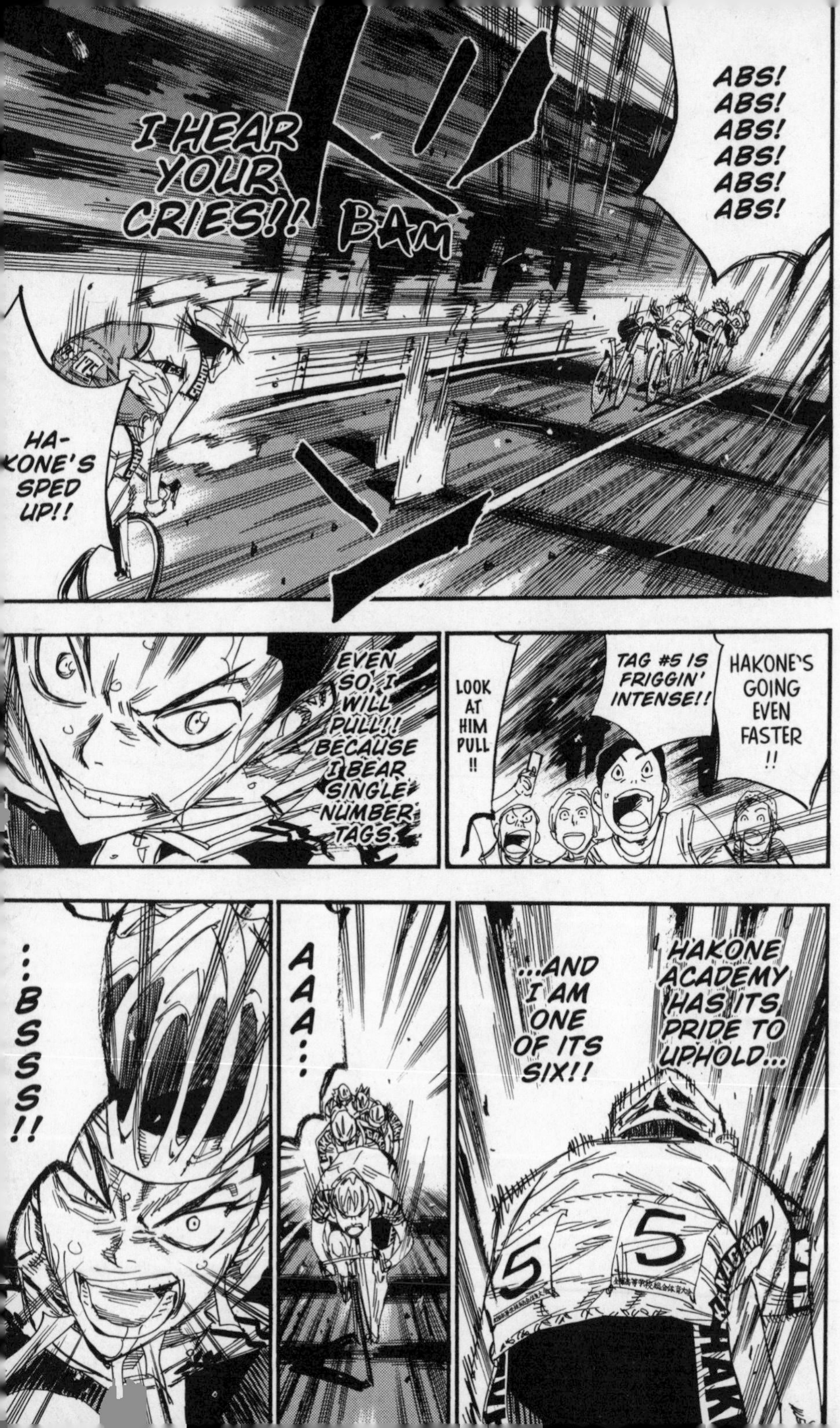
ABS! ABS! ABS! ABS! ABS! ABS!
I HEAR YOUR CRIES!!
BAM
HA-KONE'S SPED UP!!
HAKONE'S GOING EVEN FASTER!!
TAG #5 IS FRIGGIN' INTENSE!!
LOOK AT HIM PULL!!
EVEN SO, I WILL PULL!! BECAUSE I BEAR SINGLE NUMBER TAGS.
HAKONE ACADEMY HAS ITS PRIDE TO UPHOLD...
...AND I AM ONE OF ITS SIX!!
AAA...
...BSSS!!

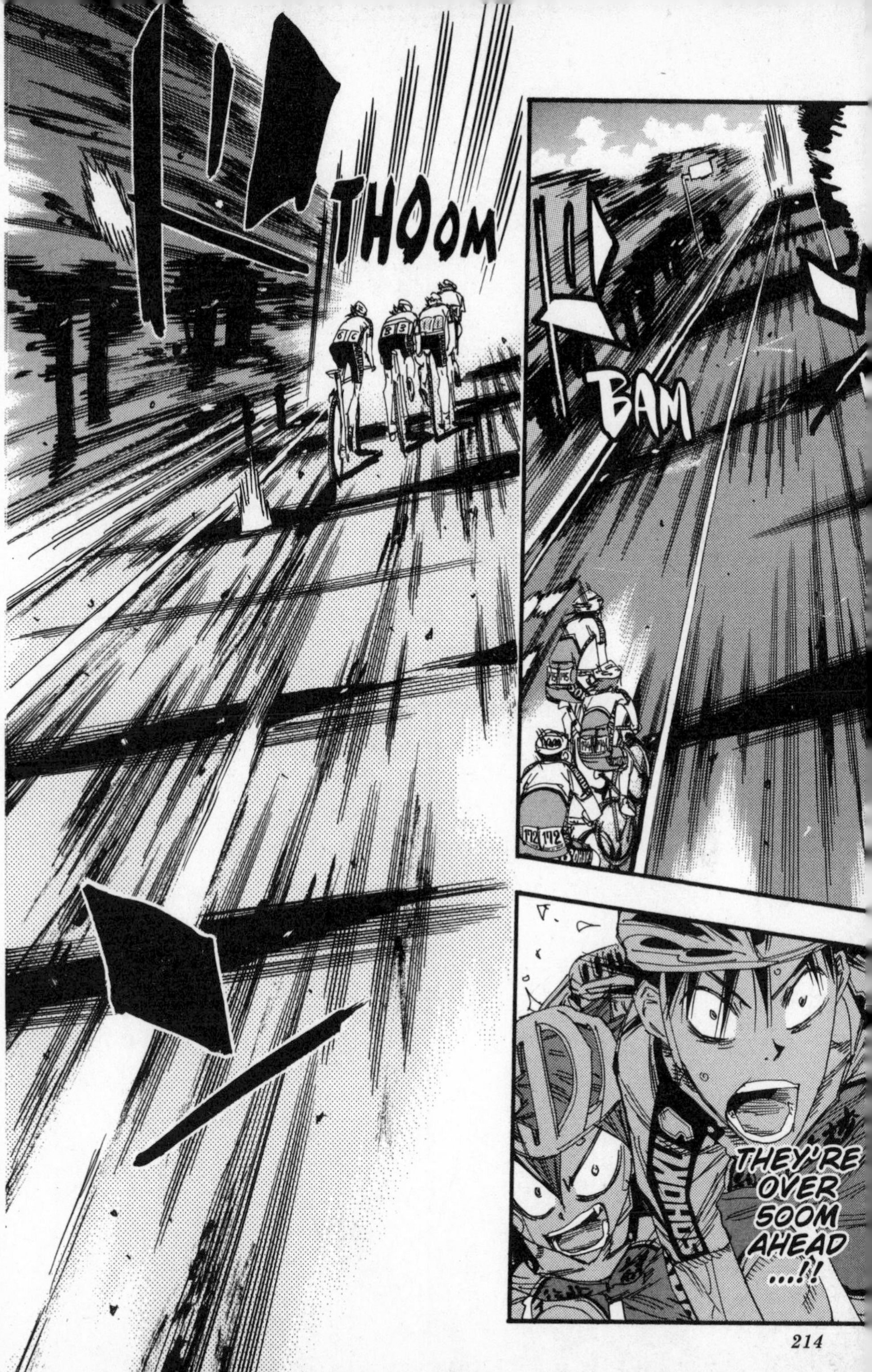
BAM
THEY'RE OVER 500M AHEAD ...!!
THOOM

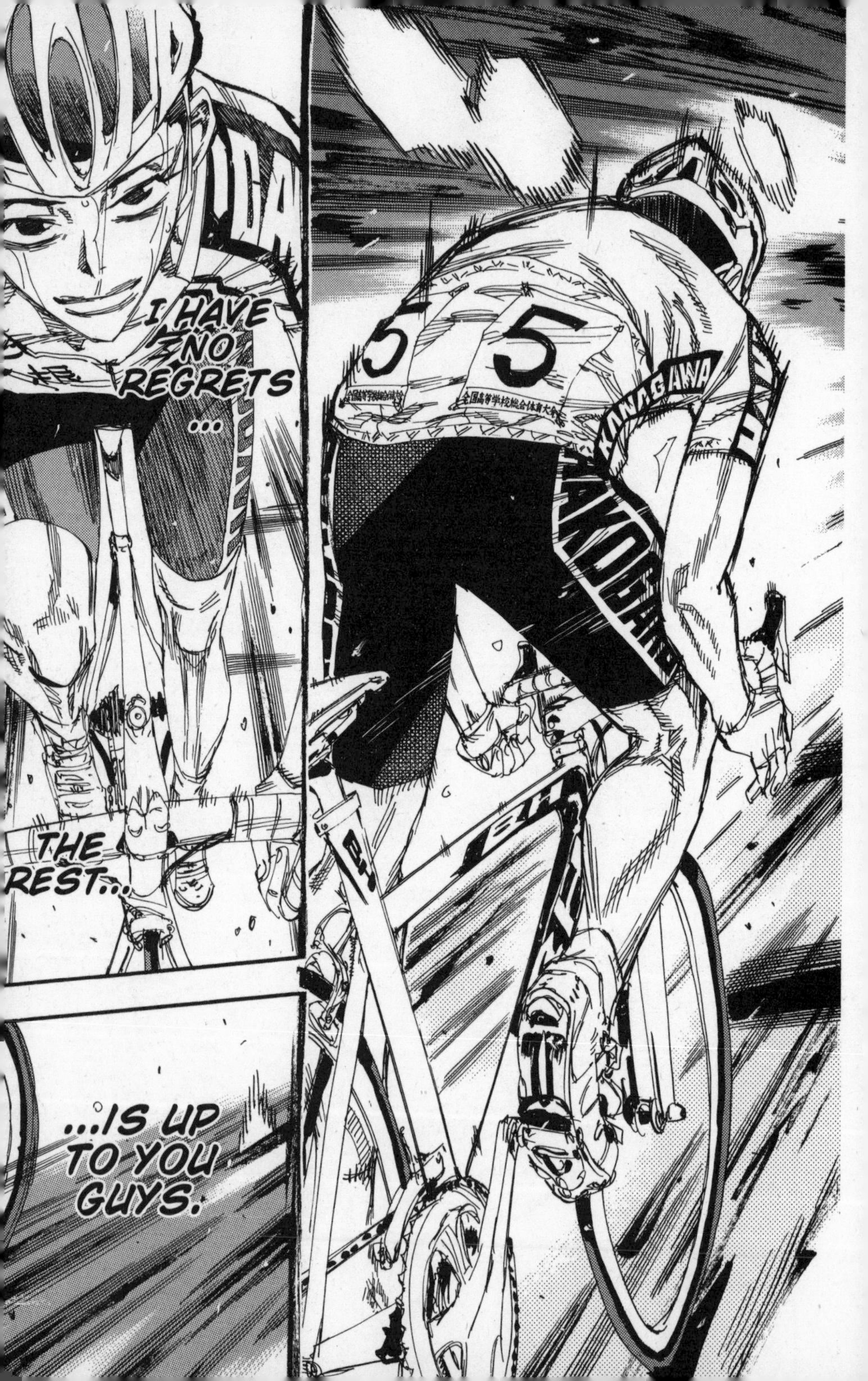
KANAGAWA
I HAVE NO REGRETS...
THE REST...
...IS UP TO YOU GUYS.

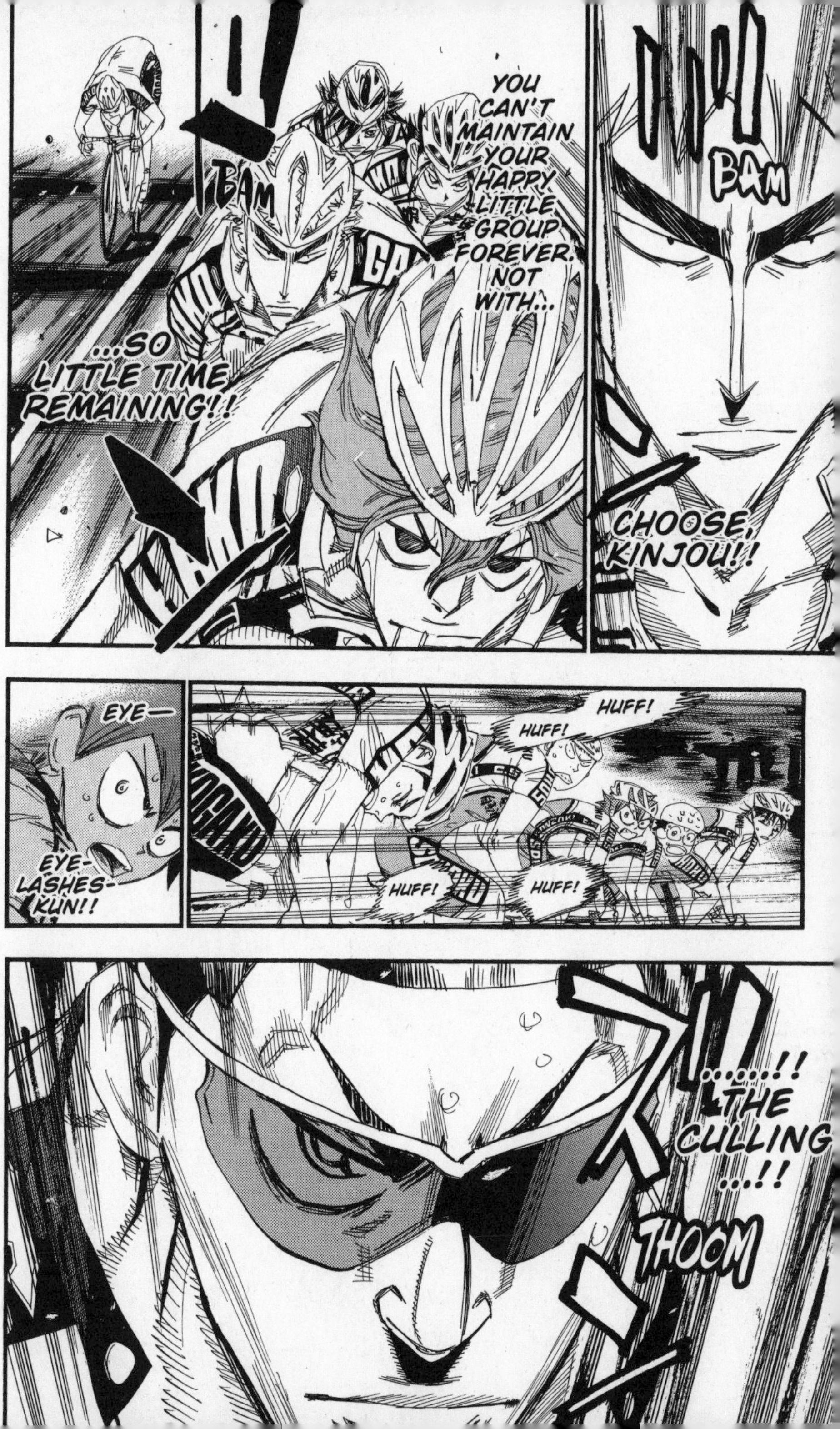
BAM
CHOOSE, KINJOU!!
YOU CAN'T MAINTAIN YOUR HAPPY LITTLE GROUP FOREVER. NOT WITH...
BAM
...SO LITTLE TIME REMAINING!!
HUFF!
HUFF!
HUFF!
HUFF!
EYE—
EYE-LASHES-KUN!!
......!! THE CULLING...!!
THOOM

RIDE.183 IZUMIDA'S PRIDE

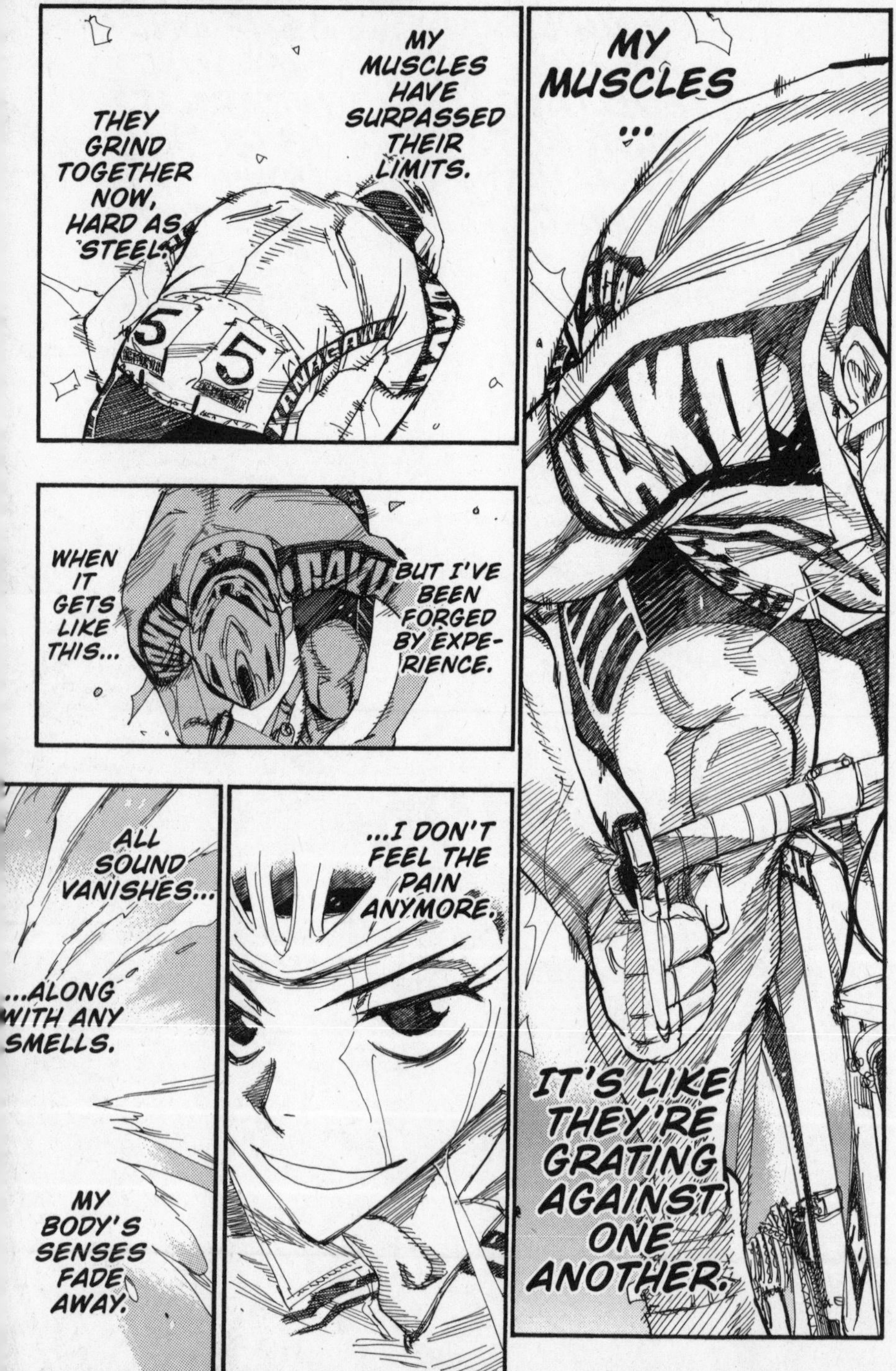
MY MUSCLES...
IT'S LIKE THEY'RE GRATING AGAINST ONE ANOTHER.
MY MUSCLES HAVE SURPASSED THEIR LIMITS.
THEY GRIND TOGETHER NOW, HARD AS STEEL.
BUT I'VE BEEN FORGED BY EXPERIENCE.
WHEN IT GETS LIKE THIS...
...I DON'T FEEL THE PAIN ANYMORE.
ALL SOUND VANISHES...
...ALONG WITH ANY SMELLS.
MY BODY'S SENSES FADE AWAY.

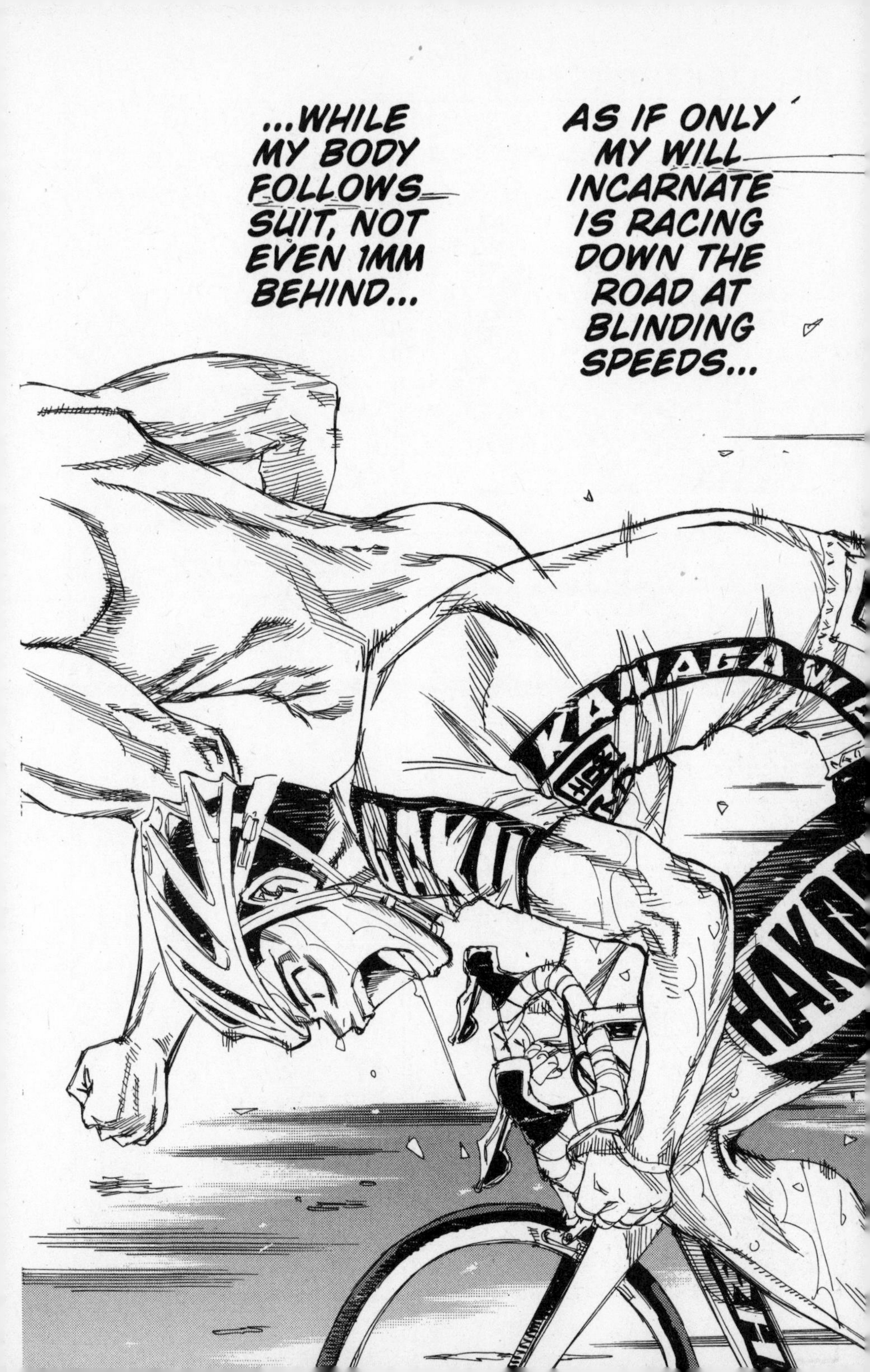
AS IF ONLY MY WILL INCARNATE IS RACING DOWN THE ROAD AT BLINDING SPEEDS...
...WHILE MY BODY FOLLOWS SUIT, NOT EVEN 1MM BEHIND...

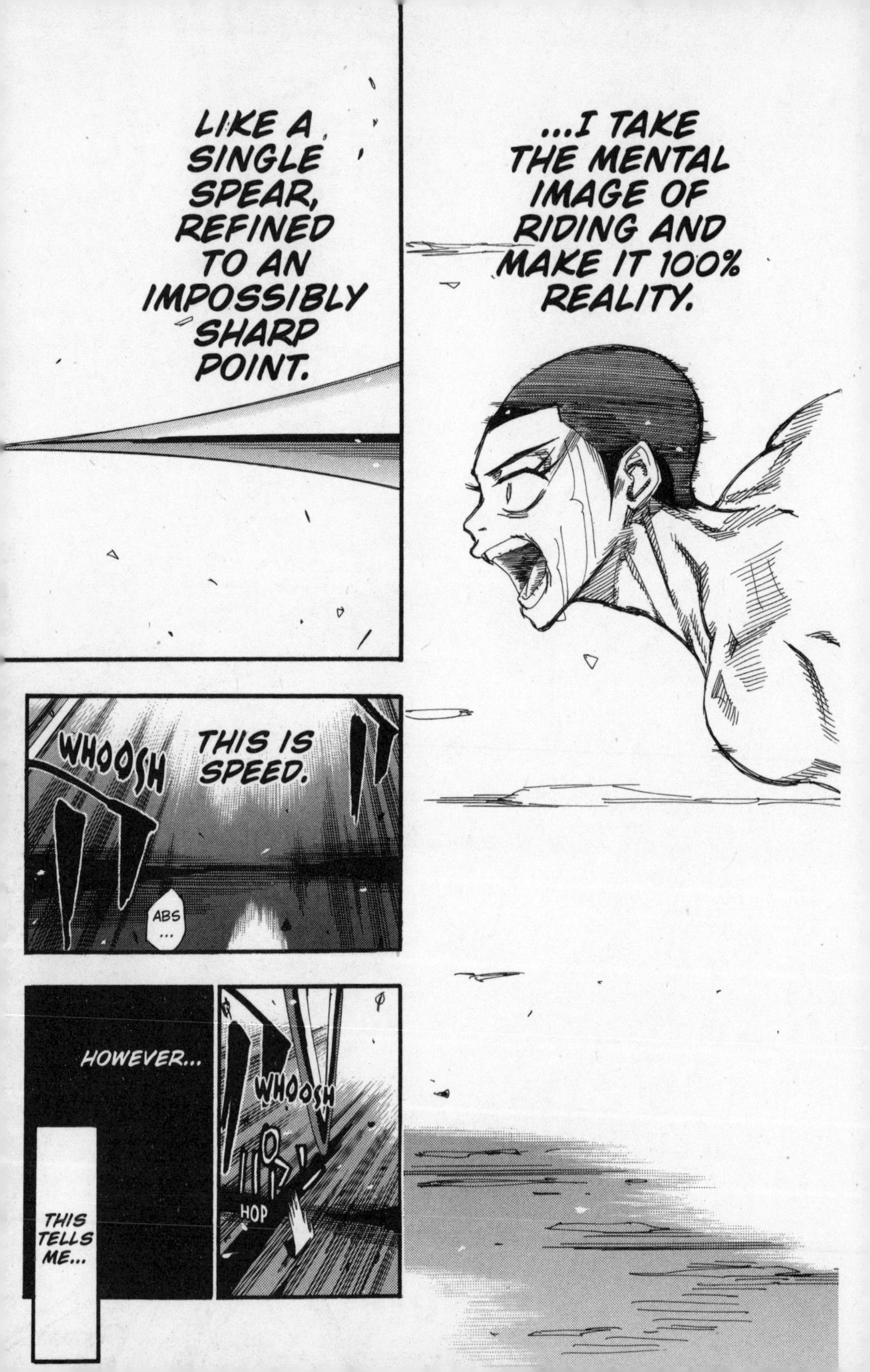
...I TAKE THE MENTAL IMAGE OF RIDING AND MAKE IT 100% REALITY.
LIKE A SINGLE SPEAR, REFINED TO AN IMPOSSIBLY SHARP POINT.
WHOOSH
THIS IS SPEED.
ABS ...
WHOOSH
HOP
HOWEVER...
THIS TELLS ME...

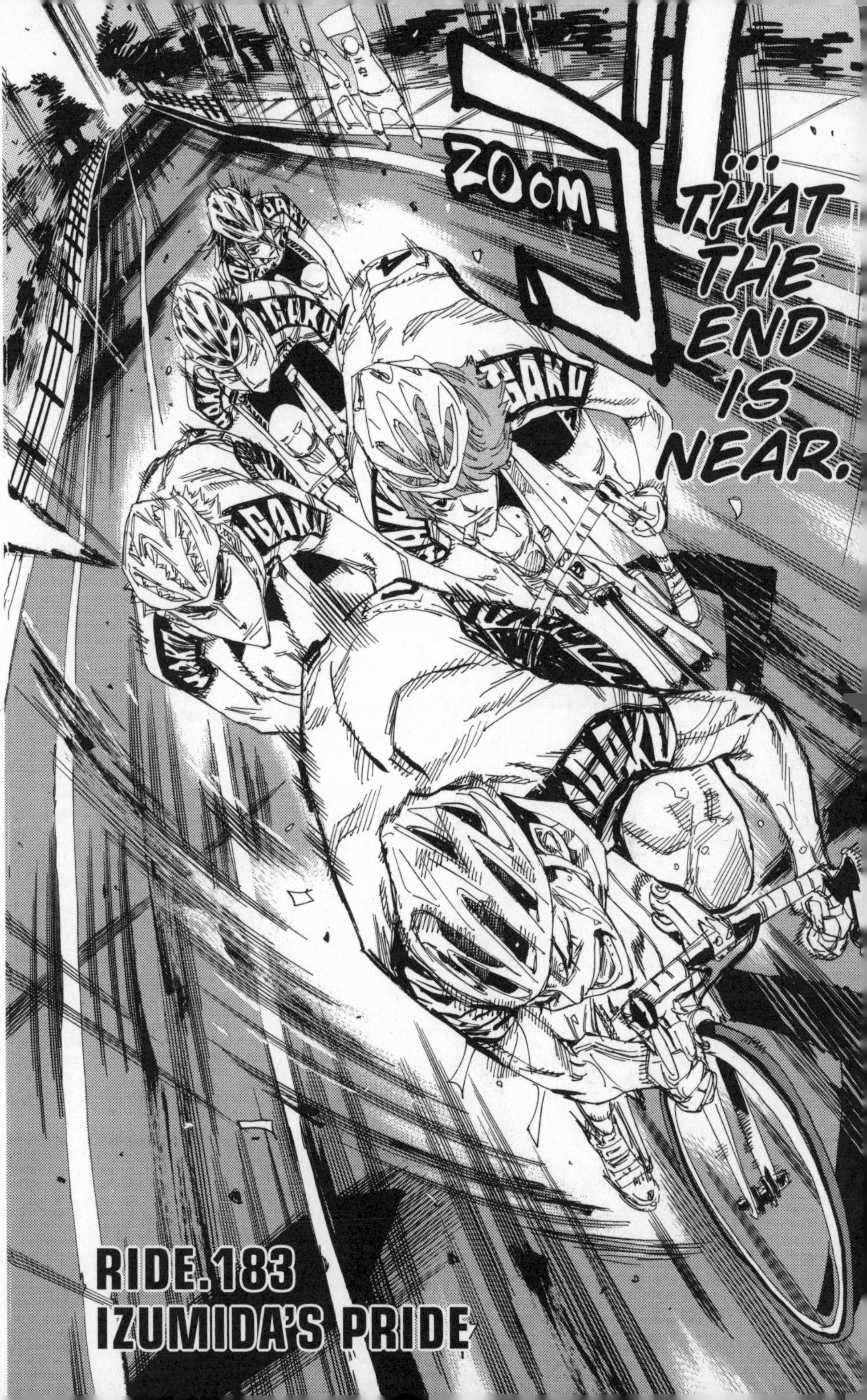
...THAT THE END IS NEAR.
ZOOM

RIDE.183 IZUMIDA'S PRIDE

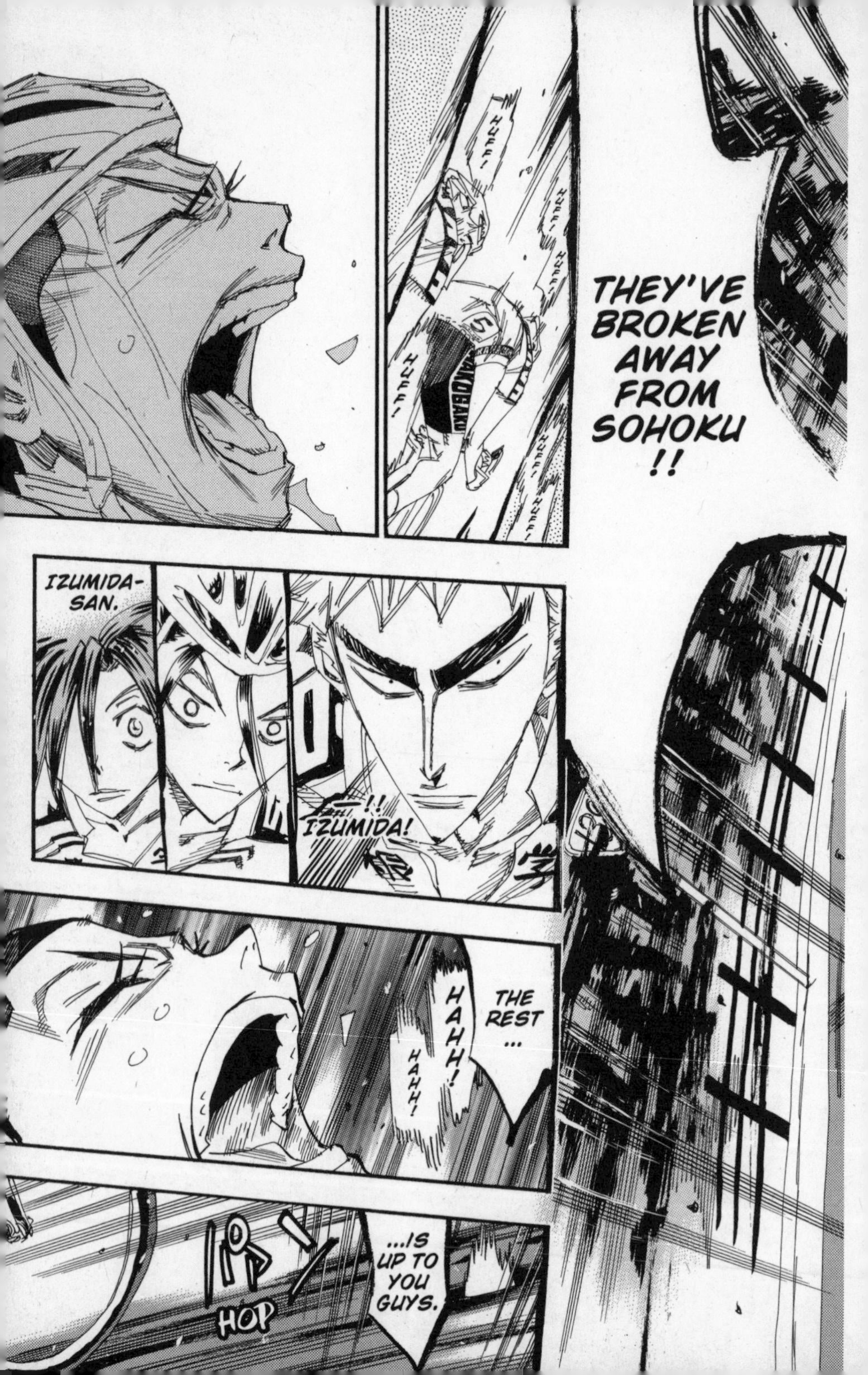
THEY'VE BROKEN AWAY FROM SOHOKU!!
HUFF!
HUFF!
HUFF!
HUFF!
HUFF!
HUFF!
HUFF!
—!! IZUMIDA!
IZUMIDA-SAN.
THE REST...
HAHH!
HAHH!
...IS UP TO YOU GUYS.
HOP

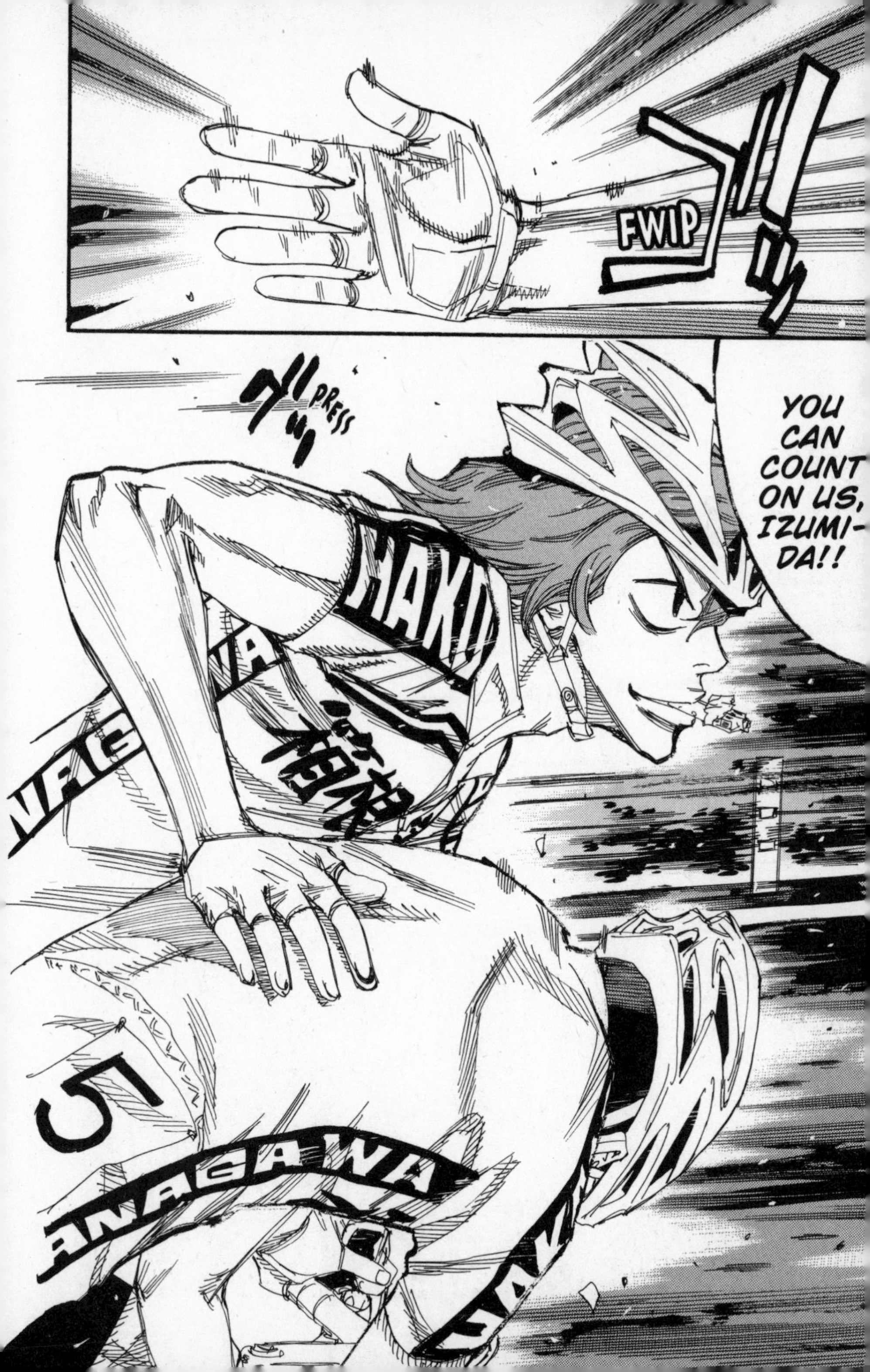
FWIP
YOU CAN COUNT ON US, IZUMI-DA!!
PRESS

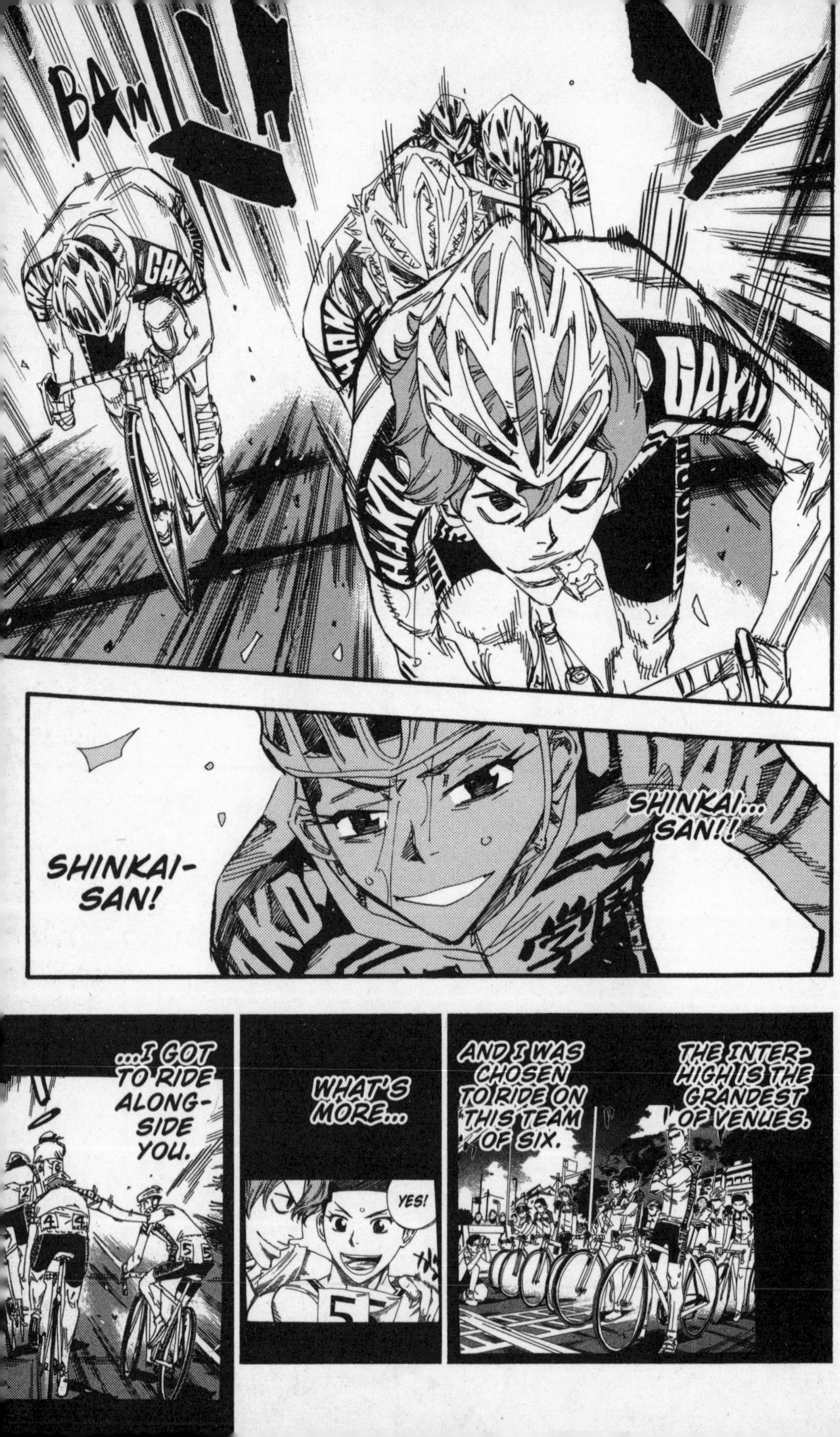
BAM
SHINKAI... SAN!!
SHINKAI-SAN!
THE INTER-HIGH IS THE GRANDEST OF VENUES.
AND I WAS CHOSEN TO RIDE ON THIS TEAM OF SIX.
WHAT'S MORE...
YES!
...I GOT TO RIDE ALONG-SIDE YOU.

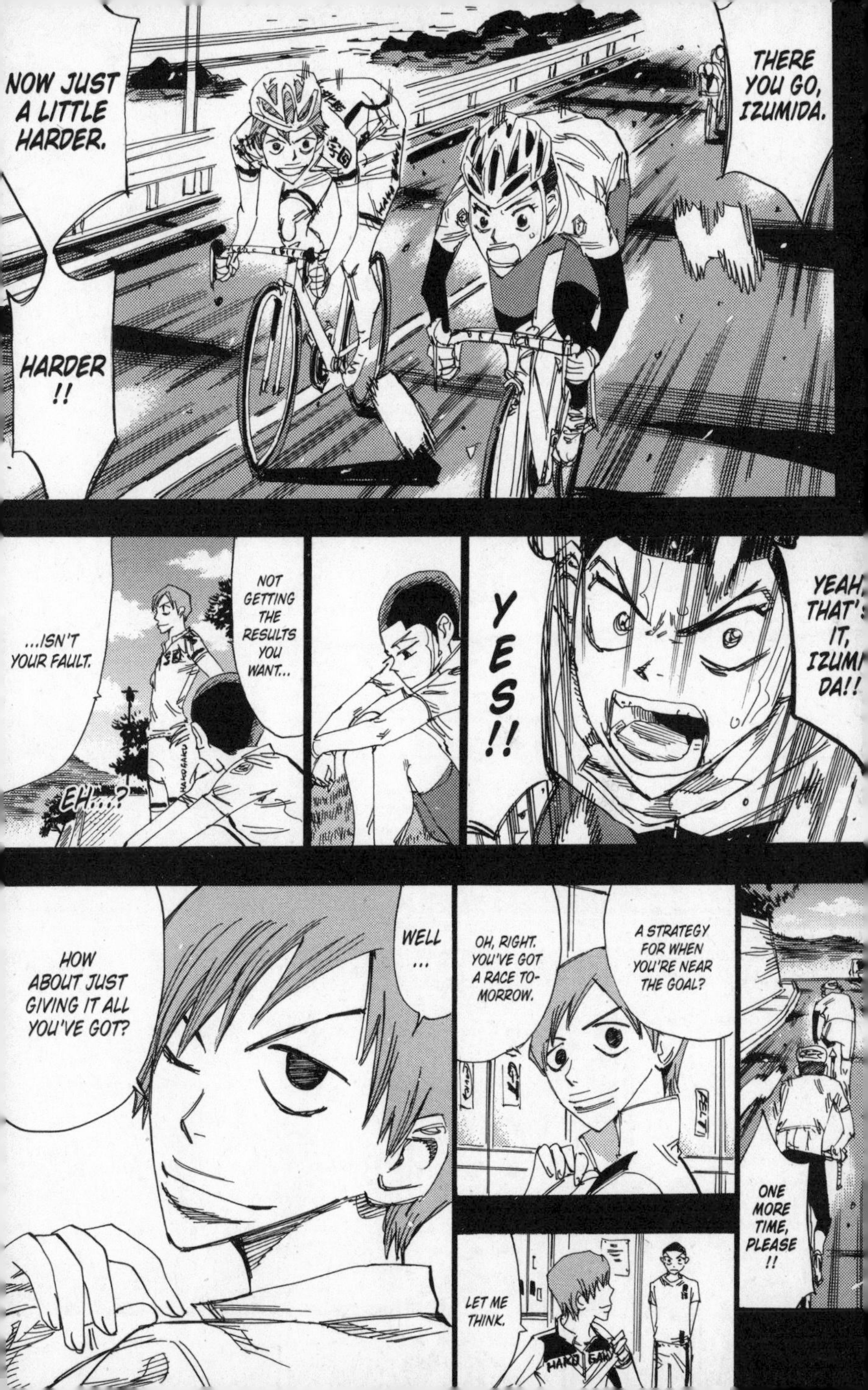
THERE YOU GO, IZUMIDA.
NOW JUST A LITTLE HARDER.
HARDER!!
YEAH, THAT'S IT, IZUMIDA!!
YES!!
NOT GETTING THE RESULTS YOU WANT...
...ISN'T YOUR FAULT.
EH...?
ONE MORE TIME, PLEASE!!
A STRATEGY FOR WHEN YOU'RE NEAR THE GOAL?
OH, RIGHT. YOU'VE GOT A RACE TO-MORROW.
LET ME THINK.
WELL...
HOW ABOUT JUST GIVING IT ALL YOU'VE GOT?

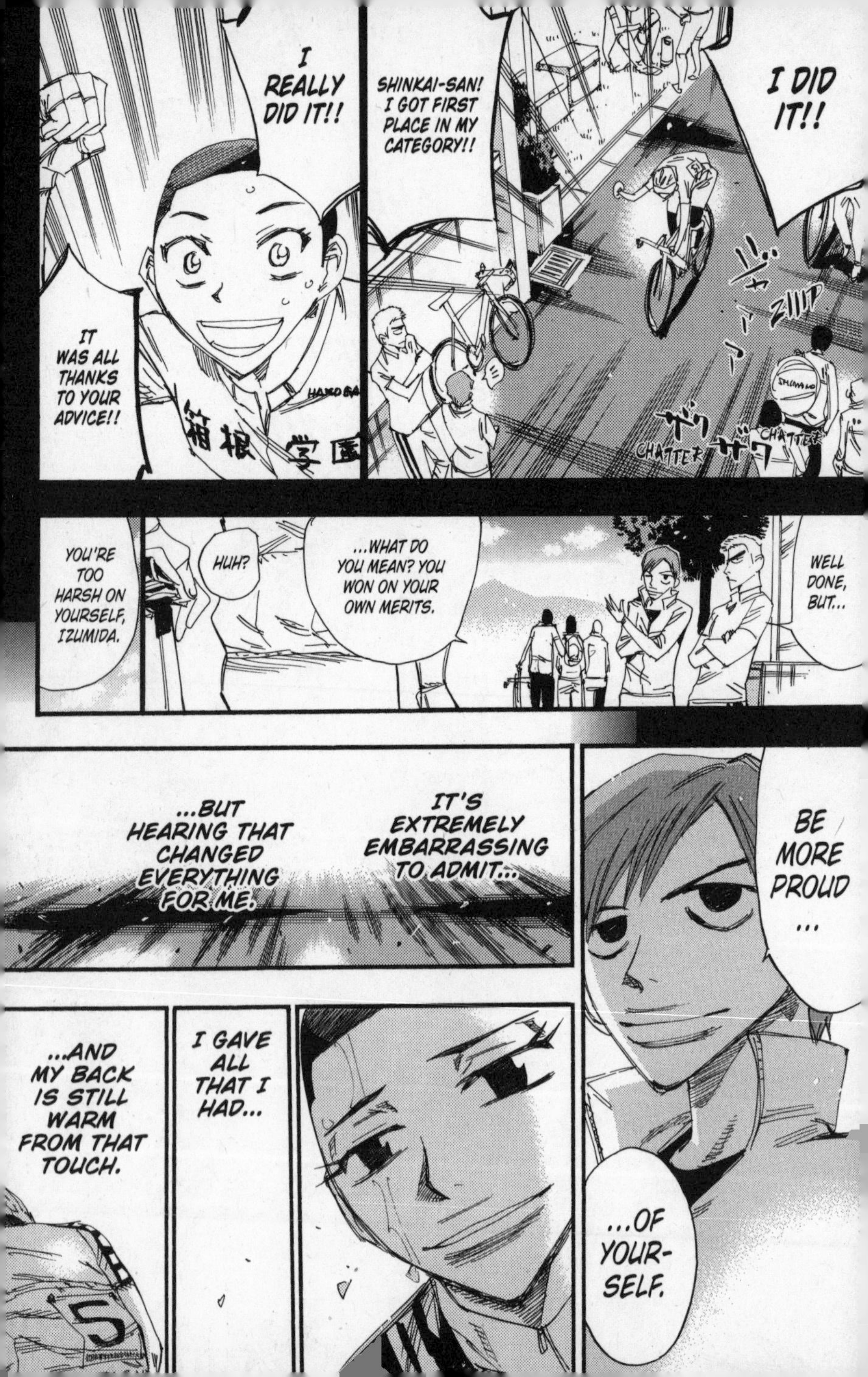
I DID IT!!
ZIIIP
CHATTER
CHATTER
SHINKAI-SAN! I GOT FIRST PLACE IN MY CATEGORY!!
I REALLY DID IT!!
IT WAS ALL THANKS TO YOUR ADVICE!!
WELL DONE, BUT...
...WHAT DO YOU MEAN? YOU WON ON YOUR OWN MERITS.
HUH?
YOU'RE TOO HARSH ON YOURSELF, IZUMIDA.
BE MORE PROUD...
...OF YOURSELF.
IT'S EXTREMELY EMBARRASSING TO ADMIT...
...BUT HEARING THAT CHANGED EVERYTHING FOR ME.
I GAVE ALL THAT I HAD...
...AND MY BACK IS STILL WARM FROM THAT TOUCH.

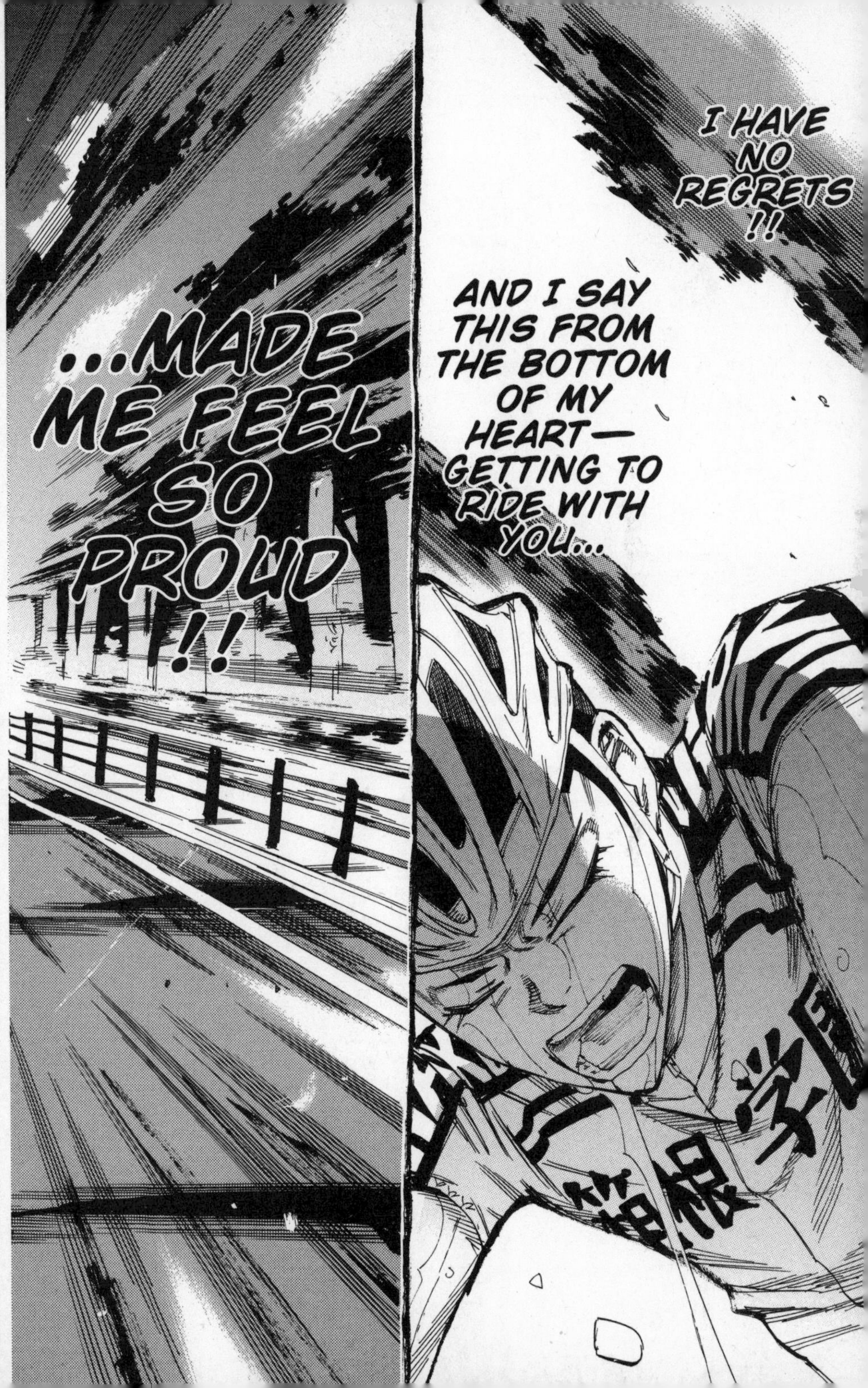
I HAVE NO REGRETS!!
AND I SAY THIS FROM THE BOTTOM OF MY HEART—GETTING TO RIDE WITH YOU...
...MADE ME FEEL SO PROUD!!

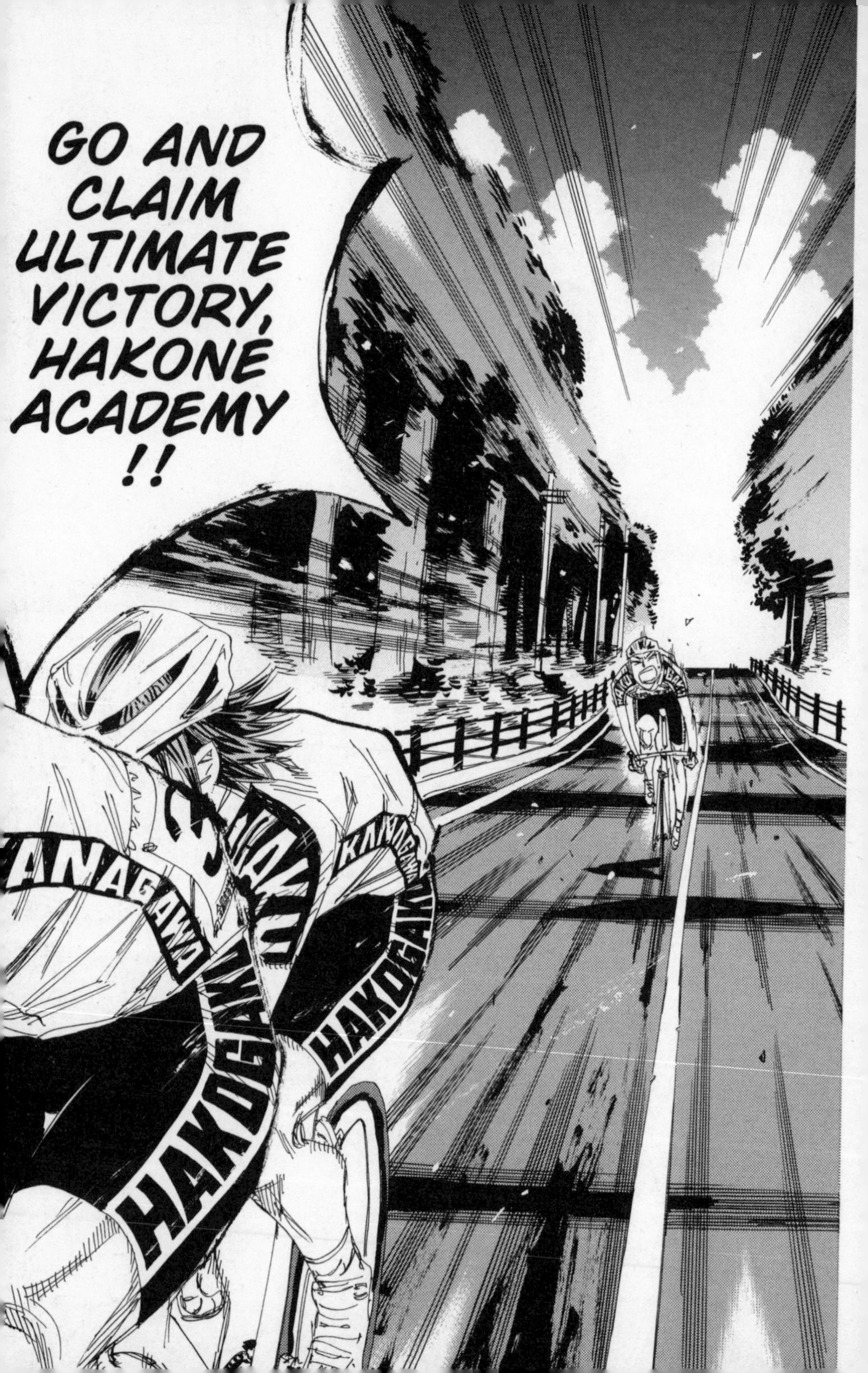
GO AND CLAIM ULTIMATE VICTORY, HAKONE ACADEMY!!
KANAGAWA
HAKOGAKU
KANAGAWA
HAKOGAKU

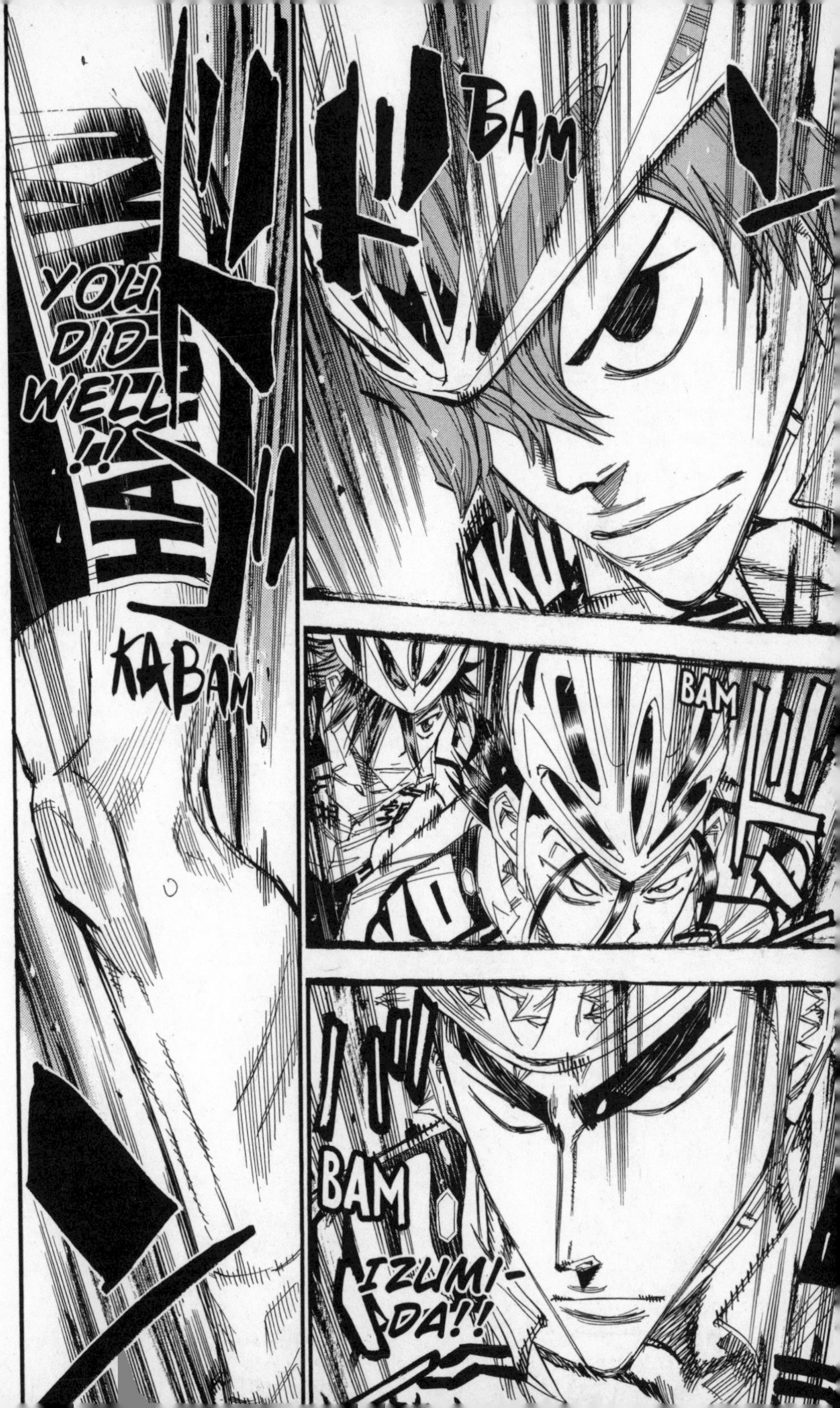
BAM
BAM
BAM
IZUMI-DA!!
YOU DID WELL!!
KABAM

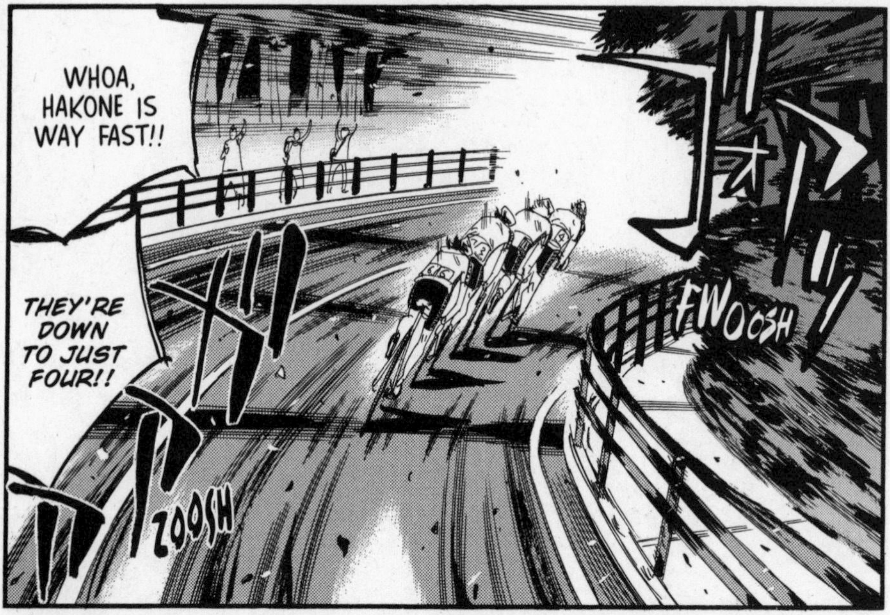
FWOOSH
WHOA, HAKONE IS WAY FAST!!
THEY'RE DOWN TO JUST FOUR!!
ZOOSH
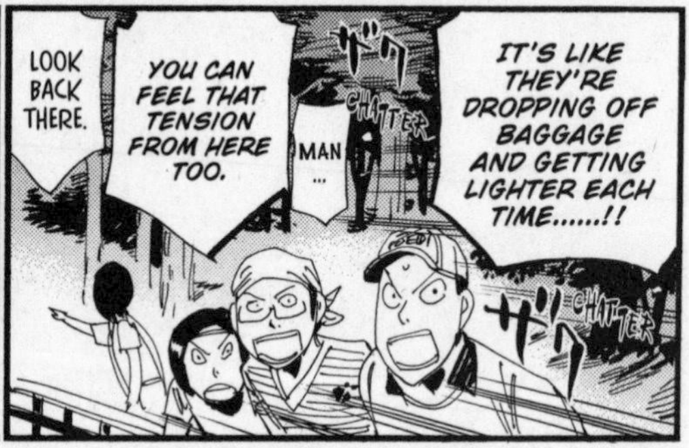
IT'S LIKE THEY'RE DROPPING OFF BAGGAGE AND GETTING LIGHTER EACH TIME......!!
CHATTER
CHATTER
MAN...
YOU CAN FEEL THAT TENSION FROM HERE TOO.
LOOK BACK THERE.
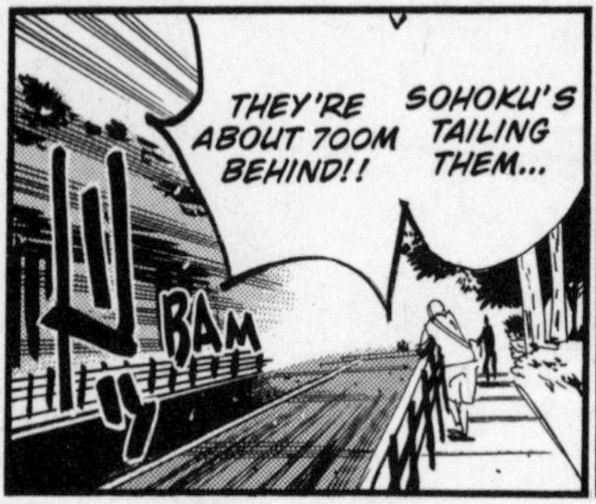
SOHOKU'S TAILING THEM...
THEY'RE ABOUT 700M BEHIND!!
BAM
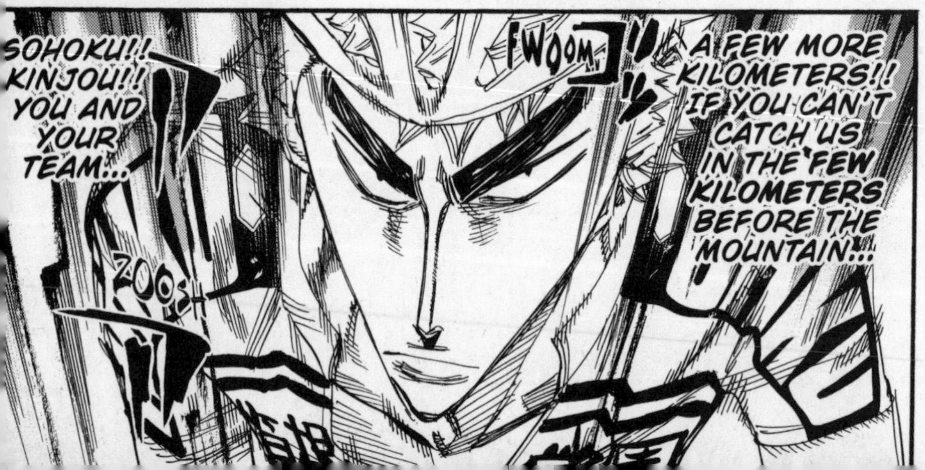
A FEW MORE KILOMETERS!! IF YOU CAN'T CATCH US IN THE FEW KILOMETERS BEFORE THE MOUNTAIN...
FWOOM
SOHOKU!! KINJOU!! YOU AND YOUR TEAM...
ZOOSH

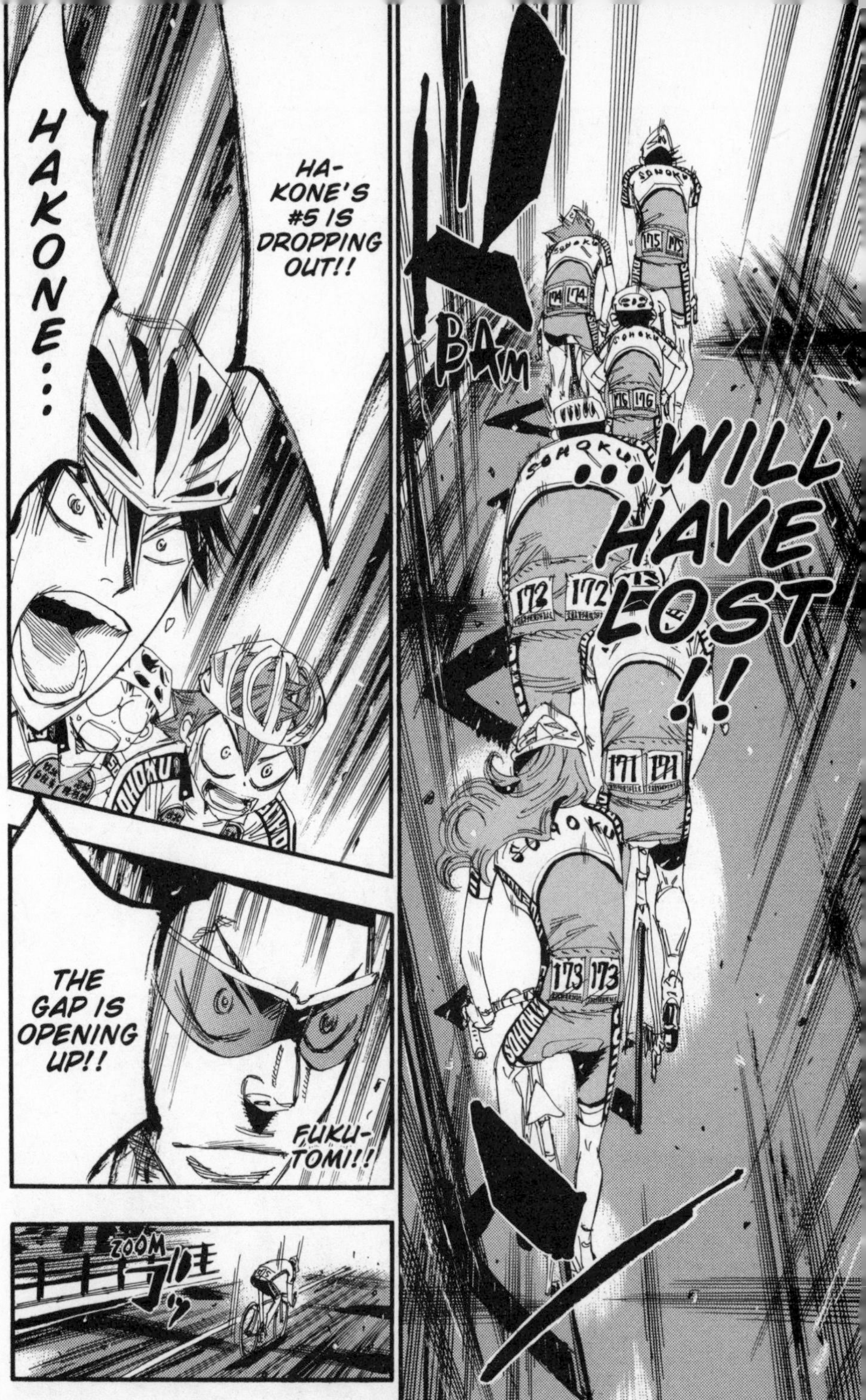
BAM
...WILL HAVE LOST!!
HA-KONE'S #5 IS DROPPING OUT!!
HAKONE...
THE GAP IS OPENING UP!!
FUKU-TOMI!!
ZOOM

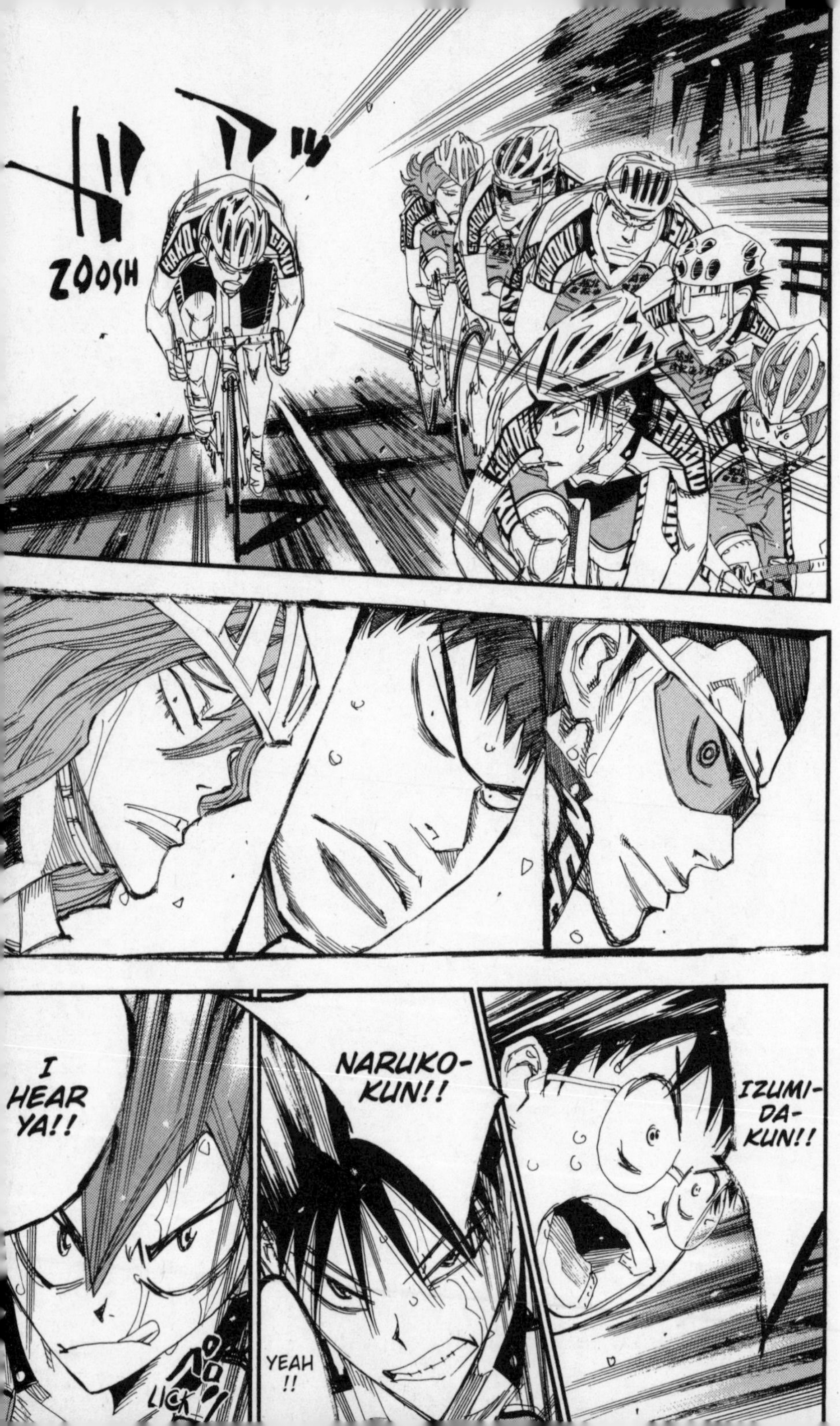
ZOOSH
IZUMI-DA-KUN!!
NARUKO-KUN!!
YEAH !!
I HEAR YA!!
LICK

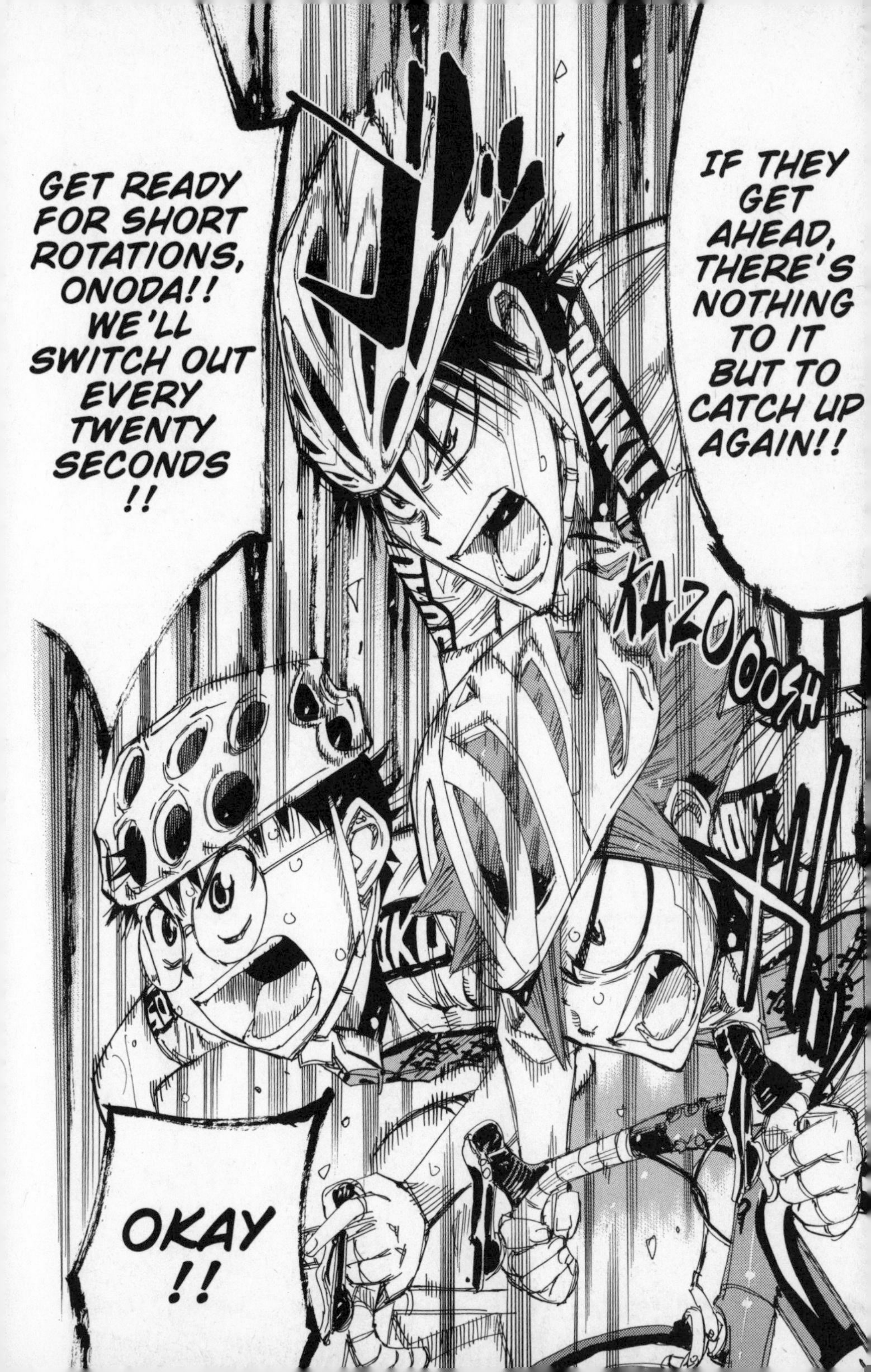

IF THEY GET AHEAD, THERE'S NOTHING TO IT BUT TO CATCH UP AGAIN!!
GET READY FOR SHORT ROTATIONS, ONODA!! WE'LL SWITCH OUT EVERY TWENTY SECONDS!!
KAZOOOOSH
OKAY!!

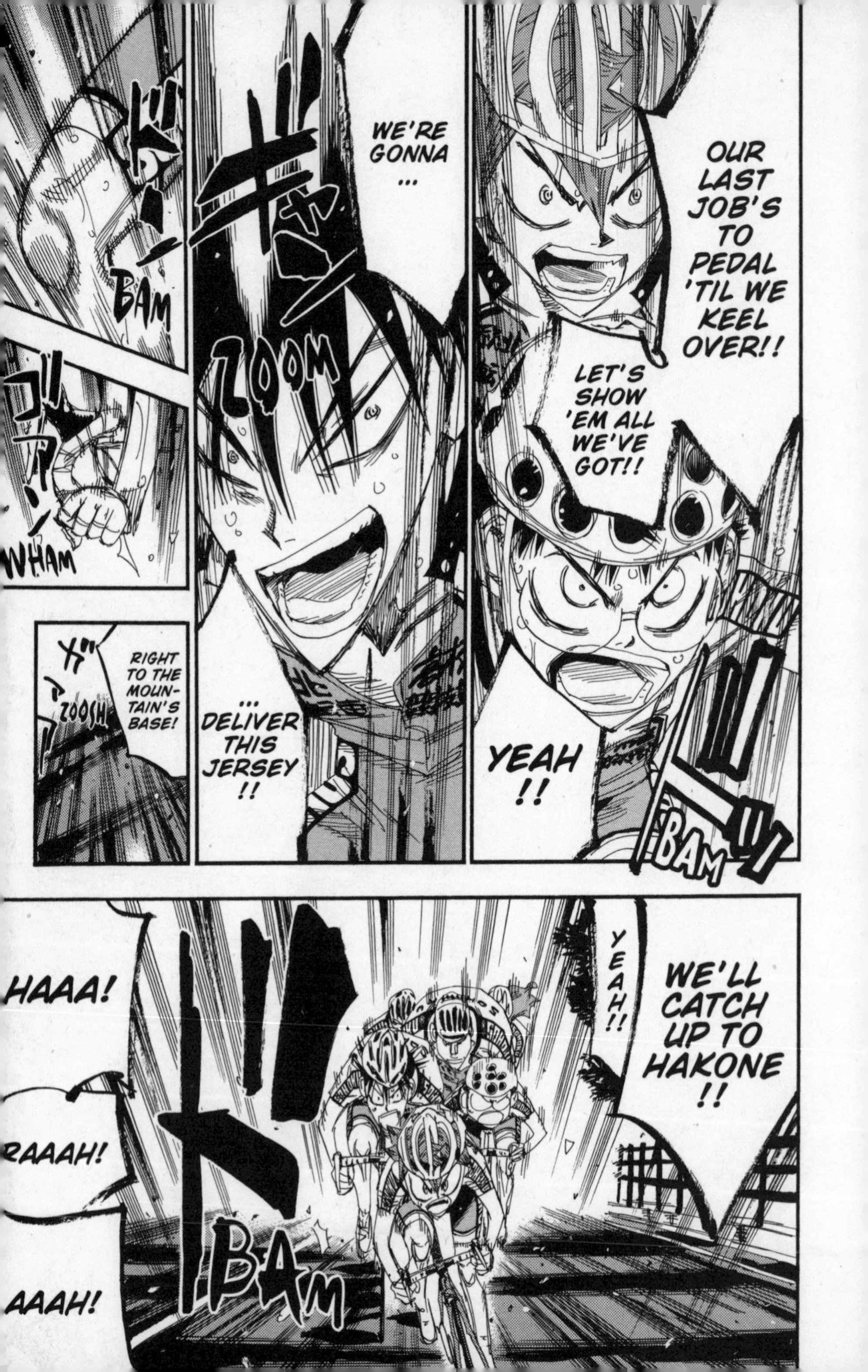
OUR LAST JOB'S TO PEDAL 'TIL WE KEEL OVER!!
LET'S SHOW 'EM ALL WE'VE GOT!!
YEAH !!
BAM
WE'RE GONNA ...
ZOOM
... DELIVER THIS JERSEY !!
BAM
WHAM
RIGHT TO THE MOUN-TAIN'S BASE!
ZOOSH
WE'LL CATCH UP TO HAKONE !!
YEAH!!
BAM
HAAAA!
RAAAH!
AAAH!

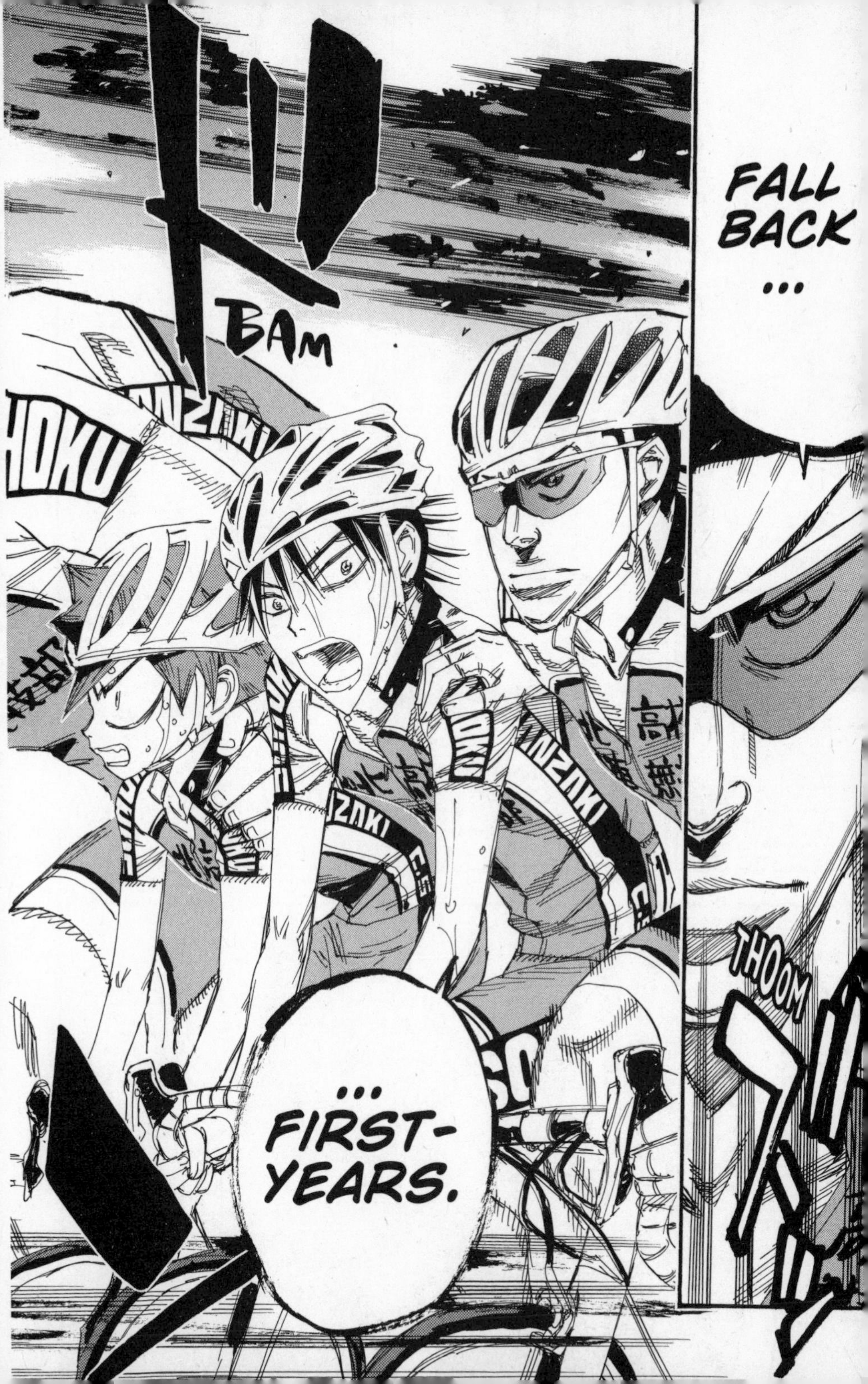
FALL BACK ...
THOOM
BAM
... FIRST-YEARS.

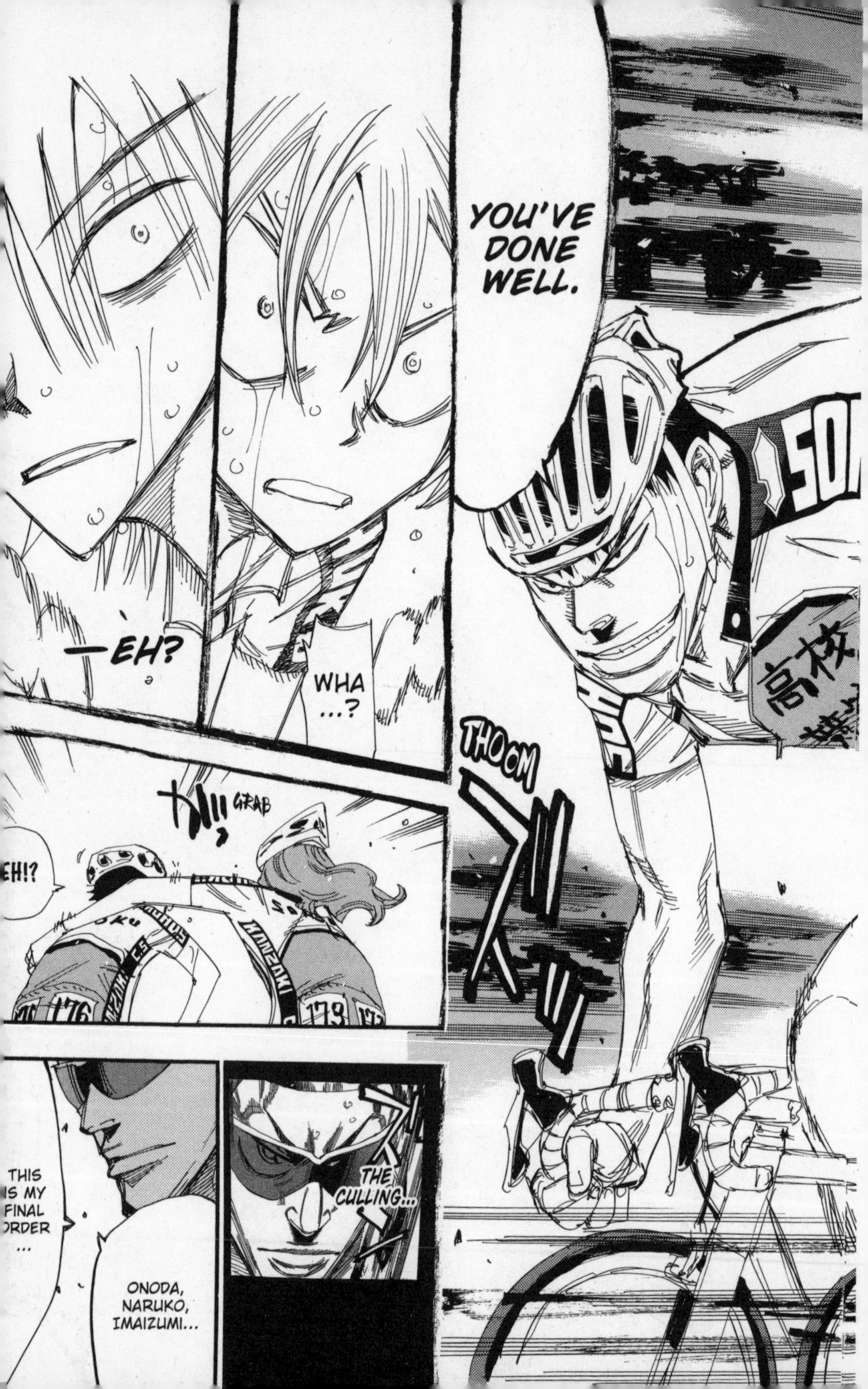

YOU'VE DONE WELL.
THOOM
WHA ...?
—EH?
GRAB
EH!?
THE CULLING...
THIS IS MY FINAL ORDER ...
ONODA, NARUKO, IMAIZUMI...

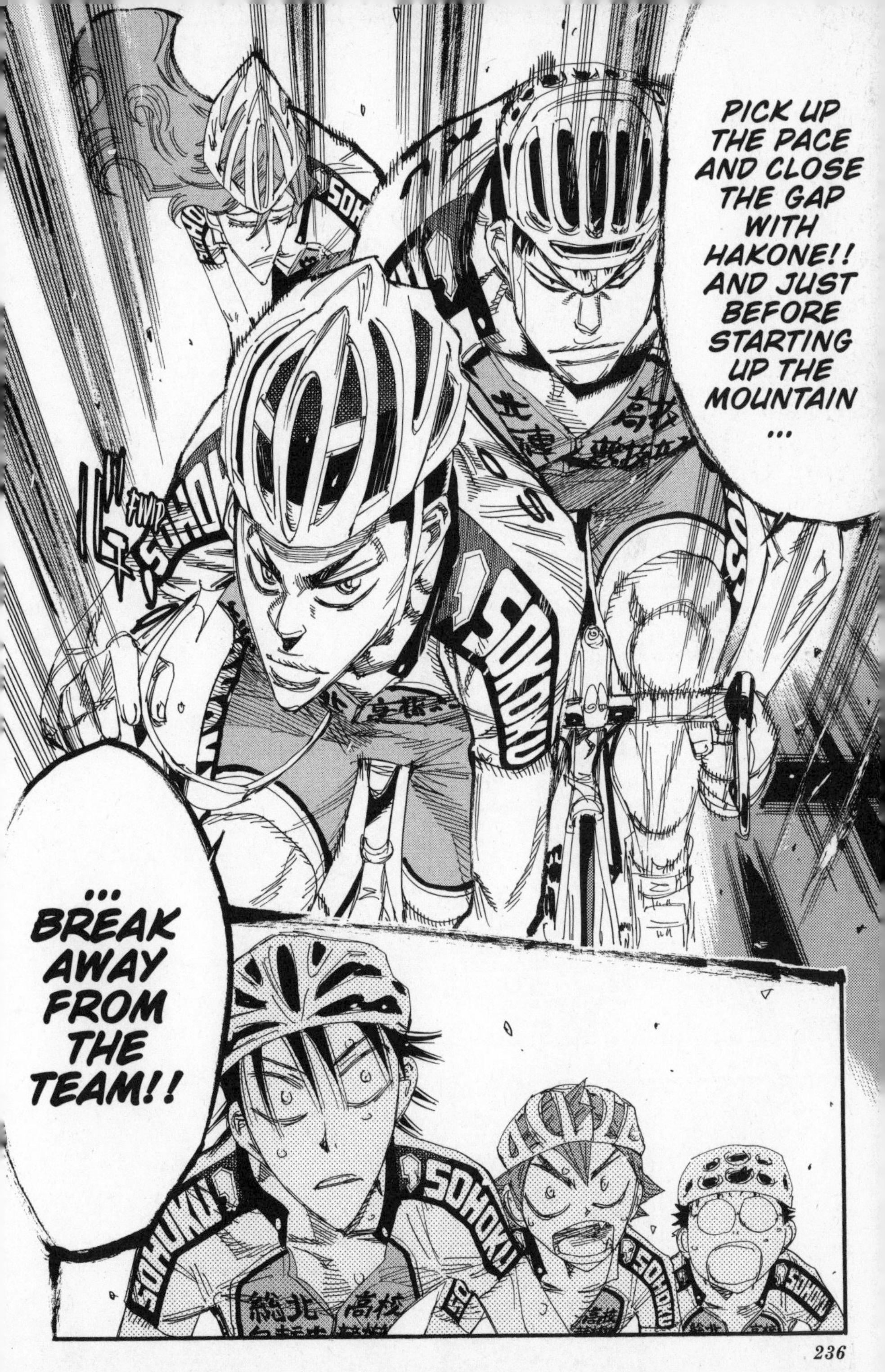
PICK UP THE PACE AND CLOSE THE GAP WITH HAKONE!! AND JUST BEFORE STARTING UP THE MOUNTAIN ...
FWIP
... BREAK AWAY FROM THE TEAM!!

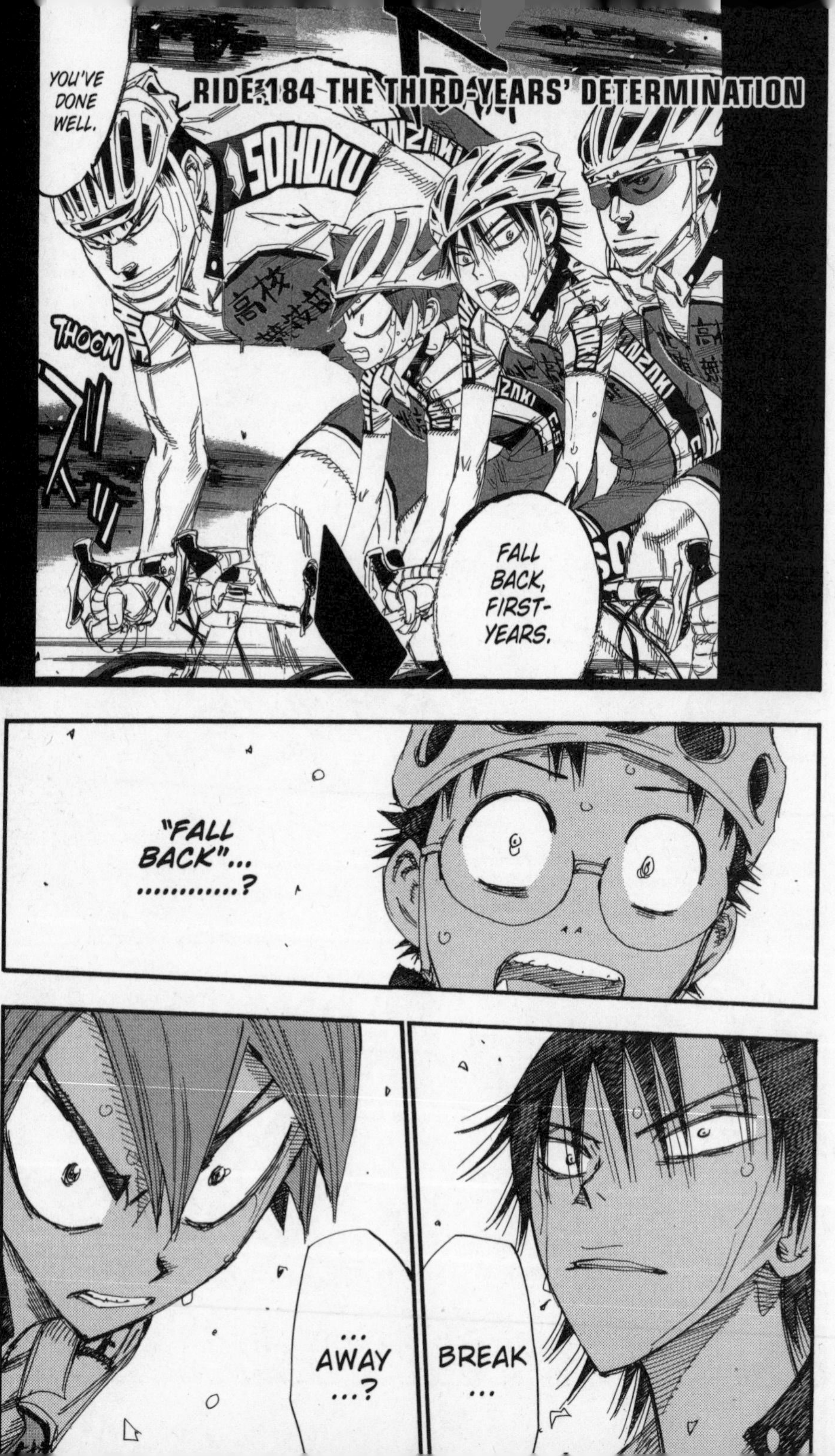
RIDE.184 THE THIRD-YEARS' DETERMINATION
YOU'VE DONE WELL.
THOOM
FALL BACK, FIRST-YEARS.
"FALL BACK"... ....?
BREAK ...
... AWAY ...?

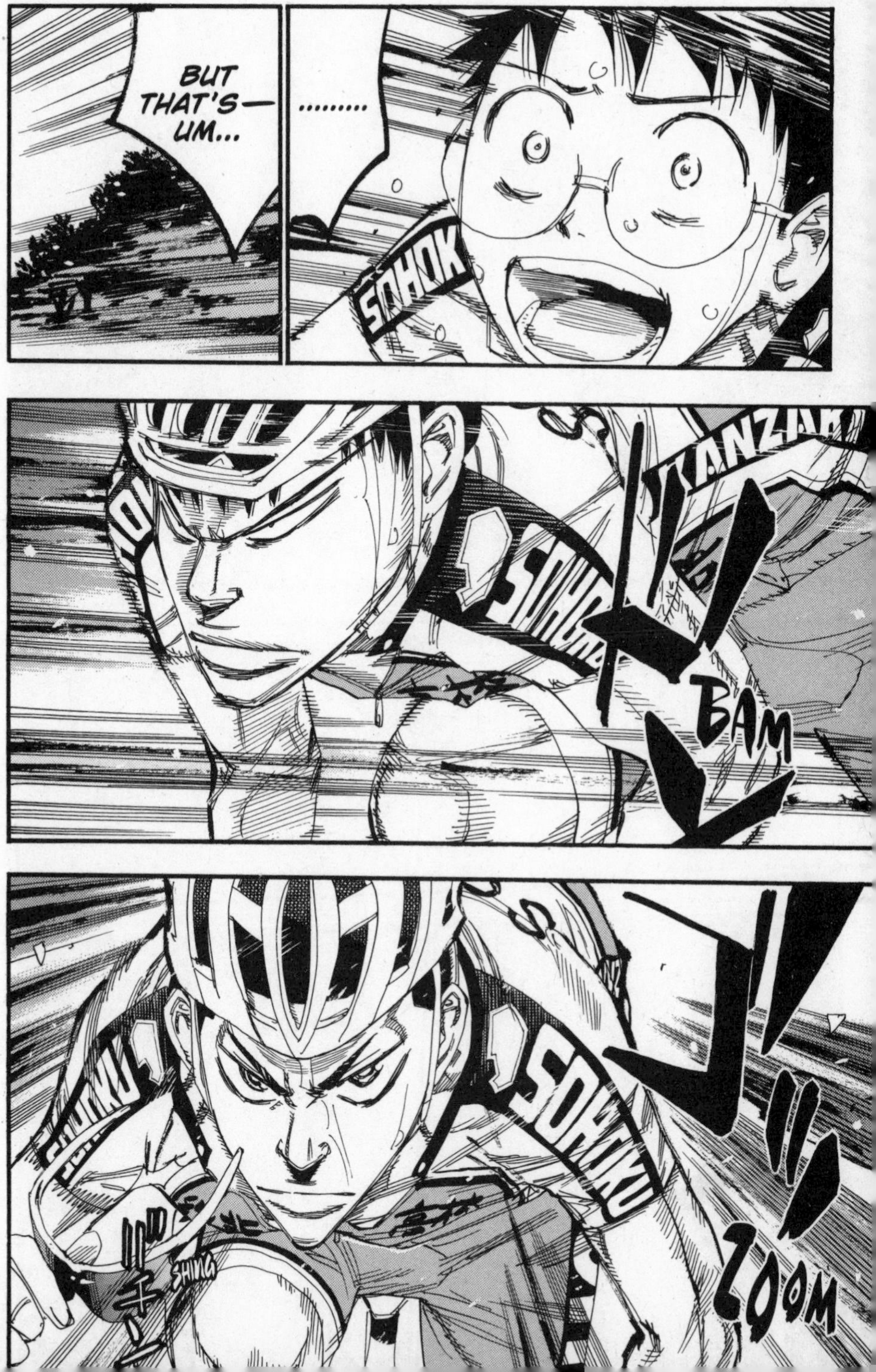
....
BUT THAT'S—
UM...
BAM
SHING
ZOOM

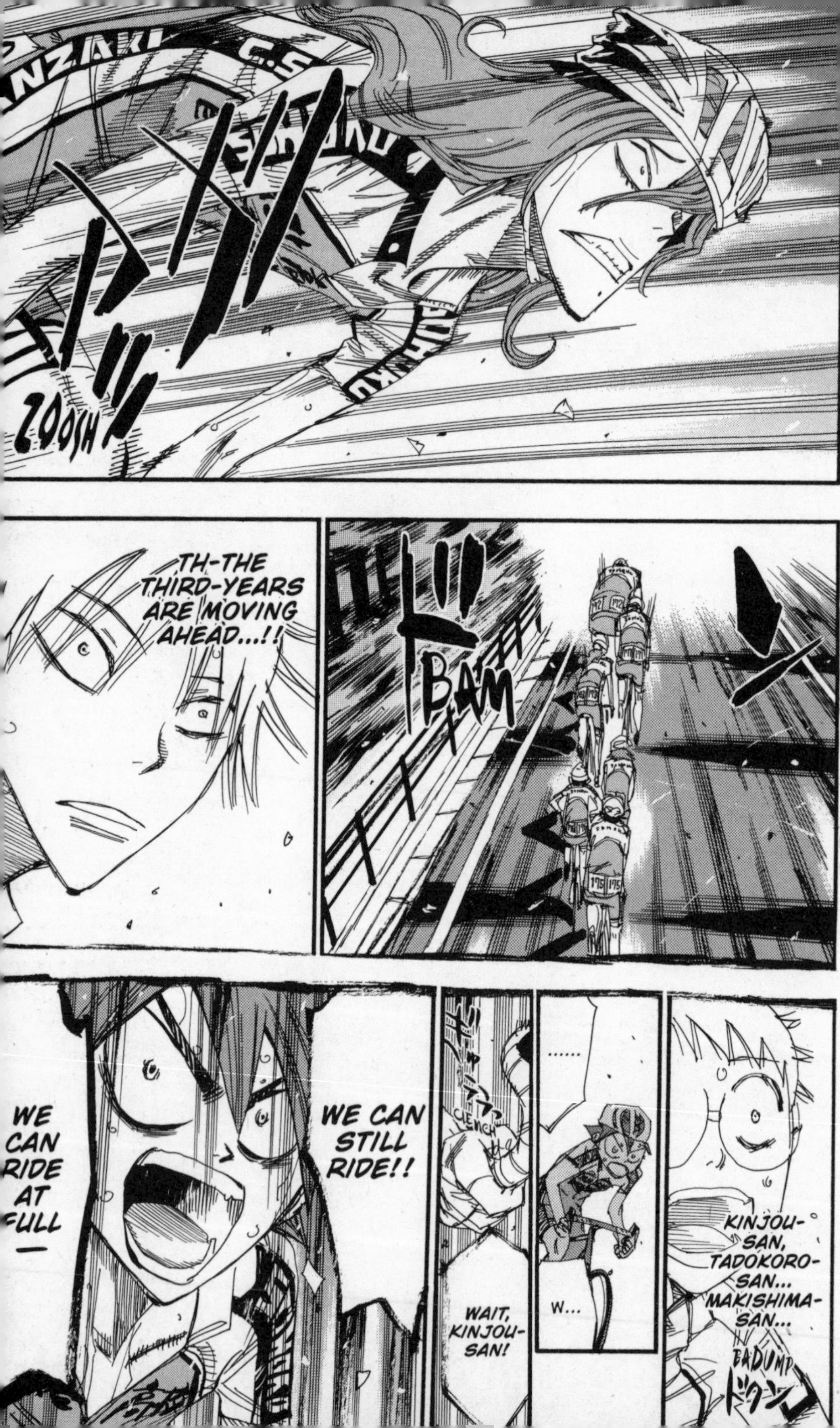
ZOOSH
BAM
TH-THE THIRD-YEARS ARE MOVING AHEAD...!!
KINJOU-SAN, TADOKORO-SAN... MAKISHIMA-SAN...
BADUMP
......
W...
CLENCH
WAIT, KINJOU-SAN!
WE CAN STILL RIDE!!
WE CAN RIDE AT FULL—

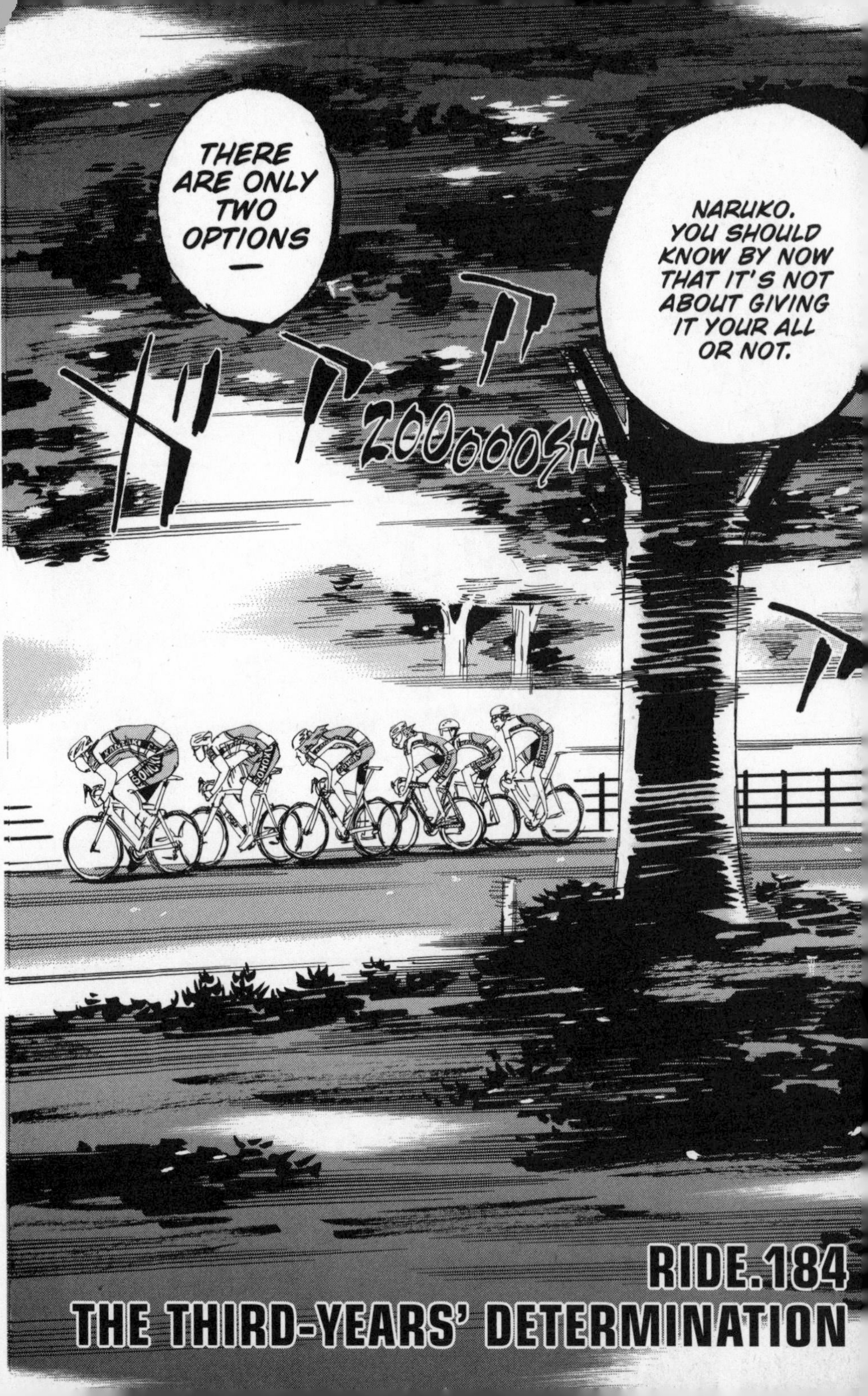
NARUKO. YOU SHOULD KNOW BY NOW THAT IT'S NOT ABOUT GIVING IT YOUR ALL OR NOT.
THERE ARE ONLY TWO OPTIONS —
ZOOOOOOSH
RIDE.184
THE THIRD-YEARS' DETERMINATION

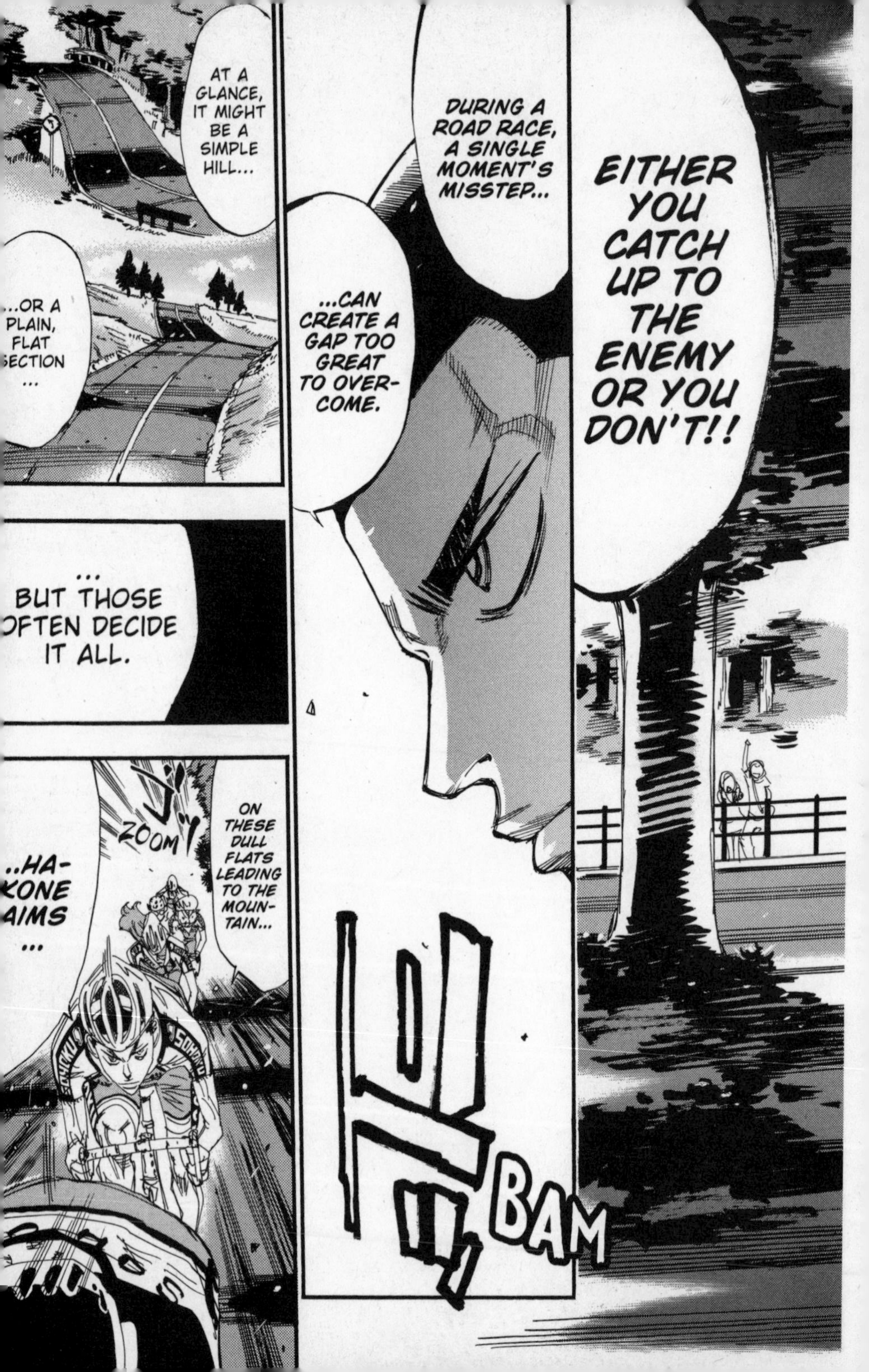

EITHER YOU CATCH UP TO THE ENEMY OR YOU DON'T!!
DURING A ROAD RACE, A SINGLE MOMENT'S MISSTEP...
...CAN CREATE A GAP TOO GREAT TO OVER-COME.
BAM
AT A GLANCE, IT MIGHT BE A SIMPLE HILL...
...OR A PLAIN, FLAT SECTION ...
... BUT THOSE OFTEN DECIDE IT ALL.
ZOOM
ON THESE DULL FLATS LEADING TO THE MOUN-TAIN...
..HA-KONE AIMS ...

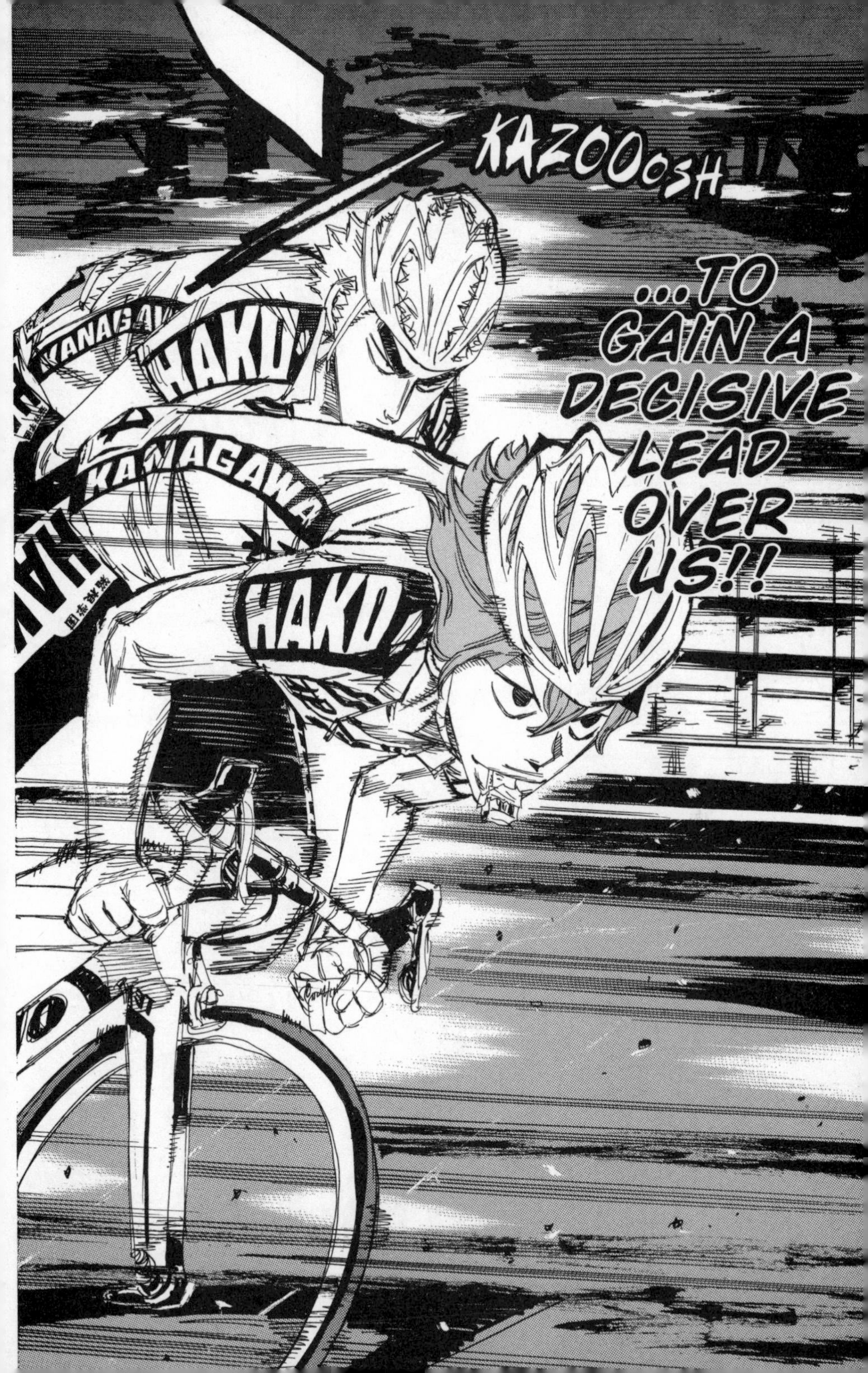
KAZOOOOSH
...TO GAIN A DECISIVE LEAD OVER US!!

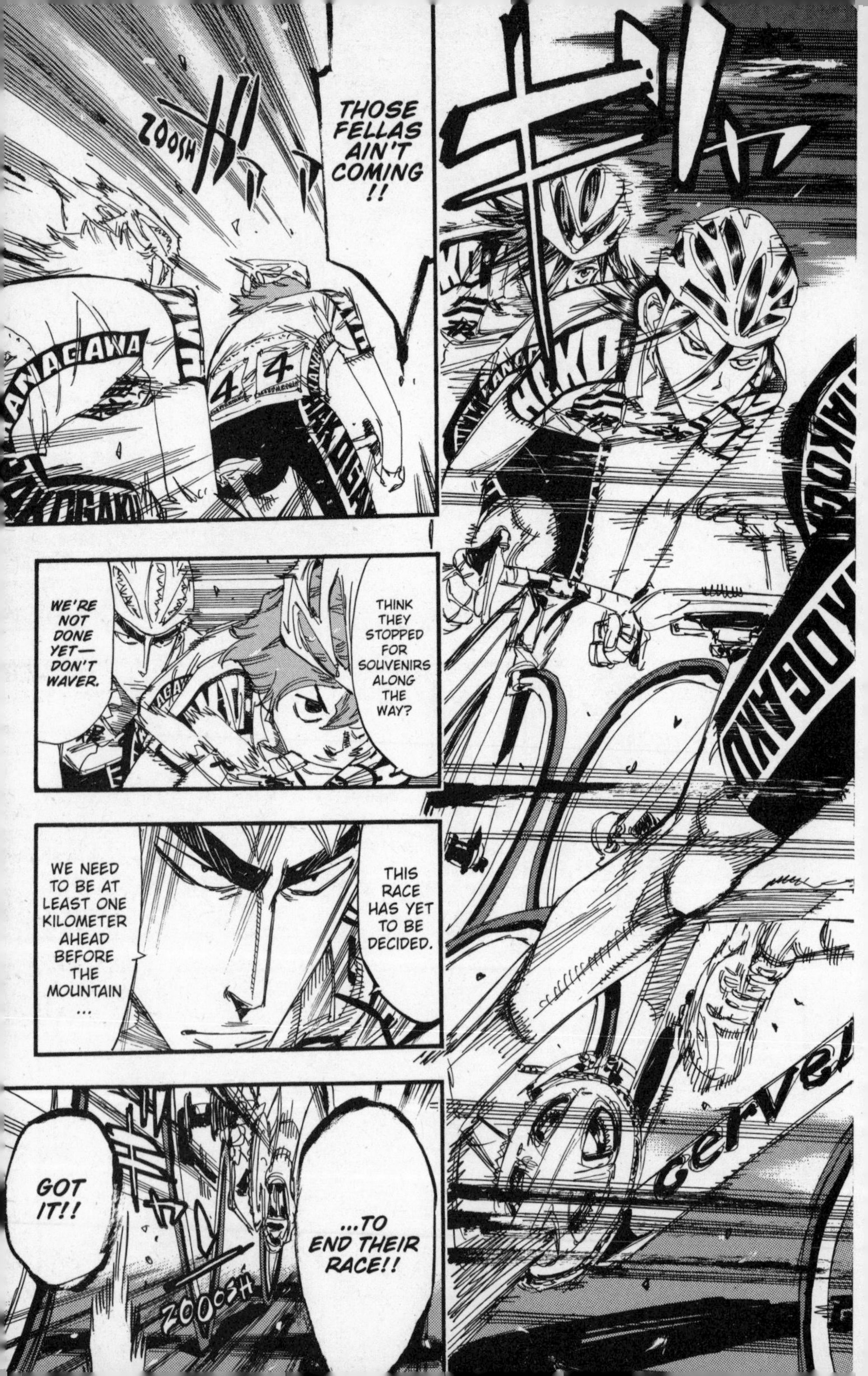
THOSE FELLAS AIN'T COMING!!
ZOOSH
THINK THEY STOPPED FOR SOUVENIRS ALONG THE WAY?
WE'RE NOT DONE YET— DON'T WAVER.
THIS RACE HAS YET TO BE DECIDED.
WE NEED TO BE AT LEAST ONE KILOMETER AHEAD BEFORE THE MOUNTAIN ...
...TO END THEIR RACE!!
GOT IT!!
ZOOOSH

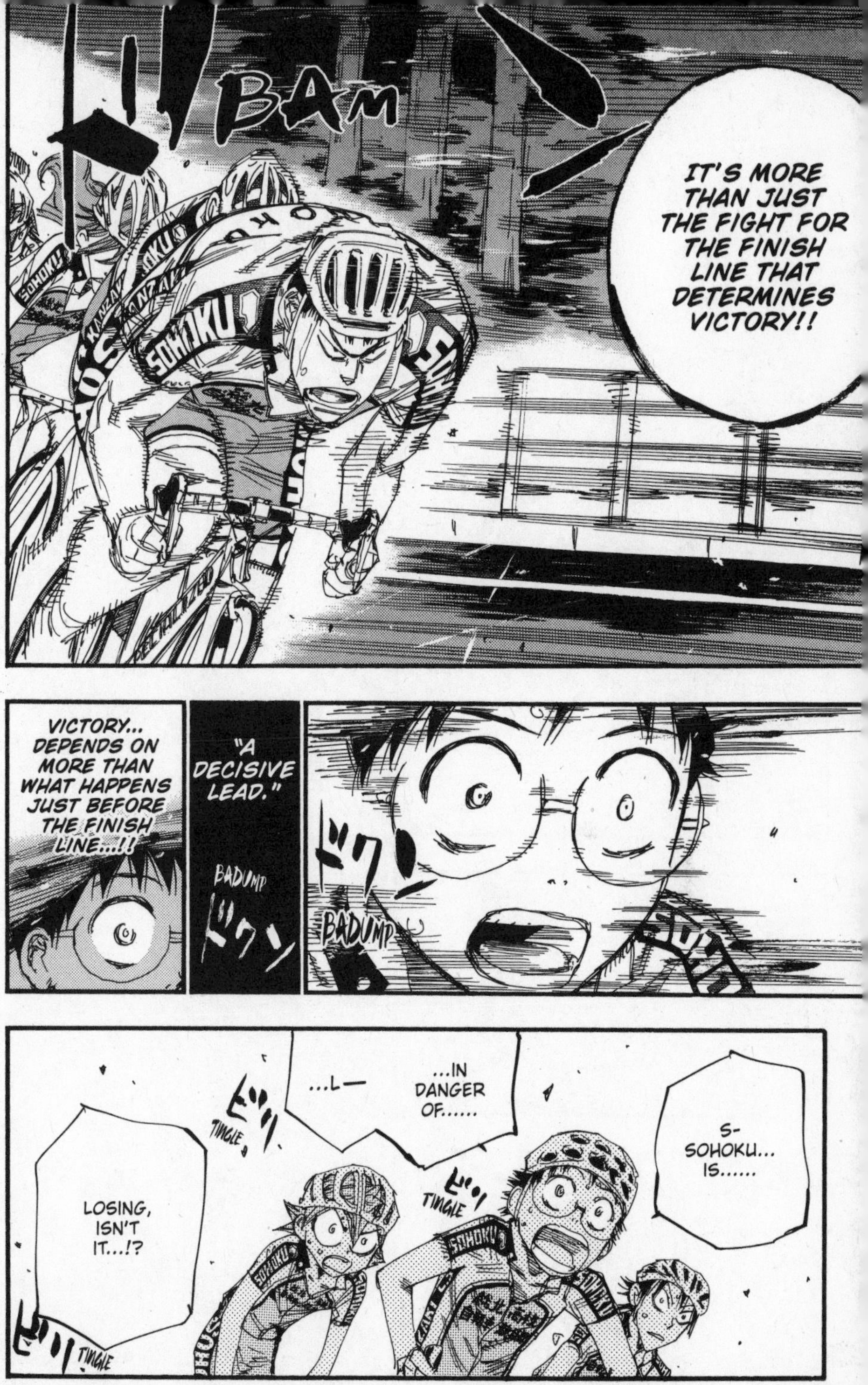
BAM
IT'S MORE THAN JUST THE FIGHT FOR THE FINISH LINE THAT DETERMINES VICTORY!!
BADUMP
"A DECISIVE LEAD."
BADUMP
VICTORY... DEPENDS ON MORE THAN WHAT HAPPENS JUST BEFORE THE FINISH LINE...!!
S-SOHOKU... IS......
TINGLE
...IN DANGER OF......
...L—
TINGLE
LOSING, ISN'T IT...!?
TINGLE

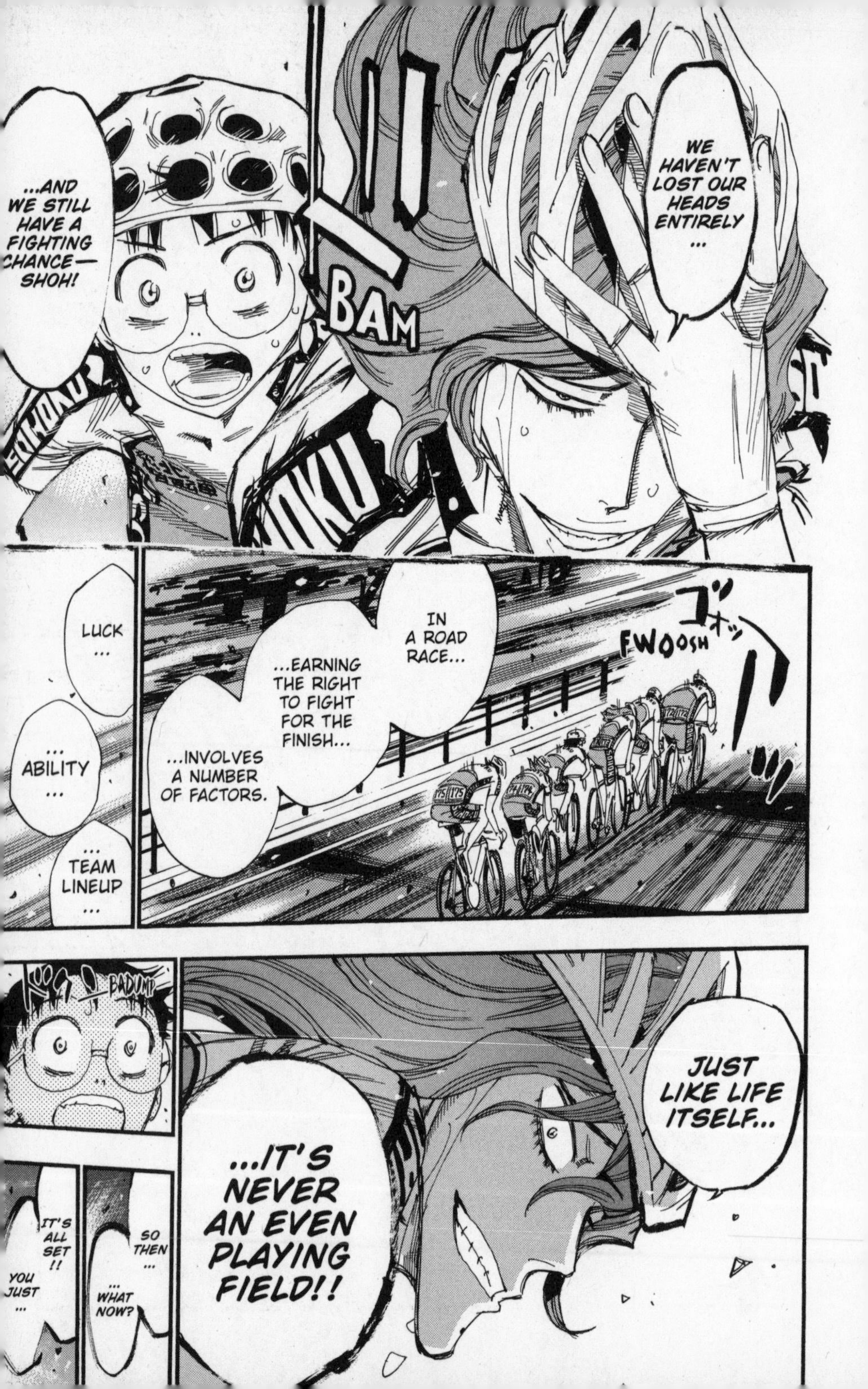
WE HAVEN'T LOST OUR HEADS ENTIRELY...
BAM
...AND WE STILL HAVE A FIGHTING CHANCE—SHOH!
FWOOSH
IN A ROAD RACE...
...EARNING THE RIGHT TO FIGHT FOR THE FINISH...
...INVOLVES A NUMBER OF FACTORS.
LUCK...
...ABILITY...
...TEAM LINEUP...
JUST LIKE LIFE ITSELF...
...IT'S NEVER AN EVEN PLAYING FIELD!!
BADUMP
SO THEN...
...WHAT NOW?
IT'S ALL SET!!
YOU JUST...

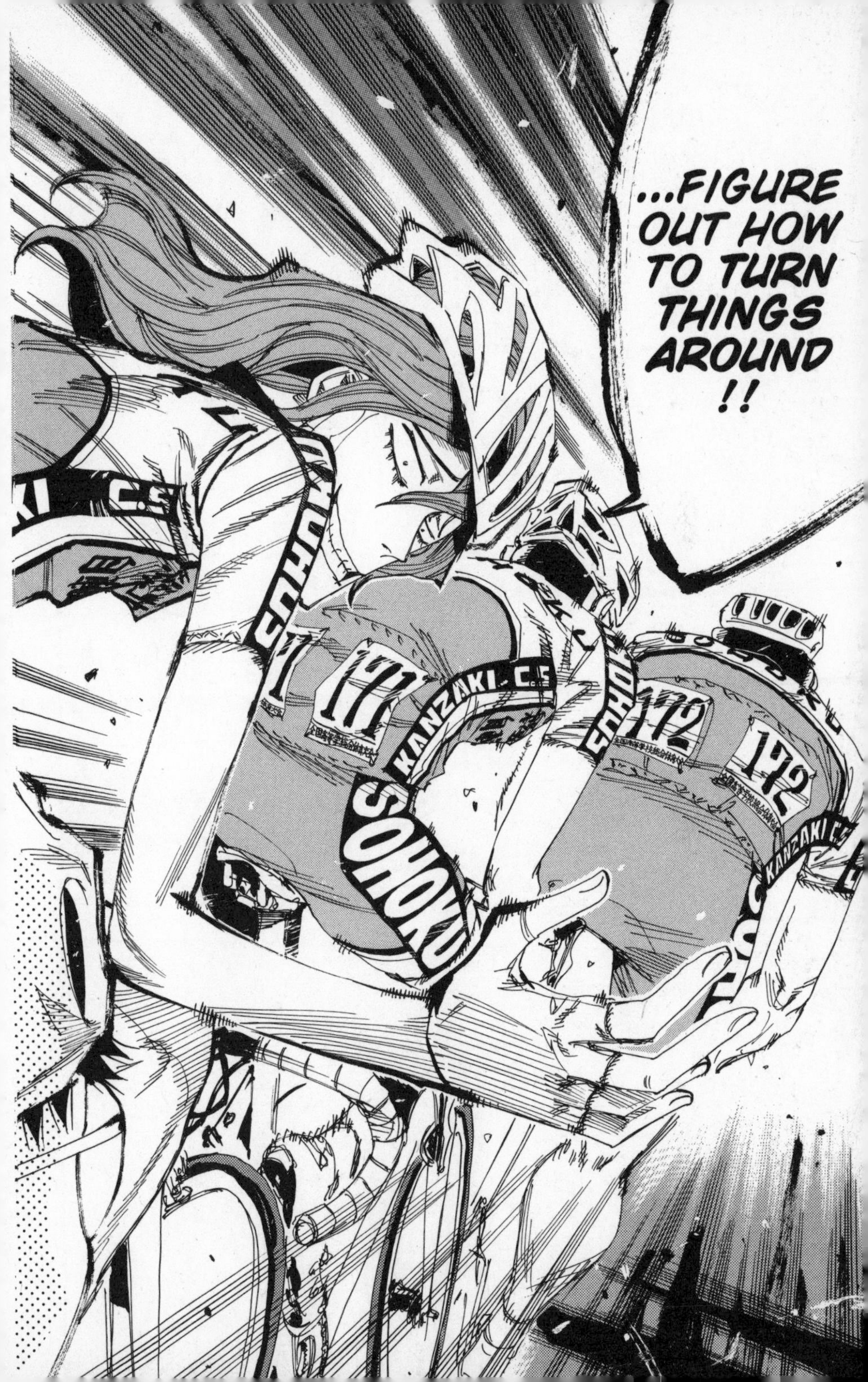
...FIGURE OUT HOW TO TURN THINGS AROUND !!
SOHOKU
KANZAKI C.S
171
172

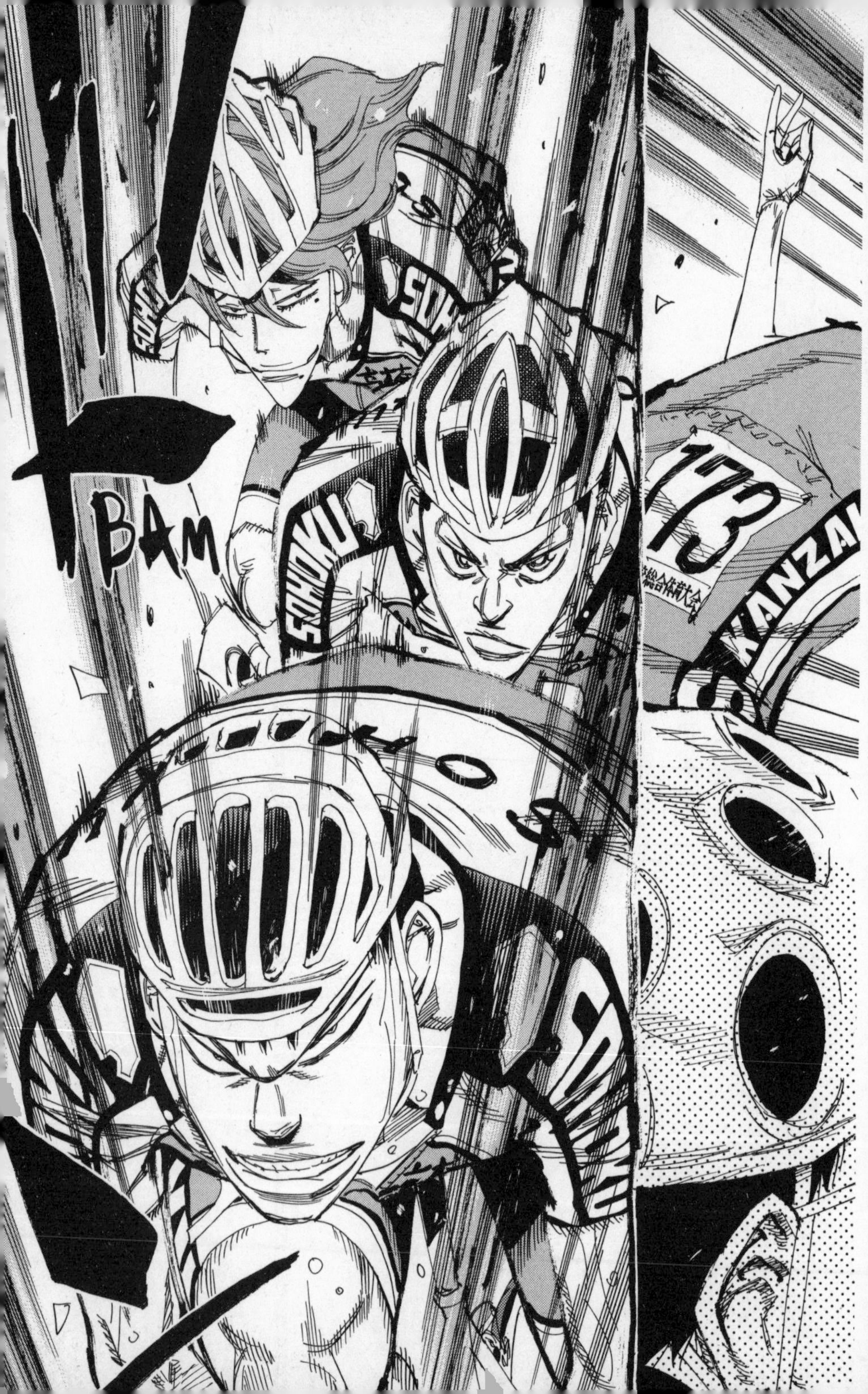
173
KANZA
BAM
SOHOKU

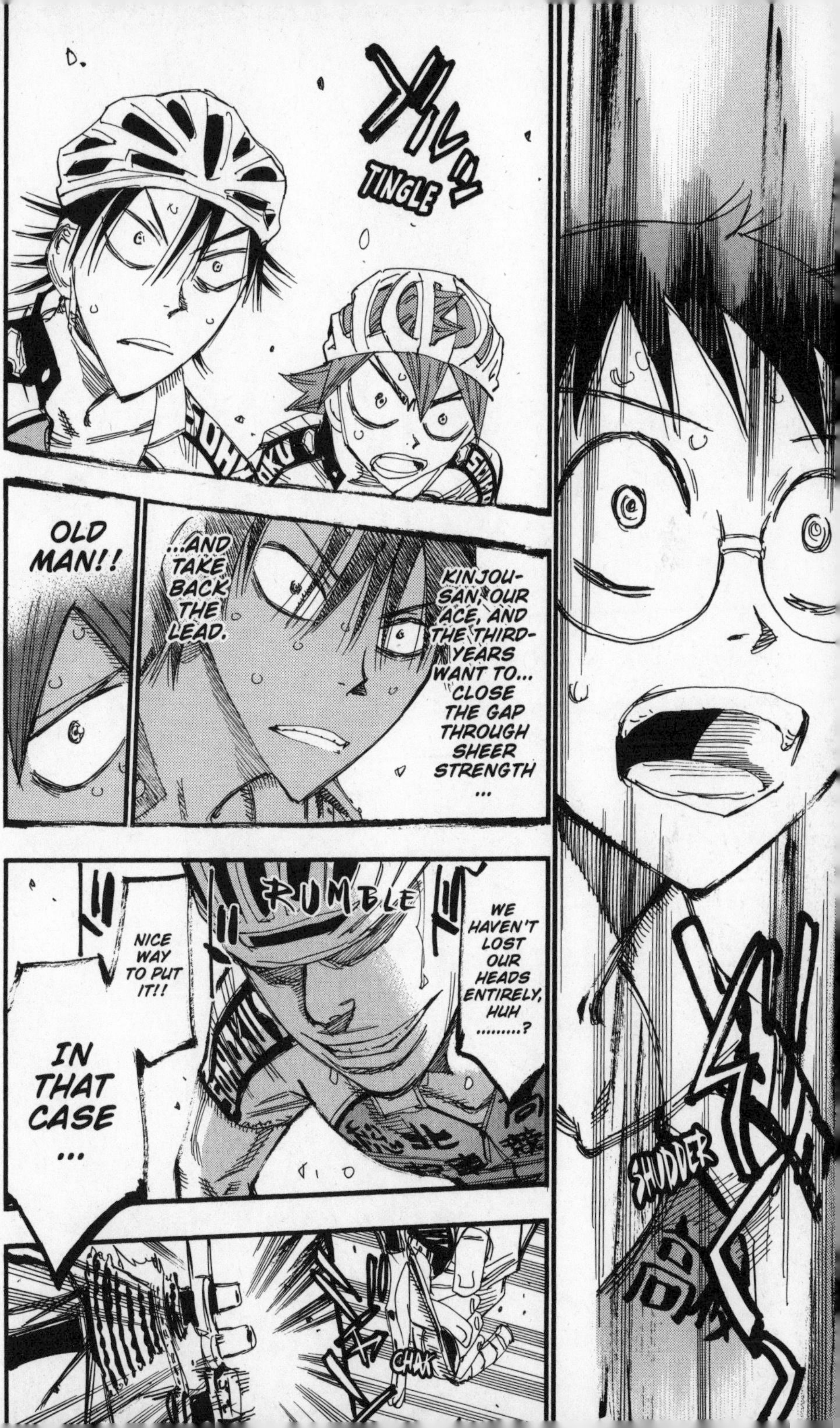
SHUDDER
TINGLE
KINJOU-SAN, OUR ACE, AND THE THIRD-YEARS WANT TO... CLOSE THE GAP THROUGH SHEER STRENGTH ...
...AND TAKE BACK THE LEAD.
OLD MAN!!
RUMBLE
WE HAVEN'T LOST OUR HEADS ENTIRELY, HUH ....?
NICE WAY TO PUT IT!!
IN THAT CASE ...
CHAK

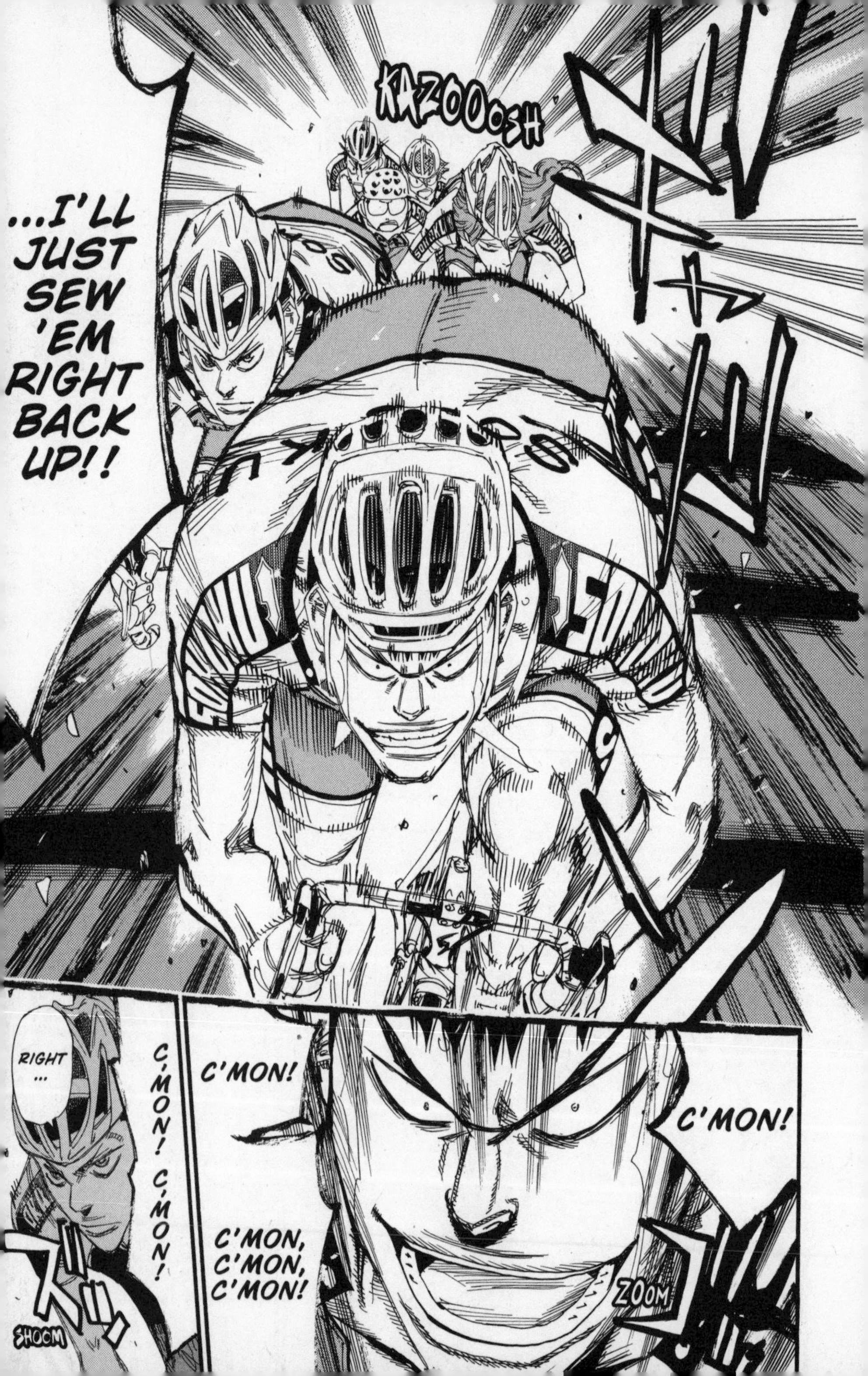
KAZOOOSH
...I'LL JUST SEW 'EM RIGHT BACK UP!!
C'MON!
C'MON!
C'MON, C'MON, C'MON!
ZOOM
C'MON! C'MON! C'MON!
RIGHT ...
SHOOM

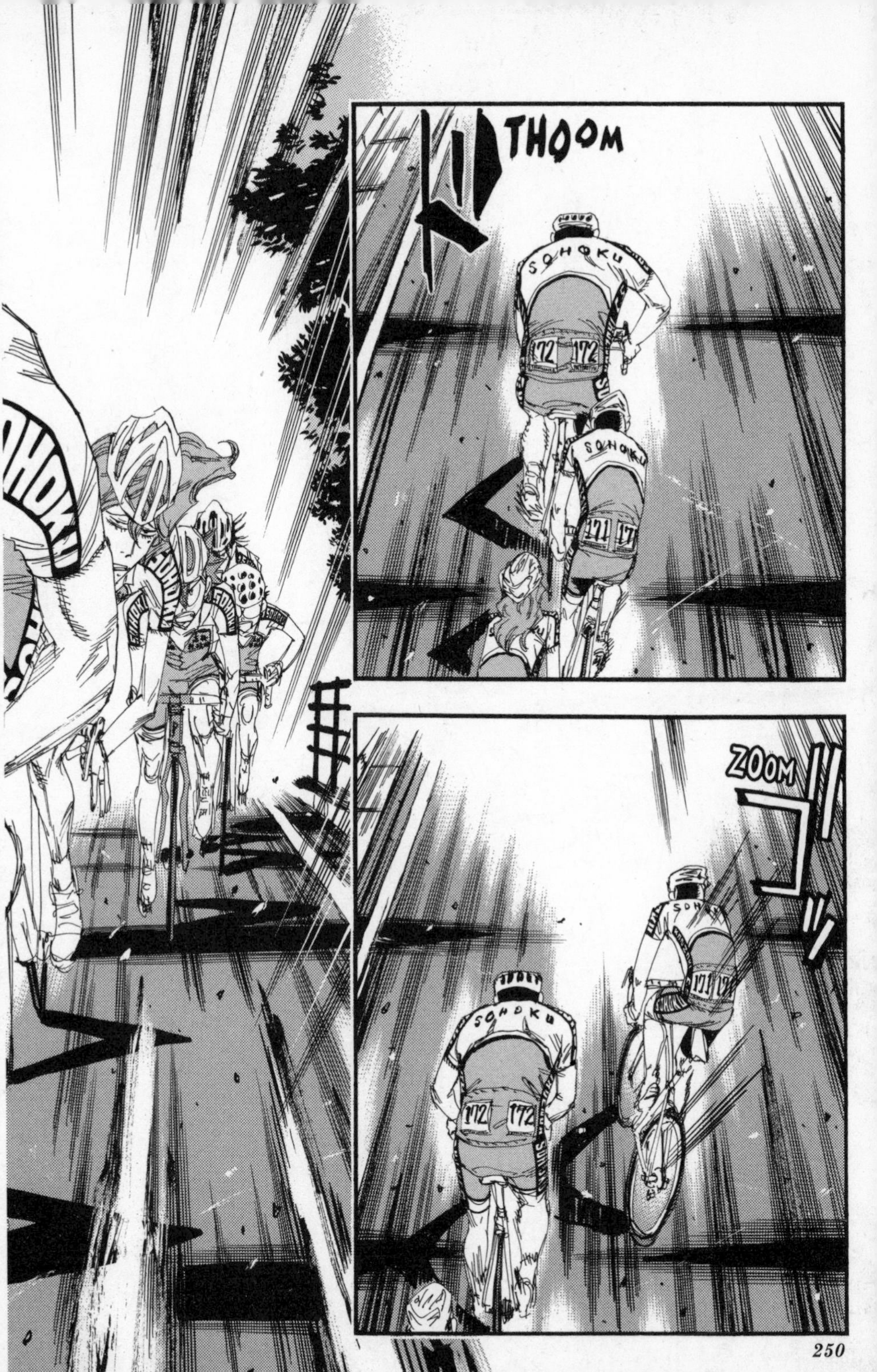
THOOM
ZOOM

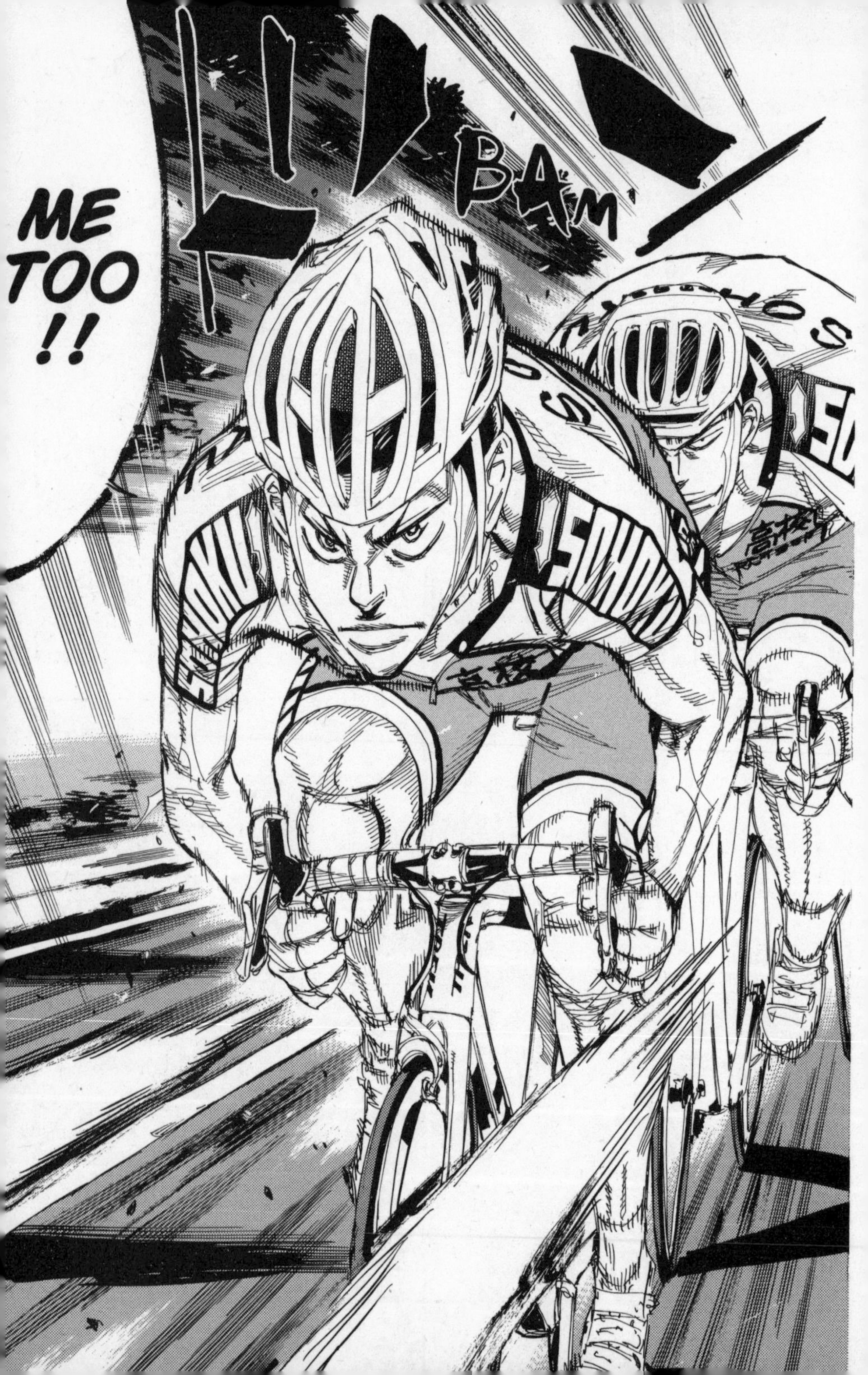
BAM
ME TOO!!

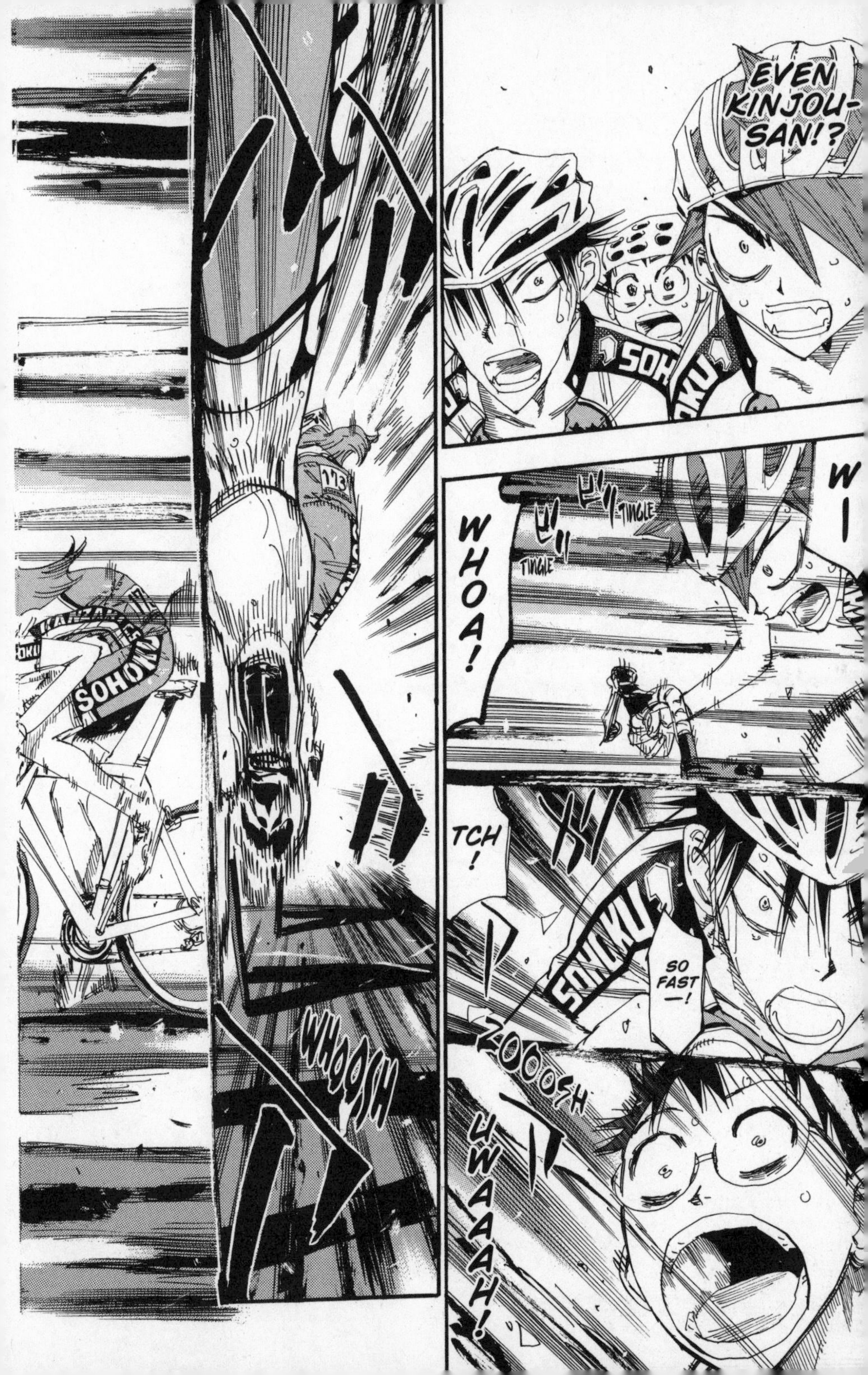
EVEN KINJOU-SAN!?
SOHOKU
SOHOKU
WI
TINGLE
TINGLE
WHOA!
TCH!
SOHOKU
SO FAST—!
ZOOOSH
UWAAAAH!
WHOOSH
113
SOHOKU

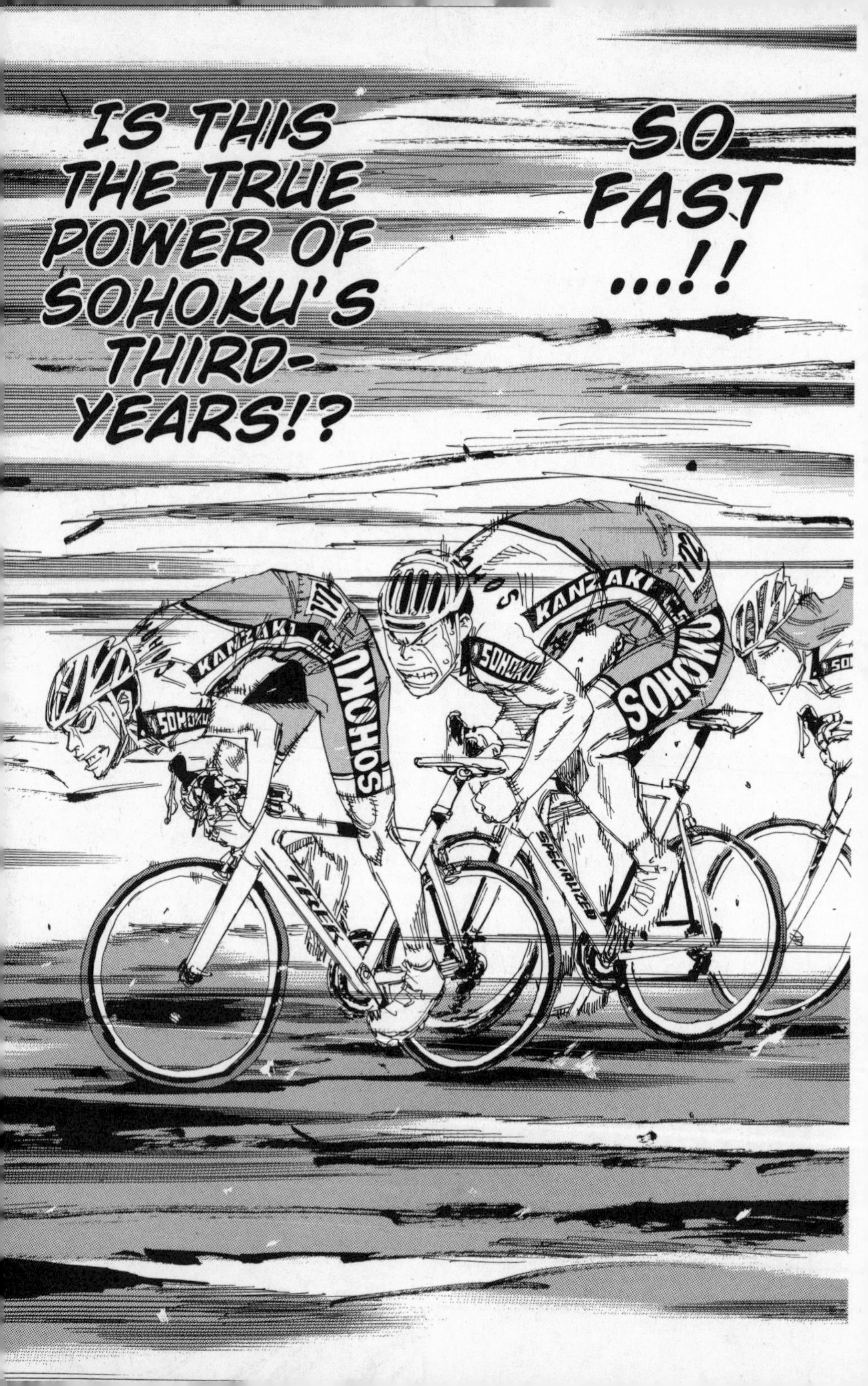
SO FAST ...!!
IS THIS THE TRUE POWER OF SOHOKU'S THIRD-YEARS!?

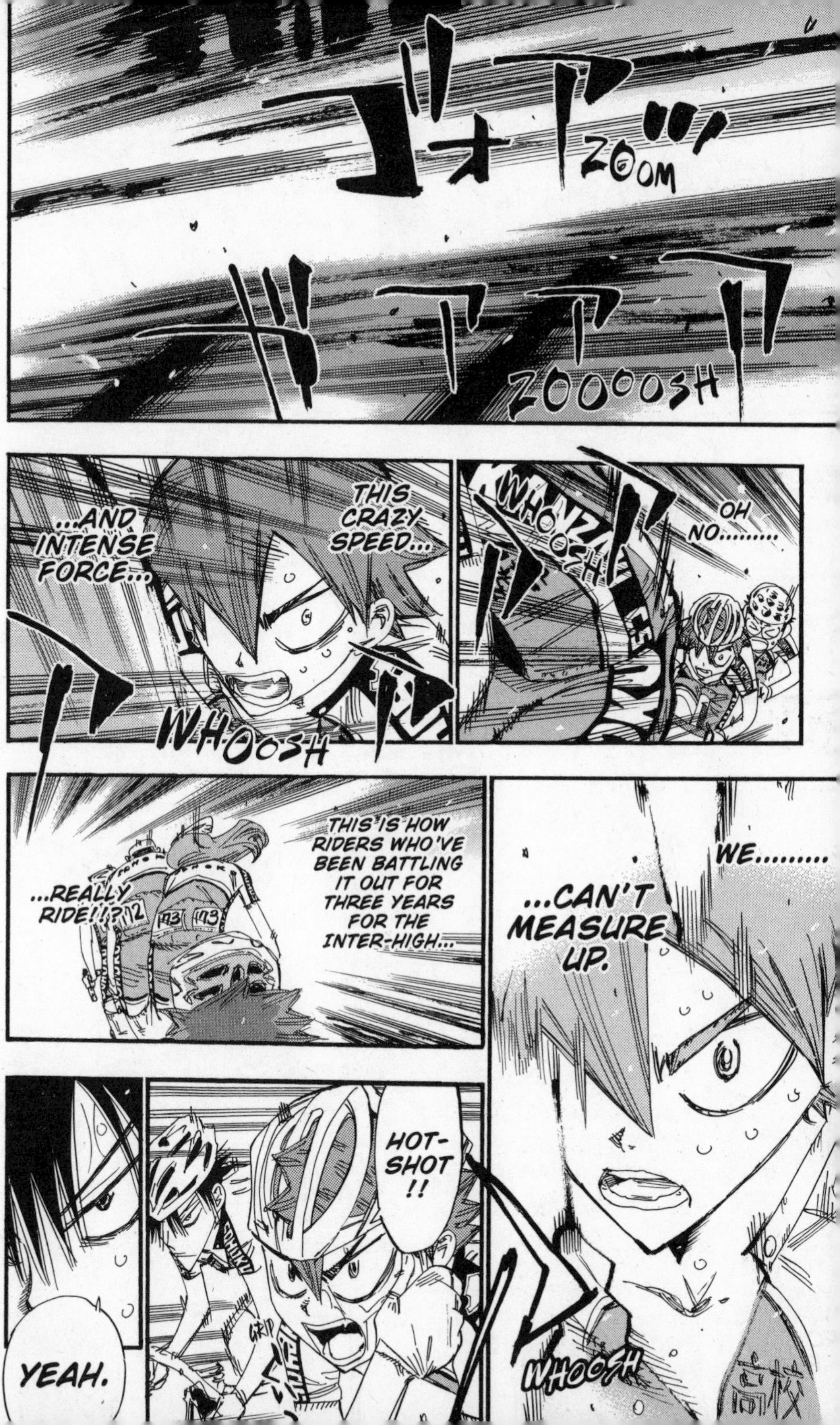
ZOOM
ZOOOOSH
WHOOSH
OH NO..........
THIS CRAZY SPEED...
...AND INTENSE FORCE...
WHOOSH
WE.........
...CAN'T MEASURE UP.
WHOOSH
THIS IS HOW RIDERS WHO'VE BEEN BATTLING IT OUT FOR THREE YEARS FOR THE INTER-HIGH...
...REALLY RIDE!!?
HOT-SHOT!!
GRIP
YEAH.

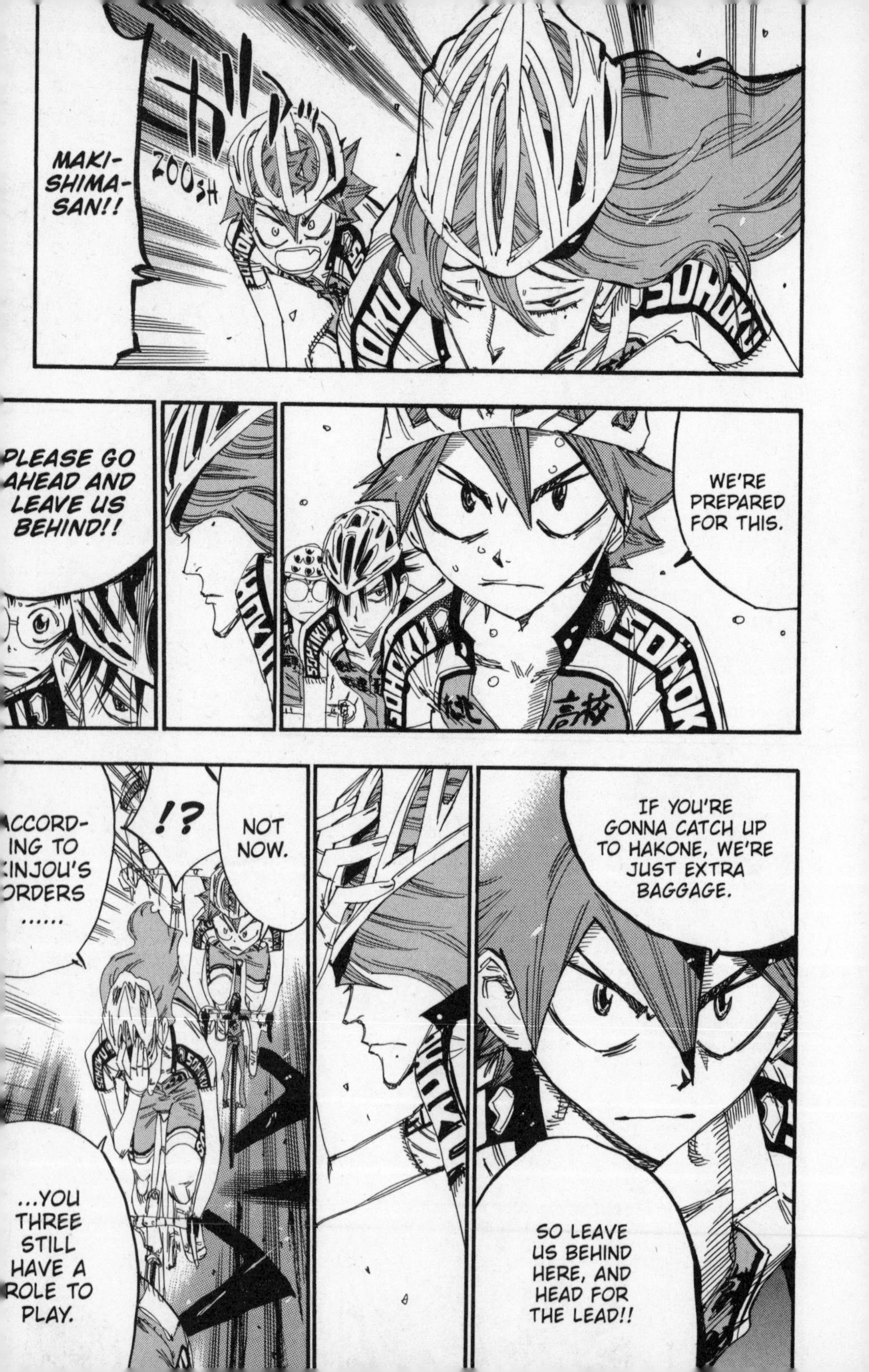
ZOOSH
MAKI-SHIMA-SAN!!
WE'RE PREPARED FOR THIS.
PLEASE GO AHEAD AND LEAVE US BEHIND!!
IF YOU'RE GONNA CATCH UP TO HAKONE, WE'RE JUST EXTRA BAGGAGE.
SO LEAVE US BEHIND HERE, AND HEAD FOR THE LEAD!!
NOT NOW.
!?
ACCORD-ING TO KINJOU'S ORDERS ......
...YOU THREE STILL HAVE A ROLE TO PLAY.

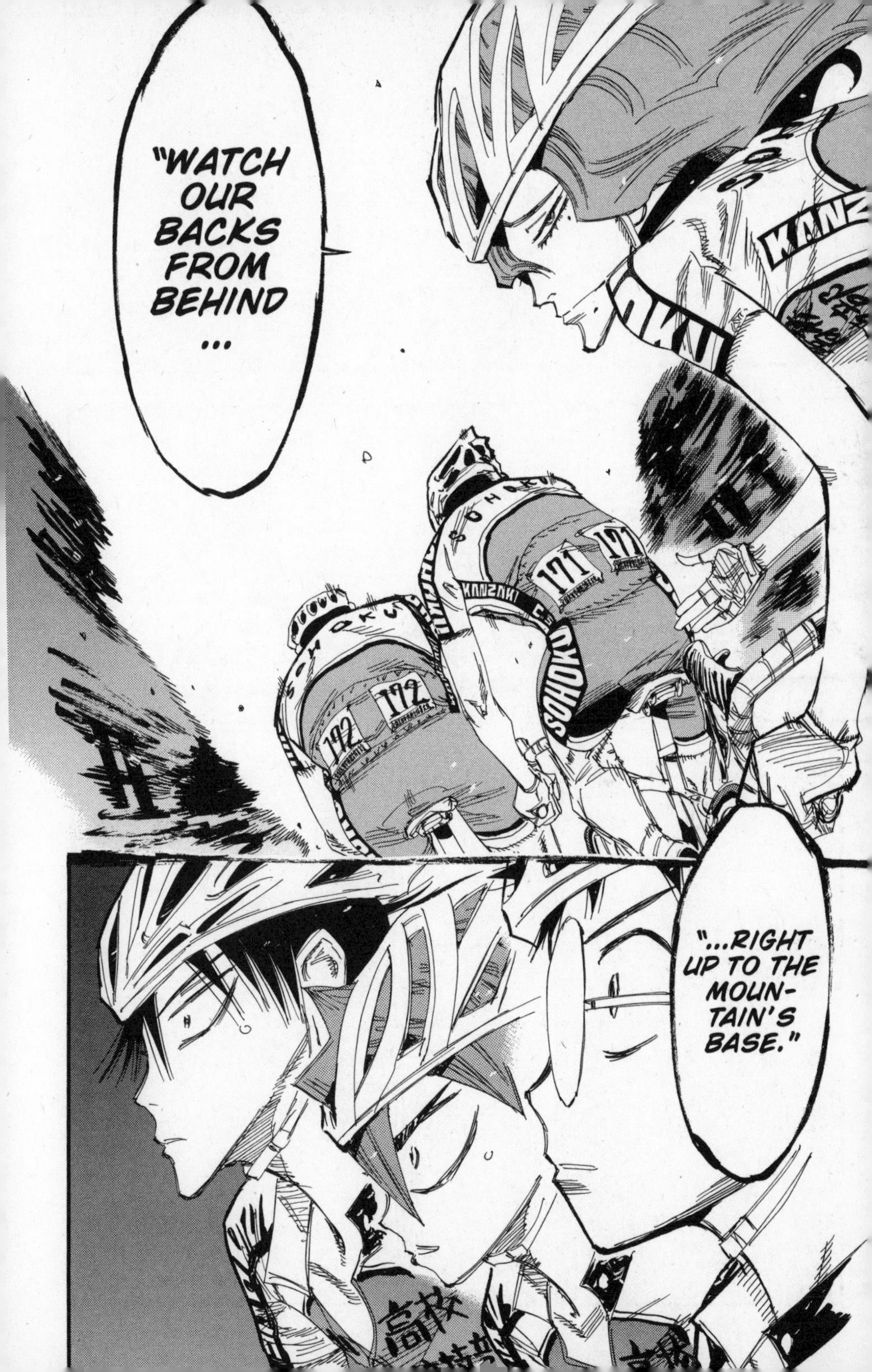
"WATCH OUR BACKS FROM BEHIND ...
"...RIGHT UP TO THE MOUN-TAIN'S BASE."

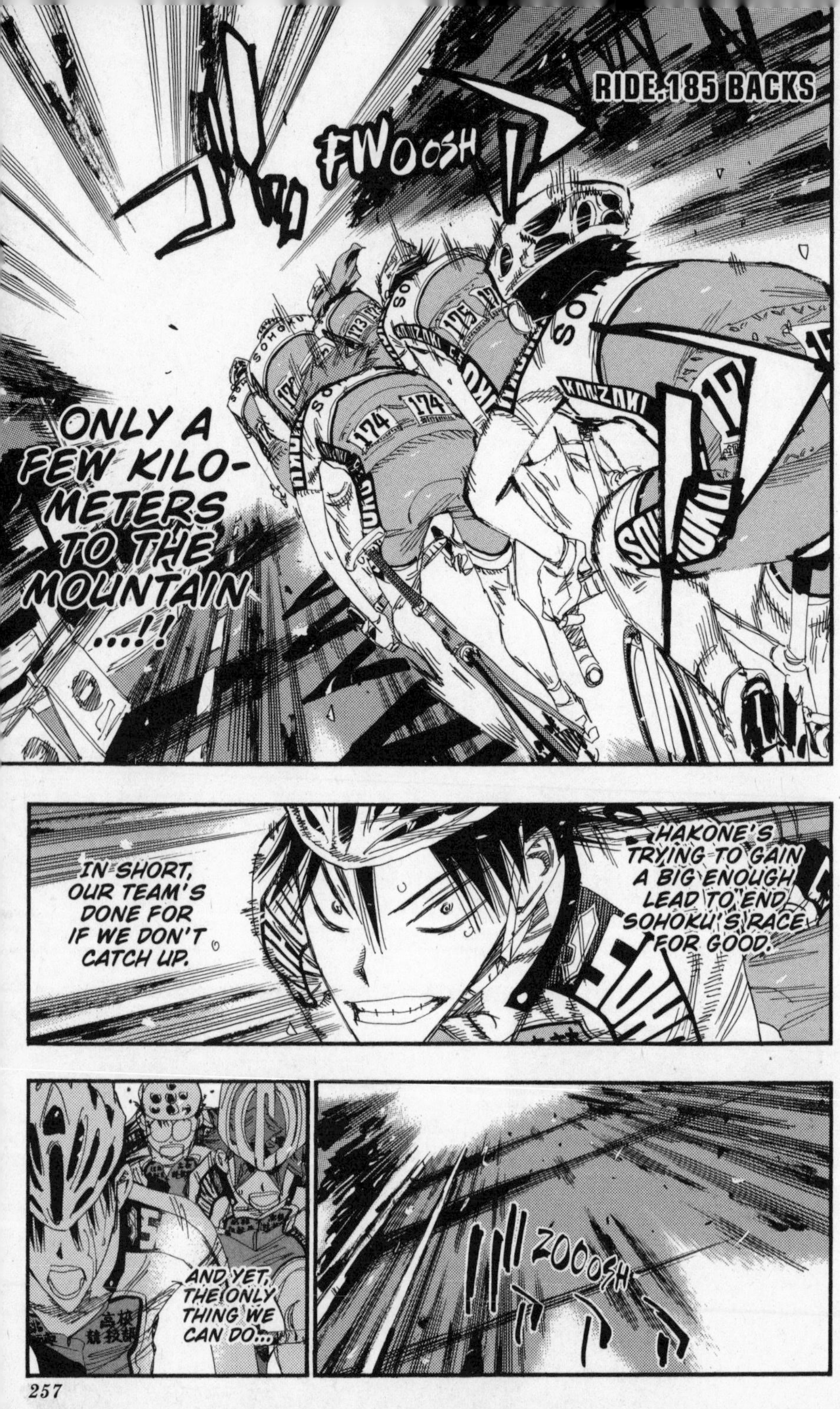
RIDE.185 BACKS
FWOOSH
ONLY A FEW KILO-METERS TO THE MOUNTAIN ...!!
HAKONE'S TRYING TO GAIN A BIG ENOUGH LEAD TO END SOHOKU'S RACE FOR GOOD.
IN SHORT, OUR TEAM'S DONE FOR IF WE DON'T CATCH UP.
ZOOOSH
AND YET, THE ONLY THING WE CAN DO...

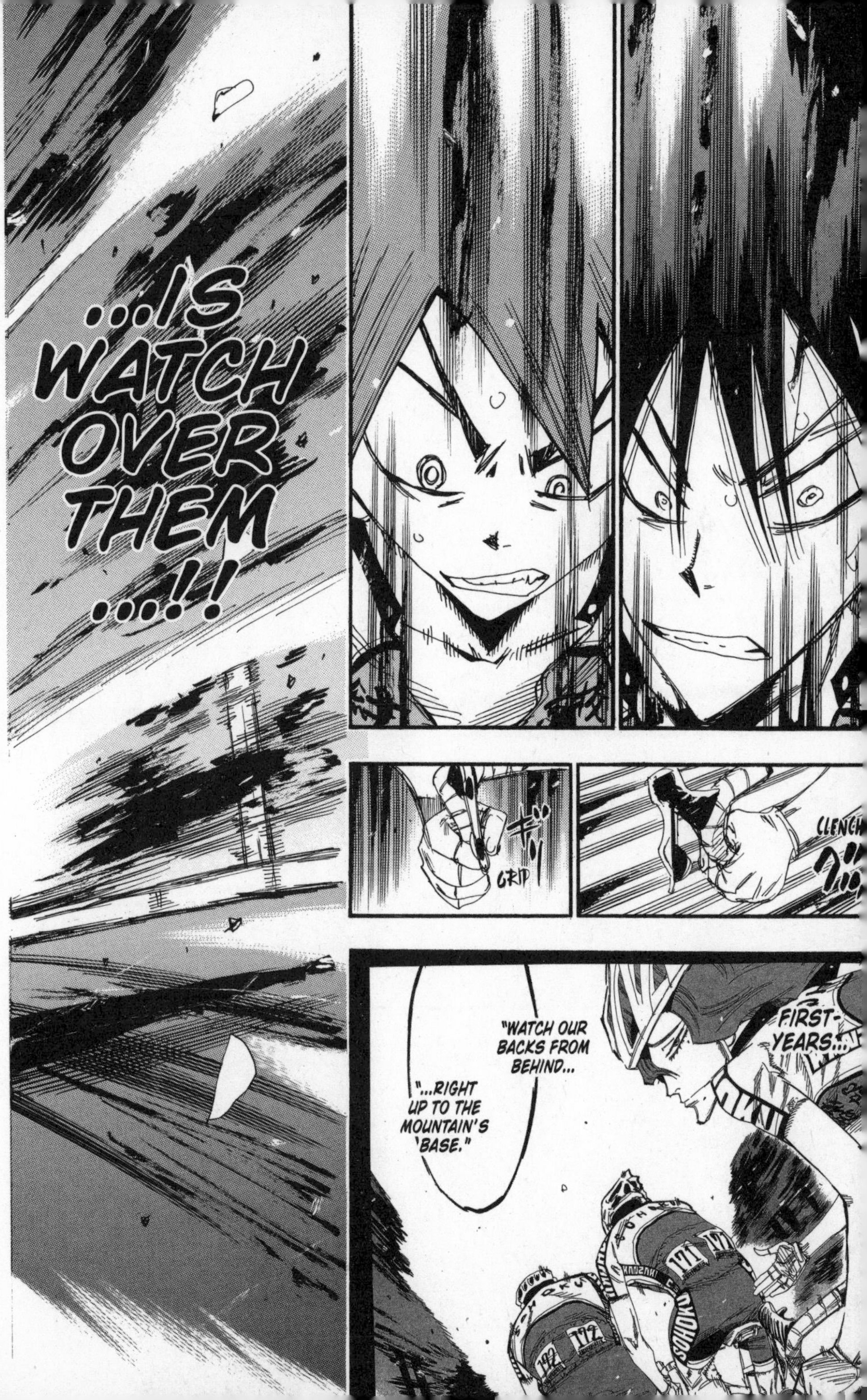
CLENCH
GRIP
FIRST-YEARS...
"WATCH OUR BACKS FROM BEHIND...
"...RIGHT UP TO THE MOUNTAIN'S BASE."
...IS WATCH OVER THEM...!!

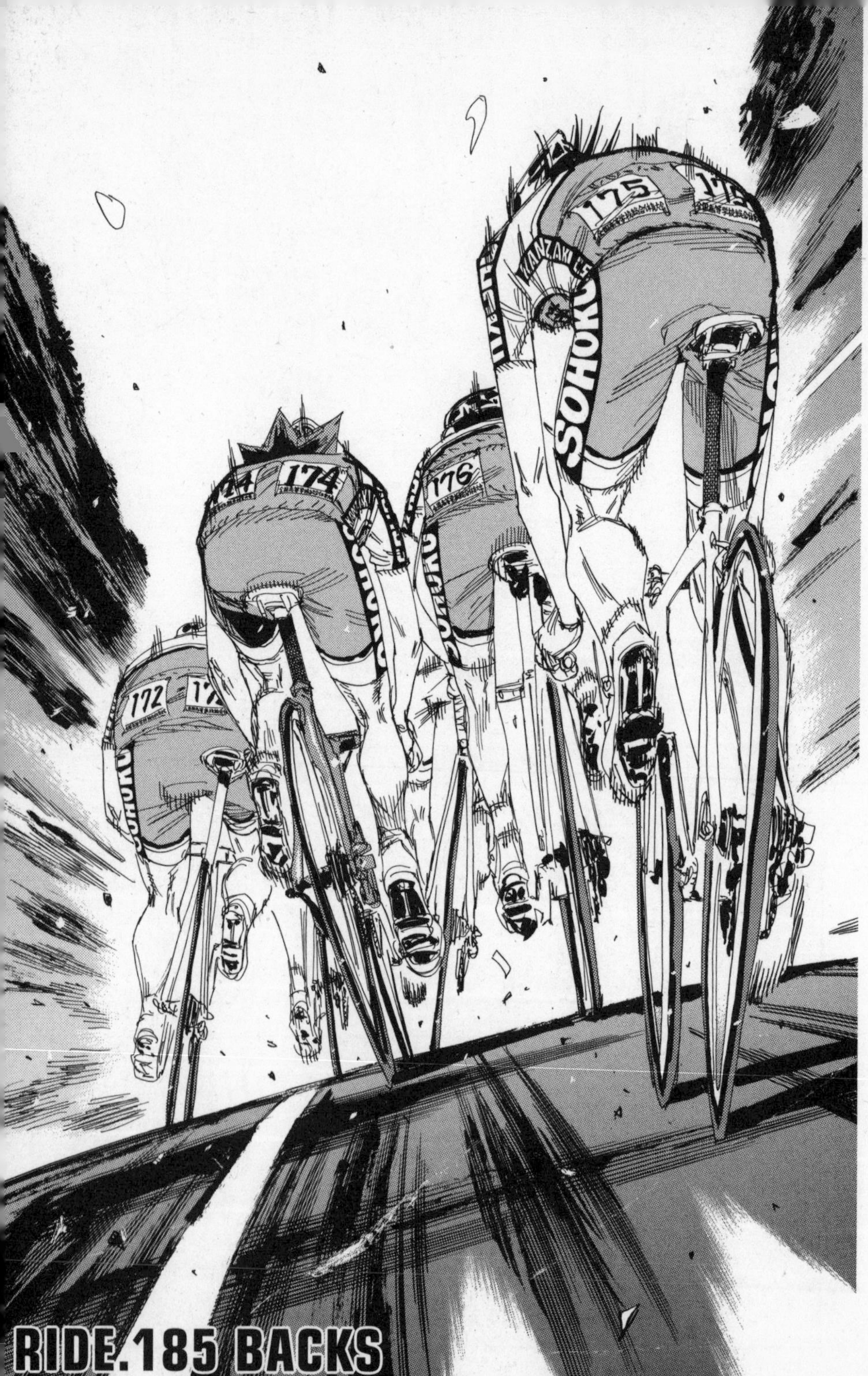

RIDE.185 BACKS

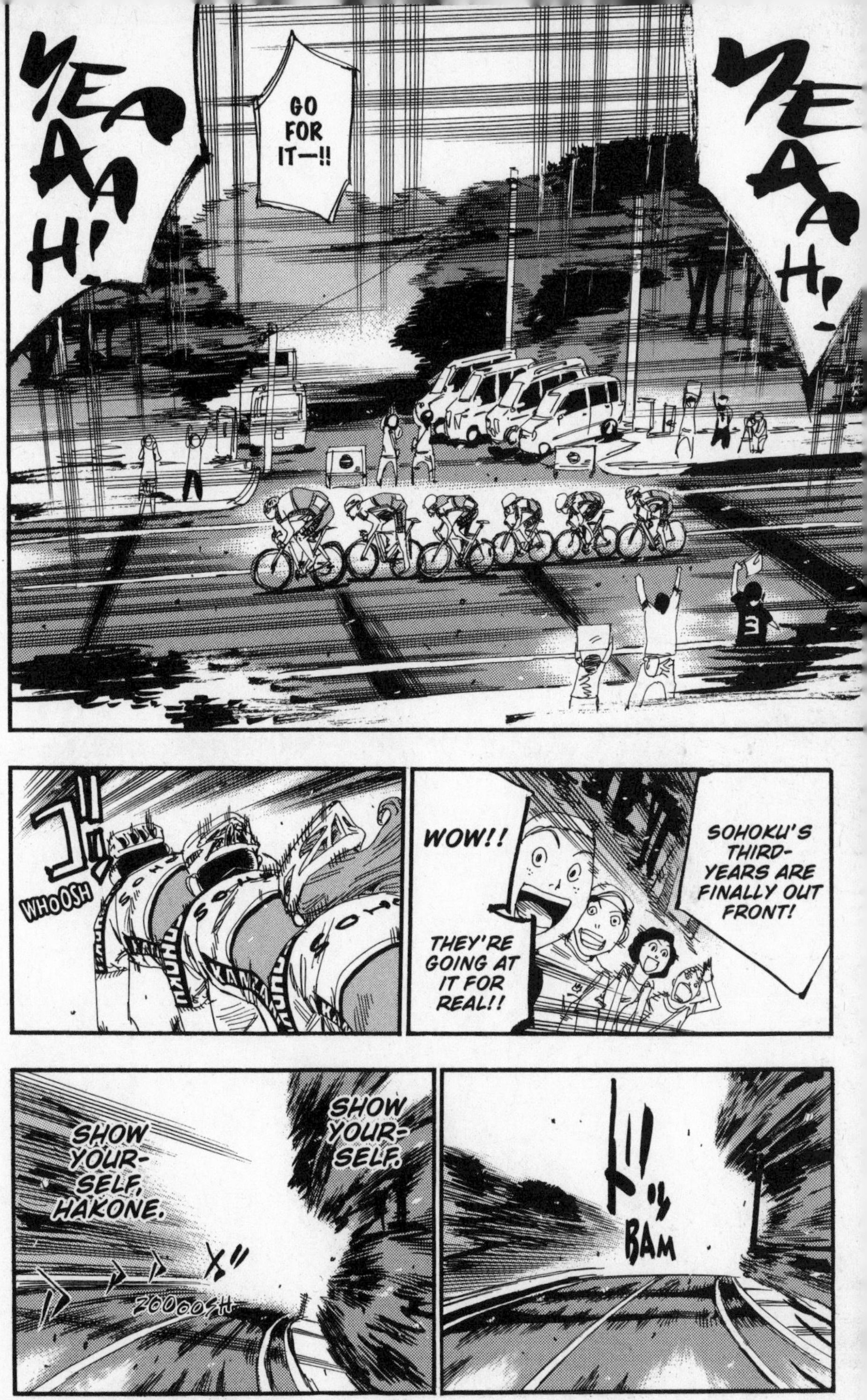
YEAAAH!
GO FOR IT—!!
YEAAAH!
SOHOKU'S THIRD-YEARS ARE FINALLY OUT FRONT!
WOW!!
THEY'RE GOING AT IT FOR REAL!!
WHOOSH
BAM
SHOW YOUR-SELF.
SHOW YOUR-SELF, HAKONE.
ZOOOOSH

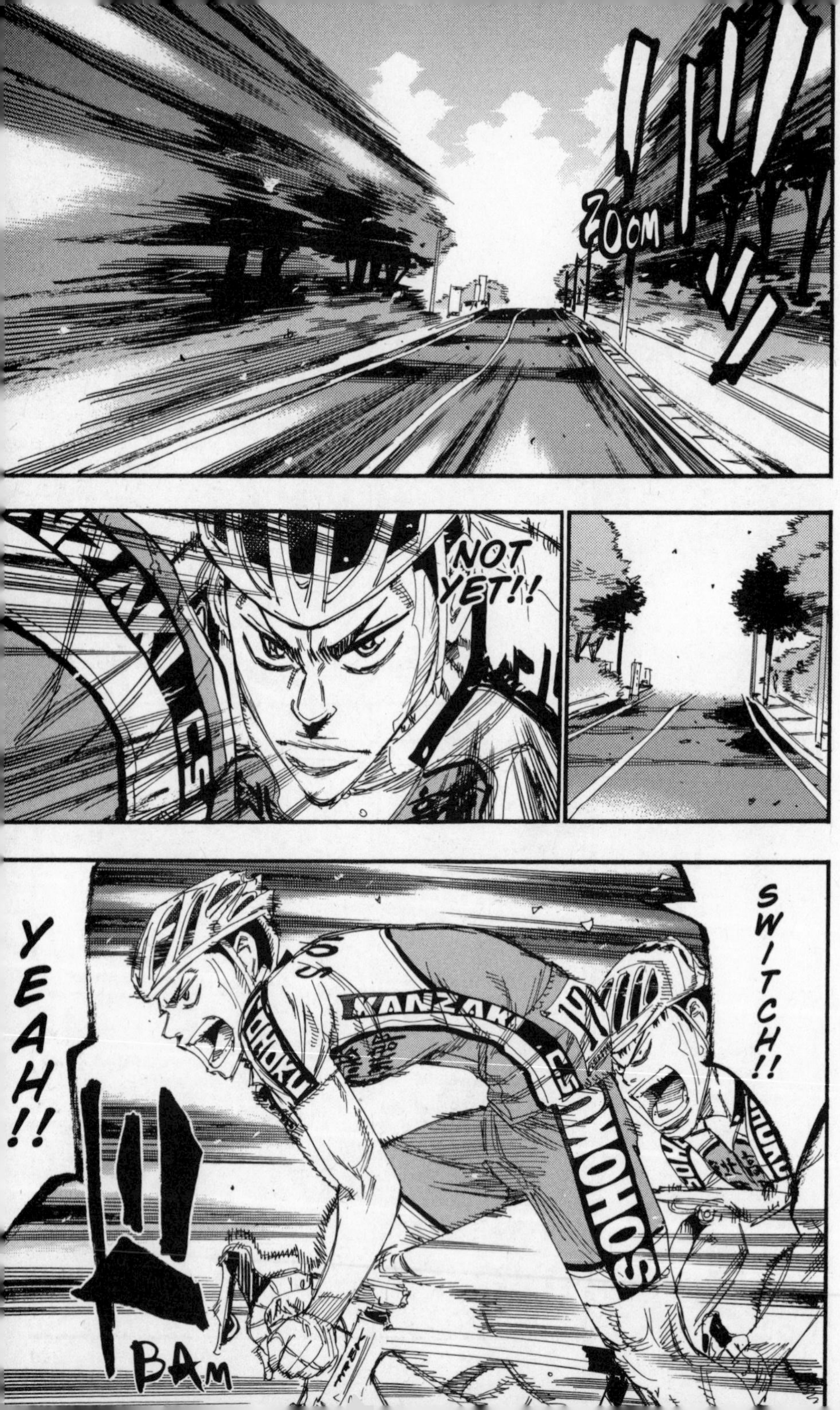
ZOOM
NOT YET!!
SWITCH!!
YEAH!!
BAM

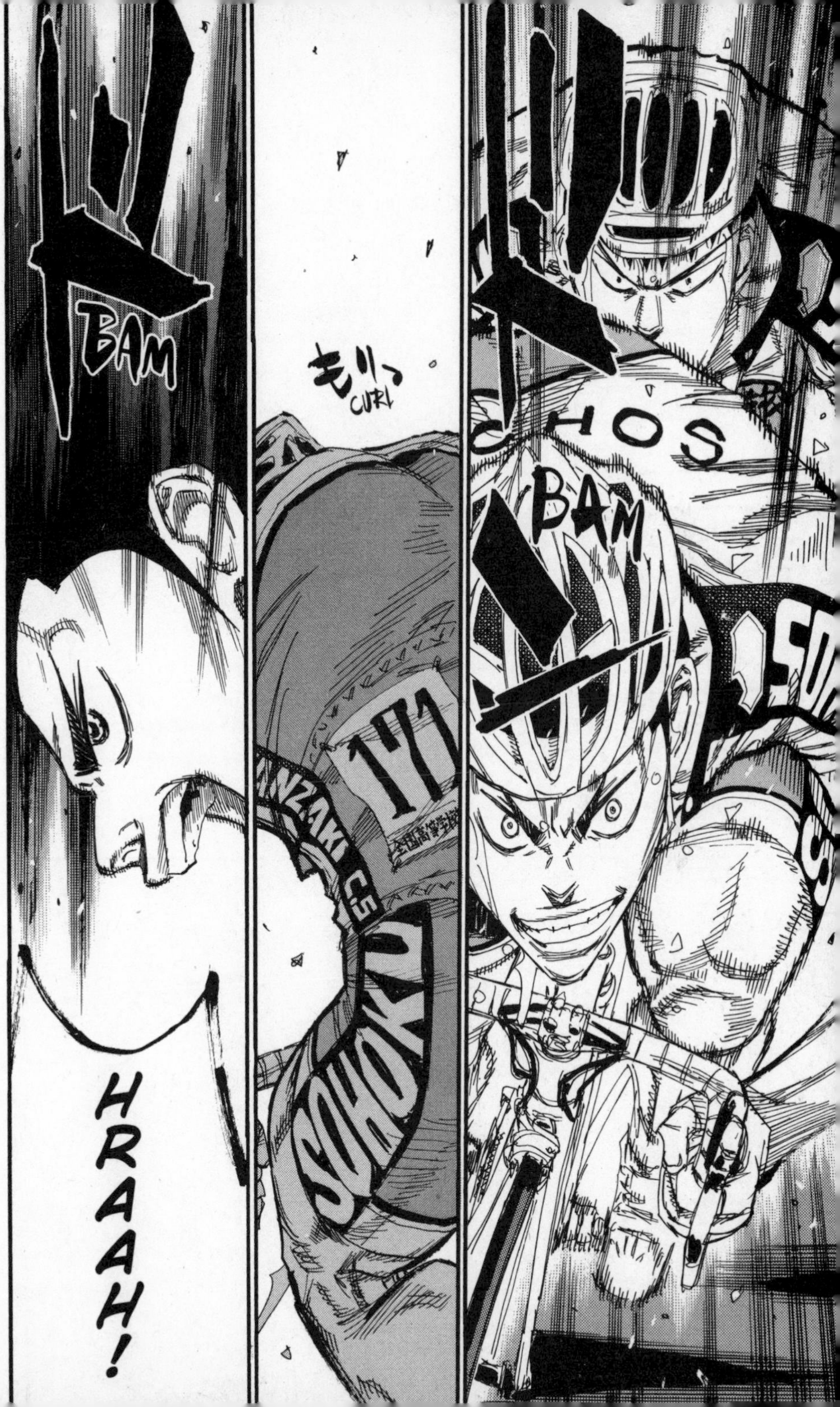
BAM
もりっ
CURL
SOHOKU
171
BAM
HRAAAH!

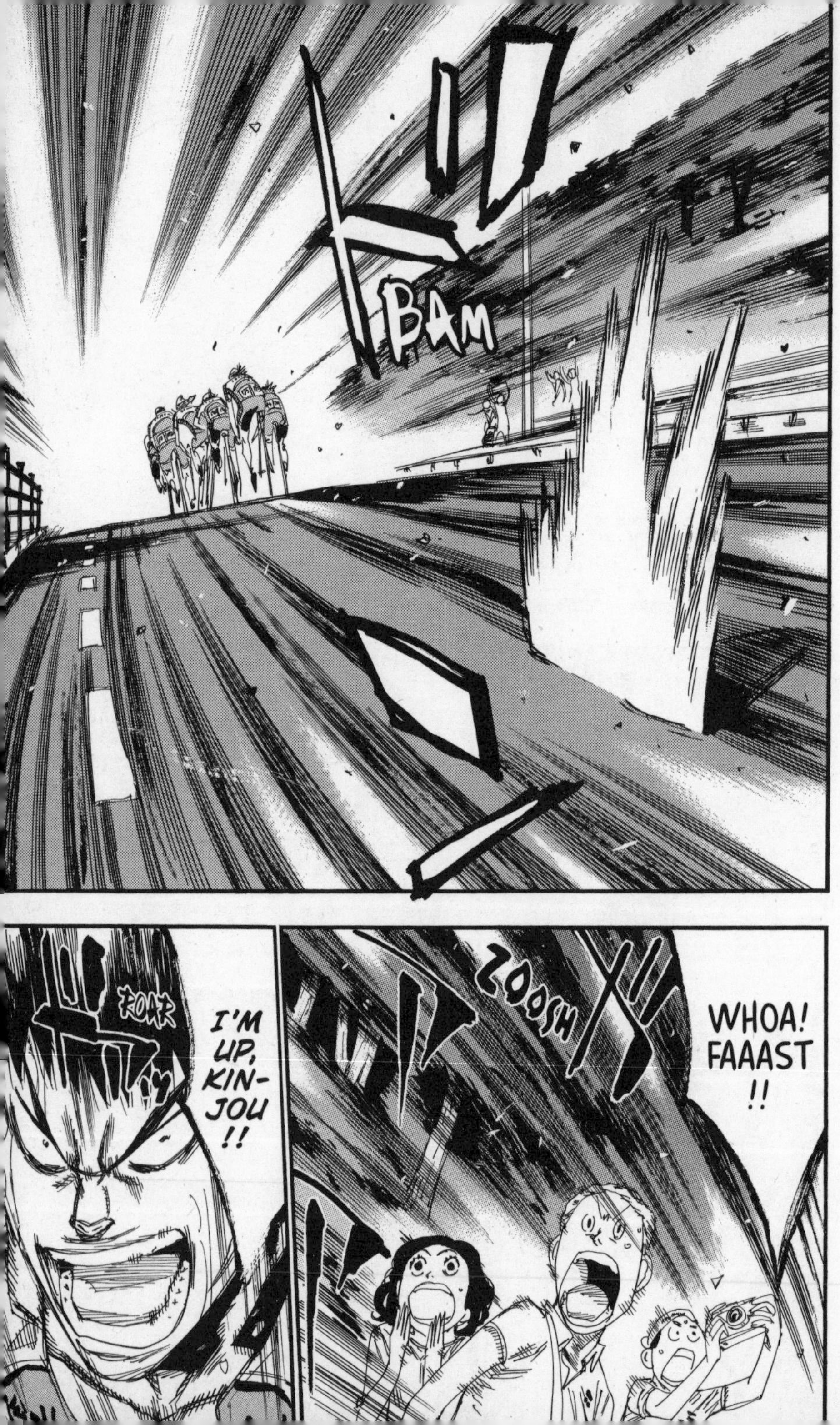
BAM
WHOA! FAAAST !!
ZOOSH
I'M UP, KIN-JOU !!
ROAR

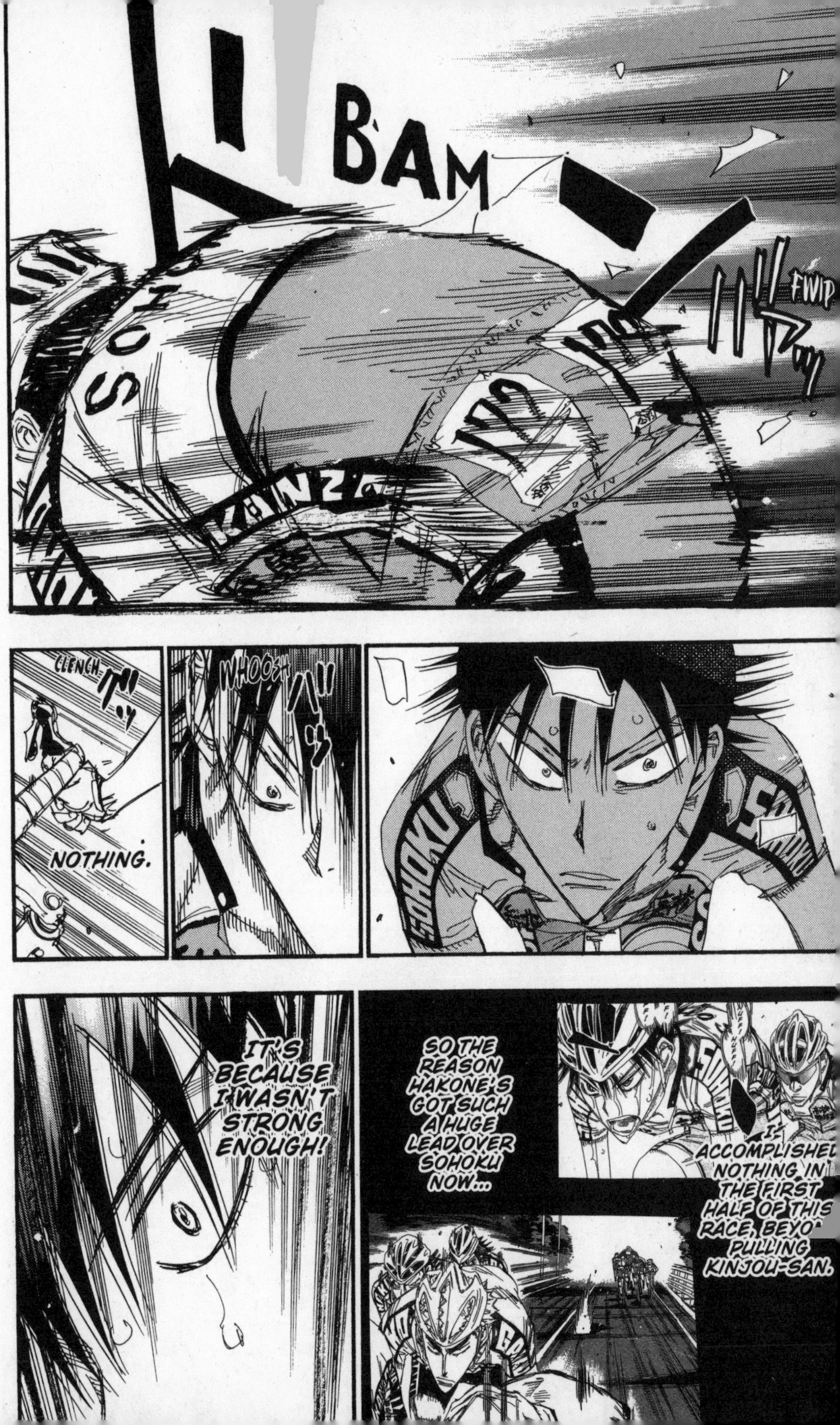
BAM
FWIP
WHOOSH
CLENCH
NOTHING.
I ACCOMPLISHED NOTHING IN THE FIRST HALF OF THIS RACE, BEYO PULLING KINJOU-SAN.
SO THE REASON HAKONE'S GOT SUCH A HUGE LEAD OVER SOHOKU NOW...
IT'S BECAUSE I WASN'T STRONG ENOUGH!

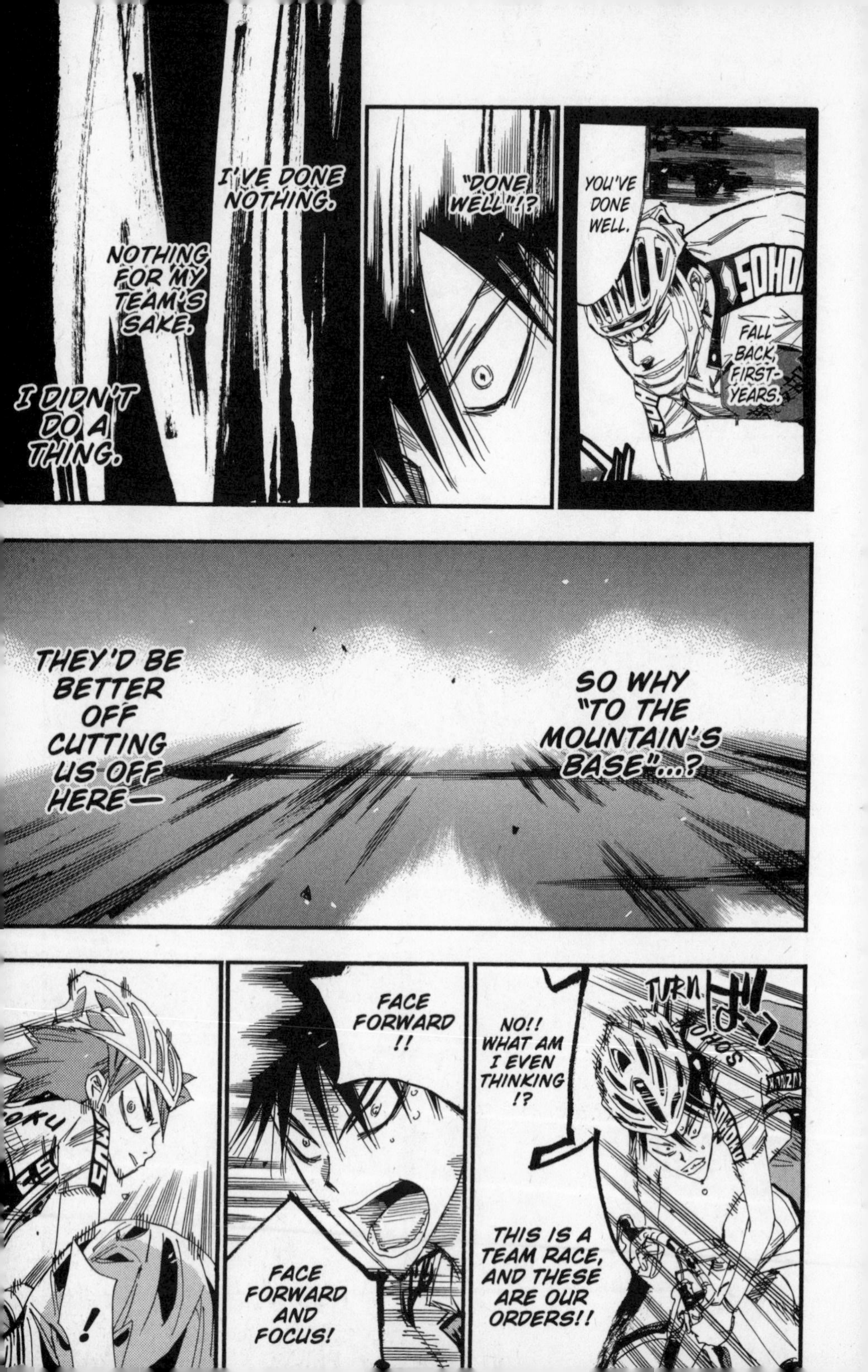
YOU'VE DONE WELL.
FALL BACK, FIRST-YEARS.
"DONE WELL"!?
I'VE DONE NOTHING.
NOTHING FOR MY TEAM'S SAKE.
I DIDN'T DO A THING.
SO WHY "TO THE MOUNTAIN'S BASE"...?
THEY'D BE BETTER OFF CUTTING US OFF HERE—
TURN
NO!! WHAT AM I EVEN THINKING !?
THIS IS A TEAM RACE, AND THESE ARE OUR ORDERS!!
FACE FORWARD !!
FACE FORWARD AND FOCUS!
!

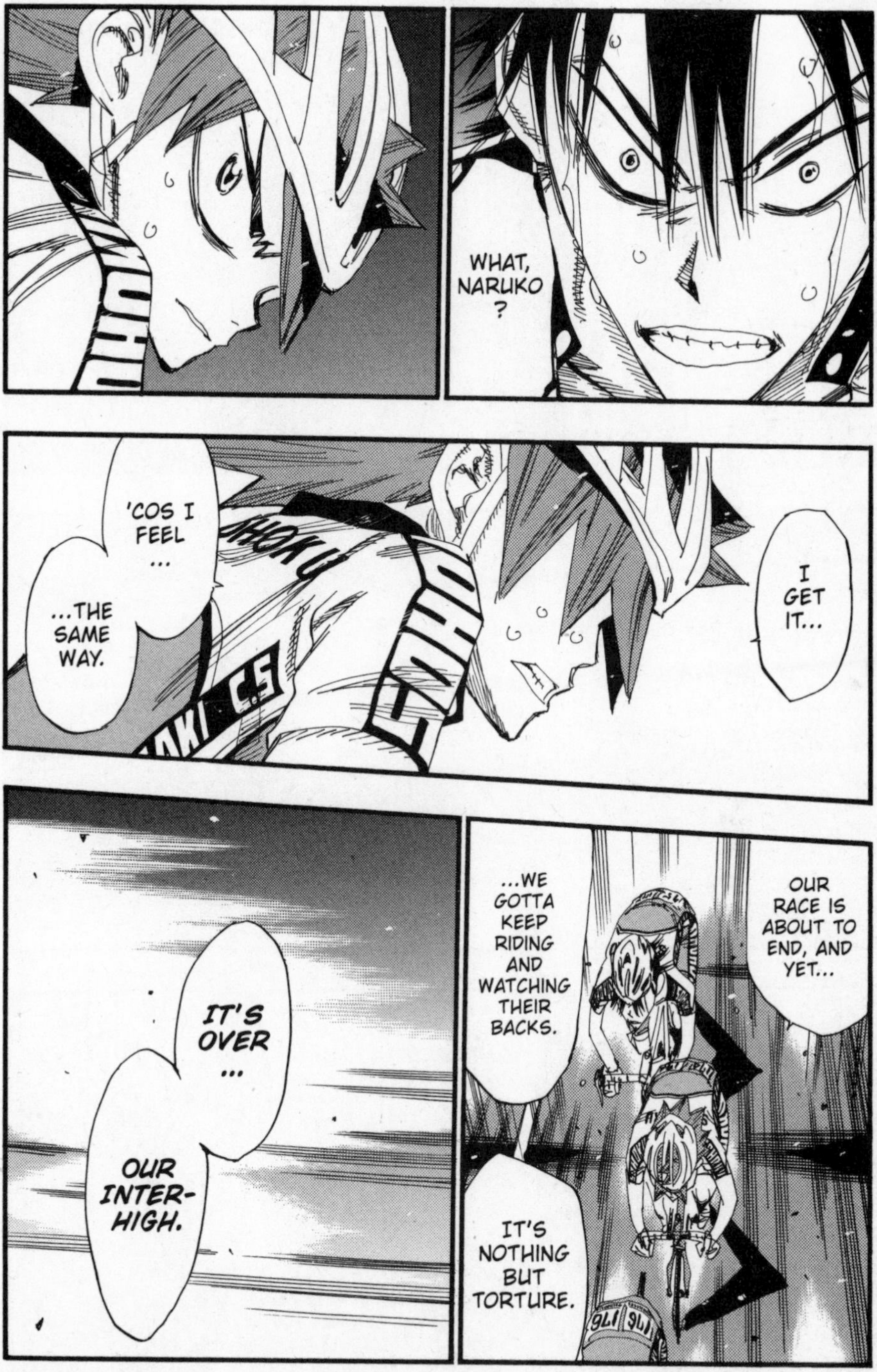
WHAT, NARUKO?
I GET IT...
'COS I FEEL...
...THE SAME WAY.
OUR RACE IS ABOUT TO END, AND YET...
...WE GOTTA KEEP RIDING AND WATCHING THEIR BACKS.
IT'S NOTHING BUT TORTURE.
IT'S OVER...
OUR INTER-HIGH.

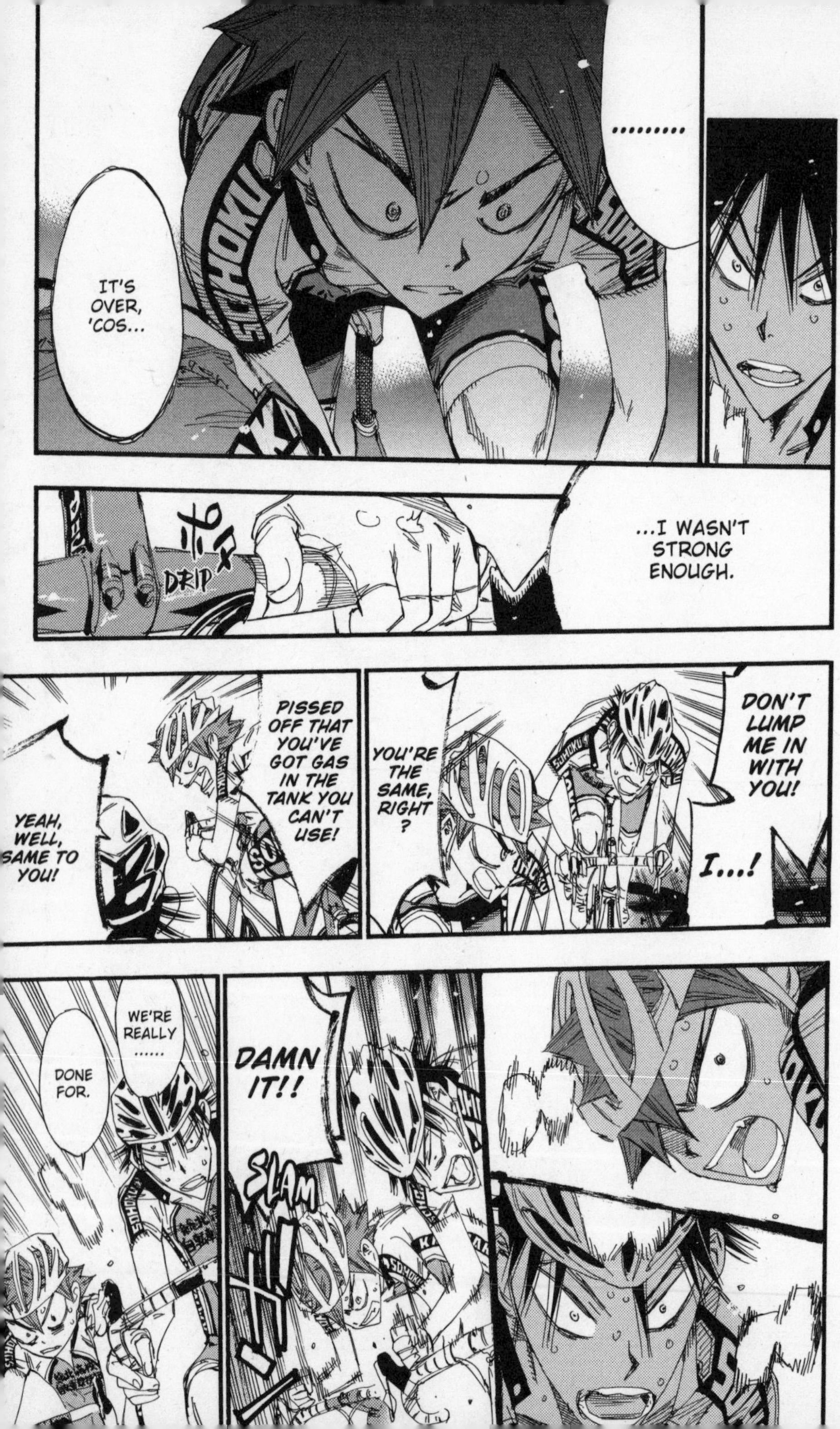
....
IT'S OVER, 'COS...
...I WASN'T STRONG ENOUGH.
DRIP
DON'T LUMP ME IN WITH YOU!
I...!
YOU'RE THE SAME, RIGHT?
PISSED OFF THAT YOU'VE GOT GAS IN THE TANK YOU CAN'T USE!
YEAH, WELL, SAME TO YOU!
DAMN IT!!
SLAM
WE'RE REALLY ......
DONE FOR.

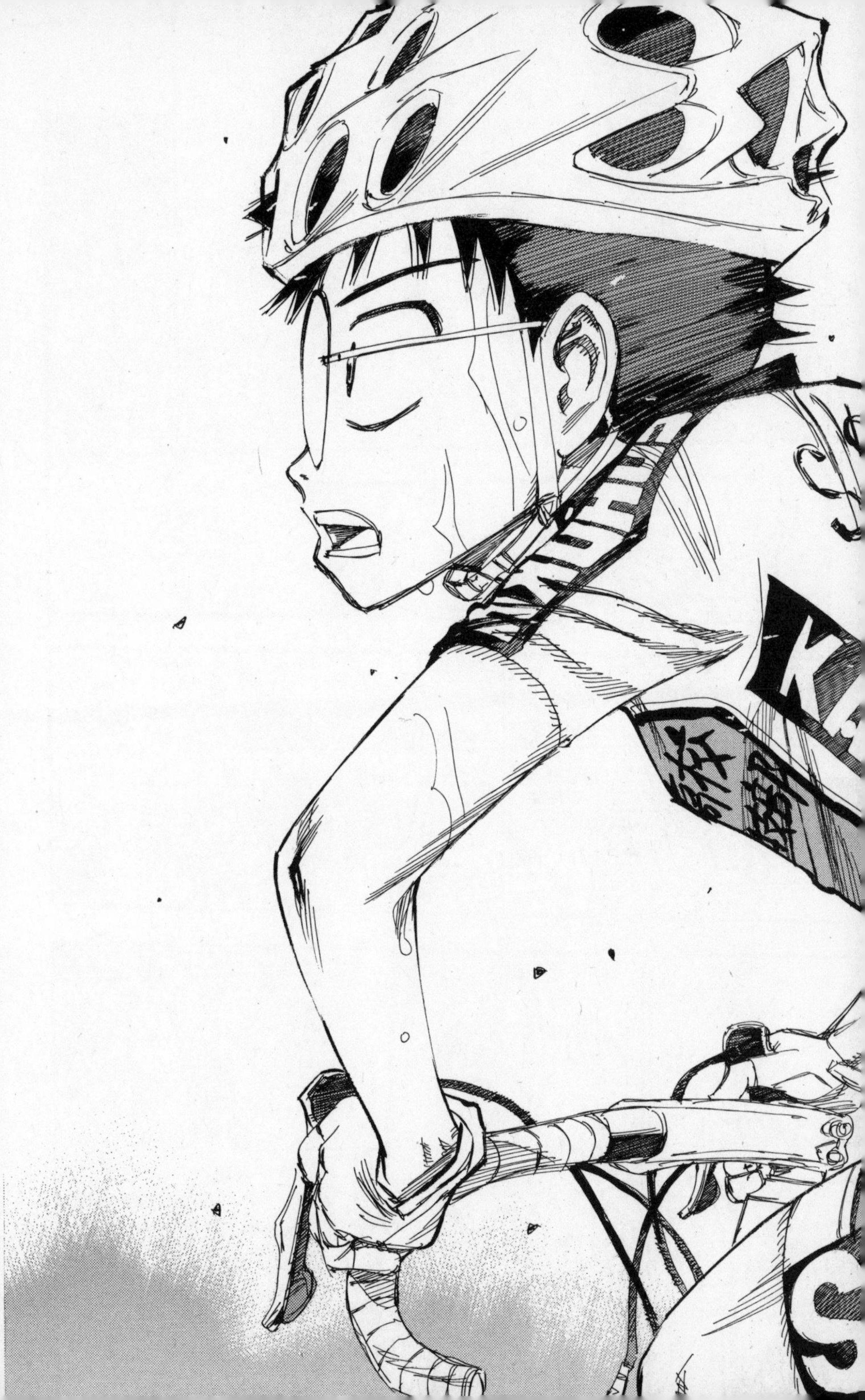

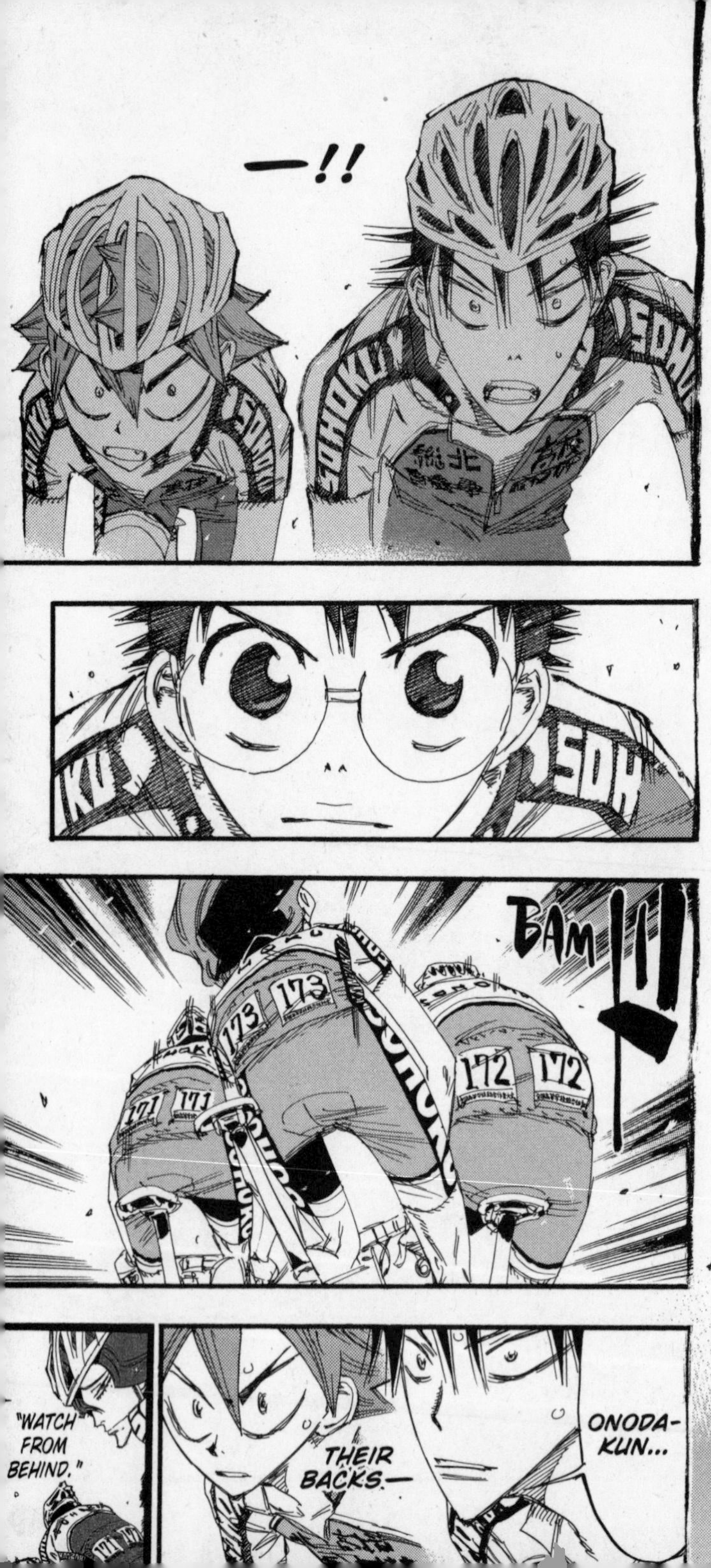
—!!
BAM
ONODA-KUN...
THEIR BACKS.—
"WATCH FROM BEHIND."

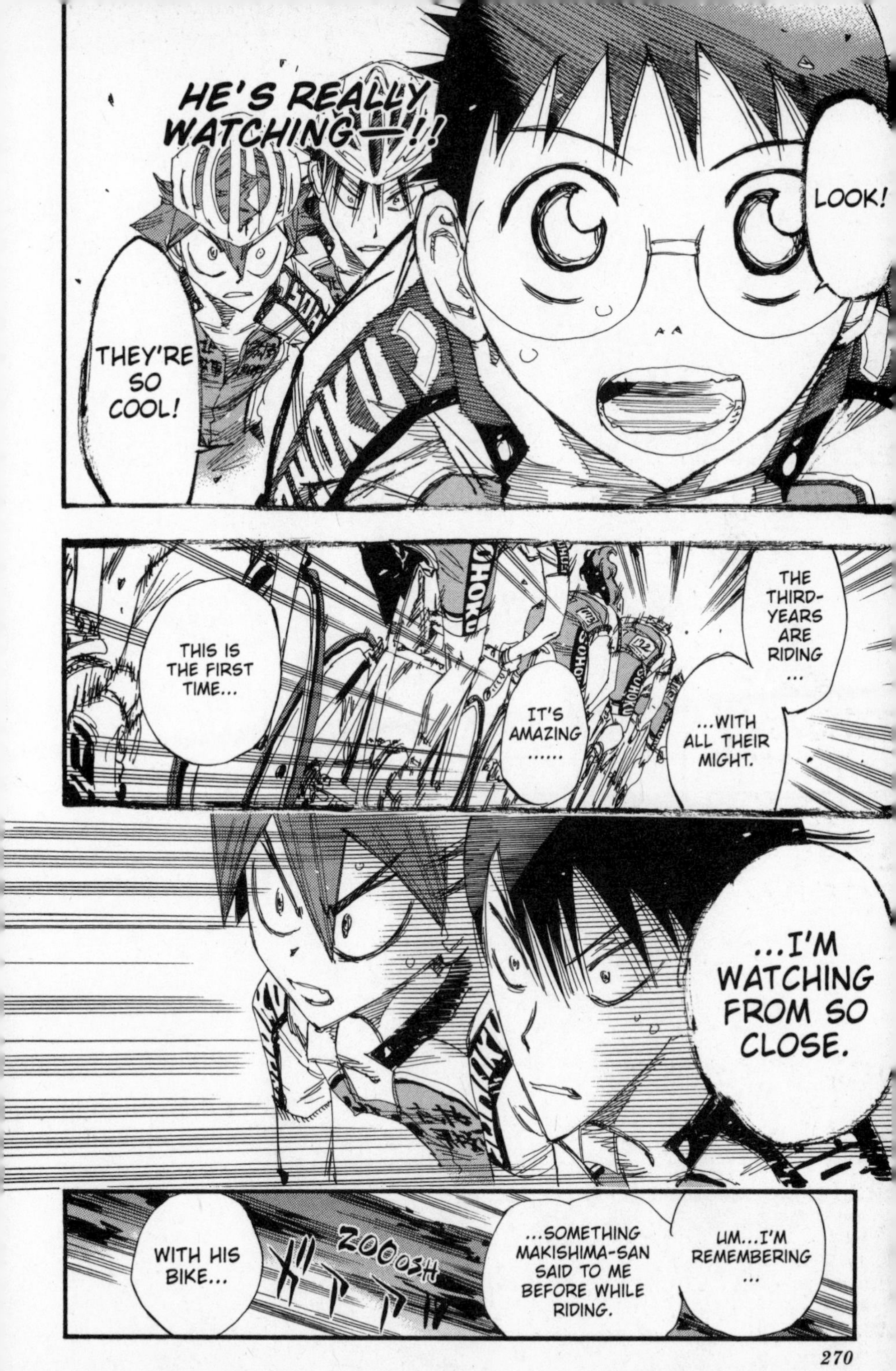
LOOK!
HE'S REALLY WATCHING—!!
THEY'RE SO COOL!
THE THIRD-YEARS ARE RIDING...
...WITH ALL THEIR MIGHT.
IT'S AMAZING......
THIS IS THE FIRST TIME...
...I'M WATCHING FROM SO CLOSE.
UM...I'M REMEMBERING...
...SOMETHING MAKISHIMA-SAN SAID TO ME BEFORE WHILE RIDING.
ZOOOSH
WITH HIS BIKE...

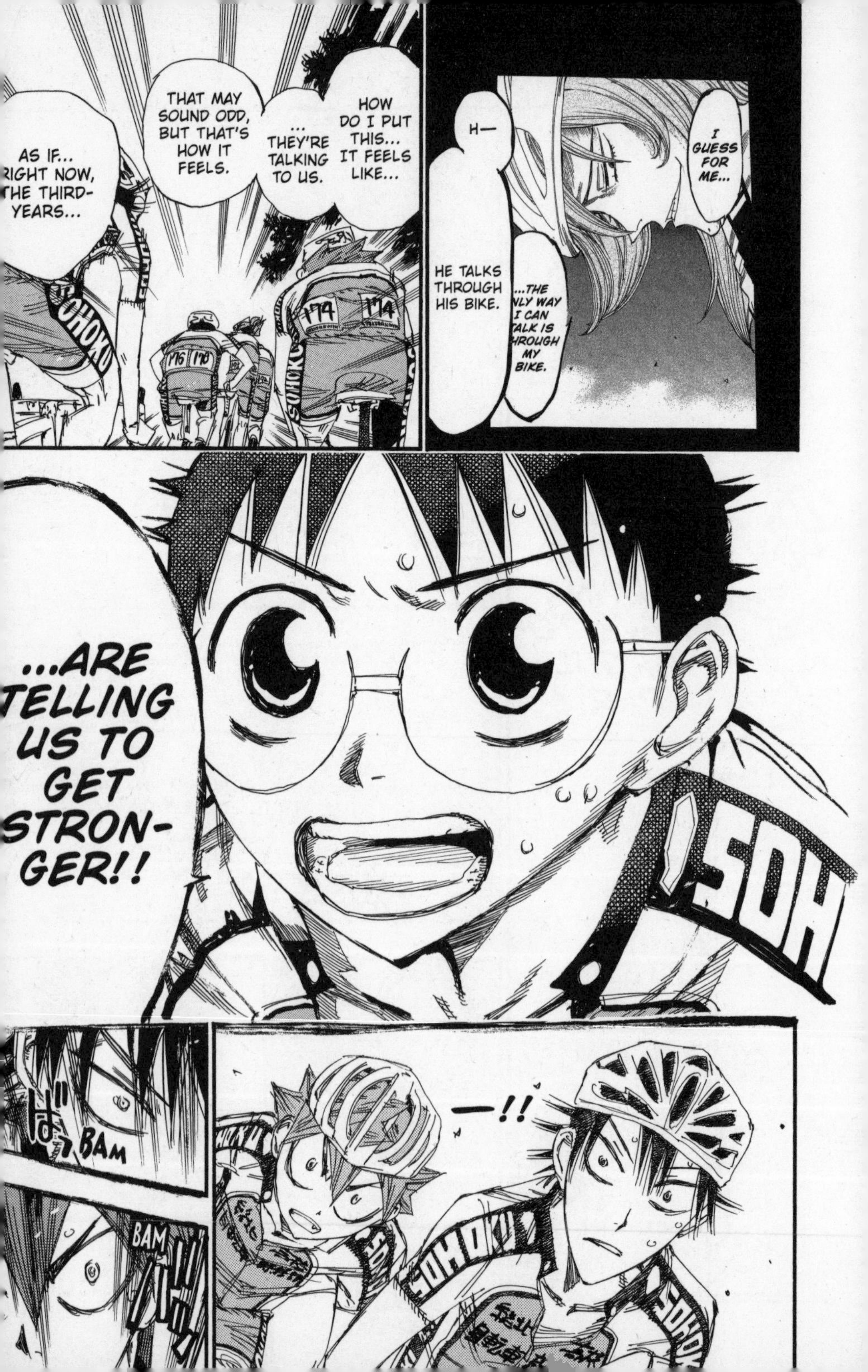

I GUESS FOR ME...
...THE NLY WAY I CAN TALK IS HROUGH MY BIKE.
H—
HE TALKS THROUGH HIS BIKE.
HOW DO I PUT THIS... IT FEELS LIKE...
...THEY'RE TALKING TO US.
THAT MAY SOUND ODD, BUT THAT'S HOW IT FEELS.
AS IF... RIGHT NOW, THE THIRD-YEARS...
...ARE TELLING US TO GET STRON-GER!!
—!!
BAM
BAM

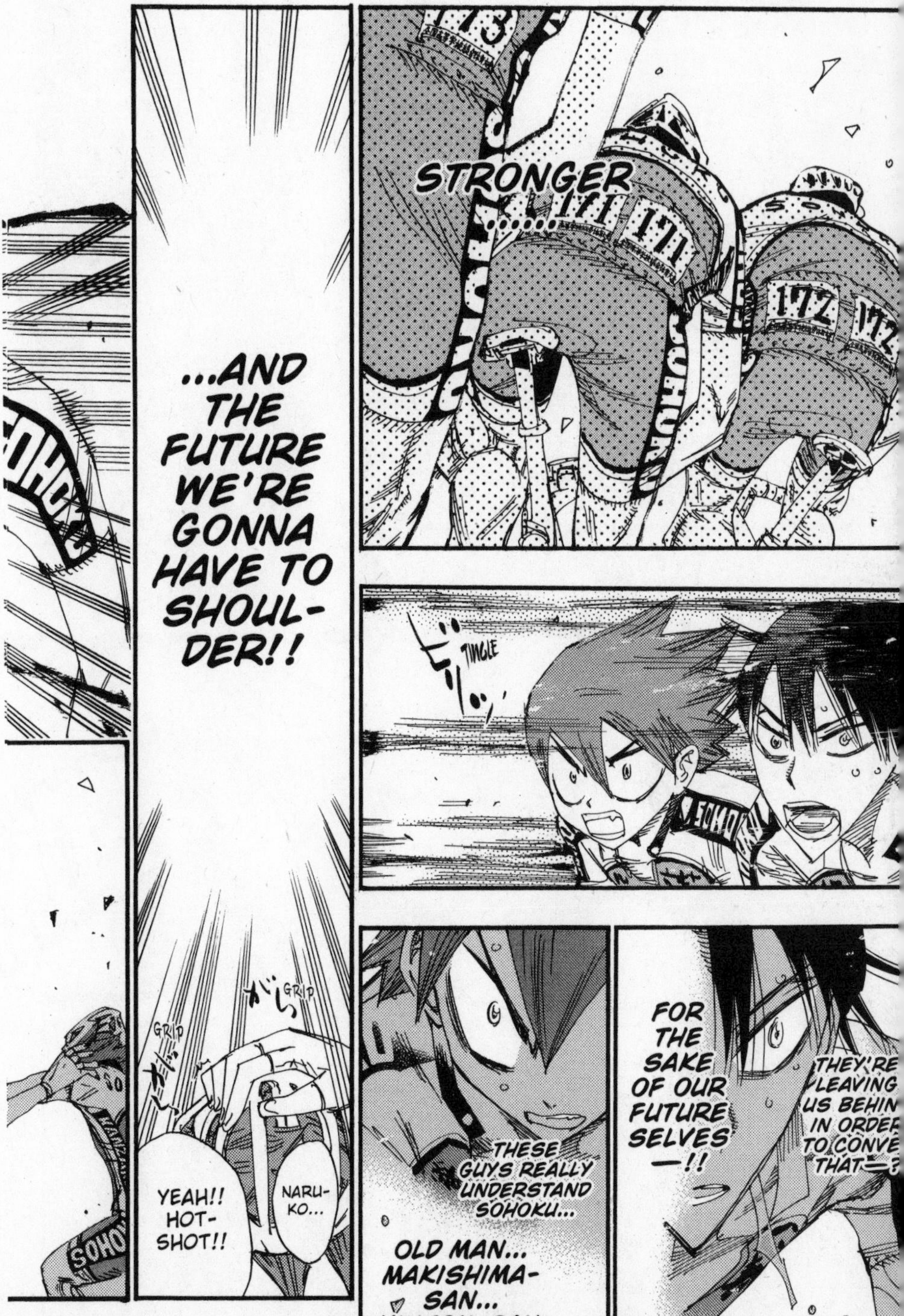
STRONGER ......
TINGLE
THEY'RE LEAVING US BEHIN IN ORDER TO CONVE THAT—?
FOR THE SAKE OF OUR FUTURE SELVES—!!
THESE GUYS REALLY UNDERSTAND SOHOKU...
OLD MAN... MAKISHIMA-SAN... KINJOU-SAN.
...AND THE FUTURE WE'RE GONNA HAVE TO SHOUL-DER!!
GRIP
GRIP
NARU-KO...
YEAH!! HOT-SHOT!!

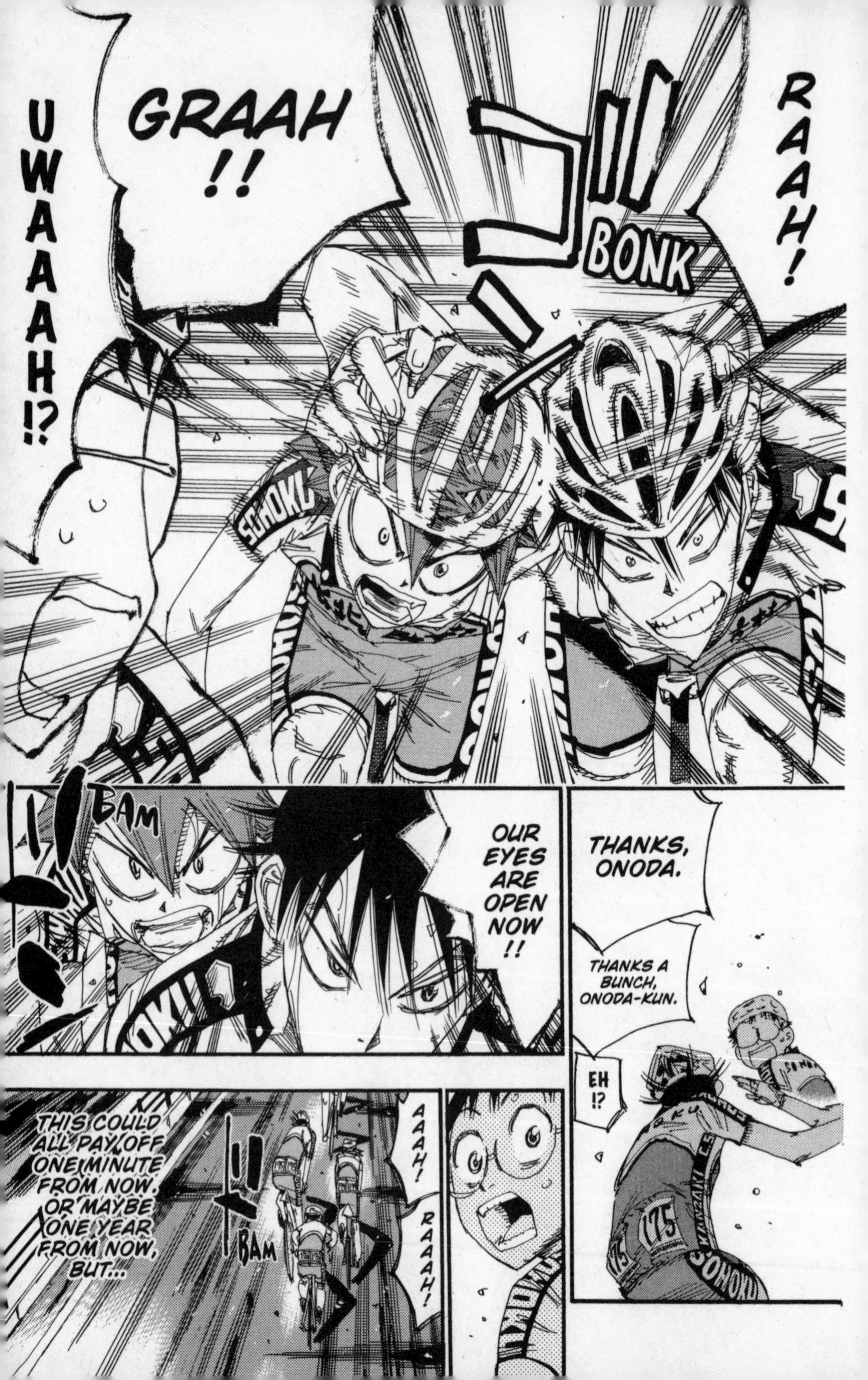
RAAAH!
BONK
GRAAH!!
UWAAAAH!?
THANKS, ONODA.
THANKS A BUNCH, ONODA-KUN.
EH!?
OUR EYES ARE OPEN NOW!!
BAM
AAAH!
RAAAH!
BAM
THIS COULD ALL PAY OFF ONE MINUTE FROM NOW. OR MAYBE ONE YEAR FROM NOW, BUT...

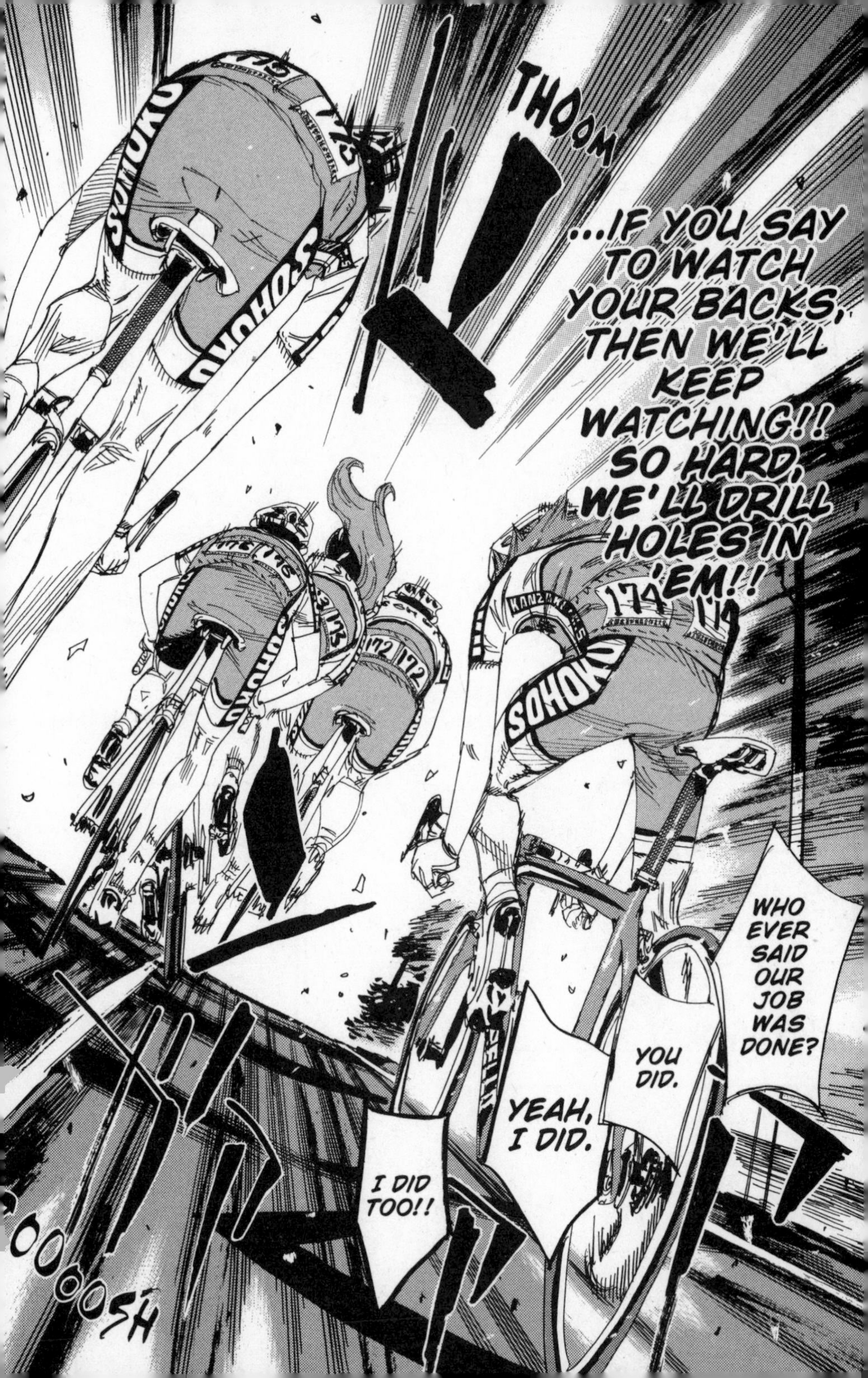
THOOM
...IF YOU SAY TO WATCH YOUR BACKS, THEN WE'LL KEEP WATCHING!! SO HARD, WE'LL DRILL HOLES IN 'EM!!
WHO EVER SAID OUR JOB WAS DONE?
YOU DID.
YEAH, I DID.
I DID TOO!!
OOOOSH

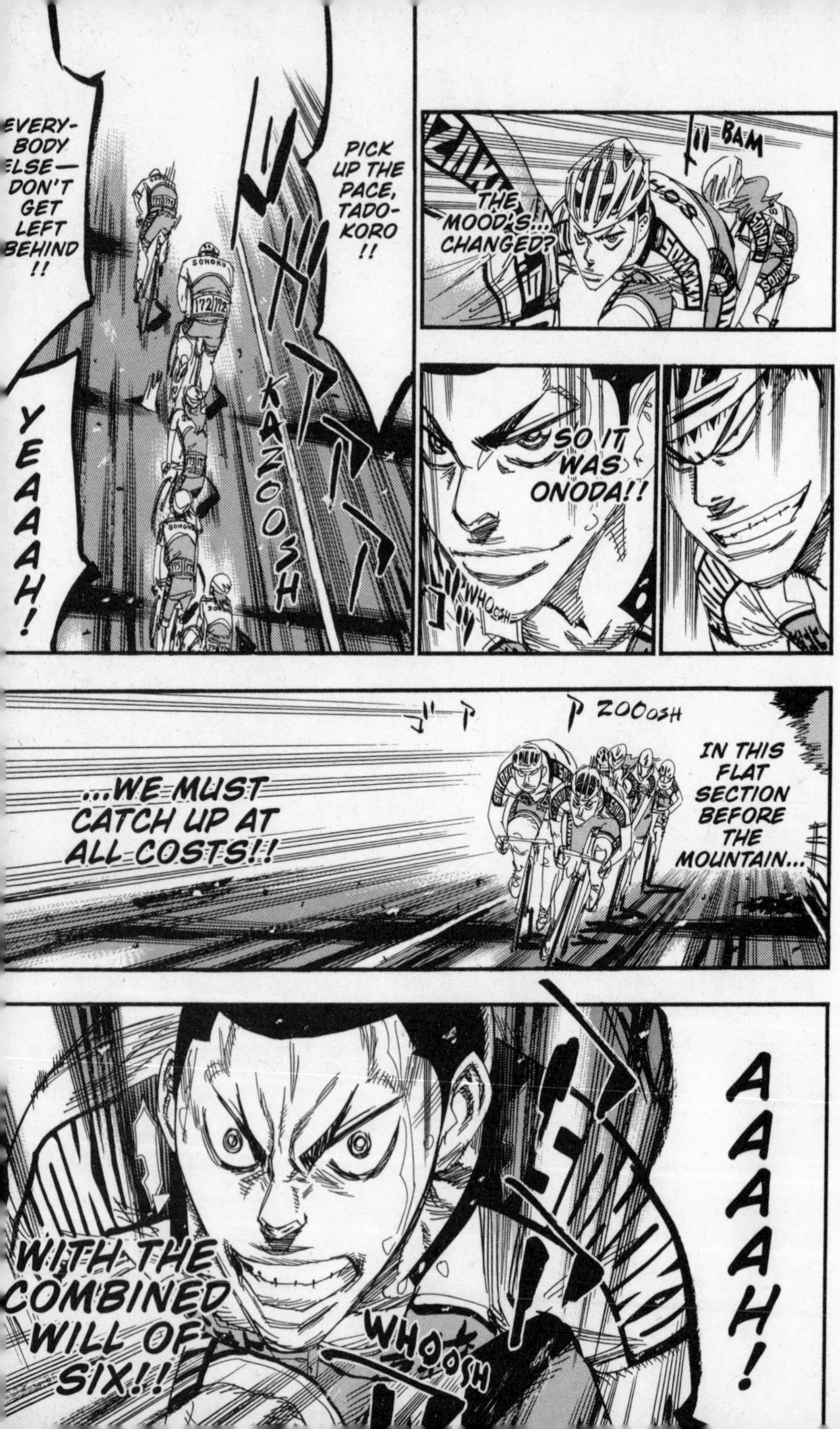
BAM
THE MOOD'S... CHANGED?
SO IT WAS ONODA!!
WHOOSH
PICK UP THE PACE, TADOKORO!!
EVERYBODY ELSE—DON'T GET LEFT BEHIND!!
KAZOOOSH
YEAAAAAH!
ZOOOSH
IN THIS FLAT SECTION BEFORE THE MOUNTAIN...
...WE MUST CATCH UP AT ALL COSTS!!
AAAAAH!
WHOOSH
WITH THE COMBINED WILL OF SIX!!

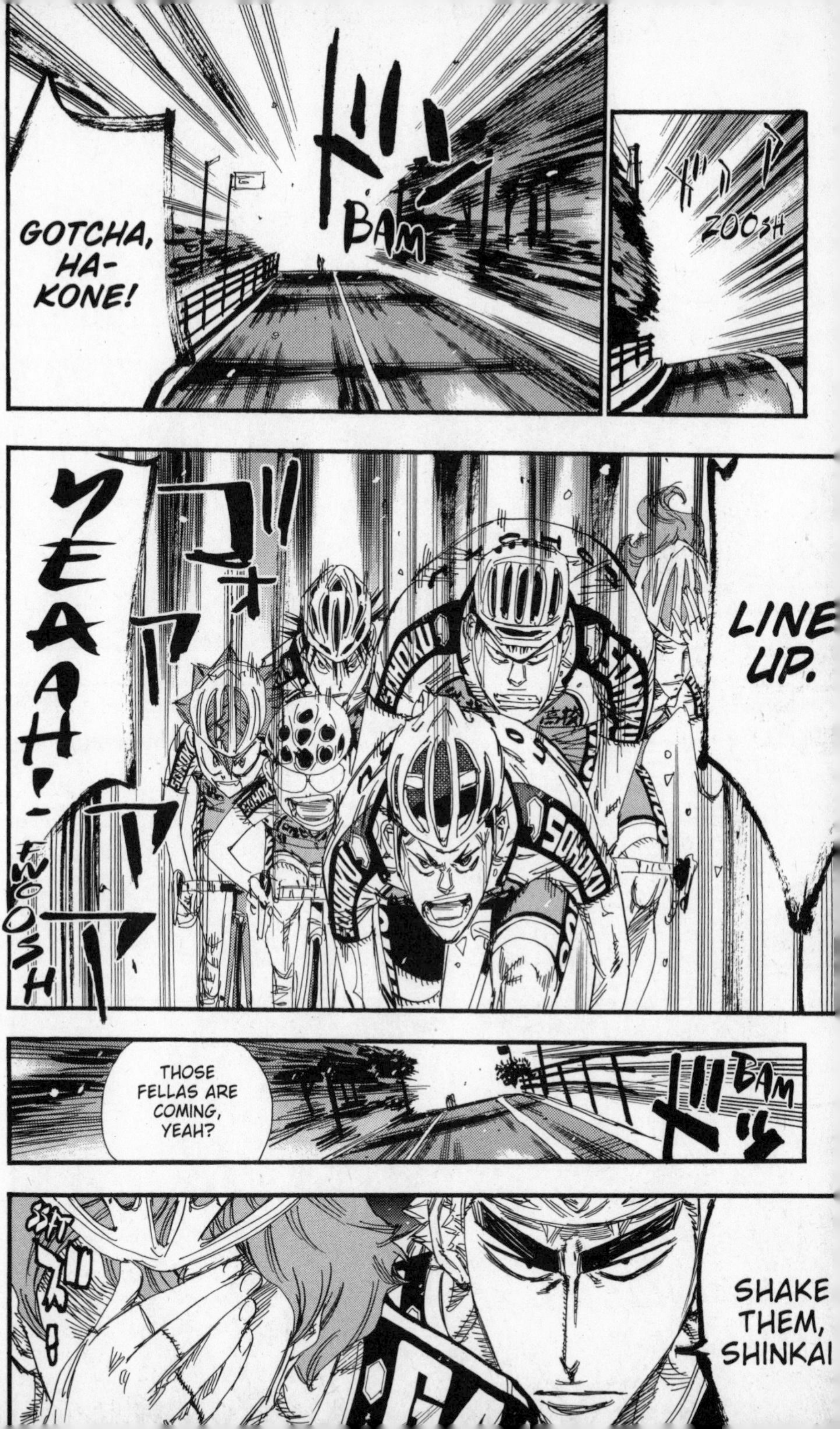
ZOOSH
BAM
GOTCHA, HA-KONE!
LINE UP.
YEAH AH!
WOOSH
BAM
THOSE FELLAS ARE COMING, YEAH?
SHAKE THEM, SHINKAI

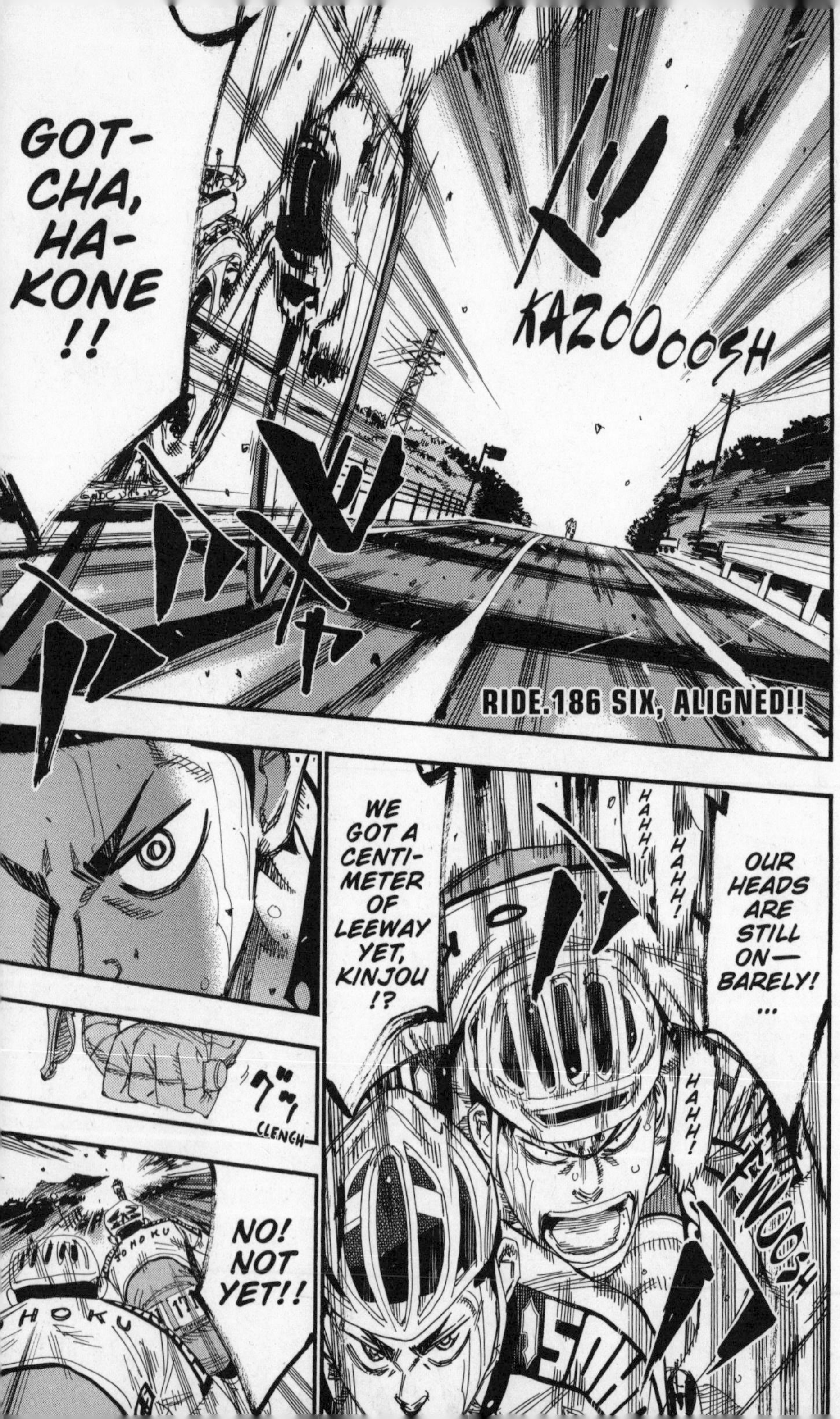
KAZOOOOOSH
GOT-CHA, HA-KONE!!
RIDE.186 SIX, ALIGNED!!
OUR HEADS ARE STILL ON—BARELY! ...
HAHH! HAHH!
WE GOT A CENTIMETER OF LEEWAY YET, KINJOU!?
HAHH!
FWOOSH
CLENCH
NO! NOT YET!!

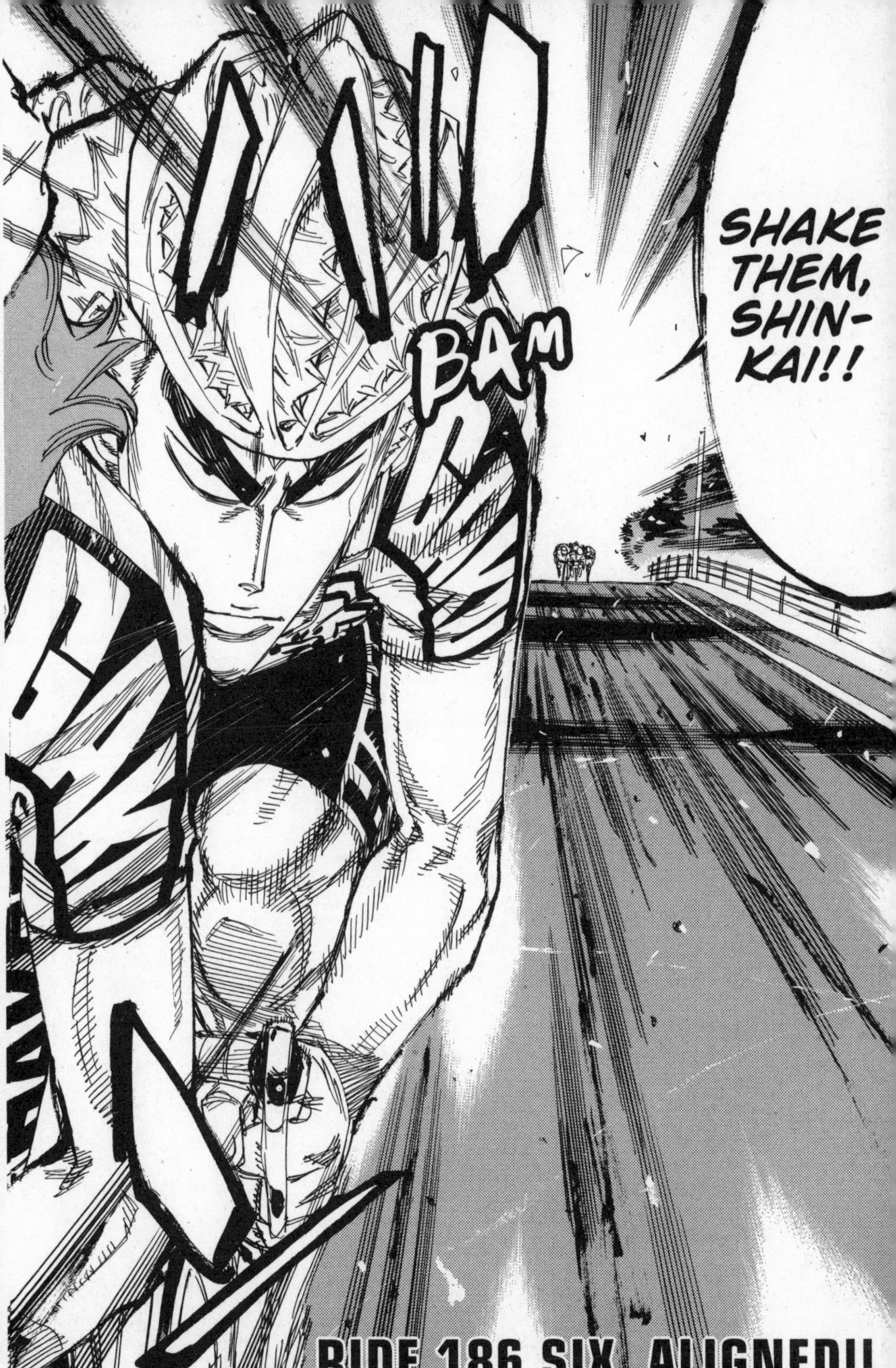
SHAKE THEM, SHIN-KAI!!
BAM

RIDE.186 SIX, ALIGNED!!

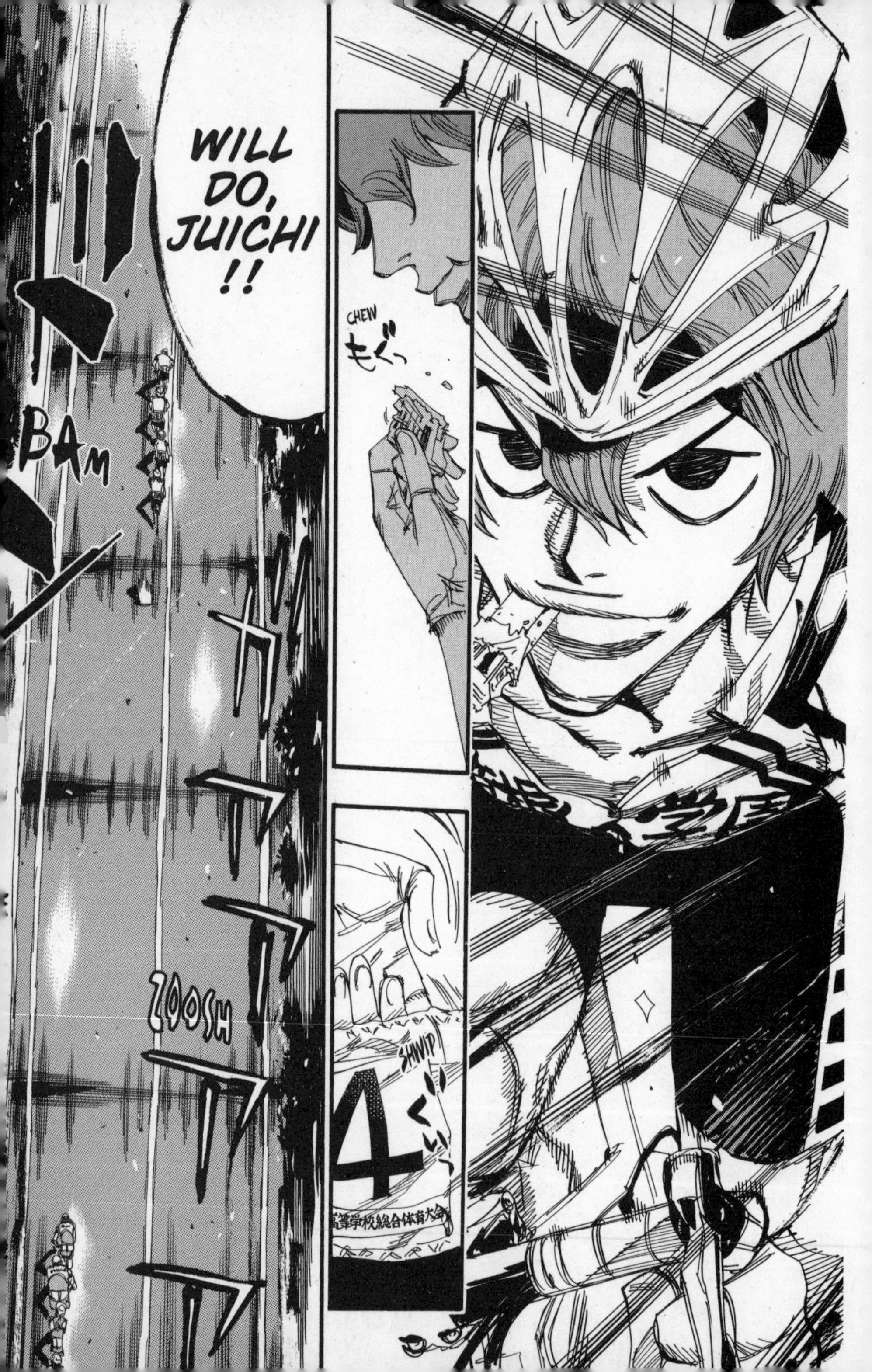
CHEW
もぐっ
SHWIP
ぐいっ
4
高等学校総合体育大会
WILL DO, JUICHI!!
BAM
ZOOSH

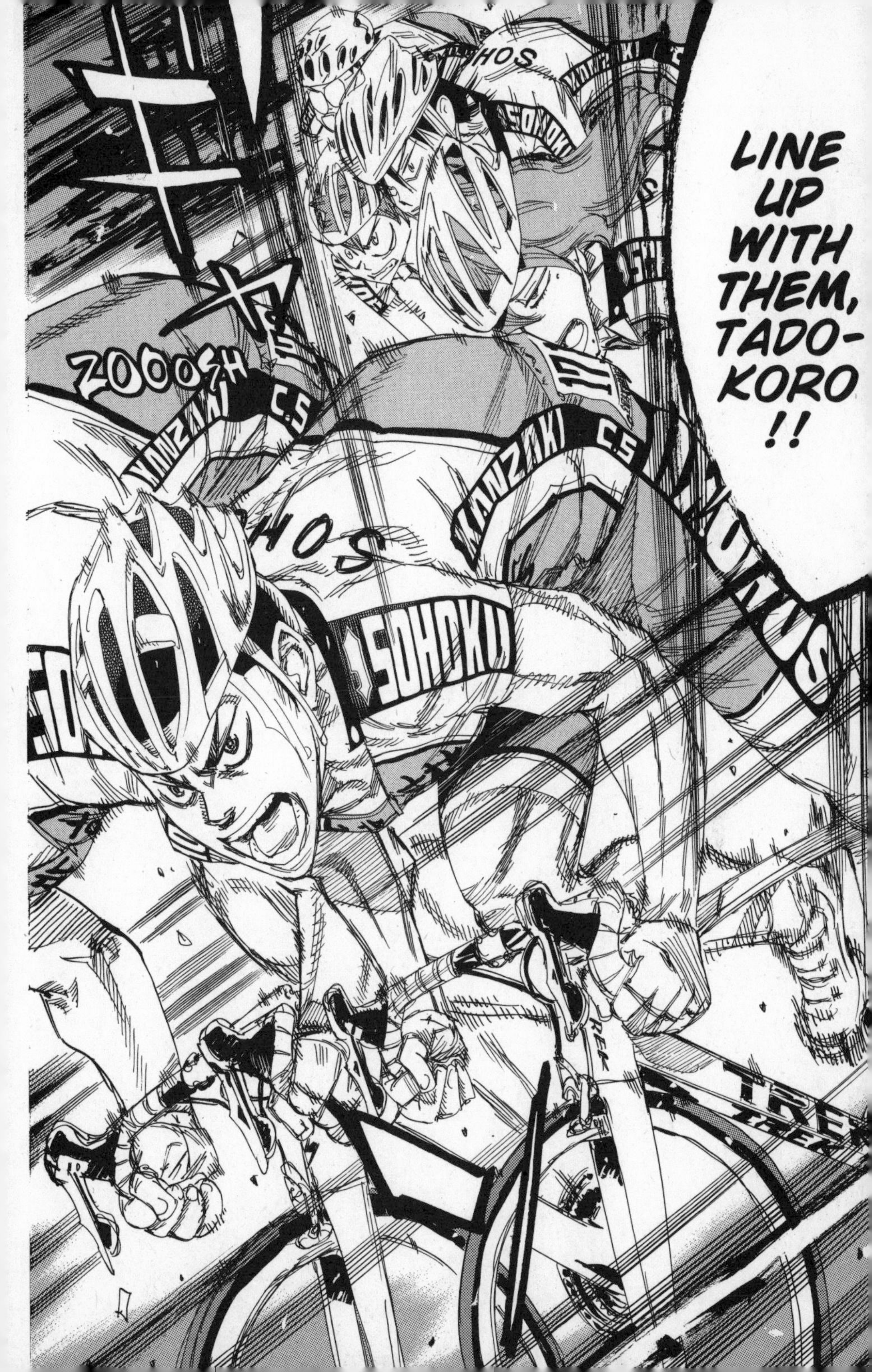
LINE UP WITH THEM, TADO-KORO!!
ZOOOSH

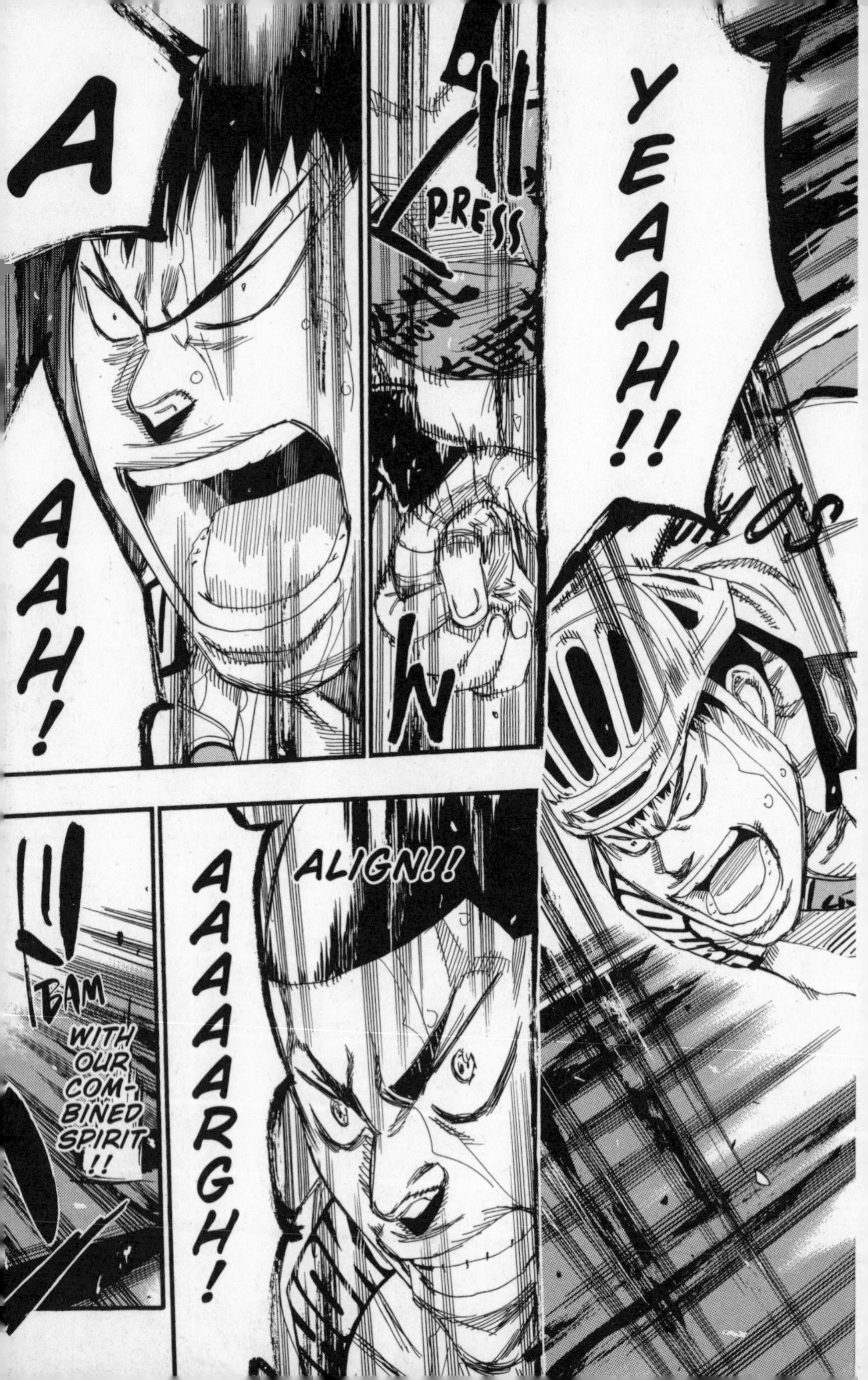
YEAAAH!!
PRESS
A
AAH!
ALIGN!!
AAAAAARGH!
BAM
WITH OUR COM-BINED SPIRIT!!

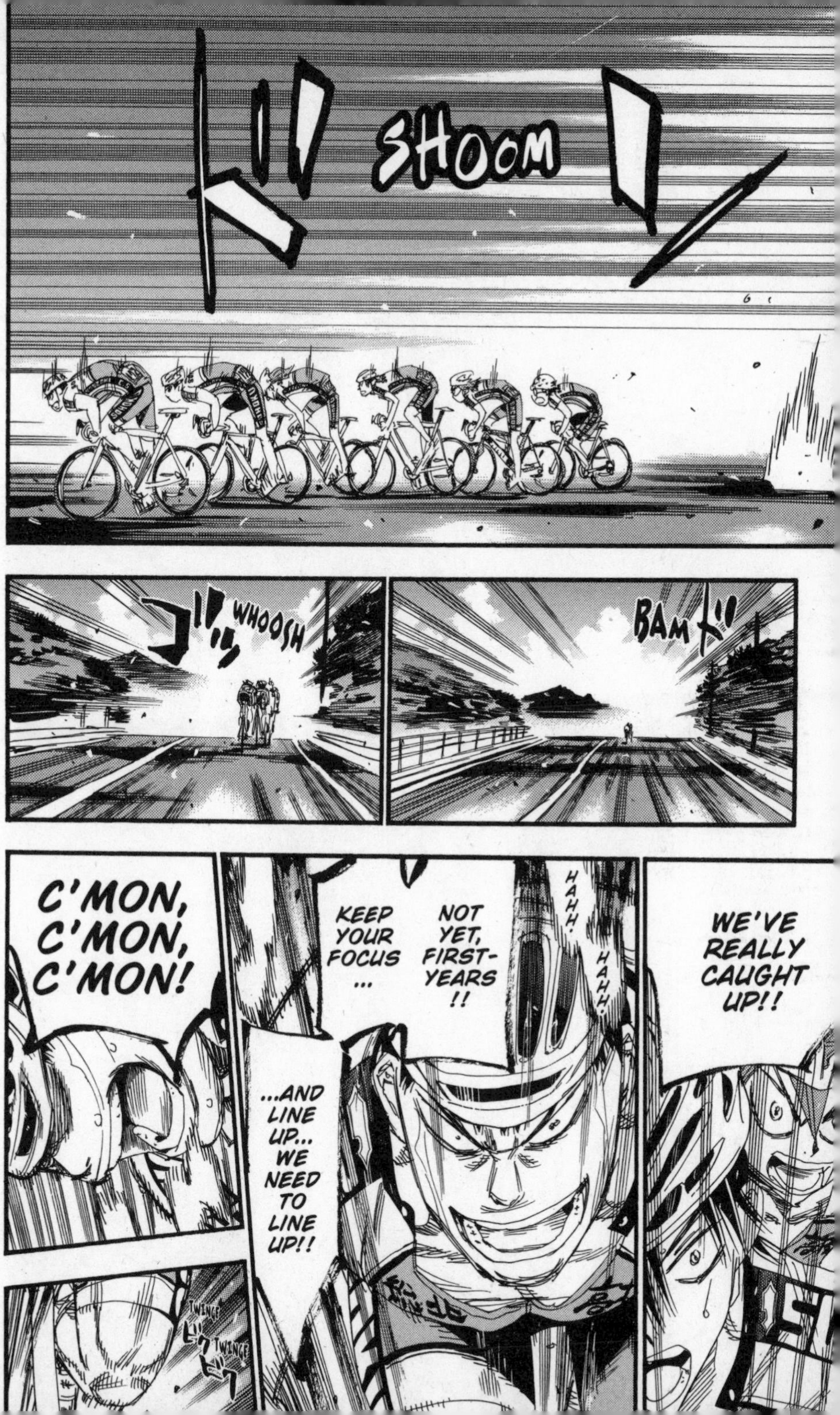
SHOOM
BAM
WHOOSH
WE'VE REALLY CAUGHT UP!!
HAHH HAHH
NOT YET, FIRST-YEARS!!
KEEP YOUR FOCUS...
...AND LINE UP... WE NEED TO LINE UP!!
C'MON, C'MON, C'MON!
TWINGE TWINGE

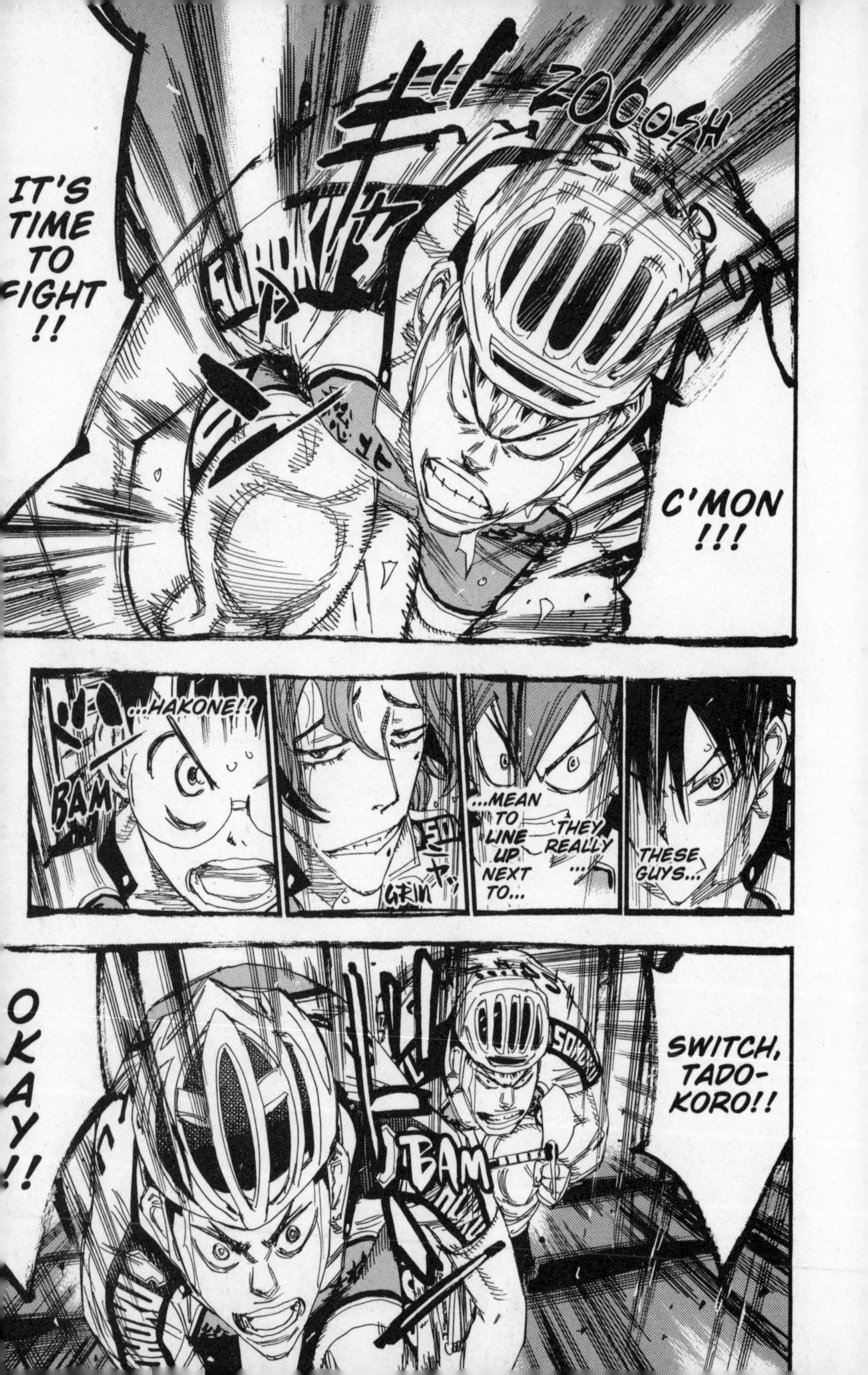
ZOOOSH
C'MON!!!
IT'S TIME TO FIGHT!!
THESE GUYS...
THEY REALLY...
...MEAN TO LINE UP NEXT TO...
GRIN
...HAKONE!!
BAM
SWITCH, TADOKORO!!
BAM
OKAY!!

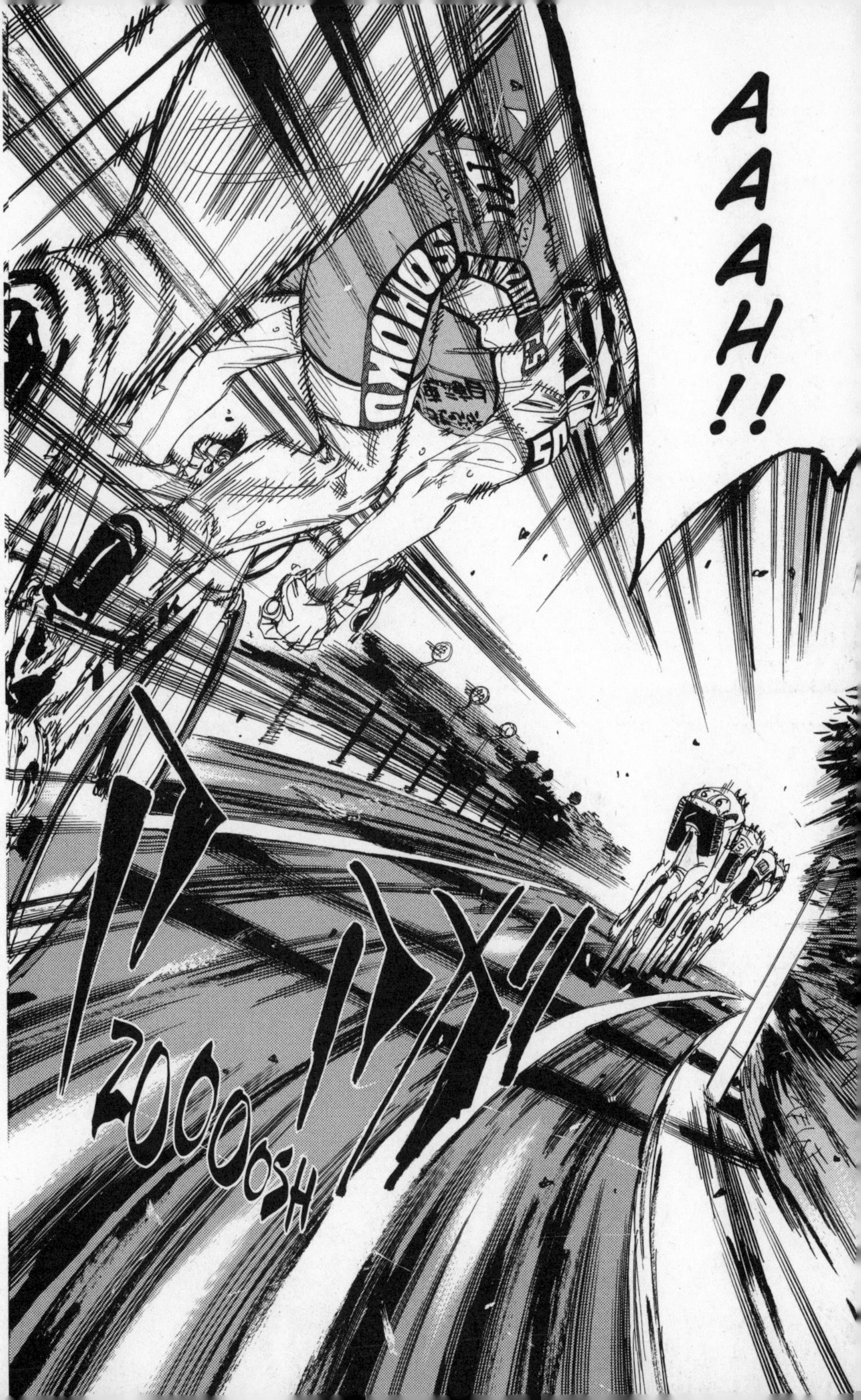
AAAAH!!
ZOOOOSH

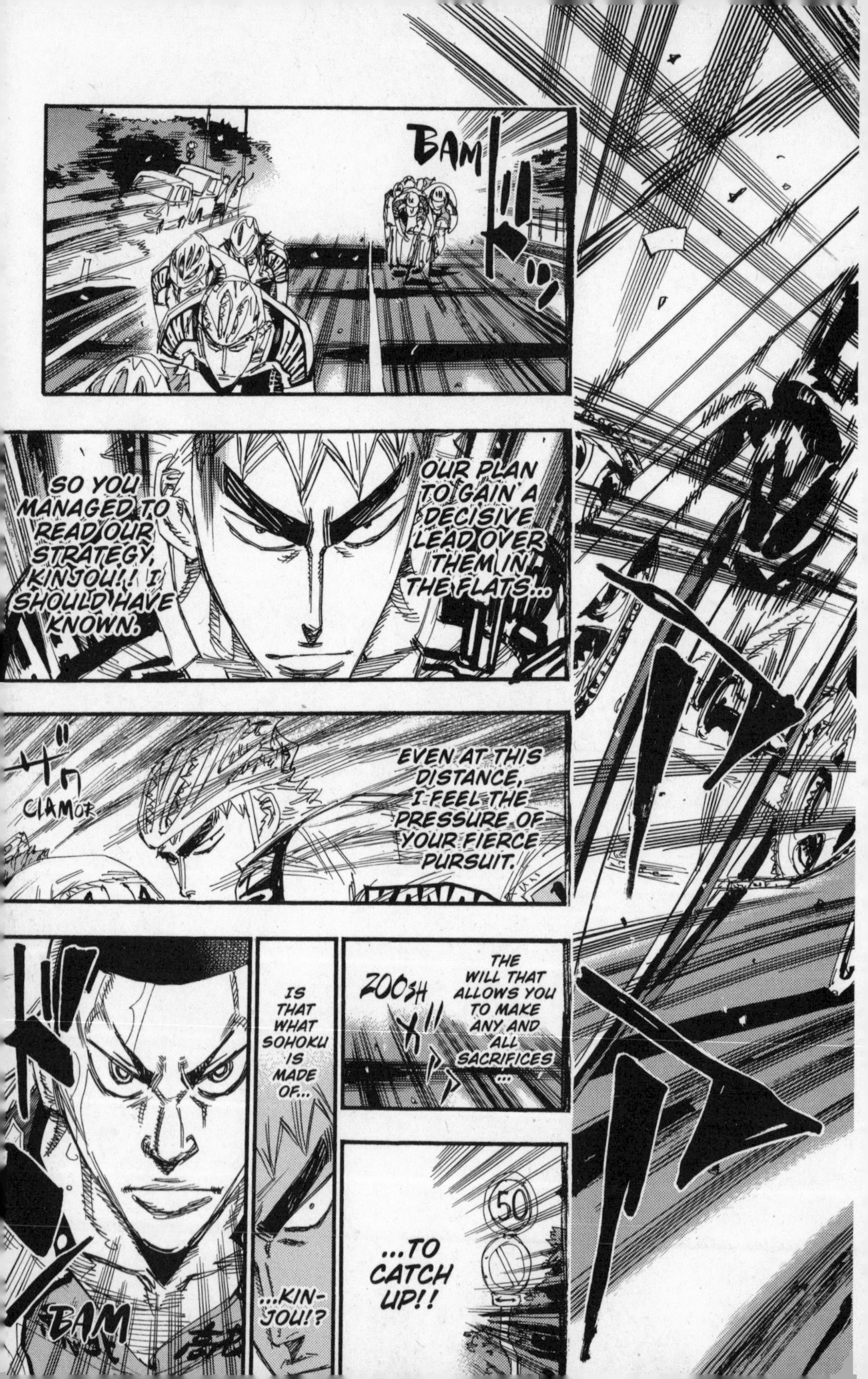
BAM
OUR PLAN TO GAIN A DECISIVE LEAD OVER THEM IN THE FLATS...
SO YOU MANAGED TO READ OUR STRATEGY, KINJOU!! I SHOULD HAVE KNOWN.
EVEN AT THIS DISTANCE, I FEEL THE PRESSURE OF YOUR FIERCE PURSUIT.
CLAMOR
THE WILL THAT ALLOWS YOU TO MAKE ANY AND ALL SACRIFICES...
ZOOSH
...TO CATCH UP!!
50
IS THAT WHAT SOHOKU IS MADE OF...
...KIN-JOU!?
BAM

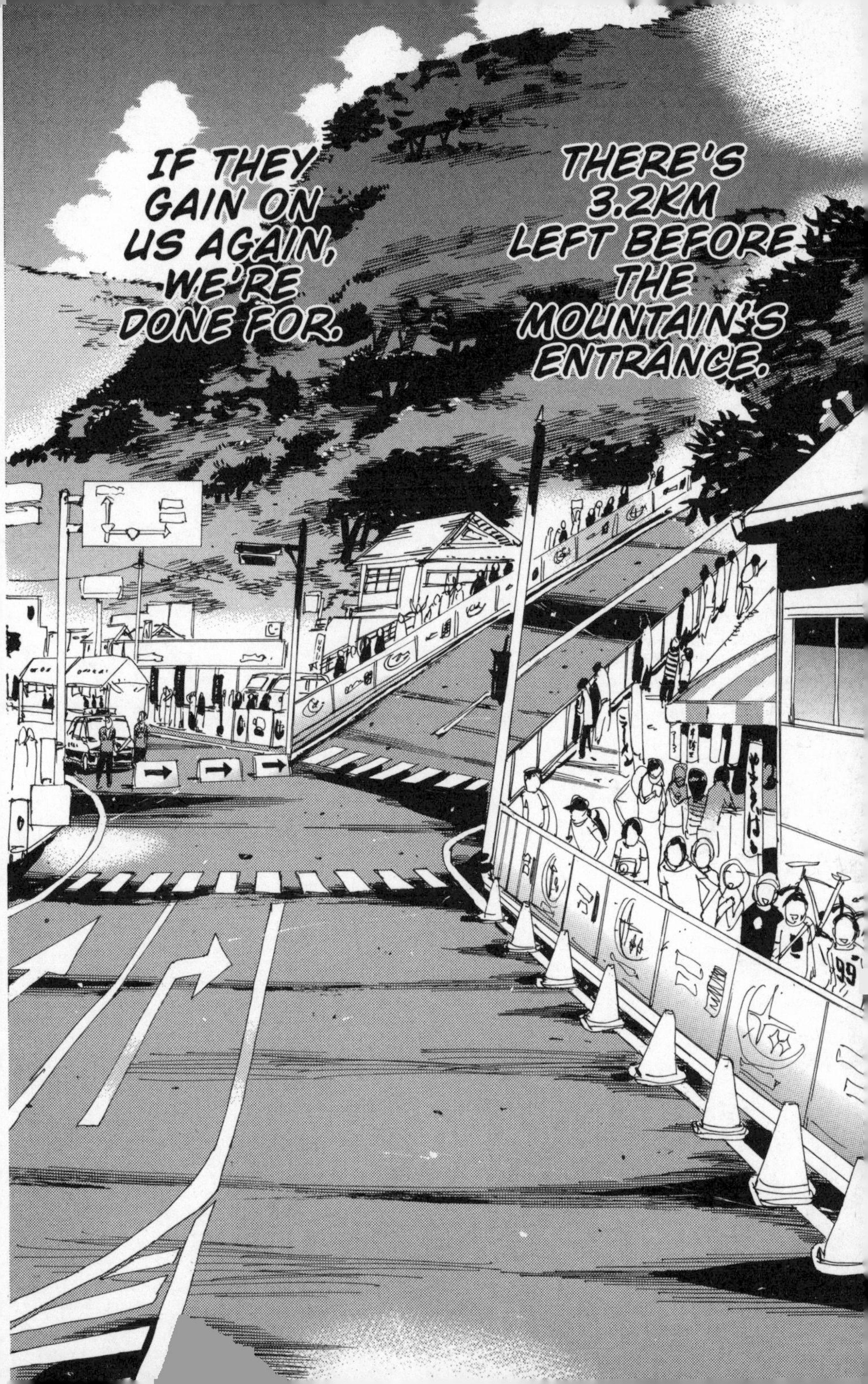
THERE'S 3.2KM LEFT BEFORE THE MOUNTAIN'S ENTRANCE.
IF THEY GAIN ON US AGAIN, WE'RE DONE FOR.

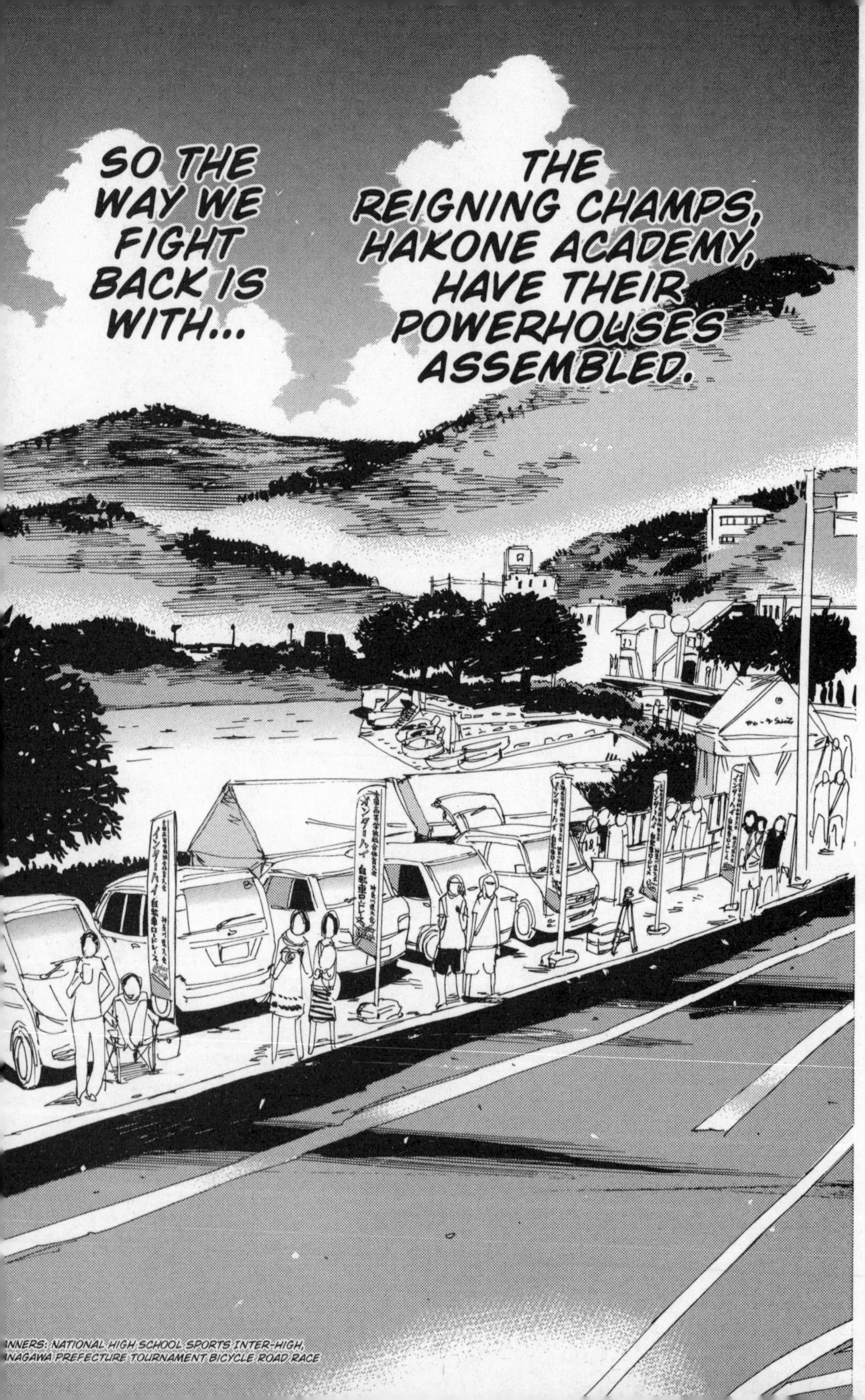
THE REIGNING CHAMPS, HAKONE ACADEMY, HAVE THEIR POWERHOUSES ASSEMBLED.
SO THE WAY WE FIGHT BACK IS WITH...
NNERS: NATIONAL HIGH SCHOOL SPORTS INTER-HIGH, NAGAWA PREFECTURE TOURNAMENT BICYCLE ROAD RACE

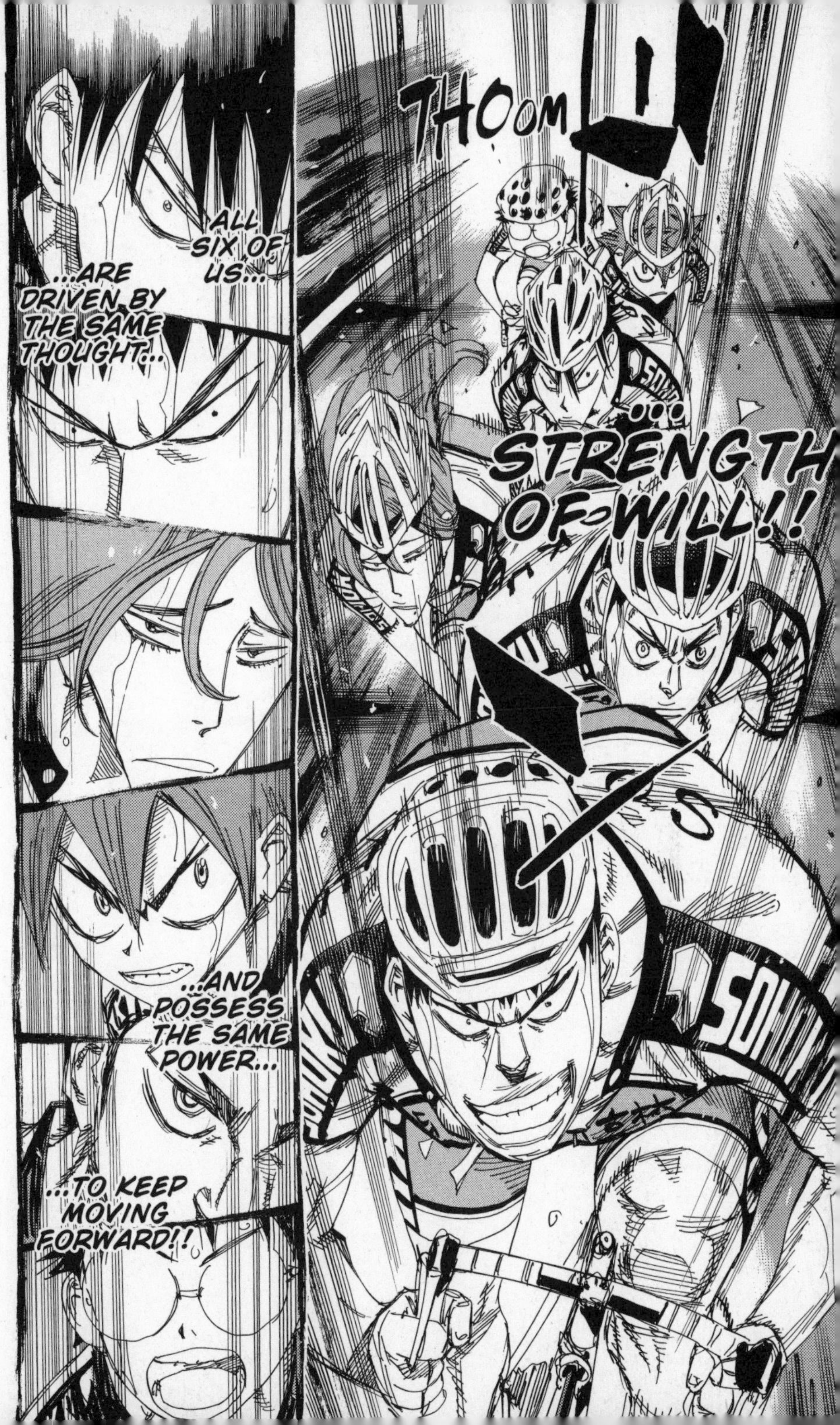
ALL SIX OF US...
...ARE DRIVEN BY THE SAME THOUGHT...
...AND POSSESS THE SAME POWER...
...TO KEEP MOVING FORWARD!!
THOOM
...STRENGTH OF WILL!!

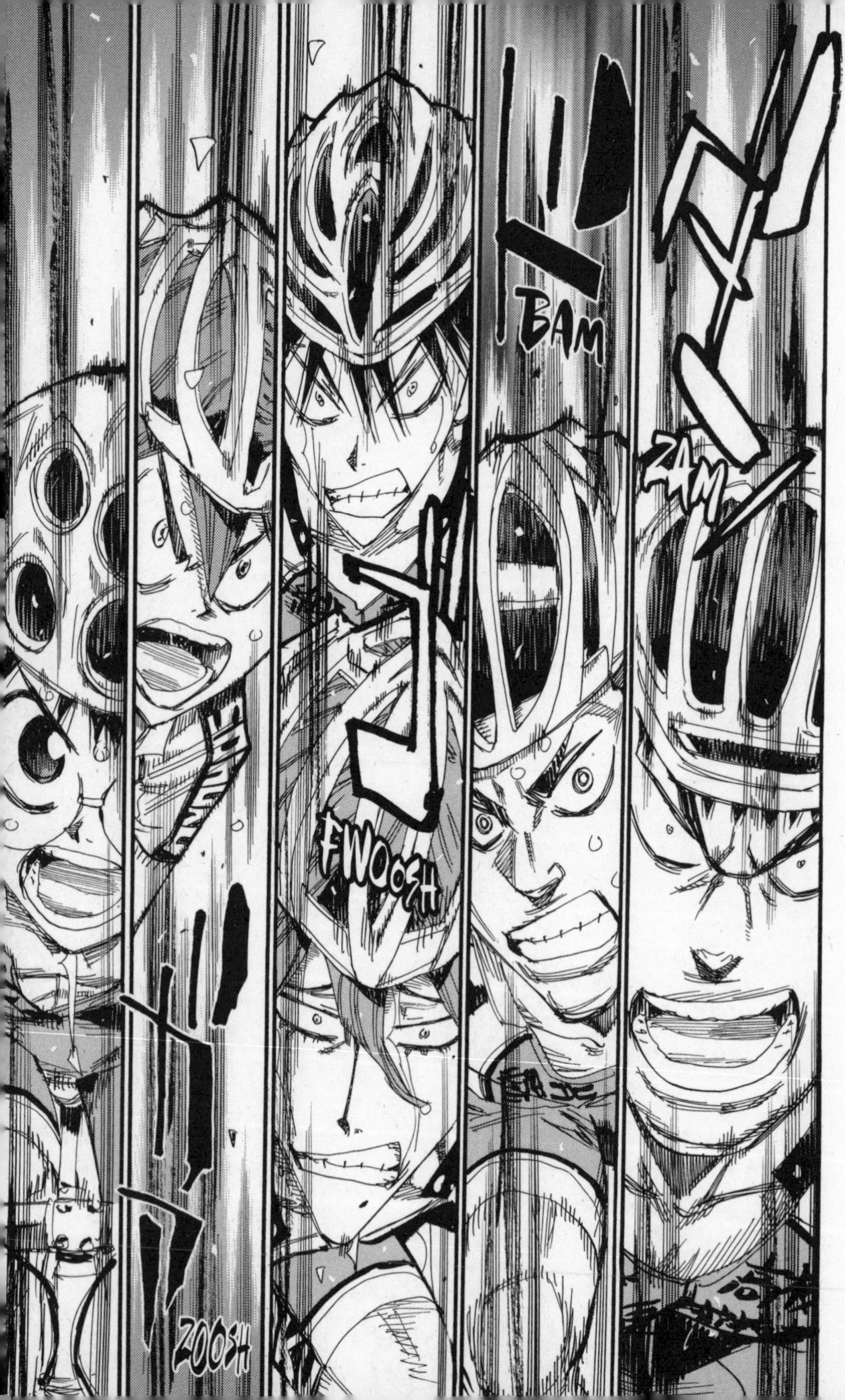
ZAM
BAM
FWOOSH
ZOOSH

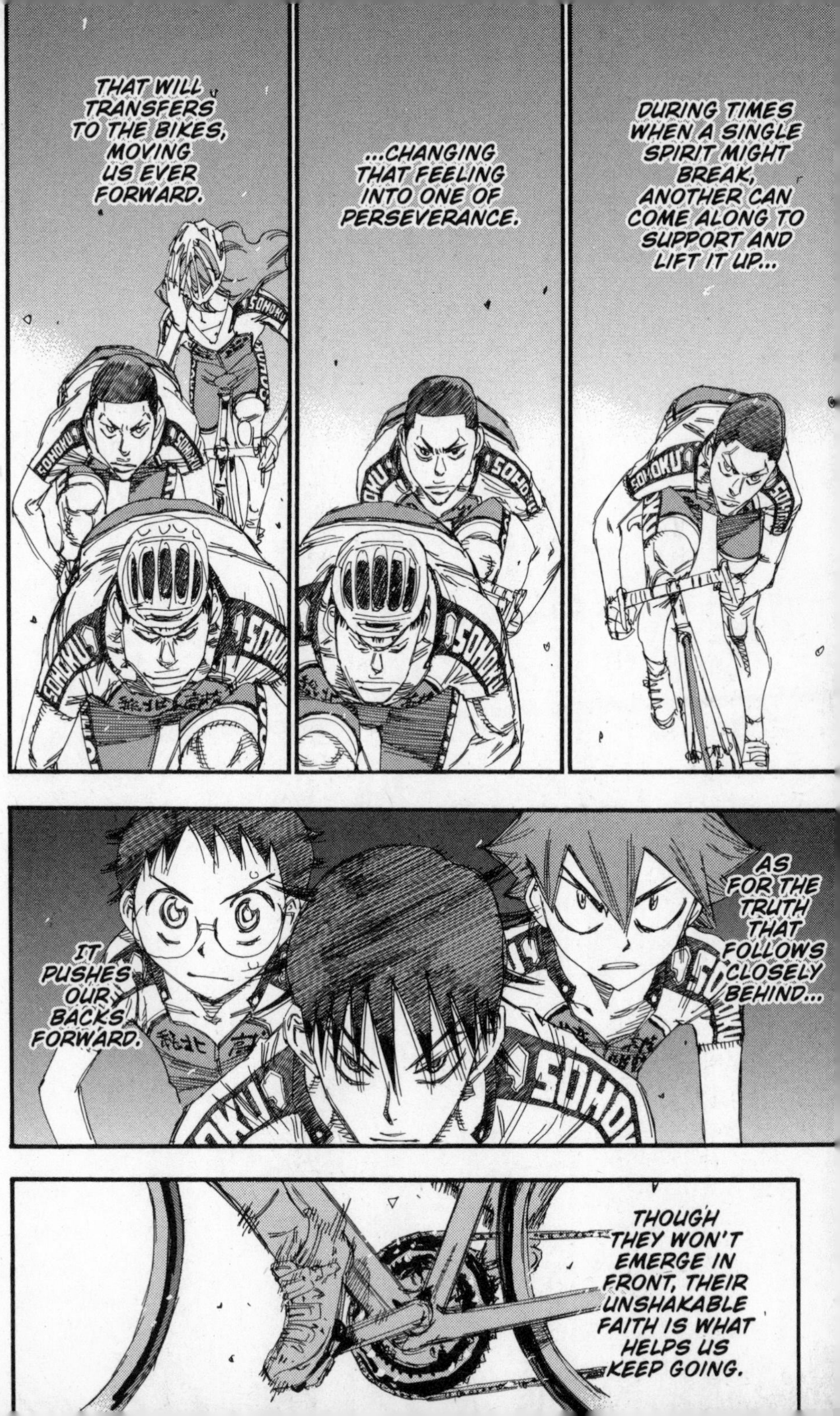
DURING TIMES WHEN A SINGLE SPIRIT MIGHT BREAK, ANOTHER CAN COME ALONG TO SUPPORT AND LIFT IT UP...
...CHANGING THAT FEELING INTO ONE OF PERSEVERANCE.
THAT WILL TRANSFERS TO THE BIKES, MOVING US EVER FORWARD.
AS FOR THE TRUTH THAT FOLLOWS CLOSELY BEHIND...
IT PUSHES OUR BACKS FORWARD.
THOUGH THEY WON'T EMERGE IN FRONT, THEIR UNSHAKABLE FAITH IS WHAT HELPS US KEEP GOING.

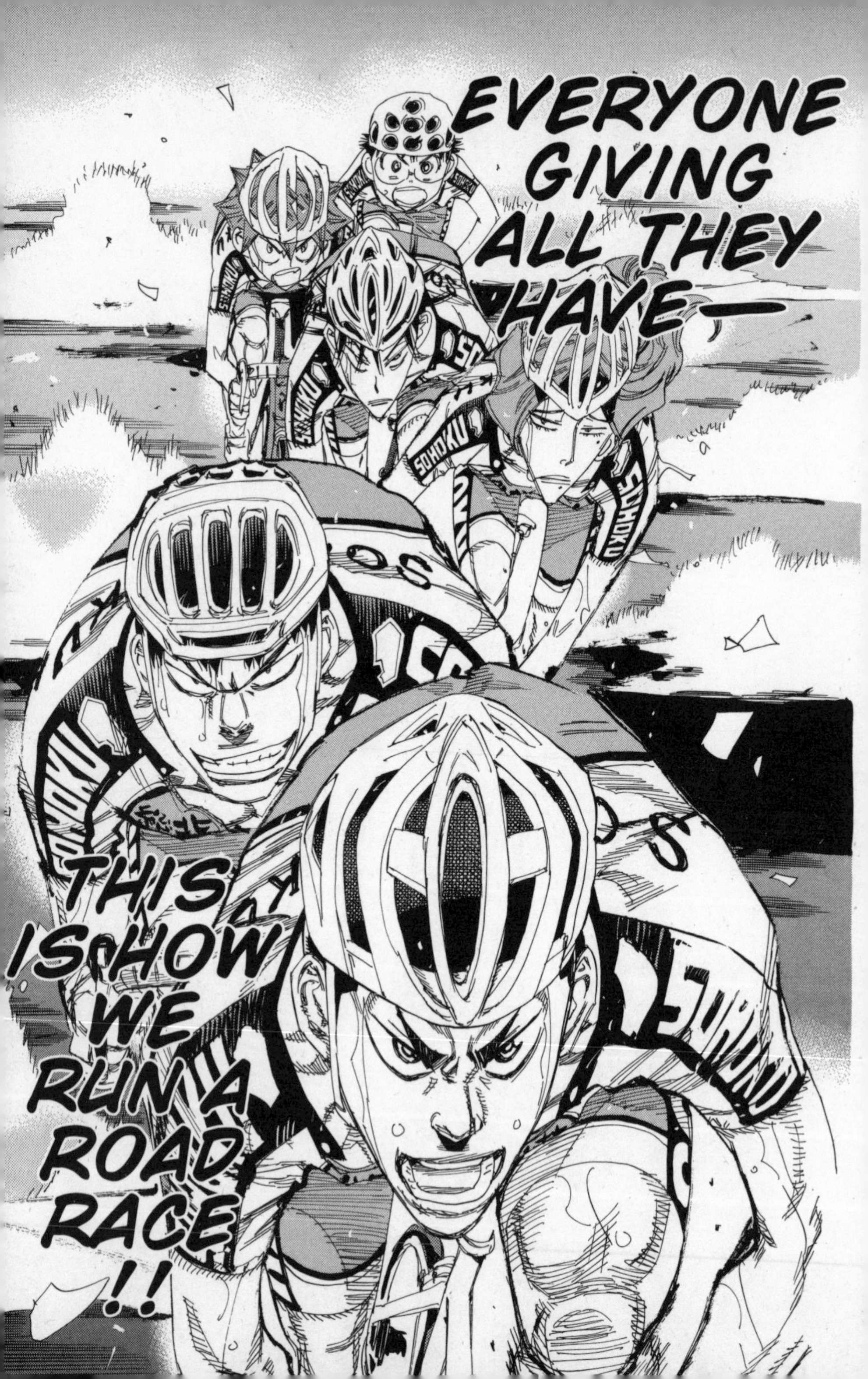
EVERYONE GIVING ALL THEY HAVE—
THIS IS HOW WE RUN A ROAD RACE!!

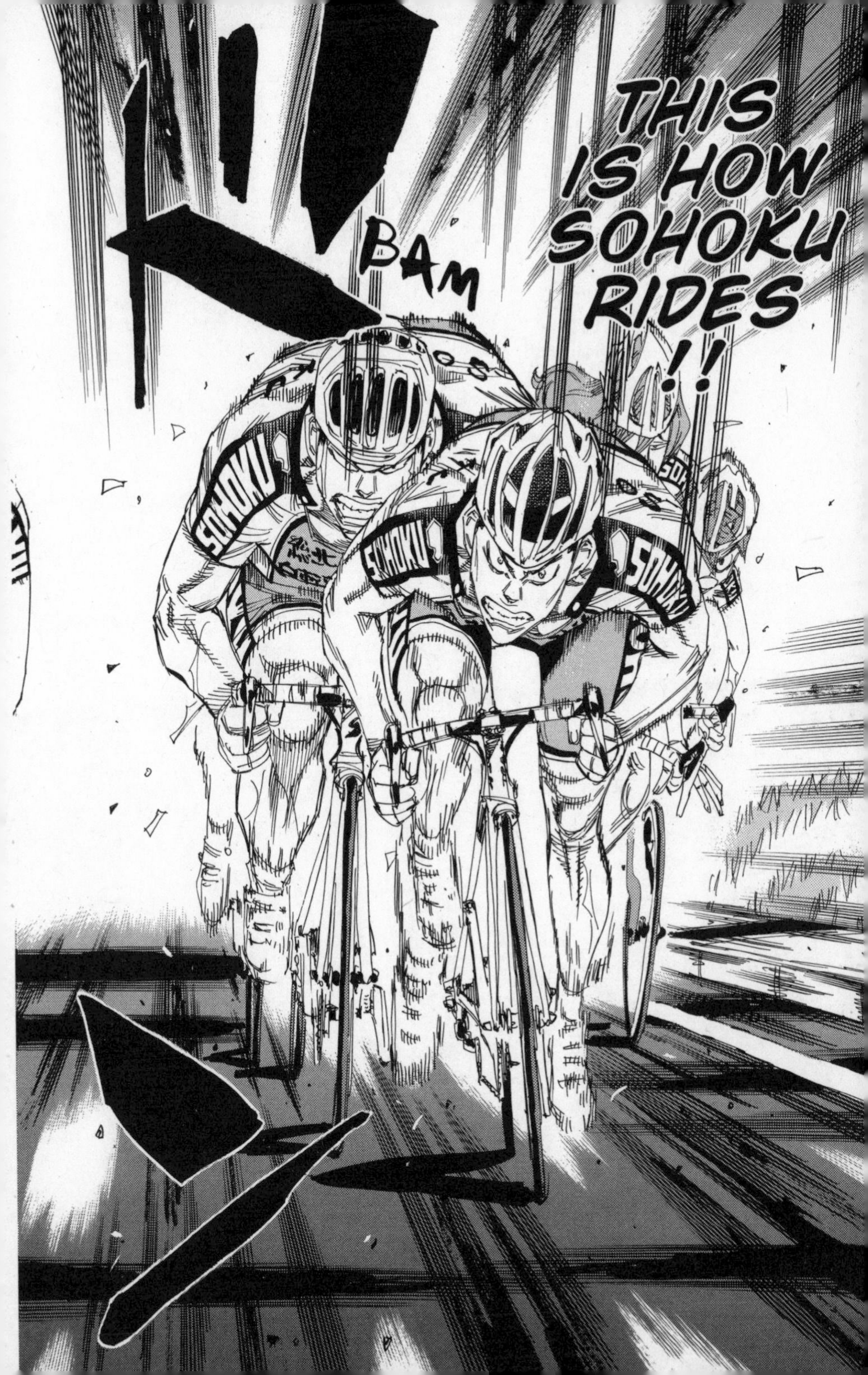
THIS IS HOW SOHOKU RIDES!!
BAM

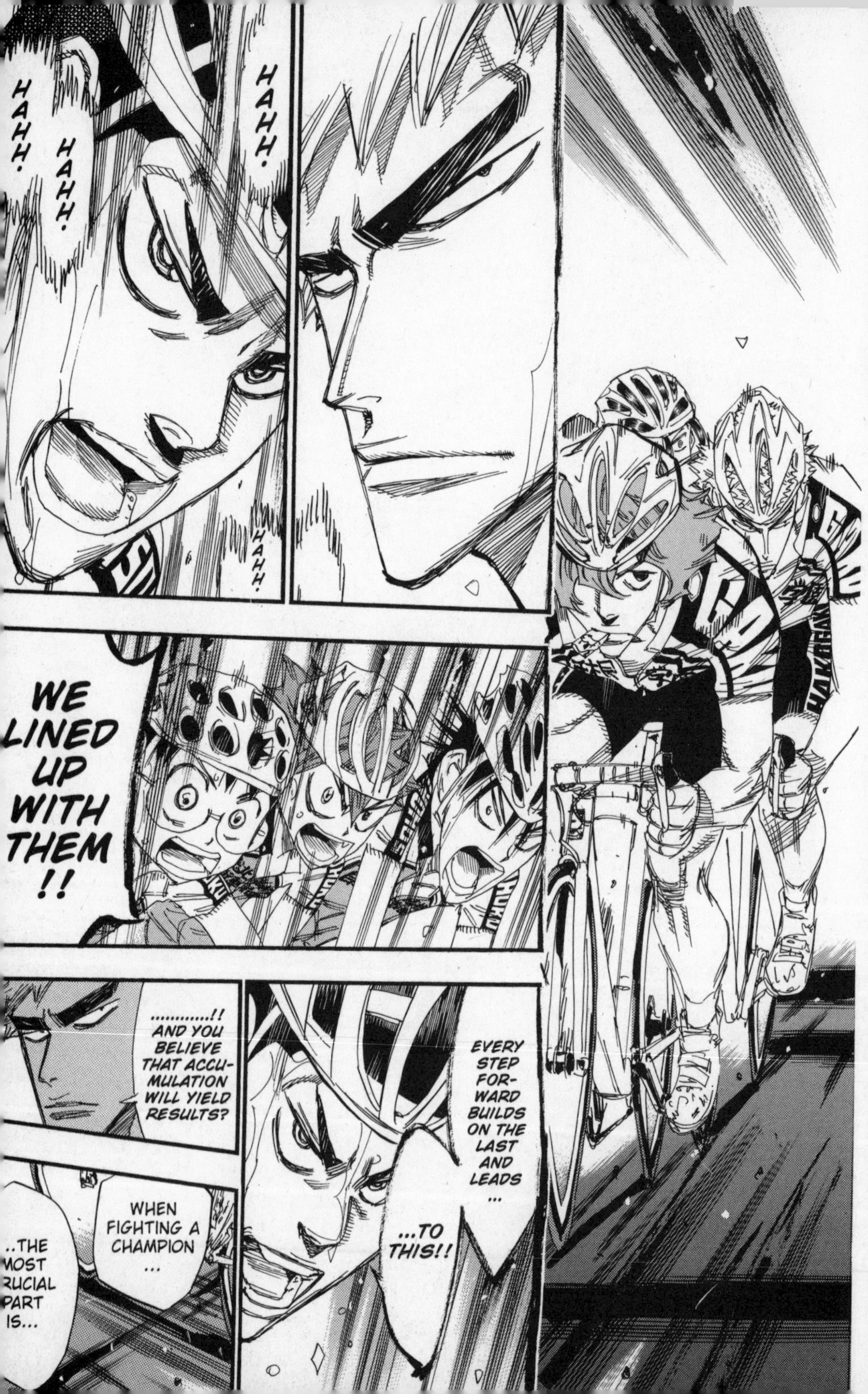
HAHH!
HAHH!
HAHH!
HAHH!
WE LINED UP WITH THEM!!
EVERY STEP FORWARD BUILDS ON THE LAST AND LEADS ...
...TO THIS!!
...........!! AND YOU BELIEVE THAT ACCUMULATION WILL YIELD RESULTS?
WHEN FIGHTING A CHAMPION ...
..THE MOST RUCIAL PART IS...

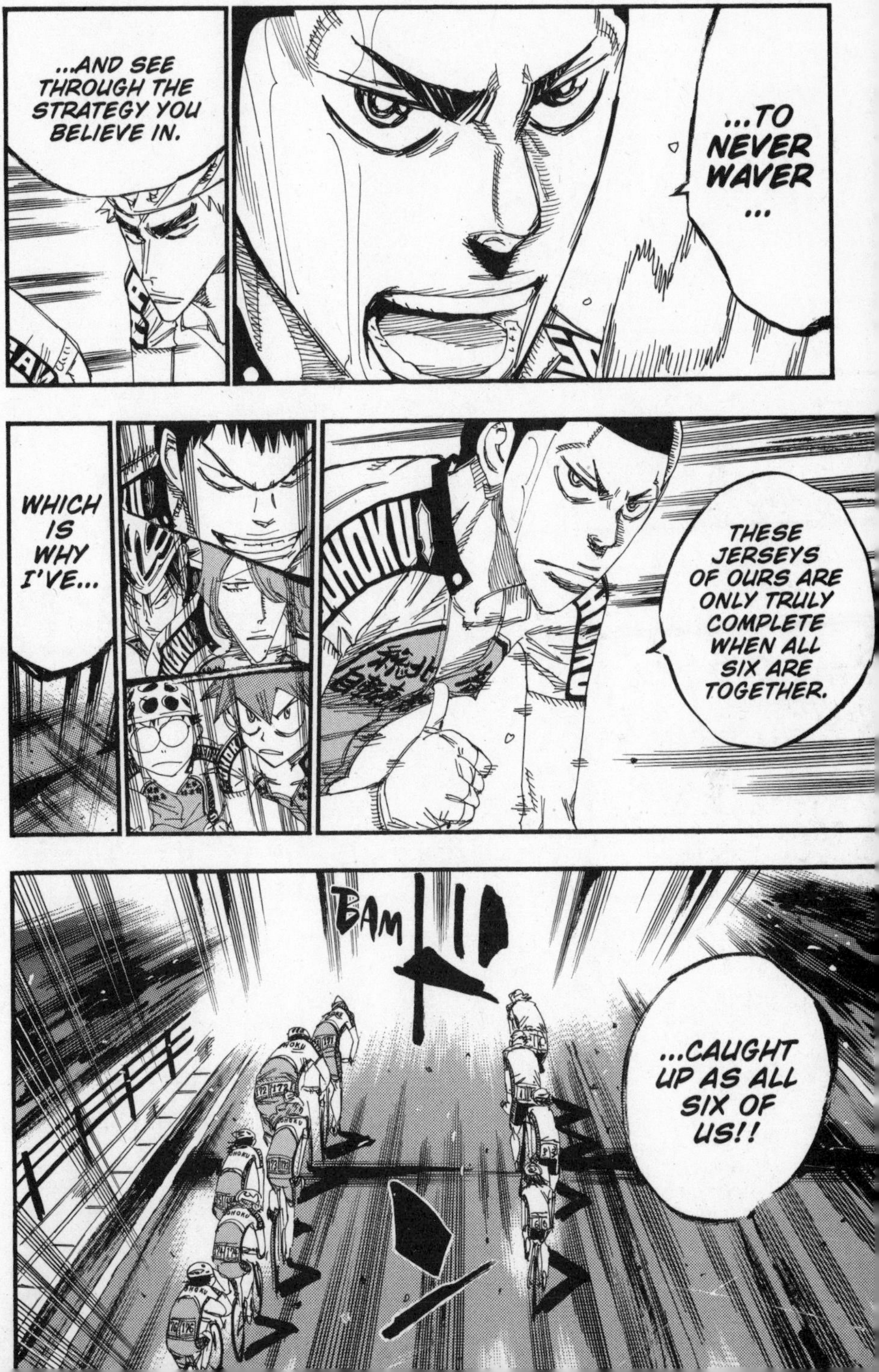
...TO NEVER WAVER ...
...AND SEE THROUGH THE STRATEGY YOU BELIEVE IN.
THESE JERSEYS OF OURS ARE ONLY TRULY COMPLETE WHEN ALL SIX ARE TOGETHER.
WHICH IS WHY I'VE...
BAM
...CAUGHT UP AS ALL SIX OF US!!

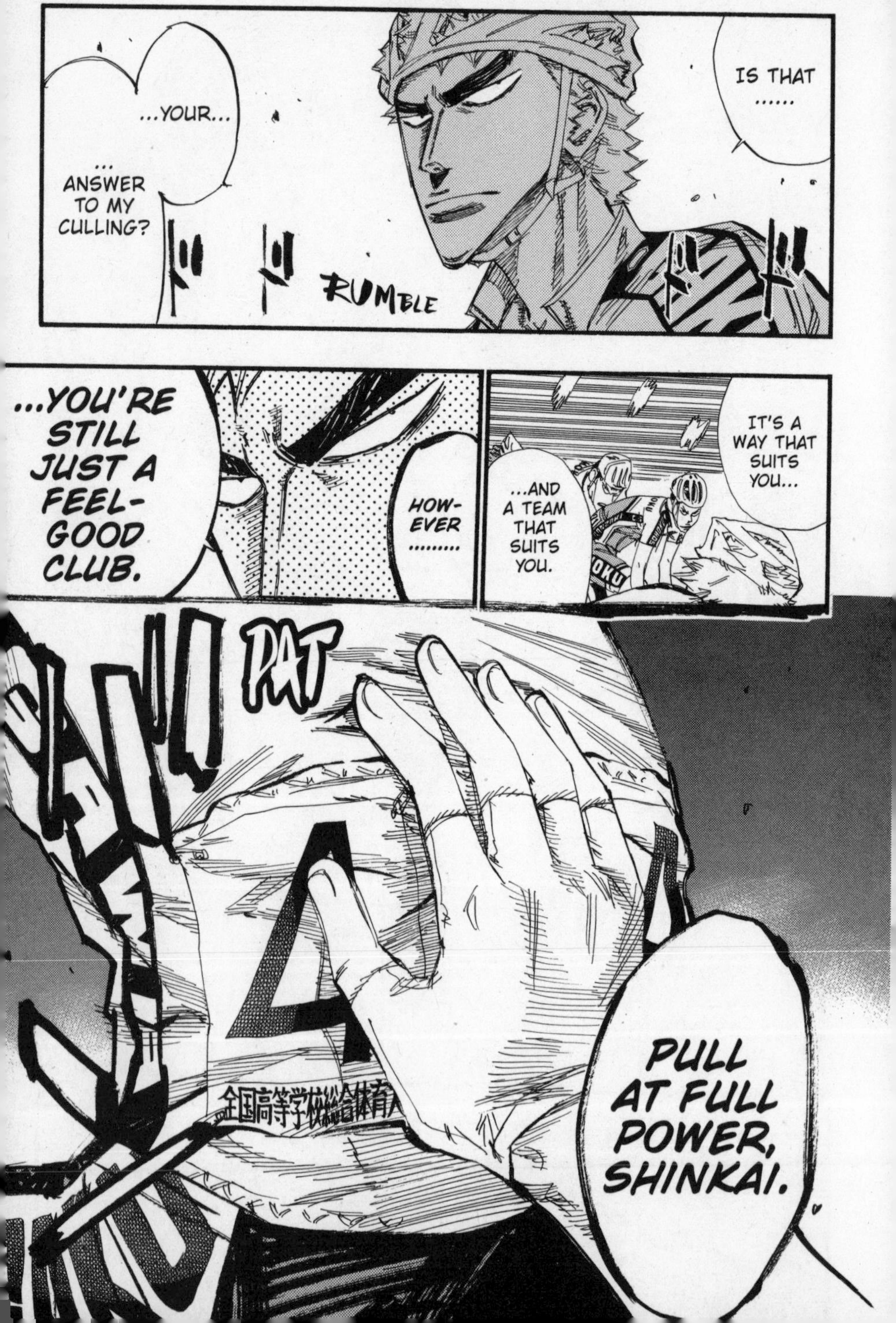
IS THAT ......
...YOUR...
... ANSWER TO MY CULLING?
RUMBLE
IT'S A WAY THAT SUITS YOU...
...AND A TEAM THAT SUITS YOU.
HOW-EVER ....
...YOU'RE STILL JUST A FEEL-GOOD CLUB.
PAT
全国高等学校総合体育
PULL AT FULL POWER, SHINKAI.

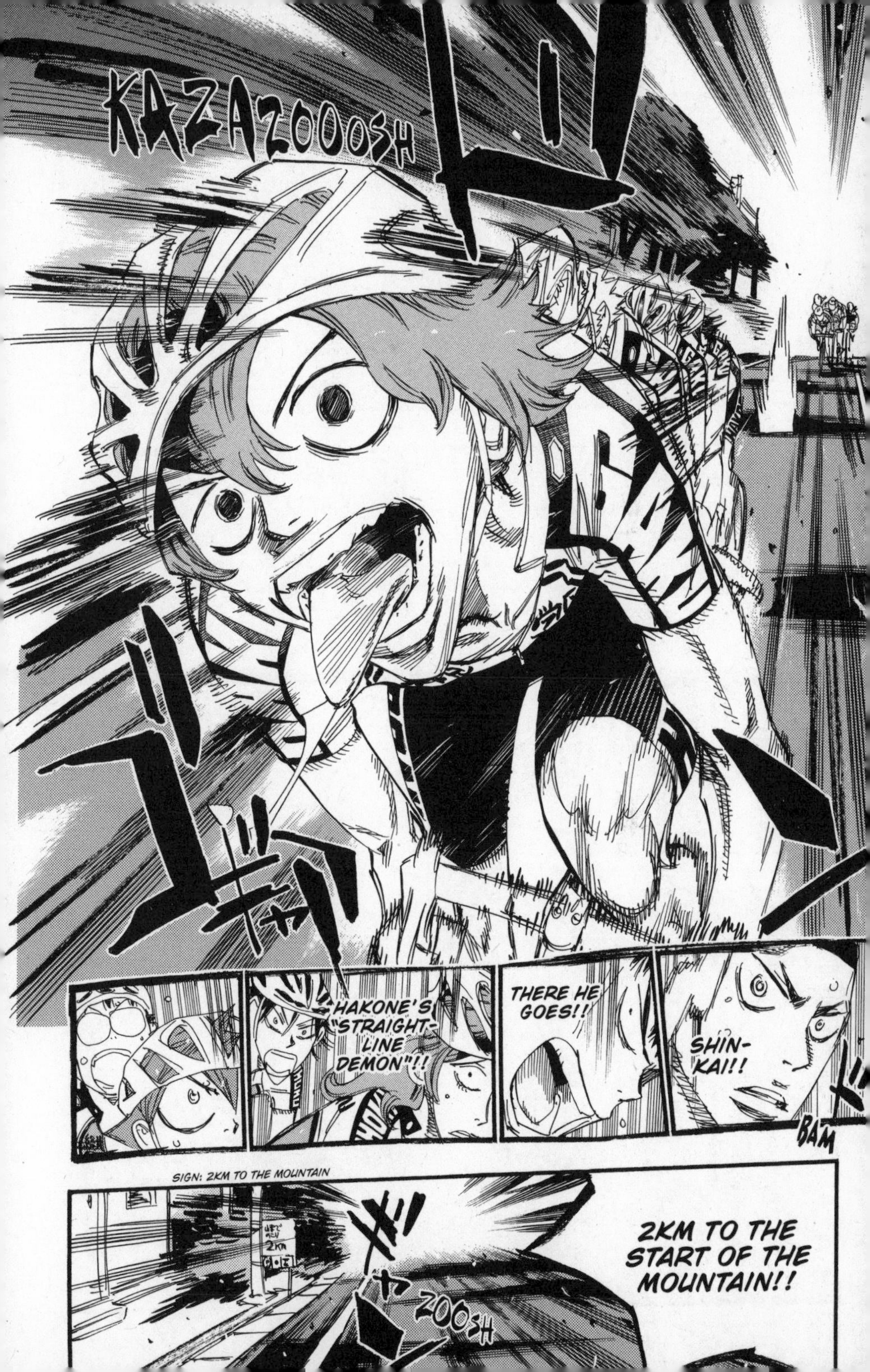
KAZAZOOOSH
SHIN-KAI!!
BAM
THERE HE GOES!!
HAKONE'S "STRAIGHT-LINE DEMON"!!
SIGN: 2KM TO THE MOUNTAIN
2KM TO THE START OF THE MOUNTAIN!!
ZOOSH

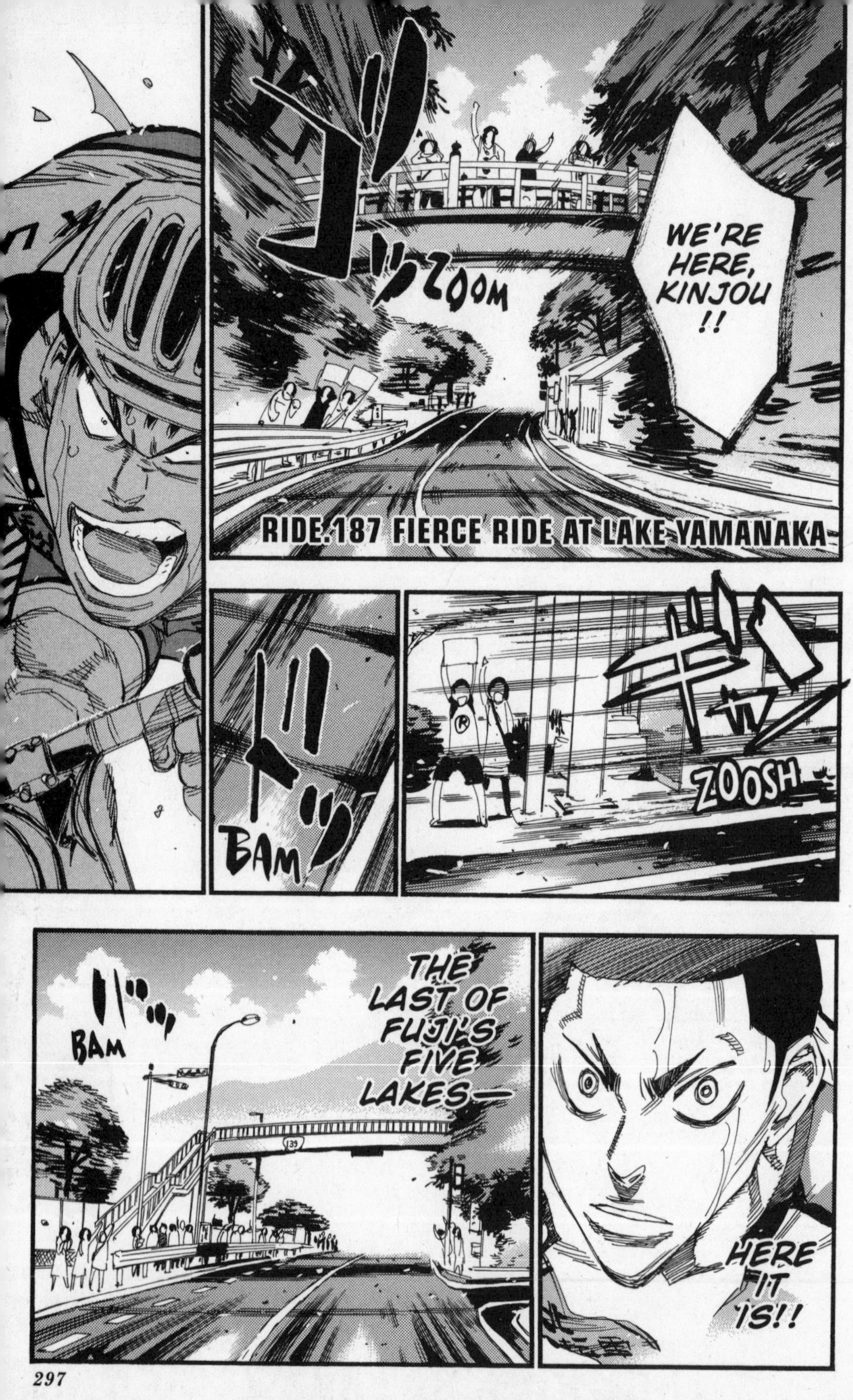
ZOOM
WE'RE HERE, KINJOU!!
RIDE.187 FIERCE RIDE AT LAKE YAMANAKA
ZOOSH
BAM
HERE IT IS!!
THE LAST OF FUJI'S FIVE LAKES—
BAM

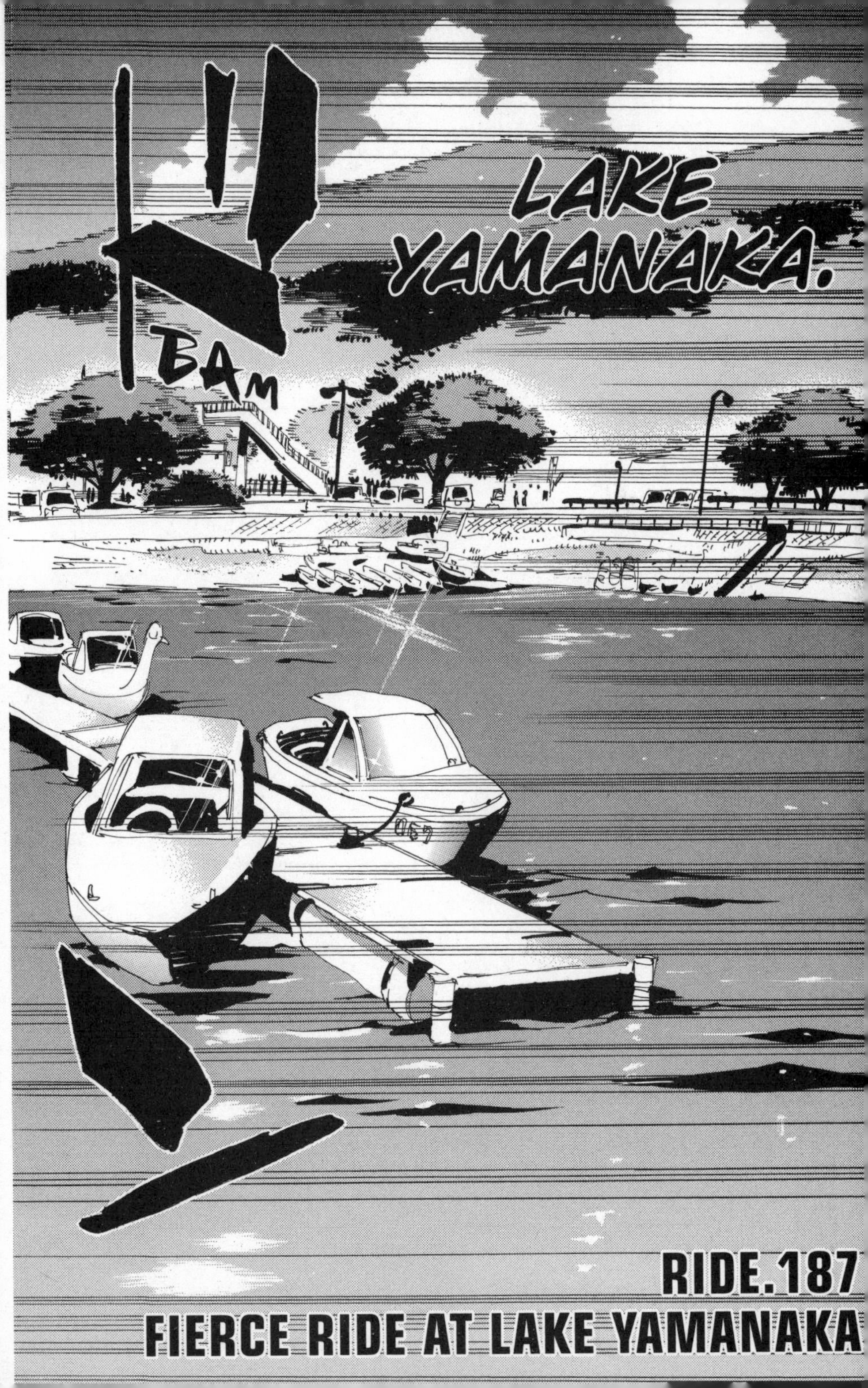
LAKE YAMANAKA.
BAM
RIDE.187
FIERCE RIDE AT LAKE YAMANAKA

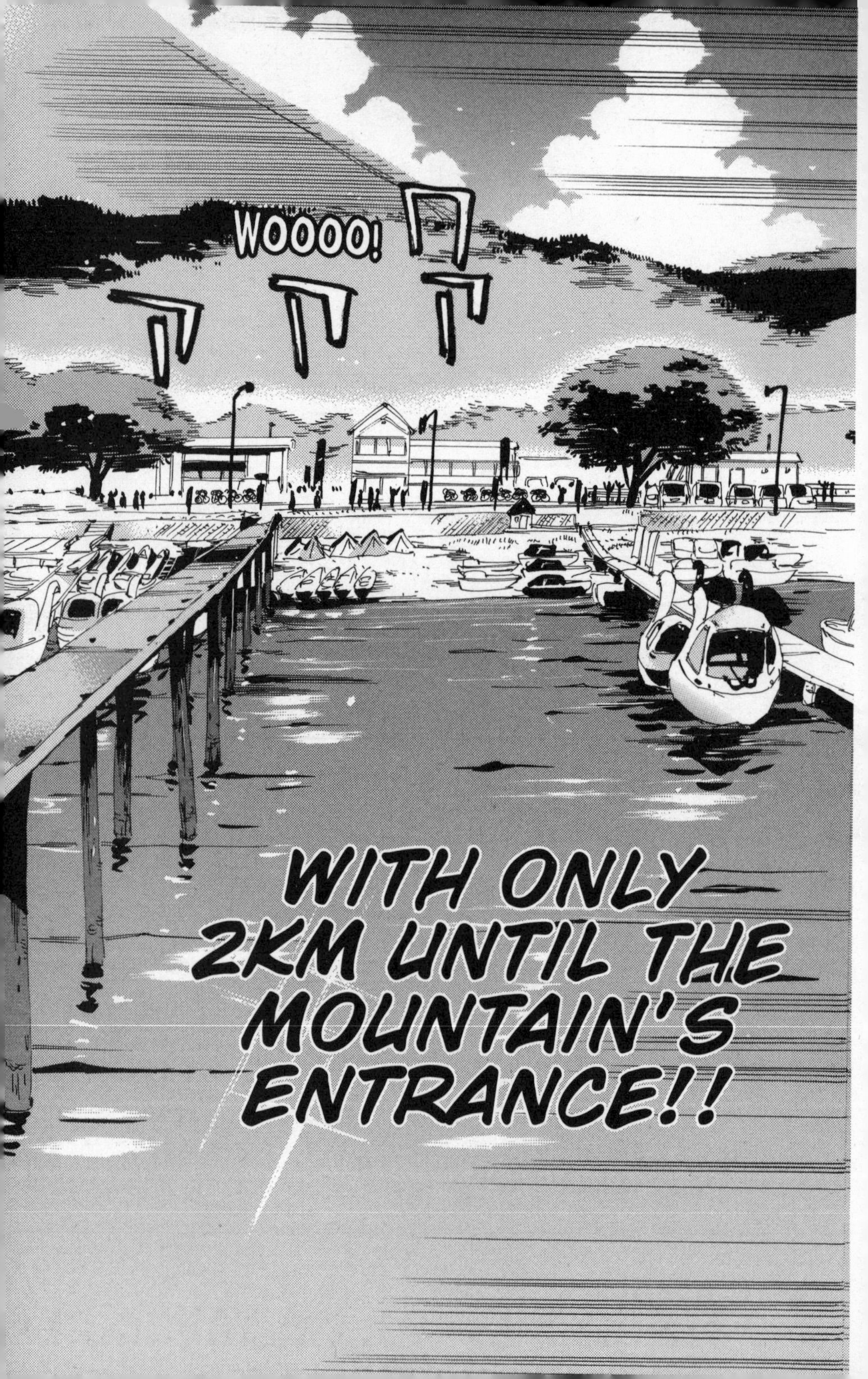
WOOOO!
WITH ONLY 2KM UNTIL THE MOUNTAIN'S ENTRANCE!!

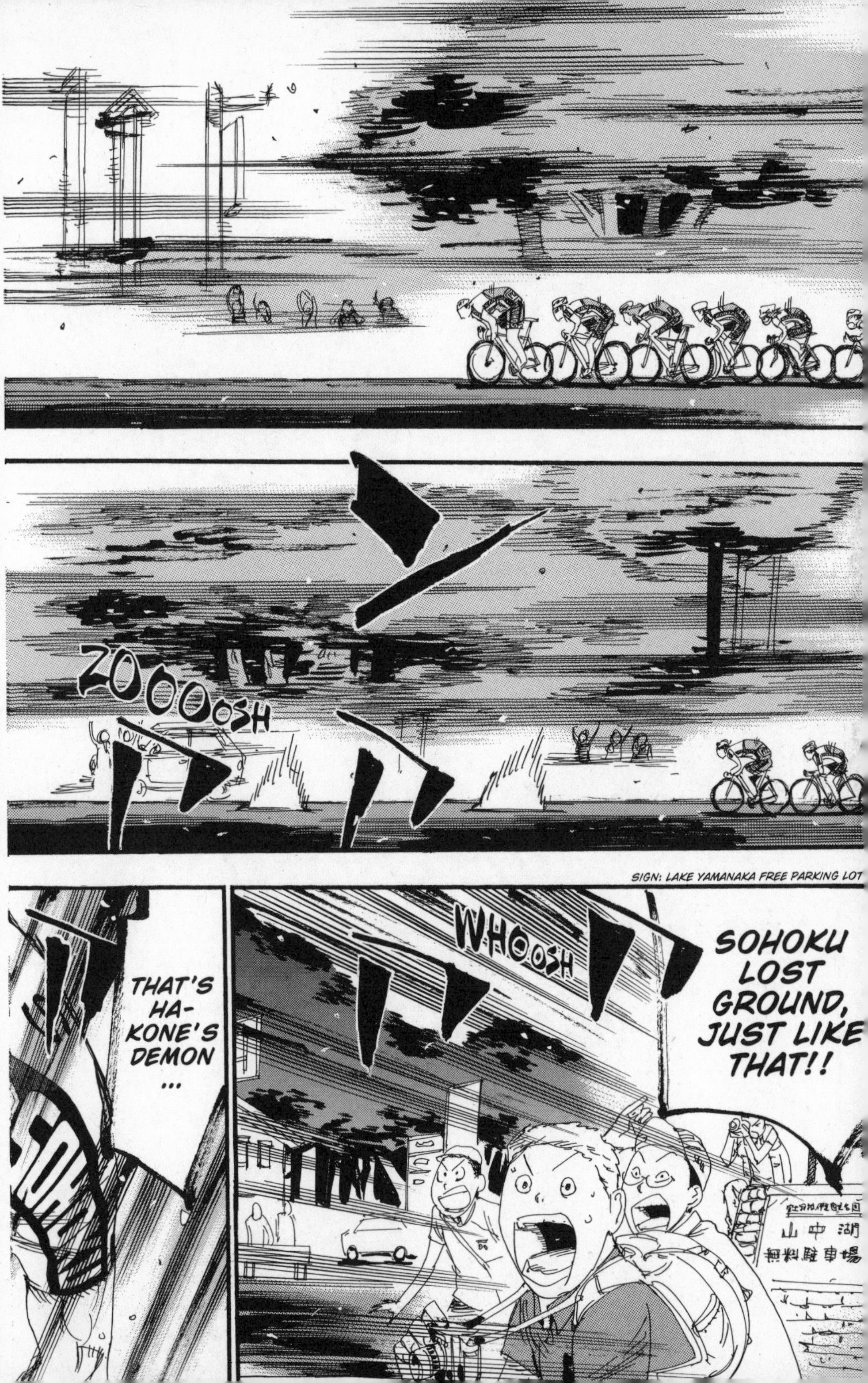
ZOOOOOSH
SIGN: LAKE YAMANAKA FREE PARKING LOT
WHOOSH
SOHOKU LOST GROUND, JUST LIKE THAT!!
山中湖
無料駐車場
THAT'S HA-KONE'S DEMON ...

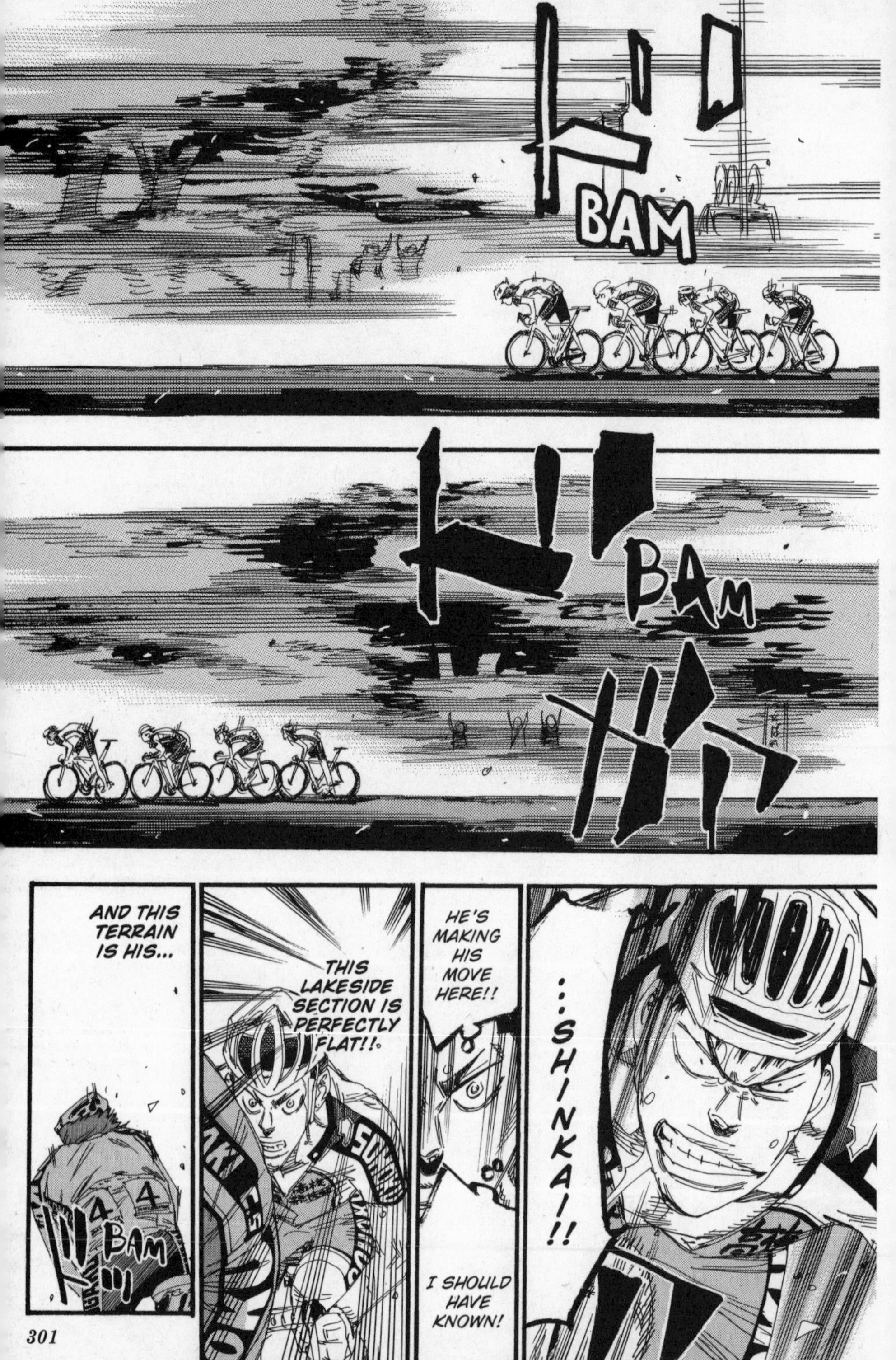
BAM
BAM
...SHINKA!!
HE'S MAKING HIS MOVE HERE!!
I SHOULD HAVE KNOWN!
THIS LAKESIDE SECTION IS PERFECTLY FLAT!!
AND THIS TERRAIN IS HIS...
BAM

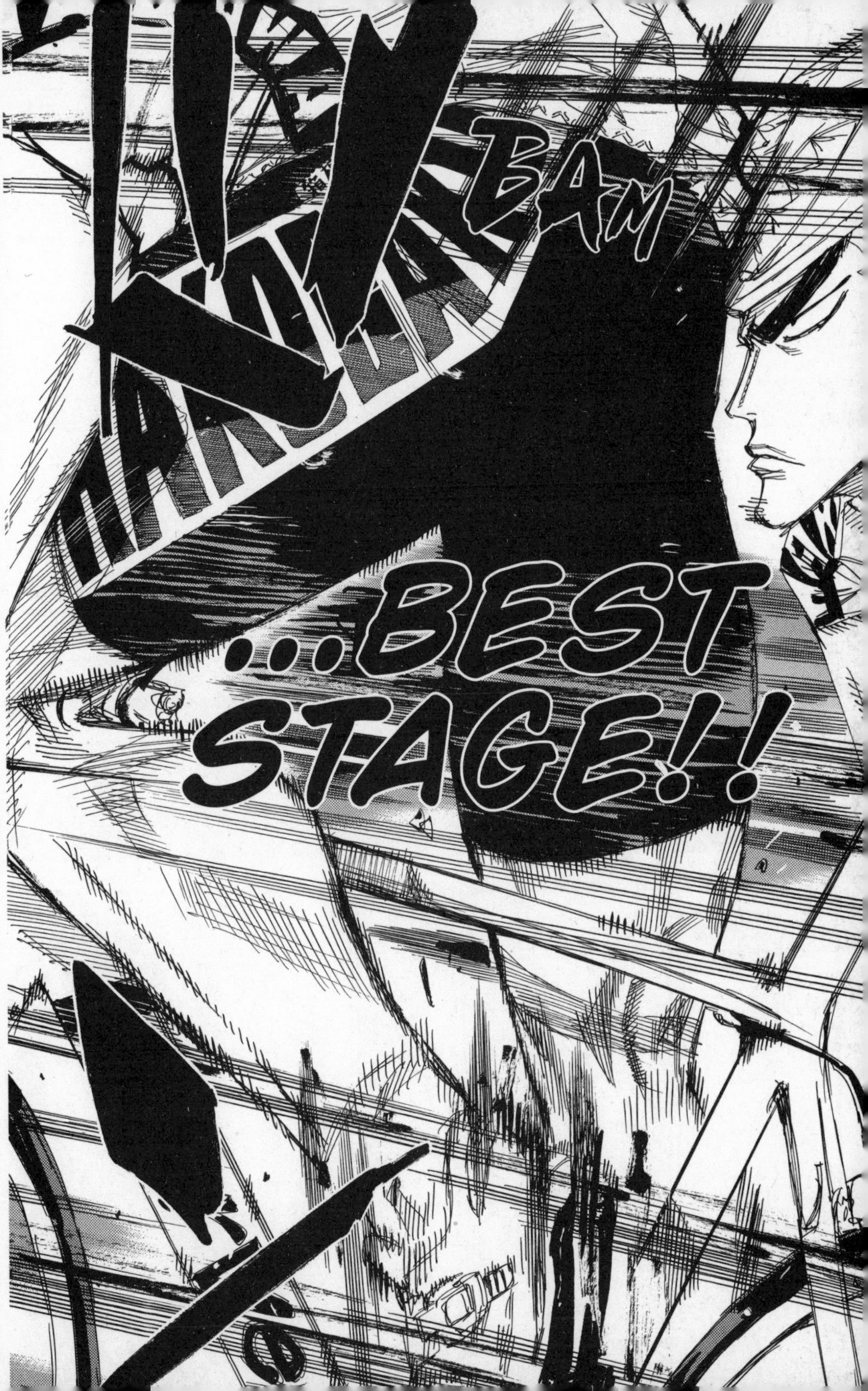
BAM
...BEST STAGE!!

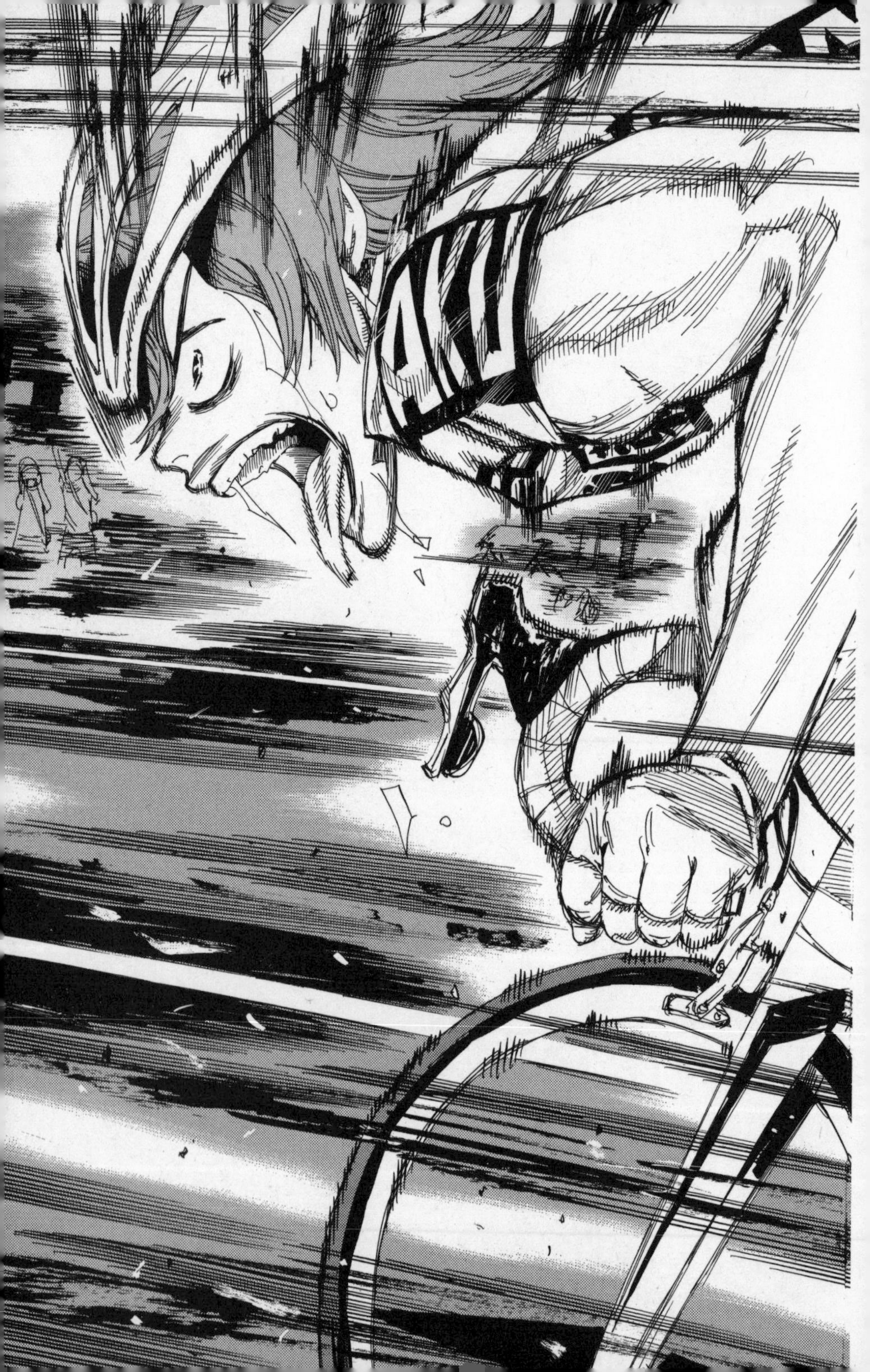

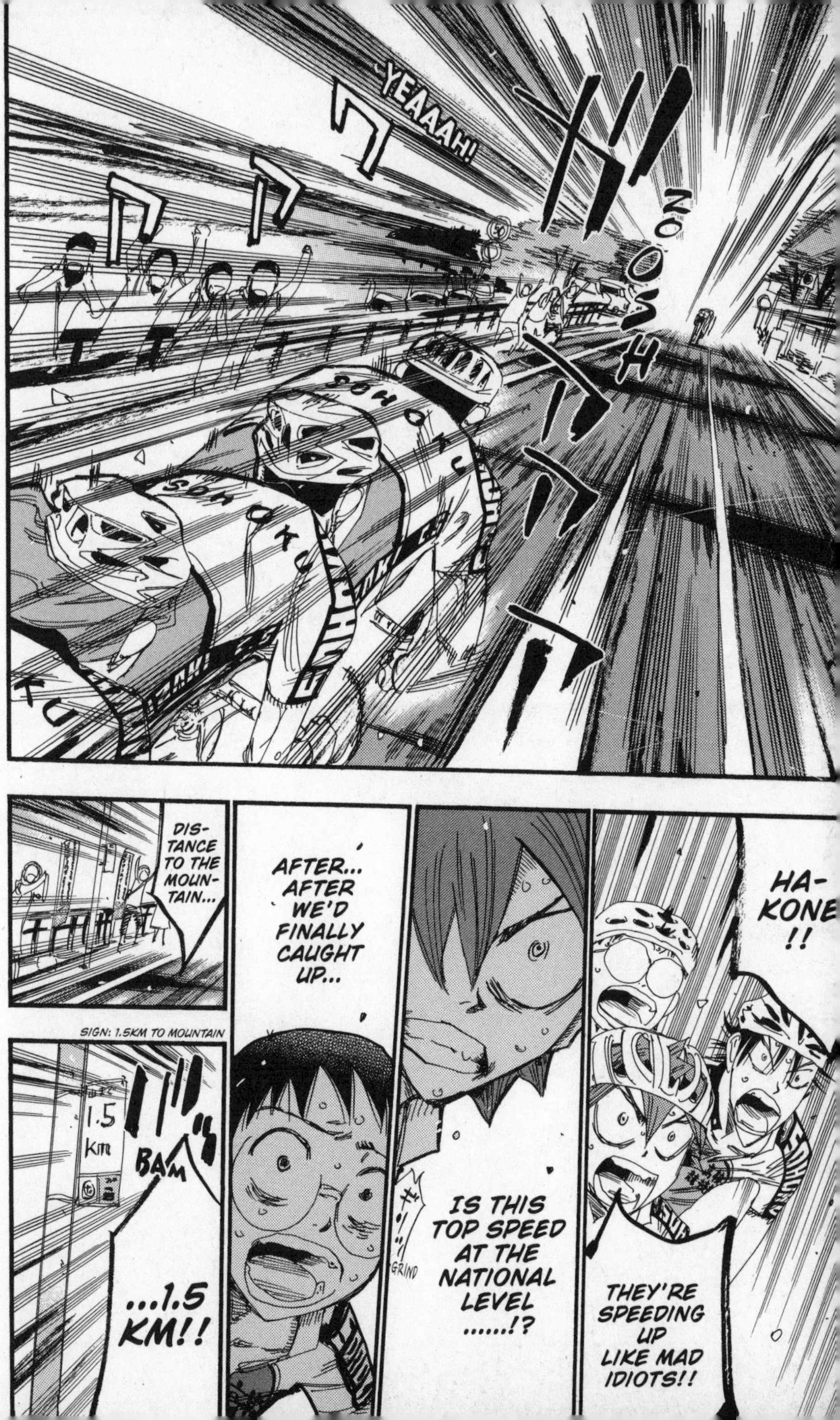
YEAAAH!
ZOOOOSH
HA-KONE!!
THEY'RE SPEEDING UP LIKE MAD IDIOTS!!
IS THIS TOP SPEED AT THE NATIONAL LEVEL ......!?
GRIND
AFTER... AFTER WE'D FINALLY CAUGHT UP...
DIS-TANCE TO THE MOUN-TAIN...
1.5 km
BAM
...1.5 KM!!
SIGN: 1.5KM TO MOUNTAIN

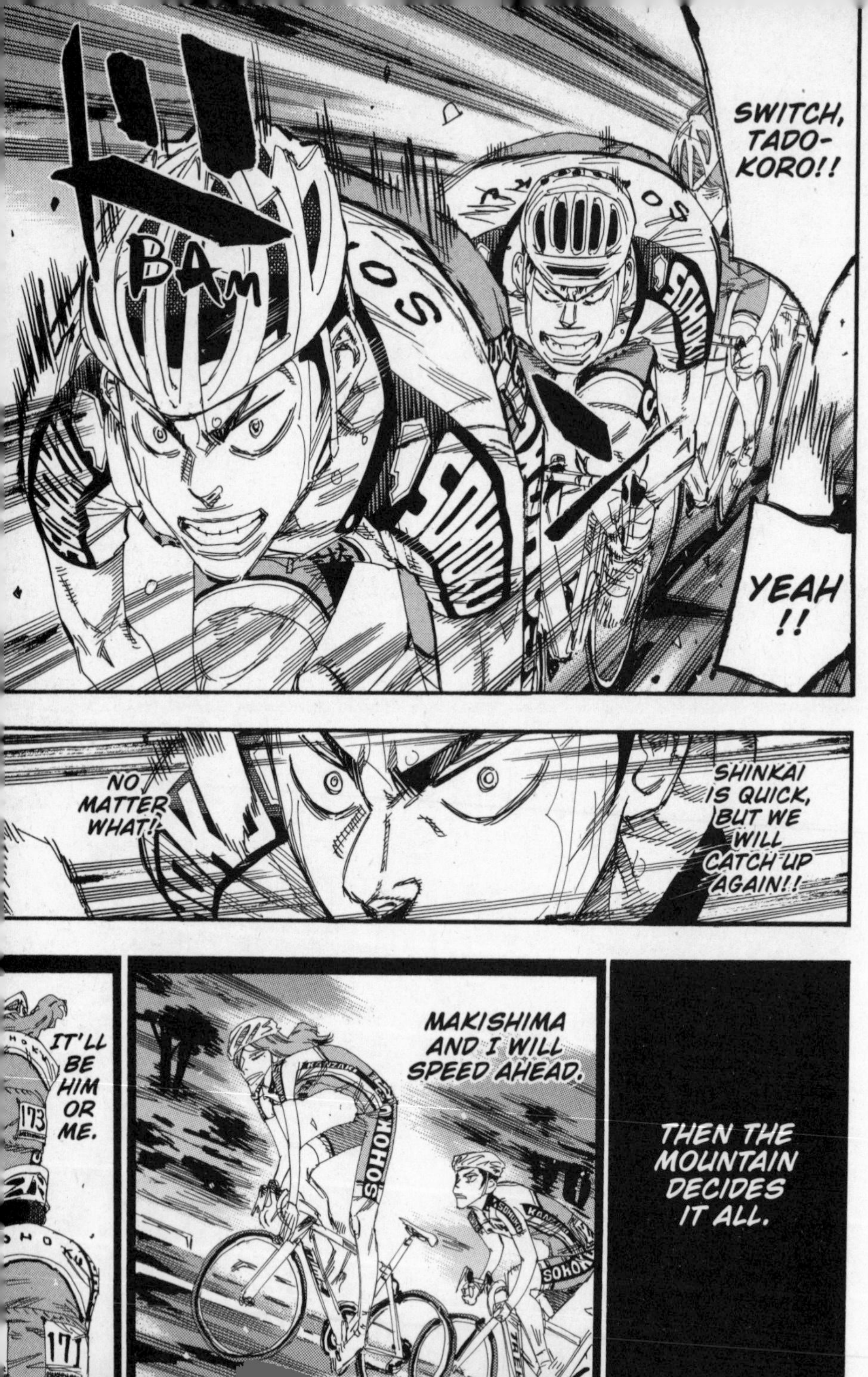
SWITCH, TADO-KORO!!
BAM
YEAH!!
SHINKAI IS QUICK, BUT WE WILL CATCH UP AGAIN!!
NO MATTER WHAT!
THEN THE MOUNTAIN DECIDES IT ALL.
MAKISHIMA AND I WILL SPEED AHEAD.
IT'LL BE HIM OR ME.

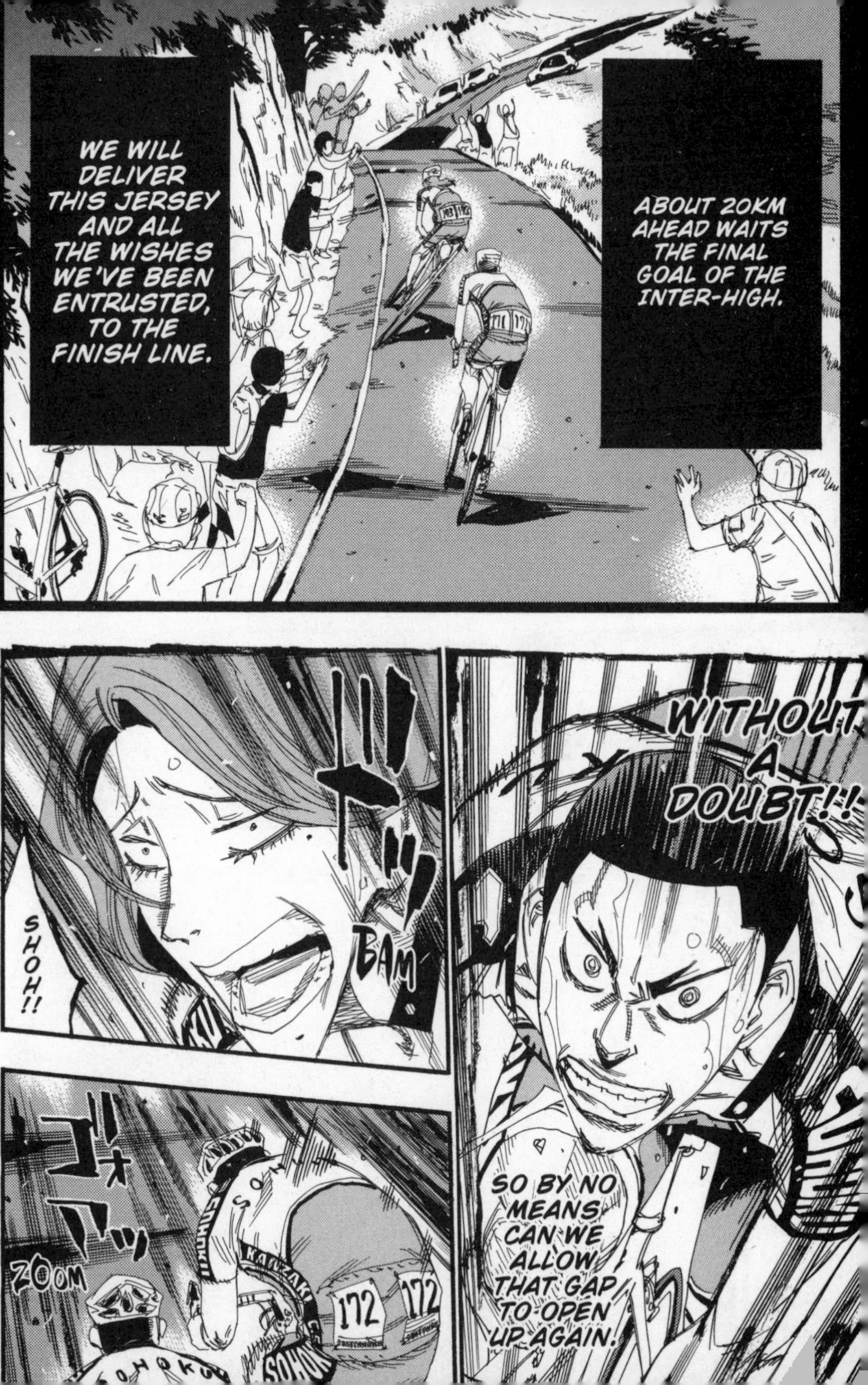
ABOUT 20KM AHEAD WAITS THE FINAL GOAL OF THE INTER-HIGH.
WE WILL DELIVER THIS JERSEY AND ALL THE WISHES WE'VE BEEN ENTRUSTED, TO THE FINISH LINE.
183
171 172
WITHOUT A DOUBT!!
SO BY NO MEANS CAN WE ALLOW THAT GAP TO OPEN UP AGAIN.
BAM
SHOH!!
ZOOM
172 172

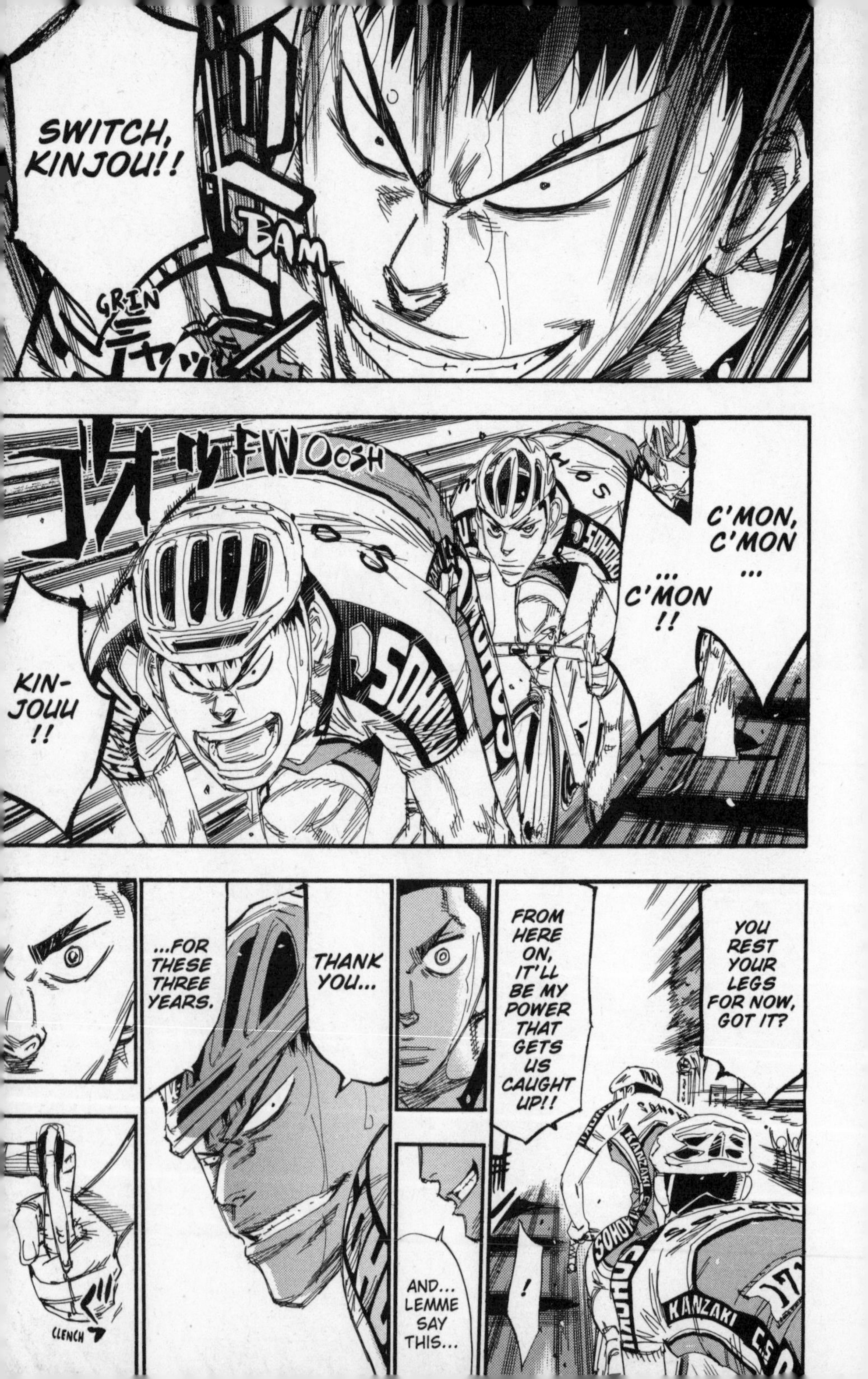
SWITCH, KINJOU!!
BAM
GRIN
C'MON, C'MON ... ... C'MON !!
FWOOSH
KIN-JOUU !!
YOU REST YOUR LEGS FOR NOW, GOT IT?
FROM HERE ON, IT'LL BE MY POWER THAT GETS US CAUGHT UP!!
!
AND... LEMME SAY THIS...
THANK YOU...
...FOR THESE THREE YEARS.
CLENCH

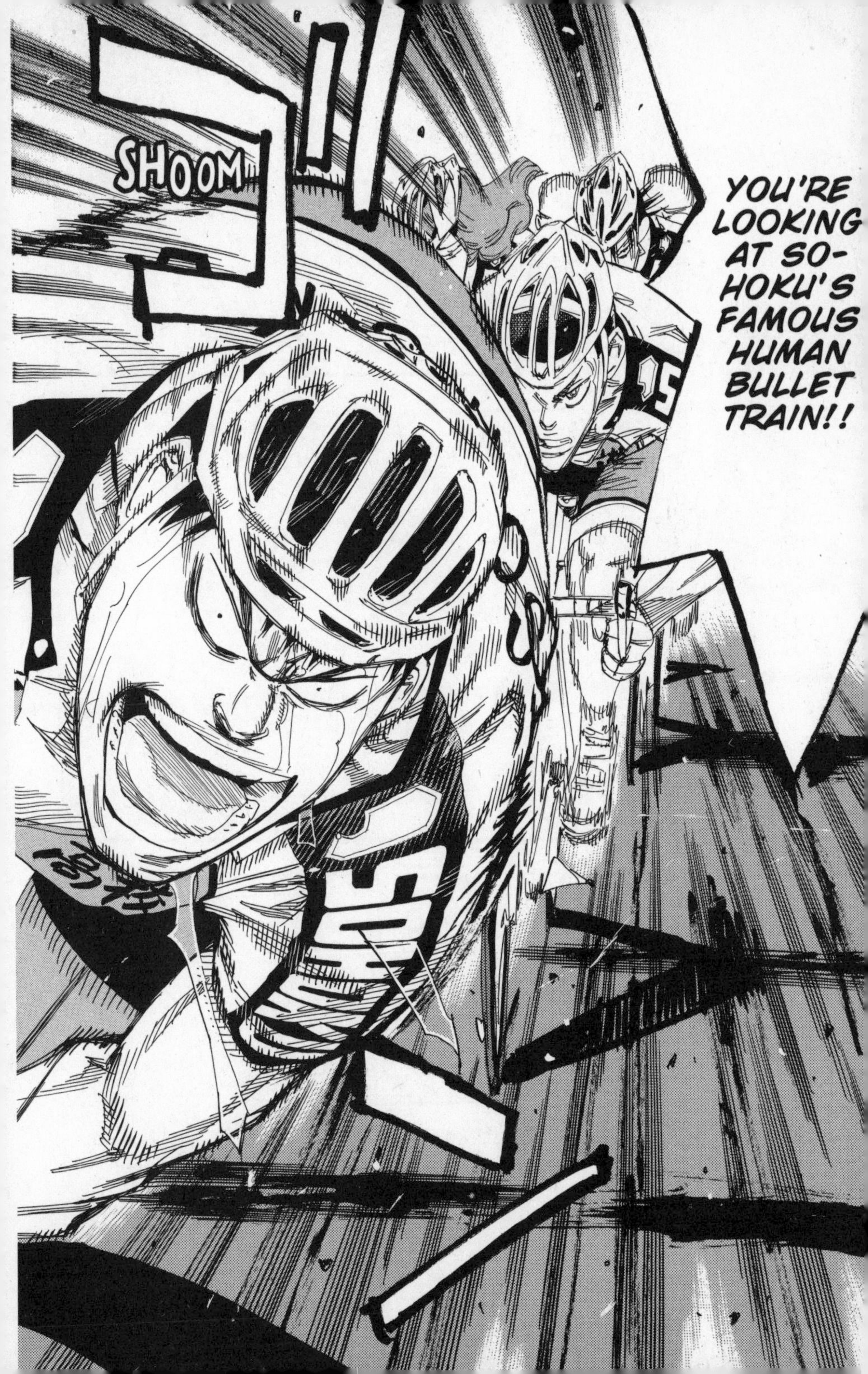
YOU'RE LOOKING AT SO-HOKU'S FAMOUS HUMAN BULLET TRAIN!!
SHOOM

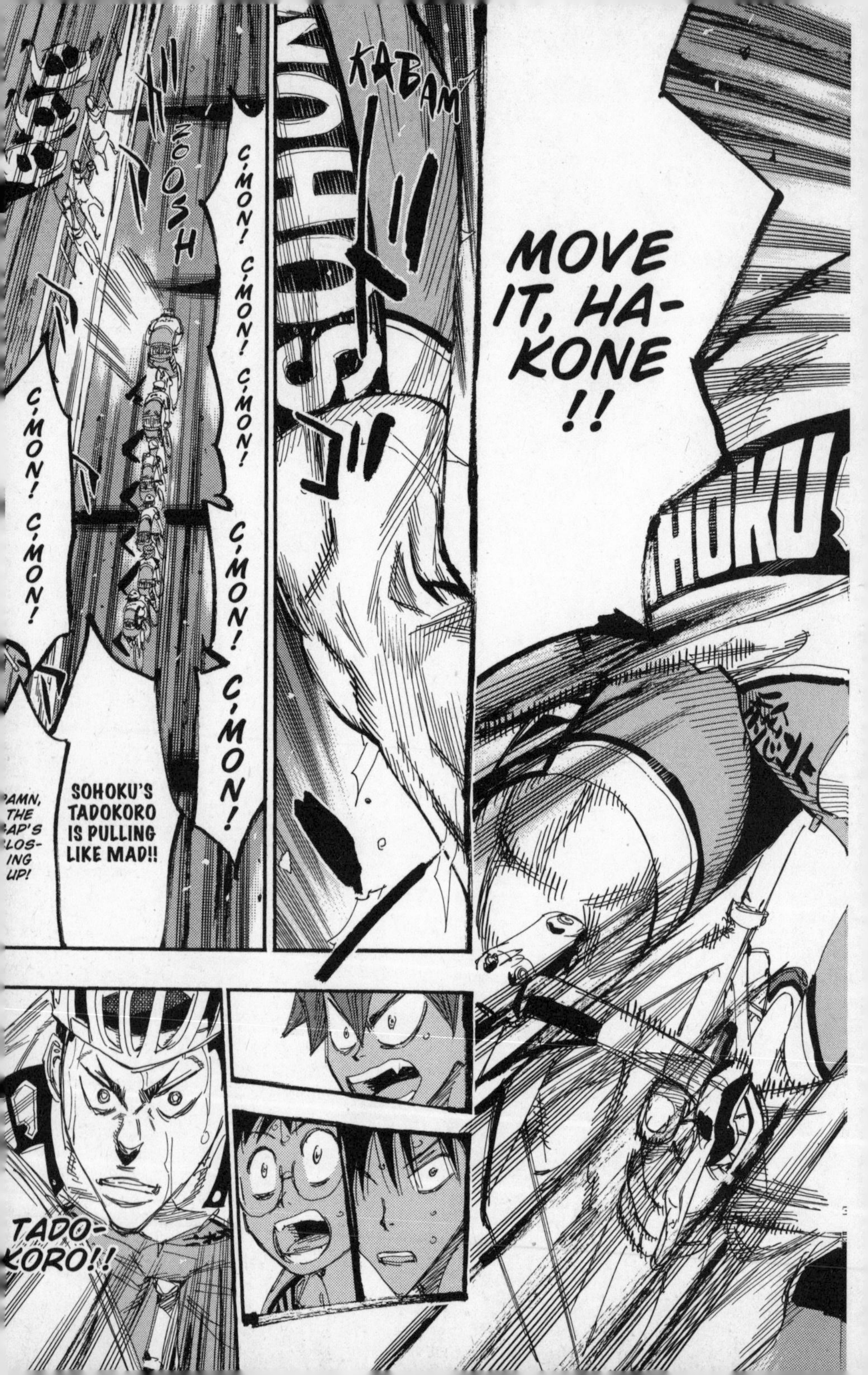
MOVE IT, HA-KONE!!
HOKU
KABAM
C'MON! C'MON! C'MON! C'MON!
C'MON! C'MON! C'MON!
ZOOSH
C'MON! C'MON! C'MON!
SOHOKU'S TADOKORO IS PULLING LIKE MAD!!
AMN, THE AP'S LOS-ING UP!
TADO-KORO!!

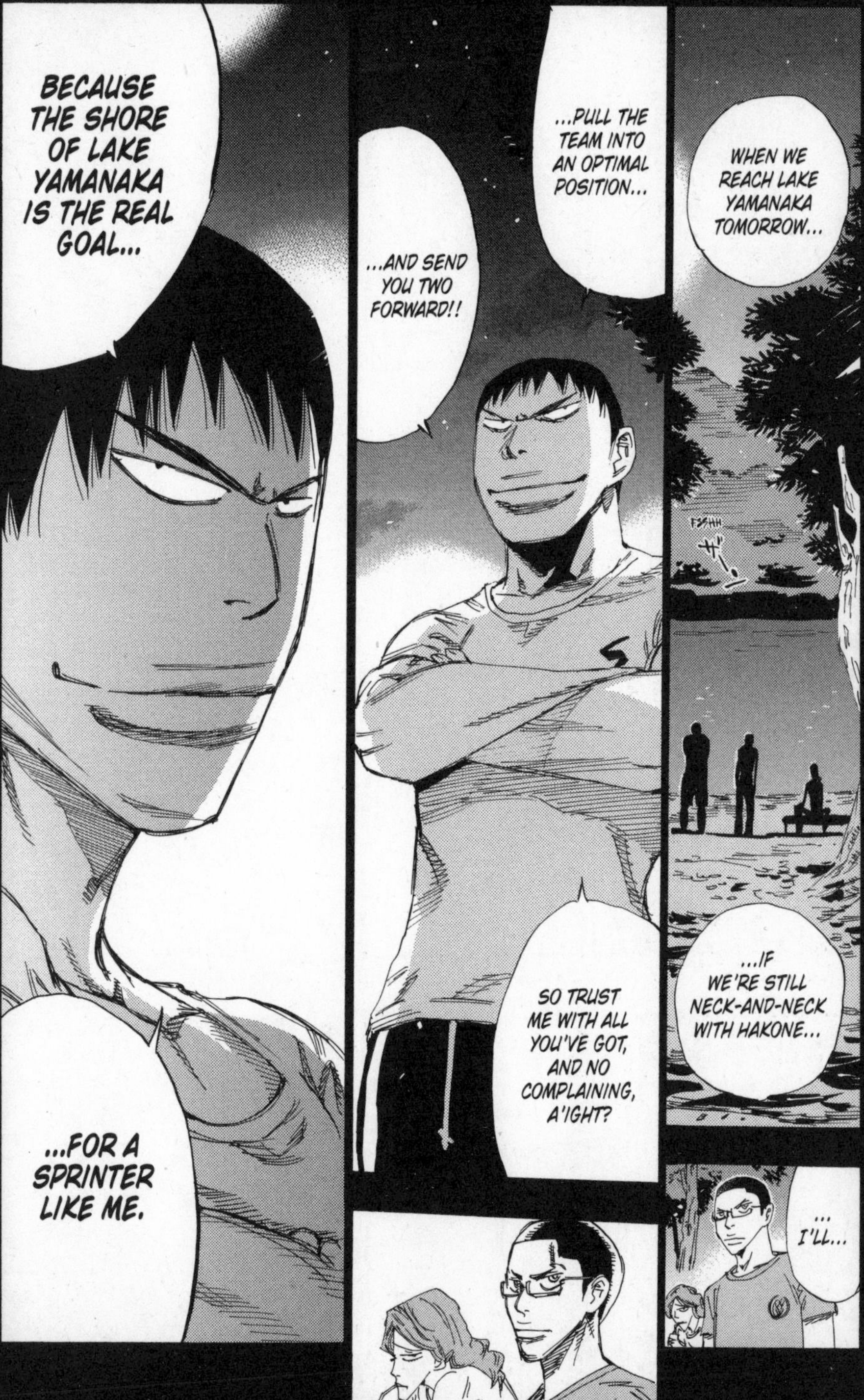
WHEN WE REACH LAKE YAMANAKA TOMORROW...
FSHHH
...IF WE'RE STILL NECK-AND-NECK WITH HAKONE...
... I'LL...
...PULL THE TEAM INTO AN OPTIMAL POSITION...
...AND SEND YOU TWO FORWARD!!
SO TRUST ME WITH ALL YOU'VE GOT, AND NO COMPLAINING, A'IGHT?
BECAUSE THE SHORE OF LAKE YAMANAKA IS THE REAL GOAL...
...FOR A SPRINTER LIKE ME.

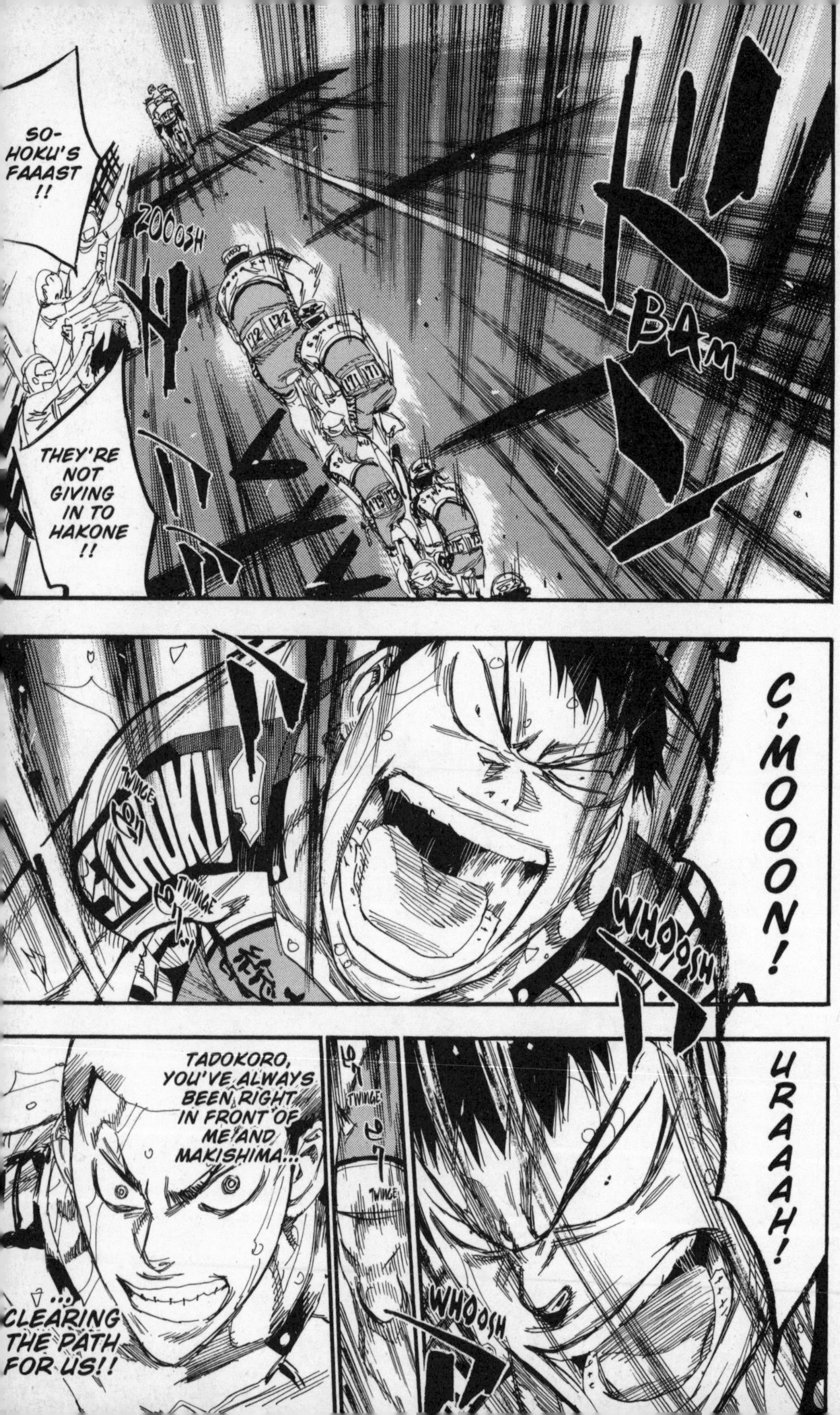
BAM
ZOOOSH
SO-HOKU'S FAAAST!!
THEY'RE NOT GIVING IN TO HAKONE!!
C'MOOOON!
WHOOSH
TWINGE
TWINGE
URAAAH!
TWINGE
TWINGE
TADOKORO, YOU'VE ALWAYS BEEN RIGHT IN FRONT OF ME AND MAKISHIMA...
...CLEARING THE PATH FOR US!!
WHOOSH

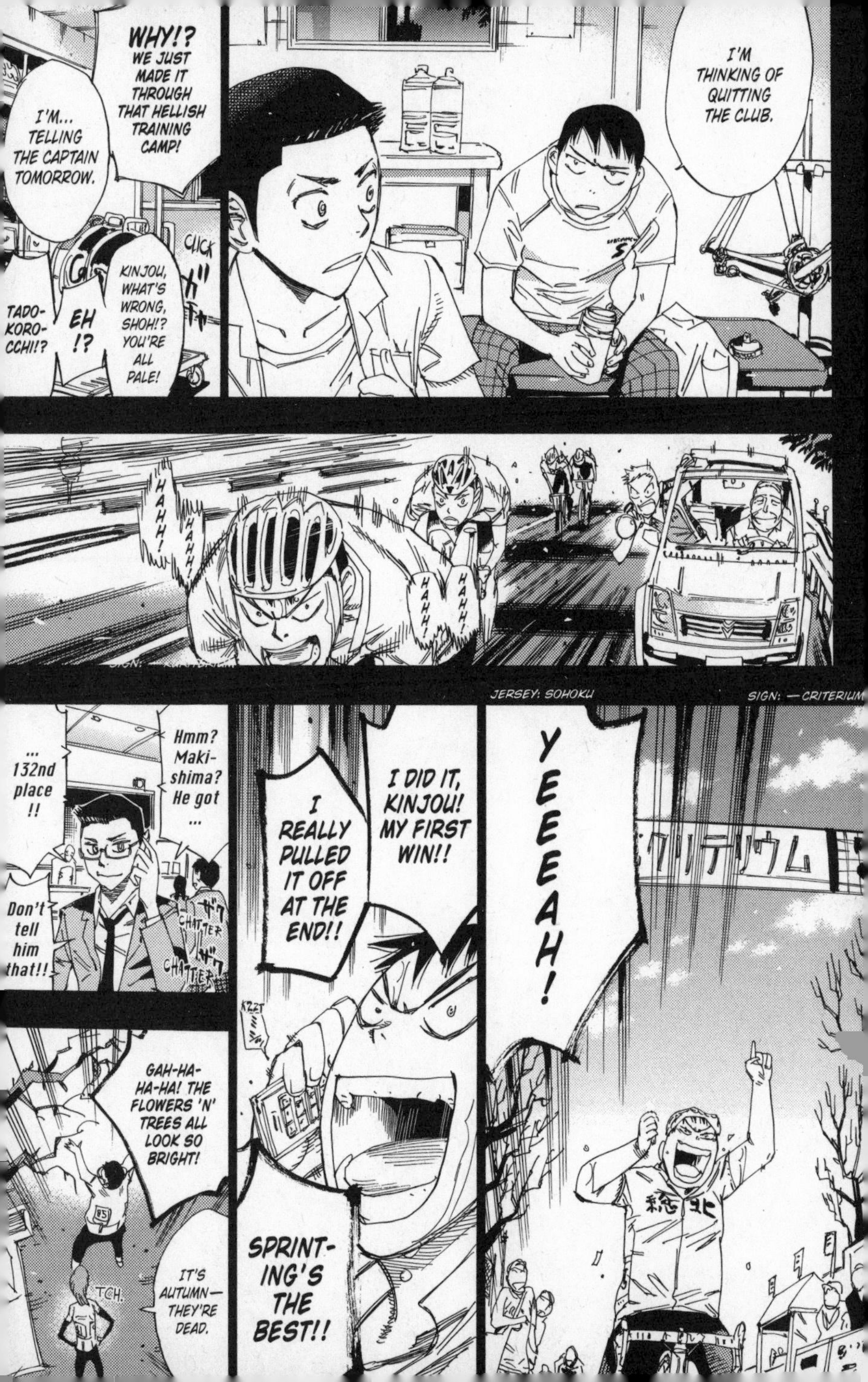
I'M THINKING OF QUITTING THE CLUB.
WHY!? WE JUST MADE IT THROUGH THAT HELLISH TRAINING CAMP!
I'M... TELLING THE CAPTAIN TOMORROW.
CLICK
KINJOU, WHAT'S WRONG, SHOH!? YOU'RE ALL PALE!
EH !?
TADO-KORO-CCHI!?
HAHH! HAHH! HAHH! HAHH!
JERSEY: SOHOKU
SIGN: —CRITERIUM
YEEEEAH!
クリテリウム
総北
I DID IT, KINJOU! MY FIRST WIN!!
I REALLY PULLED IT OFF AT THE END!!
KZZT
SPRINT-ING'S THE BEST!!
Hmm? Maki-shima? He got ...
... 132nd place !!
Don't tell him that!!
CHATTER CHATTER
GAH-HA-HA-HA! THE FLOWERS 'N' TREES ALL LOOK SO BRIGHT!
IT'S AUTUMN— THEY'RE DEAD.
TCH.

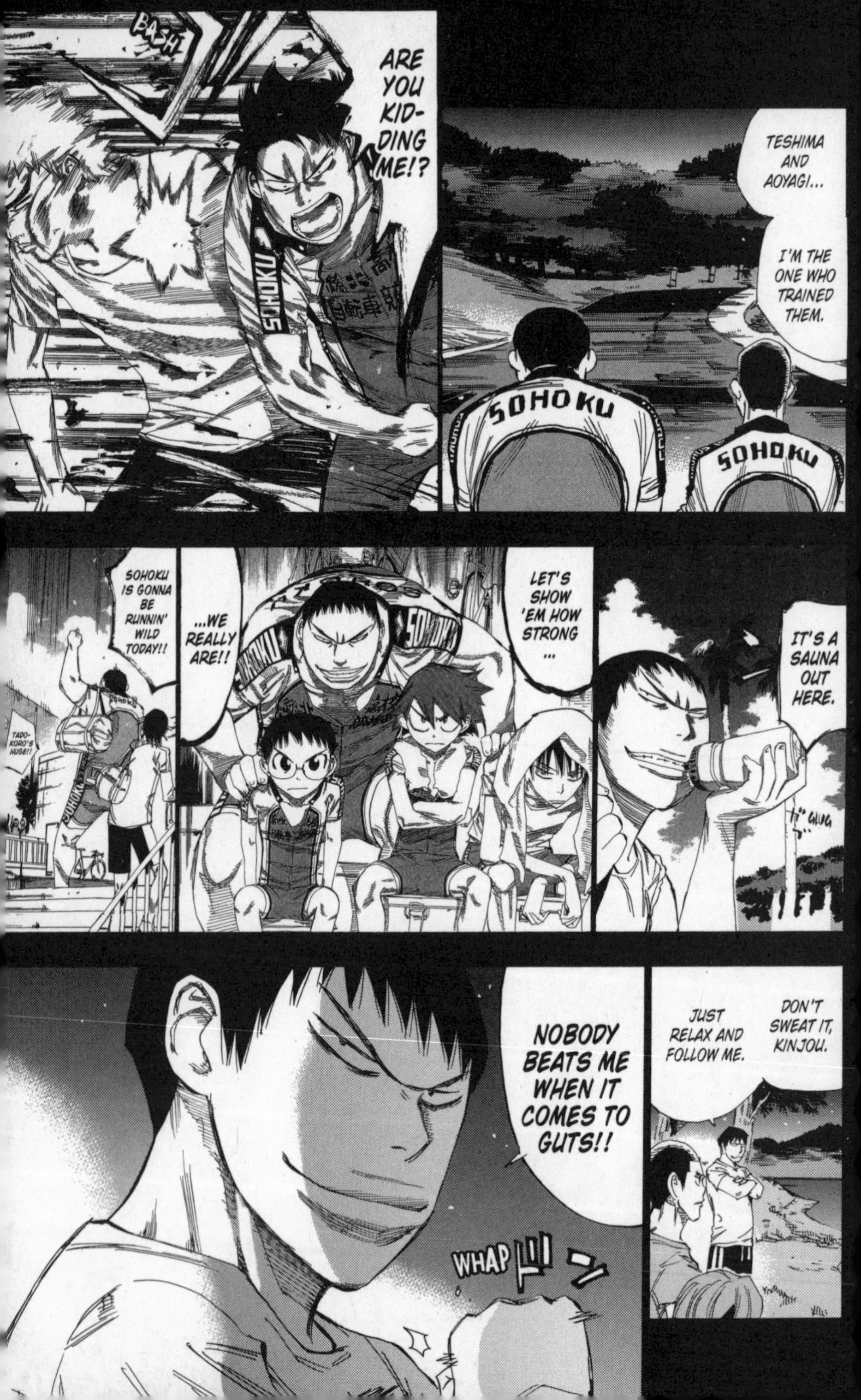
TESHIMA AND AOYAGI...
I'M THE ONE WHO TRAINED THEM.
BASH
ARE YOU KID-DING ME!?
IT'S A SAUNA OUT HERE.
GLUG
LET'S SHOW 'EM HOW STRONG ...
...WE REALLY ARE!!
SOHOKU IS GONNA BE RUNNIN' WILD TODAY!!
TADOKORO'S HUGE!!
DON'T SWEAT IT, KINJOU.
JUST RELAX AND FOLLOW ME.
NOBODY BEATS ME WHEN IT COMES TO GUTS!!
WHAP

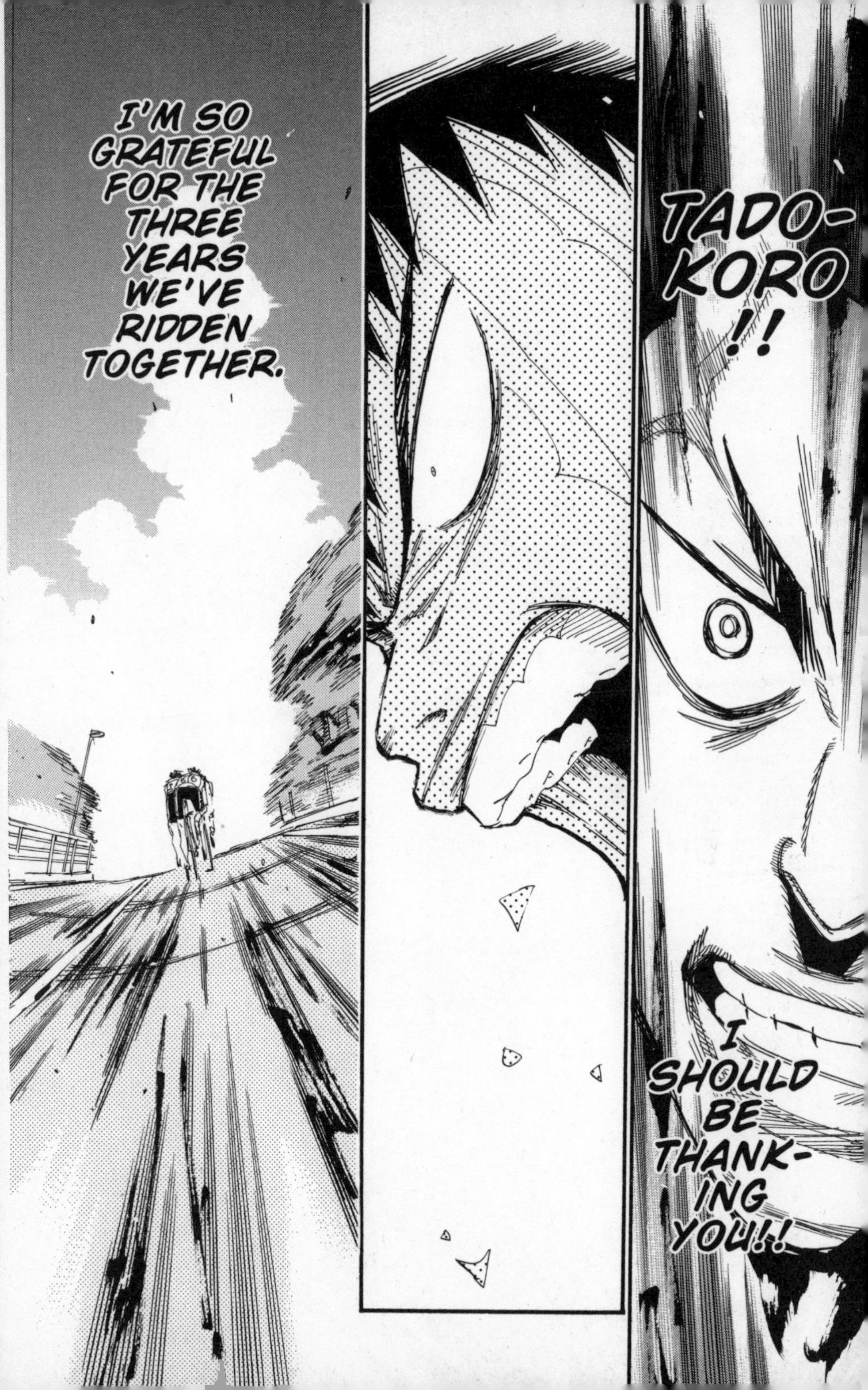
TADO-KORO!!
I SHOULD BE THANK-ING YOU!!
I'M SO GRATEFUL FOR THE THREE YEARS WE'VE RIDDEN TOGETHER.

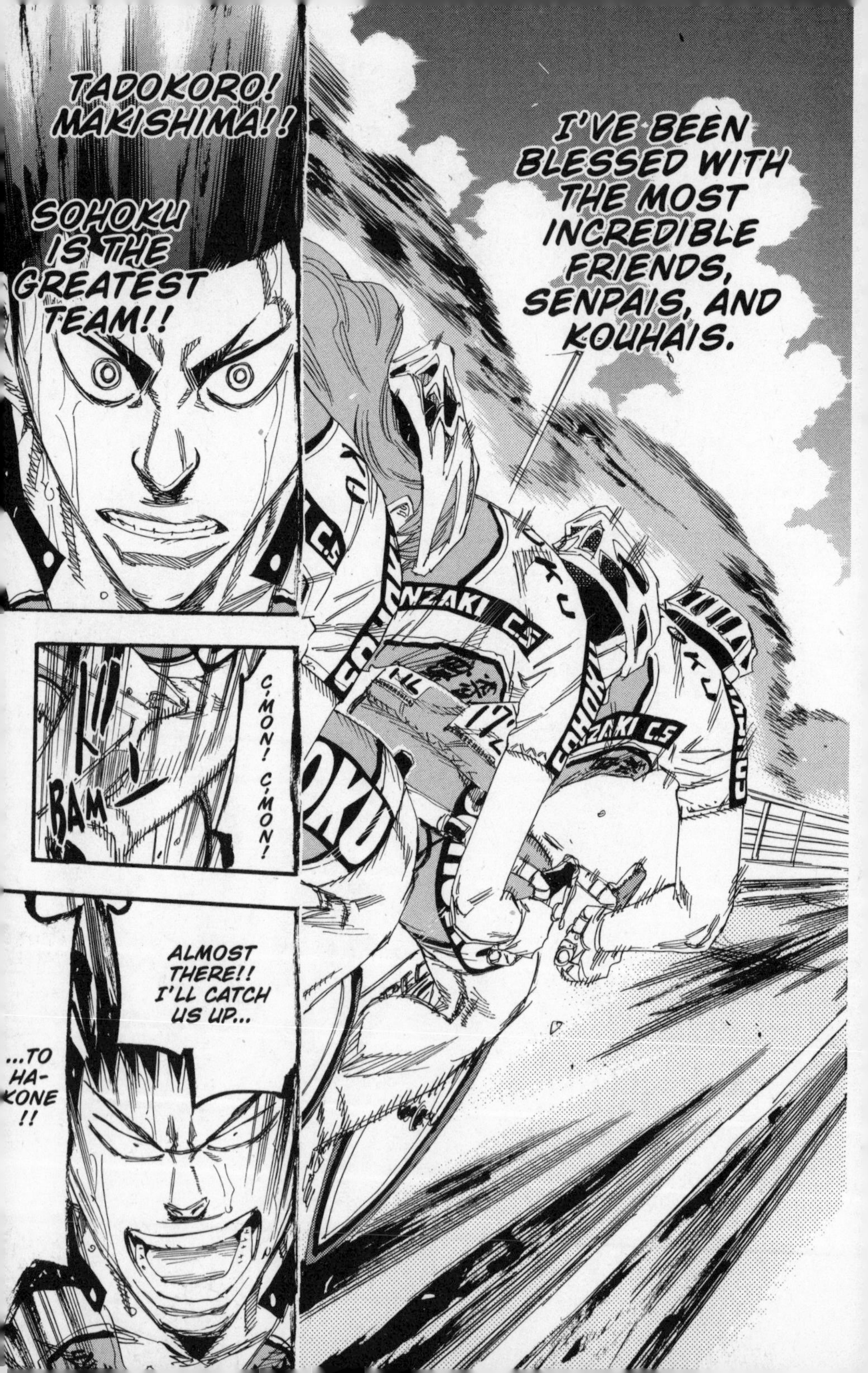
I'VE BEEN BLESSED WITH THE MOST INCREDIBLE FRIENDS, SENPAIS, AND KOUHAIS.
TADOKORO! MAKISHIMA!!
SOHOKU IS THE GREATEST TEAM!!
C'MON! C'MON!
BAM
ALMOST THERE!! I'LL CATCH US UP...
...TO HA-KONE!!

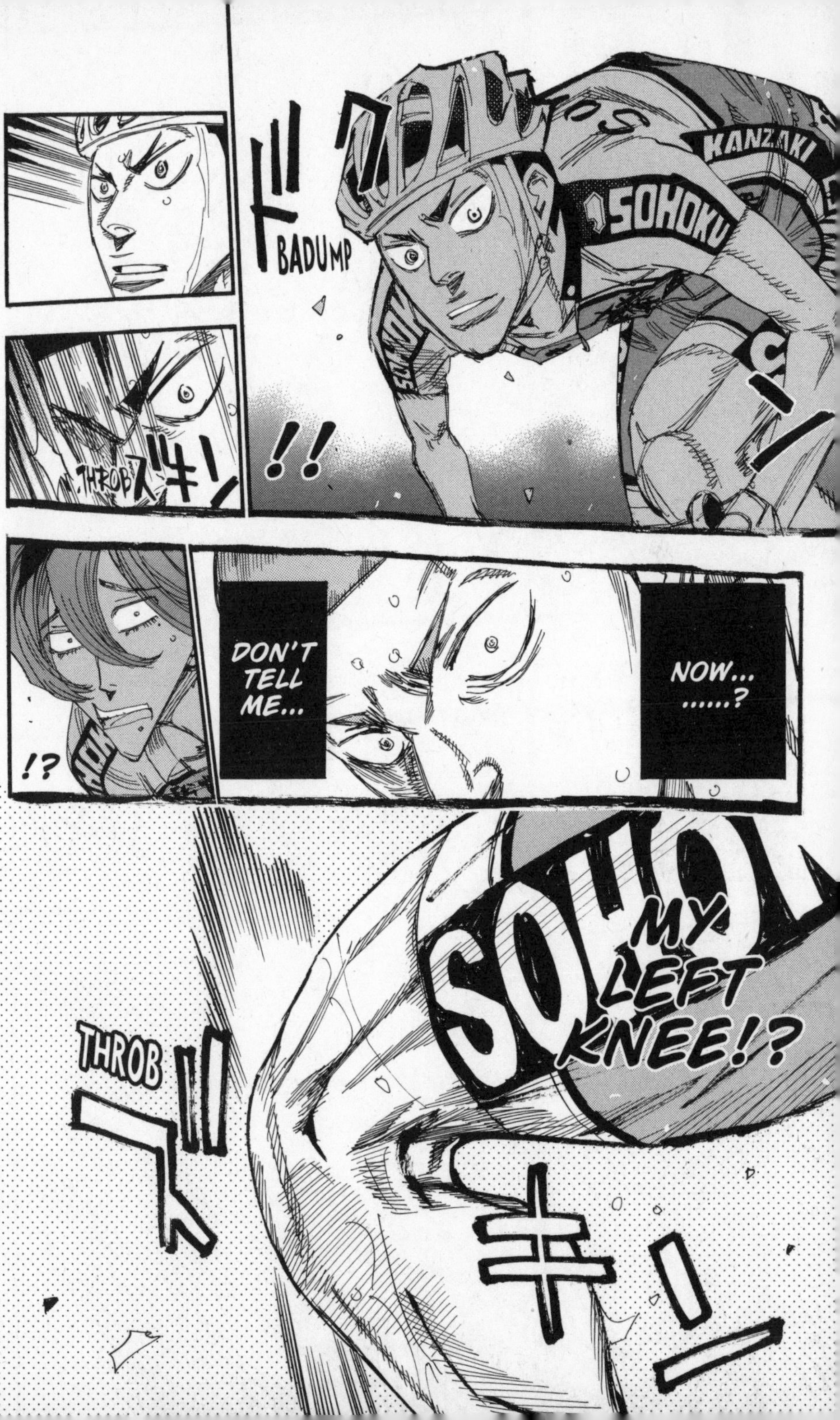
BADUMP
!!
THROB
NOW... ......?
DON'T TELL ME...
!?
MY LEFT KNEE!?
THROB

RIDE.188 TADOKORO'S LAST SPRINT

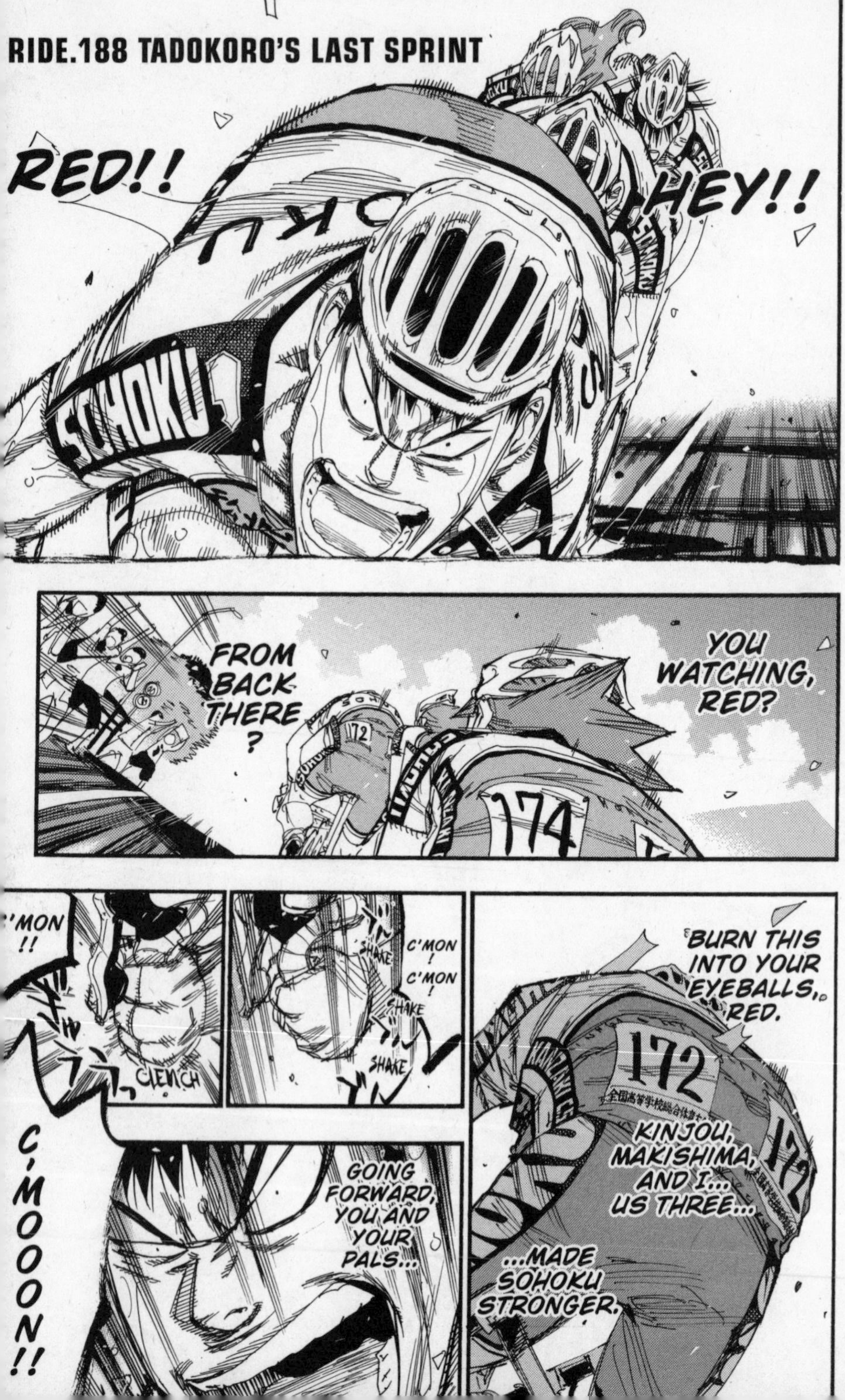
HEY!!
RED!!
YOU WATCHING, RED?
FROM BACK THERE?
BURN THIS INTO YOUR EYEBALLS, RED.
KINJOU, MAKISHIMA, AND I... US THREE...
...MADE SOHOKU STRONGER.
C'MON! C'MON!
SHAKE
SHAKE
SHAKE
C'MON!!
CLENCH
GOING FORWARD, YOU AND YOUR PALS...
C'MOOOON!!

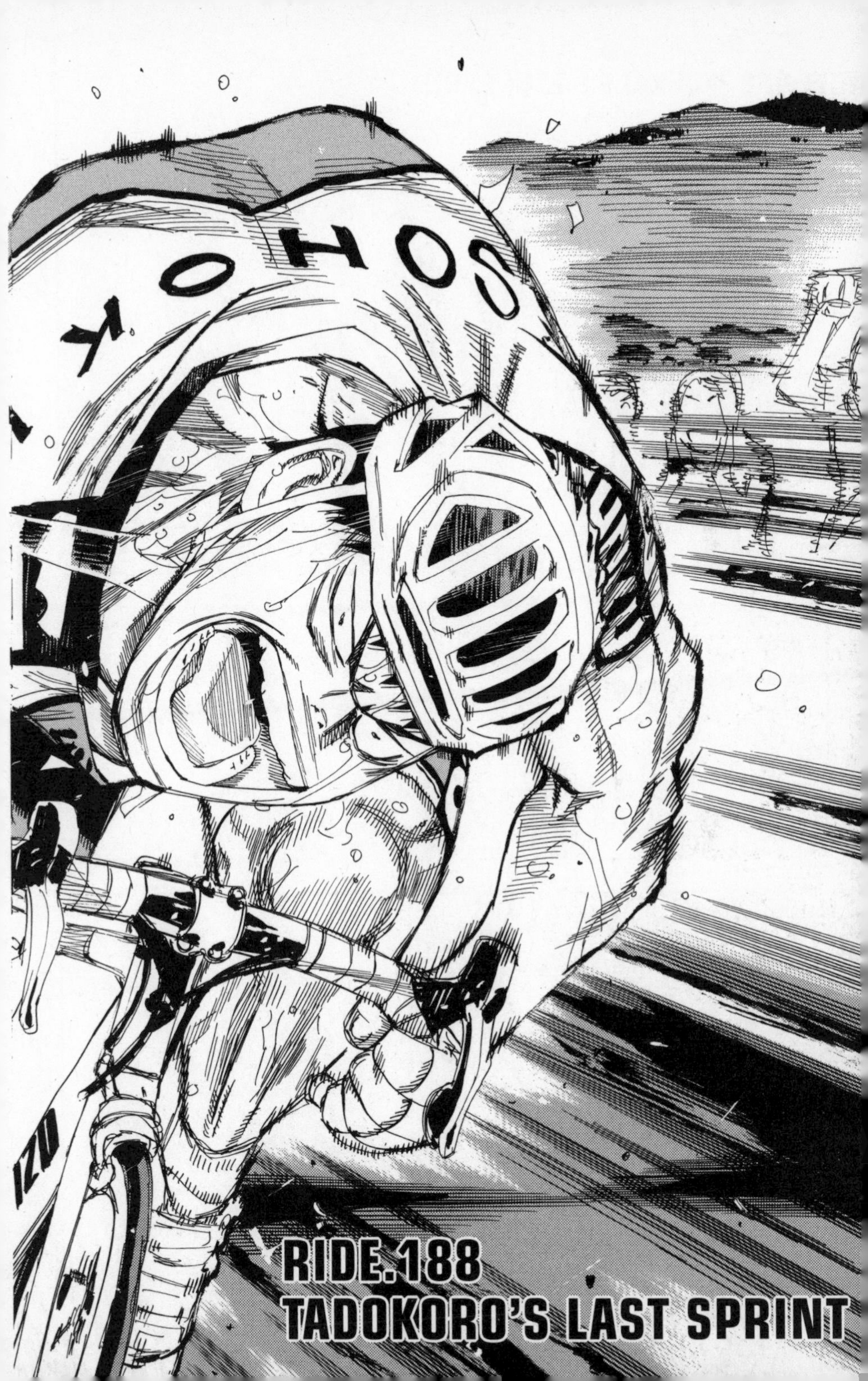

RIDE.188 TADOKORO'S LAST SPRINT

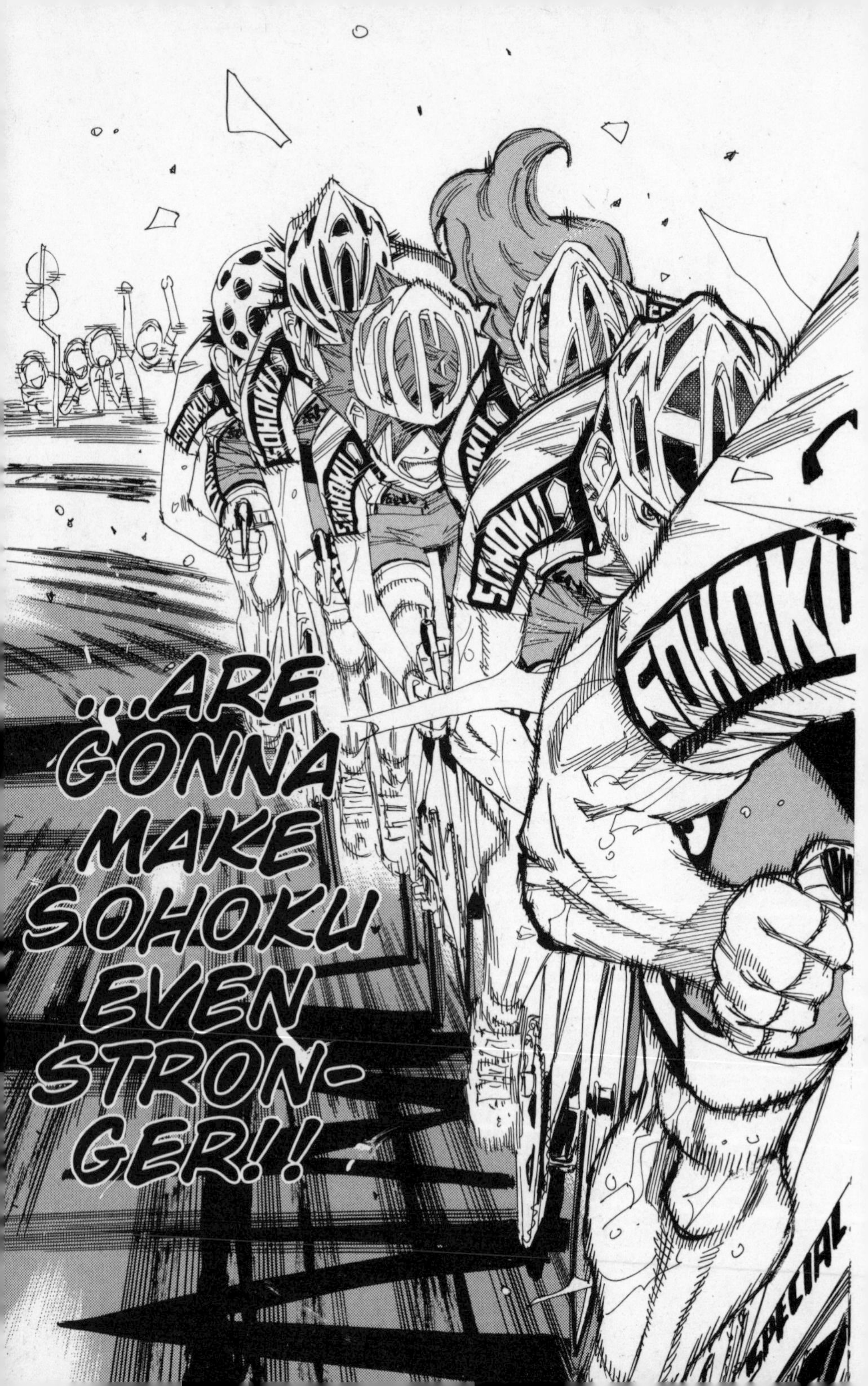
...ARE GONNA MAKE SOHOKU EVEN STRON-GER!!

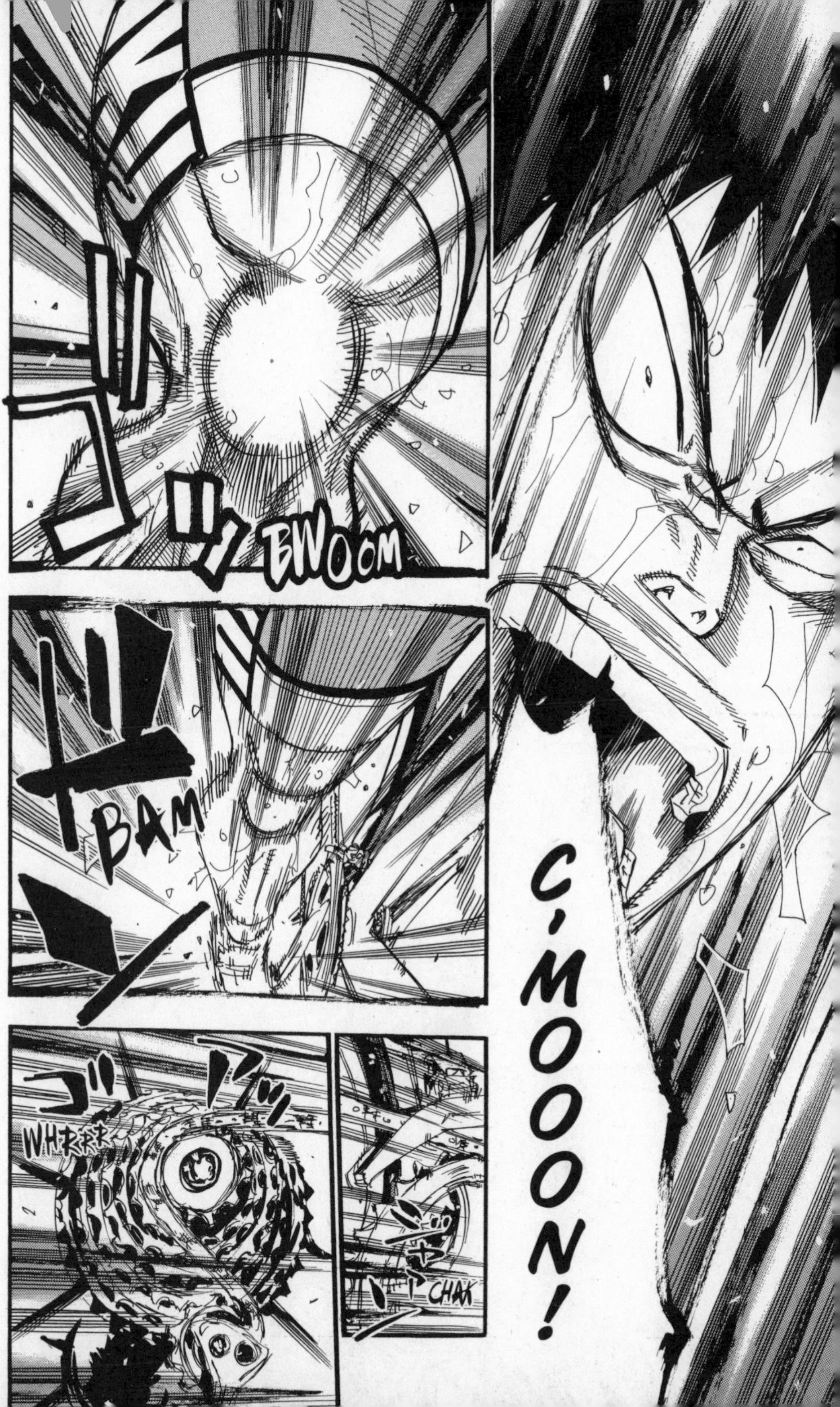
C'MOOOON!
BWOOM
BAM
CHAK
WHRRR

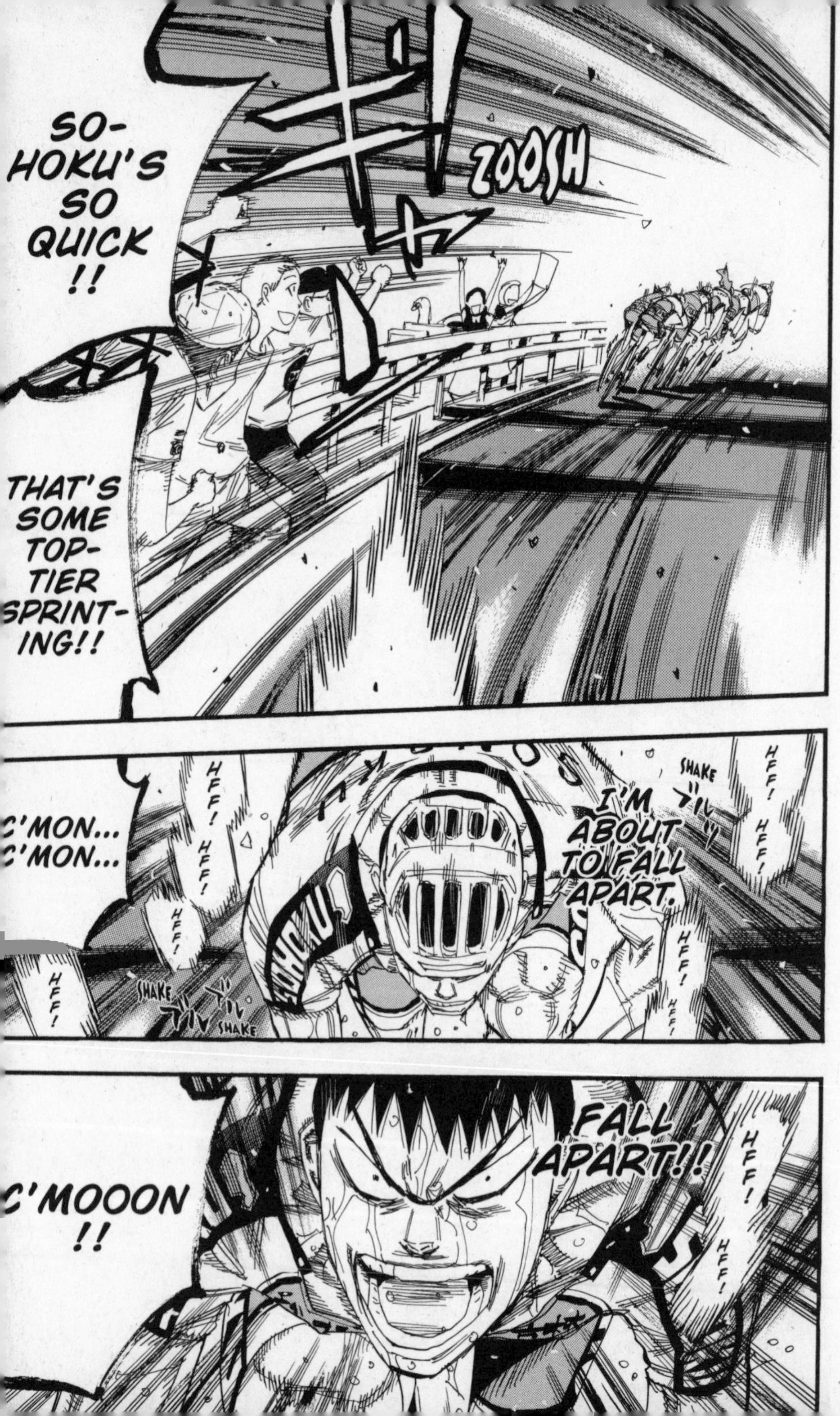
ZOOSH
SO-HOKU'S SO QUICK!!
THAT'S SOME TOP-TIER SPRINTING!!
HFF! HFF!
SHAKE
I'M ABOUT TO FALL APART.
HFF! HFF!
C'MON... C'MON...
HFF! HFF!
SHAKE SHAKE
HFF! HFF!
FALL APART!!
C'MOOON!!

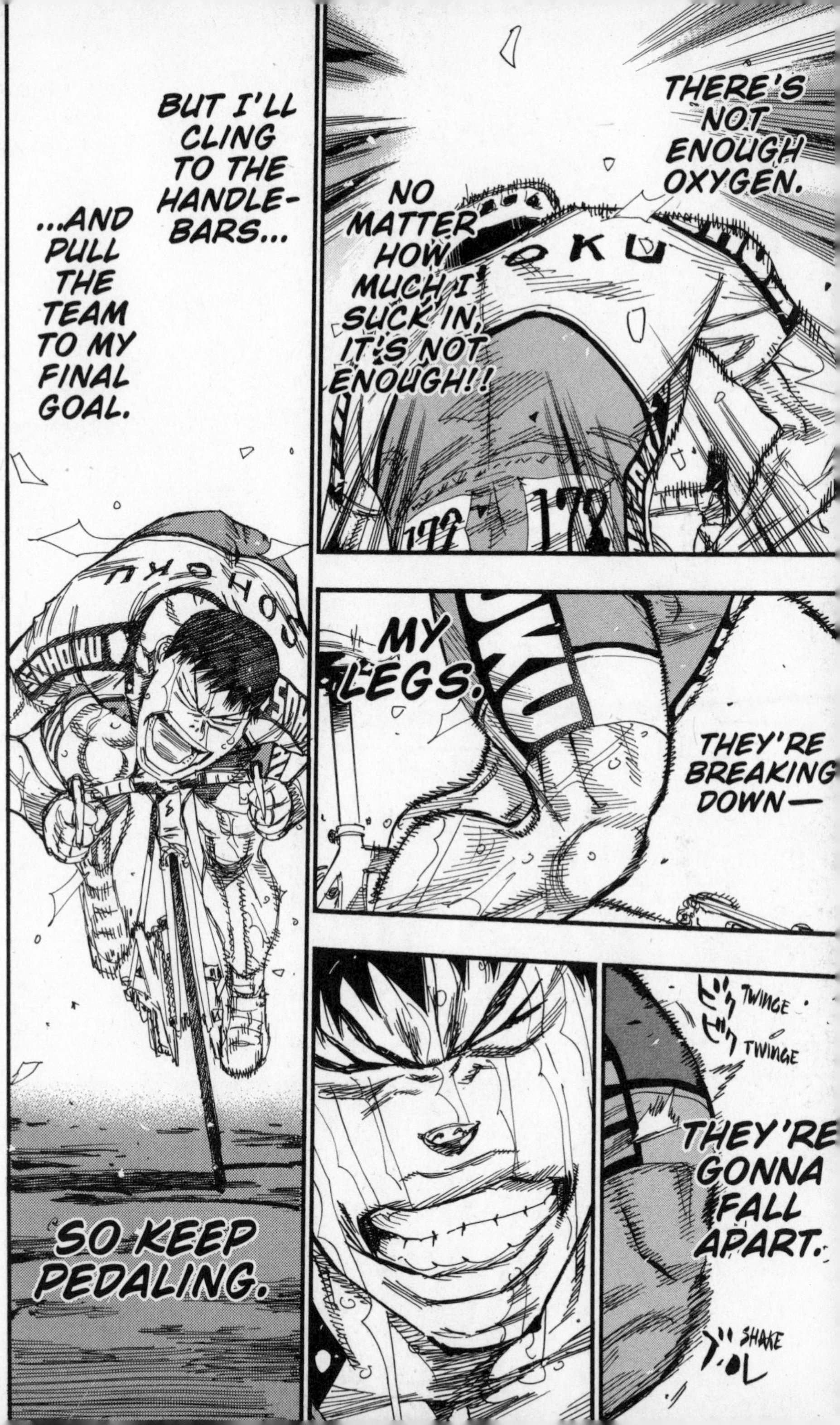
THERE'S NOT ENOUGH OXYGEN.
NO MATTER HOW MUCH I SUCK IN, IT'S NOT ENOUGH!!
MY LEGS.
THEY'RE BREAKING DOWN—
TWINGE
TWINGE
THEY'RE GONNA FALL APART.
SHAKE
BUT I'LL CLING TO THE HANDLE-BARS...
...AND PULL THE TEAM TO MY FINAL GOAL.
SO KEEP PEDALING.

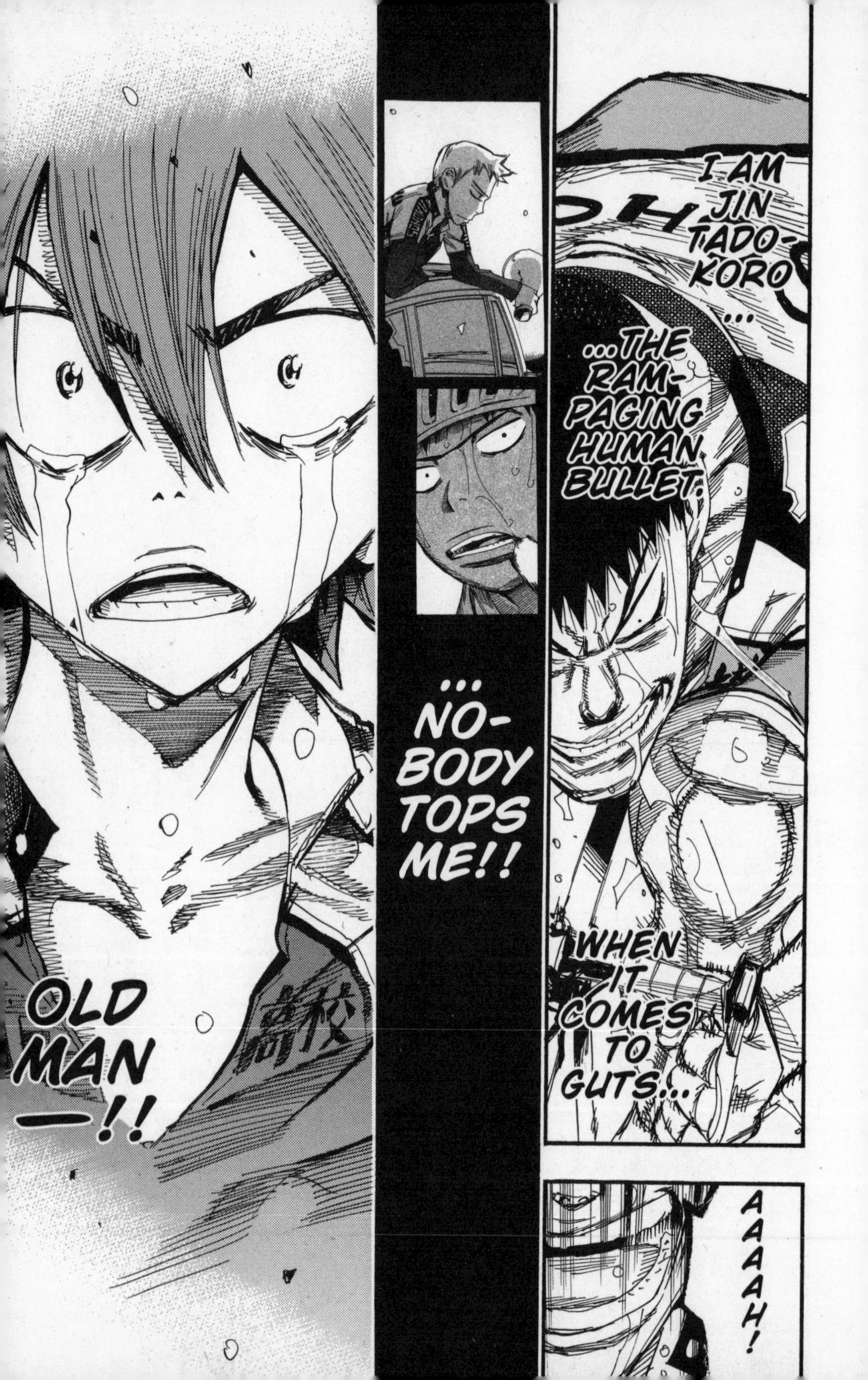
I AM JIN TADO-KORO...
...THE RAM-PAGING HUMAN BULLET.
WHEN IT COMES TO GUTS...
AAAAH!
...NO-BODY TOPS ME!!
OLD MAN—!!

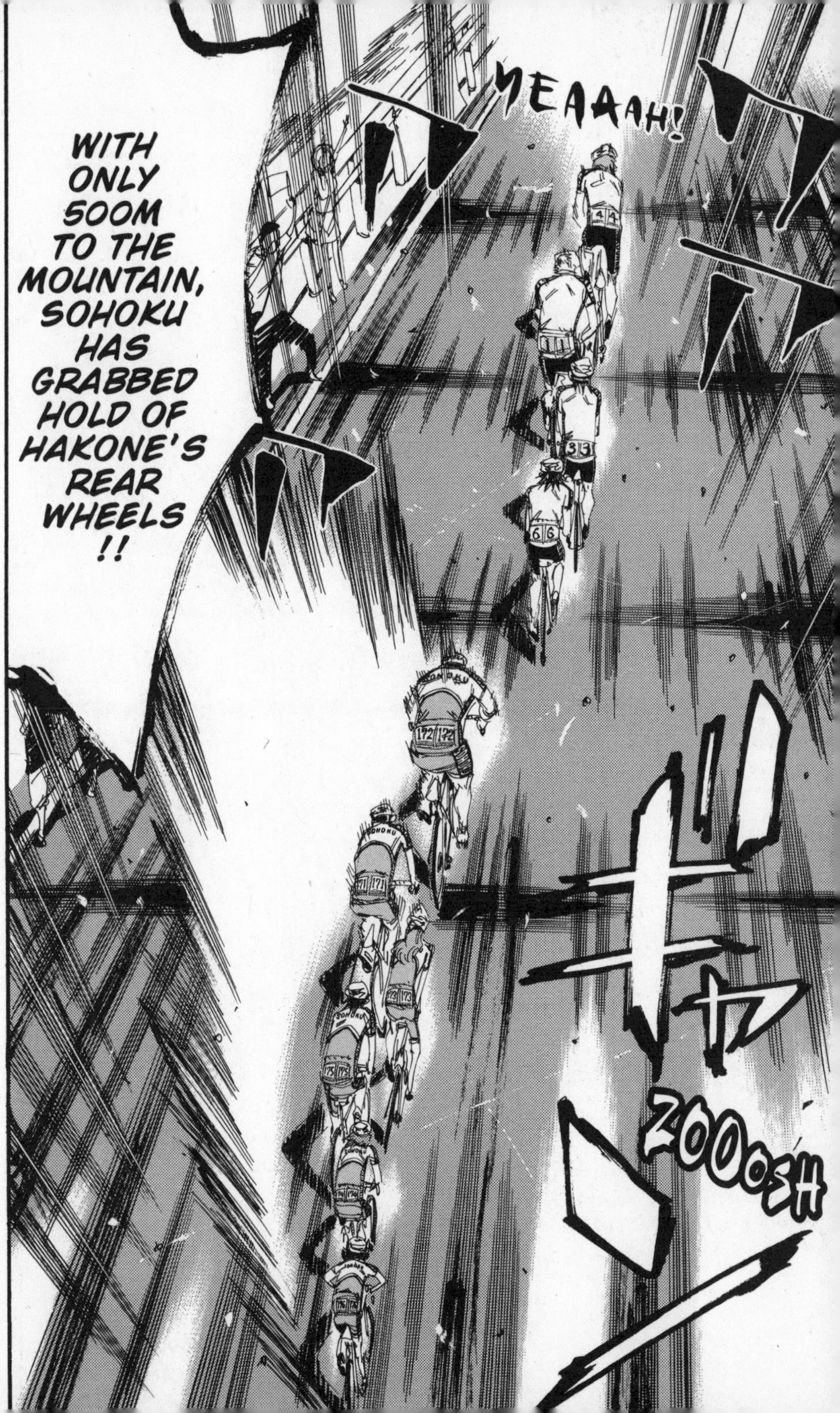
YEAAAH!
WITH ONLY 500M TO THE MOUNTAIN, SOHOKU HAS GRABBED HOLD OF HAKONE'S REAR WHEELS!!
ZOOOSH

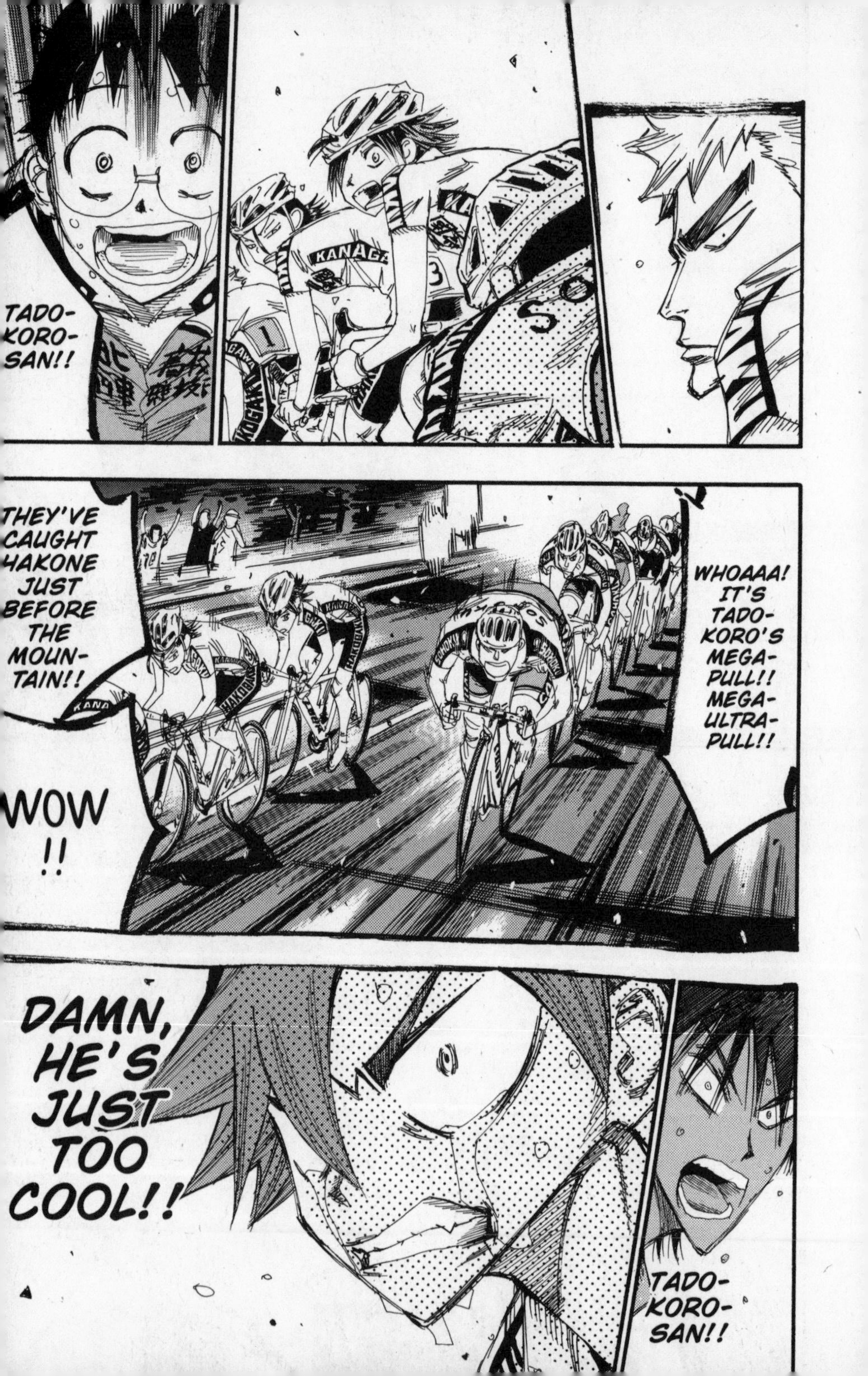
TADO-
KORO-
SAN!!
WHOAAA!
IT'S
TADO-
KORO'S
MEGA-
PULL!!
MEGA-
ULTRA-
PULL!!
THEY'VE
CAUGHT
HAKONE
JUST
BEFORE
THE
MOUN-
TAIN!!
WOW
!!
TADO-
KORO-
SAN!!
DAMN,
HE'S
JUST
TOO
COOL!!

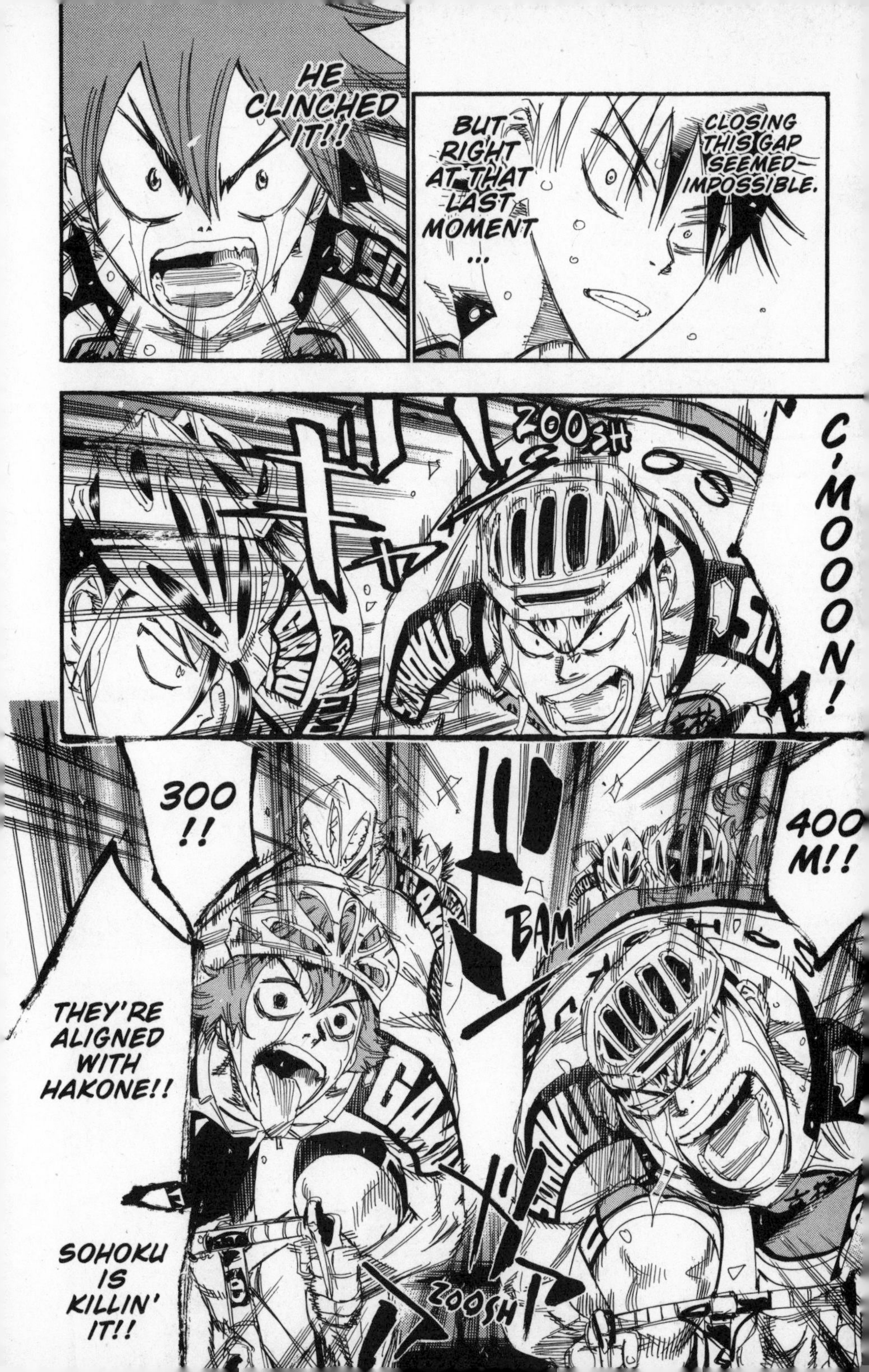
CLOSING THIS GAP SEEMED IMPOSSIBLE.
BUT RIGHT AT THAT LAST MOMENT...
HE CLINCHED IT!!
ZOOSH
C'MOOOON!
400 M!!
300!!
BAM
THEY'RE ALIGNED WITH HAKONE!!
SOHOKU IS KILLIN' IT!!
ZOOSH

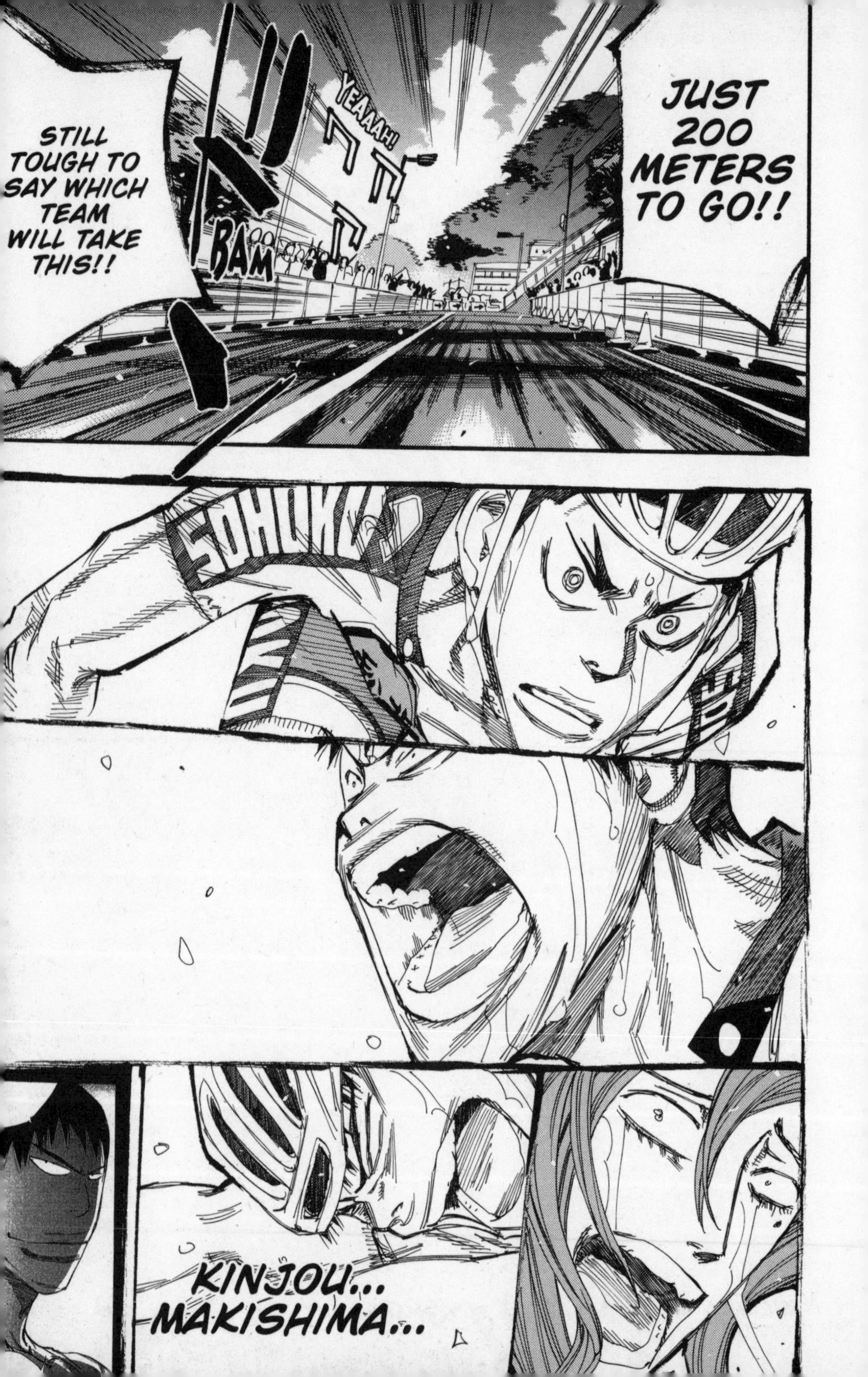
JUST 200 METERS TO GO!!
YEAAAAH!
BAM
STILL TOUGH TO SAY WHICH TEAM WILL TAKE THIS!!
SOHOKU
KINJOU... MAKISHIMA...

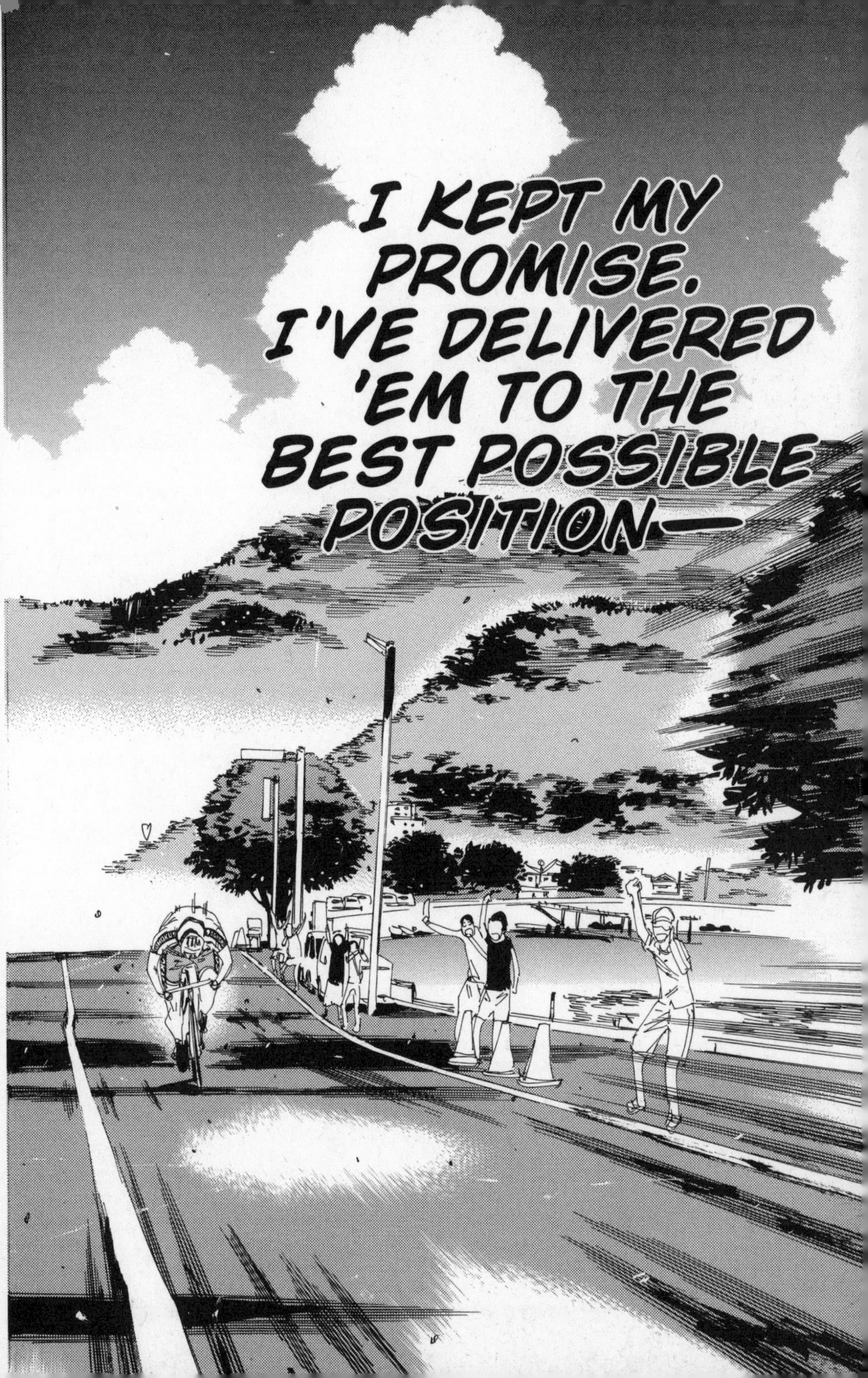
I KEPT MY PROMISE. I'VE DELIVERED 'EM TO THE BEST POSSIBLE POSITION—

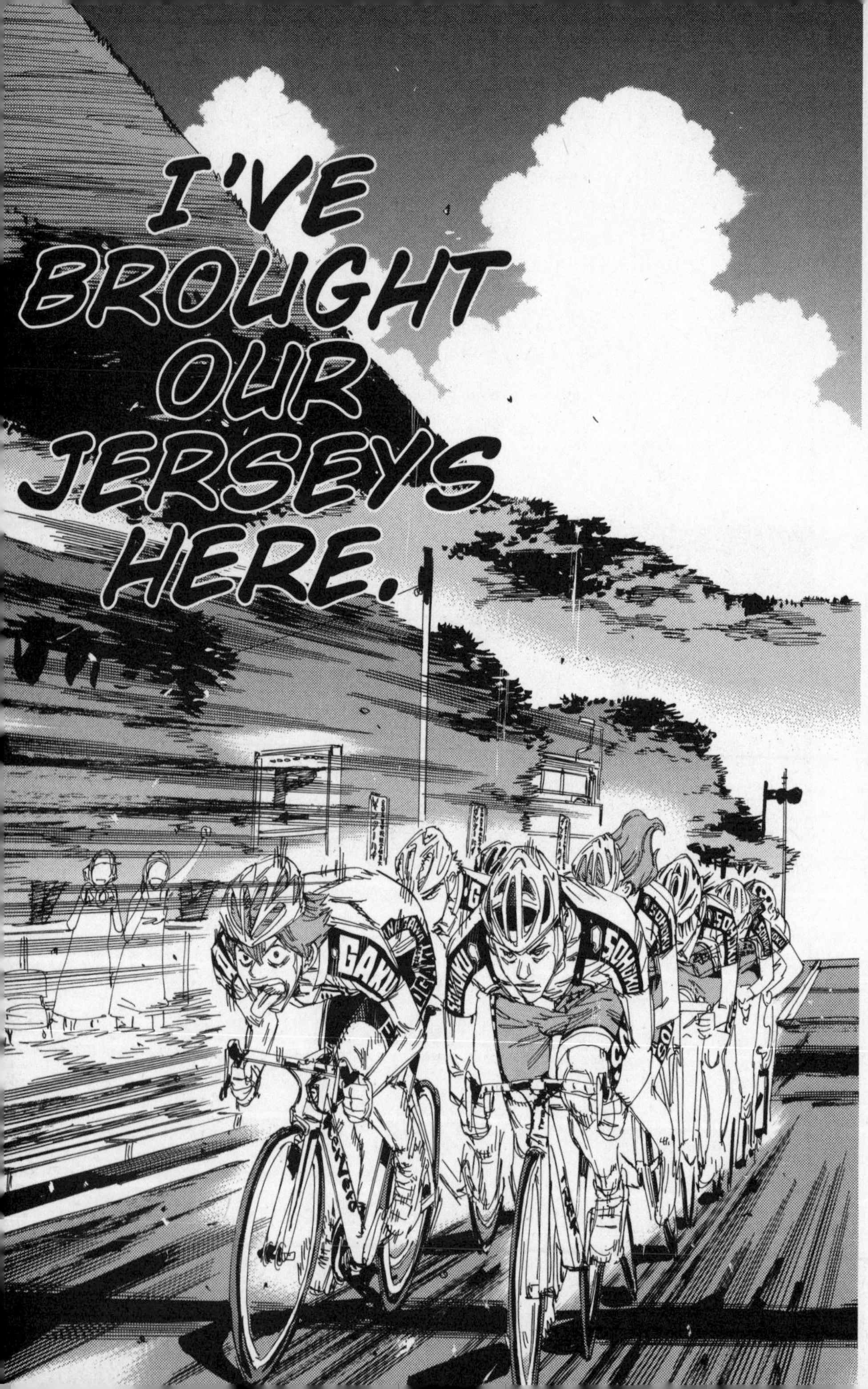
I'VE BROUGHT OUR JERSEYS HERE.

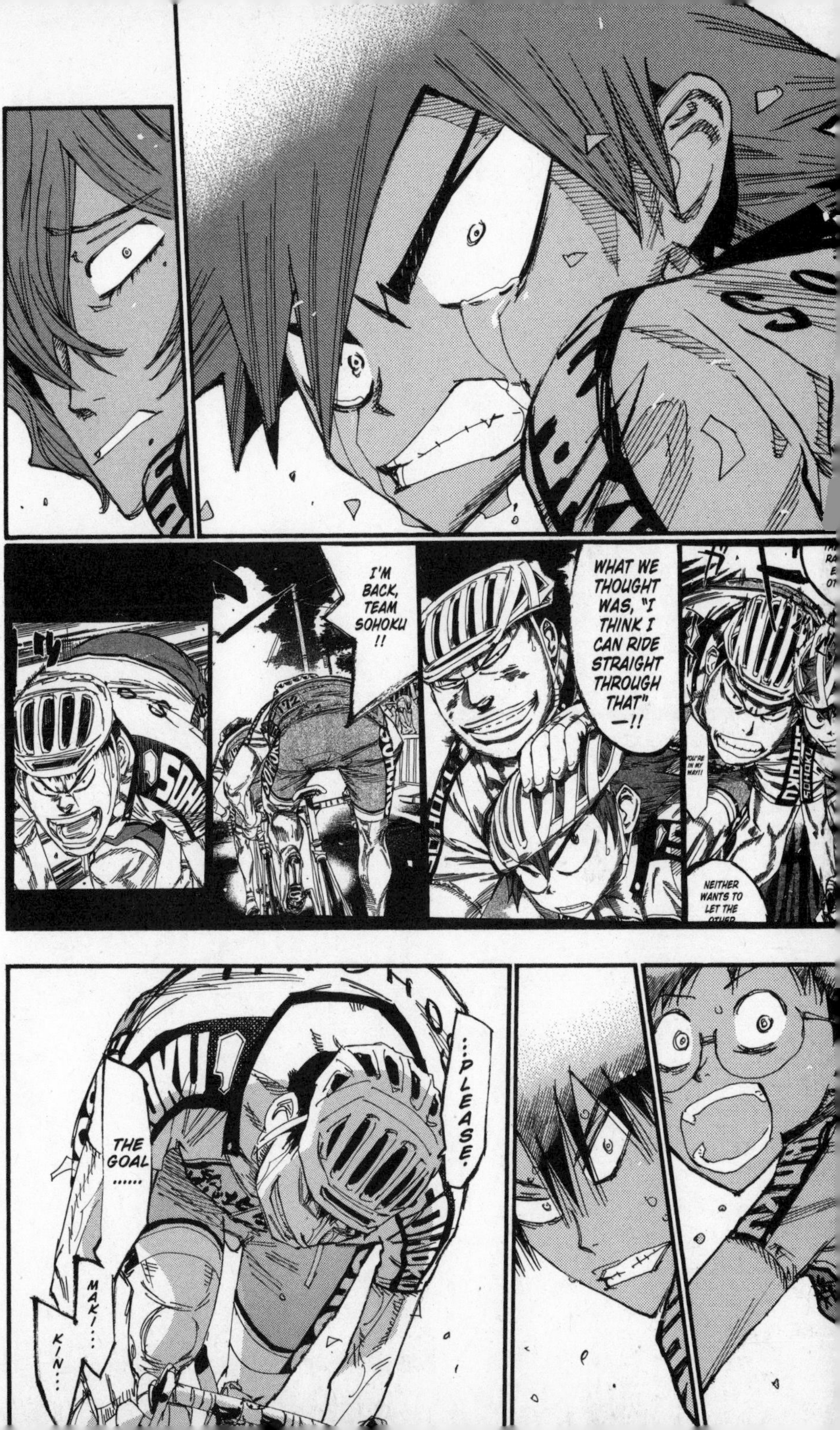
YOU'RE IN MY WAY!!
NEITHER WANTS TO LET THE
WHAT WE THOUGHT WAS, "I THINK I CAN RIDE STRAIGHT THROUGH THAT"—!!
I'M BACK, TEAM SOHOKU!!
...PLEASE.
THE GOAL ......
MAKI...
KIN...

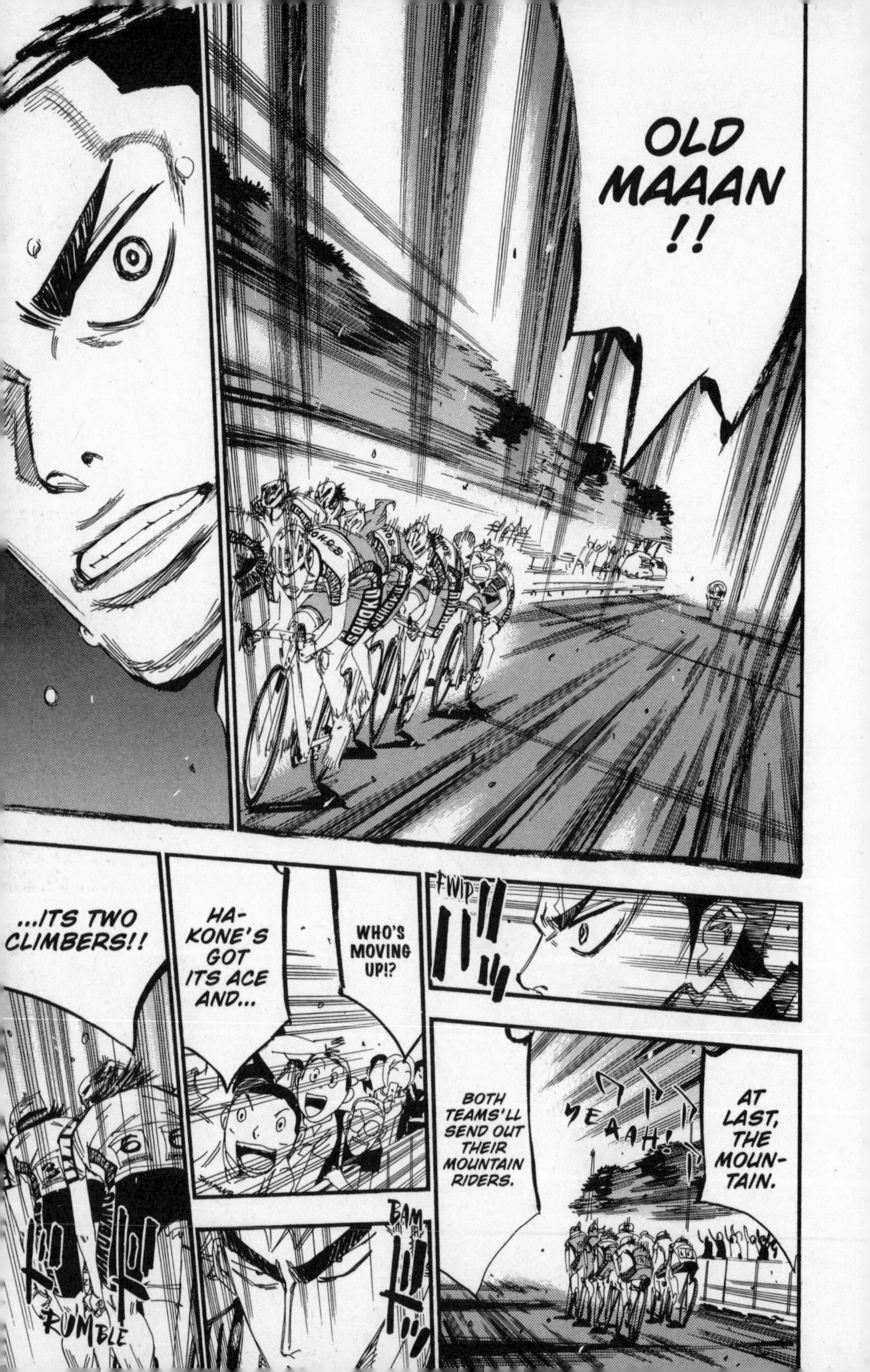
OLD MAAAN!!
FWIP
AT LAST, THE MOUNTAIN.
BOTH TEAMS'LL SEND OUT THEIR MOUNTAIN RIDERS.
YEAAH!
WHO'S MOVING UP!?
HA-KONE'S GOT ITS ACE AND...
...ITS TWO CLIMBERS!!
RUMBLE
BAM

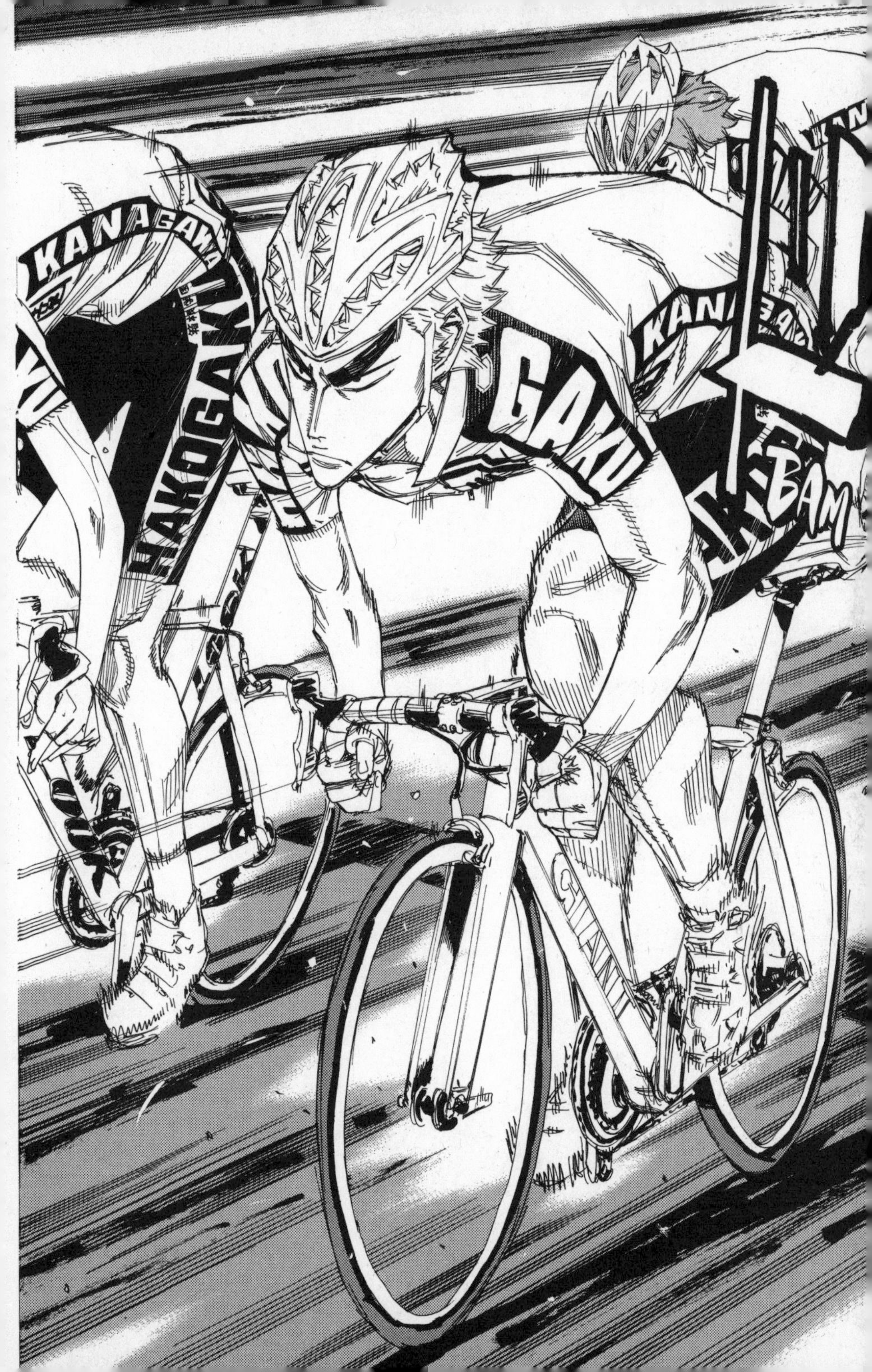
BAM

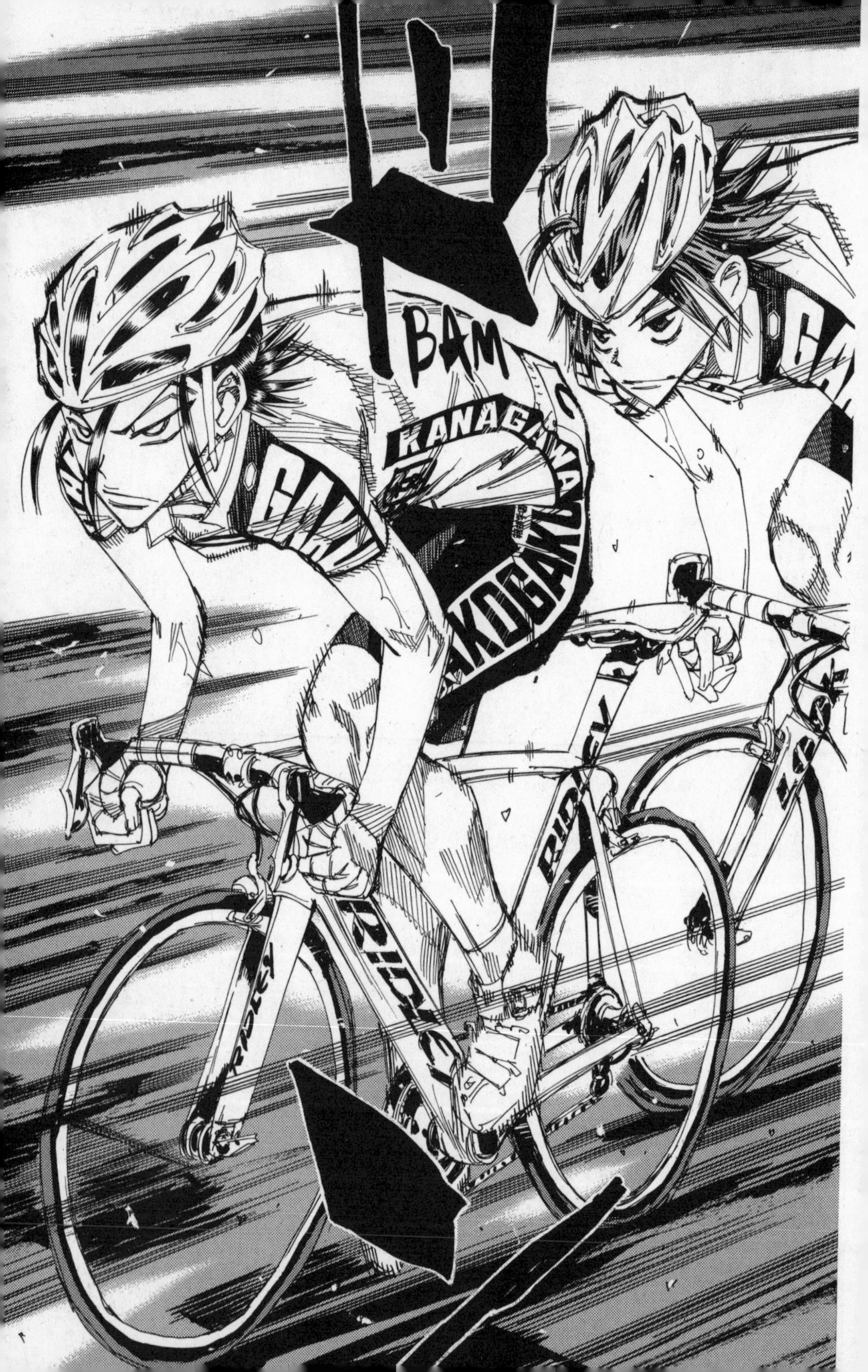
BAM
KANAGAWA

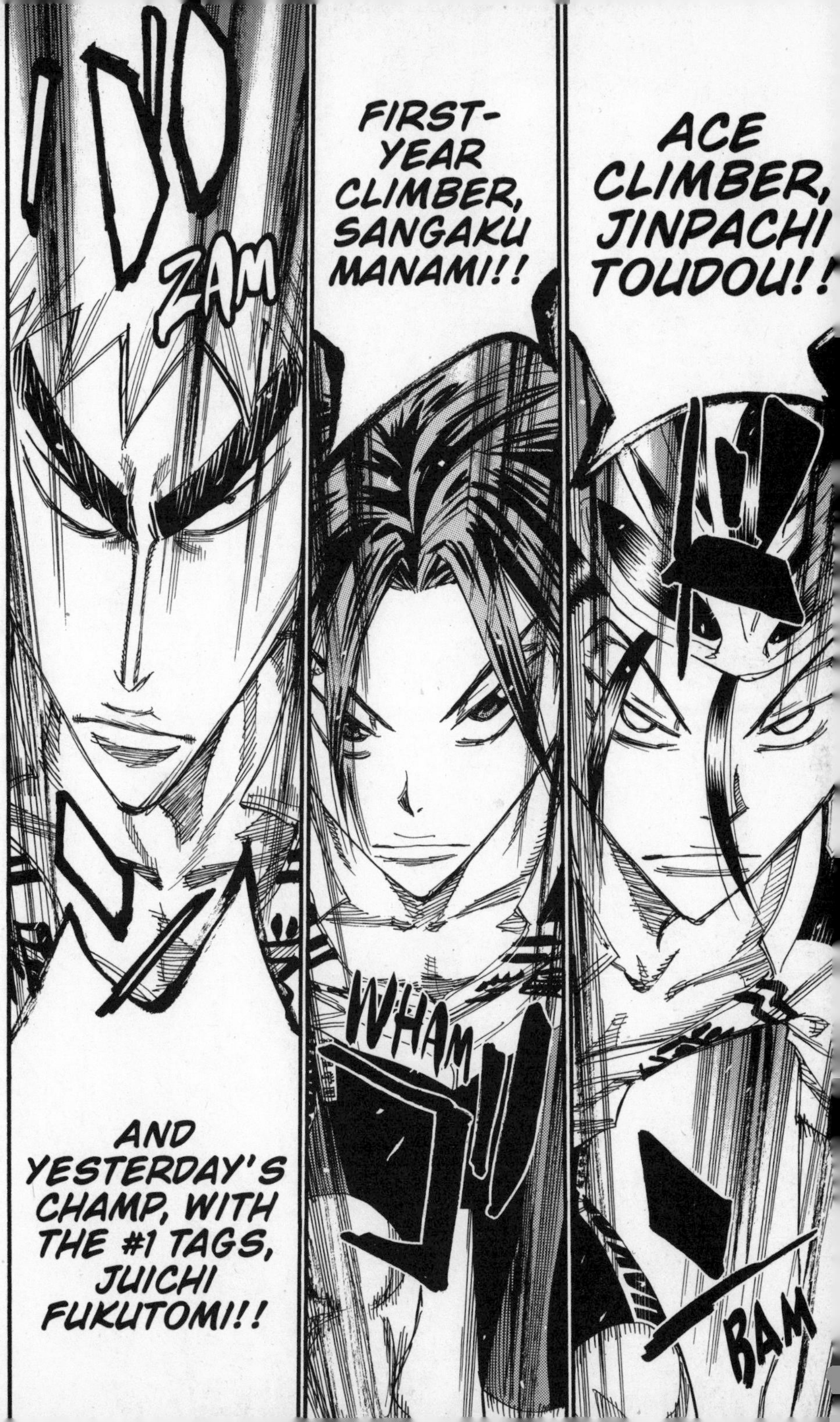
ACE CLIMBER, JINPACHI TOUDOU!!
BAM
FIRST-YEAR CLIMBER, SANGAKU MANAMI!!
WHAM
ZAM
AND YESTERDAY'S CHAMP, WITH THE #1 TAGS, JUICHI FUKUTOMI!!

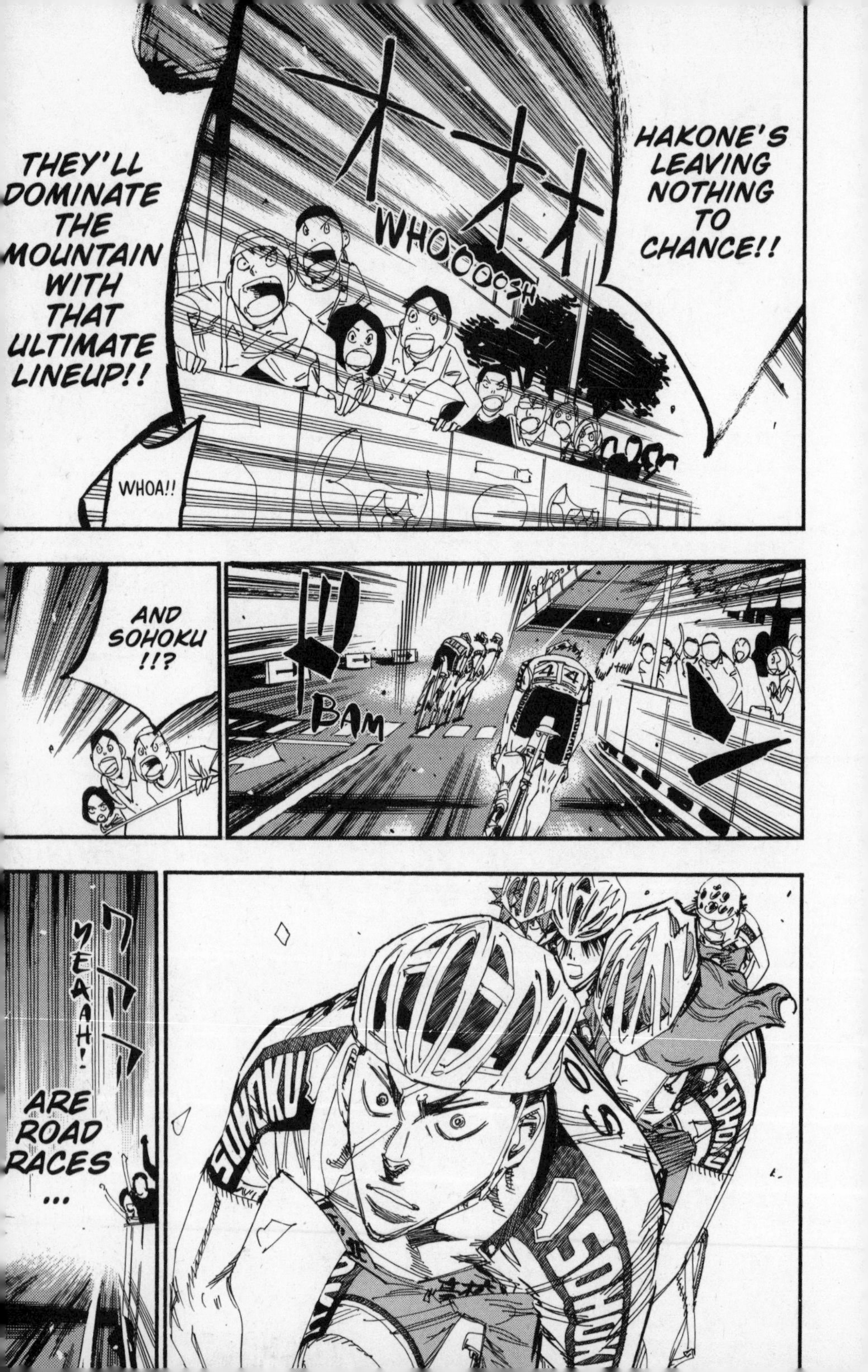
HAKONE'S LEAVING NOTHING TO CHANCE!!
THEY'LL DOMINATE THE MOUNTAIN WITH THAT ULTIMATE LINEUP!!
WHOOOOSH
WHOA!!
BAM
AND SOHOKU!!?
YEAAAH!
ARE ROAD RACES ...

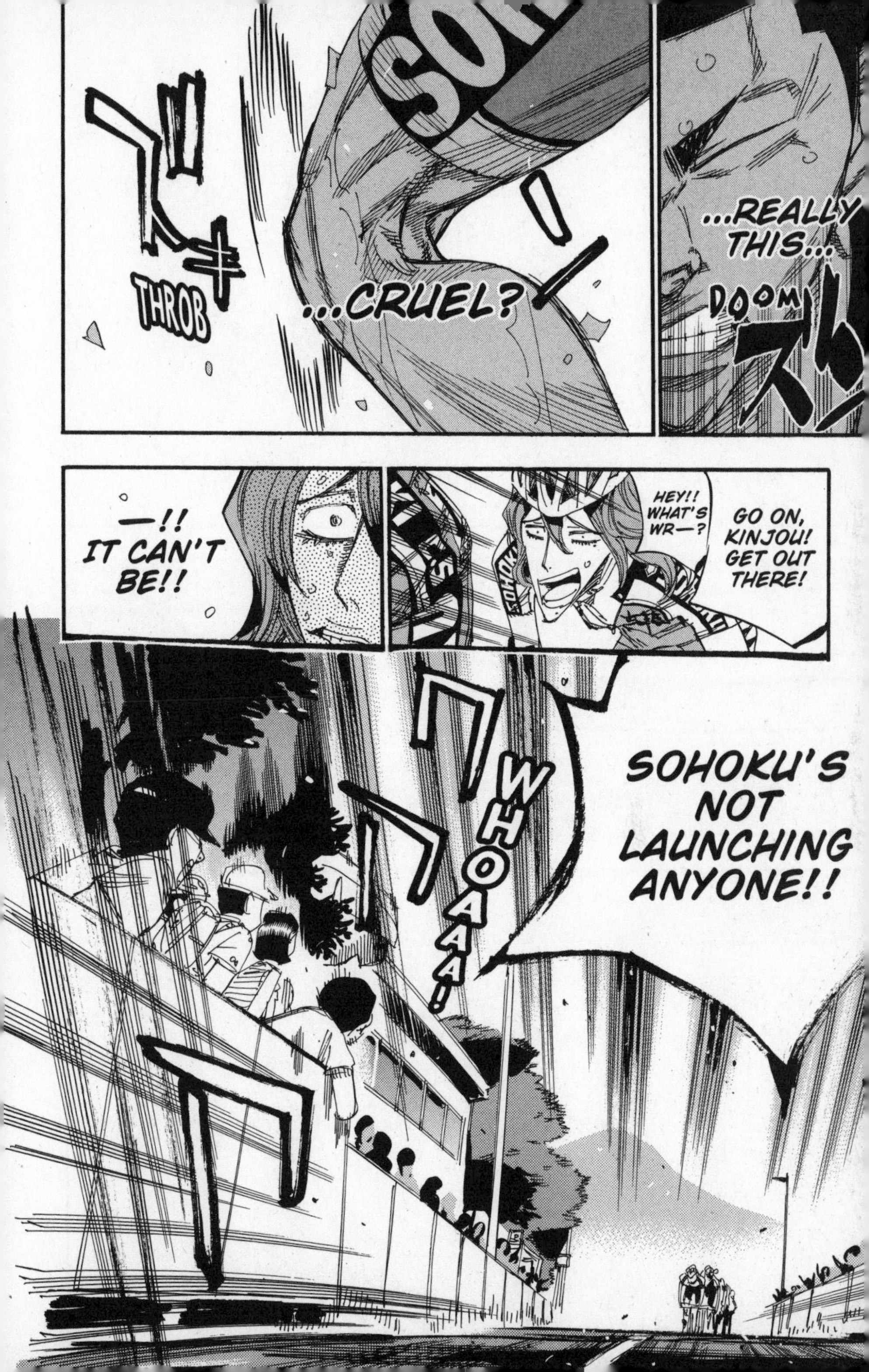
...REALLY THIS...
DOOM
...CRUEL?
THROB
GO ON, KINJOU! GET OUT THERE!
HEY!! WHAT'S WR—?
—!! IT CAN'T BE!!
SOHOKU'S NOT LAUNCHING ANYONE!!
WHOAAAA!

RIDE.189 THE ACE'S END

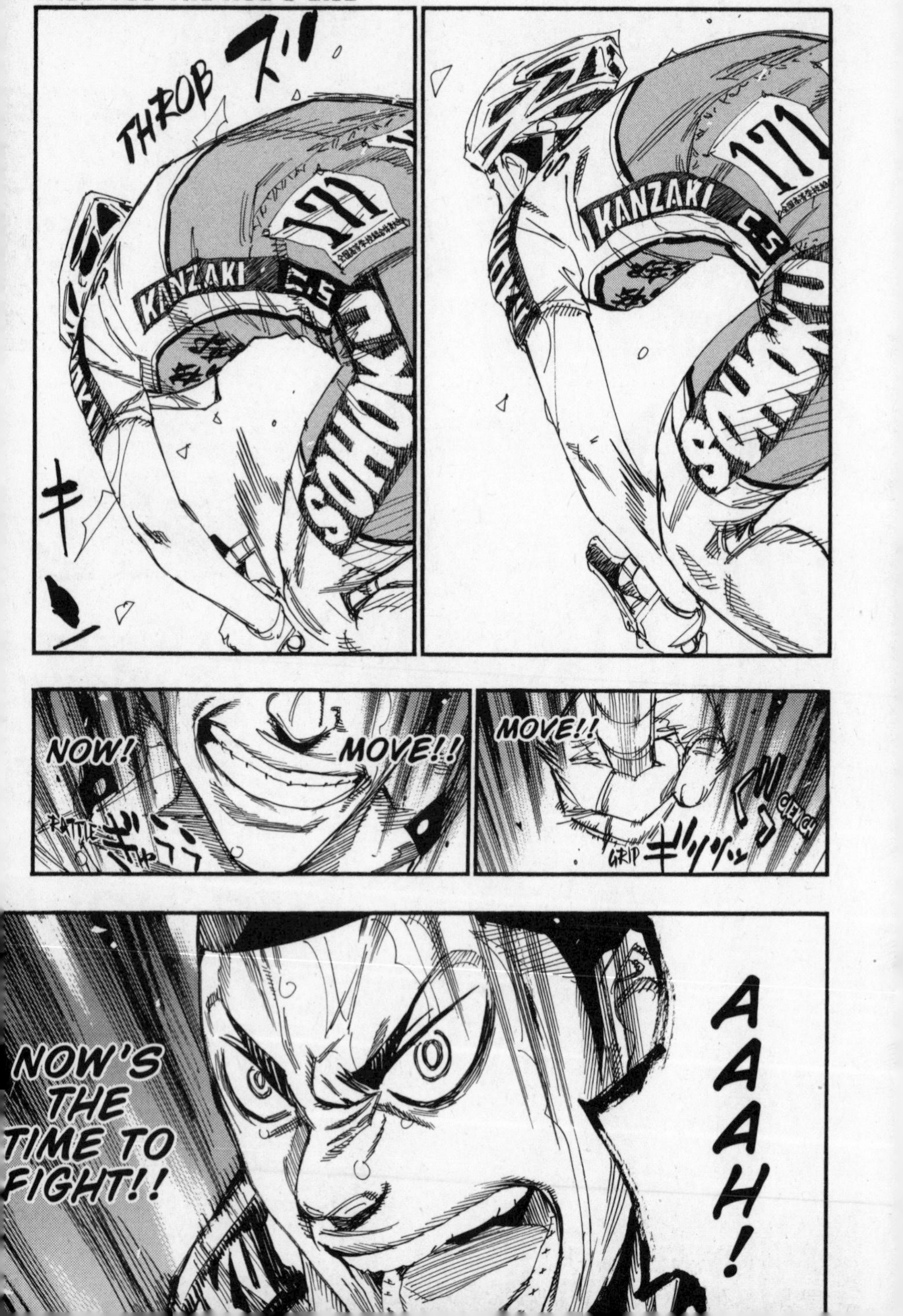
THROB
KANZAKI
SOHOKU
MOVE!!
CLENCH
GRIP
NOW!
MOVE!!
RATTLE
AAAH!
NOW'S THE TIME TO FIGHT!!

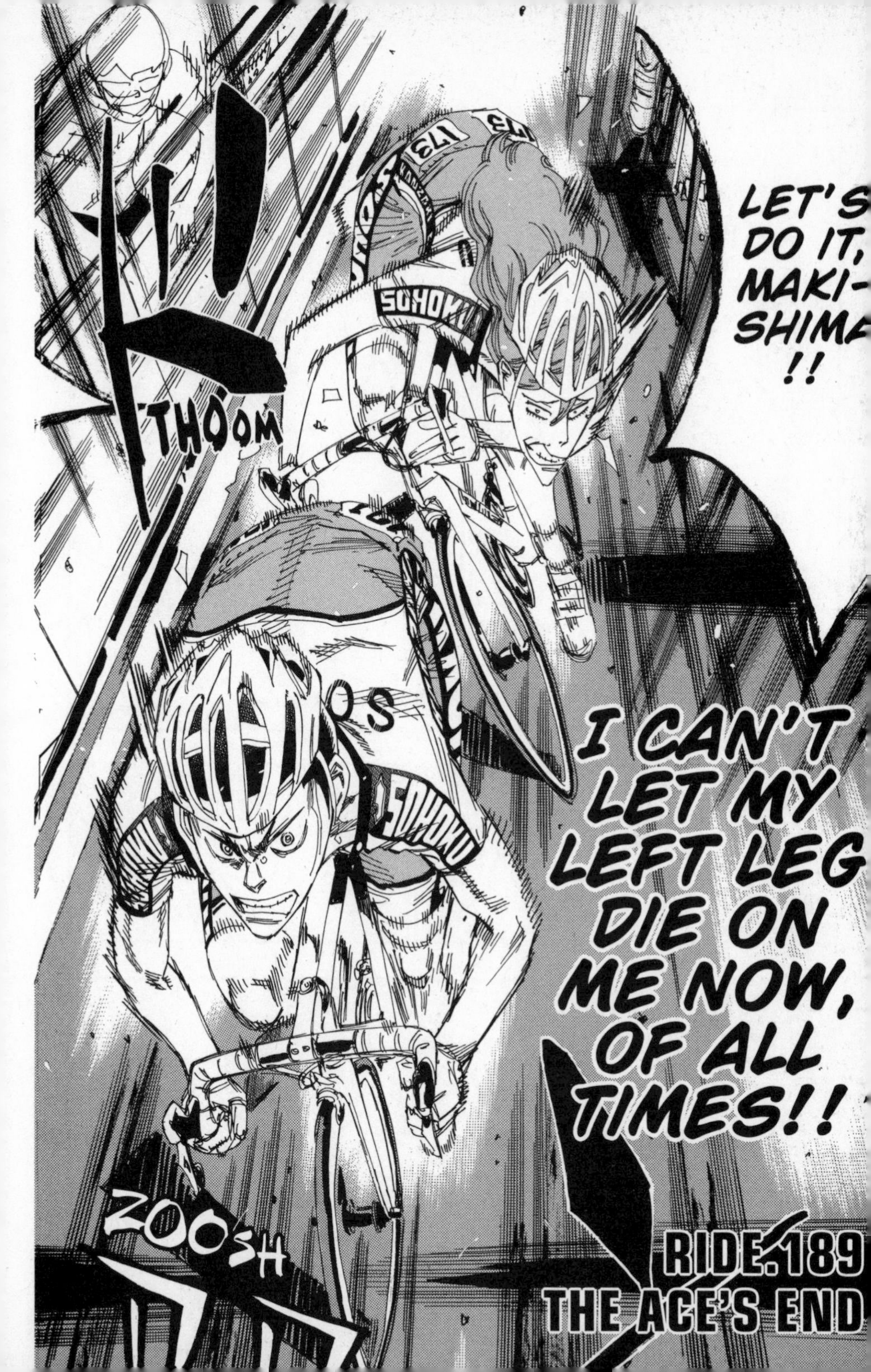
LET'S DO IT, MAKI-SHIMA!!
THOOM
I CAN'T LET MY LEFT LEG DIE ON ME NOW, OF ALL TIMES!!
ZOOSH
RIDE.189
THE ACE'S END

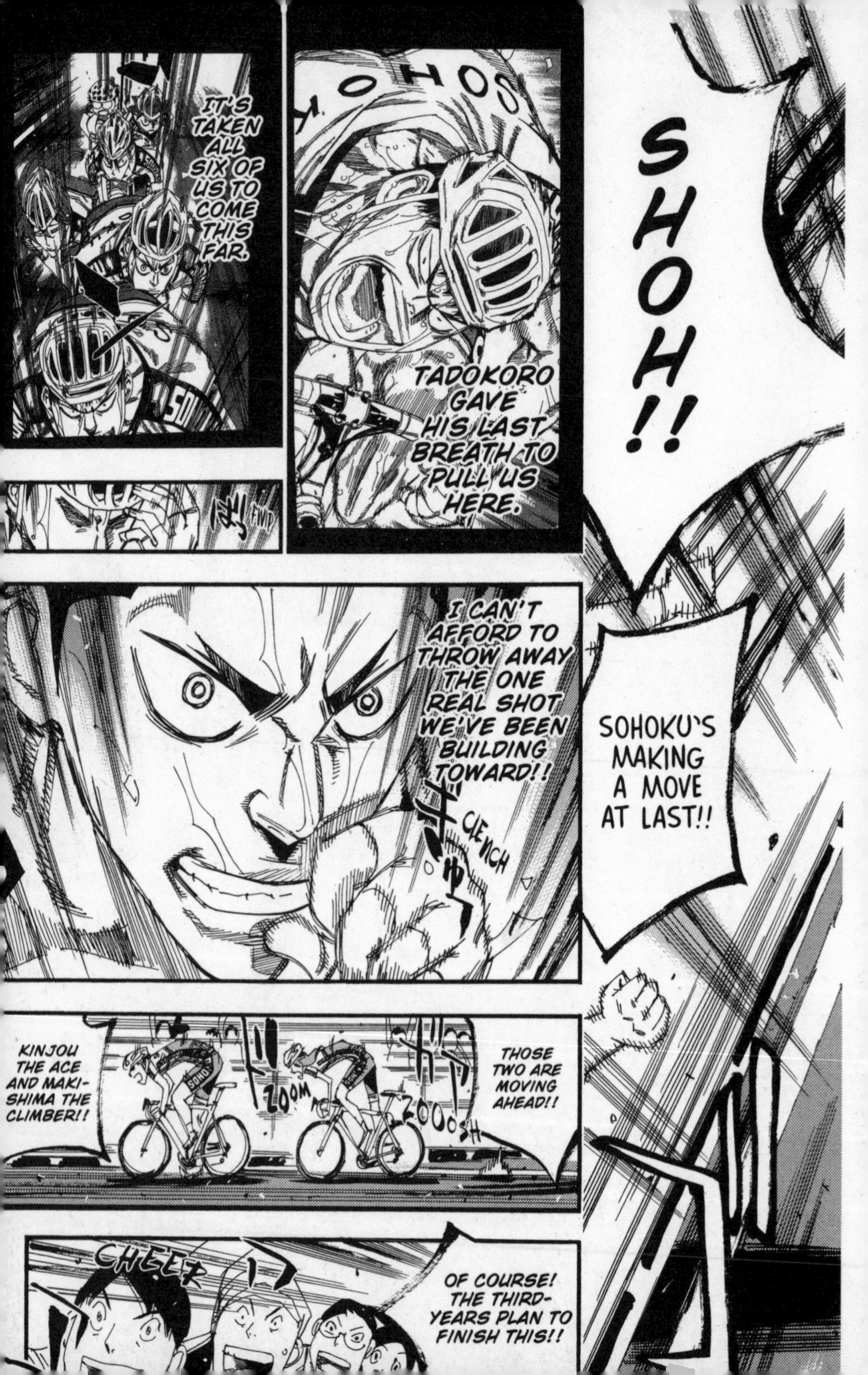
SHOH!!
SOHOKU'S MAKING A MOVE AT LAST!!
TADOKORO GAVE HIS LAST BREATH TO PULL US HERE.
IT'S TAKEN ALL SIX OF US TO COME THIS FAR.
FWIP
I CAN'T AFFORD TO THROW AWAY THE ONE REAL SHOT WE'VE BEEN BUILDING TOWARD!!
CLENCH
THOSE TWO ARE MOVING AHEAD!!
ZOOOSH
ZOOM
KINJOU THE ACE AND MAKI-SHIMA THE CLIMBER!!
OF COURSE! THE THIRD-YEARS PLAN TO FINISH THIS!!
CHEER

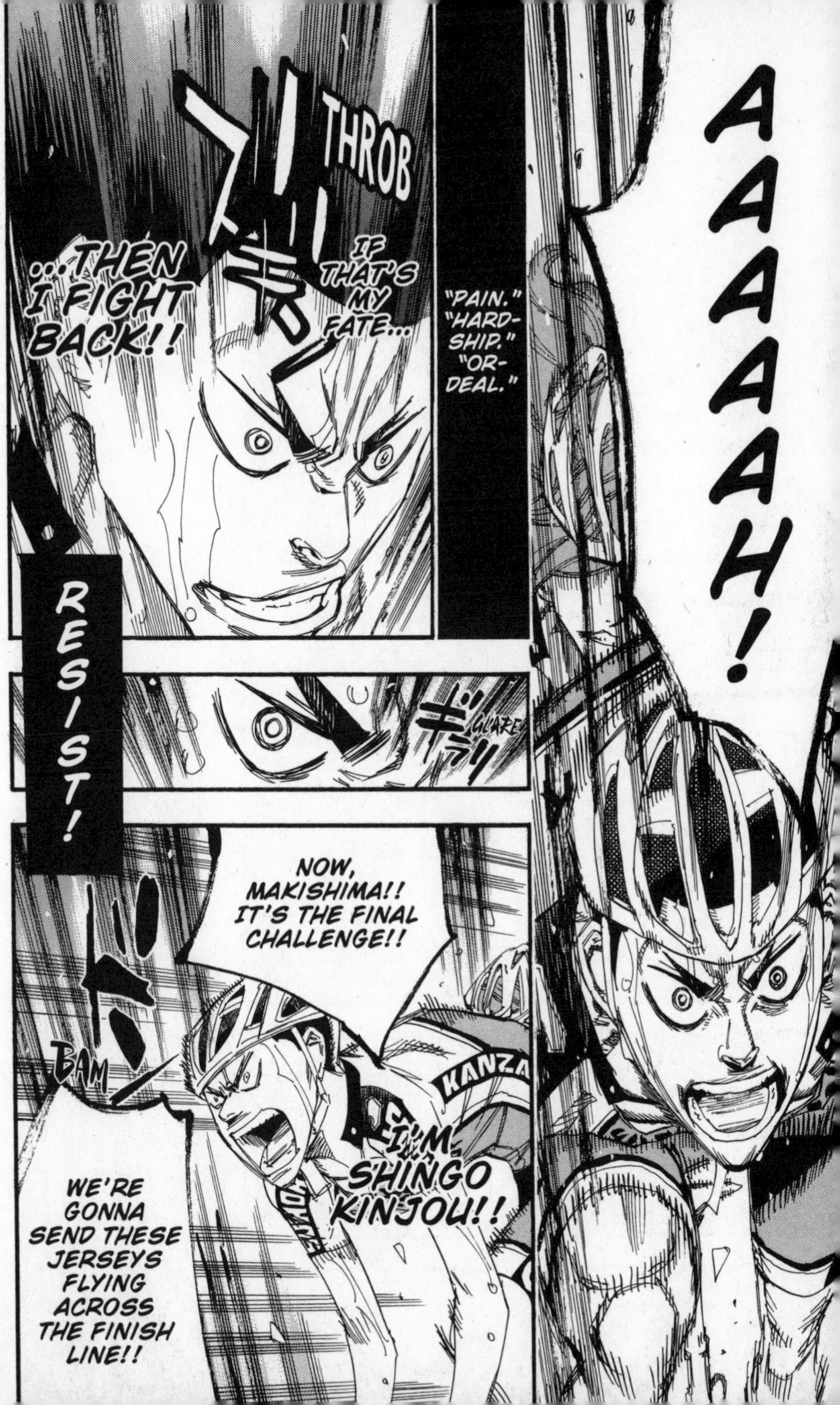
AAAAAH!
"PAIN." "HARD-SHIP." "OR-DEAL."
THROB
IF THAT'S MY FATE...
...THEN I FIGHT BACK!!
RESIST!
GLARE
NOW, MAKISHIMA!! IT'S THE FINAL CHALLENGE!!
KANZA
BAM
I'M SHINGO KINJOU!!
WE'RE GONNA SEND THESE JERSEYS FLYING ACROSS THE FINISH LINE!!

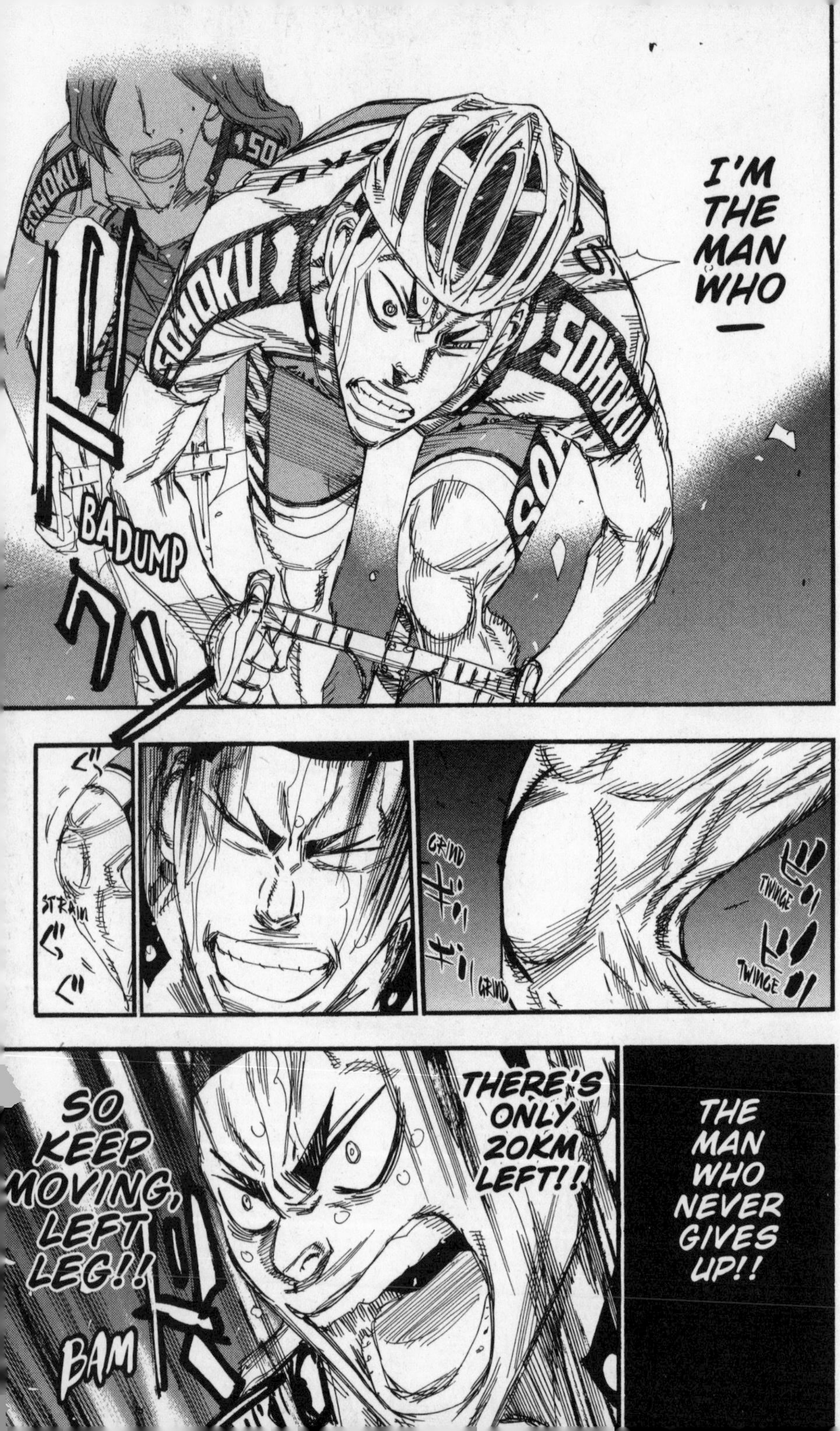
I'M THE MAN WHO—
BADUMP
TWINGE
TWINGE
GRIND
GRIND
STRAIN
THE MAN WHO NEVER GIVES UP!!
THERE'S ONLY 20KM LEFT!!
SO KEEP MOVING, LEFT LEG!!
BAM

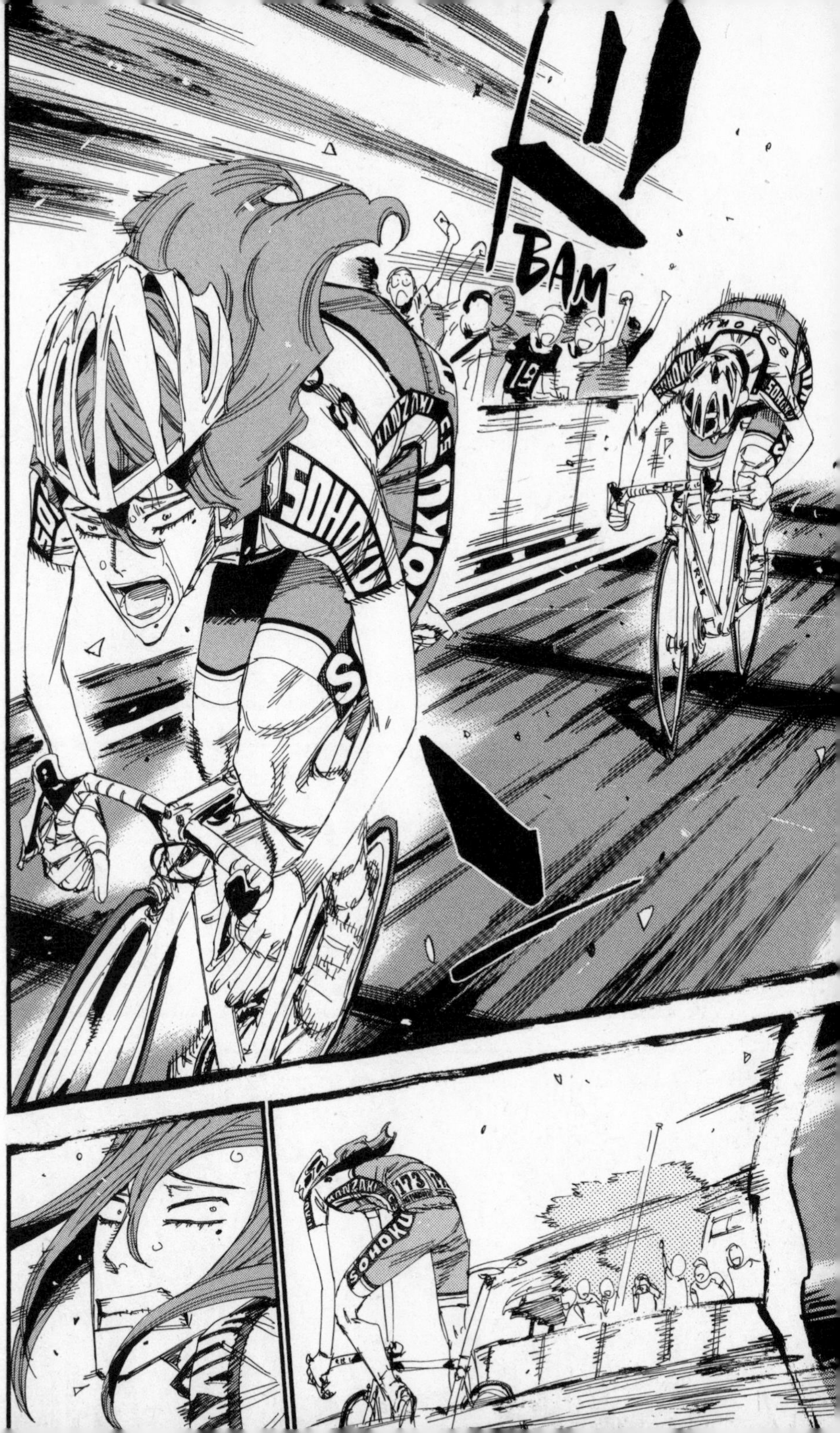
BAM

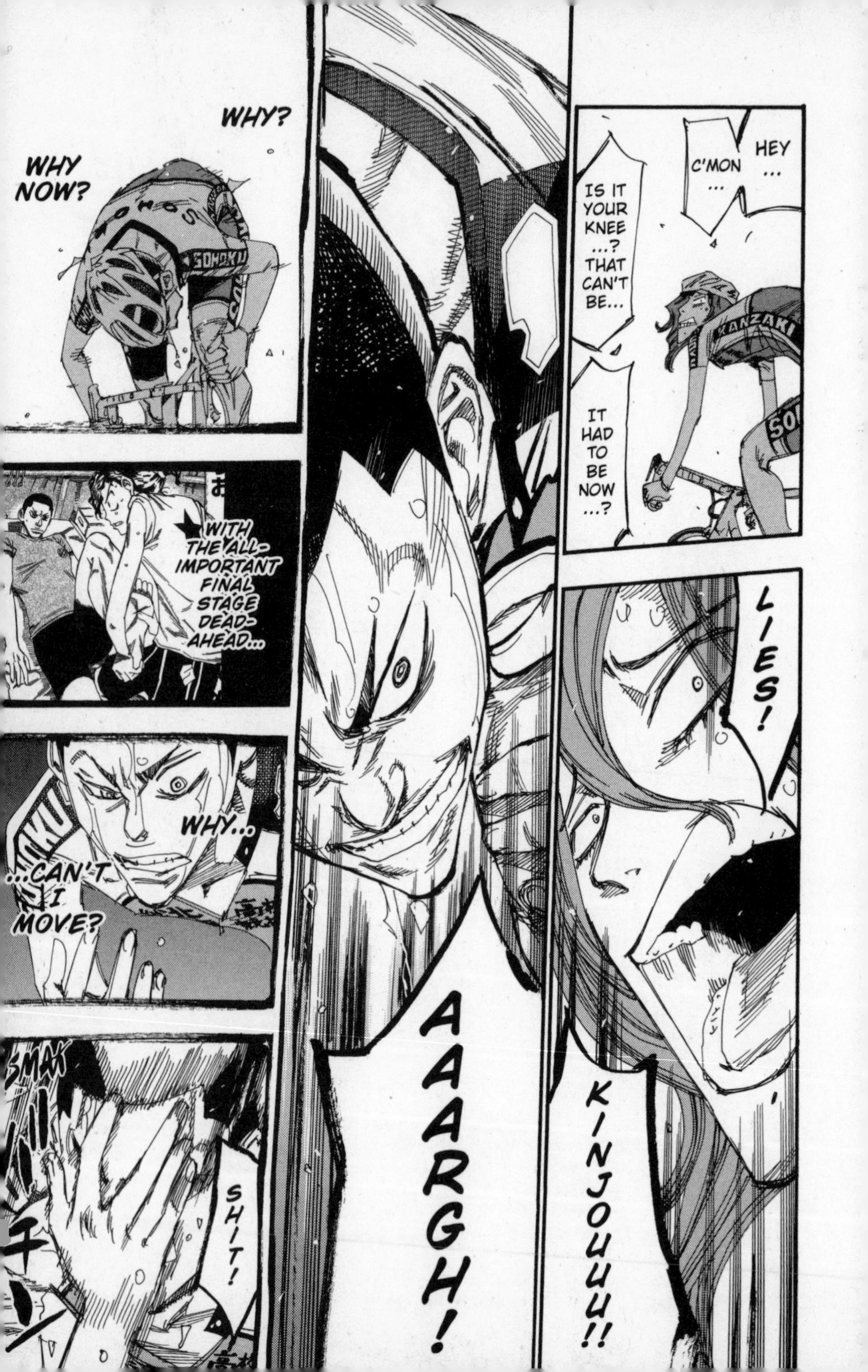
HEY ...
C'MON ...
IS IT YOUR KNEE ...? THAT CAN'T BE...
IT HAD TO BE NOW ...?
LIES!
KINJOUUU!!
AAARGH!
WHY?
WHY NOW?
WITH THE ALL-IMPORTANT FINAL STAGE DEAD-AHEAD...
WHY...
...CAN'T I MOVE?
SHIT!

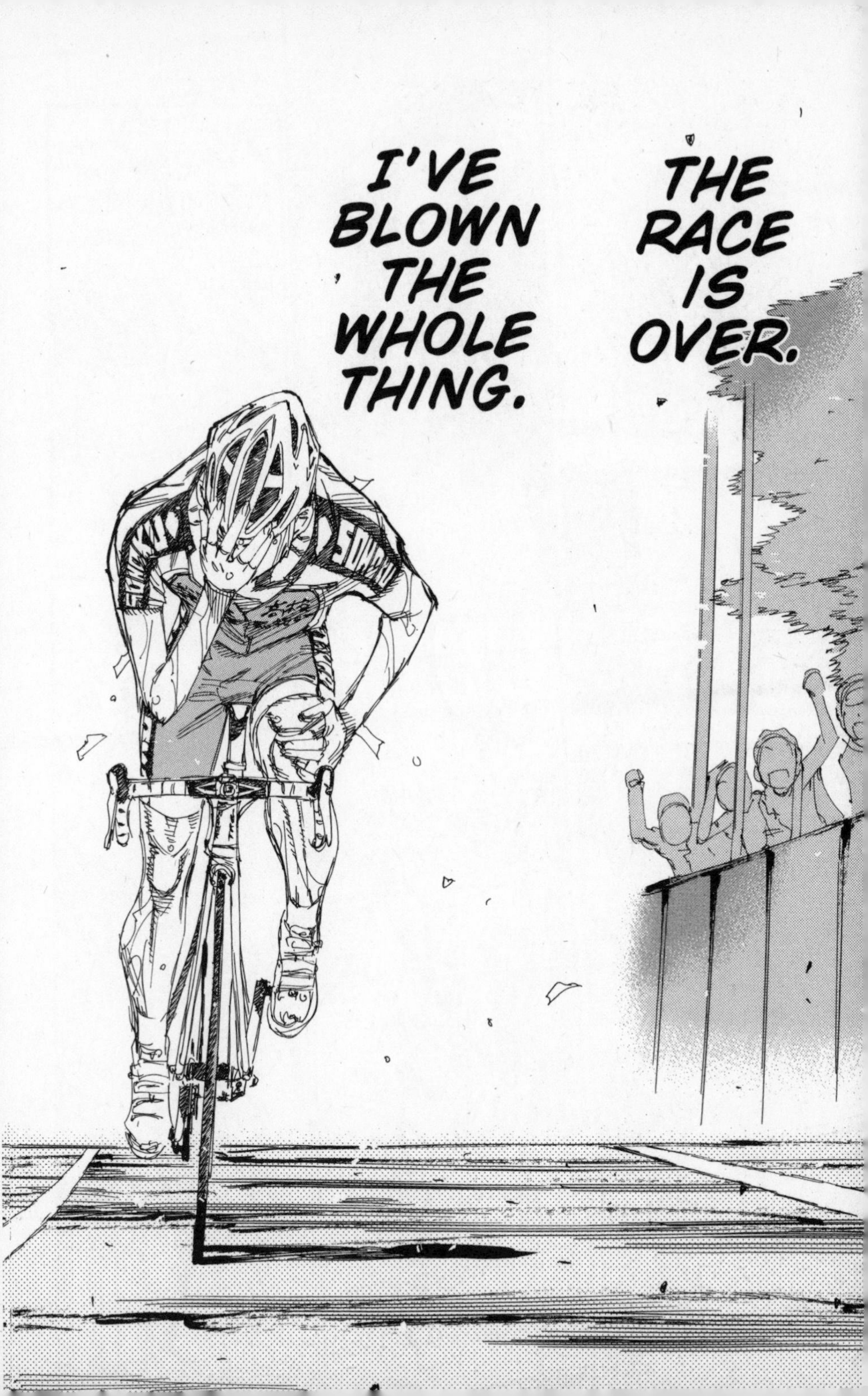
THE RACE IS OVER.
I'VE BLOWN THE WHOLE THING.

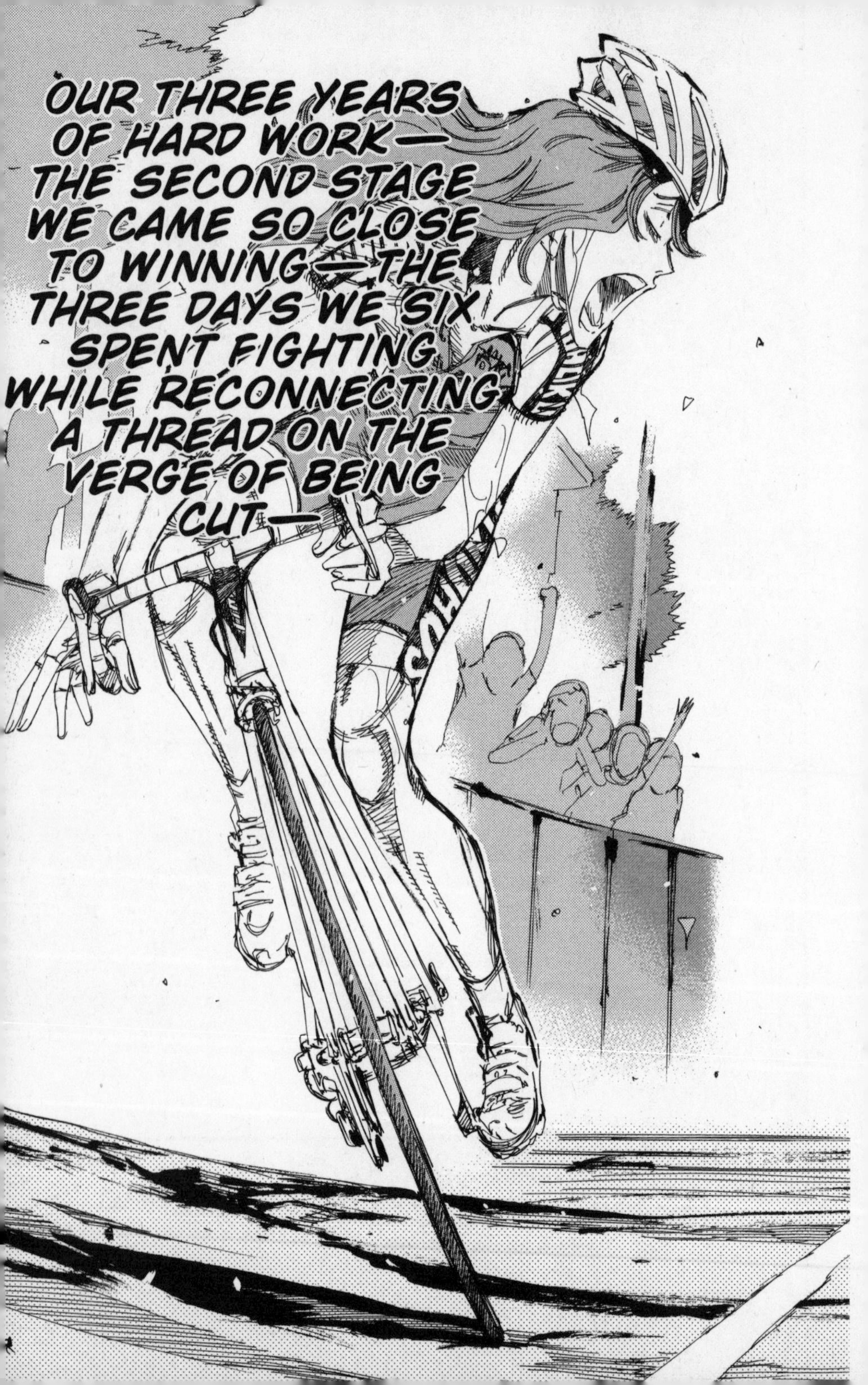
OUR THREE YEARS OF HARD WORK— THE SECOND STAGE WE CAME SO CLOSE TO WINNING— THE THREE DAYS WE SIX SPENT FIGHTING WHILE RECONNECTING A THREAD ON THE VERGE OF BEING CUT—

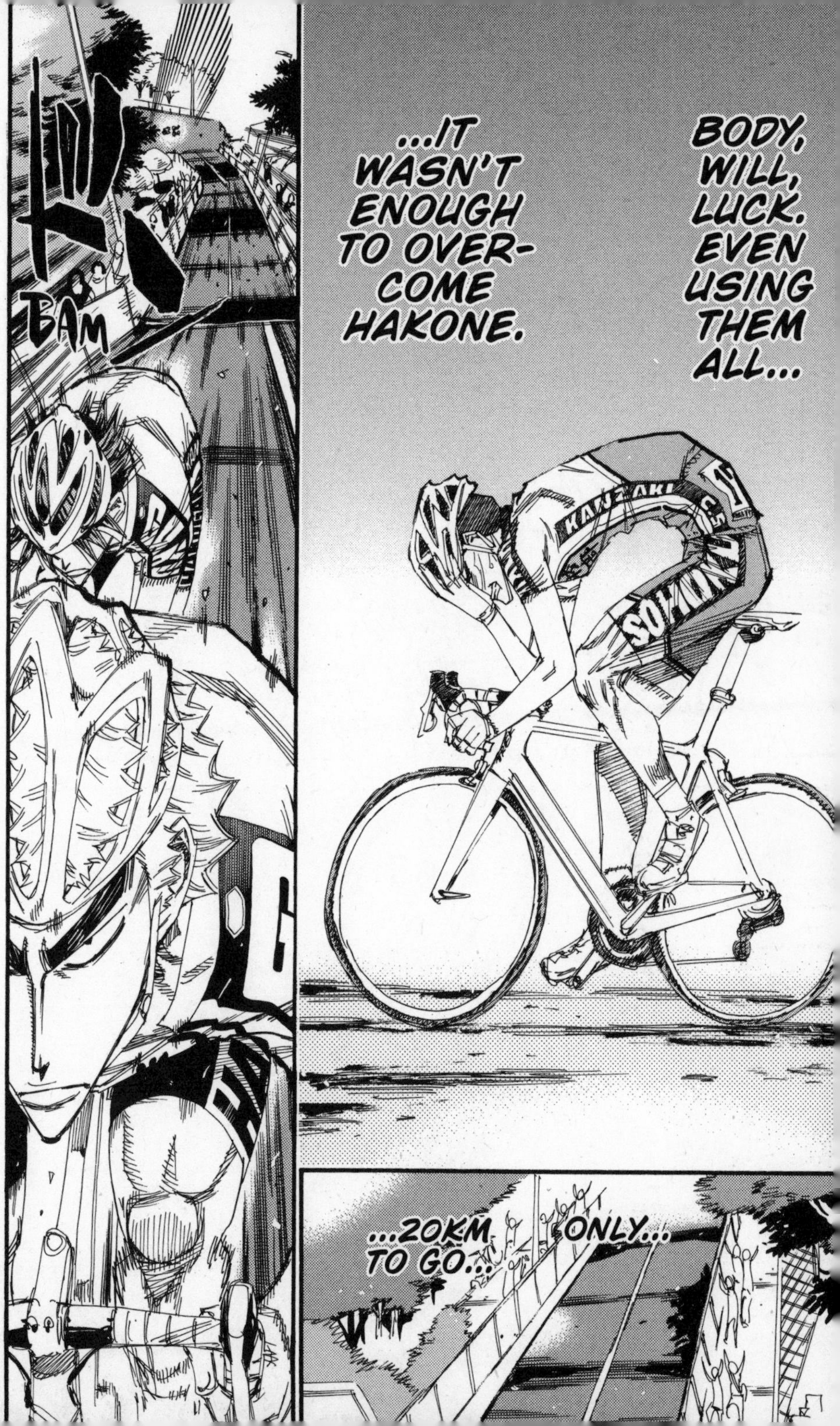
BODY, WILL, LUCK. EVEN USING THEM ALL...
...IT WASN'T ENOUGH TO OVER-COME HAKONE.
ONLY...
...20KM TO GO...
BAM

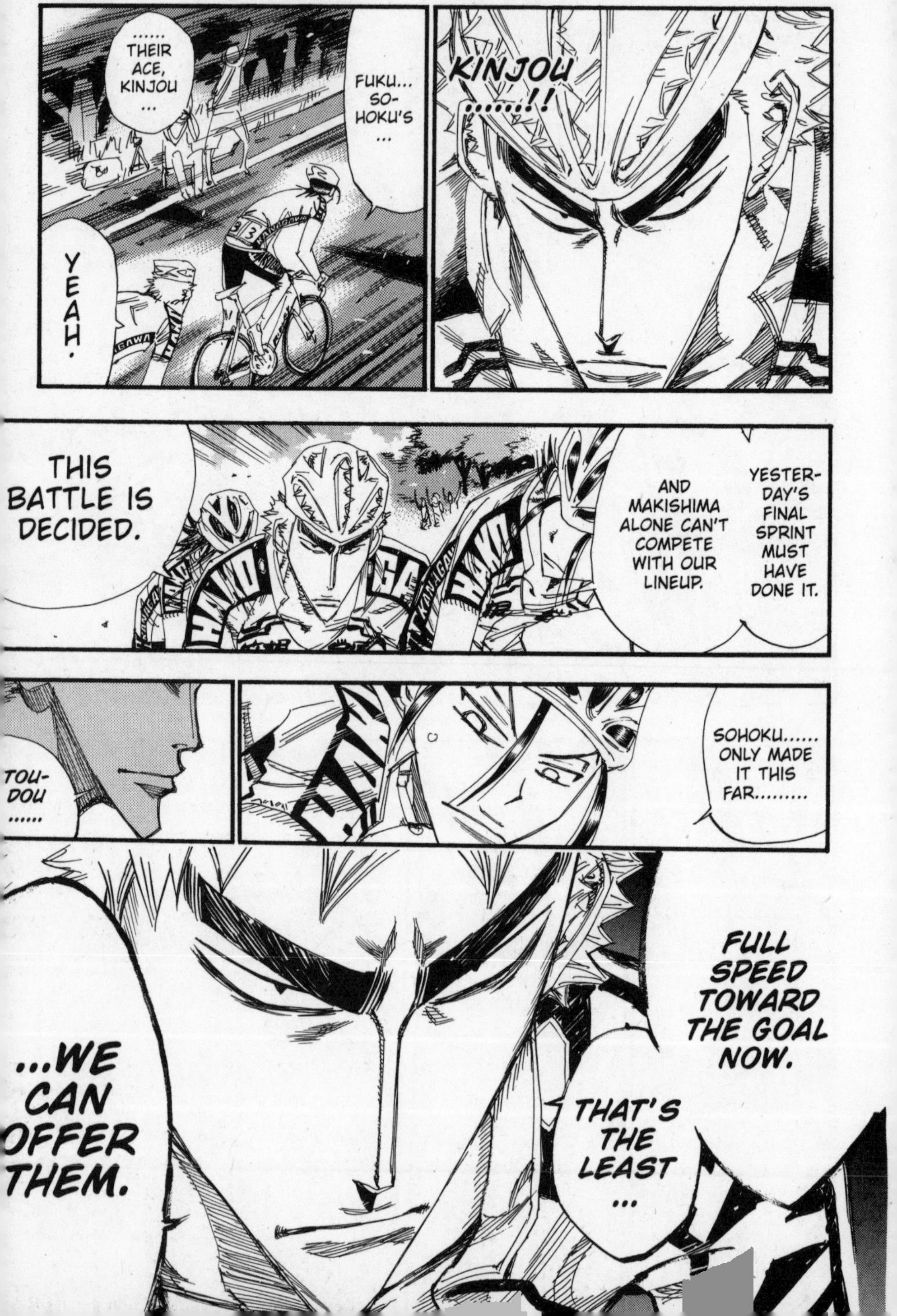
KINJOU ......!!
FUKU... SO-HOKU'S ...
...... THEIR ACE, KINJOU ...
YEAH.
YESTER-DAY'S FINAL SPRINT MUST HAVE DONE IT.
AND MAKISHIMA ALONE CAN'T COMPETE WITH OUR LINEUP.
THIS BATTLE IS DECIDED.
SOHOKU...... ONLY MADE IT THIS FAR.........
TOU-DOU ......
FULL SPEED TOWARD THE GOAL NOW.
THAT'S THE LEAST ...
...WE CAN OFFER THEM.

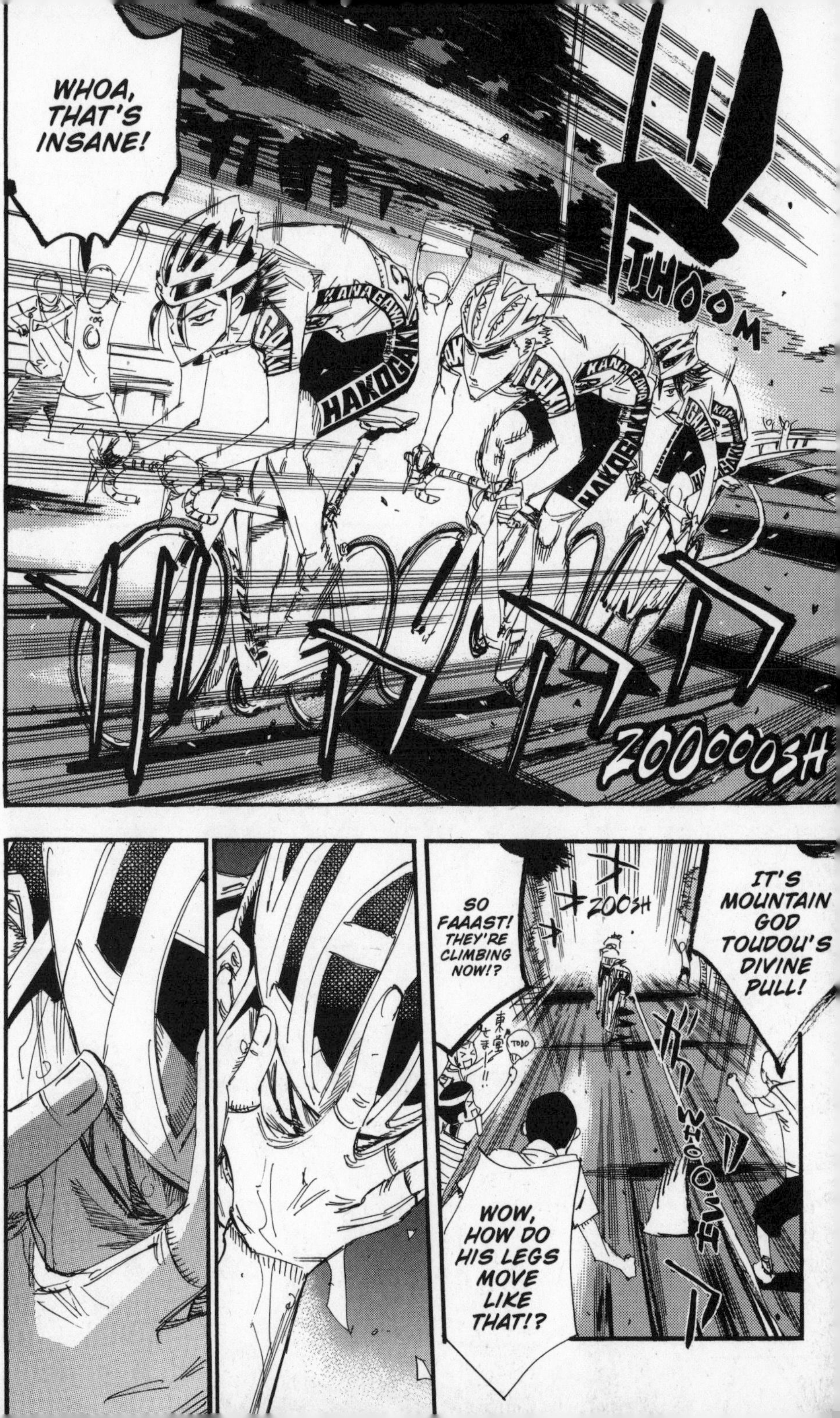
THOOM
WHOA, THAT'S INSANE!
ZOOOOOOSH
IT'S MOUNTAIN GOD TOUDOU'S DIVINE PULL!
ZOOSH
SO FAAAST! THEY'RE CLIMBING NOW!?
東堂さま!!
TODO
WHOOSH
WOW, HOW DO HIS LEGS MOVE LIKE THAT!?

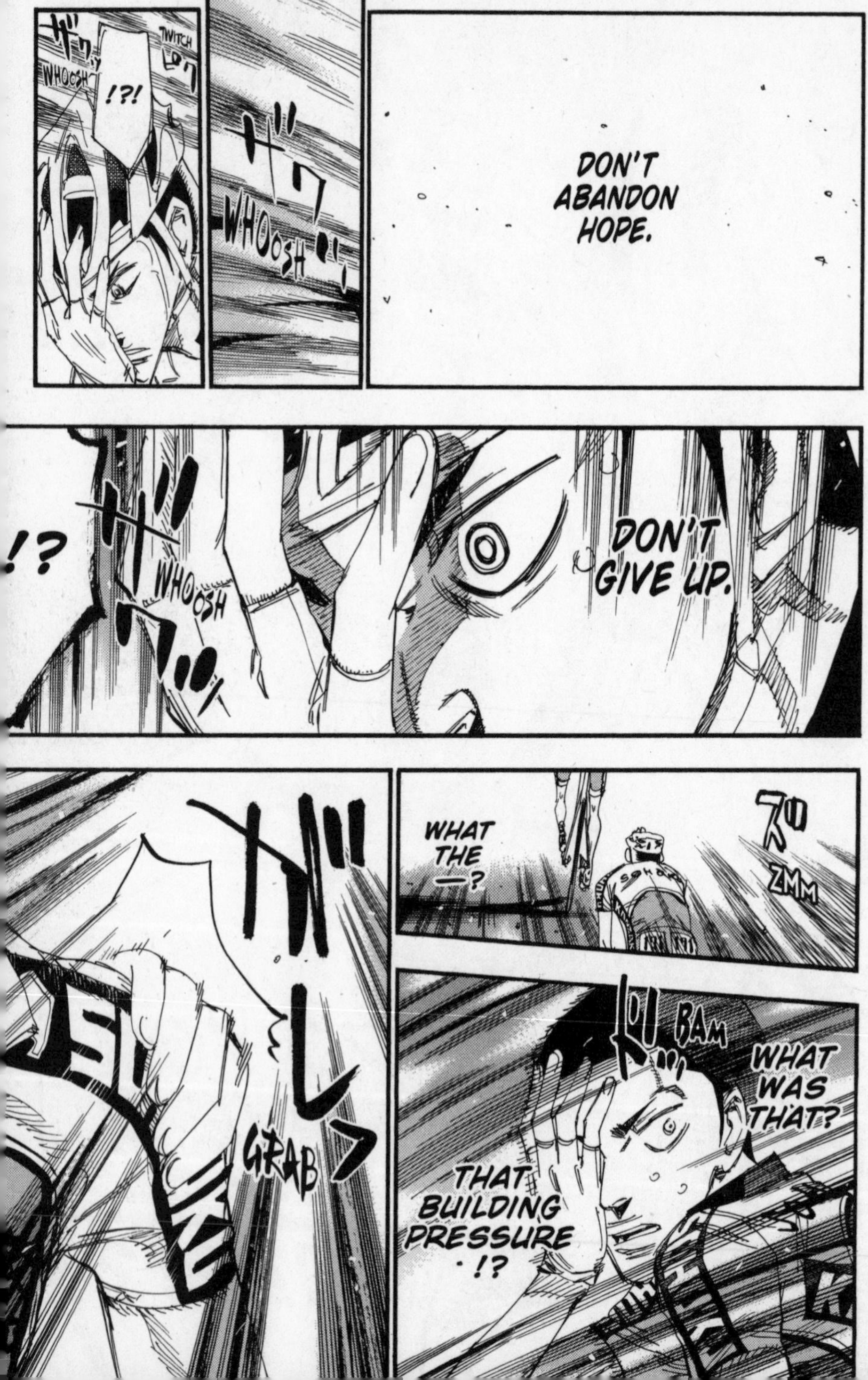
DON'T ABANDON HOPE.
WHOOSH
TWITCH
WHOOSH
!?!
DON'T GIVE UP.
WHOOSH
!?
ZMM
WHAT THE—?
BAM
WHAT WAS THAT?
THAT BUILDING PRESSURE!?
GRAB

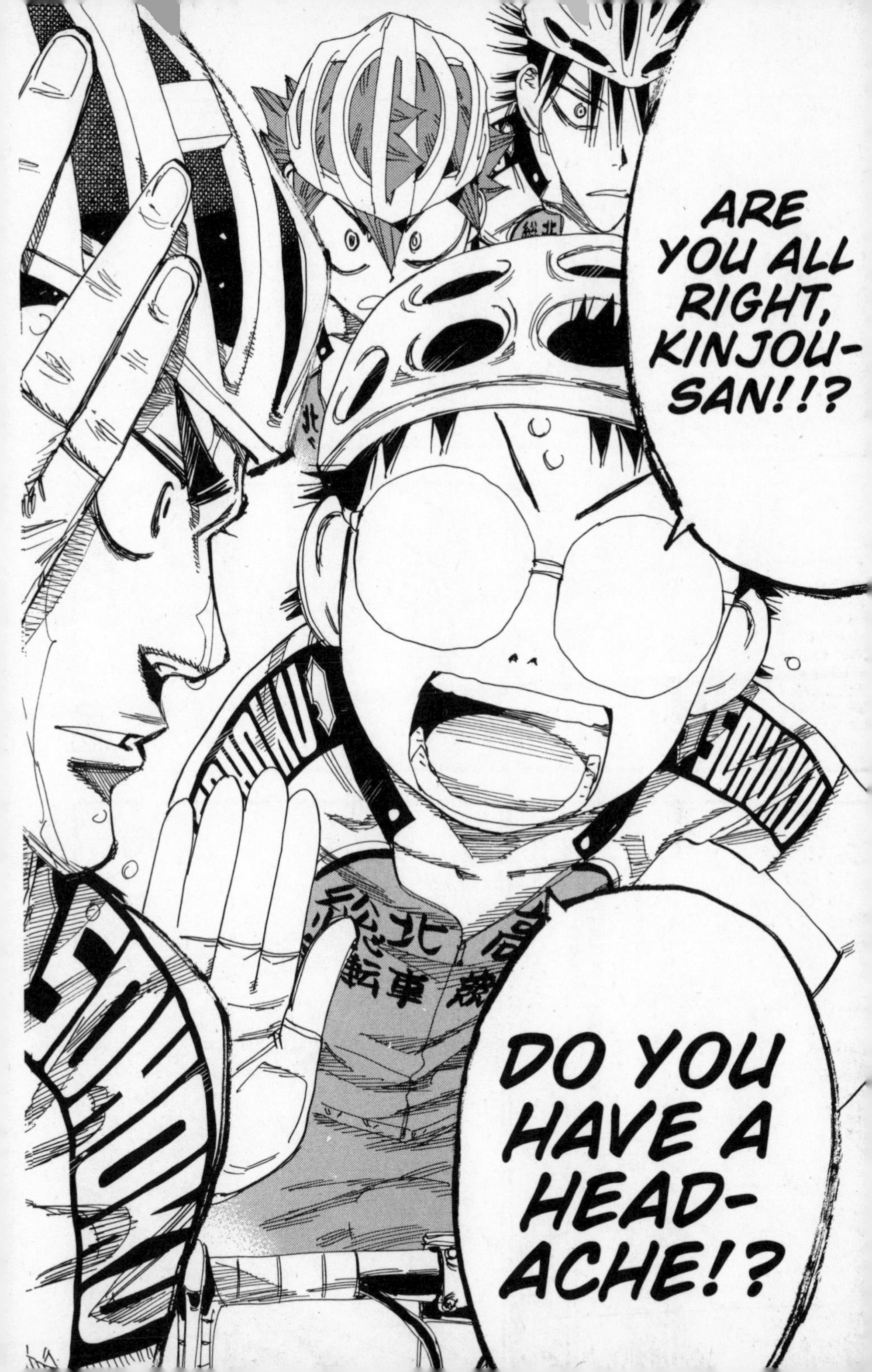
ARE YOU ALL RIGHT, KINJOU-SAN!!?
DO YOU HAVE A HEAD-ACHE!?

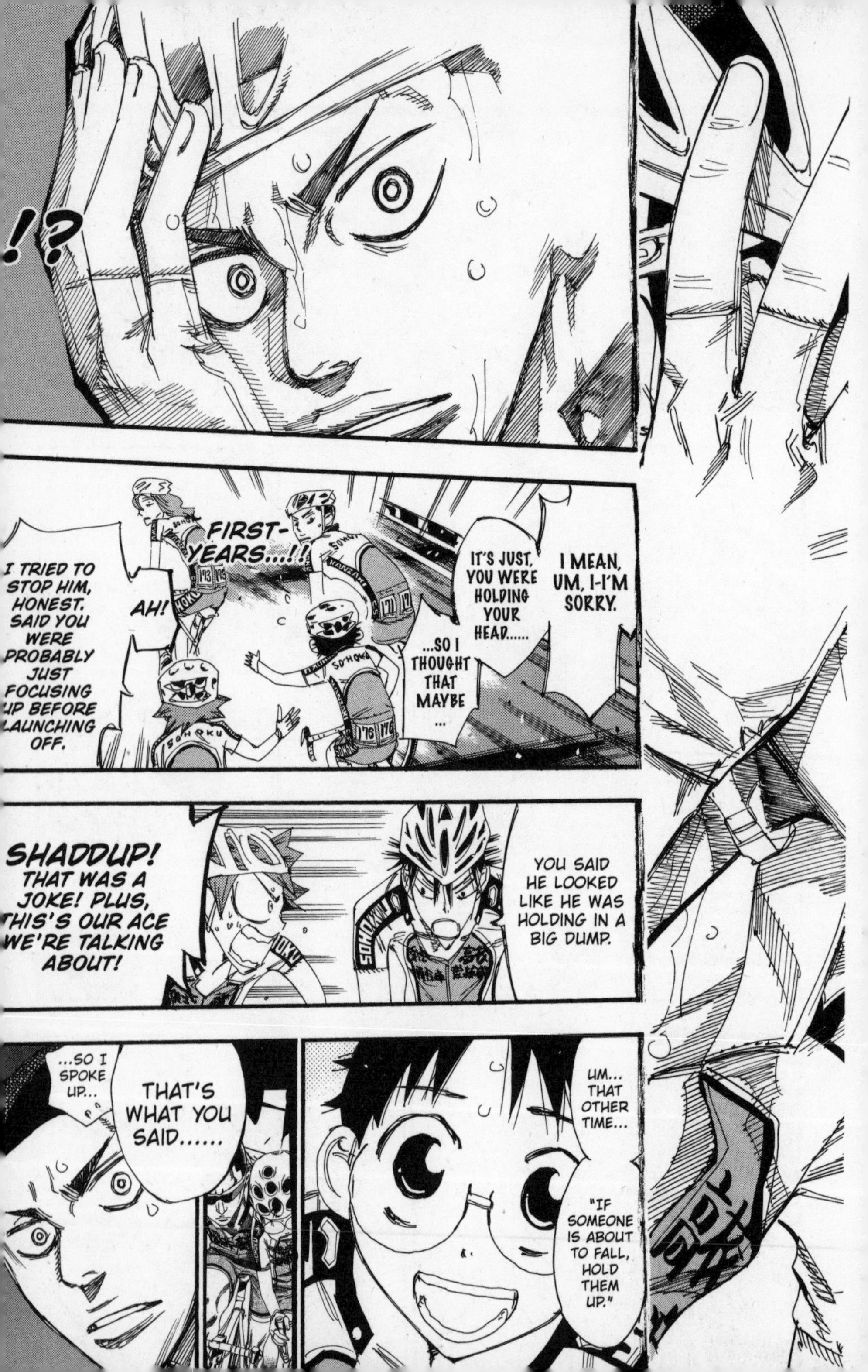
!?
I MEAN, UM, I-I'M SORRY.
IT'S JUST, YOU WERE HOLDING YOUR HEAD......
...SO I THOUGHT THAT MAYBE ...
FIRST-YEARS...!!
AH!
I TRIED TO STOP HIM, HONEST. SAID YOU WERE PROBABLY JUST FOCUSING UP BEFORE LAUNCHING OFF.
YOU SAID HE LOOKED LIKE HE WAS HOLDING IN A BIG DUMP.
SHADDUP! THAT WAS A JOKE! PLUS, THIS'S OUR ACE WE'RE TALKING ABOUT!
UM... THAT OTHER TIME...
"IF SOMEONE IS ABOUT TO FALL, HOLD THEM UP."
THAT'S WHAT YOU SAID......
...SO I SPOKE UP...

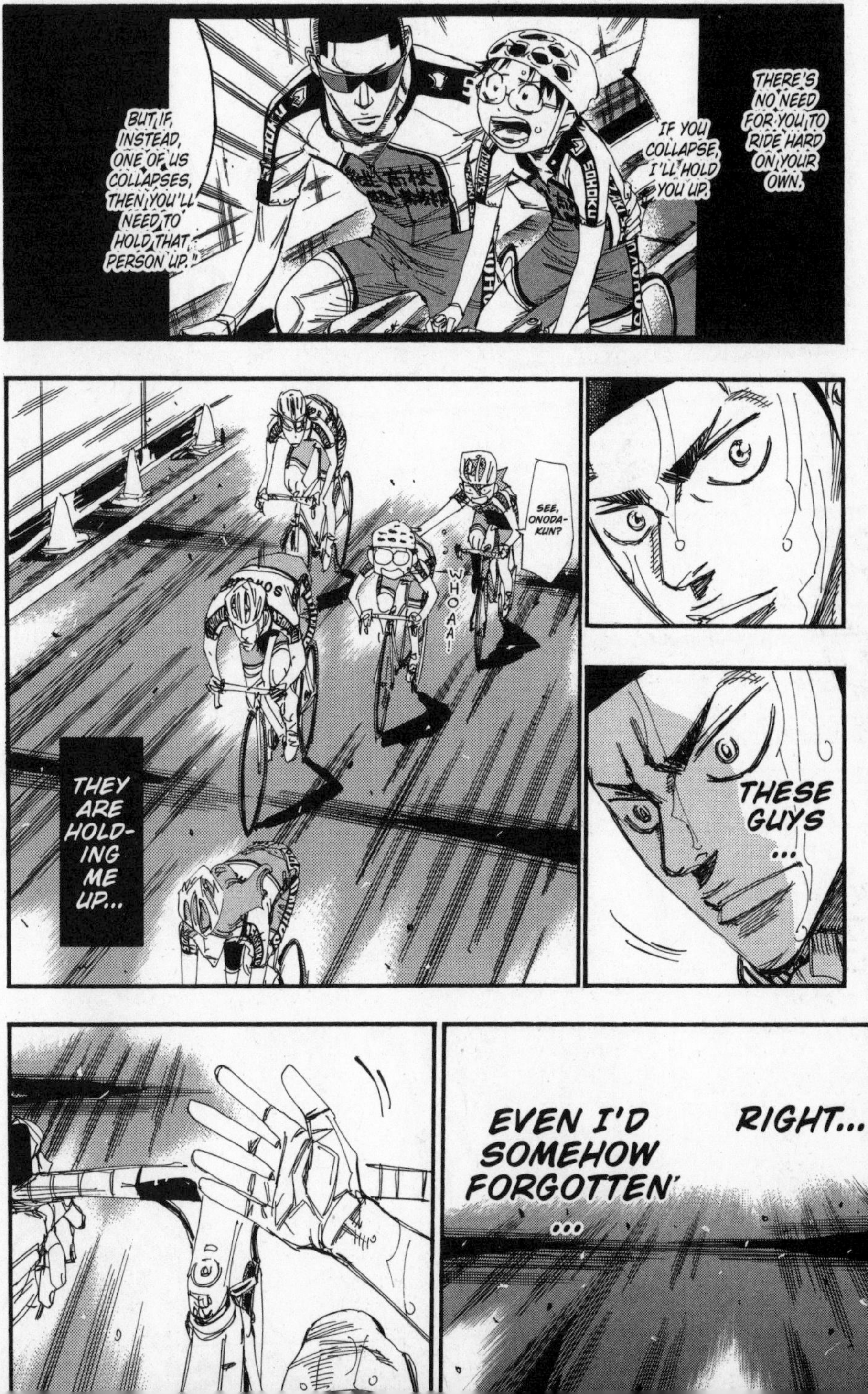
THERE'S NO NEED FOR YOU TO RIDE HARD ON YOUR OWN.
IF YOU COLLAPSE, I'LL HOLD YOU UP.
BUT IF, INSTEAD, ONE OF US COLLAPSES, THEN YOU'LL NEED TO HOLD THAT PERSON UP."
THESE GUYS ...
SEE, ONODA-KUN?
WHOAA!
THEY ARE HOLDING ME UP...
RIGHT...
EVEN I'D SOMEHOW FORGOTTEN' ...

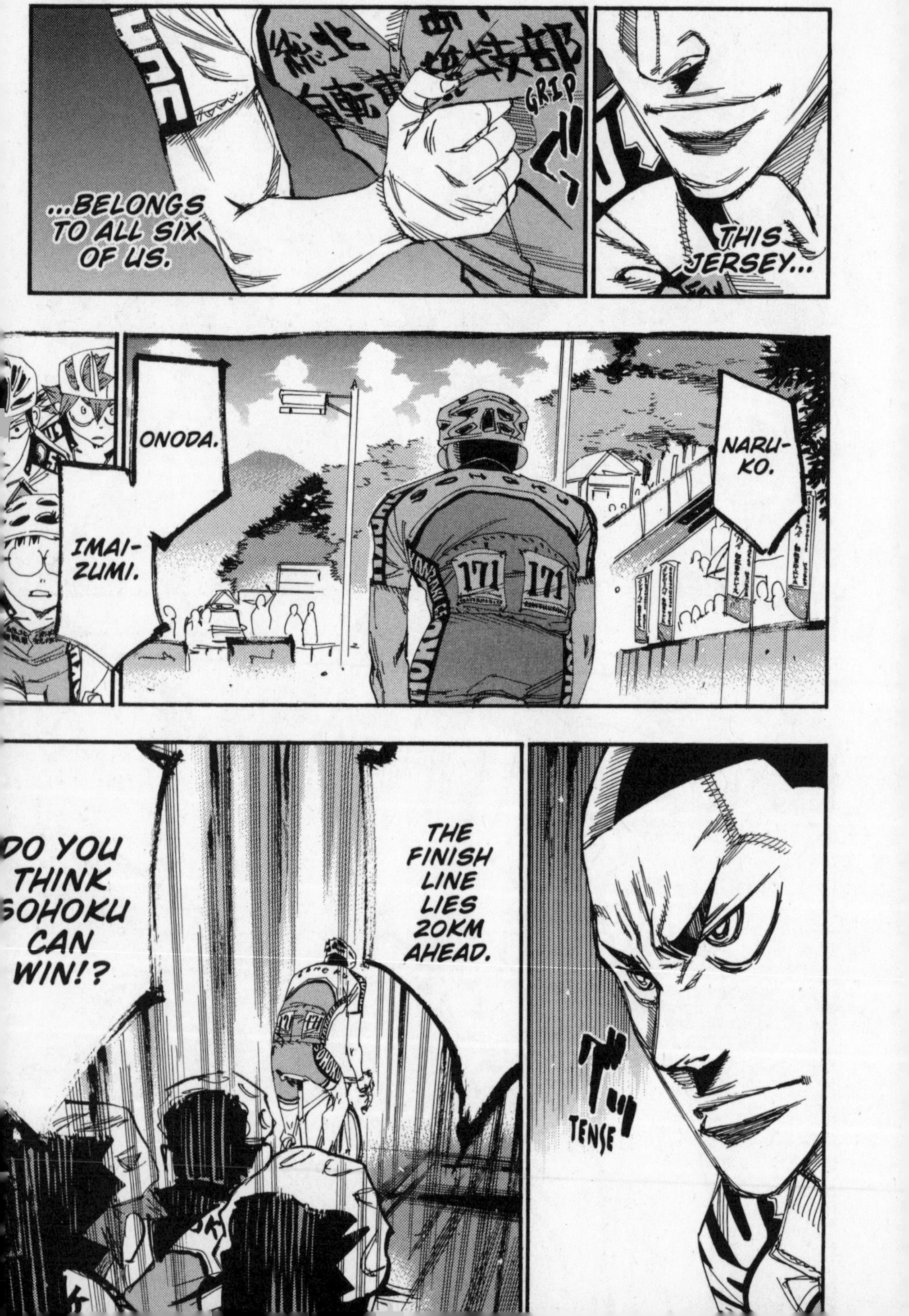
THIS JERSEY...
GRIP
...BELONGS TO ALL SIX OF US.
NARU-KO.
ONODA.
IMAI-ZUMI.
TENSE
THE FINISH LINE LIES 20KM AHEAD.
DO YOU THINK SOHOKU CAN WIN!?

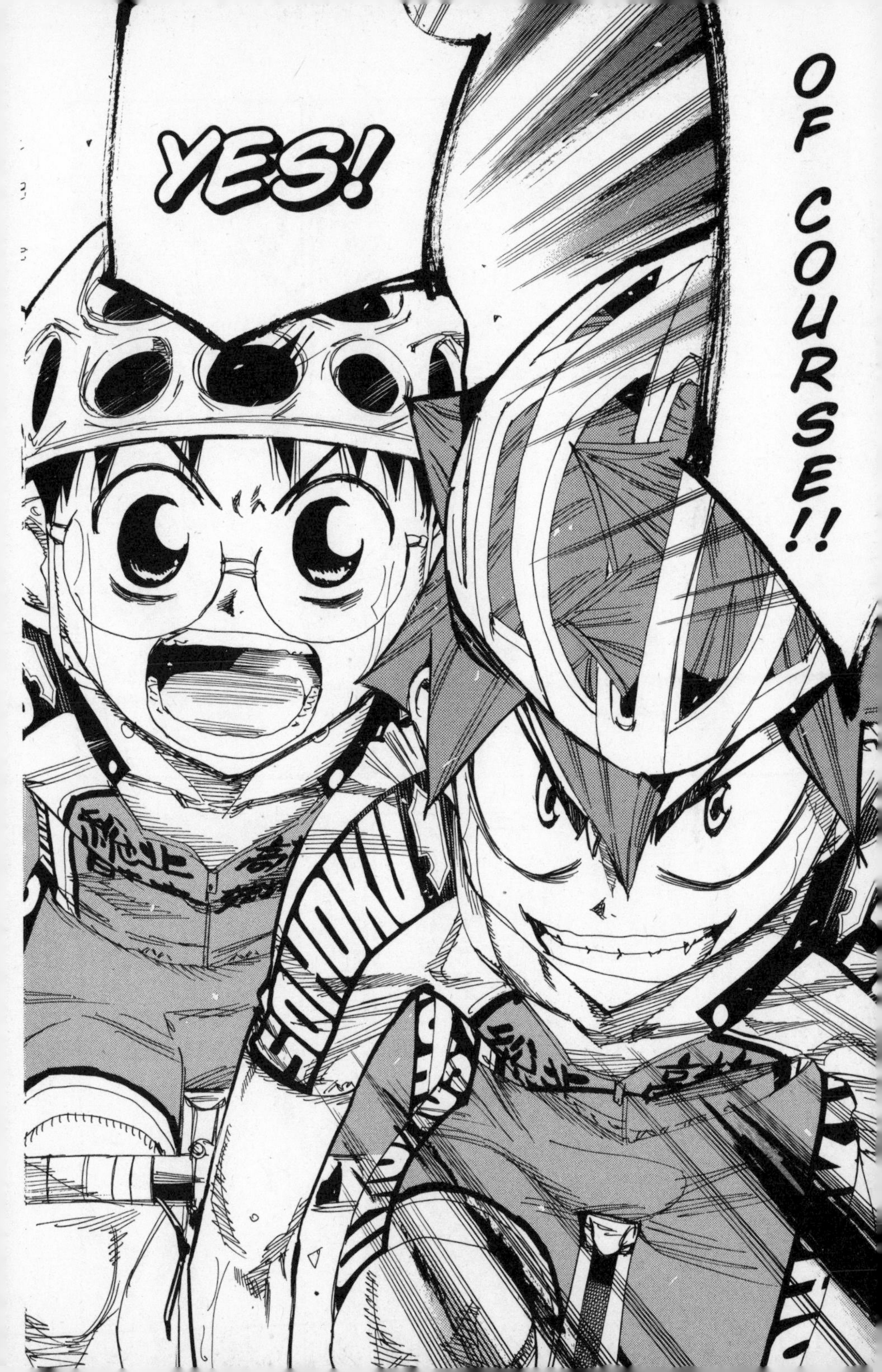
OF COURSE!!
YES!

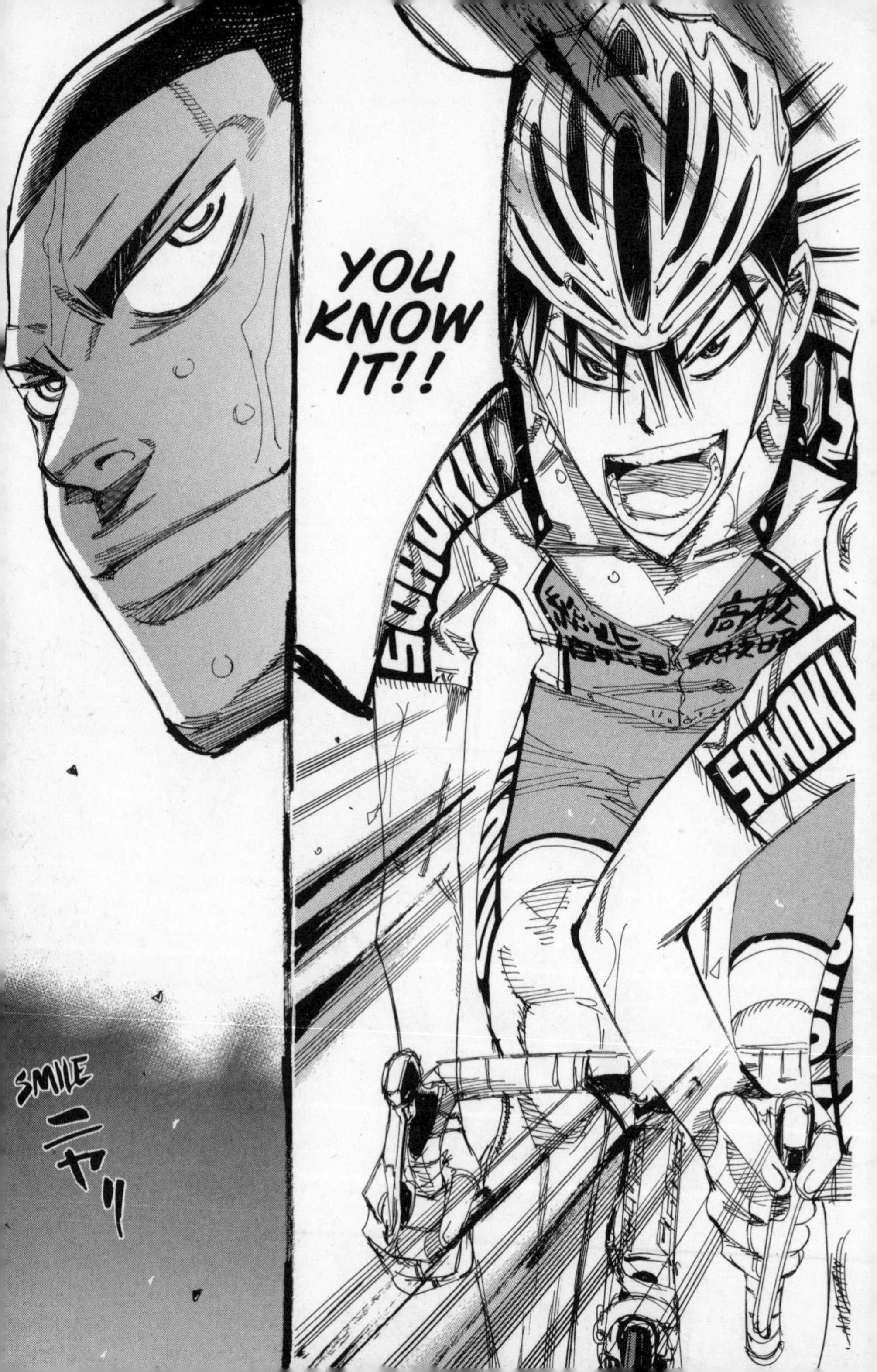
YOU KNOW IT!!
SMILE
ニヤリ

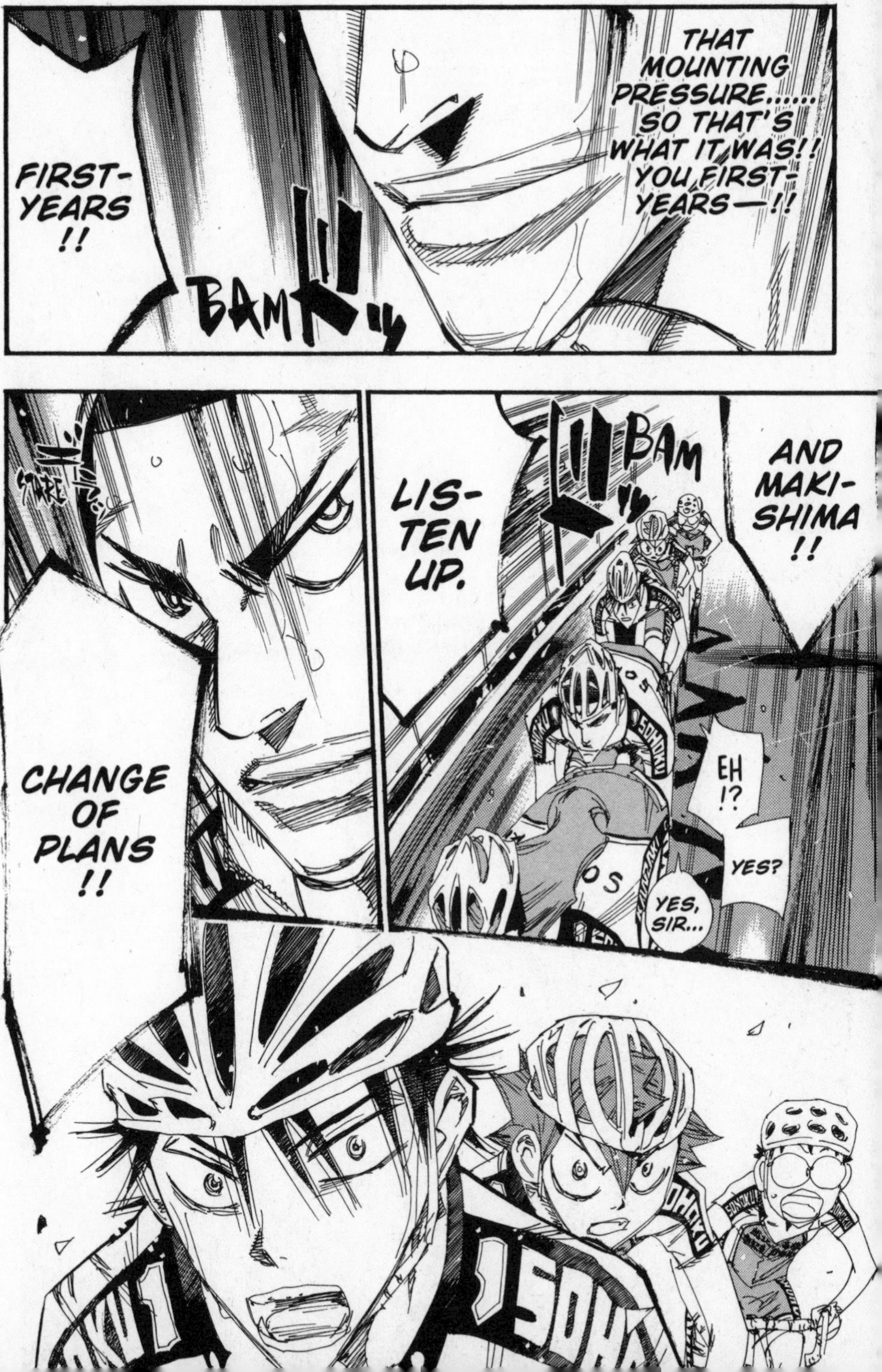
THAT MOUNTING PRESSURE...... SO THAT'S WHAT IT WAS!! YOU FIRST-YEARS—!!
FIRST-YEARS!!
BAM
AND MAKI-SHIMA!!
BAM
LIS-TEN UP.
EH!?
YES?
YES, SIR...
STARE
CHANGE OF PLANS!!

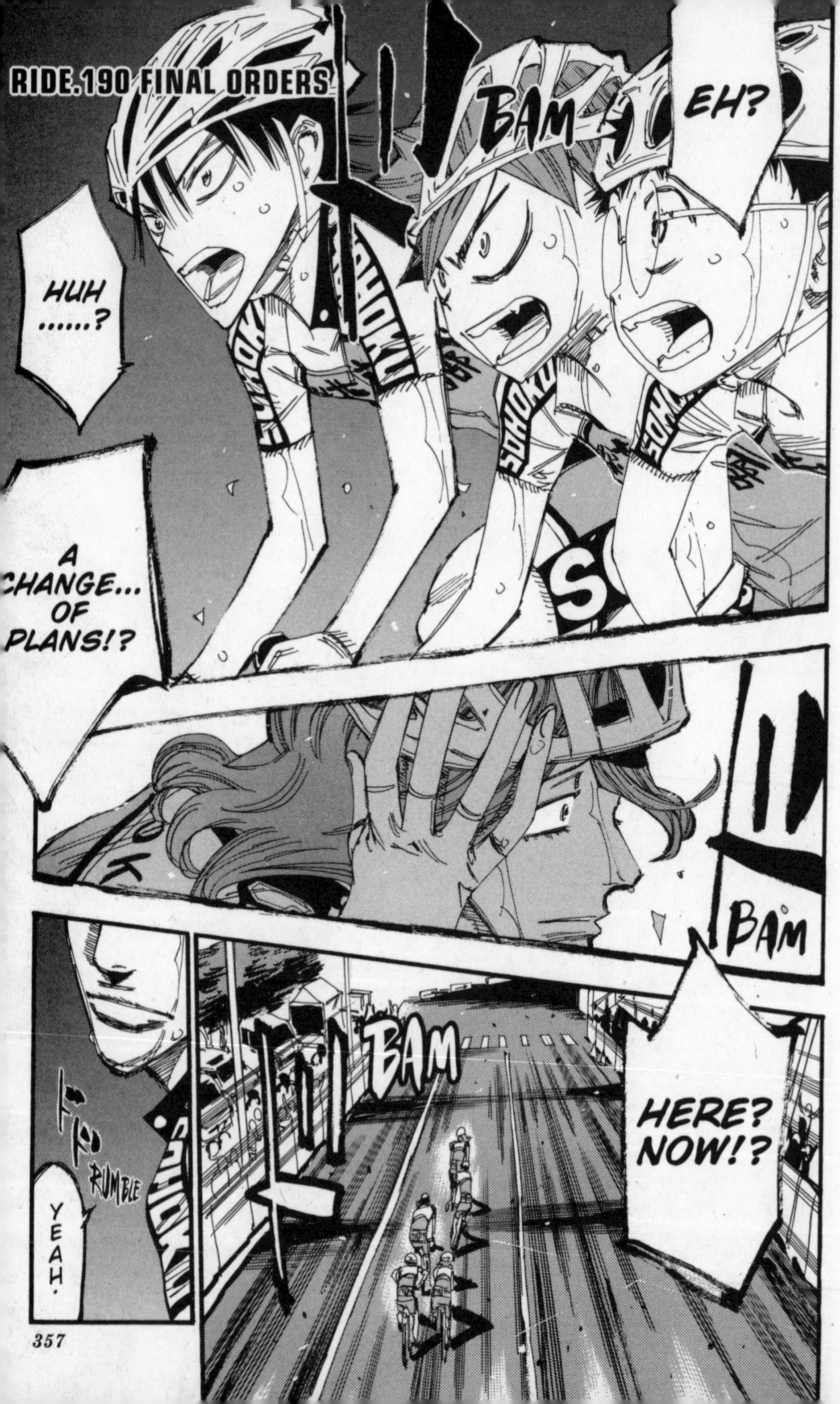
RIDE.190 FINAL ORDERS
EH?
BAM
HUH ......?
A CHANGE... OF PLANS!?
BAM
HERE? NOW!?
BAM
RUMBLE
YEAH.

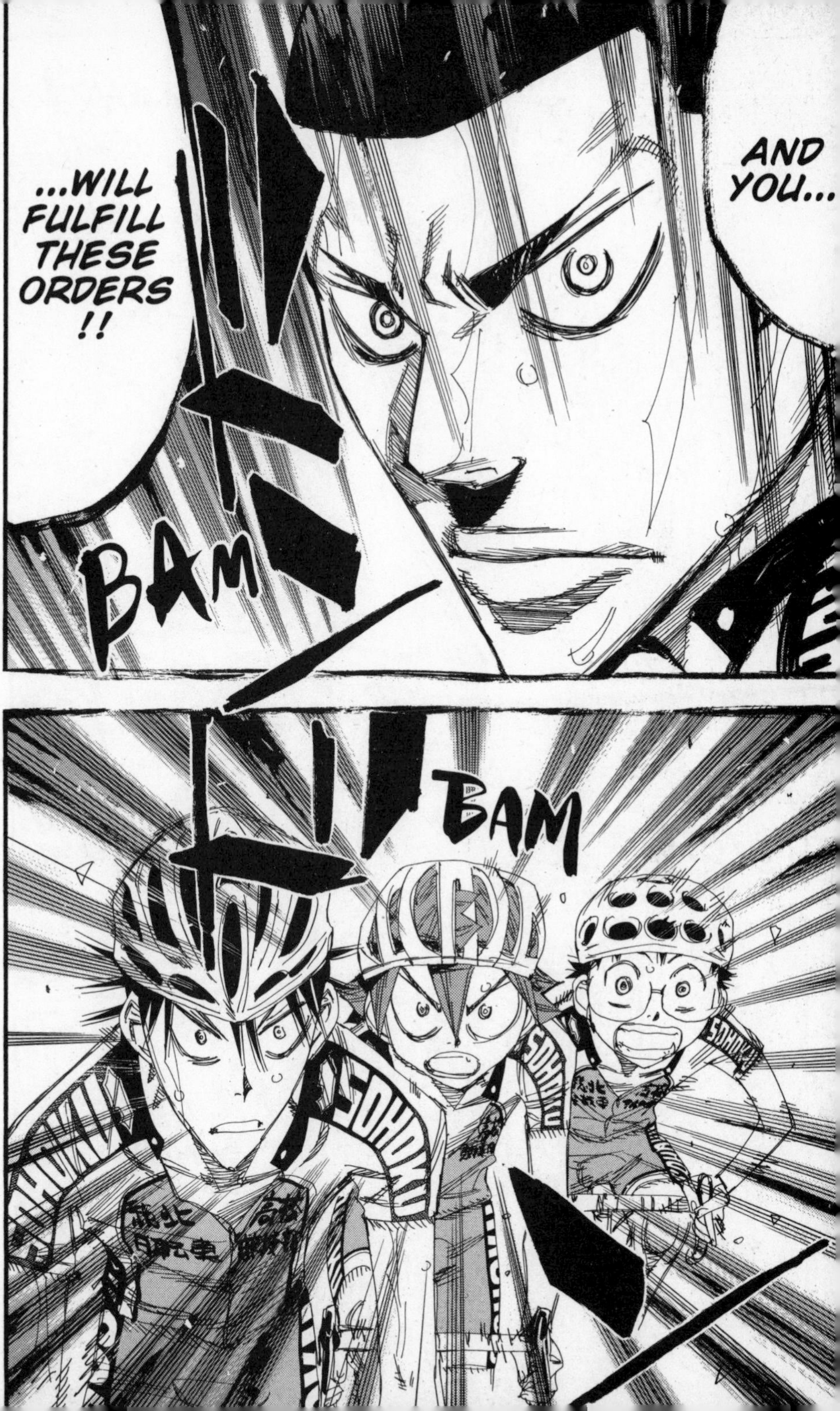
AND YOU...
...WILL FULFILL THESE ORDERS !!
BAM
BAM

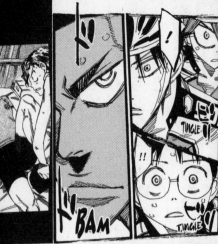

BAM

TINGLE

TINGLE

GRIP

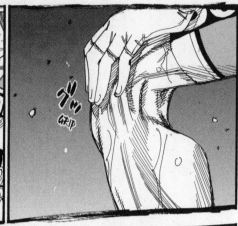

TINGLE

KINJOU-SAN!! —IS THAT WHY!?

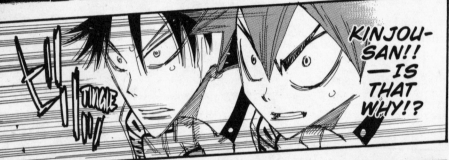

BAM BAM BAM BAM

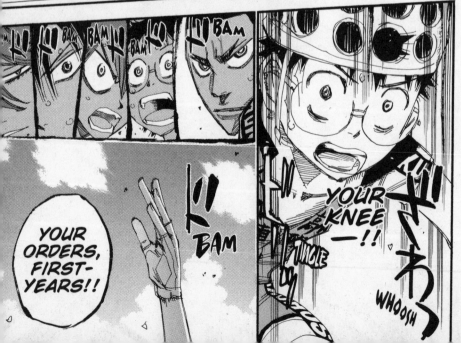

YOUR ORDERS, FIRST-YEARS!!

BAM

YOUR KNEE —!!

TINGLE

WHOOSH

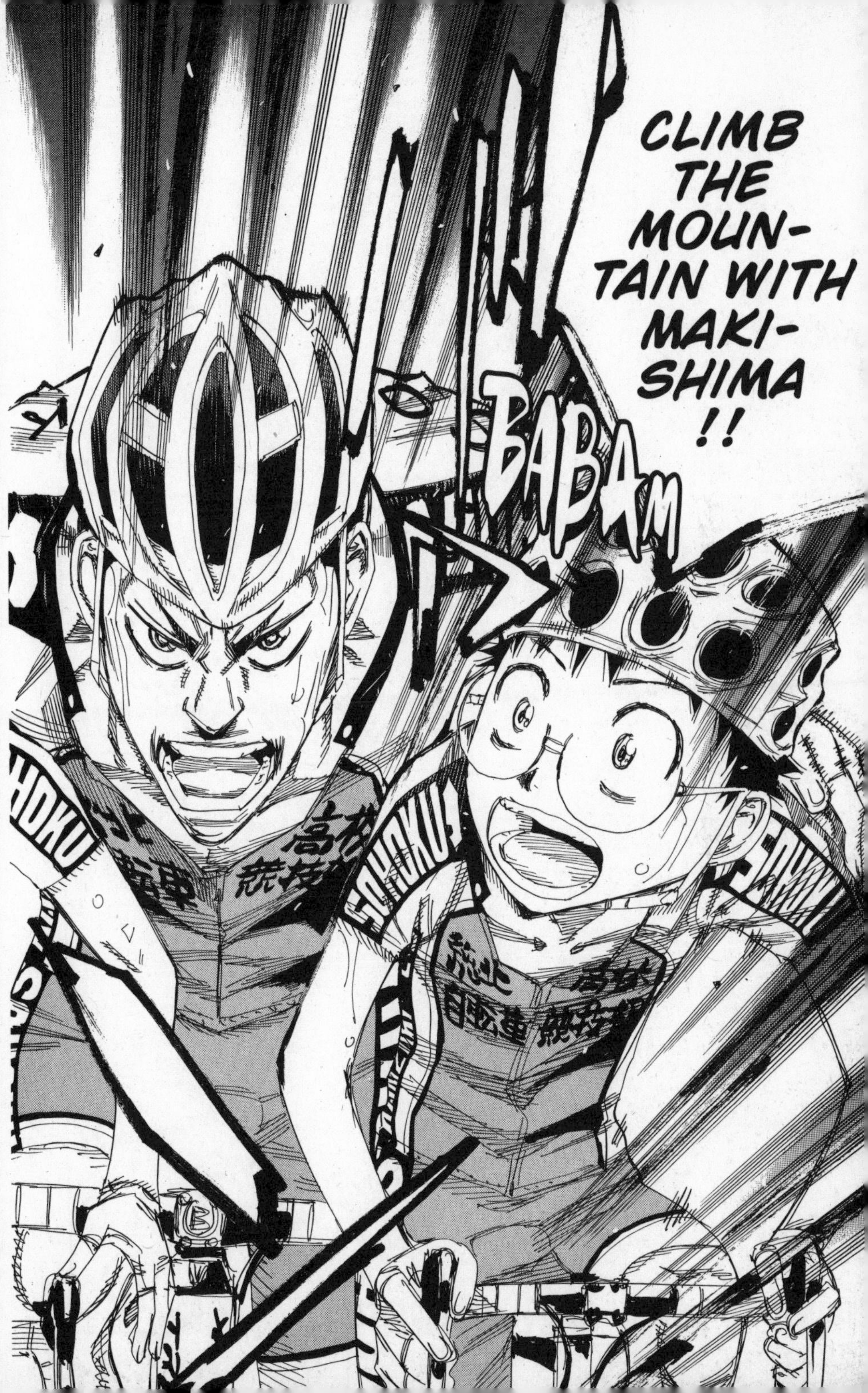
CLIMB THE MOUNTAIN WITH MAKISHIMA!!
BABAM

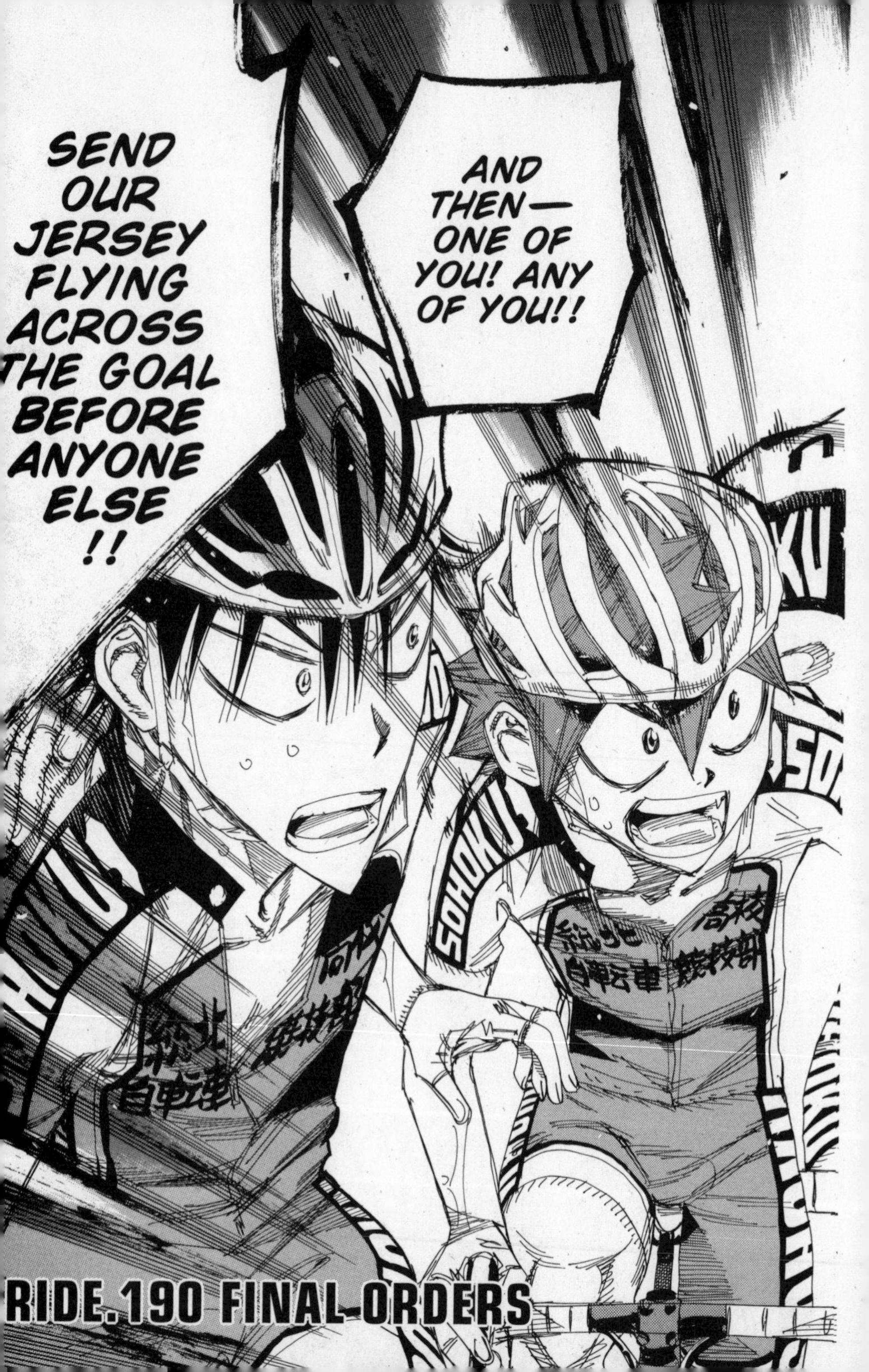
AND THEN— ONE OF YOU! ANY OF YOU!!
SEND OUR JERSEY FLYING ACROSS THE GOAL BEFORE ANYONE ELSE !!
RIDE.190 FINAL ORDERS

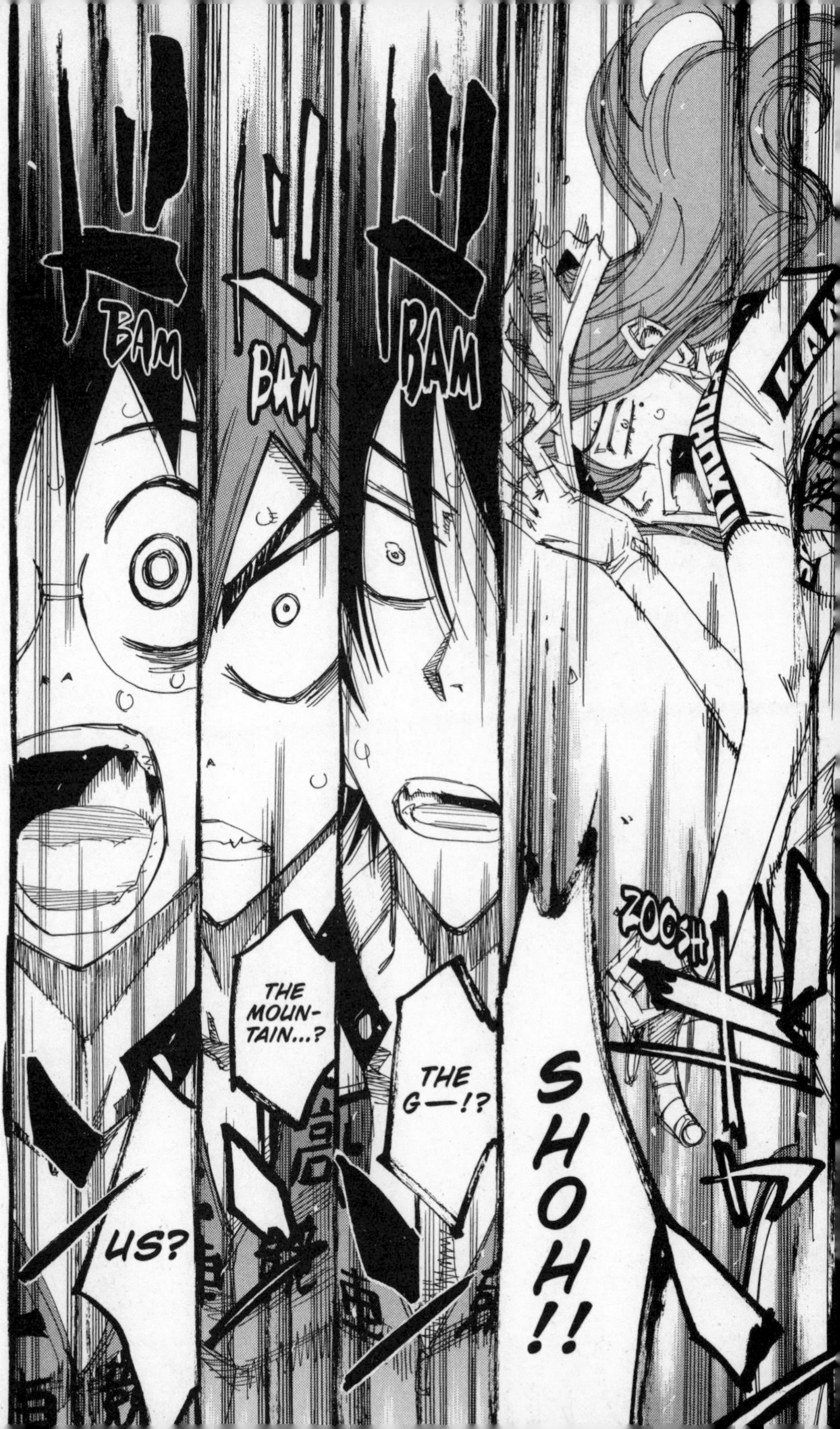
ZOOSH
SHOH!!
BAM
THE G—!?
BAM
THE MOUN-TAIN...?
BAM
US?

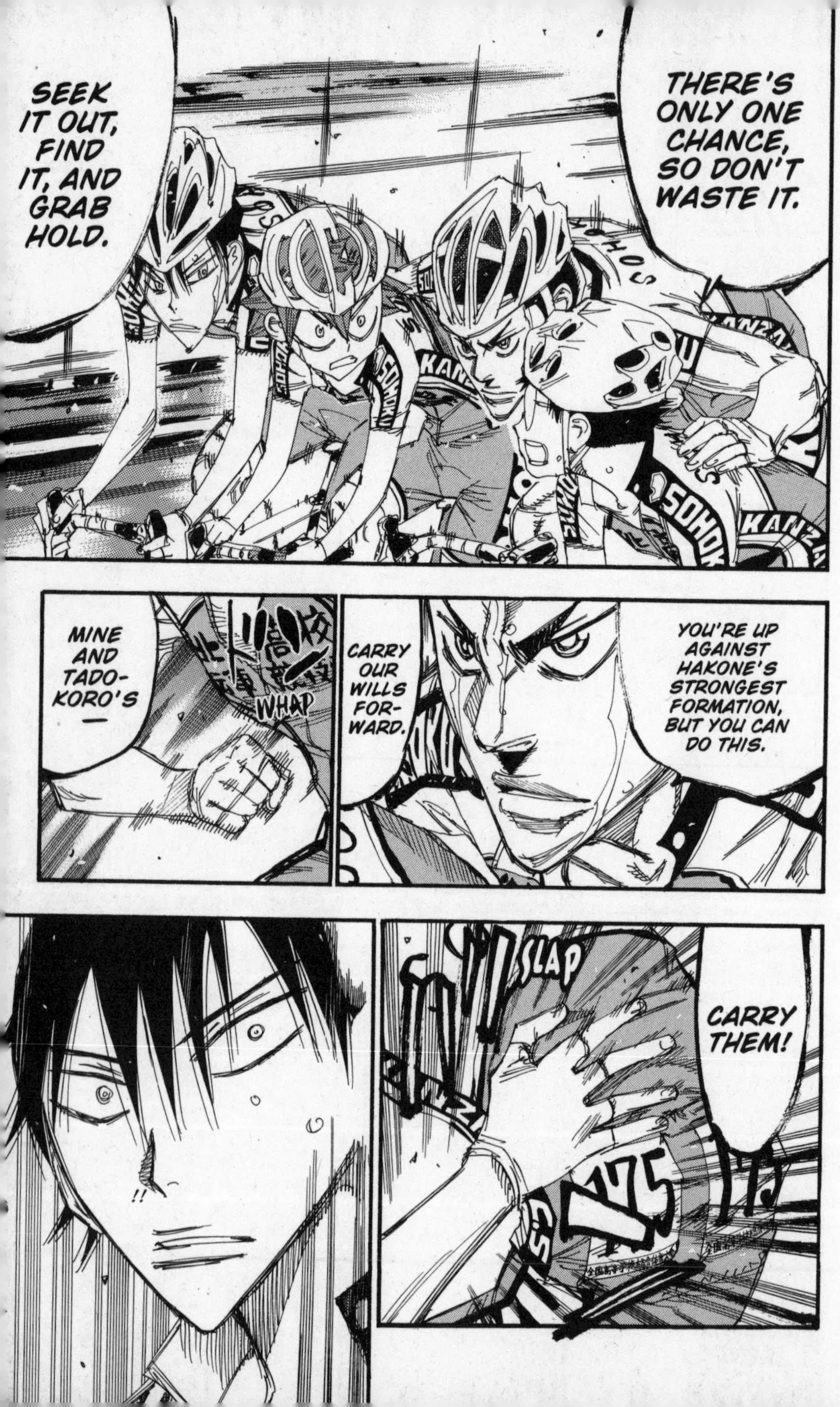
THERE'S ONLY ONE CHANCE, SO DON'T WASTE IT.
SEEK IT OUT, FIND IT, AND GRAB HOLD.
YOU'RE UP AGAINST HAKONE'S STRONGEST FORMATION, BUT YOU CAN DO THIS.
CARRY OUR WILLS FOR-WARD.
MINE AND TADO-KORO'S —
WHAP
SLAP
CARRY THEM!
!!

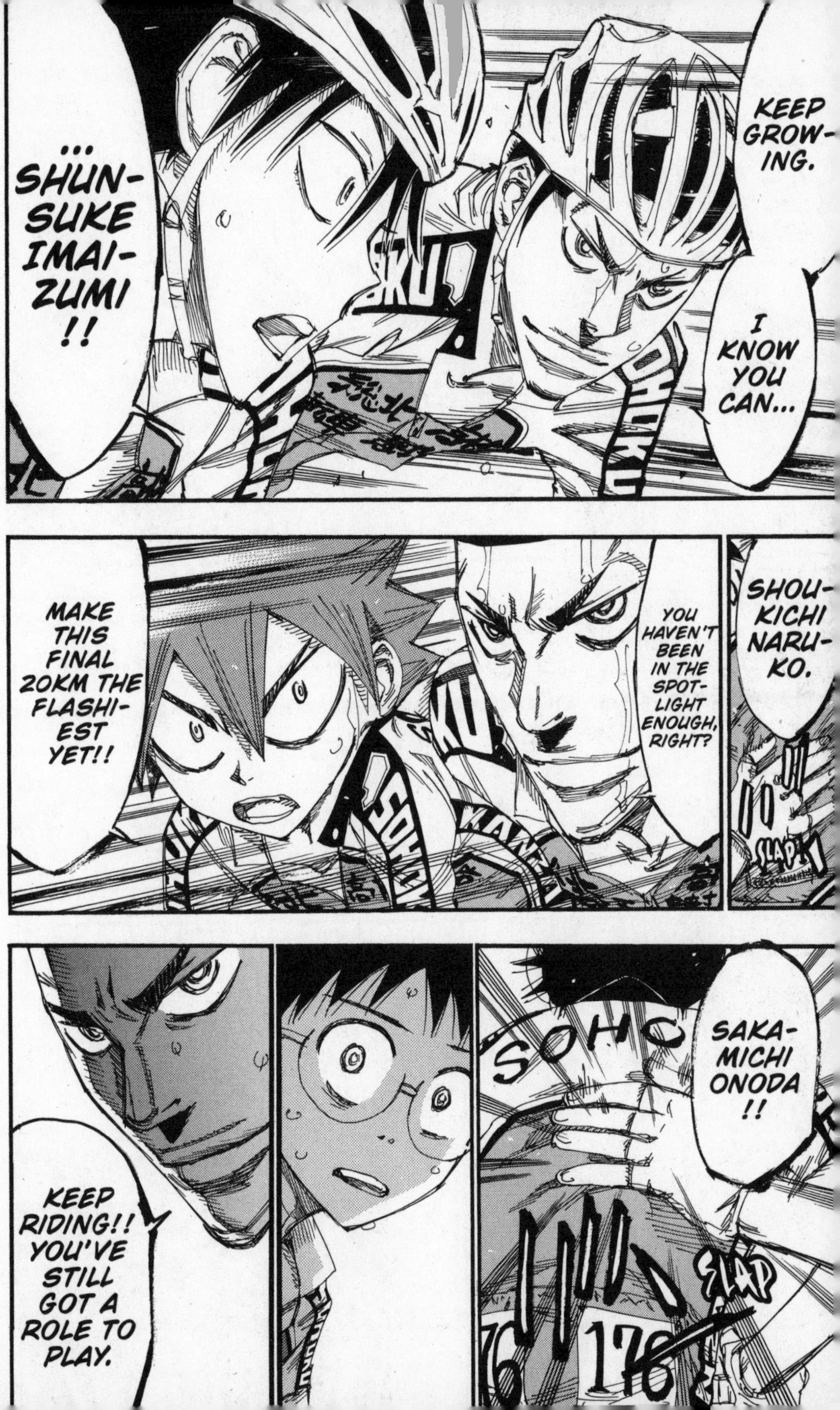
KEEP GROWING.
I KNOW YOU CAN...
...SHUNSUKE IMAIZUMI!!
SHOUKICHI NARUKO.
SLAP
YOU HAVEN'T BEEN IN THE SPOTLIGHT ENOUGH, RIGHT?
MAKE THIS FINAL 20KM THE FLASHIEST YET!!
SAKAMICHI ONODA!!
SLAP
KEEP RIDING!! YOU'VE STILL GOT A ROLE TO PLAY.

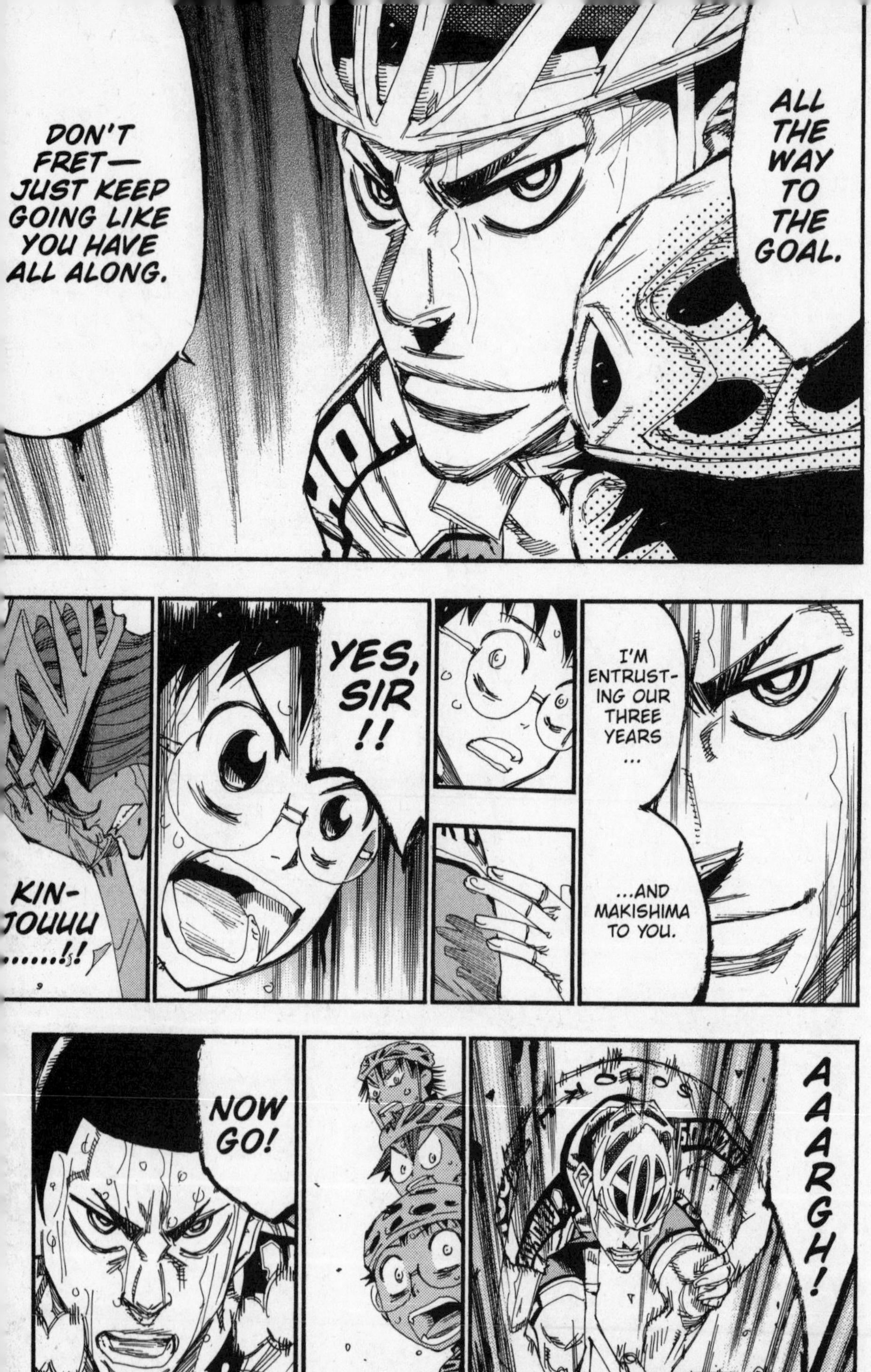
ALL THE WAY TO THE GOAL.
DON'T FRET—JUST KEEP GOING LIKE YOU HAVE ALL ALONG.
I'M ENTRUST-ING OUR THREE YEARS...
...AND MAKISHIMA TO YOU.
YES, SIR!!
KIN-TOUUU......!!
AAAARGH!
NOW GO!

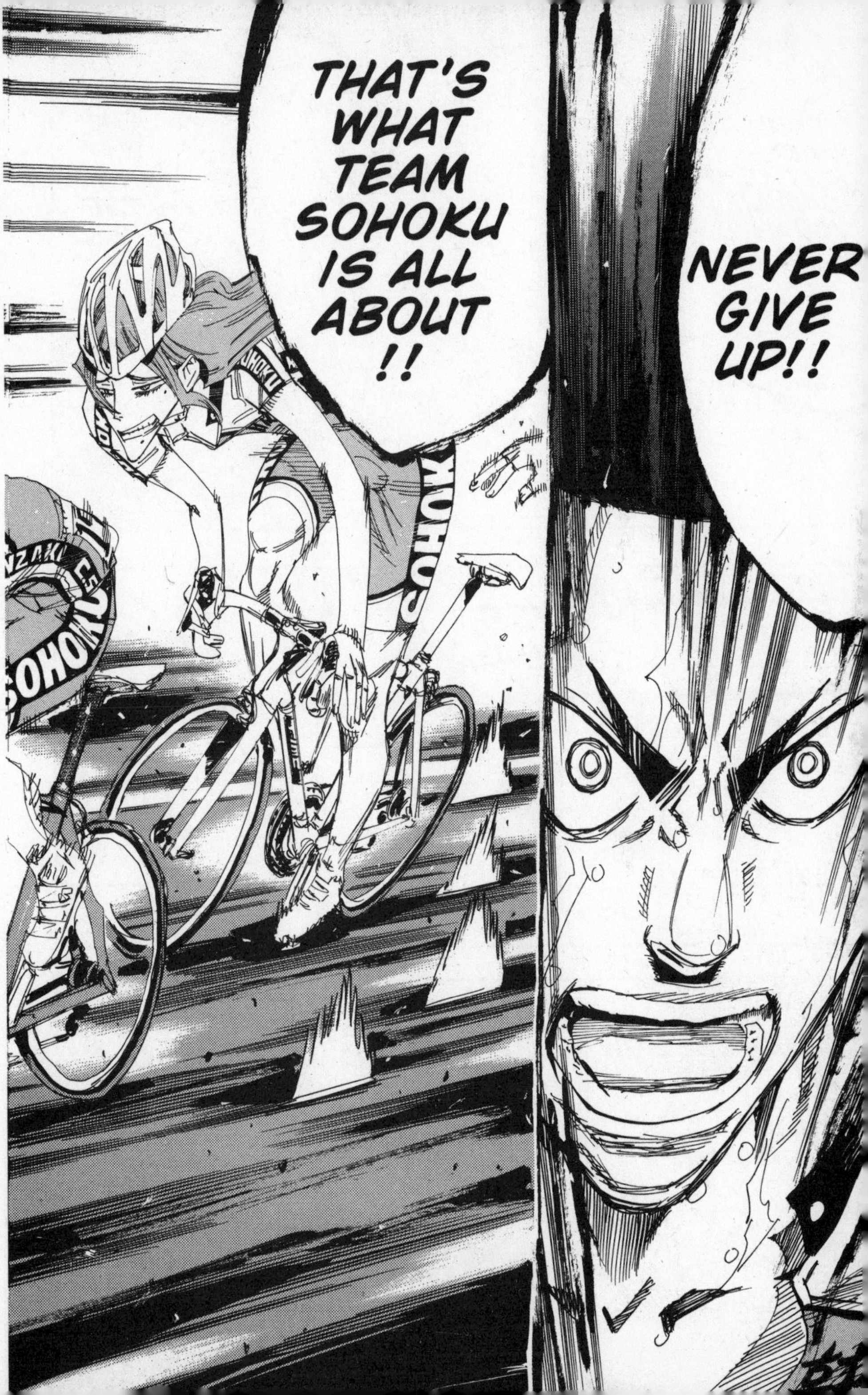
NEVER GIVE UP!!
THAT'S WHAT TEAM SOHOKU IS ALL ABOUT!!

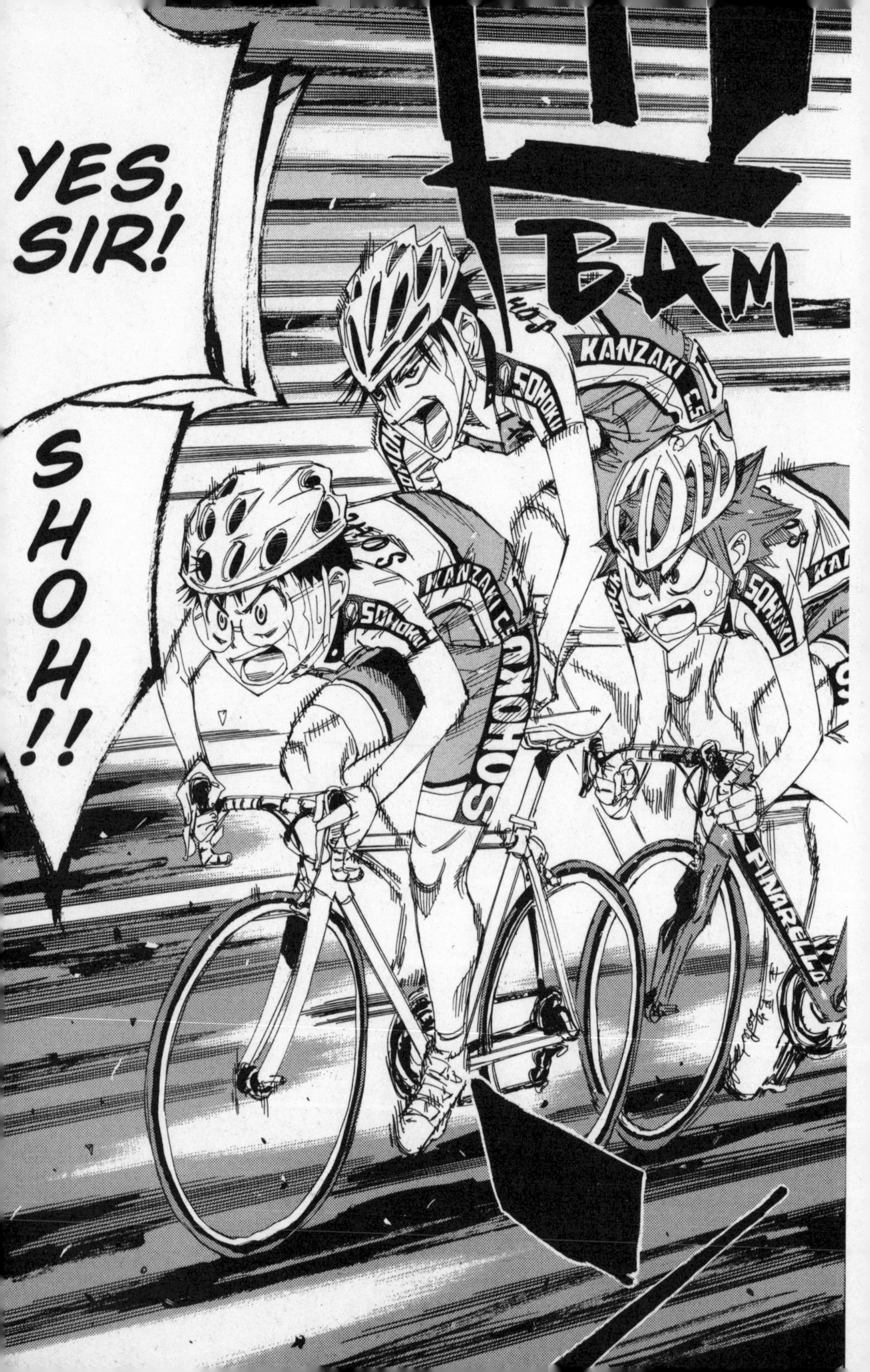
BAM
YES, SIR!
SHOH!!

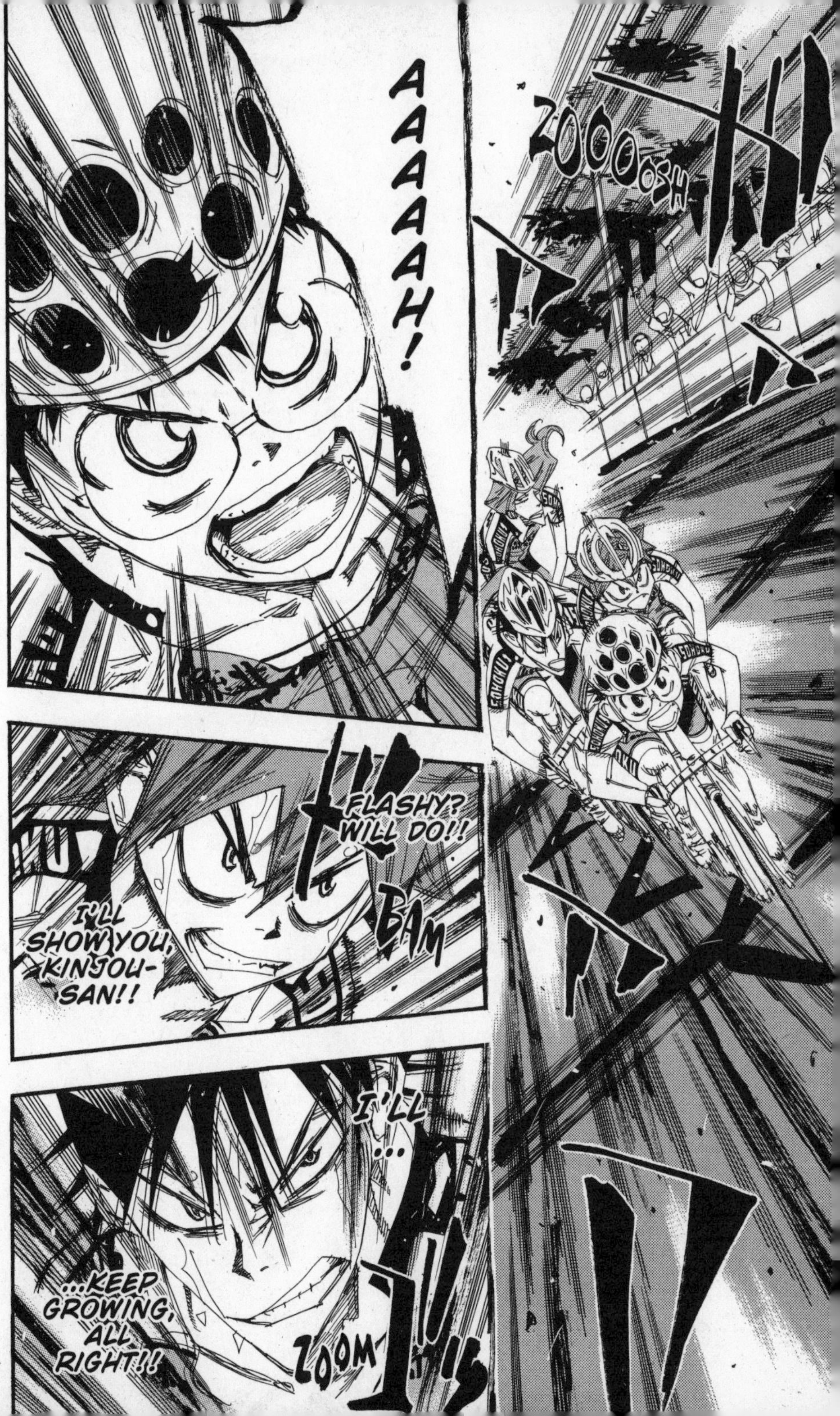
ZOOOOSH
AAAAAH!
FLASHY? WILL DO!!
BAM
I'LL SHOW YOU, KINJOU-SAN!!
I'LL...
...KEEP GROWING, ALL RIGHT!!
ZOOM

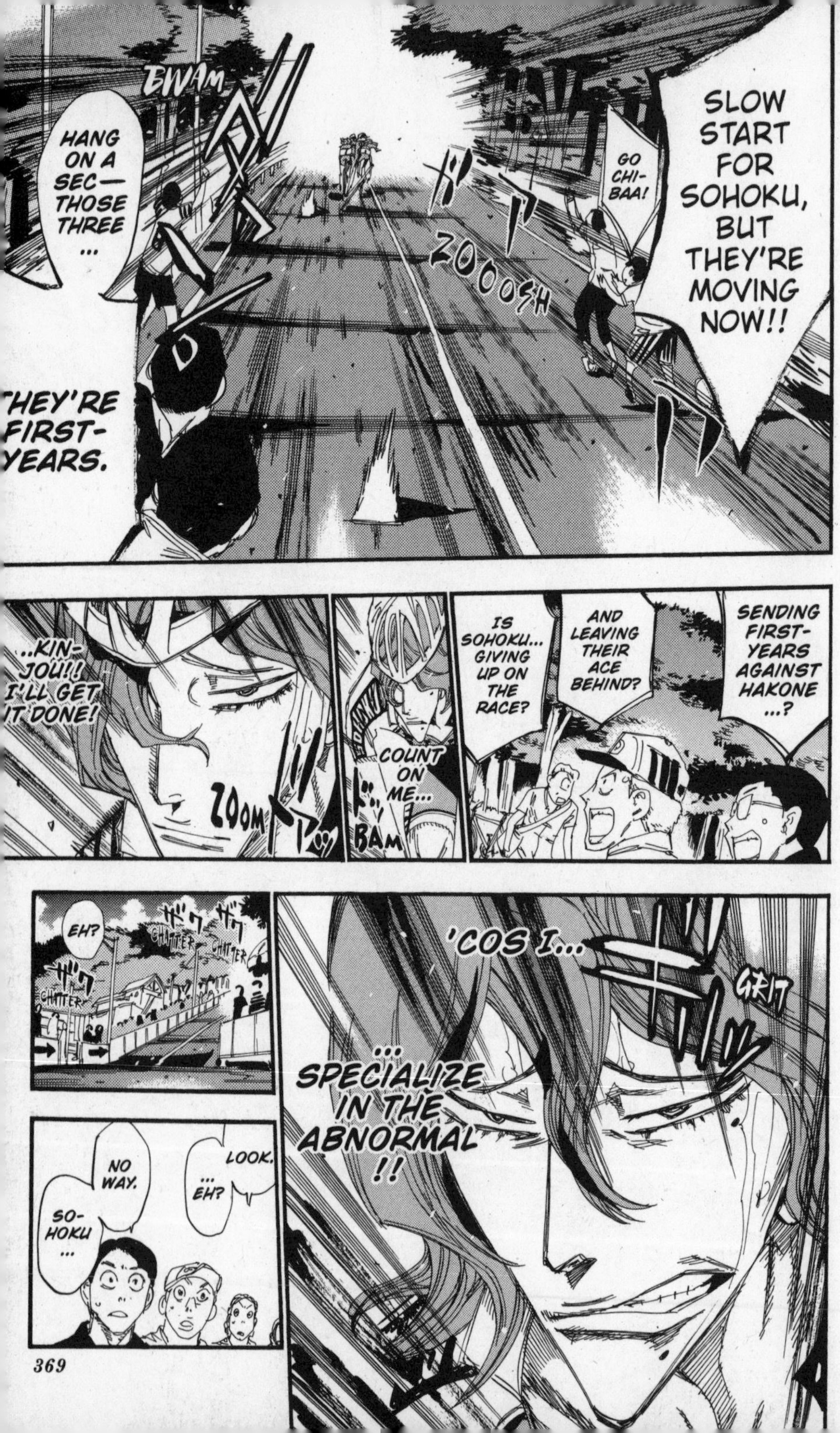
SLOW START FOR SOHOKU, BUT THEY'RE MOVING NOW!!
GO CHIBAA!
ZOOOSH
BWAM
HANG ON A SEC— THOSE THREE ...
THEY'RE FIRST-YEARS.
SENDING FIRST-YEARS AGAINST HAKONE ...?
AND LEAVING THEIR ACE BEHIND?
IS SOHOKU... GIVING UP ON THE RACE?
COUNT ON ME...
BAM
...KIN-JOU!! I'LL GET IT DONE!
ZOOM
'COS I...
GRIT
... SPECIALIZE IN THE ABNORMAL !!
EH?
CHATTER
CHATTER
CHATTER
LOOK.
... EH?
NO WAY.
SO-HOKU ...

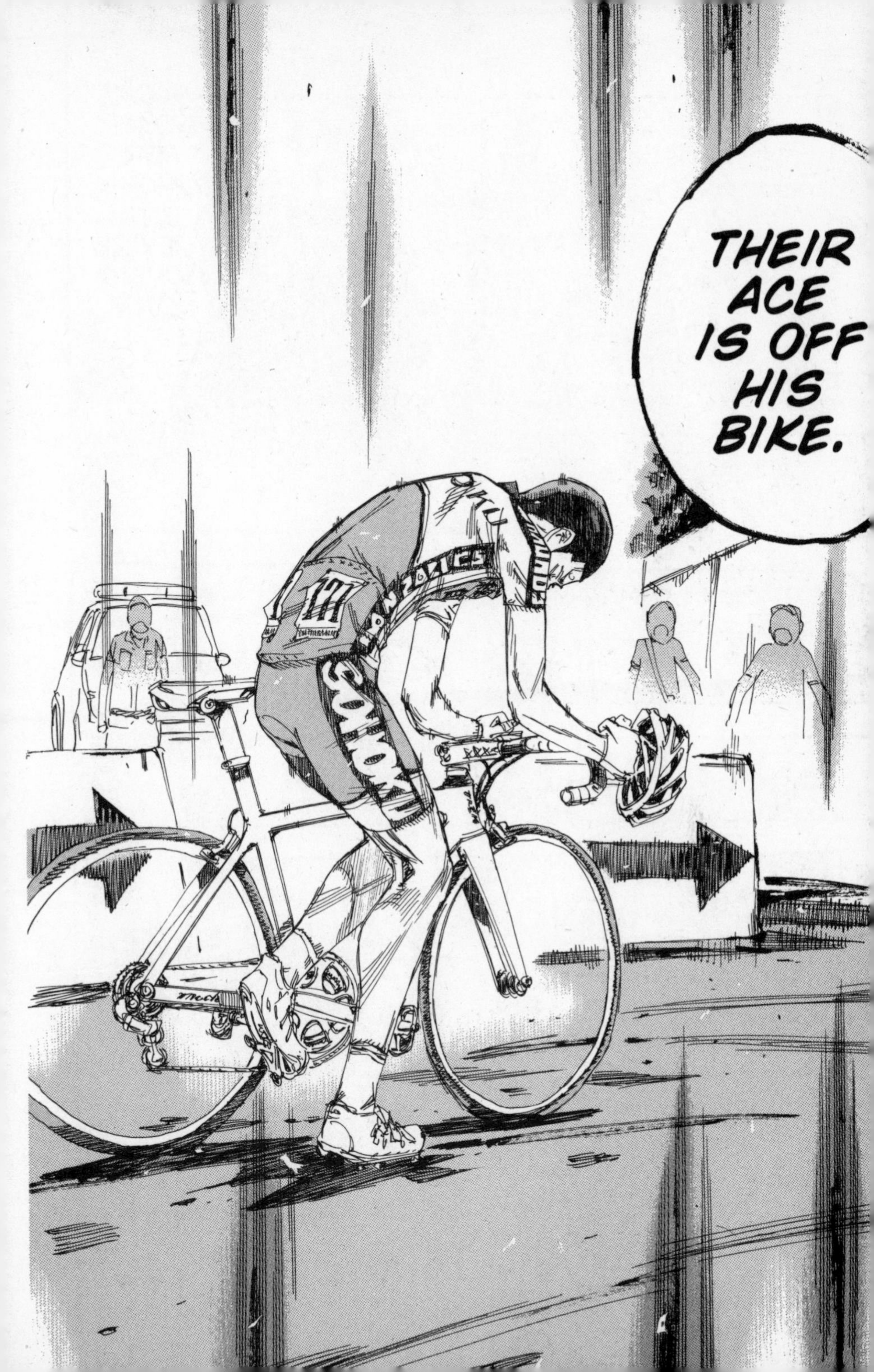
THEIR ACE IS OFF HIS BIKE.

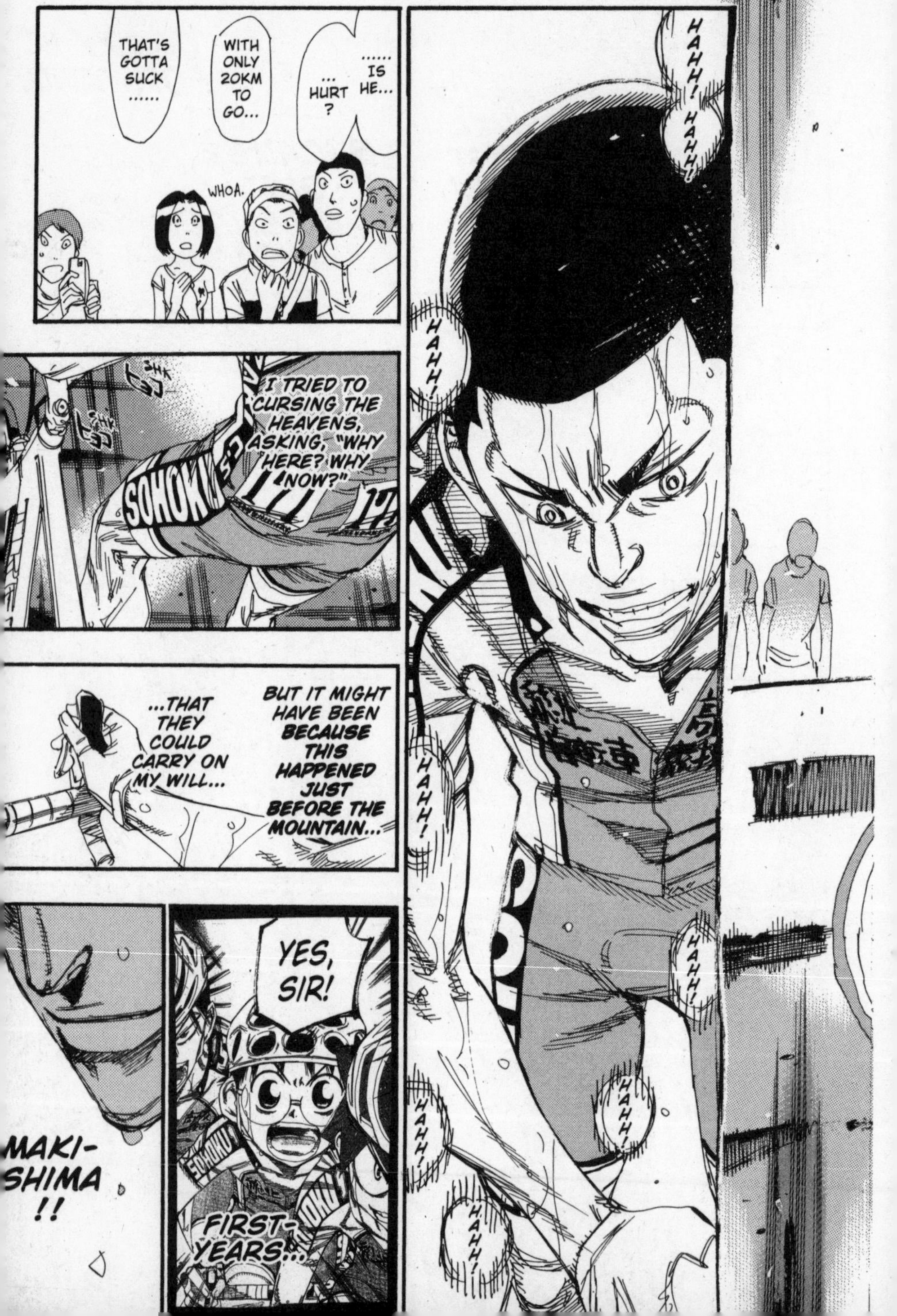
HAHH! HAHH!
HAHH!
HAHH!
HAHH!
HAHH!
HAHH!
......IS HE...
...HURT?
WITH ONLY 20KM TO GO...
THAT'S GOTTA SUCK ......
WHOA.
SHK
SHK
I TRIED TO CURSING THE HEAVENS, ASKING, "WHY HERE? WHY NOW?"
BUT IT MIGHT HAVE BEEN BECAUSE THIS HAPPENED JUST BEFORE THE MOUNTAIN...
...THAT THEY COULD CARRY ON MY WILL...
YES, SIR!
FIRST-YEARS...
MAKI-SHIMA!!

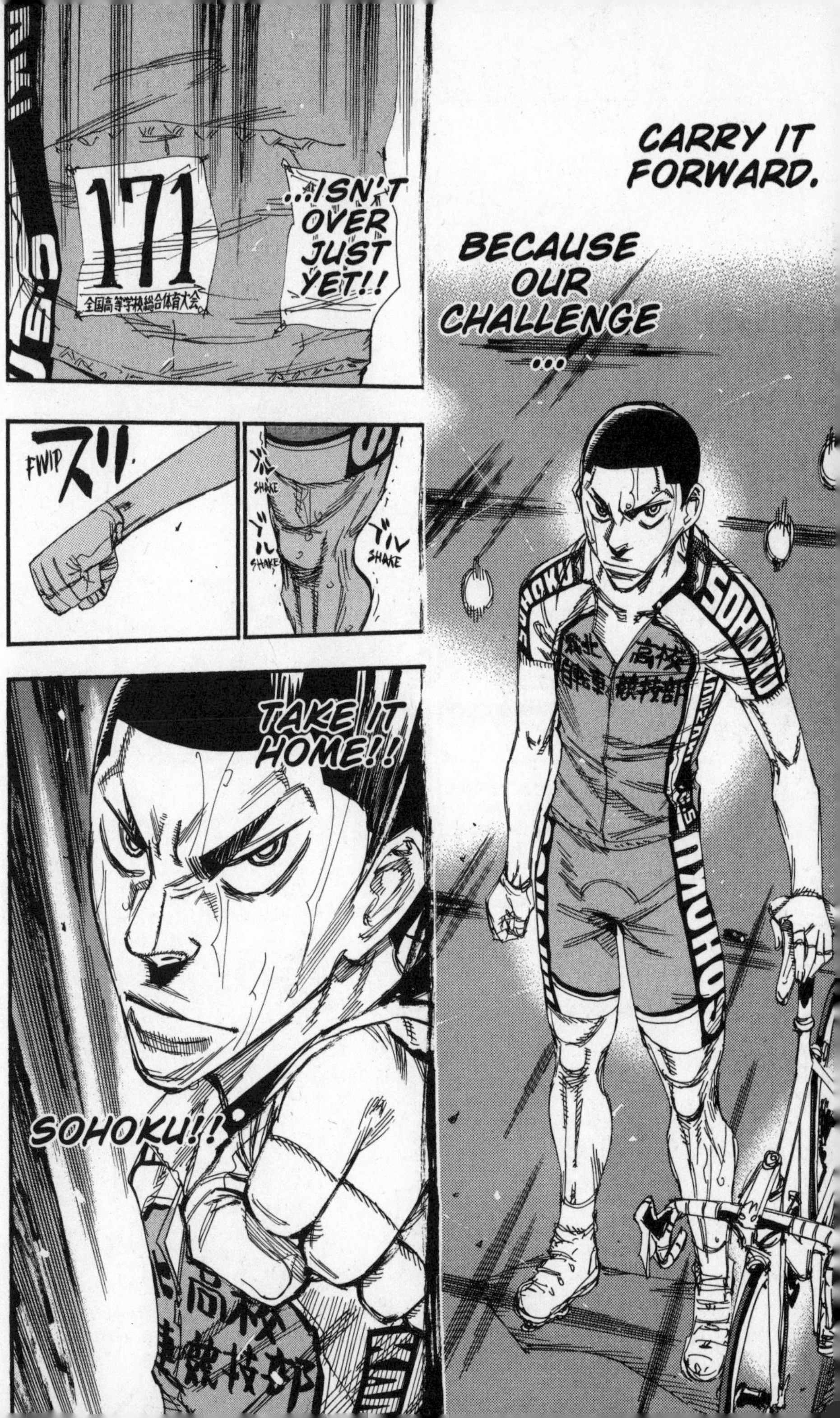
CARRY IT FORWARD.
BECAUSE OUR CHALLENGE...
SOHOKU
総北 高校
自転車 競技部
171
全国高等学校総合体育大会
...ISN'T OVER JUST YET!!
ブル
SHAKE
ブル
SHAKE
ブル
SHAKE
FWIP スリ
TAKE IT HOME!!
SOHOKU!!

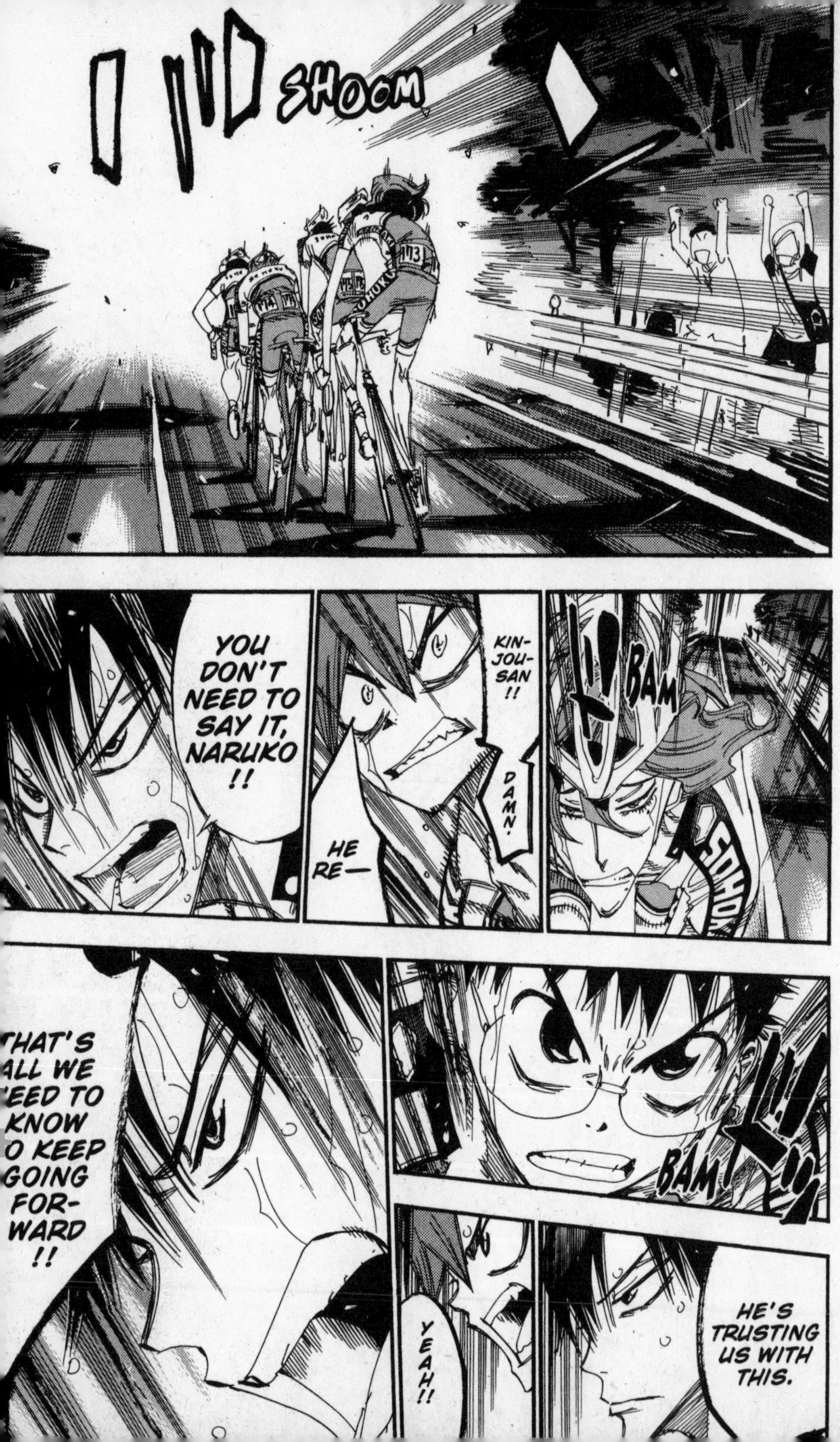

SHOOM
BAM
KIN-JOU-SAN!!
DAMN.
HE RE—
YOU DON'T NEED TO SAY IT, NARUKO!!
BAM
HE'S TRUSTING US WITH THIS.
YEAH!!
THAT'S ALL WE EED TO KNOW O KEEP GOING FOR-WARD!!

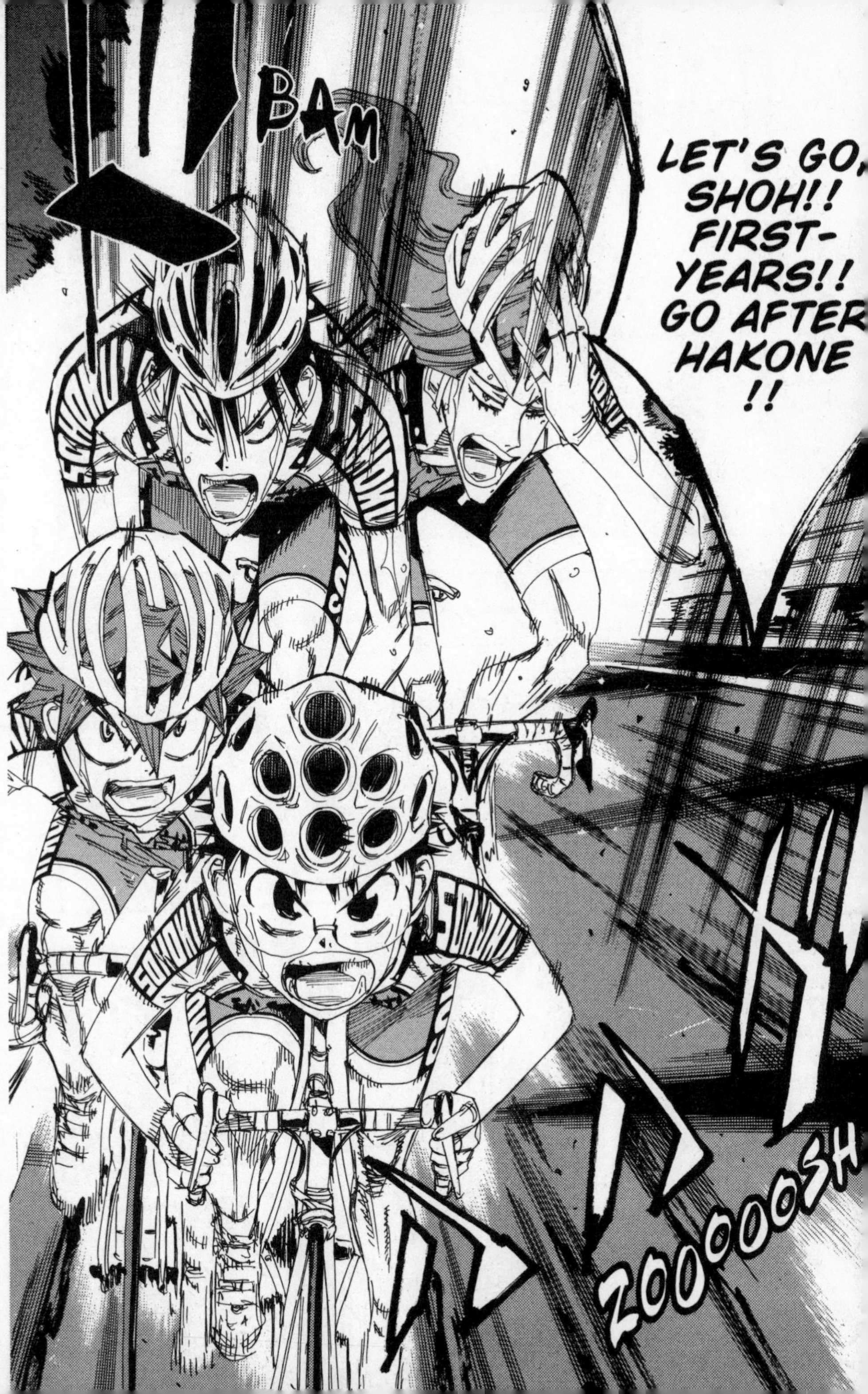
BAM
LET'S GO, SHOH!! FIRST-YEARS!! GO AFTER HAKONE!!
ZOOOOOSH

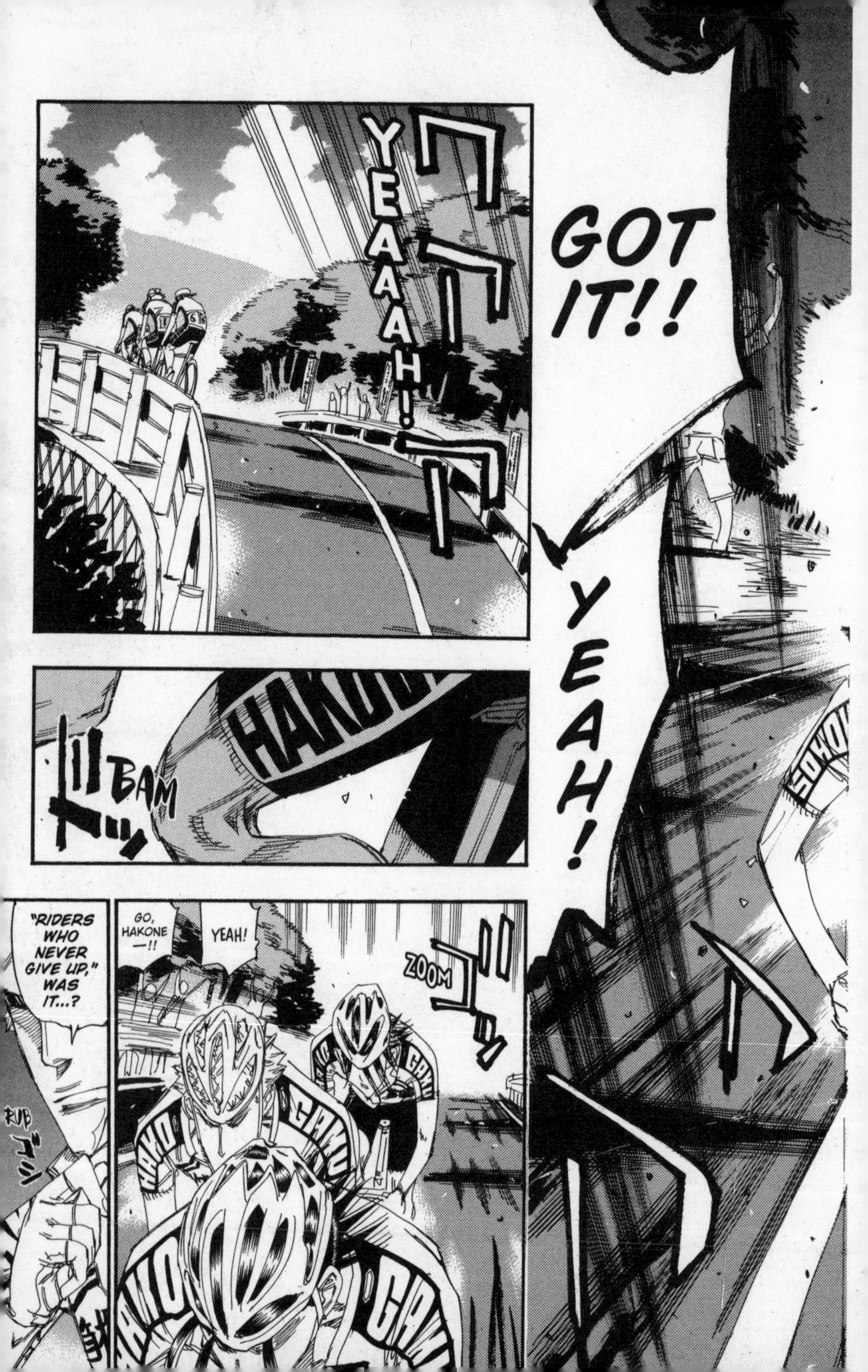
GOT IT!!
YEAH!
YEAAAAH!
BAM
ZOOM
YEAH!
GO, HAKONE—!!
"RIDERS WHO NEVER GIVE UP," WAS IT...?
RUB

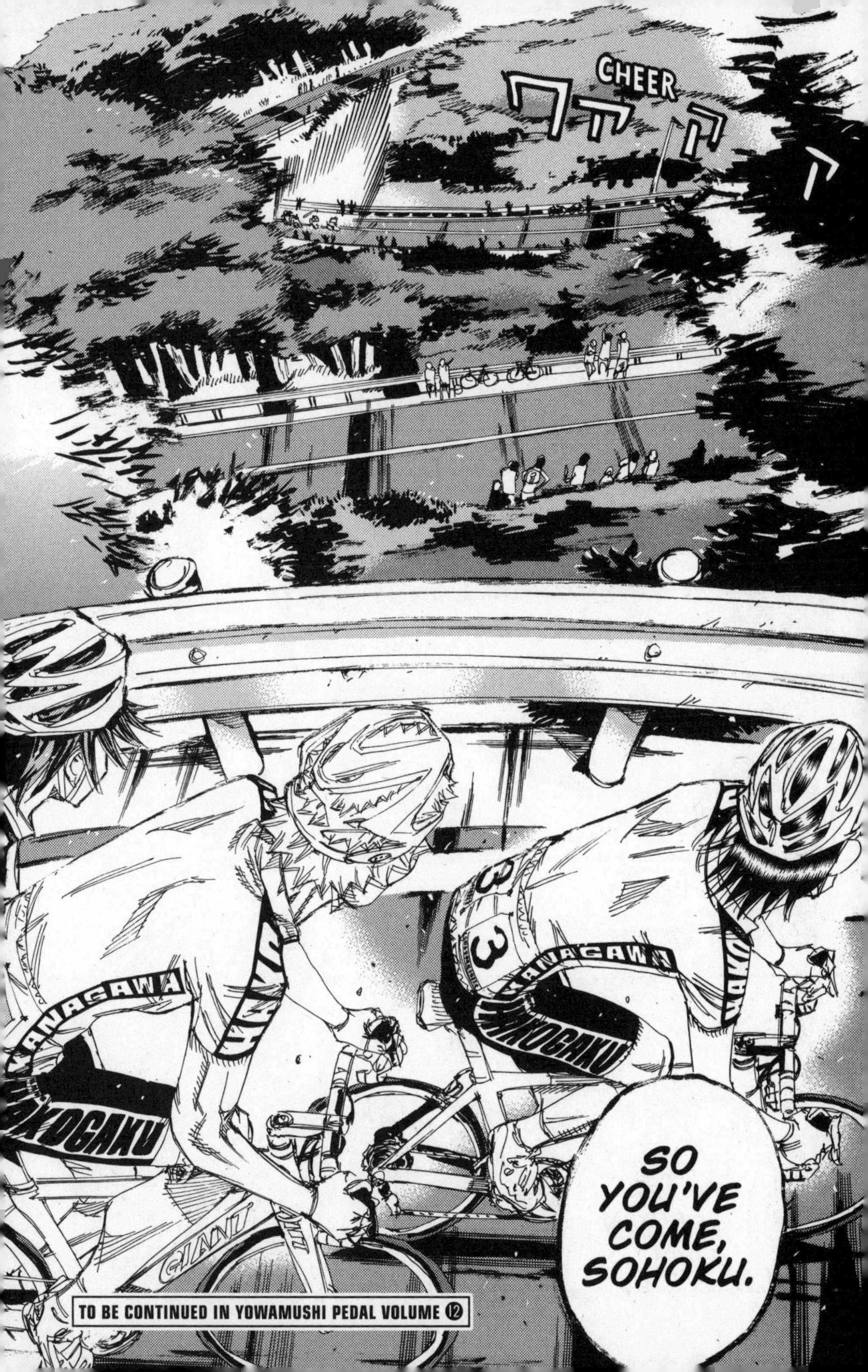
CHEER
SO YOU'VE COME, SOHOKU.
TO BE CONTINUED IN YOWAMUSHI PEDAL VOLUME 12

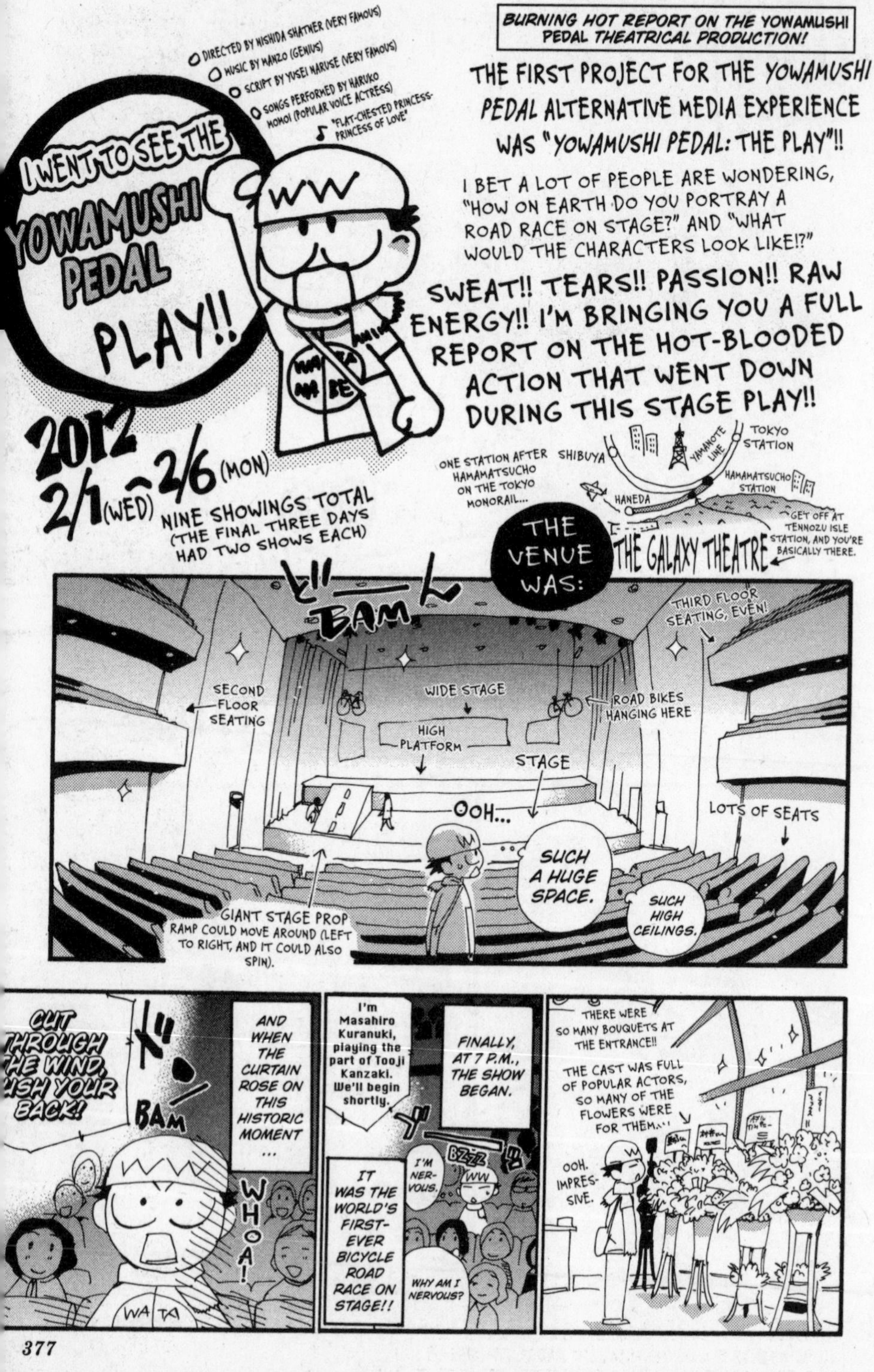
BURNING HOT REPORT ON THE YOWAMUSHI PEDAL THEATRICAL PRODUCTION!
THE FIRST PROJECT FOR THE YOWAMUSHI PEDAL ALTERNATIVE MEDIA EXPERIENCE WAS "YOWAMUSHI PEDAL: THE PLAY"!!
I BET A LOT OF PEOPLE ARE WONDERING, "HOW ON EARTH DO YOU PORTRAY A ROAD RACE ON STAGE?" AND "WHAT WOULD THE CHARACTERS LOOK LIKE!?"
SWEAT!! TEARS!! PASSION!! RAW ENERGY!! I'M BRINGING YOU A FULL REPORT ON THE HOT-BLOODED ACTION THAT WENT DOWN DURING THIS STAGE PLAY!!
I WENT TO SEE THE YOWAMUSHI PEDAL PLAY!!
DIRECTED BY NISHIDA SHATNER (VERY FAMOUS)
MUSIC BY MANZO (GENIUS)
SCRIPT BY YUSEI NARUSE (VERY FAMOUS)
SONGS PERFORMED BY HARUKO MOMOI (POPULAR VOICE ACTRESS)
"FLAT-CHESTED PRINCESS-PRINCESS OF LOVE"
WW
WATA NABE
AMI
TOKYO STATION
YAMANOTE LINE
SHIBUYA
ONE STATION AFTER HAMAMATSUCHO ON THE TOKYO MONORAIL...
HAMAMATSUCHO STATION
HANEDA
GET OFF AT TENNOZU ISLE STATION, AND YOU'RE BASICALLY THERE.
THE VENUE WAS:
THE GALAXY THEATRE
2012 2/1 (WED) ~ 2/6 (MON)
NINE SHOWINGS TOTAL (THE FINAL THREE DAYS HAD TWO SHOWS EACH)
BAM
THIRD FLOOR SEATING, EVEN!
ROAD BIKES HANGING HERE
WIDE STAGE
SECOND FLOOR SEATING
HIGH PLATFORM
STAGE
LOTS OF SEATS
OOH...
SUCH A HUGE SPACE.
SUCH HIGH CEILINGS.
GIANT STAGE PROP RAMP COULD MOVE AROUND (LEFT TO RIGHT, AND IT COULD ALSO SPIN).
THERE WERE SO MANY BOUQUETS AT THE ENTRANCE!!
THE CAST WAS FULL OF POPULAR ACTORS, SO MANY OF THE FLOWERS WERE FOR THEM...
OOH. IMPRESSIVE.
FINALLY, AT 7 P.M., THE SHOW BEGAN.
I'm Masahiro Kuranuki, playing the part of Tooji Kanzaki. We'll begin shortly.
BZZZ
I'M NERVOUS.
IT WAS THE WORLD'S FIRST-EVER BICYCLE ROAD RACE ON STAGE!!
WHY AM I NERVOUS?
AND WHEN THE CURTAIN ROSE ON THIS HISTORIC MOMENT...
BAM
CUT THROUGH THE WIND, USH YOUR BACK!
WHOA!
WA TA

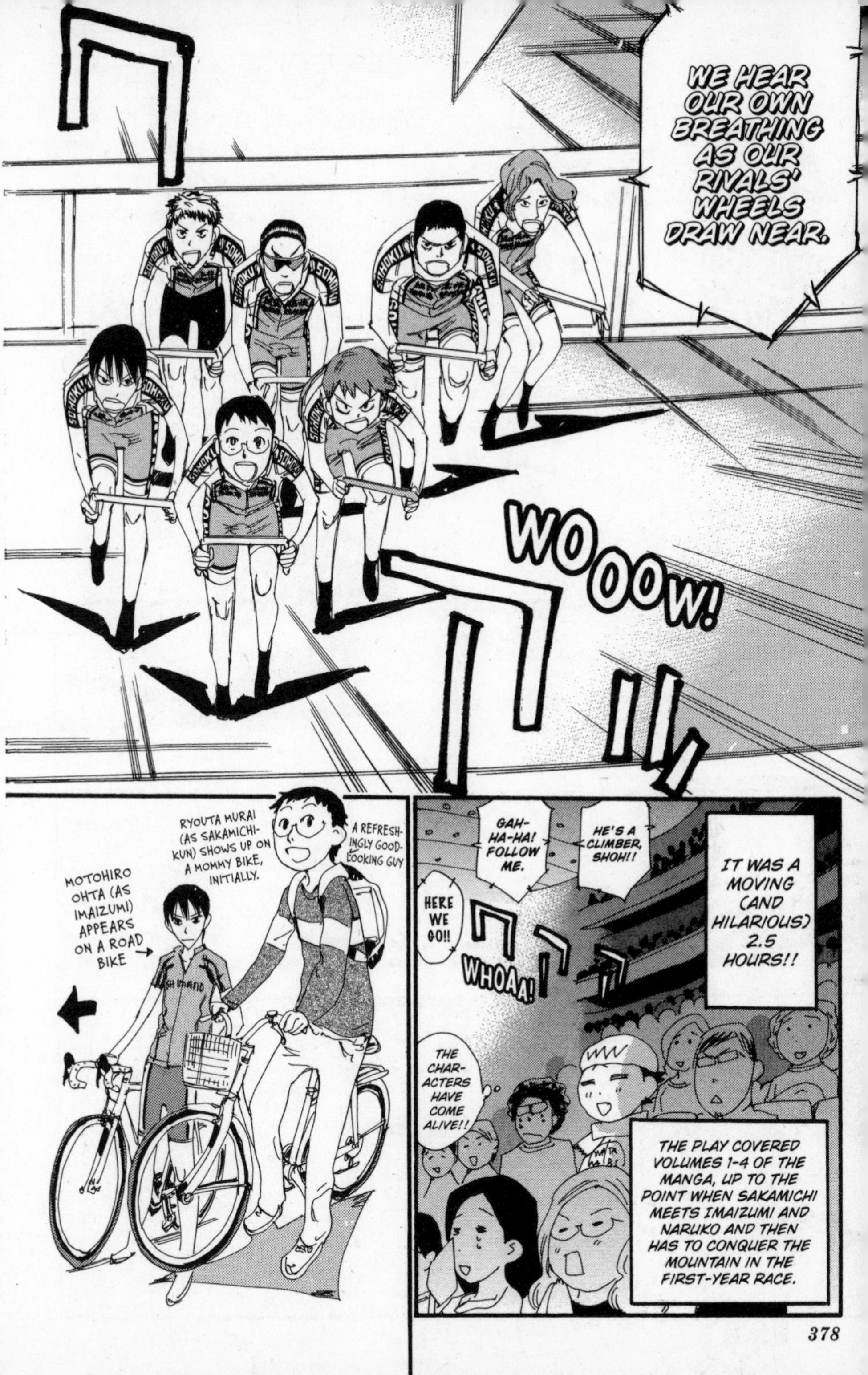
WE HEAR OUR OWN BREATHING AS OUR RIVALS' WHEELS DRAW NEAR.
WOOOOW!
IT WAS A MOVING (AND HILARIOUS) 2.5 HOURS!!
HE'S A CLIMBER, SHOH!!
GAH-HA-HA! FOLLOW ME.
HERE WE GO!!
WHOAA!
THE PLAY COVERED VOLUMES 1-4 OF THE MANGA, UP TO THE POINT WHEN SAKAMICHI MEETS IMAIZUMI AND NARUKO AND THEN HAS TO CONQUER THE MOUNTAIN IN THE FIRST-YEAR RACE.
THE CHARACTERS HAVE COME ALIVE!!
A REFRESHINGLY GOOD-LOOKING GUY
RYOUTA MURAI (AS SAKAMICHI-KUN) SHOWS UP ON A MOMMY BIKE, INITIALLY.
MOTOHIRO OHTA (AS IMAIZUMI) APPEARS ON A ROAD BIKE

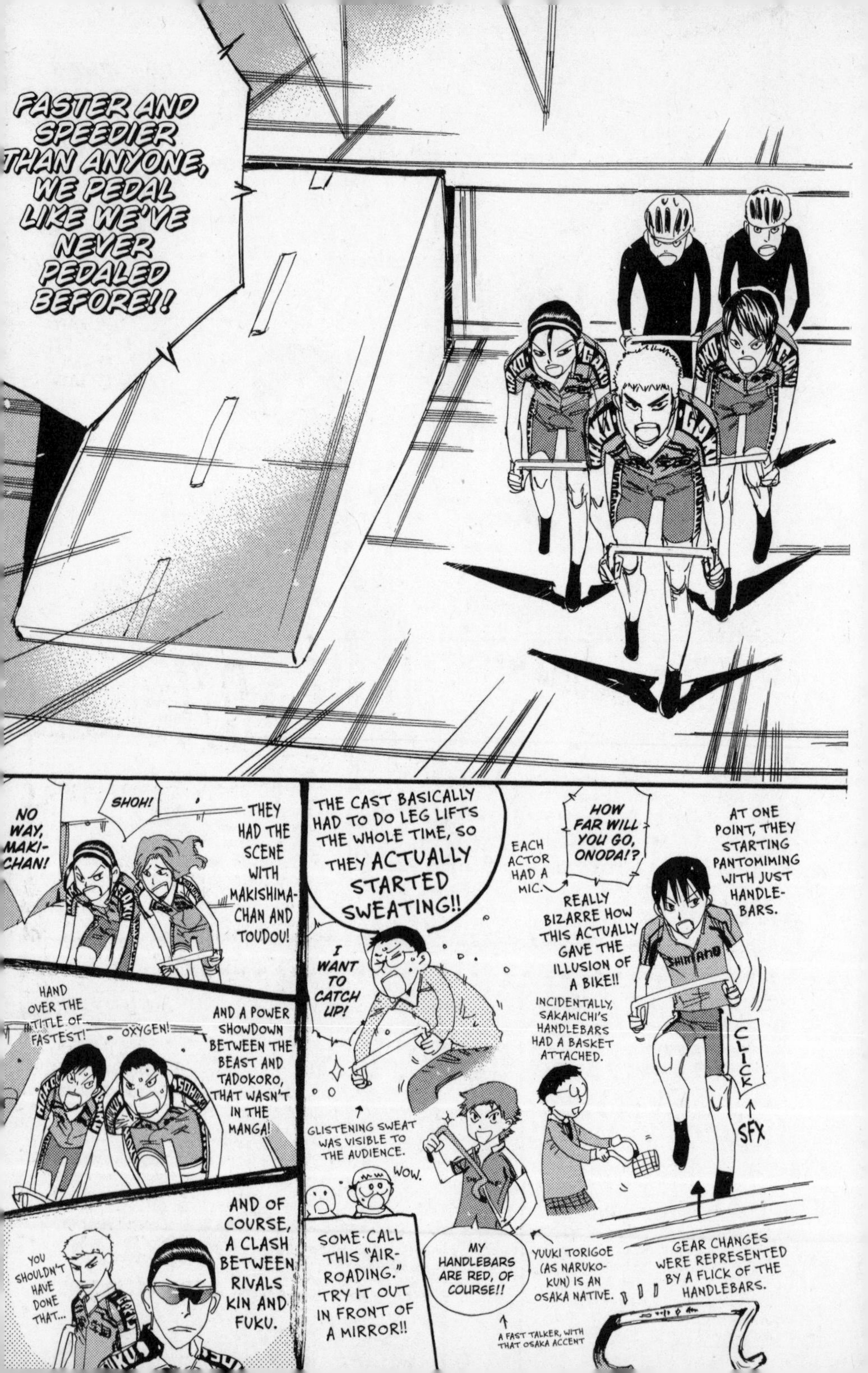
FASTER AND SPEEDIER THAN ANYONE, WE PEDAL LIKE WE'VE NEVER PEDALED BEFORE!!
AT ONE POINT, THEY STARTING PANTOMIMING WITH JUST HANDLEBARS.
HOW FAR WILL YOU GO, ONODA!?
EACH ACTOR HAD A MIC.
THE CAST BASICALLY HAD TO DO LEG LIFTS THE WHOLE TIME, SO THEY ACTUALLY STARTED SWEATING!!
REALLY BIZARRE HOW THIS ACTUALLY GAVE THE ILLUSION OF A BIKE!!
INCIDENTALLY, SAKAMICHI'S HANDLEBARS HAD A BASKET ATTACHED.
CLICK
SFX
I WANT TO CATCH UP!
GLISTENING SWEAT WAS VISIBLE TO THE AUDIENCE.
WOW.
GEAR CHANGES WERE REPRESENTED BY A FLICK OF THE HANDLEBARS.
YUUKI TORIGOE (AS NARUKO-KUN) IS AN OSAKA NATIVE.
MY HANDLEBARS ARE RED, OF COURSE!!
A FAST TALKER, WITH THAT OSAKA ACCENT
SOME CALL THIS "AIR-ROADING." TRY IT OUT IN FRONT OF A MIRROR!!
THEY HAD THE SCENE WITH MAKISHIMA-CHAN AND TOUDOU!
SHOH!
NO WAY, MAKI-CHAN!
AND A POWER SHOWDOWN BETWEEN THE BEAST AND TADOKORO, THAT WASN'T IN THE MANGA!
OXYGEN!
HAND OVER THE TITLE OF FASTEST!
AND OF COURSE, A CLASH BETWEEN RIVALS KIN AND FUKU.
YOU SHOULDN'T HAVE DONE THAT...

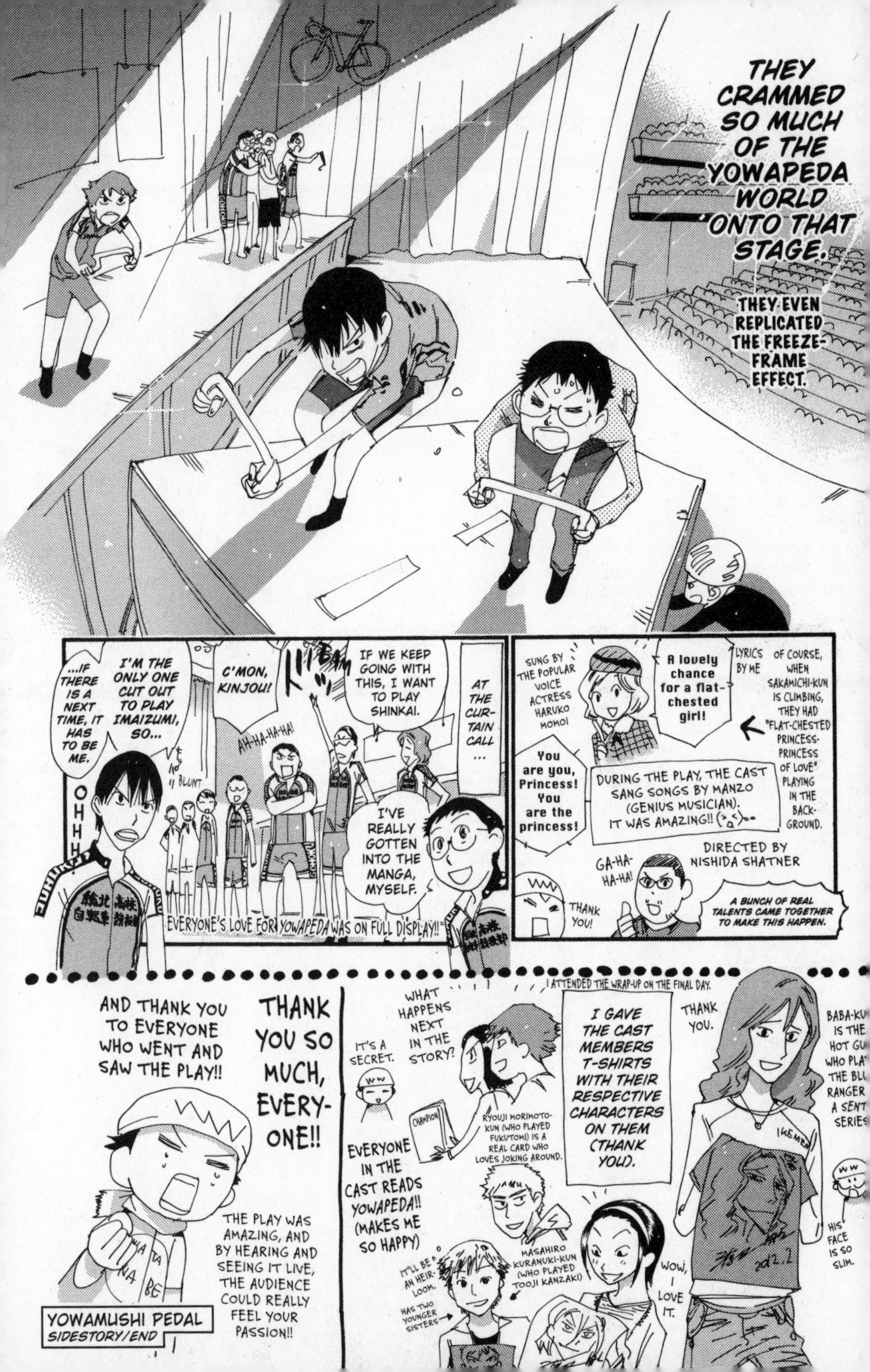
THEY CRAMMED SO MUCH OF THE YOWAPEDA WORLD ONTO THAT STAGE.
THEY EVEN REPLICATED THE FREEZE-FRAME EFFECT.
OF COURSE, WHEN SAKAMICHI-KUN IS CLIMBING, THEY HAD "FLAT-CHESTED PRINCESS-PRINCESS OF LOVE" PLAYING IN THE BACKGROUND.
LYRICS BY ME
A lovely chance for a flat-chested girl!
SUNG BY THE POPULAR VOICE ACTRESS HARUKO MOMOI
You are you, Princess! You are the princess!
DURING THE PLAY, THE CAST SANG SONGS BY MANZO (GENIUS MUSICIAN). IT WAS AMAZING!! (>_<)
DIRECTED BY NISHIDA SHATNER
GA-HA-HA-HA!
A BUNCH OF REAL TALENTS CAME TOGETHER TO MAKE THIS HAPPEN.
THANK YOU!
AT THE CURTAIN CALL...
IF WE KEEP GOING WITH THIS, I WANT TO PLAY SHINKAI.
BAM
C'MON, KINJOU!
I'M THE ONLY ONE CUT OUT TO PLAY IMAIZUMI, SO...
...IF THERE IS A NEXT TIME, IT HAS TO BE ME.
AH-HA-HA-HA!
BLUNT
OHHH
I'VE REALLY GOTTEN INTO THE MANGA, MYSELF.
EVERYONE'S LOVE FOR YOWAPEDA WAS ON FULL DISPLAY!!
I ATTENDED THE WRAP-UP ON THE FINAL DAY.
BABA-KU IS THE HOT GU WHO PLA THE BLU RANGER A SENT SERIE
THANK YOU.
I GAVE THE CAST MEMBERS T-SHIRTS WITH THEIR RESPECTIVE CHARACTERS ON THEM (THANK YOU).
WHAT HAPPENS NEXT IN THE STORY?
IT'S A SECRET.
CHAMPION
RYOUJI MORIMOTO-KUN (WHO PLAYED FUKUTOMI) IS A REAL CARD WHO LOVES JOKING AROUND.
EVERYONE IN THE CAST READS YOWAPEDA!! (MAKES ME SO HAPPY)
HIS FACE IS SO SLIM.
WOW, I LOVE IT.
MASAHIRO KURANUKI-KUN (WHO PLAYED TOOJI KANZAKI)
IT'LL BE AN HEIRLOOM.
HAS TWO YOUNGER SISTERS
THANK YOU SO MUCH, EVERYONE!!
AND THANK YOU TO EVERYONE WHO WENT AND SAW THE PLAY!!
THE PLAY WAS AMAZING, AND BY HEARING AND SEEING IT LIVE, THE AUDIENCE COULD REALLY FEEL YOUR PASSION!!
WATANABE
YOWAMUSHI PEDAL SIDESTORY/END

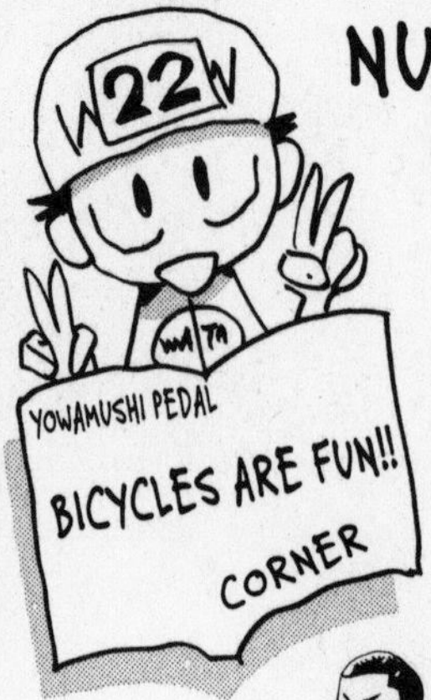

YOWAMUSHI PEDAL
BICYCLES ARE FUN!!
CORNER

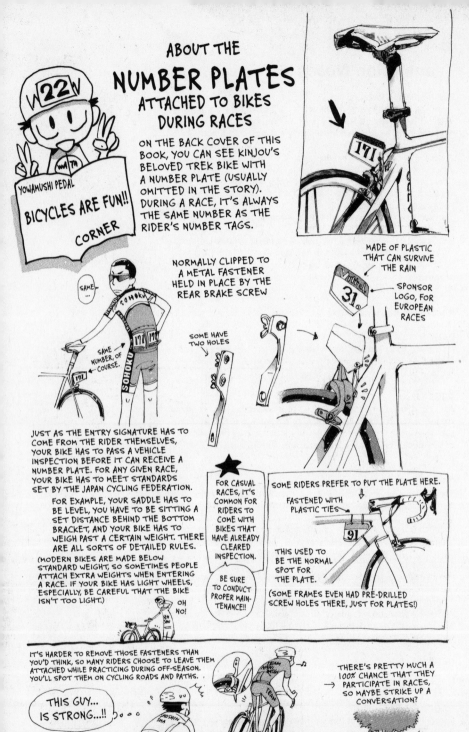

ABOUT THE NUMBER PLATES ATTACHED TO BIKES DURING RACES

ON THE BACK COVER OF THIS BOOK, YOU CAN SEE KINJOU'S BELOVED TREK BIKE WITH A NUMBER PLATE (USUALLY OMITTED IN THE STORY). DURING A RACE, IT'S ALWAYS THE SAME NUMBER AS THE RIDER'S NUMBER TAGS.

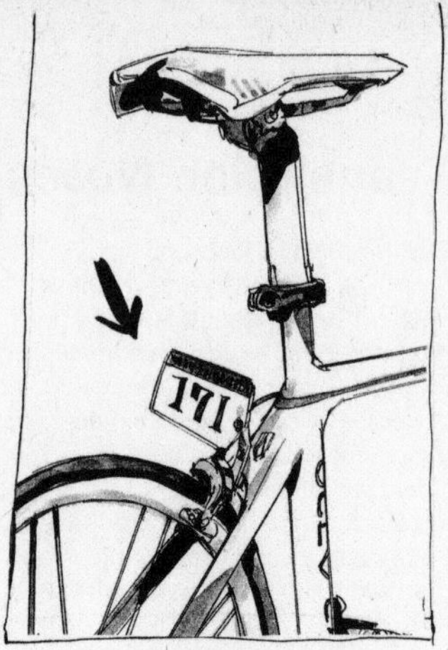

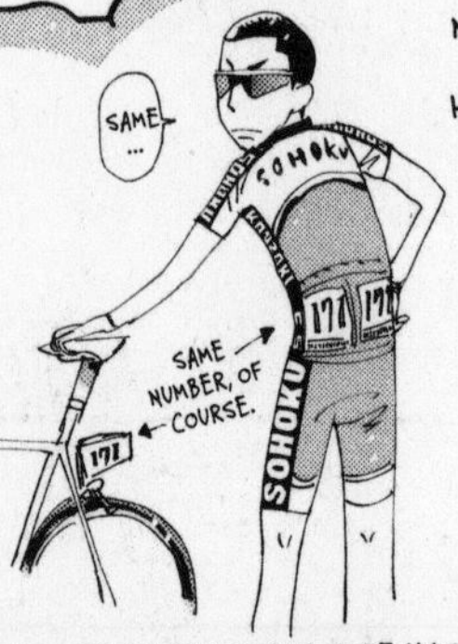

SAME...
SAME NUMBER, OF COURSE.

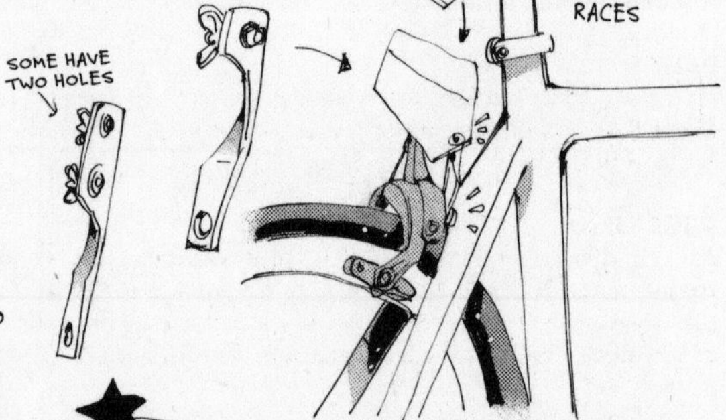

NORMALLY CLIPPED TO A METAL FASTENER HELD IN PLACE BY THE REAR BRAKE SCREW
MADE OF PLASTIC THAT CAN SURVIVE THE RAIN
SPONSOR LOGO, FOR EUROPEAN RACES
SOME HAVE TWO HOLES

JUST AS THE ENTRY SIGNATURE HAS TO COME FROM THE RIDER THEMSELVES, YOUR BIKE HAS TO PASS A VEHICLE INSPECTION BEFORE IT CAN RECEIVE A NUMBER PLATE. FOR ANY GIVEN RACE, YOUR BIKE HAS TO MEET STANDARDS SET BY THE JAPAN CYCLING FEDERATION.

FOR EXAMPLE, YOUR SADDLE HAS TO BE LEVEL, YOU HAVE TO BE SITTING A SET DISTANCE BEHIND THE BOTTOM BRACKET, AND YOUR BIKE HAS TO WEIGH PAST A CERTAIN WEIGHT. THERE ARE ALL SORTS OF DETAILED RULES.

(MODERN BIKES ARE MADE BELOW STANDARD WEIGHT, SO SOMETIMES PEOPLE ATTACH EXTRA WEIGHTS WHEN ENTERING A RACE. IF YOUR BIKE HAS LIGHT WHEELS, ESPECIALLY, BE CAREFUL THAT THE BIKE ISN'T TOO LIGHT.)

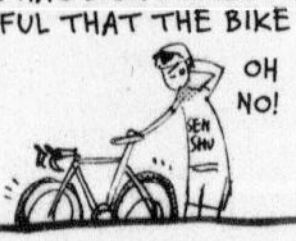

OH NO!

★ FOR CASUAL RACES, IT'S COMMON FOR RIDERS TO COME WITH BIKES THAT HAVE ALREADY CLEARED INSPECTION.

BE SURE TO CONDUCT PROPER MAIN-TENANCE!!

SOME RIDERS PREFER TO PUT THE PLATE HERE.

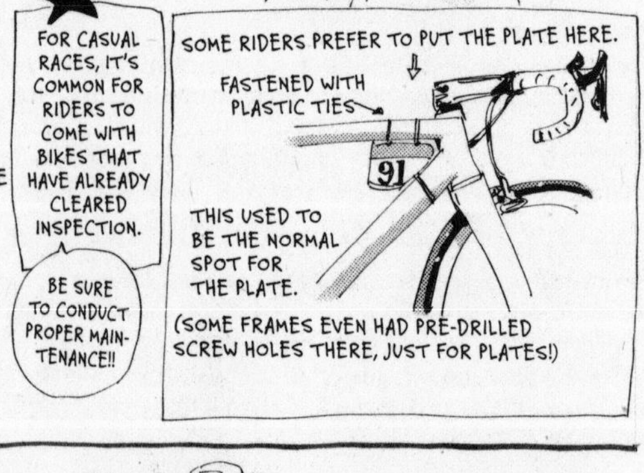

FASTENED WITH PLASTIC TIES

THIS USED TO BE THE NORMAL SPOT FOR THE PLATE.

(SOME FRAMES EVEN HAD PRE-DRILLED SCREW HOLES THERE, JUST FOR PLATES!)

IT'S HARDER TO REMOVE THOSE FASTENERS THAN YOU'D THINK, SO MANY RIDERS CHOOSE TO LEAVE THEM ATTACHED WHILE PRACTICING DURING OFF-SEASON. YOU'LL SPOT THEM ON CYCLING ROADS AND PATHS.

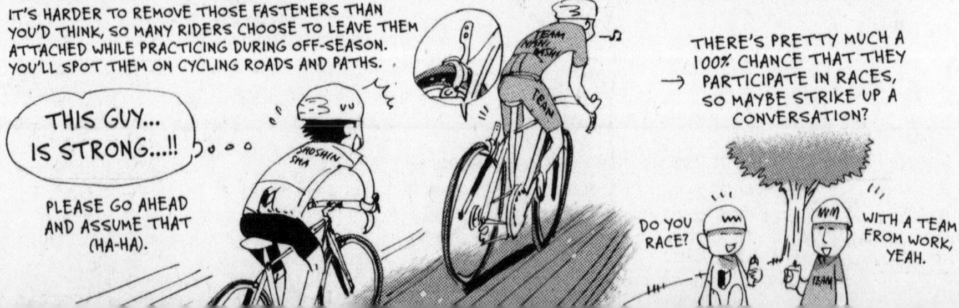

THIS GUY... IS STRONG...!!
PLEASE GO AHEAD AND ASSUME THAT (HA-HA).
THERE'S PRETTY MUCH A 100% CHANCE THAT THEY PARTICIPATE IN RACES, SO MAYBE STRIKE UP A CONVERSATION?
DO YOU RACE?
WITH A TEAM FROM WORK, YEAH.

Translation Notes

Common Honorifics
-san: The Japanese equivalent of Mr./Mrs./Miss. If a situation calls for politeness, this is the fail-safe honorific.
-kun: Used most often when referring to boys, this indicates affection or familiarity. Occasionally used by older men among their peers, but it may also be used by anyone referring to a person of lower standing.
-chan: An affectionate honorific indicating familiarity used mostly in reference to girls; also used in reference to cute persons or animals of either gender.
-senpai: A suffix used to address upperclassmen or more experienced co-workers.
-shi: A more formal version of *san* common to written Japanese, it's the default honorific used in newspapers.
no honorific: Indicates familiarity or closeness; if used without permission or reason, addressing someone in this manner would constitute an insult.

A kilometer is approximately .6 of a mile.

PAGE 9
Hakone: A town located in a mountainous area of Kanagawa Prefecture, it's popular among tourists for its scenic views and hot springs.

PAGE 20
Arakita: Arakita's name is made up of characters *ara*, meaning "rough" or "rude," and *kita*, meaning "north." Here, Onoda uses the word *arappoi* to describe Arakita's remarks, which consists of the same character *ara* to describe a rude, ill-mannered person.

PAGE 41, 43
Two-wheeler, junk: In Japanese, *chari* and *jitensha* both translate to "bike." Arakita uses *chari* to describe Fukutomi's bike, which gives the impression that his bike is like a toy for little kids, or like Onoda's mommy bike. Fukutomi uses the more formal term, *jitensha*.

PAGE 93
Hiroshima: A populous city located on the island of Honshu, Japan. The city was the target of the first atomic bombing of World War II, which led to major devastation in its infrastructure and the deaths of thousands of innocent civilians. It is known for its peace memorial, which stands a remaining marker of the war.

PAGE 94
Peloton: A cycling term for the "pack," or the main group of riders in a race.

PAGE 160
Kyoto: Former capital of Japan located in the Kansai region. It's known for its plethora of traditional Japanese architecture, having come out of World War II relatively unscathed.

PAGE 192
In the Japanese version, Watanabe wrote an author's note that appeared on the cover flap. It has been translated below.

I attended a Cycle Mode, a annual bicycle event held in both Tokyo and Osaka. For the event, we made special T-shirts and *sacoche* bags, and all four hundred of them sold out instantly! We donated all our profits. To those who participated—thank you very much!

I also took part in a panel talk where I spoke passionately about bicycle pedals.

Look forward to reading more about that in future volumes!

PAGE 243
Fellas: In Japanese, Shinkai refers to the Sohoku riders as *yakkosan*, which is a friendly and casual form of address.

PAGE 245
"Lost our heads": In the Japanese version, Makishima says *kubi no kawa ichi mai*, where *kubi no kawa* refers to the skin on one's neck and *ichi mai* means "one sheet." A similar phrase to this in English might be "to hang by a thread," but *kubi no kawa ichi mai* also suggests that there is still a glimmer of hope even in the worst situation.

PAGE 312
Criterium: A one-day bike race held within a closed course where the winner must cross the finish line first without being outdistanced.

ENJOY EVERYTHING.

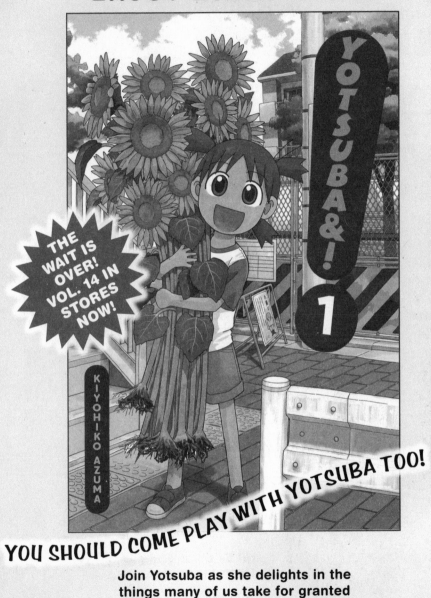

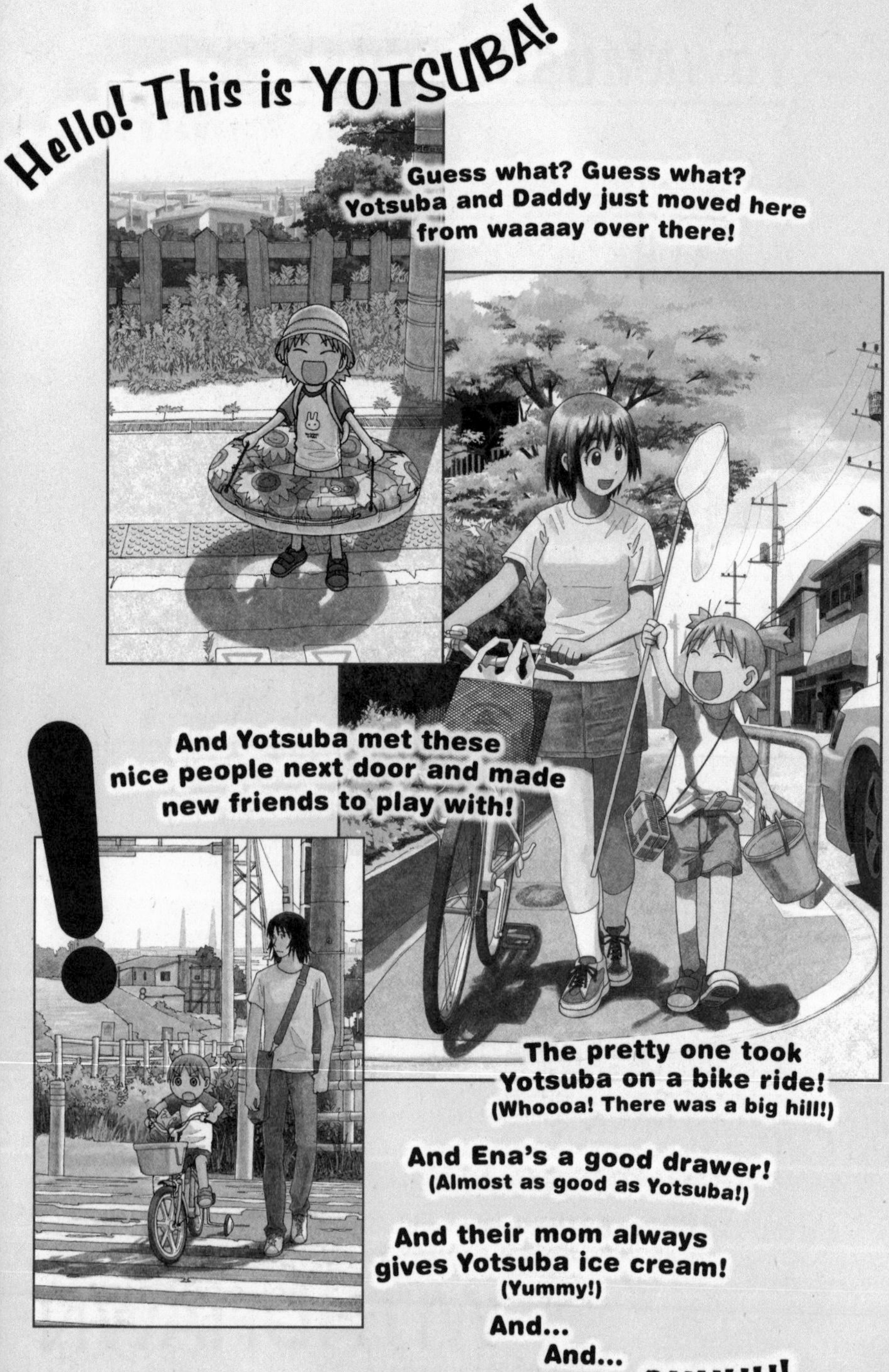
Hello! This is YOTSUBA!
Guess what? Guess what? Yotsuba and Daddy just moved here from waaaay over there!
And Yotsuba met these nice people next door and made new friends to play with!
!
The pretty one took Yotsuba on a bike ride!
(Whoooa! There was a big hill!)
And Ena's a good drawer!
(Almost as good as Yotsuba!)
And their mom always gives Yotsuba ice cream!
(Yummy!)
And...
And...
OHHHH!

7508

YOWAMUSHI PEDAL ⑪

WATARU WATANABE

Translation: Caleb D. Cook

Lettering: Lys Blakeslee, Rachel J. Pierce

This book is a work of fiction. Names, characters, places, and incidents are the product of the author's imagination or are used fictitiously. Any resemblance to actual events, locales, or persons, living or dead, is coincidental.

YOWAMUSHI PEDAL Volume 21, 22
© 2012 Wataru Watanabe
All rights reserved.
First published in Japan in 2012 by Akita Publishing Co., Ltd., Tokyo.
English translation rights arranged with Akita Publishing Co., Ltd. through Tuttle-Mori Agency, Inc., Tokyo.

English translation © 2019 by Yen Press, LLC

Yen Press
1290 Avenue of the Americas
New York, NY 10104

Visit us at yenpress.com
facebook.com/yenpress
twitter.com/yenpress
yenpress.tumblr.com
instagram.com/yenpress

First Yen Press Edition: April 2019

Yen Press is an imprint of Yen Press, LLC.
The Yen Press name and logo are trademarks of Yen Press, LLC.

The publisher is not responsible for websites (or their content) that are not owned by the publisher.

Library of Congress Control Number: 2015960124

ISBNs: 978-0-316-52095-9 (paperback)
        978-0-316-52097-3 (ebook)

10 9 8 7 6 5 4 3 2 1

WOR

Printed in the United States of America

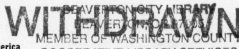